JUVENILE DELINQUENCY
Concepts and Control

Funds for this Book were Donated by:

Chapter 15 North Bay Counties
INTERNATIONAL FOOTPRINT ASSOCIATION

I.F.A. is a social association established
in 1929 to promote respect, fellowship and
mutual understanding between law enforcement officers and civilians.

JUVENILE

second edition

DELINQUENCY

Concepts and Controls

ROBERT C. TROJANOWICZ

Michigan State University

with the assistance of
JOHN M. TROJANOWICZ

Volkwagen Manufacturing Corporation of America

Prentice-Hall, Inc., *Englewood Cliffs, New Jersey 07632*

Library of Congress Cataloging in Publication Data

Trojanowicz, Robert C (date)
  Juvenile delinquency.

  Bibliography: p.
  1. Juvenile delinquency. 2. Rehabilitation of
juvenile delinquents. I. Trojanowicz, John M., joint
author. II. Title.
HV9069.T84 1978   364.36   77–23768
ISBN 0–13–514331–4

Juvenile Delinquency: Concepts and Control
second edition

Robert C. Trojanowicz

Printed in the United States of America

10 9 8 7 6 5 4 3 2

Prentice-Hall International, Inc., *London*
Prentice-Hall of Australia Pty. Limited, *Sydney*
Prentice-Hall of Canada, Ltd., *Toronto*
Prentice-Hall of India Private Limited, *New Delhi*
Prentice-Hall of Japan, Inc., *Tokyo*
Prentice-Hall of Southeast Asia Pte. Ltd., *Singapore*
Whitehall Books Limited, *Wellington, New Zealand*

Dedicated to

my son Eric and my daughter Elise

Contents

PREFACE   xiii

chapter 1

SOCIAL DEVIANCE   1

Human Behavior and Social Control
Cultural Considerations
Modern Society and Social Control
The Categorization of Deviance
Juvenile Delinquency as a Form of Deviant Behavior
Summary
Questions and Projects

chapter 2

THEORIES OF DELINQUENCY CAUSATION   29

Contemporary Theories of Criminality: An Overview
Major Sociological Theories
Conclusions from Sociological Theories

Major Psychological Theories
Conclusions from Psychological Theories
Summary
Questions and Projects

chapter 3

THE FAMILY AND JUVENILE DELINQUENCY   68

Psychology and the Family
Sociology and the Family
The Environment of the Family
The Contemporary Family
Conclusion
Summary
Questions and Projects

chapter 4

THE ADOLESCENT   94

A Cultural Perspective of Adolescence
The Normal Adolescent
Childhood Development
The Struggle of Dependence versus Independence
The Delinquent Adolescent
Working with the Adolescent
Adolescent Drug Abuse
Summary
Questions and Projects

chapter 5

FEMALE DELINQUENCY   132

The Nature and Extent of Female Delinquency
Female Crime and Delinquency: Theoretical Explanations
Female Delinquents in the Juvenile Justice System
Dispositions for Female Delinquents
New Directions
Summary
Questions and Projects

chapter 6

HANDLING THE JUVENILE DELINQUENT
WITHIN THE JUVENILE JUSTICE SYSTEM   151

Origin and Development of the Juvenile Court
Juvenile Court Legislation Today
Status Offenses
The Police and the Juvenile
The Juvenile Court—Intake and Processing
The Intake Division of the Juvenile Court
Juvenile Court Processing Beyond Intake
Conclusion
A Case Study
Summary
Questions and Projects

chapter 7

CHILD ABUSE AND NEGLECT   187

The Problem
Causes
Child Abuse and Law Enforcement
Child Protective Services
History of Child Protection
Child Protective Methods and Programs
Prevention
Summary
Questions and Projects

chapter 8

DELINQUENCY PREVENTION PROGRAMS   210

Delinquency Prevention: An Overview
Pure Prevention Programs
Rehabilitative Prevention Programs
Summary
Questions and Projects

chapter 9

METHODS OF TREATMENT   263

Psychotherapy
Social Casework
Reality Therapy
Transactional Analysis
Vocational Counseling
Behavior Therapy
Behavioral Contracts
Crisis Intervention
Individual and Group Counseling
Group Therapy
Social Group Work
Group Psychotherapy
Activity Therapy
Guided Group Interaction
Milieu Therapy
Social Environment Therapy
Direct Home Intervention
Family Crisis Counseling
Summary
Questions and Projects

chapter 10

THE NEED FOR RESEARCH
IN DELINQUENCY PREVENTION AND TREATMENT   305

History
Changing Offender Behavior
Redefinition of Recidivism
Research Methods and Strategies
Research Findings
Summary
Questions and Projects

chapter 11

AN EXAMPLE:
COMMUNITY-BASED TREATMENT PROGRAMS   323

Halfway Houses
Problems Involved in Operating a Halfway House Program

Solutions to the Problems: Developing a New Organizational and Philosophical
(Criminological) System
Evaluation of the Program
Guiding Principles for Operating a Halfway House
Recommendations for Standards and Guidelines for Community-Based Programs
Summary
Questions and Projects

chapter 12

DELINQUENCY PREVENTION
THROUGH CITIZEN INVOLVEMENT   354

The Present Ineffectiveness of Informal Social Control
Citizen Involvement
Organizing Citizen Efforts
A Model for Action: Normative Sponsorship Theory
Key Elements: A Guide to Action
Conclusion
Summary
Questions and Projects

chapter 13

CRITICAL ISSUES—A LOOK TO THE FUTURE   384

Juvenile Crime
Rural Crime
Juvenile Justice Administration
Status Offenses
Future Directions
Diversion
Youth Violence
Prevention
Summary and Conclusion

BIBLIOGRAPHY   417

INTRODUCTION

INDEX   453

Preface

The main purpose of the second edition of *Juvenile Delinquency: Concepts and Control* is to provide the practitioner or the student interested in working with juveniles an overview of the juvenile delinquency phenomenon and the process involved in its causation, prevention, control, and treatment. This second edition, as the first, emphasizes a multidisciplinary approach to the problem and updates information presented in the first edition as well as including new and important material related to the complex problem of juvenile delinquency.

The most popular and prevalent interdisciplinary issues, ideas, principles, and assumptions pertaining to the phenomenon are presented. The use of numerous examples facilitates the transition from complex theoretical principles to practical application.

Not only does the book provide an overview of the many variables related to delinquency, it points out the orientation, duties, responsibilities, and functions of the agencies in the juvenile justice system that deal with the juvenile delinquent. The orientation, programs, and procedures utilized by the various juvenile justice agencies are discussed to help the reader understand the processes the delinquent goes through from the initial contact with the police to the selection of a dispositional alternative. The description and discussion of the juvenile delinquency process will facilitate the transition from theory to practice.

Almost everyone, regardless of background or professional training, has his own theories about juvenile delinquency. Often the logic and insight demonstrated by practitioners or amateur theorists is appropriate and sound, but because they are unaware of popular theoretical assumptions and current programs and practices they are unable to systematically compare their ideas with those of the

"experts." This hinders the practitioner or the "amateur" from effectively repli-
cating and refining his own most successful ideas and practices. In other words,
the practitioner or the aspiring practitioner "flies by the seat of his pants."

This book provides the reader with an exposure to the thinking of the experts in the field of juvenile delinquency, the process involved in the causation
of this phonomenon, and examples of the most successful and effective programs, procedures, and techniques for handling juveniles.

The strength of the book is that it points out the complexity of the juvenile delinquency phenomenon and the necessity of understanding the many variables related to its causation, prevention, treatment, and control—variables that
range all the way from a knowledge of "normal" adolescent behavior to an
understanding of processing procedures in handling delinquents.

The establishment of effective juvenile delinquency prevention, treatment,
and control programs can be accomplished only if the many variables identified
in the book are understood, assimilated, and then initiated into action.

Chapter 1, "Social Deviance," introduces juvenile delinquency as a subcategory of the general concept of deviancy. Whenever people unite to achieve
individual and group goals and to satisfy needs, they must also set limits and
make rules to regulate behavior. Where there are rules and regulations, there is
the potential for deviance. If the deviant act is committed by a juvenile, it is a
delinquent deviant act.

Deviant behavior has existed throughout human history and will continue
to exist as long as man is dependent on his peers for survival. Although deviancy
is usually associated with the social outcast and the criminal offender, almost
everyone has acted in a deviant manner at one time or another.

As Cohen points out, "the study of deviance cannot simply be the study
of drunkenness, narcotic drug use, prostitution, etc., for each of these in some
society and under some circumstances was socially acceptable."[1] Hence, it is
necessary to understand and recognize not only the specific deviant act but also
the entire concept.

The last part of Chapter 1 traces the history of the development of the
concept of the delinquent child and its changing image.

Just as the reader should understand the complexity and the variability of
the concept of deviancy and the ways in which juvenile delinquency is a form of
deviant behavior, he should also become acquainted with the most popular
theoretical assumptions about the etiology of behavior that manifests itself in a
delinquent form.

Chapter 2, "Theories of Delinquency Causation," discusses the many
aspects of criminology that are referred to as *theories of causation*.

Because the study of the delinquent child and the forces that contribute to
his status have taken many avenues and originated from many disciplines, Chap-

---

[1] Albert K. Cohen, *Deviance and Control* (Englewood Cliffs, N.J.: Prentice-Hall, Inc., 1966),
p. 12.

ter 2 uses a multidisciplinary focus and orientation, placing major emphasis on the psychological and sociological fields.

It is undoubtedly helpful, regardless of the theoretical orientation, to be exposed to many different viewpoints. This approach not only broadens the reader's outlook but also introduces him to the jargon and tenets of a variety of schools of thought.

Chapter 3, "The Family and Juvenile Delinquency," uses the family as a model for incorporating both psychological and sociological principles into a meaningful framework. Regardless of the particular professional or academic discipline or orientation, the family is considered the most significant factor in the development of delinquency because the family setting is the primary environment of the child. It is within the family institution that the child first interacts, and what he learns (or does not learn) there is often the model for future behavior. Chapter 3 illustrates psychological and sociological variables interacting within the family. The use of the family as an example of these processes is a logical follow-up to the discussion of theories of causation in Chapter 2.

Chapter 4, "The Adolescent," discusses the dynamic behavior and development of the youngster during the period of transition between childhood and adulthood. Just as it is important to understand the concept of deviancy and the theories of delinquency causation, it is also important to understand the myriad of factors that accompany adolescence, the period in which most juvenile delinquency occurs.

Persons working with juveniles tend to forget that the delinquent is an adolescent first and a delinquent second. They are not familiar with the wide variety of adolescent disruptive behavior that is within the normal range. Often, more is expected of the delinquent than of the normal adolescent. Unfortunately, many prevention, treatment, and control programs are predicated on the "sickness" of the delinquent and not on the "healthiness" of the adolescent. It is important to understand the normal as well as the delinquent adolescent—as much may be learned from normality as from deviancy. Chapter 4 also examines the adolescent from many perspectives, including his wide-ranging behavior, his relationships with others, his struggle with dependence versus independence, and the most effective methods of relating to him. It also presents relevant examples and a discussion of present-day adolescent problems, such as drug abuse.

Chapter 5 focuses on female delinquency. Even though many of the theories and assumptions regarding the juvenile delinquent are applicable regardless of sex, the female delinquent has unique characteristics, problems, and difficulties. The reader will gain an appreciation for the female delinquent's special situation and an understanding of how to effectively work with her.

Chapter 6, "Handling the Juvenile Delinquent within the Juvenile Justice System," discusses concrete methods and techniques in current judicial practice, and views the delinquent from the perspective, philosophy, and responsibilities of the police, the court, and other agencies.

Relevant Supreme Court decisions are also mentioned, and their implications for the handling of the delinquent are discussed. The chapter concludes by presenting a case study of a delinquent and describing the procedure for handling him under recent court decisions and recommended juvenile court rules.

"Child Abuse and Neglect," the topic of Chapter 7, is of great concern today for professionals in all phases of the juvenile justice system. The problem can no longer be viewed as "someone else's concern." Everyone, all the way from the investigating police officer to the judge who makes the final decision, must be aware of the seriousness of the problem and what can be done to remedy this unfortunate situation.

Chapter 8, "Delinquency Prevention Programs," describes programs that have been established to prevent, control, and treat delinquency. The chapter provides illustrations of how abstract theoretical concepts may be transformed into concrete programs. The problems of transition are most illuminating.

Just as there are many and varied opinions as to how programs should be established and what theory should be transformed into concrete action, there are many views regarding the most effective methods for treatment, prevention, and control.

Chapter 9, "Methods of Treatment," examines the most prevalent, accepted, and currently successful techniques of treatment. The chapter takes a multi-disciplinary orientation and views both individual and group methods, which range from very practical approaches to highly complicated methods that require a great deal of training and skill. Examples are given as to how the various techniques are used, in what types of settings, and under what circumstances, as well as the professional orientation of the persons using them.

"The Need for Research in Delinquency Prevention and Treatment," Chapter 10, has important implications for how the delinquent will be viewed, treated, and handled in the future. Effective programs must be replicated and ineffective ones eliminated so that scarce resources can be used most effectively.

Chapter 11, "An Example: Community-Based Treatment Programs," describes a halfway house program and discusses the input necessary for the establishment and operation of such a facility.

Halfway houses are discussed more extensively than other juvenile facilities because (1) halfway houses will probably eventually be the most prevalent community-based treatment facilities for juveniles, dominating other programs, such as institutions, probation, and court services, all of which are discussed in preceding chapters; (2) a discussion of the halfway house program lends itself to the incorporation of the theories, concepts, programs, and techniques that are discussed in the preceding chapters; and (3) the example of a halfway house program illustrates the numerous elements that have to be considered if programs are to achieve their intended goals.

Chapter 12, "Delinquency Prevention Through Citizen Involvement," emphasizes including the residents of the community in any decisions that relate to delinquency prevention, control, and treatment. Without community involvement, input and commitment to programs that are established to work with youngsters will be difficult to effect.

Chapter 13, "Critical Issues: A Look to the Future," identifies and discusses both contemporary and future issues that must be dealt with if the prevention, control, handling, and treatment of the delinquent youngster is to be meaningful and effective.

Finally, a complete bibliography with summaries and library call numbers is presented at the end of the book to provide an easy reference for both the student and the practitioner. An Instructor's Manual has been developted for the text to assist the teacher.

As with any endeavor, many people have contributed to the achievement of our goal. We would like to acknowledge some of the people who helped in completing the second edition: Ray Valley, Susann (Pyzik) Jude, Thomas Schooley, and Kathleen Williams for their research assistance; Dr. Forrest M. Moss for his writing help; Steven Cline and Robert Weisman of Prentice-Hall for their encouragement; Dr. Christopher Sower for his inspiration; and our families for their support and endurance.

chapter 1

Social Deviance*

The basic purpose of this book is to explore that spectrum of human behavior known as juvenile delinquency, a phenomenon which can range from school truancy and curfew violations to major violations of the criminal law. Juvenile delinquency is essentially the study of deviance and, to a large extent, crime, the primary distinction being that the label "delinquent" is selectively applied to a certain class of offenders distinguished mostly by their age. Delinquency, therefore, is the deviant activities of a defined age group. This chapter will explore the complexity of the concept of deviant behavior itself, and attempt to place it in a social and cultural context.

What constitutes deviant behavior has evolved over time and varies from society to society, even within the same society. Although various physical phenomena such as tides, volcanic eruptions, earthquakes, and so on clearly exist in nature, and can usually be consistently attributed to particular and specifiable forces, deviance is essentially a social invention, a label applied to certain behavioral options which occur under certain circumstances, and which involve a complex network of human relationships concerned with individual and group needs, goals, power, values, and environmental realities.[1] Thus, the acquisition of property may be applauded if performed by method one, frowned upon if performed by method two, or penalized under the criminal law if performed by method three. The taking of a human life will be deemed an act of heroism in one instance, an abomination in another, or of little consequence in a third social circumstance. Because social deviance is not unique in nature, does not

*Written by Forrest M. Moss in collaboration with Robert C. Trojanowicz.
[1] Richard Quinney, *The Social Reality of Crime* (Boston: Little, Brown and Company, 1970).

necessarily remain constant over time, and is always a defined activity, we are faced with difficulties in trying to specify universal causes of such behavior, predict its future occurrence, or make excessively ambitious claims for any particular causal theory.

It is critically important to acknowledge that deviation is a common feature of society and is implicit in *all* social organizations.[2] As Dinitz *et al.* point out, *deviance* is just as much a human characteristic as is *conformity.*

> Every human group no matter how cohesive, stable, and well integrated, must somehow respond to such problems as mental illness, violence, theft, sexual misconduct, as well as to other similarly difficult behaviors. Problems of deviance inevitably are defined as being a real or perceived threat to the basic "values" of the society. For whatever reasons, some persons act at times, at least, in so bizarre, eccentric, outlandish, abhorrent, dangerous, or merely unique and annoying a manner that they cannot readily be tolerated. So every society must somehow deal with its saints and its sinners, its kooks and clowns, and its dependent, disruptive, inadequate, and aberrant members. Understanding deviance involves, at a basic minimum, at least three dimensions. First, it is apparent that every society *defines* behaviors that are to be labeled as deviant and proscribed as undesirable. Second, since deviance may be commonplace and even widespread, some explanations or *theories* must be offered for the existence and persistence of such deviant behavior in the face of negative social sanction. Third, there would be little reason to define, sanction, and explain deviance without also doing something to, for, or with the deviant in order to *correct, deter, prevent,* and/or punish him. Every society then defines, explains, and acts with regard to deviance.[3]

This book will basically deal with the three issues raised in the above quotation. In this chapter we will discuss the way society *defines* certain types of behavior that it deems unacceptable and needing sanctions. The line between deviance and conformity is not always clear cut. There are differences not only in the earliest cultures but also within cultures, where no common understanding exists regarding deviant behavior and its treatment. Sanctioning of deviant behavior depends upon not only the act but also the circumstances, the social system, the community, and the prevailing attitudes. Chapter 2 will examine various *theories* of deviant behavior (juvenile delinquency in particular), its causes, and its implications.

Any discussion of the concept of deviancy and the theories of causation should include methods and programs for prevention, treatment, and control. Subsequent chapters will focus on these matters. Most issues pertinent to juvenile delinquency will be investigated in this book. They range from understand-

---

[2] David Matza, *Becoming Deviant* (Englewood Cliffs, N.J.: Prentice-Hall, Inc., 1969).

[3] From *Deviance: Studies in the Process of Stigmatization and Societal Reaction* by Simon Dinitz, Russell R. Dynes, and Alfred C. Clark. Copyright 1969 by Oxford University Press, Inc. Reprinted by permission.

ing the "normal" adolescent to developing effective methods for dealing with delinquency.

HUMAN BEHAVIOR AND SOCIAL CONTROL

It seems safe to assert that a basic behavioral dilemma exists between man and the social group in which he finds himself. In spite of the widely publicized desire and need for man to live in harmony with other societies and with members of his own society, the historical evidence does not in any way gratify the wish, and conflict seems to be the rule rather than the exception. This behavioral dilemma emerges naturally from the interaction of humans within the confines of their social setting, whether the setting is primitive or modern.

The Conservative Tendency

Society exhibits a clear tendency to conserve and protect itself—the maintenance of the status quo or the betterment of the group—by avoiding a multitude of real or perceived natural and social threats which portend an unacceptable future. Society thus identifies and promotes a behavior and a complex of social functions which most ably relate to the aspirations, needs, and conditions of that society. Acceptable and unacceptable behavior in such a social setting can be visualized as the area under a normal bell curve (see Figure 1). At the center (valued behavior) and extending narrowly or broadly to either side (the areas in Figure 1 designated with the number one), are those actions and personal attributes most in congruence with the goals, and hence the values, of society. These behaviors are normally rewarded by a series of tangible and intangible social benefits such as increased material holdings, group status, increased feelings of self-esteem, general respect, and so on. At the extremes of the curve (the areas in Figure 1 designated with the number 3) are those behaviors which, to a very substantial degree, are considered clearly of danger to social welfare and survival. Such behavior is almost certain to invoke personal or

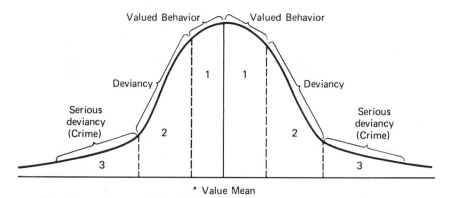

FIGURE 1. The Social Value/Behavior Curve

family retribution. Or it may be labeled as crime and punished by the state in more modern societies; whether the label identifies a violator of tribal taboos or a felon, the toleration level of society rapidly diminishes as one approaches the extremes of the bell-shaped curve.

The area which exists between valued behaviors and serious deviancy (areas designated with the number 2 in Figure 1) poses a substantial and continuing problem both to society and to criminal justice practitioners. These behaviors will be viewed, depending on the community and the particular point in time, as eccentric but harmless, eccentric and harmful, situationally appropriate or inappropriate, nonthreatening but nonetheless socially reprehensible, as fortifying or undermining the ethos or "moral" fiber of the collectivity, or even as falling within the informal purview of the criminal justice system. Such judgments about behavior are mainly cultural and class based. There are also other conditioning factors, such as the person's perception about the stability of the social structure, external and internal threats to the community, and environmental conditions, like economic prosperity or depression. Society, of course, goes to some lengths to socialize each new member so that both the valued behavior and the clearly dangerous behavioral extremes are adhered to or avoided, respectively; however, the less hazardous behavioral boundaries (area 2 in Figure 1) also require learning, adjusting and relearning throughout life since these boundaries reflect the expectations of the community at that particular point in time.

In societies which value a high degree of individual freedom, the deviancy area may be broad and the toleration of "eccentric" or "grey area" behavior high, while other societies may find the existence of behaviors in this area so unpleasant or threatening that such acts come to be defined as criminal. It is also highly probable that as the social group perceives its internal or external stability and viability to be high or low, this middle ground of behavior will be narrowed or broadened.

While society seeks to conserve and maintain itself by various sanctions directed at the reduction of deviance, it is also characteristic of most to modify those sanctions in regard to "offenders" who are presumed to have a lesser degree of responsibility because of their youth. In societies that consider age as an extenuating circumstance, the response to deviance is characteristically one aimed at the education, "resocializing," or correcting of personal or social shortcomings which were determined to have promoted the deviance in the first place. On the other hand, the specification of deviance by age group allows for the inclusion of many acts under the label "juvenile delinquency," which are clearly "normal" (or at least legal) for the adult population. In this regard later chapters discuss status offenses of juveniles.

The Inevitability of Deviance

Man, as opposed to many members of the animal kingdom, is not biologically programmed to a limited series of responses when interacting with his social or physical environment, except in a very narrow sense of the term. On the contrary, the evidence indicates that he has shown a substantial and lasting tendency to resist, reject or otherwise find inappropriate the boundaries set by society. Indeed, the actions of some juvenile offenders give rise to the question of whether even a minimal socialization process has occurred at all; other delinquents exhibit behavioral traits suggesting they have been socialized in partial or total opposition to the larger society. Furthermore, human social interaction, regardless of the complexity of the society, requires at least minimal sophistication, involving the "reading" of subtle social cues and situations so that social "rules" can be followed. Understandably, a certain amount of social deviance and crime therefore occurs because of faulty intellectual ability, ignorance, or just plain naivety, and most modern societies make some sort of allowance for acts of this nature. Finally, even under the most prosperous and congenial of social situations, man possesses an inventive and imaginative ability by which he constantly finds new ways of maximizing and changing his own social environment. This is especially true regarding increased technological knowledge and advancements.

In short, the society which makes possible the human experience also creates limits on human conduct designed to perpetuate and protect that society. Man, for a variety of reasons—many of which will be explored in detail in later chapters—often violates these limits, be they customs and traditions, social norms and roles, tribal taboos, or the formalized criminal law. Criminal justice practitioners are involved in the identification and control of serious deviancy such as murder, armed robbery, rape, and the like, as well as the formal and informal handling of a large middle-range area of deviant behavior, much of which is performed by youthful offenders. A host of rather indefinite laws relating to public safety, welfare, and order provide the legal basis for criminal justice involvement in these "grey areas" of human conduct. One of the critical questions in the study of delinquency is how individuals are "selected" into these criminal justice processes. The problem is of course compounded in this society by a heterogeneous class structure as well as the multicultural origins of our country. At a minimum, there exist diverse viewpoints in this country as to just what constitutes "right" and "wrong" behavior, many of which are often at odds with the criminal law, as well as with some of the more popular American traditions, mores, and customs.

The Variable Nature of Deviant Behavior

Because deviant behavior is not consistent in all cultures, all societies, or even all communities, what are the reference points for evaluating behavior as deviant or nondeviant, and how can the line between deviance and conformity be drawn more clearly so that the concept can be understood in more concrete terms? The major criteria or reference points utilized to determine whether or not behavior is deviant are probably those intangible guides to behavior that we call *norms*. Very simply, norms are the criteria that society utilizes to evaluate behavior.

They evolve out of the experience of people interacting with society. In turn, they guide, channel, and limit further relationships. So integral a part of human life are norms that many are unaware of their pervasiveness. Most persons are oblivious to the importance of norms in giving substance and meaning to human life. The reason for this lack of awareness is that norms become so internalized as a part of a personality, that people take them for granted. Norms are seldom consciously thought about unless they are challenged by contact with persons conforming to another normative order, perhaps foreigners, hillbillies or outsiders. This unconscious quality of norms arises from the fact that persons are rewarded for behaving in certain ways and punished for behaving in other ways until behavior according to the norms becomes almost automatic.[4]

The development and maintenance of norms, however, is related to the complexity and evolutionary growth rate of the society itself. In societies with minimal technological change, norms are usually understood and accepted by almost everyone because of the unchanging nature of the community. In modern societies, on the other hand, the phenomenal growth of technology often so changes the social mobility, occupations, communications, and values of individuals and groups that some norms come to be perceived as dysfunctional, or alternative norms may be developed by the various groups, forming the basis for norm conflict. Thus, even though clear *legal* norms may exist for society *en masse*, they may be perceived by some as meaningless or even offensive, they may in fact be unenforceable, or they may be in direct conflict with the developed norms of social subgroups or subcultures. Clinard has observed that as an example of the latter, norms of subgroups which conflict with legal norms may be those of certain age groups, social classes, occupations, neighborhoods, or regions.[5] Lee concurrently notes that the child's conditioning to a given society may differ drastically from the general norms, thus allowing for a certain amount of predictability of behavioral deviancy.[6] On the other hand, individuals and groups may, for a variety of reasons, find themselves in positions where obtaining their share of the "good life" (a goal directly relatable to perceptions of self-worth and esteem), is extremely difficult simultaneous with adhering to general social and legal norms. The result may be the seeking of personal satisfaction through socially unacceptable means and the development of deviant norms.[7]

Deviancy (and especially juvenile deviancy)—already an elusive concept—is further compounded to the extent that expectations within the same society may conflict, and deviancy itself can often be situationally defined. Failure to

---

[4] From *Deviance: Studies in the Process of Stigmatization and Societal Reaction* by Simon Dinitz, Russell R. Dynes, and Alred C. Clark, p. 4. Copyright 1969 by Oxford University Press, Inc. Reprinted by permission.

[5] Marshall B. Clinard, *Sociology of Deviant Behavior* (New York: Rinehart and Company, Inc., 1957), p. 24.

[6] Alfred McClung Lee, *Multivalent Man* (New York: George Braziller, Inc., 1966).

[7] Harry C. Bredemier and Jackson Toby, *Social Problems in America—Costs and Casualties in the Acquisitive Society* (New York: John Wiley and Sons, Inc., 1965).

recognize this problem often leads observers to seek (and often find) simplistic answers as to what causes delinquency. The fact of the matter is basically that the line between conformity and deviant behavior is very fine indeed, and the concept itself cannot be correlated directly with certain social, psychological, or other variables.

> Further confusion arises in the minds of some observers when they per-
> ceive that certain factors are associated with the occurrence of deviant
> behavior. They often jump to the conclusion that two phenomena are
> related when they may have no connection. When it is noted, for example,
> that delinquency and bad housing are often associated, the causal rela-
> tionship may be presumed to exist. Others may perceive that delinquents
> read comic books so they conclude that comic books can cause delinquen-
> cy. In both instances, the observer has failed to take into account how set
> situations may cause delinquency. Most important, however, they may
> have failed to observe that these same factors, bad housing and comic
> books, affect a large proportion of our population without necessarily
> producing deviant behavior. Although most delinquency occurs in so-
> called slum areas where housing is poor, the relation has little direct con-
> nection with any theory of human behavior and must be discounted as
> an error in perception. Moreover, delinquency does occur in areas of
> good housing. Hence, if the same logic is used, this situation might be
> attributed to the adequacy of the housing situation. In studying deviant
> behavior, it is always necessary to consider whether similar influences are
> affecting nondeviants. Therefore, some theory of human behavior must
> be devised which will account for the differential effects if they exist.[8]

Deviance is not always the result of the same processes. The individual can become deviant because of something he is reacting to in his environmental situation or because of conflicts that exist in his psychic mechanism. The labeling can also be the result of political, economic, and religious factors.

Lofland states that there are two types of deviant acts, *defensive* and *adventurous*. The defensive deviant act is a response to a sense of either perceived or real threat from the environment or individuals. The deviant act is justified on these grounds. For example, a youngster in the inner city may feel threatened by a group or gang within his environment. He reacts to the threat by "attacking before being attacked," which results in his inflicting bodily injury on his real or imagined attacker. According to Lofland, the adventurous deviant act occurs because all mammals, including human beings, enjoy manageable fear, frustration, and anxiety. The typical and mundane features of human societies are the most important contributors to deviant action. The act is committed to relieve boredom, or in the case of a delinquent, as a reaction to a "dare" or a desire to impress the group. All deviant behavior is not necessarily detrimental, however, nor should it be completely expunged

[8] Clinard, *op. cit.*, p. 38.

by the society, the community, or the organization. Exceptions in social behavior are necessary for social evolution. If some individuals did not presume themselves to be different, to develop new ideas, and to persevere in behavior that was not accepted at one particular point in time, social change and new modes of behavior that enhance the quality of life would not result.[9]

Normative Bias

Norms then constitute the social criteria by which deviancy is identified. Each individual's normative structure conditions his or her perceptions and actions and all of us usually have biases regarding the nature of deviancy and its underlying causes. Regardless of the "rightness" or "wrongness" of such biases, failure to recognize them may endanger an open study of the problem of deviancy.

A personal examination of one's own value system is often a salutory first step in investigating the problems of human behavior, social control, and deviancy. Our own social values are seldom examined. They are more usually accepted without question as "givens." These "givens" often condition our acceptance or rejection of theory and ideas about deviant behavior. As a general rule, those ideas and theories which are perceived as being *intuitively* true fall within this personal normative (value) realm, and merely reflect our own biases. These biases are predicated on a host of pleasant and unpleasant social experiences, the cultural, social and psychological conditioning to which each of us, in a unique sense, is exposed.

The conflict between personal bias and the various schemes of explanation for criminal behavior poses problems for all students and in particular those intending a career in criminal justice. Criminal justice practitioners do not function as autonomous arbiters of value and conduct, nor should they, since to do so would represent the very worst variety of situational and personal tyranny. In any operational situation, the practitioner will be confronted with his own value and behavioral norms, the value and behavioral norms of the citizen(s) (clients) with whom he interacts, and the value and behavioral mandates of the jurisdiction he is representing. While substantial consensus may exist relative to a central core of criminal activity such as murder, rape, arson, and so on, the vast majority of conduct confronted by the criminal justice system falls outside this central core, and it is this realm of "lesser" behaviors which most frequently promotes conflict between practitioners and the public they serve. This is an especially serious problem at the police level, where officers are seldom allowed even the luxury of sufficient time in which to make complex judgments, but it is also a very real problem for anyone who aspires to make a positive contribution to resolving the serious delinquency problems in this society.

For all students and practitioners, then, the best approach to the study

[9] John Lofland, *Deviance and Identity* (Englewood Cliffs, N.J.: Prentice-Hall, Inc., 1969).

of juvenile delinquency will be at an intellectual level somewhat removed from intuitive considerations. While this will not free him from having to make personal and/or professional value and behavioral judgments, it is hoped that it will sensitize him to the full spectrum of theoretical (and value) positions not necessarily in congruence with his own, and help him to achieve an operational performance more appropriate to the real complexity of the problem.

CULTURAL CONSIDERATIONS

The cultural aspects of any society provide one of the basic frameworks in which deviant behavior must be studied. While the exact definition of culture is subject to a wide range of debate, there can be no doubt that every society develops and operates within a cultural context that shapes and controls values, social control, and the identification of deviancy. A survey of several hundred definitions of culture has led two researchers to conclude that:

> . . . the essential core of culture consists of traditional (i.e., historically derived and selected) ideas and especially their attached values; culture systems may, on one hand, be considered as products of action, on the other as conditioning influences on future action.[10]

Cultural development may be thought of as the process by which social response to the environment institutionalizes customs, norms of behavior, role tradition, moral law, and so on, and thereby lends significance to particular behavior, that is, legitimates, tolerates, or condemns them. The process may include the construction of a complex methodology, a history which lauds and glorifies prior acts of a certain nature or particular moral stance and a symbolic linkage with the past, all gathered into a network of artifacts, attitudes, and values that engender a unique way of viewing the physical world and reacting to it. Although *categories* of behavior may vary little from society to society in the elemental areas of life, cultural techniques even in these areas vary greatly. The noticeable social reticence of the English, the social volatility of some Southern European cultures, the differences maintained in physical distance during conversations among Asians as opposed to Westerners, eating and working habits, the way time itself is conceptualized and utilized—these are but a few of the more mundane social techniques which can be laid at the doorstep of culture. At a more substantial level (for example, cultural values relative to the sanctity of life, property, sexual practices, and so on), specific cultural institutions arise which are designed to inculcate the "rules" and to insure a high degree of compliance with them. Where mystical or religious considerations provide the basis of the "rules," more secular forms of control are often utilized

---

[10] A. L. Kroeber and Clyde Kluckhahn, "Culture: A Critical Review of Concepts and Definitions." *Papers of the Peabody Museum of Archaeology and Ethnology* (Cambridge, Mass.) Vol. 47, No. 1.

to insure this compliance. Whether identified as tribal taboos or criminal laws, it is within a cultural context that the identification of deviant behavior will occur, and it is culture that conditions the sanctions appropriate to deviants.

Ezra Park, the founder of the School of Human Ecology (1864-1944), perceived society as the natural adaptation of the human group to the environment with the natural emergence of primary functions such as protection, food gathering, and so on. Human society differs, however, from the adaptation of plants and animals to environment, in that, in addition to a response to purely biological forces, human society develops an institutional structure which results in a cultural context as well.

> There is a symbiotic (biologically interdependent) society based on competition and a *cultural* society based on communications and consensus. As a matter of fact the two societies are merely different aspects of one society, which, in the vicissitudes and changes to which they are subject, remain, nonetheless, in some sort of mutual dependence each upon the other. The cultural superstructure rests on the basis of the symbiotic substructure. . .[11] (Parenthetic material and emphasis added)

This emphasis on the practical or functional basis of culture has many adherents in contemporary anthropology. One scholar, studying the cultural patterns of the various Mediterranean tribes, has asserted that the elaborate code of family integrity, especially relating to the honor (virginity) of young women of the tribes, is functionally related to the fact that these nomadic tribes do not own the land upon which their herds graze nor do they have any real territorial integrity. As a result, these tribes have transferred the rather elaborate cultural values concerned with real property—well known in the American experience—to the only clear "property" each of these tribes possesses (and which can be traded in the free market): the reproductive capacity of their women. This reproductive capacity then becomes a resource to be guarded and protected through the development of a cultural system of honor and sanctions, until and unless suitable marriage negotiations have been completed.[12] Prostitutes, interestingly enough, do exist in these societies and fulfill an important function (besides the obvious), in that by their presence they provide a negative example to the ideal of virginity and reinforce the virginal ideal by providing living proof of "failure."

A recurring theme which runs throughout the fabric of most, if not all, societies, and which is exemplified in the preceding example of cultural development, is that often behavior which is functional to some members of the society, but which violates explicit cultural values, is tolerated as long as

---

[11] Robert Ezra Park, "Human Ecology," *American Journal of Sociology,* XL11, No. 1 (1936), p. 3.
[12] Jane Schneider, "Of Vigilance and Virgins: Honor, Shame and Access to Resources in Mediterranean Societies," in *Law and Welfare Studies in the Anthropology of Conflict,* Paul Bohannan, Ed. (New York: The National History Press, 1967).

the deviance occurs under "agreed upon" conditions. These "agreed upon" conditions constitute, of course, just another aspect of the same cultural situation. Such behavior may be tolerated precisely because it provides a reference point against which "right" behavior may be identified, contrasted, and rewarded. One has only to reflect upon the various homilies to which we were all exposed in childhood concerning the prohibitions of stealing, sexual promiscuity, drinking, and so on, and especially the vivid examples used to make the point, to see their importance as an aid in the socialization process.

Robert K. Merton has also observed that entire deviant substructures may form in societies where cultural values are not matched by social opportunity. He describes organized crime as a "sub-population where the cultural emphasis upon pecuniary success has been absorbed, but where there is little access to conventional and legitimate means for attaining such success;" that such activity represents "the triumph of amoral intelligence over morally prescribed failure."[13] Just how much delinquent behavior is the result of this process is a moot point, although some gang behavior may constitute a close parallel.

More importantly, it should be borne in mind that the cultural development of societies conditions both the nature of deviance, the priority of sanctions, and the conditions under which deviance is either ignored or condemned. To the extent that adolescence is merely a time of testing and experimentation with these cultural "boundaries," a certain level of deviance can be expected. It is the reaction to that deviance, as much as anything, which will determine whether or not serious deviance will continue into adulthood.

Institutional Lag

One of the problems that confronts all cultures is just how meaningful custom, tradition, norms, and laws are in terms of social realities. Paul Bohannan advises that the law, which "may be regarded as a custom that has been restated in order to make it amenable to the activities of legal institutions," is always out of phase with society;

> Indeed, the more highly developed the legal institutions, the greater the lack of phase, which not only results from the constant reorientation of the primary institutions, but which is magnified by the very dynamics of the legal institutions themselves.[14]

One of these dynamics is the social requirement, in most organized societies, that the judicial process exhibit some degree of constancy. Much of the Ameri-

---

[13] Robert K. Merton, *Social Theory and Social Structure* (New York: The Free Press, 1968), pp. 126–135. See also Chapter Six.

[14] Paul Bohannan, "The Differing Realms of the Law," in *Law and Welfare: Studies in the Anthropology of Conflict,* Paul Bohannan, Ed. (New York: The Natural History Press, 1967), pp. 43–56.

can system of jurisprudence rests on what is commonly described as the traditional model; that, is a reliance on prior court decisions (*stare decisis*), historical principle, and philosophy in rendering current legal decisions. In short, a reliance on the past to guide the present. Such a reliance should not be shortchanged, since at a minimum it decreases the probability of capricious judgments, and the consistency with which American law is applied has made it a proud accomplishment of our civilization. This is not to say, however, that such constancy does not also bring with it rather severe phase problems, and in the end it may promote the labeling as criminal, behavior which is not so clearly considered criminal by large factions of the general public. The current dilemma over the use and possession of marihuana is considered by some a traumatic but rather clear example of just such lag.

Social Control in the Primitive Setting

It has been tempting and often just a little arrogant for modern observers to describe primitive societies (preliterate, pretechnical) in simplistic terms wherein individual members of that society had only to avoid a few taboos and otherwise conform to a minimum of social expectations in order to insure their own well-being. In the extreme, primitive man was even denied the concession of having a unique personality of his own. Malinowski points out that the basic assumption about primitive societies has often been that primitive man was totally conditioned by and subject to the group, acting only out of group sentiments and instincts.[15] This view does not do justice to the complexities which exist in any human group. On the contrary, any society exhibits four primary dynamics. First, all societies are aligned and develop roles related to survival needs. Second, there is the requirement that some system of social control be in effect. Third, society requires a set of social procedures (means). And fourth, society requires some communicative system so that socialization and group continuity can be assured.[16]

The traditional method of analyzing social control in primitive settings has been to identify the customs present in the society in question and the physical and/or supernatural sanctions which were imposed when someone deviated from these customs. Of course, it has always been recognized that some customs were more binding than others. It cannot be assumed that primitive societies were unable to make subtle distinctions when it came to types of and responses to deviancy. Malinowski found, in his studies of the Trobriand Islanders, that a wide range of middle-range behavior was governed by a system of economic and social reciprocity, and was in many ways, a corollary to our present-day civil law.[17]

---

[15] B. Malinowski, *Crime and Custom in Savage Society* (Paterson, N.J.: Littlefield, Adams and Co., 1964), p. 3.
[16] Raymond Firth, *Elements of Social Organization* (Boston: Beacon Press, 1963), pp. 41–79.
[17] Malinowski, *op. cit.,* pp. 63–68.

This "civil law" was based on a system of mutual obligation, reinforced through tribal ritual, and was rewarded by economic reciprocity, respect, and appeal to personal vanity. The binding force of this law was the possibility of the breaking of the reciprocity contract, as well as the loss of face in the community through advertisement of social failure. Villagers often helped the process along by physical means such as beatings. Even simple social isolation, however, was more often than not more than sufficient for the task. Thus, while it cannot be doubted that appeals to supernatural powers played a major role in primitive social control, in the main it seems that primitive man was also quite the pragmatist, and given the conditions under which he lived (a virtual total dependence upon his social group for physical survival), such pragmatism was thoroughly justified.

How social control was effected in primitive societies revolves around two primary characteristics of these societies; (1) the extensive network of kinship and primary relationships, and (2) the general lack of a centralized authority empowered by the social body to use coercive force on behalf of the society in response to deviancy. In other words, deviancy was a family matter, involving family responsibility and reaction even though such reaction was often "passed" upon by tribal leaders.

Kinship and Primary Relations

The essence of any primitive existence is the establishment of an extensive network of kinship and face-to-face personal (primary) relationships, as opposed to the host of impersonal and specialized social interactions (secondary relationships), which have become the hallmark of modern societies. Such relationships are natural where communities are isolated or restricted, where great mutual interdependence is necessary in order to survive, and where mobility opportunities are severely restricted. Much of the power of social control is vested in the power of these primary and kin relationships. Wrongs of the individual are often deemed to be wrongs of the kin group, and retaliation or demands for monetary recompense often become a collective responsibility of the group or even the tribe itself. Thus, while in a primitive setting deviant behavior can be viewed as a private matter—as opposed to an offense against the state—to be settled in one manner or another between those concerned, more often than not deviant behavior involves a substantial degree of group interaction as well.

What effect do these characteristics have on the identification of deviance and the quality (or consistency) of justice in primitive society? There can be little doubt that both depend upon situation, status of offender, negotiation, and many of the elements that are more easily recognized in a modern society. Lucy Mair found that one of the primary functions of the kin group was tribal survival. A monetary value was often placed on the loss of a life so that the tribe could receive some kind of compensation.[18]

[18] Lucy Mair, *Primitive Government* (Baltimore: Penguin Books, 1970).

> Among the Nuers, the killing of one tribal member by an outsider is just call for an equal response by members of the injured tribe, but as often, compensation is payable, in cattle, for the loss.[19]
>
> . . . the deadliest of Nuer weapons, the spear, is not used against close neighbors; if the fight is between two men of the same village or cattle camp, they use clubs, and bystanders will do what they can to separate them. (In reference to a dispute over adulterous conduct.)[20]

Again, even the breaking of a major tribal rule does not always automatically bring disaster to the offender. Malinowski describes the obligation of *talion* (the obligation to reciprocate, in kind), relative to a homicide in Melanesia as:

> . . . obligatory only in cases of a male adult of rank or importance; and even then it is considered superfluous when the deceased had met his fate for a fault clearly his own.[21]

Even when taboos are involved, punishment is dependent upon circumstance. Malinowski describes the suicide of a 16-year old boy who had violated the taboo against exogamy; in this case, specifically, sexual intercourse with his maternal cousin. Unfortunately for the boy, his misdeeds had been advertised throughout the community.

> . . . if you were to inquire . . . you would find that all statements confirm the axiom, that the natives show horror at the idea of violating the rules of exogamy and that . . . sores, disease and even death might follow clan incest.
>
> When it comes to the application of morality and ideal to real life, however, things take on a different complexion . . . I found out that the breach of exogamy—as regards intercourse—is by no means a rare occurrence, and public opinion is lenient, though decidedly hypocritical. If the affair is carried on sub rosa with a certain amount of decorum, and if no one in particular stirs up trouble, public opinion will gossip, but not demand any harsh punishment. If, on the contrary, scandal breaks out, everyone turns against the guilty pair and by ostracism and insults one or the other may be driven to suicide.[22]

The fact that suicide was often resorted to by the offenders is ample testimony to the impact of group rejection, especially where ostracism means total social isolation. The above examples also tend to confirm that social control among the "primitives" experiences the same value lag already discussed.

---

[19] *Ibid.,* pp. 35–38
[20] *Ibid.,* pp. 35–38.
[21] Malinowski, *op. cit.,* p. 118.
[22] *Ibid.,* pp. 77–81.

Central Authority

Where intense kinship ties exist and where deviance is privatized to a considerable extent, central authority is usually lacking in any real sense, and may serve only in a mediating role. It is probable that the former does not "cause" the latter, but that after the formation of a formal governing body, internal control by the state becomes the next step. E. E. Schattschneider maintains that government and the centralized authority is a reaction by a society to external forces which are perceived by society's members to constitute a threat to its continued existence, and that government is thereby best described as "a shelter organization shielding the community within."[23] In such a situation, which always involves questions of population and territory, community members willingly promote and establish a central governing structure, in the process giving up individual or group prerogatives in the greater cause of community survival. It is only after the establishment of a governing structure that deviant behavior comes to be defined as crime.

> In principle, crimes are acts that are considered by those in authority to be sufficiently inimical to the general welfare as to warrant official interdiction and punishment.[24]

More specifically:

> A crime is any act or omission prohibited by public law for the protection of the public and made punishable by the state in a judicial proceeding in its own name.[25]

These definitions certainly do not describe primitive society, yet authority structures *do* exist in these collectives and are used in resolving conflict. It is the *level* of centralized authority, power, and structural sophistication, coupled with the retention of punitive prerogatives by the people, that distinguishes primitive authority structures from those of the modern state. Even in primitive societies, the variations are great and no simple definitions are possible. Among the Kikuyus, in property disputes, kin group elders from both sides gather and negotiate the problem. Having reached a decision, they *impose* their will on both parties.[26] Among the Nkole and the Ganda tribes, a recognized and powerful ruler exists, having the power of life and death over his subjects. Neverthe-

---

[23] E. E. Schattschneider, *Two Hundred Million Americans in Search of a Government* (New York: Holt, Rinehart and Winston, Inc., 1969), p. 36.

[24] Albert Morris, "The Concept of Crime," in *Criminology*, Clyde B. Vedder, Samuel Koenig, and Robert E. Clark, Eds. (New York: The Dryden Press, 1955), p. 21.

[25] William L. Marshall and William L. Clark, "The Legal Definitions of Crime and Criminal," in *The Sociology of Crime and Delinquency*, Marvin E. Wolfgang, Leonard Savitz and Norman Johnston, Eds. (New York: John Wiley and Sons, Inc., 1962), p. 14.

[26] Mair, *op. cit.*, pp. 56–57.

less, the rights of blood revenge remain intact among individuals and families within these tribes.[27] Both the Kikuyu and the Kamba people have a procedure which has been described as "organized lynching."[28] This is a procedure in which a community member, whose presence has become so extremely offensive as to be intolerable (through such behavior as exercising witchcraft, nonpayment of large debts, and so on), is publicly lynched by those against whom the offense has been committed. This lynching requires a positive vote by the village elders in support of the proposed action, as well as the consent of the offender's nearest relative. Other societies have leaders and/or consultative bodies of elders who pass clear judgments and have the ability to fix fines and enforce their judgments. Some African societies have definitive legal procedures and a highly formal quality in the way some forms of deviance are sanctioned.

This very abbreviated survey of social control in the primitive setting has strongly suggested that there has never been a simple formula for deviance and its control, that definitions and responses have never been universally applied nor are they particularly consistent. Ideally, a consideration of the primitive situation has also revealed that the same dynamics that condition contemporary identification and response to deviance have been essentially consistent in the development of human society, although the range of deviancy and the organization for control have changed rather drastically in the modern setting. The following section will consider some of these changes.

MODERN SOCIETY AND SOCIAL CONTROL

Major Characteristics

Modern society is perhaps best described in a comparative manner by contrasting it with the primitive setting we have already discussed. Although primitive societies exhibit some variation in the identification of types of deviance and in the development and application of social techniques to repress it, in the main the primitive existence is highly integrated if for no other reason than the brutal imperative to survive. In addition, only so many kinds of deviancy are possible; mobility is virtually nil in most cases, and nonconformity does not generally offer the success opportunities in a primitive social setting that may be perceived in a highly mobile modern society. Relatively, then, a clearer moral consensus *does* exist in primitive societies, and is maintained consistent with the conditions which promote primitiveness. Modern society has several major characteristics, however, which demand new labels and definitions of deviant behavior and the development of a state organization for control of that behavior.

Technology. The almost geometric growth of knowledge in the past century has drastically changed the face of the world. As knowledge increases, so do the

[27] *Ibid.,* p. 59.
[28] *Ibid.,* pp. 59–60.

action alternatives available to all citizens—law abiding and criminal alike. New variations of crime are constantly being discovered and exploited. New and highly sophisticated techniques to commit the more traditional crimes are employed. Communications and transportation improvements provide boundless opportunity for interstate and international exploitation. Profit potential has increased while deterrent techniques seem to have fallen behind.

Multiple Social Groupings. Differentiation is the hallmark of a modern society. From relatively few occupations and functions (often based purely on sexual identification or physical strength), modern man has developed literally thousands of highly specialized occupations. Intricate status and role hierarchies have formed, and are constantly being reformed around this system of specialties, any one of which can be elevated to critical social importance and power depending upon internal and external events. The need for coordination, control, planning, and routinization has accompanied this development, thus the emergence of a variety of institutions which provide—for want of a better description—a constant input of standardized human bodies and human minds, educated and socialized to "fit" into this complex and highly interdependent life structure with a minimum of personal difficulty and system dysfunction. Such is the essence of the socialization process.

Modern society and its structural components may be compared to the inner workings of a very intricate clock. Seldom, however, does society "keep time" in a very efficient or effective manner. Social classes develop, each with its own ideas of the proper scheme of things; occupational groupings combine to maximize their own particular interests; power seekers find in the social structure a free-wheeling opportunity to indulge their ambitions; and in general, human ingenuity knows no bounds. In the end, more citizens are employed in coordinating, planning, overseeing, and scrutinizing than are engaged in goods-producing activity. Good or bad, this activity seems to be necessary, and the process is nowhere near complete. Furthermore, as specialization proliferates, so does regulation. A certain portion of that regulation always falls under the umbrella of the criminal law. As a result, modern man as an individual has neither the physical resources nor the basic information necessary to cope with current criminal activity, and since internal stability is a primary function of any organized society, a specialized institutional structure has emerged for the purpose of insuring social order and enforcing the criminal law.

Political/Structural/Territorial Integrity. All modern societies reflect a major tendency to establish political, structural, and territorial boundaries. In fact, the major function of government is to do just that. These boundaries, in turn, reflect the normative systems we have already discussed. The more boundaries one creates, however, the more deviance one creates. Thus, regardless of how necessary those boundaries may be, the boundary-making propensity impacts inevitably at the criminal justice level and the increased identification of deviants. As a society we have made woefully little progress in determining at what point organization, specialization, and boundary-making itself becomes dysfunctional to a full and satisfying human experience, preferring instead a headlong rush into increased complexities.

Organization for the Control of Criminal Deviance. The characteristics of modern society pose a dilemma. It is difficult to define the exact parameters of behavior considered sufficiently threatening to society so that criminal behavior can be easily defined and labeled. It is difficult to determine the exact social consequences that may accrue to particular deviant acts. Where complex systems have been developed, such as the American criminal justice system, there is still no assurance that the systems will be well coordinated and effective. In the United States, the legislature defines deviance and provides resources, the executive enforces social order, and the judiciary is concerned with the proper application of deviancy labels and the disposition of those so labeled. Although each serves the same client—the public—each has special and unique goals and organizational tensions. Each experiences a different intensity of public exposure and may be reactive to particular public pressure and trends. The result may be inappropriate laws, archaic judgments, over- or underenforcement, inappropriate treatment of the offender; in short, actions which may even promote the criminal deviance that the system is designed to deter. Even at this late date, primary questions concerned with the proper goals of the criminal justice system remain to be systematically explored, as well as the appropriate techniques to be utilized in achieving these goals. This is at least partly traceable to an ambivalence on the part of the general public relative to punishment, treatment, toleration levels of criminal activity, and the level of resources to be made available to the criminal justice system. The multiplicity of jurisdictions in this country—around 40,000 in all—each with its own political goals and realities, results in severe fragmentation of effort, which only compounds the problem.

THE CATEGORIZATION OF DEVIANCE

One of the most basic social techniques is the categorization process, during which labels are applied to things, groups of activity, people, and every variety of phenomena. By labeling, we ascribe characteristics, and having assumed the existence of these characteristics, we are able to react to people, activities, and things in ways we deem to be appropriate to our continued social viability. Labels connoting deviance—criminal, addict, homosexual, felon, "doper," pervert, delinquent—are bandied about both within and outside the criminal justice system, for a variety of good and bad reasons. Often these labels are used unthinkingly, with very little insight into the way in which they condition social interaction, both for the person so labeled and the person applying the label. For example, an individual labeled a "criminal" because of a conviction for a drug offense during his college days may find that future employers, neighbors, and professional associates may not make any fine distinctions as to just how much of a "criminal" that person really is, preferring to ascribe, instead, the most negative potentialities imaginable to his future conduct. This constricts the possibility for totally successful social interaction among the parties concerned.

Social interaction can become so constrained by the use and abuse of deviancy labels, that few action alternatives *except* more deviancy may be perceived as being available to the person (or group) so labeled. Richard Quinney has constructed a theoretical model of crime causation in which the labeling process plays a major part:

> During experiences shared by the criminal definers and the criminally defined, personal action patterns develop among the criminally defined because they are so defined . . . furthermore, those who have been defined as criminal begin to conceive of themselves as criminal.[29]

Labels are not, of course, always innocently applied. From a social-psychological standpoint, social interaction involves an assessment by all parties of the interaction of the social "investments" each brings to the exchange.[30] These investments may include age, sex, race, occupational expertise, social status, and reputation; and the application of labels can clearly alter the nature of the social exchange that takes place. Obviously, the same applies to group categorizations. Being labeled a "nigger" and conceiving of oneself in that context can go a long way toward the maintenance of a superior/inferior social relationship.

While labels may sometimes constitute a necessary device, especially when time does not allow for finer differentiations, the dangers in using them are infinite, and extreme care should be exercised. There are several major categories of labels which bear further discussion.

Legal Deviance

In modern societies, law becomes exceedingly complex, and the number of individuals identified and convicted of violating the civil or criminal law is almost directly related to the amount of emphasis government and the public are willing to place on detection and prosecution. Conviction of any single offense, however, connotes a very limited and precise form of social deviance, and there is no general principle in jurisprudence demanding the assumption that conviction for one criminal offense presumes a *field* of deviant propensities. Criminal justice practitioners and the public often fail to take note of this. An exception is the habitual-offender statutes which most jurisdictions have enacted. This legal device, however, is not applied until a series of serious criminal offenses has occurred. Even one offense is often more than sufficient for the public to assume future criminal propensities. The result:

[29] Quinney, *op. cit.,* p. 21.
[30] See, for example, George Homann, *Social Behavior: Its Elementary Forms* (New York: Harcourt, Brace and World, Inc., 1961).

Former offenders (including delinquents) face restrictions in 350 different occupations, ranging from fortune telling to junk dealing to practicing
medicine and law.[31]

Further, where serious legal deviance coincides with concepts of moral deviance,
the assumption of future criminal acts is intensified.

Moral Deviance

We have already spoken of the problem of moral deviance and the impact
our value systems have on our lives and the judgments we make. In the sphere
of interpersonal relations, much of the moral consensus which typified our
colonial development is now diffused, yet a central core of laws in this society
is a direct reflection of moral codes establishing the bounds of proper action
relative to the use of force, property rights, sexual conduct, and so on. Legal
violations in these and other areas can and do, therefore, often call up labels
of moral deviance as well as legal. Social sanctions include exclusion from certain
occupations and social exclusion from various segments of the community. At
what point does a police officer's or a lawyer's conduct indicate that he is morally
unfit to practice his occupation? Sexual proclivities of public school teachers,
the "unethical" activities of elected public officials, the commonly assumed
immoral tendencies of various subcultural groups within this society—all raise
the specter of the moral labeling process. Moral labeling is easy to do and difficult to refute. Morality is usually based on articles of faith, thus the process of
moral labeling is at once self-sufficient and slightly self-serving: self-serving in
that it assumes a position of moral superiority and capacity by the person or
group doing the labeling; self-sufficient in that the premises upon which the
judgments are made are not really open to examination or proof. Again, the
action guide should be extreme caution.

Biological Deviance

A substantial amount of deviant activity doubtlessly occurs because of
mental incompetence and a host of physical disabilities which render the personality structure incomplete. These same incapacities also impact on the
individual's ability to cope with social change and stress, and may even pre-
dispose the individual to illegal action. Biological deviance does not automatically equate with either moral or legal deviance, however, and the application
of either of those labels may limit whatever minimal level of social efficiency
has been achieved by such individuals. American society in general has made
considerable strides in recognizing concepts of intent and capacity in judging
deviancy from a legal standpoint, although the question of legal insanity is
still in a state of flux.

---

[31] *Juvenile Justice Digest,* Vol. 1, No. 3 (June 1973), p. 10.

Normative Deviance

Normative deviance is essentially being cast in the role of an "outsider." Thus, one can be normatively deviant if he performs certain social acts in other than the "accepted" way. In short, one group's preferred life style is another group's idea of deviance. In the end, how the dilemma is resolved may hinge on which group exercises social power. More often than not, normative deviance does little except impede social interaction. Where normative deviance is seen to threaten dominant social groups, however, such deviance can become the subject of legal action by being transferred to the realm of criminality. An example of this concerns the way native Americans greeted the influx of immigrants to this country in the eighteenth and nineteenth centuries. At a minimum, these outsiders had to be "resocialized" to a work ethic; at the extreme they were seen as an uncivilized "horde," requiring close supervision and control. Vagrancy, loitering and drunk laws, and even Prohibition may be viewed, in part, as a dominant group response to perceived normative deviance.

Normative deviance and dominant group reaction to such deviance may be of special importance to societies such as America, where a variety of cultural groups have combined to form a new society. The Melting Pot theory of cultural assimilation asserts that each of the ethnic groups coming into this society combines and unites with the others to form a unique and new "American" identity. This theory may be mostly myth, and its validity has been increasingly called into question. Glazer and Moynihan have observed that:

> . . . the adoption of a totally new ethnic identity by dropping whatever one is to become simply American, is inhibited by strong elements in the social structure of the United States. It is inhibited by a subtle system of identifying, which ranges from brutal discrimination and prejudice to merely naming.[32]

Michael Novak, writing about ethnic groups coming to this country from Eastern Europe, flatly asserts that ethnic identity is on the rise in this country and will impact on the future goals and structure of this society.[33] Hawkins and Lorinskas have compiled a convincing series of empirical studies which strongly suggest that a variety of "ethnics" have not been totally assimilated and do manifest distinctive political preferences and forms.[34] What has all of this to do with deviant behavior? Simply, that to the extent unique cultural elements are actually present in this country, either in or out of power in any specific social situation, a social milieu is created in which normative conflict is the

[32] Nathan Glazer and Daniel Moynihan, *Beyond the Melting Pot* (Cambridge, Mass.: The MIT Press, 1970), Preface p. xxxiii.
[33] Michael Novak, *The Rise of the Unmeltable Ethnics* (New York: Macmillan Publishing Co., Inc., 1971).
[34] Brett W. Hawkins and Robert A. Lorinskas, Eds., *The Ethnic Factor in American Politics* (Columbus, Ohio: Charles E. Merrill Publishing Co., 1970).

status quo. This conflict may be at least as serious as the normative conflict which exists between the various social classes. Considerations of normative deviancy will thereby condition what acts are identified as criminal and what citizens have the greater probability of being selected into the criminal justice process; in addition, cultural antecedents will have to be considered as another class of variables in explaining why such acts were committed.

JUVENILE DELINQUENCY AS A FORM OF DEVIANT BEHAVIOR

Thus far we have discussed in some detail the concept of deviancy, its social and cultural origins, and some specific categories of deviance. Juvenile delinquency, a specific form of deviance, is a social and cultural innovation of relatively recent vintage. This section will examine the historical development of this innovation in an American context.

History

Cultural factors can play a part in explaining juvenile delinquency and crime because in most instances the culture determines what will be considered crime as well as how the child will be viewed and handled. In developing a definitive concept of juvenile delinquency, Gibbens and Ahrenfeldt cite three stages of cultural change. The first stage is the tribal culture, which has little delinquency. In this setting, crime is defined in terms of adult behavior. The norms of the community control most delinquency. In some cases, as in Laos, where juveniles are treated harshly, adults are reluctant to report delinquent acts for fear of severe punishment for the youngster and therefore much of the difficulty is handled within the local neighborhood. The second stage of cultural change relates to the rapidly developing countries of Africa and the East, where urbanization is disrupting the stability of the family. This also took place in the United States and England when rapid industrialization precipitated the growth of large urban centers. It is during this stage that separate juvenile laws usually originate. In the third stage, a preventive approach becomes more prevalent and the definitions of delinquency become ambiguous. In addition to juvenile law, which originates in the second stage, great emphasis is placed on determining the psychological and sociological factors that contribute to crime causation. The countries of Western Europe and the United States would be considered as being in this stage at present.[35]

Much of American history relating to crime and delinquency is tied to the English judicial system. No distinction was made between adult crime and juvenile delinquency in either early English or American history. If the young-

[35]T. C. N. Gibbens and R. H. Ahrenfeldt, *Cultural Factors in Delinquency* (London: J. B. Lippincott Co., 1966), p. 21.

ster was involved in the commission of a criminal act, he was tried in an adult court and was usually subjected to the same criteria for processing and determining guilt. There were "young criminals," but no "delinquent children." As a result of greater urbanization and the emerging behavioral sciences, however, the public became increasingly aware that youngsters should not be treated like adult offenders or incarcerated with them because of the *contamination* effect and the child's lack of life experiences and lack of maturity.[36]

The first juvenile court was established in 1899 in Cook County, Illinois. The social conditions and the social conscience of the people at that time provided a great impetus for the development of the court and the treating of children in a manner different from that of adults.

> The juvenile court, then, was born in an era of reform and it spread with amazing speed. The conception of the delinquent as a "wayward child" first specifically came to life in April 1899 when the Illinois Legislature passed the Juvenile Court Act creating the first state-wide court especially for children. It did not include a new court; it did include most of the features that have since come to distinguish the juvenile court. The original act and amendments to it that shortly followed brought together under one jurisdiction cases of dependency, neglect, and delinquency—the last comprehending incorrigibles and children threatened by immoral associations as well as criminal law breakers. Hearings were to be informal and nonpublic, records confidential, children detained apart from adults, a probation staff appointed. In short, children were not to be treated as criminals nor dealt with by the process used for criminals. A new vocabulary symbolized the new order: Petition instead of complaint, summons instead of warrant, initial hearing instead of arraignment, finding of involvement instead of conviction, disposition instead of sentence. The physical surroundings were important, too: They should seem less imposing than a courtroom with the judge at a desk or table instead of behind a bench, fatherly and sympathetic while still authoritative and sobering. The goals were to investigate, diagnose, and prescribe treatment, not to adjudicate guilt or fix blame. The individual's background was more important than the facts of a given incident, specific conduct relevant more as symptomatic of a need for the court to bring its helping powers to bear than as prerequisite to exercise of jurisdiction. Lawyers were unnecesary—adversary tactics were out of place for the mutual aim of all was not to contest or object, but to determine the treatment plan best for the child. That plan was to be devised by the increasingly popular psychologists and psychiatrists: delinquency was thought of almost as a disease to be diagnosed by specialists with the patient kindly but firmly diagnosed.[37]

[36]Robert G. Caldwell, "The Juvenile Court: Its Development and Some Major Problems," in *Juvenile Delinquency, A Book of Readings,* Rose Giallombardo, Ed. (New York: John Wiley & Sons, Inc., 1966), p. 356.

[37]*Task Force Report: Juvenile Delinquency and Youth Crime, Report on Juvenile Justice and Consultants Papers,* The President's Commission on Law Enforcement and Administration of Justice (Washington, D.C.: Government Printing Office, 1967).

The juvenile court has since become *the* primary judicial agency for dealing with juvenile delinquency. Even though the juvenile court cannot be thought of apart from the rest of the criminal justice system, it nevertheless plays the major role in processing, handling, and treating the juvenile offender. In the spirit of the above quotation, the concept of the juvenile court and the handling of youngsters was taken from the English concept of the role of the king acting as the parent when no parents existed to protect the rights of the child. The concept is better known as *parens patriae.*

> Parens Patriae, the state substituting for the king, invested the juvenile court with the power to act as parent for the child. The judge was to assume the fatherly role, protecting the juvenile in order to cure and save him. The juvenile court withheld from the child a procedure of safeguards granted to adults because it viewed him as having a right to custody rather than a right to liberty and juvenile proceedings were civil not criminal.[38]

Under this spirit, the American courts perpetuated the concept of *parens patriae,* or the court acting in the best interests of the child. Dispositions made are theoretically considered to be in the best interests of the child as well as the community. The child is found delinquent, but not criminal, and is therefore incapable of committing a crime in the conventional sense.

The Term Delinquent Is Ambiguous

Bloch and Flynn discuss delinquency and mention that even though the development of the juvenile court system, which by the year 1941 existed in every state of the Union, did much to protect the rights of the child and extract him from the domain of adult criminality, the term *delinquent* itself still remained ambiguous, with varying connotations and definitions depending upon the legal jurisdiction and the community in which the child lived. There is both a *legal* and a *social* definition of delinquency. To be legally delinquent, the youngster must have violated a statute of some governmental jurisdiction. Many of these statutes, however, involve moral judgments, such as incorrigibility and willful disobedience. Even though there is much more consistency and objectivity today in defining juvenile delinquency, many differences still exist in the way children are handled in various jurisdictions and the way they are treated by the agencies within a community. As for the social definition of delinquency, the ramifications can be even more devastating than the legal ones. For example, the child may be barred from certain groups, may be labeled delinquent, and may thus be considered unacceptable in some circles. He may elicit disapproval from the community and be forced to associate with groups and persons who are less conducive to the transmitting of socially acceptable norms. Because of

---

[38] C. E. Reasons, "Gault: Procedural Change and Substantive Effort," *Crime and Delinquency,* Vol. 16, No. 2 (April 1970).

the ambiguousness of the term *delinquent,* it has come to mean all things to all men. A quick perusal of various state statutes shows that delinquency can encompass almost any type of youthful deviant behavior. Even a youngster who has not come in formal contact with courts, the police, or the social agencies, but is merely considered "different" by his community, can also be labeled delinquent. The economic status of the youngster as well as other factors can affect the way he is handled in the criminal justice system and viewed by the community.

> . . . whether a child becomes a delinquent or not will frequently depend upon the general attitudes of the community toward children and families with certain behavioral problems, upon the character of the social agencies in the community, and more specifically, upon the community's policies of referral for such children. Oftentimes other factors are involved in the handling of delinquents. For example, a child whose deeply disturbed emotional state manifests itself in chronic physical assaults may be taken by his middle-class parents to a child psychiatrist or possibly to a boarding school. The same emotional state in a slum child may result in his being brought summarily to the children's court. While the first child scarcely ever figures as a statistic in our compilation of data on delinquency, the second may account for a prominent part of such data.[39]

Because of such factors as economics and the quantity and quality of community service agencies, some youngsters are stigmatized with the label of delinquency. This of course can have negative ramifications for the youngster.

> The judgment against a youth that he is delinquent has a serious reflection upon his character and habit. The stain against him is not removed merely because the statute says no judgment in this particular proceeding shall be deemed a conviction of crime or so considered. The stigma of conviction will reflect upon him for life. It hurts his self-respect. It may at some inopportune, unfortunate moment rise to destroy his opportunity for advancement and blast his ambition to build up a character and reputation entitling him to the esteem and respect of his fellow men.[40]

Lack of appropriate and adequate community resources and indiscriminate labeling and ensuing stigmatization can be obstacles to effectively treating, preventing, and controlling delinquency.

> While the court may see its intervention as helpful and rehabilitative, prospective employers, for example, tend to view less benignly the fact

[39] Herbert A. Bloch and Frank T. Flynn, *Delinquency* (New York: Random House, Inc., 1956), p. 42.
[40] *Commonwealth* v. *Fisher,* 213 Pa 48 (1905), 85, 87.

the youth "has a record." The schools may view with suspicion the young-ster who has been pronounced delinquent. Further, it is important to draw the distinction between engaging in one delinquent act and the repetitive commission of delinquent acts. Many young people may engage in one or two delinquent acts as a relatively normal part of their adoles-cence. Occasional and minor delinquency need not presage a delinquent career. To funnel such youth into the formal juvenile justice and correc-tional system may have the unfortunate and unnecessary consequence of contributing to the development of a career in delinquency.[41]

The orientation of the agencies of the criminal justice system is also an important factor in effectively dealing with the problem of juvenile delinquency. At present some courts take a social orientation to handling the offender, while other courts are more legalistic in their approach.

The original intent and philosophy of the court was social in nature; that is, the child was to be treated rather than convicted and provided assistance and guidance rather than punished. Many times, however, court personnel as well as others within the criminal justice system did not abide by the *spirit* under which the social agency orientation was originally established. They misused their power under the guise of "helping" and made subjective judg-ments which had little legal basis and often infringed upon the child's civil rights. Because of recent U.S. Supreme Court decisions, many courts and agen-cies are taking a more legal orientation when handling youngsters. The process is growing increasingly similar to that used with adults. Even though the social agency orientation and philosophy is ideally the best approach, the abuses that have taken place have precipitated the more legalistic emphasis that exists today. The answer to the dilemma of which orientation the court and related agencies should adhere to is probably somewhere in the middle, with an empha-sis on the social "ideal" of treating the delinquent while affording him legal safeguards so that his civil liberties can be guaranteed.[42]

SUMMARY

This chapter has focused on the concept of deviancy, a concept which finds its major origins in a social and cultural context. Juvenile delinquency, and its many variables, was identified as a special subcategory of deviant behavior.

Thus far, however, this chapter has not discussed the objective extent of the juvenile delinquency problem itself. By almost any standard, it is serious and extensive. In terms of an index of *serious* crime (see Table 1), the increase in arrests of offenders under 18 has increased drastically. In 1974 alone the

[41] *Annual Report of Federal Activities,* (Washington, D.C.: U.S. Department of Health, Education, and Welfare, Social and Rehabilitation Service, Youth Development and Delin-quency Prevention Administration, 1971), p. 5.
[42] H. Warren Dunham, "The Juvenile Court: Contradictory Orientations in Processing Offenders," in Giallombardo, *op. cit.,* pp. 337–54.

TABLE 1. 1974 Arrest Rates for Persons Under Age 18 for Crime Index Offenses

Offense Charged	Percentage of Arrests of Persons Under Age 18	Increase 1960-1974 (Percent)
Murder	5.3	224
Aggravated assault	10.5	211
Forcible rape	10.1	147
Robbery	17.8	307
Burglary	34.3	139
Larceny-theft	37.4	166
Motor vehicle theft	35.3	33

SOURCE: Uniform Crime Reports for 1974 (Federal Bureau of Investigation).

police reported taking into custody over 1,700,000 youths under 18, of which over 800,000 were officially referred to the juvenile court. In this same year 27 percent of arrests for any offense reported under the Uniform Crime Reporting System were of persons under 18.[43] The period 1969-1974 saw an increase in arrests of males under 18 by 35 percent. Arrests of females under 18, however, increased by 68 percent during these same years.[44] The actual increase in the number of individuals in the U.S. population does not justify these increases based on growth alone. From 1960 to 1974 the actual number of citizens under 18 increased from 64,202,000 to 69,689,000, less than a 10 percent increase.[45]

Even statistics such as these, however, probably fall far short of specifying the real nature and extent of juvenile delinquency in this society, and it is difficult to be more precise because of the imperfections in statistical technique to say nothing about that whole spectrum of delinquency which is never reported or officially reacted to by criminal justice agencies.

> The first requirement generally stated for a system of criminal statistics is to know the amount and extent of crime, and the number and kinds of criminals. Crimes can be accounted for only through those special agencies set up to enforce criminal law. Thus has come the general axiom that crimes can be counted best in terms of the known offenses reported to police agencies. Obviously, no one will ever know actually how many criminal offenses are committed. The number and extent of unknown offenses may be a subject of speculation, but not of measurement.[46]

An extensive presentation of elaborate statistics does little to solve the problem of juvenile delinquency at any rate, and is certainly secondary to an under-

[43] Clarence M. Kelly, Uniform Crime Report, 1974 (Washington, D.C.: U.S. Government Printing Office 1975), pp. 45, 177.
[44] *Ibid.,* p. 45.
[45] U.S. Census, Characteristics of the Population, Vol. 1, Part 1 (Washington, D.C.: U.S. Government Printing Office), pp. 1-287.
[46] R. H. Beatie, "Problems of Criminal Statistics in the United States," *The Journal of Criminal Law, Criminology, and Police Science,* 46, No. 2 (July 1955), 178.

standing of the many variables which impact on and condition the behavior itself, and relate to delinquency causation, prevention, control, and treatment. The following chapters address these complex issues.

QUESTIONS AND PROJECTS

Essay Questions

1. How can labeling be avoided when working with juveniles?

2. How much "deviance" should be allowed in a society?

3. Why do most persons conform even though it is relatively easy to get away with deviant behavior?

4. Why is there a need for a juvenile court?

5. Explain why the concept of juvenile delinquency is variable in nature.

Projects

1. Develop a juvenile court model that incorporates both the social and the legal orientation to the delinquent youngster.

2. Develop a plan for realistically and objectively gathering accurate statistics on the amount and kind of juvenile delinquency in your community.

3. Develop a list of the legal and social criteria that are usually used when labeling a youngster "delinquent."

chapter 2

Theories of Delinquency Causation

This chapter will discuss the many aspects of criminology that are referred to as *theories of causation*. It is sometimes assumed that criminology embodies one specific set of principles and codified knowledge when in fact it includes a wide variety of criminological thought as well as contributing disciplines. Because of the complex nature of the delinquency phenomenon, no single theory exists that can explain all crime and delinquency, nor can one single cause of delinquency be specifically determined and applied in all cases. Because of the varied nature of causation factors and the complexity of the problem, it will be necessary to examine a variety of explanations and schools of thought in relation to delinquency causation. The reader will be exposed to a wide range of views taken mostly from the fields of psychology and sociology.

Before the last half of the nineteenth century, little scientific research was done to investigate the many factors that contribute to delinquency and crime. Most attempts at criminological explanation took the form of moralistic pronouncements or unscientific personal generalizations. Not until the end of the nineteenth century did scientific criminological inquiry begin to emerge in this country. With the onset of the discipline of sociology, academic courses that dealt with crime and criminality began to appear. Even at the present time the major discipline concerned with criminality and delinquency is the field of sociology, although in the latter part of the nineteenth century, psychology, psychiatry, and to a lesser degree, other related disciplines became more concerned with the problem and interested in its causation, control, prevention, and treatment.[1]

---

[1] Donald R. Cressey, "Crime," in *Contemporary Social Problems,* Robert K. Merton and Robert A. Nisbet, Eds. (New York: Harcourt, Brace and World, Inc., 1966), p. 160.

Because of the variety of disciplines studying criminology, there are many different and often opposing philosophies regarding delinquency and crime. To help clarify the diffferent orientations, we shall discuss briefly the two major schools of criminological thought and the orientation that each takes when viewing the criminal offender. These two schools of thought, which give the *classical* and the *positive* views of criminology, provide the basis for past and contemporary criminological assumptions and principles of delinquency and criminality.

Classical and Positive Criminology

The differences in the theoretical orientation of the classical and positive schools of thought have implications for the way offenders are perceived and "treated."

The *classical* school of thought, developed by Cesare Beccaria, an Italian nobleman (1738-1794), conceived of man as a free agent, pursuing hedonistic aims, and able to rationally decide on all or most courses of action.[2]

The offender was viewed as possessing free will and being no different from the nonoffender except that he "willed" to commit the crime. As a natural consequence of this philosophy punishment was expected to be harsh and immediate so that the offender would "unwill" to commit future crimes. The offender's mental makeup, background and extenuating circumstances were irrelevant.[3]

Because the offender was viewed as being very rational, the pleasure–pain principle was invoked as the major method of dealing with him. The pleasure-pain principle proposed that if the punishment for the particular act produced negative consequences that were more severe than the pleasures derived from committing the act, the potential offender would be discouraged from being deviant. The offender was presumed to be rational enough and have enough "good sense" to choose right from wrong since most of his behavior was supposedly guided by his desire to seek pleasure and to avoid pain. If the punishment produced enough pain, then the potential offender would decide not to become involved in unlawful behavior. The punishment was also supposed to fit the crime and such factors as age of the offender or background characteristics were not to be considered. If a person was apprehended for committing an illegal offense not only was the punishment painful, it often included incarceration so that the offender could contemplate and decide—or "unwill"—to commit future crimes.[4]

Succinctly stated, the classical school said that,

> . . . crime involves a moral guilt, because it is due to the free will of the
> individual who leaves the path of virtue and chooses the path of crime,

[2] George B. Vold, *Theoretical Criminology* (New York: The Oxford University Press, 1968). See Chapter 2.
[3] Martin R. Haskell and Lewis Yablonsky, *Crime and Delinquency* (Chicago: Rand McNally and Co., 1970), p. 344.
[4] *Ibid.*

and therefore it must be suppressed by meeting it with a proportionate quantity of punishment.[5]

The purpose of the classical orientation was to make the system of criminal prosecution and punishment rational and consistent, so that society could be protected and the offender could "change his ways."

The *positive* school of criminology, founded by Cesare Lombroso, emphasizes the criminal offender's personal and background characteristics rather than just the rational thought process and "free will."

> The positive school of criminology maintains, on the contrary, that it is not the criminal who wills; in order to be a criminal it is rather necessary that the individual should find himself permanently or transitorily in such personal, physical, and moral conditions, and live in such an environment, which becomes for him a chain of cause and effect, externally and internally, that disposes him toward crime.[6]

The positive school rejected the classical school's belief that man exercises reason, is capable of choice and free will, and that the offender is no different from the nonoffender.[7]

In effect the offender is "sick" and his behavior merely reflects the various determinants in his background. The determinants would be the offender's biological, psychological, sociological, cultural, and physical environments.

Treatment would include altering one or more of the determinant factors that contributed to the unlawful behavior. Even though almost all modern theories have emanated, in one way or another, from the positive school, Lombroso's work did not incorporate sociological and psychological considerations as we know them today. His *scientific investigations* emphasized the biological differences of offenders.

Basically, Lombroso felt that (1) criminals were a distinctive type at birth, (2) they could be recognized by certain stigmata, that is, such distinguishing characteristics as "a long, lower jaw," and "a low sensitivity to pain," (3) these stigmata or physical characteristics did not cause crime but enabled identification of criminal types, and (4) only through severe social intervention could born criminals be restrained from criminal behavior. The Lombrosian school of thought relied heavily on biological determinism.[8]

As pointed out earlier there are other determinants of behavior that extend beyond biological determinism. For example, Gabriel Tarde refuted Lombroso's biological emphasis by focusing on *social determinism*. In other words, criminal behavior was the result of factors in the environment of the offender and not due to biological makeup. The disagreement between Lom-

[5] Enrico Ferri, *The Positive School of Criminology*, Stanley E. Guipp, Ed. (Pittsburg: The University of Pittsburg Press, 1968), p. 54.
[6] *Ibid.*, p. 24.
[7] David Matza, *Delinquency and Drift* (New York: John Wiley & Sons, Inc., 1964), p. 11.
[8] Haskell and Yablonsky, *op. cit.*, p. 345.

broso and Tarde, however, related solely to what factors determined or caused the criminal behavior. They did not disagree on the question of free will versus determinism. They both agreed that explanations of criminal behavior should extend beyond the classical school's free will emphasis. They parted ways when it came to specifically identifying which deterministic behavior (biological or social) provided the key for explaining criminal behavior.[9]

Even though Lombroso's biological determinism was refuted by some of his "students" he began the scientific investigation into the "causes and cures" of criminal behavior. His principles aren't even "far fetched" for many modern day theorists. Ernest Hooton in the 1930s extensively studied Lombroso's principles and developed biological typologies. Sheldon extended Lombroso and Hooton's concepts and incorporated psychological factors. As a result of his investigations Sheldon arrived at three body classifications—*endomorph, mesomorph,* and *ectomorph*—which combine certain physical characteristics with temperament characteristics. For example, the endomorph is a rotund person with characteristics of jovialness and outgoingness. He is considered an extrovert. The mesomorph is muscular, with characteristics of aggressiveness, competitiveness, and physical drive. The ectomorph is slender and slight. Temperamentally he is aloof and withdrawn, and he is considered an introvert. In evaluating an individual according to these characteristics, Sheldon developed a numerical scale. An individual could receive a classification of, for example, 5-3-1, which would indicate that on a 10-point scale, he had a score of 5 for endomorphy, 3 for mesomorphy, and 1 for ectomorphy. Sheldon felt that of the three classifications, delinquents and criminals adhered most closely to his mesomorph classification with the corresponding temperament traits of aggressiveness, competitiveness, and so on. The biological, or body-type, approach to studying criminality and deviant behavior has been attacked on many grounds. The results at best have been superficial and the theorists themselves have contradicted each other. For example, Hooten felt that criminals and criminal types were inferior physically, whereas Sheldon felt that they were superior. There has been little scientific substantiation of the findings of the relationship of body type to criminality. Most of the studies have been performed on institutionalized populations, without the benefit of control groups. Even though Sheldon created some new enthusiasm with his approach, the biological school of crime causation is not generally popular at present.[10] Studies have been conducted, however, that some researchers feel point to differences in chromosome makeup between offenders and nonoffenders. The XYY chromosome discussion has received popular attention, although many of the findings are inconclusive.

XYY Man. Recently there has been new emphasis on determining criminality through biological investigation, especially through investigation of chromo-

[9]Cressey, *op. cit.,* p. 161.
[10]Marshall B. Clinard, *Sociology of Deviant Behavior* (New York: Holt, Rinehart and Winston, Inc., 1963), p. 120.

somes. Since the early 1940s it has been recognized that some possible sex chromosome combinations are not normal: XO, XXY, XXX, and XYY and the rare combinations XXXX, XXYY, and XXXXY. All these combinations, except the XYY, had been described and identified prior to 1961. The August 26, 1961, issue of *Lancet* contained a preliminary report of the identification of an XYY man, which pointed out that this man had two abnormal children, one a mongoloid, and one whose internal sex organs had not developed.[11]

After the 1961 discovery of the XYY chromosome abnormality, further studies were conducted. It was not until 1965, however, that a comprehensive report of the incidence of XYY males among mentally subnormal male patients with dangerous violent or criminal propensities, who had been institutionalized, was released. Jacobs, Brienton, and Melville reported that men with an additional Y chromosome presented a rather striking clinical picture. Of 197 patients examined, twelve were found to have chromosomal abnormality. Of this number, seven were XYY types. One outstanding characteristic of the XYY male was that he was at least six inches taller than the general male population. This was the only unusual feature noted about the XYY man at that time.[12]

In 1966, follow-up research was conducted at the same mental hospital, and nine additional cases of the XYY syndrome were identified. Of the nine, eight were considered to be mentally retarded, one was schizophrenic, and all had criminal records. In addition, six of the nine were over six feet tall, although no other physical abnormality was present. Upon additional investigation the researchers found that all nine XYY patients were suffering from a severe degree of personality disorder, though none had a history of any form of brain damage, epilepsy, or psychosis. In general, their personalities showed extreme instability. They had little goal orientation and a low frustration tolerance. The researchers felt that family background was not a significant factor in the XYY man's criminal behavior. In addition, only one of the thirty-one siblings of the nine XYY men had been convicted of a criminal offense. A control group used for comparison showed that XYY males differed in many ways from other incarcerated offenders—they had little skill in crime, their gain from crime was minimal, and they usually came from stable homes.[13]

Since the initial survey in 1965, eighteen other studies have been conducted in the Western world on inmates incarcerated because of criminality, mental illness, and retardation. The various surveys have pointed out that XYY men are much taller than the normal population, as well as possessing other physical abnormalities. The excessive height has been the one prominent characteristic that has been identified in every study, whereas some other physical abnormali-

[11] *The Lancet* (August 26, 1961). Note: The research on the XYY man (references 10-14) was done by Roland Burnham, a graduate paper, School of Criminal Justice, Michigan State University, East Lansing.
[12] Patricia A. Jacobs, M. Brienton, and M. Melville, *Nature* (December 25, 1965), pp. 1351-52.
[13] W. W. Price, J. A. Strong, P. B. Whatmore, and W. F. McClemont, *British Medical Journal,* 1 (1968), pp. 533-36. Also, *The Lancet* (March 12, 1966), pp. 565-66.

ties, such as abnormal genitals—although being identified in most studies—have not shown up in every case.

Research, as Burnham relates, has also indicated that the presence of an extra Y chromosome in any combination appears to greatly increase the probability of psychiatric problems, although an extensive review of available literature revealed no consistent trend toward any one type of psychological disorder in XYY males. No two studies agreed exactly on the psychological profile of the XYY male. The only consistency in the studies was that some type of psychological disorder or personality disturbance was present in all XYY males examined. These findings should be viewed with reservation, however, because of the inaccuracy of much psychological testing. Most testing, regardless of population, will reveal a certain percentage of individuals with some personality abnormality. Even in some studies of the XYY man where control groups have been used, there was little significant difference between the two groups. Research on the XYY man, although interesting, has been sketchy and in many cases inconclusive. Richard G. Fox, in the *Journal of Criminal Law, Criminology, and Police Science,* aptly sums up the present status of the XYY man:

> Although it will be shown that the research findings are less significant than reports first suggested and that there are strong psychological reasons for interest in the topic, the flurry of recent attention has at least provoked criminologists into reexamining the hitherto largely neglected field of criminal biology. The new biological research is not simply a revamping of Lombroso or Hooton, but is rather a continuation and an extension of the work of Kretschmer, Sheldon, and the Gluecks on the relationship between body type, temperament, and criminality. And in the final analysis its importance lies less in the weight of the current findings than in the fact that the attempt to identify the behavioral correlates of particular genetic defects represents one of the important first steps toward the elimination of undesirable traits in human beings by genetic manipulation. The attainment of this goal, however frightening it may appear to be, is no fanciful dream; its realization has been seriously predicted for the first decade of the new century, and with the recently reported isolation of a single gene by a Harvard scientist, this prediction may already require updating.[14]

Determinism and Modern Theory

Modern crime causation theory, in the main, is all deterministic insofar as it posits a statistical relationship among man, his various environments, and deviant activity. Such theory, while it seemingly depreciates by implication the premise of free will, does not and need not attack that concept directly, since most theory is stated in the form of probabilistic propositions. In other words,

[14] Richard G. Fox, "The XYY Offender: A Modern Myth?" *The Journal of Criminal Law, Criminology, and Police Science,* 52, No. 1 (March 1971), p. 62.

if variables A and B, for example, are present in individual #1's environment and interact with individual #1, there is a given probability that acts of a specified nature will occur. Thus, free will—to the extent that one subscribes to that concept—may exist in any specific behavioral situation. It is only in the "long run" that the deterministic laws or propositions will be proven. Other forms of modern theory assert relationships only, in which behavior A is related to behavior B, but there is no assertion that behavior A "causes" behavior B.[15]

CONTEMPORARY THEORIES OF CRIMINALITY: AN OVERVIEW

The preceding discussion has attempted to illustrate briefly the transition and the historical development criminology has taken from the older classical school of thought to the present emphasis on theories whose assumptions are based on the postive school of criminology. This section will present the views of the major sociological and psychological theorists who have contributed to the present body of criminological knowledge.

Albert Cohen points out that sociological explanations of criminality do not oppose psychological explanations in that they are not rival answers to the same question, but they answer different questions about the same sort of behavior. Psychological theories are concerned mainly with motivation and those factors that contribute to the individual manifesting behavior in either deviance or conformity.

> Sociological inquiry or theory is concerned with identifying variables and processes in the larger social system that in turn shape those that are involved in motivation and that determine their distribution within the system . . . actions are not only events in the biographies of individuals (psychological theory)—things that people do; they are also events located somewhere in a social system or structure—in a family, a neighborhood, a city, a region, an organization, a country. Different kinds of deviant acts are variously distributed within a given social structure, and these distributions differ from one time to another and from one structure to another. It also makes sense to ask: What is it about social structures— their organization, their cultures, their histories—that accounts for differences within and between them?[16]

To simplify the distinction between psychological and sociological theories, it may help the reader to remember that the psychologist takes a more individualistic, specific view of human behavior and the personal internal factors

---

[15] Forrest M. Moss, unpublished paper, Michigan State University, East Lansing, Michigan, 1976.

[16] Albert K. Cohen, *Deviance and Control* (Englewood Cliffs, N.J.: Prentice-Hall, Inc., 1966), pp. 45–47.

that contribute to criminality. The sociologist takes a more general view, looking at the external environment in which the individual lives. The sociologist is concerned with the distribution of crime within the environment and the factors in the system that affect the crime rates. The sociologist can usually accurately predict the amount of crime that will be committed in certain areas, but he is unable to pinpoint specific potential offenders.

MAJOR SOCIOLOGICAL THEORIES

As pointed out earlier, sociology was the first major discipline to study criminology and criminal causation. The sociological approach to crime causation is concerned with the effects the social system or the environment has on the development of attitudes, group patterns of behavior, and other social factors. Translating these broad abstract concepts into variables that can give some indication of how the individual acquires criminal behavior (in a discussion of motivation) is usually the domain of the psychologist. Theorists who make the connection between abstract general sociological theory and the more specific motivational aspects of psychological theory are called social psychologists. They consider both social and psychological factors in relation to crime and crime causation.[17]

Group and Structure-based Theory[18]

Group and structure-based theory is generally the special concern of sociology, and focuses on the impact of social organization on behavior. The hard sociological position is that to know the structure of society is to identify its values, and to know the values and goals of the group is to know all, since it is the group which clearly shapes and directs the activities and values of the individual. The structure of society reflects the dominant values of that society, which are mediated, in turn, by the various groups which comprise the functional elements of the social system. One of the primary functions of the group is to transmit to new members its hierarchy of roles, statuses, and norms; that is, to socialize the individual. Unfavorable environmental conditions either directly or indirectly contribute to crime and delinquency.

The primary group, the family, inculcates in the individual his basic orientation to society, and thus plays a major role in the socialization process. The individual internalizes a system of roles, statuses, and norms transmitted by his parents. The problems usually start when the individual begins to interact in the larger social arena, the world of secondary groups—the institutional superstructure of the society. He may experience discrepancies between his internal-

---

[17]Donald R. Taft, *Criminology* (New York: Macmillan Publishing Co., Inc., 1956), p. 84. Also Richard R. Korn & Lloyd W. McCorkle, *Criminology and Penology* (New York: Holt, Rinehart and Winston, Inc., 1966), pp. 273–74.

[18]The section on group and structure-based theory was written by Forrest M. Moss, unpublished paper, Michigan State University, East Lansing, Michigan, 1976.

ized norms and the norms of others; or he may not have the opportunity to achieve particular social standings. A neglected childhood may have left him with an ambiguous norm structure, or he may experience frustration when confronted with multinorm/role situations. Criminal deviancy can occur for a variety of reasons. The individual may have been raised in an environment where the roles and norms were criminal, as defined by a dominant social group or even the entire society. His frustration at not being able to achieve in a manner consistent with his internalized norms and goals may prompt him to resort to criminal methods for similar ends. He may become situationally deviant, dependent upon association with deviant subgroups in the society.

That sociology is a highly normative area of social science is understandable, because talking about social organization, social opportunity, and social values invites discussing the results of organization, opportunity structure, and value systems, proposing alternatives, and taking sides. John Horton has provided a valuable analysis of sociological thinking, which may aid the student in his future study of this theory. Horton sees sociological thinking as falling into two main value camps, with analysis based either on (1) the premise that the existing basic social structure is appropriate, or (2) that repressive social structure is the cause of criminal behavior.[19]

Order-based theorists, as would be expected, take the structural conditions they find, and seek to explain social disorder and criminal deviance as the result of the bad alignment of various elements within the system, that is, we may need to increase economic opportunities in one part of the community, increase educational opportunity in another part, decrease control in yet another section of the community.

Conflict-based theorists, on the other hand, reject the basic social structure, since they find it naturally repressive and deem it the cause of deviancy. Deviants are not people who have been poorly socialized and are without norms. Rather, they are people who have become alienated by a repressive system in which the only healthy response is system rejection. System rejection can take the form of criminal activity.

These are obviously dichotomous positions. Horton sums them up, to wit: ". . . the conflict theorist invariably questions the legitimacy of existing practice and values; the order theorist accepts them as the standard of health."[20] In further summary, it is well to remember that sociological declarations about criminal behavior are apt, at times, to become somewhat emotional, and the student should exercise care in his own evaluation of these theories.

A major criticism of sociological theory is that it does not explain why the majority of people, both juveniles and adults, who live under unfavorable environmental conditions do *not* become delinquent or criminal.[21] Sociological theory obviously does not answer all the questions relating to crime causation.

---

[19] John Horton, "Order and Conflict Theories of Social Problems as Competing Ideologies," *American Journal of Sociology* (May 1966).

[20] *Ibid.*

[21] Walter C. Reckless, *The Crime Problem* (New York: Appleton-Century-Crofts, 1967), p. 387.

The way the sociologist views crime causation and the perspectives and assumptions that underly his thinking have been discussed. The following section will present the views of the major theorists within the field of sociology who have contributed to an increased understanding of delinquent behavior and adult criminality. These theorists are by no means the only writers who have had something to say about crime causation. They have been selected mainly because of their specific contributions or because their viewpoints are similar to those of other theorists.

Anomie Theory—Emile Durkheim

Durkheim was one of the earliest sociologists to talk about the social system and environment and how it affects the individual. His primary emphasis focused on suicide and the differential rates of this occurrence depending on such factors as isolation and a feeling of not being a part of the community. His early investigations into suicide rates led him to conclude that if persons do not feel a part of a group and are isolated from the mainstream of interaction and positive peer support, then a reaction to this situation would be some sort of deviant behavior. His technical terminology for this phenomenon was *anomie*—a feeling of isolation or, more specifically, normlessness. Durkheim's concept of anomie has implications for delinquency and crime; and Robert Merton extended Durkheim's significant contribution, even though he did not focus on these social problems.[22]

Social Structure and Anomie—Robert Merton

The main thrust of Merton's efforts was "in discovering how some social structures exert a definite pressure upon certain persons in a society to engage in nonconformist rather than conformist conduct."[23] He made a threefold distinction in his theory of deviant behavior, which was similar to Durkheim's analysis of suicide causation. They are (1) the cultural goals or aspirations that men learn from their culture, (2) the norms that men employ when attempting to achieve the goals, and (3) the institutionalized means or the facilities that are available for goal achievement.[24]

When there is a discrepancy between the institutionalized means that are available within the environment and the goals that individuals have learned to aspire to in their environment, strain or frustration is produced, norms break down, and deviant behavior can result. For example, if a ghetto child is exposed by the mass media to success symbols and a life style that are difficult for him to attain because of a lack of institutionalized means—such as adequate schools

---

[22] Emile Durkheim, *Suicide: A Study in Sociology,* translated by John A. Spaulding and George Simpson (Glencoe, Ill.: The Free Press, 1951).
[23] Robert Merton, "Social Structure and Anomie," *American Sociological Review,* 3 (October 1938), p. 672.
[24] *Ibid.,* pp. 672-74.

and employment opportunities—this, Merton feels, will create strain and frustration. This strain and frustration can produce behavior that is deviant and contrary to the norms or the rules that generally govern behavior. The delinquency of the ghetto child would be explained by Merton as being the result of a discrepancy between the goals that the child has internalized and the means that were available to achieve these goals in a socially acceptable manner.

All societies differ in the way wealth is distributed and the way opportunities present themselves. Merton saw our society as being extremely productive, but at the same time creating frustration and strain because all groups do not have equal access to the institutionalized means of legitimately achieving goals.

In his article "Social Structure and Anomie," Merton states:

> It is only when a system of cultural values extols, virtually above all else, certain common symbols of success for the population at large while its social structure rigorously restricts or completely eliminates access to approved modes of acquiring these symbols for a considerable part of the same population that anti-social behavior ensues on a considerable scale. The "end justifies the means" doctrine becomes a guiding tenet for action when the cultural structure unduly exalts the end and the social organization unduly limits possible recourse to approved means.[25]

Merton also charts the alternative modes of behavior that may result when there is a disjunction between goals, means, and institutionalized norms, and when there is an overemphasis on goals or means. For example, when both societal goals and institutionalized means are adhered to, there is *conformity.* If the means are followed but the goal is lost sight of, there will be *ritualism.* The bureaucrat who becomes so engrossed with following the rules that he forgets that the rules are only a means to goal achievement, and not an end in themselves, is an example of ritualistic behavior. Another of Merton's alternatives, *innovation,* is emphasis on the goal and disregard for the institutionalized means. An example of this type of adaptive behavior would be a professional thief who wanted material rewards and success but did not want to follow the prescribed means, namely through legitimate employment, to achieve his goal. Merton discusses two other alternatives: *retreatism,* which is a rejection of both goals and means and which can result in drug culture involvement; and *rebellion,* which is a withdrawal of all allegiance to the social system and an attempt to reconstruct a new one. An example of rebellion would be revolutionaries. Merton's approach is essentially sociological because he does not discuss individual motivational factors as they relate to the selection of a particular alternative. His emphasis is on the strain produced by the system and the culture, and on the position occupied by individuals, which will depend on the

---

[25] *Ibid.*

alternative they are forced to select. Merton's theory increases our understanding of the effects of strain produced by the system, but it does little to increase our understanding of why all persons in similar situations do not choose the same alternative, that is, why some perform acts of deviance.

Gang Theory—Frederick Thrasher

At about the same time that Merton was positing his views on deviant behavior, Frederick Thrasher was exploring the subject of group delinquency. Many theorists have studied the group and its effect on delinquent behavior. Processes whereby a group takes on certain behavior characteristics and then transmits them to its members are intriguing for both the theorist and the layman. Although other theorists, such as Cohen, Ohlin and Cloward, and Miller, include gang behavior in their studies on delinquency, Thrasher is considered the foremost authority on gang behavior because of his extensive research on the subject.

Thrasher's study

> is not advanced as a thesis that the gang is a cause of crime. It would be more accurate to say that the gang is an important contributing factor facilitating the commission of crime and greatly extending its spread and range. The organization of the gang and the protection which it affords, especially in combination with a ring or a syndicate, makes it a superior instrument for the execution of criminal enterprises. Its demoralizing influence on its members arises through the dissemination of criminal techniques and a propagation through mutual excitation of interests and attitudes which make it easier (less inhibited) and more attractive.[26]

Thrasher felt that gangs originate naturally during the adolescent years from spontaneous play groups. The major factor that transforms a play group into a gang is conflict with other groups. As a result of the conflict, it becomes mutually beneficial for individuals to band together in the form of a gang to protect their rights and to satisfy needs which their environment and their family cannot. By middle adolescence, the gang has distinctive characteristics, such as a name, a particular mode of operation, and usually an ethnic or a racial distinction.

Thrasher is probably best known for the systematic way he analyzed gang activity and gang behavior. His rigorous attempt at analyzing all facets of gang activity has probably never been equaled. He studied the local community to determine what influence it has on gang behavior. He found that the environment is permissive, lacks control, and facilitates gang activity. The presence of adult crime within these communities also influences gang behavior because many of the adults who have high status in the community are adult criminals.

---

[26] Frederick Thrasher, *The Gang* (Chicago : University of Chicago Press, 1936), p. 381.

Even though most of the gang's activities are not illegal, the environment is supportive of illegal gang behavior. Local businessmen will act as fences for stolen goods, and local citizens are readily available customers for the stolen property. Local politics also contribute to gang behavior—political pull was often the only way that rewards could be obtained because of the extreme poverty conditions that existed at the time of this study.

Thrasher also studied gangs at the level of the adolescent and determined what activities are normal for adolescents and what activities are unique to gang members. He showed that gang behavior is enticing, rewarding, and supported within the environment. He emphasized that not all gang activities are necessarily devious and that much of the gang members' time is spent in normal athletic activities as well as in other teen-age endeavors.

Thrasher, like Durkheim and Merton, described how the environment can be conducive to delinquent behavior. The more the environment is supportive of and conducive to delinquency, the more delinquency will exist. Durkheim's example of suicide as a reaction to the strain produced by the environment, as well as Merton's description of alternatives available to strain, can be correlated with Thrasher's discussion of gang behavior as a mode of adaptation to environmental pressure. The following theorists shed some light on why crime rates and criminal activity are inordinately high in certain environments and sections of the community.

Cultural Transmission—Clifford Shaw and Henry McKay

In attempting to account for the distribution of delinquency in American cities, Shaw and McKay concluded that because the high rate of delinquency that existed in Chicago from 1900 to 1906 had not changed a great deal from 1917 to 1923, even though demographic changes had taken place, delinquency and crime were learned and transmitted from one group to another and from one generation to the next and were fairly stable within the central part of large cities. The core of their theory was that crime was transmitted through personal and group contacts and that lack of effective social control agencies also contributed to the high incidence of crime in these areas.

> In some parts of the city, attitudes which support and sanction delinquency are, it seems, sufficiently extensive and dynamic to become the controlling forces in the development of delinquent careers among a relatively large number of boys and young men. These are the low income areas where delinquency has developed in the form of the social tradition inseparable from the life of the local community.[27]

The authors state that delinquency often becomes enticing because of the contact that the youngster has with persons in his environment. They feel that

[27] Clifford R. Shaw and Henry D. McKay, *Juvenile Delinquency and Urban Areas* (Chicago: University of Chicago Press, 1969), p. 316.

from the point of view of the delinquent's immediate social world he is
not necessarily disorganized, maladjusted, or antisocial. Within the limits
of his social world and in terms of his norms and expectations, he may
be a highly organized and well adjusted person.[28]

According to Shaw and McKay, economic status has a great deal to do
with the rates of delinquent behavior. The greater the economic deprivation,
the greater the delinquency. The less the economic deprivation, the less the
delinquency. Like Durkheim and Merton, Shaw and McKay feel that persons
living in disadvantaged environments often have the same material aspirations
as persons living in areas that have social and economic advantages. Residents
in disadvantaged areas soon learn, however, that legitimate access to their goals
is difficult. The disparity between their goals and the means available for legitimately achieving them therefore creates a situation conducive to deviancy,
delinquency, and crime in urban areas.

The authors sum up their propositions as follows:

> it may be said, therefore, that the existence of a powerful system of
> criminal values and relationships in low income urban areas is a product
> of a cumulative process extending back into the history of the com-
> munity and of the city. It is related both to the general character of the
> urban world and to the fact that the population in these communities
> has long occupied a disadvantageous disposition.[29]

Furthermore,

> it is the assumption of this volume that many factors are important in
> determining whether a particular child will become involved in delin-
> quency. Even in those communities in which a system of delinquent
> and criminal values exist, individual and personality differences as well
> as differences in family relationships and in contacts with other insti-
> tutions and groups no doubt influence greatly his acceptance or rejec-
> tion of opportunities to engage in delinquent activities. It may be said,
> however, that if the delinquency tradition were not present and the boys
> were not, thus, exposed to it the preponderance of those who become
> delinquent in low income areas would find their satisfaction in activities
> other than delinquency.[30]

Shaw and McKay do acknowledge that other factors may cause certain
youngsters to become involved in delinquent activities, but they feel that these
individual factors are secondary to the economic and social factors that exist
in the community and have little bearing on actual rates of delinquency. The
authors' emphasis on crime and delinquency as a phenomenon learned while

---

[28] *Ibid.*
[29] *Ibid.*, p. 320.
[30] *Ibid.*, p. 321.

living in an environment conducive to deviant activity is further defined and elaborated in a theory developed by Edwin Sutherland.

Differential Association—Edwin Sutherland

Sutherland's theory of differential association is probably one of the most systematic and complete theories of delinquency causation that has yet been constructed. The theory states that (1) criminal behavior is learned; (2) criminal behavior is learned in interaction with other persons in the process of communication; (3) the principal part of learning of criminal behavior occurs within intimate personal groups; (4) when criminal behavior is learned, the learning includes not only techniques for committing the crime, which are sometimes very complicated, sometimes very simple, but also a specific direction of motives, drives, rationalizations, and attitudes; (5) the specific direction of motives and drives is learned from definitions of legal codes as favorable and unfavorable—in American society, these definitions are almost always mixed and consequently there is culture conflict in relation to the legal codes; (6) a person becomes delinquent because of an excess of definitions favorable to violation of law over definitions unfavorable to violation of law; (7) differential association may vary in frequency, duration, priority, and intensity; and (8) the process of learning criminal behavior by association of criminal and anticriminal patterns involves all of the mechanisms that are involved in any other learning.[31]

An important principle of differential association is that delinquent behavior will be predictable if there is an excess of definitions within the environment favorable to the violation of laws versus those definitions that are unfavorable to the violation of laws. When the former set of definitions takes precedence over the latter, the stage is set for the commission of crime. If an individual associates mostly with criminals, chances are that he will become involved in delinquent activity. Conversely, if an individual associates mostly with noncriminals, chances are that he will not become involved in delinquent activity. Sutherland's concepts of *frequency, duration, priority,* and *intensity* in relation to the quality and quantity of relationships help explain the effects of differential association. If an individual has many contacts with criminals over a long period of time and if they are important to him, as well as intense, he will probably become involved in delinquent activity.

The major criticism of Sutherland's theory is that it is difficult to empirically test the principles and objectively measure "associations" and the priority, intensity, duration, and frequency of relationships. In their book, *Principles of Criminology,* Sutherland and Cressey admit that "the statement of differential association process is not precise enough to stimulate rigorous empirical test, and it therefore has not been proved or disproved. This defect is shared with broader social psychological theory."[32] Even though Sutherland's

[31] Edwin Sutherland, *The Sutherland Papers,* Albert K. Cohen, Alfred R. Lindesmith, and Karl F. Schuessler, Eds. (Bloomington: University of Indiana Press, 1956), pp. 8–10.
[32] Edwin Sutherland and Donald R. Cressey, *Principles of Criminology* (New York: J. B. Lippincott Co., 1966), p. 98.

theory of differential association is one of the most complete and systematic theories that exists regarding the way criminality is learned and transmitted, he does not adequately handle the problem of why some persons in the same environment incorporate and assume criminality as a mode of behavior while their peers do not. Role theory provides a part of the explanation and adds another piece to the puzzle of crime causation.

Self-Role Theory—George Herbert Mead

Mead lends new insight into why an individual takes on certain types of behavior (roles), becomes comfortable with them, and develops a characteristic life style.[33] Role theory helps explain why only a limited number of persons assume criminal identities while the majority of people remain law abiding. Cohen adequately sums up the concept of role theory when he states that

> it assumes, like differential association theory, that we do not learn anything without first being exposed to it. It also assumes, however, that whether we take notice of it, remember, and make it our own depends on whether it matters to us . . . from the standpoint of role theory, the central issue in the problem of learning deviant behavior becomes the process of acquiring and becoming committed to roles.[34]

Hence, becoming delinquent and assuming a criminal identity involves more than merely associating with law violators. The associations have to be meaningful to the individual and supportive of a role and self-concept that he wants to become committed to. Durkheim, Merton, Thrasher, and Shaw and McKay all emphasize the effect that the environmental system has on producing strain and, ultimately, deviant behavior. Sutherland explains how criminality is learned and transmitted. Mead tells us why it is incorporated into an identity and perpetuated as a role. The following theorists build upon the contributions of the above-mentioned theorists and blend them with their own.

Working-Class Boy and
Middle-Class Measuring Rod—Albert Cohen

Cohen feels that the problem of delinquency is mainly a working-class phenomenon. He states that

> the working class boy, particularly if his training and values be those of the working class, is more likely than his middle class peers to find himself at the bottom of a status hierarchy whenever he moves into the middle class world whether it be of adults or children. To the degree to which he

---

[33] George Herbert Mead, "The Psychology of Punitive Justice," *American Journal of Sociology,* 23 (March 1918), 577–602.
[34] Cohen, *op. cit.,* p. 101.

values middle class status either because he values the good opinion of middle class persons or because he has, to some degree, internalized middle class standards himself, he faces the problem of adjustment and is in the market for a solution.[35]

He further states that

a delinquent subculture is a way of dealing with the problems of adjustment. . . . These problems are chiefly status problems; certain children are denied the respect of society because they cannot meet the criteria of the respectable status system. A delinquent subculture deals with these problems by providing criteria of status which these children can meet.[36]

In other words, Cohen feels that working-class boys have not been equipped to deal with the competitive struggle that takes place in middle-class institutions. They have not learned the type of behavior that will contribute to their success and therefore are not comfortable when they come in contact with these institutions. As a result of this frustration they react against those institutions that they feel represent an environment that is too demanding, given the preparation they have received. "The hallmark of the delinquent subculture is the explicit and wholesale repudiation of middle class standards and the adoption of their very antithesis."[37]

Group or gang delinquent activity legitimizes and supports aggression against middle-class institutions. The collective support of the group is important to the boy if he persists in delinquent activity, because he is not convinced, at least unconsciously, that his hostile reaction is normal. As long as the group supports his actions he can continue to blame the external middle-class institutions and ward off internal feelings of inadequacy.

Cohen's work, like that of Ohlin and Cloward, the next theorists that will be discussed, combines the work of the sociologists previously mentioned. In addition, Cohen invades the realm of psychology when he talks about the delinquent's having problems of self-esteem and feelings of inadequacy. Cohen can be considered one of the theorists who attempt to bridge the gap between sociology and psychology.

Success Goals and Opportunity Structures— Lloyd Ohlin and Richard Cloward

To cope with some of the discrepancies presented by anomie theory, role theory, and differential association, Ohlin and Cloward expand upon these precise concepts to give a more comprehensive explanation of the types of

---

[35] Albert Cohen, *Delinquent Boys, The Culture of the Gang* (Glencoe, Ill.: The Free Press, 1955), p. 119.
[36] *Ibid.*, p. 121.
[37] *Ibid.*, p. 130.

alternatives available as a result of strain. They also point out that the environmental system produces strain as a result of a lack of legitimate alternatives to satisfy needs.

> The disparity between what lower class youths are led to want and what is actually available to them is a source of a major problem of adjustment. Adolescents who form delinquent subcultures have internalized an emphasis upon conventional goals. Faced with limitations on legitimate avenues of access to these goals and unable to revise their aspirations downward, they experience intense frustrations and exploration of nonconformist alternatives may be the result.[38]

Ohlin and Cloward go on to say that

> when pressures from unfulfilled aspirations and blocked opportunity become sufficiently intense, many lower class youth turn away from legitimate channels adopting other means beyond conventional mores, which might offer a possible route to successful goals. . . . Discrepancies between aspirations and legitimate avenues thus produce intense pressures for the use of illegitimate alternatives. Many lower class persons, in short, are the victims of a contradiction between goals toward which they have been led to orient themselves and socially structured means of striving for these goals. Under these conditions, there is an acute pressure to depart from institutional norms and to adopt illegitimate alternatives.[39]

Ohlin and Cloward describe three forms of behavior adaption to environmental strain. First, the criminal subculture, which exists in areas where there is a strong adult criminal culture and where youth learn patterns of criminality at an early age and then graduate to adult criminal circles. The illegitimate response to strain in these neighborhoods takes the form of criminal apprenticeship programs. Second, the conflict subculture, which is similar to the criminal subculture in that it offers limited access to goal achievement through legitimate channels; however, no strong ties with the adult criminal subculture exist, resulting in a lack of even illegitimate opportunities for goal achievement. Criminality is more individually oriented in these neighborhoods, and behavior is more violent, and less structured and systematic. Criminal apprenticeships do not generally exist. The third form of behavioral adaption is the retreatist subculture, in which neither avenue of opportunity, legitimate, or illegitimate, exists. In addition an individual may also have certain moral inhibitions about becoming involved in a criminal type of behavior. The conflict may be resolved if the person withdraws from his environment and retreats to a drug culture.

Ohlin and Cloward's theories, like most of those that have been discussed, are difficult to test and evaluate empirically. They make assumptions about

[38] Lloyd Ohlin and Richard Cloward, *Delinquency and Opportunity, A Theory of Delinquent Gangs* (New York: The Free Press of Glencoe, 1960), p. 86.
[39] *Ibid.,* p. 105.

human behavior and reaction to strain, but there is difficulty in translating the assumptions into practical application. Even though Ohlin and Cloward, unlike the other theorists, give a more definitive description of alternatives to strain, all three forms of reaction and adjustment they described can exist within the same neighborhood. Their categories are useful for description but are not always reliable for predicting the mode of behavior and subsequent strategies for prevention, control, and treatment.

Ohlin and Cloward, Cohen, Durkheim, Merton, Shaw and McKay, and Thrasher have all either stated or implied that crime is the result of strain produced by a lack of environmental opportunity and is therefore more prevalent among the lower socioeconomic classes. The hostile manifestation of criminal behavior is generally felt to be a reaction to economic and social conditions as well as to those institutions that set normative standards. The next theorist, Walter Miller, proposes that delinquent behavior may not necessarily be a reaction to strain or a rebellion against middle-class institutions, but simply behavior that is contrary to the middle-class standards because of different learned patterns of conduct acquired from their lower-class culture.

Lower-Class Boy and Lower-Class Structure—Walter Miller

According to Miller,

> in the case of gang delinquency, the cultural system which exerts the most direct influence on behavior is that of the lower class community itself—a long established distinctively patterned tradition with an integrity of its own—rather than a so-called "delinquent subculture" which has arisen through conflict of middle class culture and is oriented to the deliberate violation of the middle class norms.[40]

The lower-class culture that Miller mentions has come about as a result of the processes of immigration, migration, and mobility. Those persons who are left as a result of these processes comprise the lower class and have developed a pattern of behavior which is distinct to that class and is not necessarily reactive against any other class. Miller states that

> expressed awareness by the actor of the element of rebellion often represents only that aspect of motivation of which he is expressively conscious; the deepest and most compelling components of motivation—adherence to highly meaningful group standards of toughness, smartness, excitement, fate, and autonomy are often unconsciously patterned. No cultural pattern as well established as the practice of illegal acts by members of lower class corner groups could persist if buttressed primarily by negative, hostile, or rejective motives; its principal motivational support, as in the case of

---

[40] Walter Miller, "Lower Class Culture as a Generating Milieu of Gang Delinquency," *Journal of Social Issues*, 14, No. 3 (1958), 6.

any persisting cultural tradition, derives from a positive effort to achieve what is valued within that tradition and to conform to its explicit and implicit norms.[41]

Miller also discusses, in addition to distinctive lower-class traits (toughness, autonomy and so on), the effects female-based households in lower-class families have on the adolescent boy's sexual identification. The street group provides him with an opportunity to act tough, become involved in other masculine activities, and reject the female orientation that has been the greater part of his life up to that point. Many of the boy's delinquent activities revolve around his desire to become a "real man." Furthermore, the excitement and free life of the streets and the gratification received from "acting out" by means of the group provide a greater return for the effort expended than can be gained by adopting the more sedentary behavior that is normative to the other socioeconomic classes. The major criticism of Miller's theory is that today, with mass communication, it is difficult to believe that the distinct lower-class culture Miller describes can exist in such a pure form—Miller's lower class will undoubtedly be influenced by the other classes, and adaption to the environment, whether legitimate or illegitimate, will include influences that extend beyond the immediate community. Miller has presented his ideas on delinquency and its relation to the lower class. Other writers have also correlated delinquency with social class.

Middle-Class Juvenile Delinquency—Edmund Vaz

Much has been written about juvenile delinquency and its prevalence in the lower-class sections of communities. Edmund Vaz is one of the few theorists to focus on middle-class delinquency. He states that

> the apparent inconsistency between the protective upbringing of middle-class children and their delinquencies is a result partly of middle-class delinquency as viewed as a function of conformity to the expectations of the role of adolescent in the middle-class youth culture and to parentally favored activities. Among middle-class teen-agers, sociability is the quickest route to acceptability and status gain. The recluse and the bookworm are seldom admired. Teen-agers expect enthusiastic participation from peers in youth cultured events. But the pursuit of status and the pull of popularity can easily lead to novel kinds of behavior variations on everyday games and practices. Perhaps much middle-class delinquency is precisely these kinds of acts. This suggests that certain kinds of delinquency are an unexpected result of institutionalized patterns of conduct, and that delinquency is spawned among the stable, cherished values, attitudes and activities of the middle-class.[42]

[41] *Ibid.*, p. 19.
[42] Edmund Vaz, *Middle-Class Juvenile Delinquency* (New York: Harper & Row, Publishers, 1967), p. 4.

Vaz emphasizes the youth culture and particularly the youth culture of late and describes how certain activities are fostered, perpetuated, and supported by adults. Parents consider it important that their children become involved in these activities which are considered normal. At the same time the child feels it is important to gain status with his peers and be an active participant in group activities. It is precisely from these group activities and group involvement that middle-class delinquency evolves. Vaz states that

> although all behavior is perhaps partly exploratory, stabs at marginal differentiation are likely to be guarded, tentative, and ambiguous and to transpire in a situation characterized by "joint exploration and elaboration" of behavior. Yet extreme conduct of any kind is apt to be strongly disapproved among sophisticated youths, and there exist strong motivations to conform to prevailing norms and patterns. But the boundaries of legitimacy are not impregnable, and it is during these legitimate, fun-ridden activities that boys are encouraged to join in, that unobtrusive acts lead gradually to unanticipated elaboration beyond the precincts of legitimacy. Since adolescent activities occur in a spirit of good-will, creative efforts are applauded, encouraged, and behavioral novelty is seldom considered delinquent.[43]

Vaz, then, is saying that as a result of normal group activities, innovation is tried and deviations that were at first slight and were considered exploratory and adventurous then become normative to the group and are ultimately taken for granted. An example of deviancy that results from normal group association is shoplifting, an activity that has become commonplace among affluent middle-class teen-agers. Younsters caught shoplifting often explain that their activity originated as a game played for excitement and novelty. The activity, then, is perpetuated for the above factors as well as for other benefits, such as material gain. The important point, however, is that the activity originated from the normal processes of group interaction and involvement. Vaz sums it up very well when he says:

> The motives for much middle-class delinquency are learned through sustained participation in everyday respectable adolescent activities. In this manner, delinquency becomes gradually routine in the middle-class youth culture.[44]

All the sociologists discussed thus far have explored the phenomenon of criminality in the tradition of the positive school of criminology. They emphasize the role of the environment in determining adaptive behavior rather than the free will and rationalism emphasized by the classical school. The next theorist to be discussed, David Matza, a modern sociologist, combines the

[43] *Ibid.,* p. 135.
[44] *Ibid.*

most relevant concepts of both the positive and the classical schools in an attempt to provide new insights into delinquent and criminal behavior.

Delinquency and Drift—David Matza

Matza attempted to blend the classical school's concept of "will to crime" with positive assumptions and methods of scientific investigation. He does not totally agree with the deterministic orientation of the positive school—that delinquent behavior is caused almost entirely by emotional and environmental factors. Matza acknowledges that environmental and emotional factors can have an effect on the individual's behavior, but he feels that other aspects contribute to making one youngster choose the delinquent route while another youngster in the same general environment does not. Matza feels that man is neither totally free, as the classical school assumes, nor totally constrained or determined, as the positive school assumes. He feels that everyone is somewhere between being controlled and being free and that everyone drifts between these two states.

> Drift stands midway between freedom and control. Its basis is an area of the social structure in which control has been loosened, coupled with the abortiveness of adolescent endeavor to organize an autonomous subculture, and thus an independent source of control, around illegal action. The delinquent transiently exists in a limbo between convention and crime, responding in turn to the demands of each, flirting now with one, now the other, but postponing commitment, evading decision. Thus, he drifts between criminal and conventional action.[45]

> Drift is a gradual process of movement, unperceived by the actor, in which the first stage may be accidental or unpredictable from the point of view of any theoretic frame of reference, and deflection from the delinquent path may be similarly accidental or unpredictable. This does not preclude a general theory of delinquency. However, the major purpose of such a theory is a description of the conditions that make delinquent drift possible and probable and not a specification of invariant conditions of delinquency.[46]

According to Matza, psychological makeup and environmental factors do not destine an individual to become delinquent. There is, however, a movement between convention and crime, and impinging factors, one of them being the individual's "will," can influence which route he ultimately chooses.

Even though most of a youngster's activities are law abiding, he can periodically drift into delinquency because the normal conventional controls that usually inhibit delinquent behavior become neutralized as a result of the drifting process. When the youngster does become involved in difficulty this is

[45] Matza, *op. cit.*, p. 28.
[46] *Ibid.*, p. 29.

not an irreversible process, however, because he can and usually does drift back to conventionality. When the youngster does drift into delinquency and when the moral commitment to conventionality is neutralized, this is when the element of "will to crime" plays an important part. "I wish to suggest that the missing element which provides the thrust or impetus of which the delinquent act is realized is will."[47]

Matza's concept of "will"provides an important element in understanding why some youngsters choose delinquent behavior while most of their peers within the same environment choose socially acceptable modes of adaption. He also explains why delinquency is not an "either-or" proposition. Most youngsters exist somewhere along the continuum between convention and crime. Total commitment to delinquency is uncommon.

Matza's theory also has important implications for fostering cooperation between the professionals who work within the criminal justice system. Police officers and social workers, the two largest professional groups within the criminal justice system, usually make different assumptions about the ethology, control, treatment, and prevention of juvenile delinquency. Police officers' assumptions are usually derived from the classical school, whereas social workers' assumptions emanate from the positive school.

It is understandable why police officers subscribe to the classical school philosophy. Their profession is commissioned with dealing with the delinquent in a practical, legalistic, objective, and expedient manner. The police officer does not have the luxury of spending a great deal of time with the offender to talk about his psychological dynamics and his environmental background. He has to be practical because of the demands of his job. Many police officers have only a high-school education and therefore have not been exposed to the popular psychological and sociological theories of juvenile delinquency, most of which have emerged from the positive school of criminology. As a result, the classical school of criminology is most appealing to them.

Those professionals oriented to the positive school are usually in social work and social service professions. They feel that the offender is sick and needs social and personal treatment. Social agency professionals subscribe to the positive school of criminology for many reasons. They do not have to deal with the immediate problems of arresting, processing, and responding to the actual delinquent act within a community. They have more time to probe into the environmental and personal background of the offender to determine why his behavior has taken an antisocial channel. Also, social workers are more thoroughly grounded in the social sciences than police officers. They have been exposed to the popular theoretical assumptions that have emerged from the positive school of criminology. As a result of these factors, most social workers quite naturally subscribe to the positive school.

The orientations of the additional community agencies in the criminal justice system in regard to criminological emphasis vary somewhere along the

[47]*Ibid.,* p. 181.

continuum between the classical and positive schools of criminology. Our emphasis will not, however, be focused as heavily on these agencies because their orientation is not reflected in as extreme a manner as police and social work agencies. Also police officers and social workers are the professionals who come in most direct contact with the delinquent offender, and it is their hand-ling of the offender that can have the most long-lasting effect on future behavior.

As for differences in criminological philosophy, David Matza has given us some important insights as to how to combine the two schools to make criminology more realistic and more acceptable to both police officers and social workers. In revising and combining the two schools of thought, Matza fits

> many of the empirical observations of positive criminology into a frame-
> work more consistent with classical assumptions and teachings. The
> classical conception of a "will to crime" is utilized in order to maintain
> the ineradicable element of choice and freedom inherent in the condition
> of delinquency.[48]

Chapter 12 will discuss the method of increasing interagency coordination and cooperation which can facilitate more effective delinquency prevention, control, and treatment. It should be mentioned here, however, that the es-tablishment of training programs that are responsive to the feelings, orientation, and needs of both professions (police and social work) would be helpful in creating a more cooperative attitude between them. Each profession needs greater insight into the other's profession. New models for training would be conducive to developing joint efforts in order to produce more effective and coordinated programs.

Differences in Organizational Perspective

The existence of conflict between criminal justice agencies is a readily accepted fact. The interesting point, however, is that even though interagency conflict is sometimes a result of power building, boundary maintenance, and professional jealousy, it also occurs somewhat unknowingly because of the different professional and theoretical organizational orientations. Differences in criminological orientation have already been discussed. In addition to the difference in philosophy between the components of the criminal justice sys-tem—police and social work agencies—there is also generally a difference in organizational structure, philosophy, and orientation. Most organizations do not fit one organizational typology in its purest form, although there is usually a major emphasis on one or the other school. When analyzing agencies within the criminal justice system it becomes obvious that police organizations, because they are paramilitary and because their functioning often necessitates discipline

[48] Matza, *op. cit.*, p. 27.

and order as well as immediate response to command, are established according to classical organization theory. They have an emphasis on ranks, a specific authority structure, a close adherence to the unity of command and span of control principles, and a delineation of functions by specialization.

Social work or social service agencies are closer to the human relations approach because of the more casual atmosphere in which they operate. They also have more specialized and advanced training and greater latitude in job functioning. Furthermore, the theoretical base upon which their profession is oriented, namely, psychological and sociological theory, presupposes that they will naturally be more concerned about interpersonal relations, participation in decision making, and emphasis on social interaction.

Differences in criminological and organizational perspective among criminal justice practitioners have been pointed out to illustrate that there are many factors, some obvious and some not so obvious, that inhibit meaningful interaction and cooperation.

CONCLUSIONS FROM SOCIOLOGICAL THEORIES

The preceding section has attempted to give the reader a general view of the major sociological theories of juvenile delinquency. All these theories have their strengths and their weaknesses. Merton and Durkheim have shown how the discrepancy between institutional means available and goals desired can produce strain which can in turn lead to delinquency. Thrasher, in a more general sense, also alludes to strain as a result of poverty and points out that an environment is conducive to delinquent behavior when ineffective social controls and inadequate models for identification exist. Shaw and McKay's and Sutherland's work also stresses the importance of the environment for determining delinquent behavior. They also point out how delinquency and crime are transmitted from one group to another and how stable criminal patterns can result because of this learning process. George Herbert Mead sheds some light on how a delinquent role is incorporated into a life-style. If delinquent behavior is supportive of a person's identity, he will incorporate it and use it. Ohlin and Cloward's and Cohen's work is similar to that of all the aforementioned theorists in that they too emphasize strain from the social system. However, the delinquent behavior they describe takes on more of a reactive nature against the dominant middle-class system and its social institutions and much of the delinquency is hostile and nonutilitarian and is used solely to vent aggression. Miller and Vaz relate delinquency to class status, Miller emphasizing the lower class and Vaz the middle class as the major departures for their theories, David Matza is important to the discussion because of his attempt to combine the most relevant concepts of both the classical and positive schools of criminology. His realistic description of the "drift" process also helps place the delinquency phenomenon in its proper perspective.

This abbreviated discussion of the major sociological concepts does not of course include all the theorists who have contributed to an understanding of juvenile delinquency. Chapter 3 will examine other concepts related to juvenile delinquency and the family.

Compared with sociological theorists, few psychologists seem to be interested in theorizing about juvenile delinquency and adult crime. Psychologists did not become interested in delinquency and criminality as a specific field of study until fairly recently. Even at the present time the study of delinquency and criminality is often considered only a secondary manifestation of the larger category of behavior termed *mental illness,* and the emphasis has been on studying mental illness in general.

MAJOR PSYCHOLOGICAL THEORIES

Whereas sociologists emphasize the environment of the social structure and its effect on crime rates and crime causation, psychologists take a more specific approach and consider the individual and his motivational patterns in an attempt to describe delinquency and criminality. The present discussion will focus on psychological factors, and the sampling of theorists will range from those who operate under Freudian assumptions to those who use testing as their major method of criminological investigation. Just as all sociologists cannot be grouped into a single category, all psychologists do not, as a group, emphasize the same areas of investigation. Some sociologists are more psychologically oriented than some psychologists, and vice versa. For descriptive purposes, however, it will be assumed that both fields have a distinct body of knowledge and method of investigation and that if a person calls himself either a sociologist or a psychologist certain assumptions can be made about his orientation to delinquency and criminality.

There are varying opinions about the quantity and the quality of the impact that psychological factors have on the causation of juvenile delinquency. Bloch and Flynn feel that

> Although wide-spread disagreement exists about the functioning of organic and environmental factors in the lives of delinquents, there is considerable unanimity on the part of most investigators about the presence of emotionally disturbed states among delinquent offenders, particularly the persistent delinquent. The precise diagnosis of these emotional states, however, is another matter and raises several vital questions—symptomatic states that appear similar need not necessarily be the same and conversely many emotional states that appear different in their manifestations originate from quite similar sources.[49]

[49] Herbert A. Bloch and Frank T. Flynn, *Delinquency* (New York: Random House, Inc., 1956), p. 153.

At present there is no single psychological theory (just as there is no single sociological theory) that has been tested empirically and totally explains, for all circumstances, juvenile delinquency and criminality. In addition, unsubstantiated overgeneralizations of human behavior have been made.

> This does not mean, however, that the search for valid hypothesis based upon demonstrated proof is not moving forward nor does it mean that the work in the field of delinquency may not be an important step in the development of an adequate personality theory.[50]

Individual-based Theory[51]

Individual-based theory focuses on man's personality as the primary variable in explaining action, be it deviant or well within the bounds of social acceptability. The way in which the personality is developed and how it comes to direct deviant acts depends upon the way in which the dynamics of personality formation are conceptualized. There are two main schools of thought, the psychoanalytic and the learned-behavior. Variations on these theoretical themes are almost without number.

Psychoanalytic Theory. Originally developed by Sigmund Freud, this theory asserts that all relevant personality formation is concluded very early in childhood, based on interaction between the child and his adult environment. The child goes through a series of sexual stages (anal, oral, phallic, and so on), during which he tries to resolve the conflicts which arise between his needs and his adult world.[52] Failure to satisfy these needs, or to find suitable alternatives to these needs, may result in his becoming stunted or fixated at a particular level of development. As the child learns, at a subconscious level, to repress, express, sublimate and otherwise emotionally "live" with both his primitive sexual urges and his adult environment, he forms a tripartite personality structure which consists of the id, the ego, and the superego. These structures correspond to the primitive instincts (id), the self-image (ego), and the conscience (superego), respectively. Where the personality structure fails to develop adequately, or the psychosexual development becomes fixated, particular and unique personality characteristics become evident. Some individuals become socially aggressive, others completely passive; some are unable to control particular impulses to action—the range of deviation is immense. Where the personality mechanisms are badly warped, in relation to what is considered a "normal" personality, antisocial actions are sure to occur, some of which fall within

---

[50] *Ibid.,* p. 84.
[51] The section on individual-based theory was written by Forrest M. Moss, unpublished paper, Michigan State University, East Lansing, Michigan, 1975.
[52] Gerald S. Blum, *Psychoanalytic Theories of Personality* (New York: McGraw-Hill Book Company, 1953).

the purview of the criminal law. Psychiatrists can explain almost all forms of criminal behavior in terms of this theory. Psychiatric therapy is the usual method of treatment, sometimes combined with tranquilizing medication.

Learned-Behavior Theory. This conceptual scheme is somewhat more mechanistic than psychoanalytic theory.[53] Man's personality develops through a process of conditioning; that is, he learns what behaviors are appropriate or inappropriate through a system of positive and negative reinforcements to his responses to stimuli received from his environment. He initially receives these reinforcements from his parents; later he is subject to conditioning by all of the individuals and institutions with which he interacts. Through associational processes, the individual classifies responses to social stimuli, and if his earlier conditioning has been appropriate, he finds that his responses are rewarded. For a variety of reasons, however, the conditioning may have been defective. It may have been internally inconsistent, too harsh or too lenient. The physiological structure of the individual may have impaired the efficacy of the process. As a result, the individual may exhibit a negative self-image, an inability to relate viably to his surroundings, a lack of ability to select appropriate responses in new situations, or an inability to defer gratification, to mention but a few of the problems which can result from inadequate conditioning.

Within this conceptual scheme, remedial conditioning becomes a distinct possibility to help the client be reconditioned to respond in a more socially acceptable manner. Learned-behavior theory has the distinction, among the social sciences, of having reached a rather sophisticated level of research, and has at its disposal an impressive array of empirical data. Learning theory engenders, concurrently, substantial opposition on ethical grounds in that, somehow, being conditioned to be productive, responsive, happy, and "good" smacks of an Orwellian world, and is less pleasing than visions of heroic and existential man against the elements.

Regardless of the particular individual based theory, delinquency and crime are viewed as an outgrowth of maladaptive experience of the particular individual. There are numerous professionals and professions, i.e., psychiatry, psychology, psychoanalysis, that use the individual approach. Generalizations will be made to include all the various groups so that discussion of psychological theories will be facilitated and a comparison between sociology and psychology will be made easier for the reader.

The most noted theorists who became interested in the study of individual characteristics of offenders were William Healy and Bernard Glueck. Several years later investigators refined many of the explorations made by Healy and Glueck. Even though many early "findings" have been refuted, the early works gave impetus to an increased focus on individual factors as they relate to crime and delinquency.[54]

---

[53] For an excellent discussion of learning theory, see B. F. Skinner, *Cumulative Record: A Selection of Papers,* third ed. (New York: Appleton-Century-Crofts, 1972).
[54] Cressey, *op. cit.,* p. 163.

August Aichhorn was the first major theorist to expand Freud's concepts and use the psychoanalytic method to treat delinquent (or dissocial) youngsters. Aichhorn has also influenced others to use the psychoanalytic technique as a treatment method.

Psychoanalytic Theory—August Aichhorn

According to Aichhorn,

Psychoanalysis enables the worker to recognize the dissocial manifestations as a result of an inner play of psychic forces, to discover the unconscious motives of such behavior and to find means of leading the dissocial back to social conformity.[55]

He further states that

dissocial behavior indicates that the psychic processes which determine behavior are not functioning harmoniously. Delinquency can now be considered as a dynamic expression; it can be attributed to the interplay of psychic forces, which have created the distortion which we call dissocial behavior.[56]

Aichhorn feels that reeducation as a result of understanding the delinquent's psychic processes is the way to solve the problem. He believes that help has to include more than just removing the delinquent symptom and that the cause of the problem has to be determined, or else the expression of the symptom will merely take another form.

Because of the conflicts that exist within delinquents, Aichhorn feels that first there has to be an understanding of the three dynamic components of the personality—the id, the ego, and the superego. As a result of understanding the interplay of these three dynamic components, conflicts can be diagnosed and the reaons for dissocial behavior understood. After this had been accomplished, psychoanalytic treatment methods along with the use of the milieu can be used to facilitate recovery. Since dissocial children have inadequate conscience structures, new positive identification models have to be provided so that the child's faulty identification with criminal parents or unacceptable persons in his environment can be altered.[57]

In reference to treatment, Aichhorn states that

re-education, however, is not achieved through words, admonition, scolding or punishment, but through what the child actually experiences. Through the milieu recreated in our institution and through our type of

[55] August Aichhorn, *Wayward Youth* (New York: The Viking Press, Inc., 1953), p. 3.
[56] *Ibid.,* p. 38.
[57] *Ibid.,* p. 171.

leadership, we had the opportunity every day to give the children experiences, the deep effect of which helped relieve their dissocial behavior.[58]

He goes on to say that

during the course of his training, the delinquent must learn that the
amount of pleasure obtained from social conformity is greater than
the sum of small pleasures derived from dissocial acts even when the
accompanying discomfort of conformity is taken into account.[59]

The following theorists, although they are not considered to be psy-
choanalysts like Aichhorn, also used individual, psychological principles to
study delinquency and crime.

The Individual Approach—W. Healy and A. Bronner

Healy and Bronner do not use the psychoanalytic method as their primary
source of investigation and treatment. They state that

in terms of a general principle, the origins of delinquency in every case
unquestionably represent the expression of desires and urges which are
otherwise unsatisfied. For the onlooker, delinquency merely signifies
misconduct. For the offender, it is just as much a response to inner drives
and outer stimuli as any other kind of conduct. Delinquency is one small
part of the total stream of the individual's life activities and in its significance represents, equally with the other behavior, a response to inner
or outer pressures. In common with all voluntary activities it is one variety of self-expression.[60]

The authors place a heavy emphasis on the child's feeling secure in his
family, being accepted by his peers and other groups, and receiving recognition
if he is going to make a satisfactory adjustment to his environment. They mention that in relation to their studies there has been

a striking finding . . . [regarding] the immense amount of discoverable
emotional discomfort that clearly has been part of the story of the origins
of delinquency. On the other hand—very few indeed of the non-delin-
quents in the same families had in their emotional lives any such frustrations—and those few had found channels other than delinquency for
modes of compensatory satisfaction.[61]

Furthermore,

[58] *Ibid.,* p. 126.
[59] *Ibid.,* p. 158.
[60] William Healy and A. Bronner, *New Light on Delinquency and Its Treatment* (New Haven,
Conn.: Yale University Press, 1936), p. 3.
[61] *Ibid.,* pp. 6–7.

when there have been no intense feelings of deprivations, inadequacies or thwartings as related to either ego impulses or desires for affection, the individual has been able to readily find sufficient satisfactions in socially acceptable behavior.[62]

The delinquent, the authors find, has almost universally been a child

who at some stage of his development has been blocked in his needs for satisfying relationships in his family circle. On the other hand, the non-delinquent has nearly always been without any such acute frustrations. His relationships with those in his immediate social environment had been much more satisfying.[63]

The authors emphasize that the delinquent feels deprived and inadequate and that he has not found socially acceptable channels for satisfying his needs. They explain why this is the case. They state that "the father or mother either had not played a role that was admired by the child or else on account of the lack of a deep love relationship, was not accepted as an ideal."[64] Furthermore,

In the lives of delinquents, the ever flowing stream of urges and wishes which, in general, follow the broader channels of socially acceptable behavior, has met obstructions or frustrations that caused part of the stream to be deflected into currents that sooner or later show the characteristics which we term delinquency. We are convinced that it is possible to discover in nearly every case the nature of these obstructions.[65]

Healy and Bronner go on to say that the nature of these obstructions can generally be discovered through psychological methods and the investigation of individual behavior. Other modern theorists, such as Scarpitti, Murray, Dinitz, and Reckless, have also made reference to psychological factors and their effect on delinquent behavior. They feel that internal factors such as lack of esteem and feelings of inadequacy contribute to delinquent behavior. More specifically, an adequate self-concept (feeling worthwhile) can be an insulating factor in repelling delinquency.

Juvenile Delinquency and Self-Concept— Frank Scarpitti, Ellen Murray, Simon Dinitz, and Walter Reckless

The authors did a longitudinal study comparing delinquent and non-delinquent boys over a four-year period to determine the relationship between a postive self-concept and delinquency.

---

[62] *Ibid.,* p. 9.
[63] *Ibid.,* p. 201.
[64] *Ibid.,* p. 10.
[65] *Ibid.,* pp. 200–201.

The follow-up study confirms our 1955 predictions and those of the teachers and mothers of the respondents, as well as of the good boys themselves, that they would remain law-abiding in the future. They continue to isolate themselves from law violating friends and acquaintances; they predict law abiding behavior for themselves and in this respect they reflect their teacher's concepts of them—In sum, they continue to define themselves as good boys and are so defined by others in spite of remaining, for the most part, in high delinquency areas—The results of this investigation may be interpreted to mean that once a favorable self-image has been internalized by preadolescents with respect to friends, parents, school, and the law, there is every reason to believe that it is difficult to alter. . . . In view of the relatively stable and cohesive families, the continued interest in and supervision of their activities by their parents, their school aspirations, and isolation from purveyors of delinquent values, it may be predicted that the good boys will persist in their law abiding behavior.[66]

This study indicates that if a youngster feels that he is not going to become delinquent and if he feels that his teachers and parents and other important adults within his environment perceive him as being adequate and not delinquent, then chances are he will not become delinquent. Conversely, if a child is perceived to be delinquent or predelinquent by his parents, teachers, and others within his environment, this will affect his own concept of himself, producing and perpetuating a negative self-image. A negative self-image or self-concept is conducive to the development of delinquent behavior.

Only a few of the major psychological theories have been examined in this section. Additional related material will be presented in the next chapter. The *multifactor* approach to studying juvenile delinquency will now be briefly examined. It incorporates both psychological and sociological principles. The work of Sheldon and Eleanor Glueck typifies this approach.

Multifactor Approach—Sheldon and Eleanor Glueck

Even though William Healy has been described as a theorist whose work incorporated psychological principles, he like the Fluecks was also influential in contributing to the multifactor approach.[67] In his studies he attempted to select all those factors that he felt explained some part of criminal behavior regardless of whether the principles originated from psychology or sociology.

Although the multifactor approach can make a valuable contribution to the understanding of criminal behavior, it is generally acknowledged that no one body of knowledge can be considered a theoretical base for this approach.

[66] Frank R. Scarpitti, Ellen Murray, Simon Dinitz, and Walter Reckless, "The Good Boy in a High Delinquency Area," in *The Sociology of Crime and Delinquency*, Marvin E. Wolfgang, Leonard Savitz, and Norman Johnston, Eds. (New York: John Wiley & Sons, Inc. 1962), p. 209.
[67] William Healy, *The Individual Delinquent* (Boston: Little, Brown, 1913).

Criticisms have been made of the multifactor approach, namely, that it is too loosely defined and that it is no more than superficial generalizations. A brief exposure to the multifactor point of view will be helpful, however, in providing a wider base of understanding of the delinquency phenomenon and how it is viewed by certain theorists.

The Gluecks state that

> persistent delinquency can be the result, not only of one specific combination or pattern of factors that markedly differentiate delinquents from non-delinquents, but of each of several different patterns. The concept of plurality of causal combinations immediately throws light on a host of puzzling problems in the study of crime causation. Just as the fact of a boy's death, although always and everywhere the same terminal event, may nonetheless be the result of various preceding sequences of conditions, so the terminal event of persistent delinquency may have in its causal pedigree and background a variety of different sequences leading to the same ultimate result of habitual antisocial behavior.[68]

In relation to the practitioner,

> many probation and parole officers, teachers, school attendants, officers, and others seem to want specific answers to the "why" of causation; that is, they want to know what the "ultimate cause" of a child's misbehavior is and how it came about. But the ultimate cause is something like a mirage. The more you approach it, the farther it seems to recede.[69]

The Gluecks used the multifactor approach in comparing five hundred delinquents with five hundred nondelinquents. The delinquents were matched by residence in underprivileged areas, age, ethnic origin, and intelligence. The Gluecks considered sociological variables (the environment) and psychological variables (internal dynamic processes). In addition they administered tests. They concluded that the delinquency of the youngsters could not be blamed on any one set of factors. The delinquent behavior was the result of a combination of intellectual, social, temperamental, and physical factors. To pinpoint any particular one would be difficult. They summarized their findings as follows:

> it is particularly in the exciting, stimulating, but little controlled, and culturally inconsistent environment of the urban underprivileged area that such boys readily tend to give expression to their untamed impulses and their self-centered desires. . . . It will be seen that virtually all the conditions enumerated are of a kind that in all probability preceded the evolution of delinquent careers, and in respect to sequence of events in time may legitimately be regarded as causally connected.[70]

[68] Sheldon and Eleanor Glueck, *Venture in Criminology* (Cambridge: Harvard University Press, 1967), p. 16.
[69] *Ibid.,* p. 17.
[70] *Ibid.,* p. 27.

Delinquency, then is the result of an interplay of many different and diverse variables as viewed from the multifactor approach. Other theorists make a more "radical" interpretation of what causes delinquent behavior. Ardry associates delinquency with animal territoriality.

Juvenile Delinquency as an Expression of Animal Territoriality—Robert Ardrey

Robert Ardrey, in his *African Genesis: A Personal Investigation into the Animal Origins and Nature of Man,* sees juvenile delinquency as the natural legacy of animal instincts. The juvenile delinquent does not see himself as sick, as do many theoreticians. Neither does Ardrey, who calls him a "natural man." He buttresses his theory by citing the studies of Sheldon and Eleanor Glueck. The Glueck studies showed the delinquent by and large superior to the non-delinquent in energy and physique. Moreover, far fewer neurotics were found among the delinquents. Conforming children also showed a greater sense of insecurity, of being unloved, unwanted, or rejected than did the delinquents.

Ardrey claims that delinquents do not possess what society regards as a conscience because conscience is a social invention. Their freedom from neuroses is attributable to the fact that their instincts are not suppressed by the inhibitions of civilization. Rather than society having rejected the delinquent, Ardrey postulates that the delinquent has rejected society. The delinquent way of life is in perfect harmony with his animal needs.[71]

> He has the security of his gang, and finds his rank among its numbers. He has sex, although it does not preoccupy him. Without any learned instruction, he creates directly from his instincts the animal institution of territory. In the defence of that territory his gang evolves a moral code, and his need to love and be loved is fulfilled. In its territorial combats, the gang creates and identifies enemies and his need to hate and be hated finds institutional expression. Finally, in assault and larceny, the gang and its members enjoy the blood and the loot of the predator. And there is always the weapon, the gleaming switch-blade which the non-delinquent must hide in a closet, or the hissing, flesh-ripping bicycle chain which the family boy can associate only with pedaling to school.[72]

> Why should the delinquent not be happy? He lives in a perfect world created solely by himself. And if caught by that larger society against which he offends, and for which he holds the most knowing, cynical, and deserved disrespect, then follows the last, vast irony. He will be excused. He will be understood. Society will blame itself.[73]

[71] Robert Ardrey, *African Genesis: A Personal Investigation into the Animal Origins and Nature of Man.* (New York: Dell Publishing Co., 1961).
[72] *Ibid.,* p. 331.
[73] *Ibid.,* p. 332.

Ardrey continues by stating:

> Every accouchement—today, tomorrow, and until the end of our species' time—presents civilization with an aspiring candidate for the hangman's noose. Yet truly to domesticate him means probably to destroy him. [74]

Ardrey considers the gang to be a manifestation of the biological nation, a form of social organization. The gang provides an identity, "Blackstone Rangers," "Hell's Angels," and so on, and gives the individual a place in the gang's hierarchy, further reinforcing his sense of identity. Moreover, struggles for power within the gang and conflicts with the legitimate power structure, with other gangs, and vandalism and thievery committed against them, fulfill the individual's need for stimulation; nothing is more intolerable, especially to young people, than boredom—or the lack of stimulation. Furthermore, the need for a certain modicum of security is provided by the numbers of his colleagues and by their claim to a certain territory, all of the defensive and offensive terrain advantages of which he knows intimately, providing him with a distinct advantage over any intruding antagonist.

David E. Davis demonstrates that rank and territory are the objects of aggression in the human gang as well as in most of animal fighting:

> A wide variety of observations suggest that fighting for rank and territoriy has innate features . . . Thus contrary to the conclusions of some authors, it seems that aggression is heavily dependent on genetics. Probably only the means of fighting and the object of attack are learned. [75]

Contemporary street gangs are thus merely acting out those instincts which proved to have survival value in the mists of the animal past.

CONCLUSIONS FROM PSYCHOLOGICAL THEORIES

Like the sociological theories discussed, the psychological theories add to an understanding and knowledge of deviant behavior, especially of the form that manifests itself in delinquency. As in sociological theory, there should be more scientific substantiation of the principles and assumptions utilized by psychologists and psychiatrists. Psychological theories and especially the psychoanalytic method have assumed certain universal uniformities about human behavior. Generalizations have been made from these assumptions, and hence conclusions

[74] Robert Ardrey, *The Territorial Imperative* (New York: Dell Publishing Co., 1966), p. 191.
[75] D. E. Davis, "The Phylogeny of Gangs," in *Roots of Behavior,* E. L. Bliss, Ed. (New York: Harper & Row, Publishers, 1962).

are not always applicable to all classes and types of behavior. Not all delinquents are mentally ill or deeply disturbed. More comparative studies using control and experimental groups have to be undertaken. Studies which investigate many different interacting variables, both social and psychological, will have to be performed.[76]

Walter Reckless has been successful in combing psychological and sociological theory in what he calls his "containment theory" to explain both conforming and deviant behavior. He feels that there are two important aspects of control, *inner control* and *outer control,* and that depending upon the balance of these control systems, the individual can take either a deviant or a conformist route. His assumption is that "strong inner and reinforcing outer containment constitutes an isolation against normative deviancy (not constitutional or psychological deviancy), that is, violation of the socio-legal conduct norms.[77]

Some of Reckless's inner containment components consist of self-control, a good self-concept, high frustration tolerance, a well-developed superego, and so on. Outer containment represents factors such as institutional reinforcement of an individual's norms, goals, and expectations and social control factors such as supervision and discipline and limits.

> In a vertical order, the pressures and pulls of the environment are at the top or the side of the containing structure, while the pushes are below the inner containment. If the individual has a weak outer containment, the pressures and pulls will then have to be handled by the inner control system. If the outer buffer of the individual is relatively strong and effective, the individual's inner defense does not have to play such a critical role. Likewise, if the person's inner controls are not equal to the ordinary pushes, effective outer defense may help hold him within bounds. If the inner defenses are of good working order, the outer structure does not have to come to the rescue of the person.[78]

Effective control, then involves both internal factors (the conscience) and external variables (the environment). One compliments the other and often each has to "pick up the slack" and exert influence and control.

Beyond Social Determinism[79]

The deterministic approach to crime and delinquency, regardless of the particular form it takes (physiological, social, psychological, and so on), is based

---

[76] Clinard, *op. cit.*
[77] Walter C. Reckless, "A New Theory of Delinquency and Crime," in *Juvenile Delinquency: A Book of Readings,* Rose Giallombardo, Ed. (New York: John Wiley & Sons, Inc., 1966), p. 223.
[78] *Ibid.,* p. 229.
[79] The section "Beyond Social Determinism" was written by William Selke, unpublished paper, Michigan State University, East Lansing, Michigan, 1976.

on the philosophy of positivism. Not to be confused with the positive school of criminology, the philosophy of positivism is the base upon which the positive school of criminology was formulated. The positive school, as it was originally hypothesized by Lombroso, is only one of numerous forms the philosophy of positivism can take. Theories of delinquency based on positivism have in common the goal of finding the causal agent of the phenomenon. Differences in beliefs regarding causal agents will obviously result in different positions with regard to the societal reaction to deviance. Thus, biological determinism suggests a severe punishment reaction, psychological determinism—individually centered treatment, and social determinism—a reform of societal structures. The next phase beyond social determinism might be loosely termed "political determinism."

The writings of Quinney have recently begun to spell out the political nature of crime and delinquency.[80] Writings of this nature have been extremely valuable in illustrating the role of politics and the political process. But the implications of Marxist-based views of crime control in capitalist societies are unclear in terms short of revolution. These ideas, however, combined with other threads running through delinquency theory, have been successful in refocusing attention on the role of the criminal law in a democratic society and the processes and institutions which are responsible for implementing the legal precepts.

A great deal of recent thinking about delinquency has yet to be formally organized into a theory of delinquency. Several of the ideas which are having visible effects on the operations of the juvenile justice system seem to be merging into a new perspective on delinquency. For example, two currently popular trends along the lines of Schur's[81] nonintervention approach—diversion from formal processing and the removal of status offenses from the juvenile codes— are based on ideas which seem to be forging a new perception of delinquency and societal reactions to it. While it is not denied by advocates of these positions that individual and/or social factors might be related to delinquent behavior in a causal manner, the underlying notions of primary interest are the way in which delinquent behavior is defined and the manner in which these sanctions are applied in society. Cavan's concept of "tolerance" implies the basic type of issue at which these writings appear to be aimed.[82] The shift is away from emphasizing the continued development of individual treatment approaches and societal reform techniques. Questions are now being raised as to the appropriateness of various delinquent definitions and the propriety of applying formal sanctions to such a wide range of juvenile behaviors. Interest is being generated by the notion of increasing community tolerance of youthful behaviors. In this manner, it is suggested that much delinquency can be informally absorbed by the com-

[80] Richard Quinney, *Critique of Legal Order* (Boston: Little, Brown and Co., 1974).
[81] Edwin M. Schur, *Radical Non-Intervention* (Englewood Cliffs, N.J.: Prentice-Hall, Inc., 1973).
[82] Ruth Shoule Caven, Ed., *Readings in Juvenile Delinquency*, second ed. (Philadelphia: J. B. Lippincott, 1969).

munity (e.g., through the development of alternative school systems) to the benefit of youths *and* the overburdened juvenile justice system.

Many controversies and problems of the adult and juvenile justice systems point out the need for clarification of some basic underlying assumptions. If, for instance, it is assumed that societal structures facilitate the development of delinquency, practices and policies would logically be aimed at improving agencies and institutions so that a broad spectrum of youth might utilize the services. But if it is assumed that contact with formal official mechanisms is likely to aggravate the already present condition, policy would likely emphasize the restriction of exposure to the process. Most issues in juvenile justice can be traced to similar shortcomings in conceptual clarity, as well as the corresponding lack of empirical evidence which necessarily follows from theoretical ambiguities. Although there is little in the way of a concrete and systematic theory, the multifactor approach to delinquency theory appears to have the greatest potential for pulling together a number of dangling concepts which are currently unaccounted for by delinquency theories. Only in this manner will a theory of delinquency evolve which comprehensively addresses both sides of the interactional process—the individual behavior and the societal reaction.

SUMMARY

This chapter has presented a sampling of the most prevalent theories of crime and delinquency causation. Because of the complexity of the problem, there is no single answer or "common cure." Many academic disciplines and theoretical approaches can contribute to a better understanding of the delinquency phenomenon and methods for its control, treatment, and prevention. Because a comprehensive knowledge of the problem necessitates an interdisciplinary approach, the next chapter uses the family as a framework for analyzing juvenile delinquency and incorporating psychological and sociological principles.

QUESTIONS AND PROJECTS

Essay Questions

1. What are the major differences between psychological and sociological theories?

2. Which school of criminological thought, the Positive or the Classical, is most appealing to you and why?

3. Is it useful to classify delinquents?

4. Why are biological theories of deliquency and crime causation not generally accepted?

5. Why do some theorists take an individual orientation to studying crime and delinquency causation, while other theorists take an environmental orientation?

Projects

1. Develop a project that puts into action one or more of the theories discussed.

2. Discuss the ways that your community can benefit from a knowledge of the theories of delinquency and crime causation.

3. Develop a checklist of psychological and sociological factors that have to be considered when trying to determine the causes of crime and delinquency in your community.

chapter 3

The Family and
Juvenile Delinquency

This chapter will use the family as a model for integrating various psychological and sociological principles into a meaningful framework and will provide an understanding of both the psychologist's and the sociologist's view of the family's importance and contribution to the phenomenon of delinquency.

Regardless of the particular professional orientation or academic discipline, theorists generally agree that the family plays an important part in the youngster's life. The family institution provides the child with his first experiences in social living, and these experiences have an effect on most of his later development. What happens in the family can have great impact on how the child behaves in other social institutions and on whether he becomes "normal" or delinquent.

Many theorists thus consider the family the most significant factor in the development of juvenile delinquency. A review of the literature reveals that theorists ranging all the way from those oriented to Freudian psychology to those in the sociological field consider the family the most important environment of the child. Socioeconomic status, class status, peer group relations, class mobility, and delinquent subculture are also important, but if analyzed closely, each is either directly or indirectly related to the family environment.

Since no theory has been developed that can adequately account for all forms of delinquent behavior, it will be helpful to isolate those factors that contribute to delinquency. The family is one of the major factors.

Much research has been done by sociologists, psychologists, and psychiatrists concerning the relationship between family and delinquency variables and many theories have been advanced to explain the relationships found. Due to a severe lack of interdisciplinary communication, however, few attempts have been made to consider both the sociological and psychiatric aspects of the family's role in delinquency.[1]

An interdisciplinary effort, viewing the family's role in delinquent behavior as a model, can therefore be helpful in examining the delinquency phenomenon. The family can provide a basis for incorporating concepts and variables from both the psychological and the sociological disciplines to give a more insightful understanding of delinquency and a comprehensive approach to the problem.

Using the family as a model for examining the delinquency phenomenon can account for delinquency in all socioeconomic classes, since unhappy home situations and resulting problems cut across class lines and economic strata.

If class were the major determinant of delinquent behavior, the great majority of urban slum children would be delinquent. The great majority of urban slum children, despite their deprived environment and lack of adequate opportunity, do not become involved in delinquent behavior. As Gold points out, child-rearing variables that effect delinquent behavior regardless of class are found to be similar in delinquent families regardless of class.[2]

Delinquency cuts across all class lines, and a great deal of hidden delinquency never comes to official attention. These are indications that delinquency is more evenly distributed throughout the classes than most official records indicate.[3]

Official records deal only with those juveniles who have come into formal contact with the criminal justice system. It is difficult to determine the number of youngsters who have been reprimanded, taken to their parents, or released as the result of some other informal disposition. Even the determining factors related to formal disposition are often correlated with the economic status of the family, the location of the child's home, and other similar variables.

Police dispositions tend to be related to demographic characteristics of offenders, thus, males, Negroes, lower income youths, and older boys are more frequently dealt with formally by court referral.[4]

Studies that are based on data from the records of officially adjudicated delinquents may lead to a theory of causation that is almost entirely related to socioeconomics (as were some of the theories discussed in Chapter 2). It is therefore preferable to seek explanations that are not linked to class. Utilizing the

[1] Hyman Rodman and Paul Grams, "Juvenile Delinquency and the Family; A Review and Discussion," *Task Force Report: Juvenile Delinquency and Youth Crime*, p. 195.
[2] Martin Gold, "Status Forces in Delinquency Boys," in Rodman and Grams, *ibid.*
[3] F. Ivan Nye, *Family Relationships and Delinquent Behavior* (New York: John Wiley & Sons, Inc., 1958), p. 23.
[4] Don C. Gibbons, *Delinquent Behavior* (Englewood Cliffs, N.J.: Prentice-Hall, Inc., 1970), p. 45.

family as a model for examining juvenile delinquency causative factors is a more logical approach.

PSYCHOLOGY AND THE FAMILY

Chapter 2 pointed out that psychological theories are mainly concerned with variables that relate to early childhood experiences which influence the formation of the personality. Psychologists feel that much early emotional deprivation is directly associated with, and related to, later psychological disturbances and emotional problems. The greater the deprivation, the greater the emotional insecurity, and therefore the greater the chance for emotional problems or deviant behavior.

August Aichhorn stresses the importance of the family in shaping the children. He feels that the family should provide the child love and security and at the same time be a haven of relief from outside pressures.[5]

Sidney Berman believes that delinquent children have often had difficulty in their early relationships with their parents.

> This implies that these children have reacted adversely to certain early life experiences which other children have been guided through more adequately. The concern, therefore, is with the psychological factors which structure this morbid behavior.[6]

The early life experiences of the child in the family lay the groundwork for the type of future behavior and the development of attitudes, values, and a life style. Parental hostility, rejection, and inconsistency can all contribute to delinquent behavior.[7] The family is the backdrop in which the child learns to deal with his emotions and drives and handle his problems in a socially acceptable manner. When the family does not help the youngster to adjust to his environment, he loses the most important means of psychological support and the most effective agent for socialization. Aichhorn states that so strong is the influence of the family in shaping behavior that pathology undoubtedly exists in all families where there is a delinquent youngster—even though families of delinquents may appear to be at least superficially normal and well adjusted, further investigation will identify some type of pathology or sickness. In addition to open hostility, there will often be shallow relationships between family members, little concern felt by parents for their children, and absence of a role model with whom the youngster can identify.[8]

---

[5] August Aichhorn, *Delinquency and Child Guidance* (New York: International Universities Press, 1969), p. 16.
[6] Sidney Berman, "Antisocial Character Disorder," in *Readings in Juvenile Delinquency*, Ruth S. Cavan, Ed. (Philadelphia: J. B. Lippincott Co., 1964), p. 142.
[7] *Ibid.*, pp. 142–43.
[8] *Ibid.* p. 132.

When parents identify with and support positive community norms and values, they will be effective socializing agents for their children. If, however, parents do not transmit positive community norms and values to their children and fail as positive identification models, the children will often come in conflict with community institutions.[9]

There is widespread consensus, then, that early family training is important in influencing future behavior. Early childhood experiences, especially those experiences within the family, determine in great part how the youngster will be molded and how he will eventually adapt to the external environment.[10] Delinquency signifies more than merely misconduct—it is the expression of desires, drives, urges, and motivations which have been greatly influenced by the youngster's early experiences in his family. If early family experiences have been positive, the youngster will be able to handle the pressures and responsibilities he will meet in adjusting to the community because his parents will have assisted him in developing problem-solving capabilities.

Psychologically oriented theories that emphasize the importance of early parent-child relationships can be helpful in identifying those factors that most directly affect the child-rearing process. The identification of these variables is important in pinpointing reasons for the abnormal expression of behavior. When the behavior is expressed in an antisocial form, juvenile delinquency is the result.

SOCIOLOGY AND THE FAMILY

Whereas the psychologist is concerned with the identification of individual variables, such as motivation, drives, values, and needs, the sociologist is concerned more with the general environment as it relates to the distribution of crime, the factors in the system that affect crime rates, and the functioning of the institutions of control that have been commissioned to deal with the offender. In other words, sociology attempts to explain the manner in which society acquires crime, the processes that contribute to crime causation, and the mechanisms developed to deal with it. Underlying sociological investigation is the assumption that unfavorable environmental conditions in the social system influence an individual's actions and, in fact, can force him into delinquency or crime. Even though sociology and psychology deal with different aspects of the crime problem (sociology stresses the system, psychology stresses the offender), both disciplines look at "control." Psychology emphasizes the process of personal or internal control that is represented by the superego (conscience). Sociology emphasizes the institutions in the community that directly influence the external social control pro-

---

[9]*Ibid.*, p. 232.
[10]Beatrice Simcox Reiner and Irving Kaufman, *Character Disorders in Parents of Delinquents* (New York: Family Service Association of America, 1959), p. 15.

cesses. Reiss views delinquency as being the result of the failure of both personal and social controls to produce behavior that conforms to social norms and is acceptable to the community.[11]

> Delinquency results when there is a relative absence of internalized norms and rules governing behavior in conformity with the norms of the social system to which legal penalties are attached, a breakdown in previously established controls, and/or a relative absence of a conflict in social rules or institutions of which the person is a member. Hence, delinquency may be seen as a function or consequence of the relationship established among the personal and social controls.[12]

The chance of delinquency becomes greater when both personal controls and social controls break down. In Chapter 2 we saw that when such community institutions of social control as the courts and the police are ineffective, delinquency and crime are more prevalent. Similarly, when the individual does not have an adequate conscience structure, internal personal control is ineffective. When there is a combined lack of *personal* and *social* control, delinquency and crime are often the result.

The family is extremely important because it can both influence the development of the internal control structure (conscience) and have an effect on the external control social process by its methods of direct control and discipline.[13] If the parents are not adequate models of identification, so that a positive conscience can develop, and if their methods of discipline are not effective, community social control institutions usually have to intervene.[14] Thus, if the youngster is going to refrain from delinquent behavior, he has to be guided by both internal and external control structures.[15] The family plays the greatest role in both these processes. Community institutions of control intervene only after the family has been unsuccessful.

THE ENVIRONMENT OF THE FAMILY

As Chapter 2 pointed out, sociological explanations of criminality and delinquency do not oppose psychological explanations because they are not rival answers to the same question but they answer different questions about the same sort of behavior.[16] The environment of the family can be appropriate for answering the "different" questions posed by both psychology and sociology.

---

[11] Albert J. Reiss, Jr., "Delinquency as the Failure of Personal and Social Controls," *American Sociological Review* (1951), pp. 196–207.
[12] *Ibid.*, p. 196.
[13] Nye, *op. cit.*, p. 72.
[14] *Ibid.*, p. 23.
[15] Gold, *op. cit.*
[16] Albert K. Cohen, *Deviance and Control* (Englewood Cliffs, N.J.: Prentice-Hall, Inc., 1966), p. 47.

This section will discuss family environmental factors that can have an impact on producing delinquent behavior—broken home, family tension, parental rejection, methods of parental control, parental emotional stability, and family economics.

Broken Homes

Sheldon and Eleanor Glueck define a stable family as one in which at least one parent has a continuous physical and affectional relationship with the children.[17] They found that a much higher proportion of nondelinquents were exposed to households where there were minimal disruptions rather than those typified by parental separation, divorce, death, or parental absence. In a substantial number of the broken homes, the youngster was under five years of age at the time of the break.

> It is probable that the first definitive breach in the organic structure of the family is crucial because it is likely to deal the greatest blow to a child's conception of the solidarity and reliability of the parental team and to disrupt his general sense of security as well as of family stability.[18]

Over half of the delinquents studied were reared by one parent, whereas only 10 percent of the nondelinquents were reared by one parent.

Toby feels that the American family has its greatest influence over the younger children in the family, and hence it is most devastating to these children when the family becomes disrupted for whatever reason.[19] The older children in the family, because they have more autonomy and have developed various patterns for coping with problems, are not as adversely affected. This view corresponds with some psychologists' contention that a child's behavior patterns and psychic structure are almost completely formed by the time he is five and that instability and physical and psychological deprivation at a very early age can be devastating to the youngster. Monahan[20] found that delinquents from broken homes were more likely to be recidivists than those from unbroken homes; Browning,[21] Gold,[22] Slocum and Stone,[23] and Peterson and Becker,[24] like the Gluecks, found that a significantly greater number of delinquents than nondelinquents were from broken or disorganized homes.

Although Sterne agrees on the fundamental importance of the family in

[17] Sheldon and Eleanor Glueck, *Delinquents and Nondelinquents in Perspective* (Cambridge, Mass.: Harvard University Press, 1968), p. 12.

[18] *Ibid.*, p. 12.

[19] Rodman and Grams, *op. cit.,* p. 196.

[20] Thomas P. Monahan, "Family Status and the Delinquent Child," *Social Forces* (1957), pp. 250–58.

[21] Charles J. Browning, "Differential Impact of Family Disorganization on Male Adolescents," *Social Problems* (1960), pp. 37–44.

[22] Gold, *op. cit.*

[23] Walter Slocum and Carol L. Stone, "Family Interaction and Delinquency," in *Juvenile Delinquency,* Herbert C. Quay, Ed. (Princeton, N.J.: D. Van Nostrand Co., Inc., 1965).

[24] Donald R. Peterson and Wesley C. Becker, "Family Interaction and Delinquency," in *Juvenile Delinquency*, Herbert C. Quay, Ed.

shaping behavior, he does not believe that a broken home is a major cause of delinquency.[25] He explains that the actual breaking up of the home is preceded by much disruption, disorganization, and tension. Therefore, because negative factors existed before the formal separation, the broken home in itself was not the major contributing factor to delinquent behavior. The tensions and problems that created and contributed to the actual breakup are the real causative factors, with the eventual breakup being only the final link in a long line of disruptive activity.[26]

Family Tension

Sterne's statement that the cluster of events preceding the formal breakup is the major contributing factor to delinquent behavior is most illuminating because this is often overlooked in studies of broken homes.[27]

Abrahamsen believes that family tension greatly contributes to delinquent behavior.[28] The tension that exists in many "intact" families of delinquents results from hostility, hatred, bickering, and the like. This type of tension-filled family environment is obviously not conducive to making the youngster feel secure and content. Long-term tension reduces family cohesiveness and affects the parents' ability to provide an atmosphere conducive to satisfactory child rearing and family problem solving.[29]

Andry found that tension in homes of delinquents is also manifested through intersibling quarrels.[30] Aichhorn states that

> the relationship [of children] to the parents has somehow become abnormal and the original relations of the children to one another, stressed as they are by competition, have not developed into a normal brotherly bond as they should have if they had been submitted to the influence of an equally divided affection toward the parents.[31]

In regard to family cohesiveness, the McCords and Zola agree that cohesive homes produce few delinquents, whereas homes where tension and hostility exist are good breeding grounds for future delinquents.[32] When a great deal of tension and hostility exists in the home, the youngster is often forced to find "peace of mind" in groups outside the family environment. When the youngster

---

[25] Richard S. Sterne, *Delinquent Conduct and Broken Homes* (New Haven, Conn.: College and University Press, 1964), p. 21.

[26] *Ibid.*, p. 28.

[27] Glueck, *op. cit.*, p. 12.

[28] David Abrahamsen, *The Psychology of Crime* (New York: Columbia University Press, 1960), p. 43.

[29] *Ibid.*, p. 46.

[30] R. G. Andry, *Delinquency and Parental Pathology* (London: Metheun, 1960), p. 64.

[31] Aichhorn, *op. cit.*, p. 154.

[32] William and Joan McCord, and Irving Zola, *Origins of Crime* (New York: Columbia University Press, 1959).

seeks relief from the constant bickering and quarrels within his family, he often flees and "takes refuge in the street."[33]

According to the McCords and Zola:

> Quarrelsome, neglecting families actually had a higher crime rate than homes in which a permanent separation had disrupted the family—conflict and neglect within the home predisposes a child to crime (even more so than broken homes).[34]

Nye shows a relationship between quarreling and delinquent behavior for girls, but not for boys.[35] He explains this by pointing out that the family is more of a focal point for girls than for boys and that the boy can often retreat to the streets or to other groups more readily than can his female counterpart.

Disruptive, quarrelsome, and tension-producing relationships between parents not only affect the marital relationship but disrupt the entire family.[36] This total family disruption can often contribute to and even produce delinquent behavior. The Gluecks found that one in three delinquent families, as compared with one in seven nondelinquent families, were disrupted when one of the parents left the family because of a tension-filled and quarrelsome relationship.[37] Aichhorn found that in all the families that he worked with that had a delinquent youngster, some kind of conflict or disturbance was present in the family relationships.[38] Slocum and Stone noted that 52 percent of delinquents studied, compared with 16 percent of nondelinquents, considered their families uncooperative—which can be another indication of conflict or tension.[39]

If, then, the family environment is unstable and if the parents quarrel most of the time and have difficulty getting along together, they will be unable to exert a positive influence on their children. When there is a great deal of conflict within the household, the child often bears the brunt of much of his parents' hostility. The youngster can get caught up in parental quarrels and be negatively affected by family disruption. The Gluecks point out that

> there is already evidence that the forces of disruption found excessively in the families of the delinquents were greater and stronger than those making for cohesiveness. In addition, it should be pointed out that less than two in ten in the families of the delinquents, compared to six in ten families of the control group, evidenced strong and steady affectional ties among the members, shared joint interests, took pride in their homes, and felt themselves to be "one for all and all for one." Thus, a highly important quality that is both expressive of loyalty to the blood group and sup-

[33] Aichhorn, *op. cit.,* p. 164.
[34] McCord, McCord, and Zola, *op. cit.,* p. 83.
[35] Nye, *op. cit.,* p. 48.
[36] Rodman and Grams, *op. cit.,* p. 198.
[37] Glueck, *op. cit.,* p. 8.
[38] Aichhorn, *op. cit.,* p. 33.
[39] Slocum and Stone, *op. cit.*

portive of the individual in his sense of security and in devotion to others, the delinquents were far more deprived than nondelinquents.[40]

Even though some disagreement may exist as to the amount of influence that the divorced versus the hostile but nondivorced family has upon delinquent behavior, it is evident that marital adjustment, family cohesiveness, and the amount of tension existing in the family are directly related to juvenile delinquency.[41]

Parental Rejection

From the psychological standpoint, emotional deprivation as the result of lack of parental love has much to do with juvenile delinquency. If a rejected or neglected child does not find love and affection, as well as support and supervision, at home, he will often resort to groups outside the family; frequently these groups are of a deviant nature. The hostile or rejecting parent is usually not concerned about the youngster's emotional welfare, nor is he concerned about providing the necessary support and guidance. In many cases, parents only become concerned about their child's activities outside the home when he becomes involved in difficulty and embarrasses them. After the youngster has been apprehended, the parent or parents often react in a pseudo-concerned manner. The hostility and the open rejection characteristic of many parents of delinquents are replaced by an appearance of concern.[42]

Nye points out that many studies have been made of parents' attitudes toward their children, but almost no research has been done to find out what children think of their parents. Youngsters' perceptions of their parents can lend insight into the behavior of rejecting or hostile parents and can contribute to a better understanding of this negative dynamic. Studies have found that mutual rejection of parent and child markedly affects positive relationships and can ultimately result in delinquent behavior. When there is mutual animosity and rejection, the chance of maladaptive behavior within the community can become commonplace.[43]

Jenkins found that parental rejection had a direct effect on the child's ultimate development and growth of a conscience.[44] He stated that the lack of an adequate conscience structure, combined with feelings of hostility for being rejected, led to general unsocialized aggression. On the other hand, socialized delinquent behavior would result when there was parental indifference rather than outright rejection. In other words, the form of aggression was less serious in

---

[40] Glueck, *op. cit.,* pp. 9–10.
[41] Rodman and Grams, *op. cit.,* p. 198.
[42] Nye, *op. cit.,* p. 73.
[43] *Ibid.,* pp. 74–75.
[44] Richard L. Jenkins, "Motivation and Frustration in Delinquency," *American Journal of Orthopsychiatry* (1957), pp. 528–37.

those youngsters whose parents showed indifference than in those youngsters whose parents showed outright rejection.

According to Andry, delinquents were the recipients of less parental love both in quantity and in quality than were nondelinquents.[45] There was also less adequate communication between child and parent in homes of delinquents. If a strong positive emotional tie does not exist between parents and children, this can produce problems. A positive atmosphere in the home is conducive to effective modeling by the parents and also increases the amount of influence that parents exert over their children. The Gluecks found that in twice as many nondelinquent homes the father showed a great deal of warmth and affection than in delinquent homes. In nondelinquent homes mothers also were much more affectionate than in delinquent homes.

> The extent to which the boy's father was acceptable as a figure with whom to identify is revealed in a finding that fewer than two out of ten of the delinquents, as contrasted with more than half of the nondelinquents, considered their father to be the kind of man that the boy himself would like to be and had respect for the father's vocational and social standing as well as having some sort of common understanding with him.[46]

Bandura and Walters, like the Gluecks, found a direct correlation between rejecting, hostile fathers and delinquent behavior.[47] Fathers of delinquents spent far less time with their sons than did the fathers of nondelinquents. Their rejection and hostility can take both direct and indirect forms. The direct forms are obvious. Indirectly, however, the parents may reject the youngsters by becoming so involved in other activities that they substitute the giving of material awards for emotional affection and security. In addition, if parents are away from the home most of the time, either because of an occupation or because of outside activities, their exposure to their children is limited.

When parents spend a great deal of time away from home, they are often tired when they get home and apathetic about their children. They can be more concerned about achieving financial or social success than about providing their children with love, affection, understanding, and realistic discipline; elements that children interpret as love and concern. The father can often be the greater abuser. In many families the father's main role is being the provider and nothing more. He may "put bread on the table," but he plays little part in providing emotional warmth and security by paying attention to his children and becoming actively involved in their lives. In addition, he is often not an adequate identification model. It then becomes more difficult for the youngster to assume a socialized internal control structure (conscience).[48]

Although somewhat skeptical of delinquency theories based solely on fam-

[45] Andry, *op. cit.*
[46] Glueck, *op. cit.*, p. 14.
[47] Abrahamsen, *op. cit.*, p. 62.
[48] *Ibid.*

ily relationships, Gibbons believes that "scientific candor compels us to conclude that the link between parental rejection and aggressive conduct is one of the more firmly established generalizations concerning delinquency."[49]

Many professionals in the fields of both psychology and sociology agree that open rejection and hostility can directly affect youngsters and ultimately produce delinquency and that the family institution has the greatest influence on the youngster's behavior in the community. Parental control is both direct and indirect. Parents indirectly control their children through the identification process, which ultimately results in the development of an adequate conscience structure. Parents exert direct control by developing a system of rewards and punishments. The method of parental control is an important aspect of child rearing.

Methods of Parental Control

Just as tension, rejection, and a broken home can affect the stability of the family structure, methods of control or processes and forms of discipline can play a part in the development of delinquent behavior.

Every parent uses some type of discipline in rearing children, even though it may differ from situation to situation and from child to child, as well as in content and form. Nye discusses discipline and its effects on child rearing and says that an authoritarian approach to discipline may affect the adolescent in his peer group relationships. The child will not be able to interact freely with his peers if his mobility is hindered by extremely strict parents. Conversely, a too permissive type of discipline will not provide the child with the necessary controls and limits so that reference points can be established to guide behavior.

> Unfair or partial discipline may be associated with an ambivalent or negative attitude toward the parent which reduces the indirect control that can be exerted by the parent. An attitude of this type toward parents is thought to make it difficult for the parents to act as an agent in the formation of an adequate conscience in the child, prevents the adults from serving as a model to be imitated by the child, and reduces the wish of the adolescent to conform to please the parent and to avoid delinquent behavior or avoid hurting the parent.[50]

The Gluecks identified differences in disciplining patterns in parents of delinquents. They found that the parents of delinquents used physical punishment more than verbal discussion. Mothers were much more permissive and less strict than fathers. Both parents were less consistent in their disciplinary measures than were the parents of nondelinquents.[51]

---

[49] Gibbons, *op. cit.,* p. 202.
[50] Nye, *op. cit.,* pp. 79–80.
[51] Glueck, *op. cit.,* pp. 15–16.

Because of this inconsistent discipline and lack of cooperation between parents, an adequate control structure does not exist within the home. The child then often rejects the entire sphere of parental influence because he loses respect for the process of control utilized by his parents.[52] Parents cannot present a united front if inconsistency and disagreement exist, and therefore the youngster will not be influenced by his parents, will often belittle their efforts, and will not develop an adequate superego (conscience). The youngster can also manipulate the inconsistent pattern of control to turn one parent against the other. The ultimate effect is that the youngster does not have benefit of consistent guidelines and limits to assist him in behaving in a socially acceptable manner.[53] The attitude of "nothing can happen to me" will develop because the youngster learns that his parents' inconsistent discipline and demands are seldom translated into coordinated action.

Nye, interestingly enough, found that unfair punishment, although not having a direct effect upon delinquency when administered by the mother, did have a marked effect when administered by the father.[54] It can be assumed that the more severe discipline is usually administered by the father and thus makes a greater impact. The McCords and Zola classified methods of disciplining youngsters under six types: (1) *love-oriented discipline*, in which reasoning is used with the child and punishment involves withholding rewards or privileges; (2) *punitive discipline*, in which a great deal of physical violence is used and there is a great deal of anger, aggression, and threat; (3) *lax discipline*, in which neither parent exerts much control; (4) *erratic discipline*, in which one parent uses love-oriented methods and the other is lax or wavers between the two types; (5) *erratic discipline* (love oriented, lax, and punitive), in which both parents waver in using the three methods, so that all three are combined; and (6) *erratic discipline* (punitive and lax), in which one parent is punitive and one parent is lax, or both parents waver between the methods.[55]

The McCords and Zola found that lax or erratic discipline involving punitive methods was strongly related to delinquency, whereas consistent discipline, either by punitive or love-oriented methods, was significantly related to nondelinquency. The erratic nature of the discipline, not the amount involved, was the major variable in producing the delinquent behavior.

Contrary to our expectations (and to findings of previous studies) we found no evidence that consistently punitive discipline leads to delinquency. In fact, we were surprised to discover that the 14 children who had been severely but consistently treated had the lowest rate of crime. Consistent use of love-oriented techniques also seems to produce noncriminality. These figures indicate that the consistency of parental behav-

[52] Nye, *op. cit.,* p. 48.
[53] Aichhorn, *op. cit.,* p. 233.
[54] Nye, *op. cit.,* p. 80.
[55] McCord, McCord, and Zola, *op. cit.,* p. 76.

ior is more important than the methods parents use for enforcing their demands.[56]

Discipline and the way in which it is administered can have a marked effect on delinquent and adolescent behavior. Consistency is extremely important, and a united approach by parents is desirable—but difficult to present if there is a broken home, a great deal of tension in the home, or parental rejection. All these factors can be important negative contributory variables in the delinquent's home. Another important aspect of the environment of the family, which can have a marked effect on how the child ultimately reacts in the community, is the emotional stability of his parents.

Parental Emotional Stability

Delinquent behavior can often be directly traced to behavioral disturbances and emotional instability in one or both of the parents. Parents who have their own emotional sickness frequently "act out" the sickness or transmit it to their children. Freeman and Savastano found that although some mothers of delinquents wanted to give their sons "adequate mothering," their own personality problems interfered with their effectiveness as mothers. If the only time the mother shows a great deal of tenderness is after she punishes the child, he will often deliberately misbehave for the express purpose of receiving the tenderness, even though it is not under the most optimal conditions. The erratic and misdirected tenderness is an important motivating factor in his negative behavior.

Children can also be the recipients of much hostility and jealousy from emotionally unstable parents.

> Mothers who are jealous of their growing daughters, cannot reconcile themselves with the loss of their own femininity; they cling abnormally to their husbands; they try exaggeratedly to limit his freedom of action and often rob him of the opportunity to exchange a few loving words with his own child; they observe suspiciously every gesture made by husband and daughter and then discharge their dissatisfaction upon the daughter alone. Consequently, the daughter feels still drawn more toward her father or step-father. Family life becomes impossible, the more so because the girl is intolerant of her mother and uses every opportunity to withdraw from the domestic environment; a reaction which exposes her to the dangers of waywardness.[57]

Conversely, if there is little love between the parents, the youngster can become the "love object" of one or the other. The inordinate amount of attention the youngster receives because he is being used as a substitute for the rejected marital

---

[56] *Ibid.,* pp. 77–78.
[57] Beatrice Freeman and George Savastano, "The Affluent Youthful Offender," *Crime and Delinquency* (1970), pp. 264–72.

partner can greatly confuse him. Freeman and Savastano reported that marital conflict was frequently expressed in the parent-child relationship. The mother gives the child a great deal of love and affection, worries about the child constantly, and does not let him have much freedom. The child can often exploit this situation by being disruptive. He knows he can get away with a great deal of misbehavior. He does not receive control from his mother because he has become a substitute love object in an entangled relationship. In addition, the lack of control creates uneasiness for the youngster because no limits are established for him, nor reference points to guide his behavior. As a reaction to this type of situation, he may "act out" further so that controls will be imposed and some type of structure developed for him. A negative cycle develops. The more "acting out" the child does, the more the mother hovers over him with her permissiveness, and then the greater the "acting out" in the hope that controls will be imposed. This type of abnormal relationship is not conducive to effective child rearing and can ultimately contribute to delinquent behavior. When the marital relationship between parents is not positive and the child is the recipient of inappropriate and exaggerated emotions, he soon learns that he is not loved for himself but is being used as an object by one or both parents to vent their hostility on each other.[58]

The type of role that the parent plays within the family can also affect the youngster's perception of his parents and ultimately his perception of himself. If the mother is domineering and aggressive and the father is weak, the modeling process of father to son is complicated and the formation of an adequate conscience is affected.[59]

In households where parents do have behavioral disturbances and manifestations of emotional immaturity, instability, or insecurity, there is frequent loss of temper and the direction of inappropriate emotions to children. Where tension, hostility, and displaced emotions exist, the family environment will not be conducive to producing children who are themselves stable and who can function effectively. In families where one or both parents have emotional disturbances— or a disease such as alcoholism—the youngster runs a much greater risk of developing problems that often manifest themselves in a delinquent activity. The Gluecks found that a significantly large number of parents of delinquents had problems themselves and came from homes that had an alcoholic in the family, mental retardation, or emotional disturbances. And mothers of delinquents, as well as fathers, were often inferior physically, intellectually, and emotionally.[60] Aichhorn also associated behavioral disturbances of parents with delinquent behavior of their children and pointed out the negative family environments that parents of delinquents often come from.

More significantly, however, such severe emotional abnormalities as psychosis, psychoneurosis, epilepsy, sex inversions, marked emotional insta-

[58] *Ibid.*
[59] *Ibid.*, p. 170.
[60] Glueck, *op. cit.*, p. 5.

bility and pronounced temperamental deviation existed in one or more members of at least one-fourth of the families from which the delinquent father sprang, compared to but one-sixth of nondelinquents' paternal families. The maternal families of delinquents were also found to be far more pathological emotionally than those of nondelinquents.[61]

Reiner and Kaufman noted that parents of antisocial character disorder children often acted out their own unconscious parental wishes through other children.[62]

Often a parent engages in overt delinquency or shows deviant attitudes that are a counterpart to the child's behavior. But even in such cases when the child gets in conflict with the law, the parent is enraged at the child's behavior. He does not condone the delinquency in the child or really condone it in himself. In some instances, one form of delinquency may be acceptable to the parent while another form is not acceptable. In these cases, we find that the parent has led the child in a particular direction by his prohibitions. The parent is afraid that his own impulses, against which he has built a rigid reaction formation, will break through, and he projects this danger onto the child.[63]

Other theorists, such as Aldrich,[64] generally agree with Reiner and Kaufman's statement that many parents receive vicarious satisfaction when their children act out unacceptable impulses. These parents have emotional disturbances themselves and have never really worked out their internal conflicts. The major energy release for their own instability comes through their children's delinquent activities.

Practitioners in the field of criminal justice can give many examples of parents who, either directly or indirectly, condone the delinquent activities of their children. In some cases, parents even encourage this negativism because they themselves harbor pent-up hostility and resentment.

The unconscious transmission of negative attitudes of parents to their children has been a subject of much discussion. Even though theorists disagree as to the amount and form that these transmissions take, they believe that much, if not most, delinquent behavior is spawned in the family. Even though Bandura and Walters in their study of adolescent aggression found no evidence that parents had displayed "consistently blatant anti-social behavior," they did find that many of the fathers of the boys had provided aggressive models for imitation.[65] Parental emotional instability can take many forms, but regardless of the form of expression, the effect on youngsters can apparently be devastating.

---

[61] Aichhorn, *op. cit.,* p. 146.

[62] Reiner and Kaufman, *op. cit.*

[63] *Ibid.,* pp. 15–16.

[64] C. Knight Aldrich, "Thief," *Psychology Today* (March 1971), pp. 67–68.

[65] Albert Bandura and Richard H. Walters, *Adolescent Aggression* (New York: Ronald Press, 1959), p. 355.

Family Economics

Families of delinquents, regardless of socioeconomic status, usually have certain characteristics that are different from those of families of nondelinquents—disruptive homes with a great deal of tension and rejection, ineffective methods of parental control, and parental emotional instability.

Even though these conditions can exist in all homes regardless of economic status, family economics can be a contributing variable to delinquency. Reiss, for example, concluded that there is an association between a family's economic dependence and a son's success on probation.[66] A family's inability to provide for the material needs of the youngster can create insecurity and affect the amount of control that the family exerts over the youngster because he often seeks material support and security outside the home.[67] Other theorists have pointed out that the homes of delinquents are often physically deteriorated, which can affect the boy's perception of himself and the attitude of the community toward his family.

According to Peterson and Becker:

> The homes in which delinquents live tend to be dirty and rundown—the homes of delinquents are often disorderly and cluttered, present routines are weakly fixed, physical space is at a premium and privacy can best be had by leaving the house—there is little order in the model delinquent home. As a physical social stimulus the typical delinquent home acts mainly as a repellent, driving people away.[68]

It should, however, be pointed out that many delinquents come from homes that do not typify the above description. Economic status and material possessions might be directly correlated with delinquent activity in some cases, but they do not explain middle- and upper-class delinquency. The economic condition of the family can be one of many contributing factors in the multiproblem family.

Barker and Adams find that almost without exception delinquents come from multiproblem homes where other siblings are in trouble and where there is a great deal of personal and family disorganization as well as some economic handicap.[69] "Too often their parents are 'losers,' unable to make a marriage go, unsuccessful in business or alcoholics, emotionally unstable, or have other problems."[70]

Tait and Hodges feel that the typical delinquent family is working under

[66] Reiss, *op. cit.*, p. 198.
[67] *Ibid.*
[68] Peterson and Becker, *op. cit.*, p. 67.
[69] Gordon H. Barker and W. Thomas Adams, "Glue Sniffers," *Sociology and Social Research* (1963), pp. 298–310.
[70] Howard James, *Children in Trouble* (New York: David McKay Co., Inc., 1969), p. 196.

many more handicaps than the average family, thus making it difficult for the child to be integrated into the family in a meaningful manner. In healthy families the youngster has a secure atmosphere and can learn socially acceptable modes of behavior and a life-style that will help him adjust effectively in the community. Conversely, in homes of delinquents, the family fails both the youngster and ultimately the community because it does not provide the proper atmosphere for helping the youngster to develop into a productive citizen.[71]

Family economics is probably one of the least meaningful variables that is directly related to delinquent behavior, although it can play a part when combined with other factors. We now examine the contemporary family and some of the problems associated with present-day child rearing.

THE CONTEMPORARY FAMILY

Adolescents present peculiar problems to their families and their communities. Because this is a topic of great interest and importance, Chapter 4 will focus on the physical, psychological, and social problems that accompany adolescence. When these problems become acute, patterns of delinquent behavior often emerge. The major purpose of discussing the adolescent in this section is to point out the gap that often exists between the generations and the effect this has on effective problem solving within the family structure.

Caplan and Lebovici postulate that whenever social and technological change accelerates, the gap between the generations increases and each succeeding generation has to deal with the accumulation of problems that develop. And because adults often have to work out methods of coping with environmental challenges without benefit of youthful input, problems between generations arise. Although parents transmit to their children both directly through communication and indirectly through modeling various patterns of behavior for coping with problems, historical and technological change often leaves the patterns that have been transmitted inadequate to solve a totally new range of problems.[72]

The Group for the Advancement of Psychiatry suggests that because of adult resistance to change and interest in maintaining the status quo, many adolescent problems are created which contribute to stressful relations between generations.[73] In complex societies such as ours where major transitions are taking place daily, the gap between the younger and the older generations increases because of a lack of meaningful communication and the inability of both generations to identify with each other's problems and problem-solving processes. The conflict and the gap between the generations seem to be increas-

---

[71] Downing Tait, Jr., and Emory F. Hodges, Jr., *Delinquents, Their Families and the Community* (Springfield, Ill.: Charles C Thomas, 1962), p. 90.

[72] Gerald Caplan and Serge Lebovici, *Adolescence: Psychosocial Perspectives* (New York and London: Basic Books, Inc., 1969), p. xi.

[73] Group for the Advancement of Psychiatry, *Normal Adolescence: Its Dynamics and Impact* (New York: Charles Scribner's Sons, 1968), pp. 95–96.

ing. Adults and youth have difficulty not only adjusting to the changes but also developing patterns of behavior that can be both meaningful and compatible. Adolescents feel that many of the changes that are occurring are the result of adult decision making in which they have not been involved, and they therefore have difficulty committing themselves to a style of life and a problem-solving process of which they do not feel a part. Often, because adults have no clear answers to their own problems in our complex society and because the experiences of their own adolescent years are far removed, they lack empathy or understanding and are unable to provide guidelines and dependable role models for youngsters. Garrison comments that tension between the generations is an inevitable consequence of the rapid rate of social change that is taking place in our society. "Since western society is above all a society of change, conflict between our society and the growing child is inherent in the development of personality."[74]

Caplan and Lebovici sum up the conflict that exists between generations and the reasons for its development as follows:

> this situation is complicated by the fact that as participants in an evolving culture, we adults have continually been adjusting to a succession of changes. We have developed selective perceptual distortions and ways of reconciling ourselves to discrepancies between feasible "reality" and our basic theories and stated values, which allow us to pursue our paths in life with relative equanimity, even though it may well be that these paths turn out to be unsuccessful. We communicate only our abstract concepts and values to our adolescents. And since they have not shared in the process whereby we insensibly adjusted these to our experience of reality, when they come relatively suddenly onto the adult scene, with open eyes, they correctly perceive the discrepancies between our precepts and our practice. Moreover, they do not have our commitment to the ways of life we have worked out or need to rely on them because of personal investment. Since adolescence is a developmental period marked by a rapid increase in the capacity for abstract conceptualization and an interest in active exploration and analysis of the world, adolescents often confront us with fundamental questions about our adult ways. Their lack of adult bias and stereotyped thinking frequently results in their seeing a situation more clearly and truly than we do. They propose valuable and innovative approaches precisely because they are not aware of those "facts of life" to which we possibly ill-advisedly have accommodated ourselves.[75]

The Group for the Advancement of Psychiatry states that adolescent questioning of adult values and refusal to accept societal institutions on faith create unpleasant feelings of doubt and anxiety in adults and renew the awareness of their own shortcomings. Outmoded approaches to life may be exposed by

[74] Karl C. Garrison, *Psychology of Adolescence* (Englewood Cliffs, N.J.: Prentice-Hall, Inc., 1965), p. 18.
[75] Caplan and Lebovici, *op. cit.,* pp. xi–xii.

adolescent skepticism. For example, parents may have evolved a precarious balance between the strict moral teachings of their youth and their own personal immoral behavior, but exposed to blunt challenges the balance may be upset. "The painful exposure and self-reappraisal caused by the 'show me,' 'prove it' attitude of the adolescent and his behaving in ways that adults may envy, but no longer allow themselves, are difficult to experience with equanimity."[76]

The Group for the Advancement of Psychiatry contends that because adults have repressed conflicts and anxieties during their own adolescent years, they are unable to share the adolescent's dilemma sufficiently to be able to empathize and help him. The attitude and rebelliousness of the adolescent often generates consternation in alarmed parents. Their attempts to reason with the adolescent in order to solve conflicts may be met with hostility. Parents often react by giving up in despair or reverting to the authority that they believe they still possess. Results of such confrontations are often alienation of the adolescent and the adult from each other. The adolescent feels he is being "managed" rather than receiving the respect due him as an individual in his own right.[77]

These findings lend new insight into the problems that parents have in influencing their youngsters in socially acceptable ways so that the conflicts that inevitably exist between the community and its residents can be minimized. The importance of the family in shaping the youngster's attitudes and behavior cannot be overemphasized. The contemporary family is faced with problems that have no historical precedent. The gap that naturally exists between parents and youngsters because of our highly complex technical society and the vast amount of change that has taken place lends itself to further difficulty and problem situations within the family constellation. We will now focus on the contemporary family and some of the problems that exist between parents and youngsters that can ultimately contribute to delinquent behavior. Many of the problem areas to be discussed are not peculiar to any socioeconomic class or ethnic group but seem to be symptoms of our present complex society.

Many people consider today's social problems an enigma because many of the communities experiencing the greatest difficulty do not have problems emanating from poverty, unemployment, or lack of education. Paradoxically, these communities seem to have problems that result from affluence, overcompetitiveness, and—in some cases—too much reliance on formal education. Contemporary parents have become so involved in daily competition for material success and rewards that they do not take time to reflect on their goals in life or evaluate the process of achieving them. Jobs and social activities become ends in themselves and not means to self and family fulfillment, and life goals become slowly and unintentionally altered because of the emphasis on material success. The result is that children often become "caught up" in this competitive process.[78]

[76] Group for the Advancement of Psychiatry, *op. cit.*, p. 98.
[77] *Ibid.*, p. 95.
[78] Caplan and Lebovici, *op. cit.*, p. xi.

Formal education has sometimes become an end in itself and not a means for improving the individual, the family, and the community. Education without practical application is like a servant without a master. Parents have lost their ability to intuitively perceive the problems of their youngsters and to effectively communicate with them. Many contemporary parents have tried to obtain the answers to their questions in textbooks or from professionals, forgetting that the cornerstone of any strong unit, and especially a family unit, is the ability of its members to be sensitive to the needs of each other. Even though material possessions and status have been achieved by many parents, their ability to relate to their children has taken a secondary position in their lives.[79]

Use of External Resources. The reliance on technical assistance from professionals and "outsiders" has become commonplace. Textbook knowledge and professional assistance is necessary, but any honest professional would be the first to point out that outside assistance should only be used to supplement the intuitive sensitivities, feelings, and judgments of parents. If parents depend exclusively on outside resources, they lose their ability to empathize and to communicate effectively with their children.

After reviewing the literature, it becomes evident that although much has been written about preadolescent child care and development, comparatively little has been written about the way parents should relate to their teen-age children. Many specialists are willing to work with preadolescents, but few of them want to work with adolescents. This is unfortunate because the teen-age years, the period of most juvenile delinquency, is a time of turbulence and the youngster is attempting to determine who he is and what his goals in life should be. He is developing a self-concept and attempting to cope with the struggle of dependence versus independence. If parents have depended exclusively on child-rearing manuals during their children's early years, they have not learned to handle their children's problems through an honest direct relationship. Instead of communicating directly in accordance with the emotion that accompanies the particular confrontation or event, the communication process becomes tempered and complicated with jargon and popular theoretical clichés. Parents often deny and repress the acceptable and common human emotions of anger and ambivalence. When these emotions are not expressed directly and honestly, they are often manifested in subtle forms that are difficult for the child to understand and accept.[80]

For example, a parent may be irritated at his child's behavior in a particular situation, but because the parent believes that the emotion of anger is abnormal, he does not express his feelings or set limits on the child's behavior. Instead, he may deny that the emotion exists. Denial is not totally effective, however, because invariably the feelings are expressed in some form which if not

---

[79] Abrahamsen, *op. cit.,* p. 43.
[80] Group for the Advancement of Psychiatry, *op. cit.,* p. 98.

expressed directly, usually takes a passive-aggressive (indirect) channel. The result is that the parents may "pick at" the child for such insignificant matters as haircuts, dress, and taste in music. The child then, because he cannot understand why his parent is "bugging" him, overreacts by going to extremes. Problems such as this can be avoided if parents can learn to handle the situation and their emotions on the spot. The child, if dealt with directly, can much more readily accept his parents' anger and understand the need for imposing limits and the rationale for the particular restriction. Expression of displaced emotions is not effective in problem solving. It only contributes to a denial of the problem and further widens the gap between generations.[81]

Parents are able to "get away with" their dependence on outside resources during the early years of the child's life because children are fairly predictable at this time and most of their difficulties revolve around physical rather than emotional problems. When the child reaches adolescence, however, there are not only limited outside resources (psychiatrists, reading material, etc.) but the child is no longer as predictable. If parents have not learned to use their intuitive feelings and good judgment to react spontaneously in a sensitive manner, they will be at a loss during the teen-age period. The problem becomes increasingly severe as a result of their increased frustration and need for help during the teenage years. Parents who have not learned to relate to their child become even more amenable to popular clichés and shallow jargon, and their effectiveness in preparing the youngster for interactions in the community becomes neutralized.[82]

Decision Making. Parents find that one of their most difficult tasks is decision making. Parents avoid making important decisions for their children in many ways. They can relegate their decision-making responsibility to others (outside resources), or they can simply avoid making them. Because an efficient and non-anxiety-provoking decision-making process is sought, simple answers to complicated child-rearing problems are often forthcoming.

Because parents do not know how to react to the adolescent struggle of dependence versus independence and are not confident of their own decision-making ability to take the adolescent problem as it comes on a case-by-case basis, they often tend to oversimplify the process by subscribing to either an extremely permissive or an extremely disciplinarian philosophy and approach to child rearing. Both extremes can have disastrous results. The strictly disciplined child rebels against the stringent demands of his parents, while the "free-floating" child does not know where he is going and may react in a delinquent manner because he fears the extensive freedom given to him so readily. Many practitioners have had delinquent adolescents tell them that they wished their parents had exerted more controls and set limits because they interpreted limits and controls

---

[81] Nye, *op. cit.,* p. 73.
[82] Clyde E. Vedder and Dora B. Summerville, *The Delinquent Girl* (Springfield, Ill.: Charles C Thomas, 1970).

as being an expression of love and concern. Extreme permissiveness can be harmful to, and misunderstood by, the child, and the family therefore becomes an ineffective agent of socialization for him. Extreme permissiveness and extreme discipline are merely different sides of the same coin. They are symptoms of the same problem—inadequate parenting. Excessive discussion and rationalizing of these symptoms may often only be a diversionary tactic that parents find useful when they do not want to examine their own motives for taking extremes rather than considering the youngster's individual situation, circumstances, and personality. Of course, when parents do take all these factors into consideration, the decision-making process becomes much more difficult than it would have been if they had merely adhered to either the permissive or the disciplinarian philosophy. It is much easier to say yes or no to the child than to analyze each situation for its merits and disadvantages.[83]

Unrecognized Immaturity. Technological advances and rapid social change have led many parents to believe that because their youngsters seem more sophisticated intellectually and socially, they are also better equipped emotionally to handle complex problems. When parents assume this, problem situations arise and the generation gap broadens. Parents often accept totally whatever their youngster says, but are not sensitive to his feelings and nonverbal communication. The youngster may say he is grown up, may sound as if he is grown up, and may look as if he is grown up, but he still vacillates between wanting to be a child and wanting to be an adult. He still seeks assistance from his parents in planning and guiding his life, but because his parents believe that what he says and what he looks like indicate his true personality, they react by giving the youngster more freedom than he is capable of handling. In other words, many youngsters grow physically and intellectually, but not emotionally. They believe that their parents want them to be sophisticated, and the parents believe that their youngsters want to be treated as sophisticated adults. This faulty communication process exists because parents have not relied on honest communication in respect to feelings, nor have they been sensitive to their children's needs and nonverbal communication. Too often parents give their children decision-making power under the guise of the children's right to individual freedom, self-destiny, and self-expression when, in fact, they want to reduce their own anxiety and indecisiveness. They therefore relinquish their own decision-making responsibility and force it on their children. This again is an undesirable assumption and process because only with the guidance of parents within a cohesive family unit can youngsters become astute decision makers.[84]

A Matter of Priorities. Parents can also lose sight of priorities in their relationship with their children. Listing priorities is a facet related to decision making

[83] John and Valerie Cowie, and Eliot Slater, *Delinquency in Girls* (London: Heinemann Educational Books, 1968).
[84] McCord, McCord, and Zola, *op. cit.*

and a process followed whether it is in the workaday world or within the family constellation. Just as sometimes a priority of means rather than ends take precedence in our daily struggle for material prosperity, so can secondary child-rearing priorities take precedence over primary priorities. For example, even though the giving of material rewards to children is a part of natural child-rearing process, this should not become an end in itself, nor a substitute for the giving of emotional security, guidance, and support. Or a parent may be a heavy smoker or drinker, but because he feels it will be harmful for his child, lies to him and tells him that he does not smoke or drink. The child may later see his parent slightly intoxicated or surreptitiously smoking. The child has caught his parent lying. The priority of not lying to the child should have taken precedence over the child's not knowing that his parent smokes or drinks. Lying can have far-reaching negative consequences. It can affect the basic relationship between parent and child, further increase the gap between generations, and neutralize the effectiveness of the family as a socializing agent.[85]

Unconscious Parental Transmissions. The subtle negative ways in which parents can influence their children's behavior can also contribute to delinquent behavior, and they are often the result of the parents' own emotional instability and neurotic method of problem solving. As was pointed out earlier, these undesirable transmissions from parents to children can be a contributing factor in the youngster's "acting out" his parents' feeling in an antiauthority, antisocial manner. When parents transmit only negative feelings or attitudes without assisting their youngsters in developing the accompanying frustration tolerance and self-control, problem situations can occur. Youngsters cannot usually handle these transmissions without support. They have not learned the accompanying controls because they have not been exposed to the necessary life experiences and are not familiar with the decision-making processes that can assist them in analyzing the total situation. Most human behavior is the result of an "attitude set," plus an evaluative process and then a decision as to what mode of behavior will be appropriate. Children who pick up negative transmissions from their parents without the accompanying controls only have the benefit of one of the variables in the decision-making process—an attitude.[86]

Parents can also transmit to children the attitude of individual rights and freedom of expression, two highly valued norms in a democratic society, without emphasizing personal responsibility and social consciousness. The use of drugs, a contemporary social problem, is an example of how children pick up their parents' transmissions without accompanying controls (see Chapter 4). Although most parents will subscribe to, and transmit to their children, the values of individual freedom of expression, most parents will not condone drug use by their children. Parents do not realistically discuss the constellation of factors involved in using drugs and may only transmit an attitude or feeling of individual

[85] Aichhorn, *op. cit.,* p. 233.
[86] Reiner and Kaufman, *op. cit.,* p. 15.

freedom of expression. Youngsters can therefore logically conclude that individual rights and freedom of expression can be extended to the individual's right to use drugs and become involved in other self-gratifying behavior. The parents' transmission of feelings and attitudes without communicating the ramifications of these feelings and attitudes and the spectrum of their life experiences gives the child only half the picture.

Persons working with juvenile delinquents can also be guilty of the same phenomenon. For example, a probation officer may personally feel that drug laws should be liberalized. He may either consciously or unconsciously transmit this to the child. The youngster, not having the accompanying controls, "acts out" the probation officer's feelings, uses drugs, is apprehended, and is convicted. The probation officer can receive vicarious satisfaction from the child's acting out against the establishment that has imposed the legal restrictions against the use of drugs. The probation officer, however, does not have to pay the penalty for the use of drugs. The delinquent youngster "pays the price"; the probation officer receives the satisfaction. If the probation officer in this example found it necessary to transmit the attitude, he should also have discussed the ramifications regarding the use of drugs, the logic behind the law, and the process for changing it. Again, as in the example of the parents and the child, the delinquent has been given only half the picture. The mere transmission of an attitude without accompanying explanations can initiate or perpetuate antisocial behavior.[87]

CONCLUSION

The complexities of the family environment and the way they contribute to the "gap" between youngsters and parents and delinquent behavior have been discussed. Specific problem areas that exist in the contemporary family were also delineated because they can affect the family environment, and the family is obviously the major agent in influencing the youngster's future behavior. Many contemporary parents have substituted clichés for feelings and have transmitted attitudes to their youngsters without accompanying explanations of the total picture. Parents often tell their children that when they were their age, they solved complicated problems very easily. This is not realistic. The problem-solving and decision-making processes, whether in the workaday world or in the family, are difficult processes at any age. A transmission to children that decision making is difficult and that only through mutual assistance can the process be effective will be helpful in presenting a realistic picture of the life process and in establishing an effective communication process between the generations. The generation gap between young and old is somewhat inevitable because of present rapid change and technological advancements. The negative effects of the generation gap can be reduced, however, if parents will take the time to pay attention

[87]Caplan and Lebovici, *op. cit.,* pp. xi–xii.

to their youngsters and help them adjust to complex problems. A realistic and empathetic approach to child rearing that includes assistance and guidance in daily decision making to prepare youngsters for future roles in their communities is much more effective than a superficial or mechanical approach that substitutes material rewards for emotional security and support.[88]

If *generation gap* means inability of adults to relate to youth and meaningfully communicate both verbally and nonverbally with the younger generation, then the gap is indeed a real problem and a cause for concern. The generation gap is not necessarily detrimental if meaningful communication does exist. A gap between the generations can have positive secondary effects. It is important that the younger generation learn from the life experiences of their elders so that they can avoid the mistakes their elders made by the trial-and-error method. Conversely, the older generation needs the vitality and idealism of the young so that social institutions can change and be responsive to the needs of all community members. Cooperative involvement between generations is the most effective approach to problem solving and self-fulfillment. The family and the total environment of the family can be much more effective in handling youngsters' problems if mutual understanding and support exist. Even though totally free communication between the generations is an idealistic goal, "peaceful coexistence" is possible and, furthermore, necessary if the many social problems that exist are to be solved.[89]

SUMMARY

This chapter has attempted to use the family as a model not only to incorporate both sociological and psychological principles but also to point out the usefulness of blending the two disciplines for a more comprehensive understanding of the delinquency phenomenon. The sampling of material presented illustrates the factors in the family environment that contribute to delinquency and the importance of a healthy family atmosphere in influencing youngsters in socially acceptable ways.

Practical suggestions have been made for increasing the effectiveness of the family in the contemporary community so that the gap between the generations can be understood and the problems contributing to hostility and resentment can be reduced. There are numerous other ideas, theories, and assumptions about the influence of the family on delinquent behavior. Gibbons points out that a typology of delinquency has to be developed that incorporates what is known about delinquent behavior into some kind of meaningful framework. At present, a "smorgasbord" approach exists. "Instead, some way must be found to judiciously put these influences into some kind of coherent order and to assign different weights to them depending on the contribution they make to delin

---

[88] Reiner and Kaufman, *op. cit.,* p. 15.
[89] Group for the Advancement of Psychiatry, *op. cit,* p. 95–96.; Garrison, *op. cit,* p. 18.

quent conduct."[90] Even though all delinquent behavior cannot be explained by studying the family, the importance of the family in regard to this phenomenon cannot be denied. It is probably the single most relevant variable that consistently plays a part in the causation of delinquent behavior. The following chapters will reemphasize this point. The next chapter focuses on adolescence and the peculiar problems that accompany this stage of development.

QUESTIONS AND PROJECTS

Essay Questions

1. Why is the family so important in the youngster's life?

2. Are economic conditions of the family directly related to delinquency causation?

3. Are teen-agers more mature or less mature today? Explain.

4. Is some form of discipline necessary in each family?

5. Will early parent-child relationships predestine the child's behavior?

Projects

1. Develop a community program that can help strengthen the families of delinquents.

2. Develop guidelines for parents to use in rearing their children.

3. State the major reasons why the older and the younger generations have difficulty communicating. How can they better understand each other?

---

[90] Gibbons, *op. cit.,* p. 93.

chapter 4

The Adolescent

Because most juvenile delinquency occurs during the adolescent stage of development, it is important to understand the dynamics of the phenomenon of adolescence. Even though all adolescents are not delinquents, all juvenile delinquents are adolescents. Therefore, to understand the juvenile delinquent it is necessary to understand the adolescent stage of development.

> Adolescence encompasses an extensive period of accelerated physical and psychological growth. Its onset can be determined by observation of physical changes—change usually begins at about the age of ten in girls and the age of twelve in boys. Clinical evidence shows that modifications of the psychological structure takes place at approximately the same time as the physical change occurs.[1]

It is easier to determine the physical changes of adolescence than the psychological changes for obvious reasons. The psychological changes and difficulties that occur during adolescence have particular ramifications regarding whether the youngster satisfactorily adjusts to his environment or reacts in a delinquent manner.

Adolescence is a phase of development that cannot be totally explained by one academic discipline.

> Marked social, psychological, and physical changes are characteristic of this age span and they do not occur unrelated to each other. The physical

[1] Irene M. Josselyn, *The Adolescent and His World* (New York: The Family Service Association of America, 1952), p. 5.

changes have definite effect on the social and psychological adjustments of the individual; social factors influence the psychological and physical changes. The psychological factors have repercussions both socially and physiologically.[2]

Much has been written concerning the so-called period of adolescence, it often being described as a very turbulent phase of development in which many problems occur and many conflicts exist. Even though it is recognized that social, psychological, and physiological changes take place, the assumptions regarding the most predominant determining variables that affect the adolescent have been many and varied. For example, Margaret Mead, in her famous study *Coming of Age in Samoa*, concluded that adolescence and the characteristics peculiar to it are culturally determined—depending on the culture, the adolescent will be happy or unhappy, constrained or uninhibited, and his state as an adolescent will be almost solely determined by the culture in which he lives. Mead felt that the Samoan culture, unlike the culture in our country, was much more conducive to the adolescent youngster's experiencing less turmoil and adjusting satisfactorily to his environment. Other writers have pointed out that American adolescents have a distinct system of shared values which are very different from the values of their parents.

> Our society has within its midst a set of small teen-age societies which focus teen-age interest and attitudes on things far removed from adult responsibilities and which may develop standards that lead away from those goals established by the larger society.[3]

Even though there is much conjecture, discussion, and theorizing from many different disciplines regarding the adolescent phase of development, it will be helpful to present some of the most prevalent ideas and views of the adolescent phenomenon. A more thorough knowledge of the characteristics and behavior of the adolescent will lend insight into the behavior of the delinquent adolescent.

A CULTURAL PERSPECTIVE OF ADOLESCENCE

The adolescent phenomenon is not the same in all cultures. The Cavans point out that a shortening or even an omission of adolescence occurs in societies where there is a well-organized family controlled by family elders. In some cultures the child's entire behavior revolves around the family, and little outside assistance supplements the material and psychological support that the child received from his family. The particular role that the youngster occupies in the family or in his community is well established, with little room for experimenta-

[2] *Ibid.*, p. 10.
[3] T. Coleman, *The Adolescent Society* (Glencoe, Ill.: The Free Press, 1961).

tion or mobility. When the youngster becomes physically mature, he is considered an adult and is given the privileges of adulthood as well as its responsibilities.

> In contrast is a situation in western industrialized societies where both the period of adolescence and a concept of juvenile delinquency exist. The family does not operate as a social, economic, or political unit. A child at an early age enters specialized agencies that compete for his loyalty and open many choices to him for present or future aspirations and goals. The passage from childhood to adulthood is not clearly and almost inevitably channeled toward a specific adult role. In the transition from early childhood in his family to later childhood in organized agencies, the child may escape incorporation into any conventional organized group and become a kind of "free lance" in his behavior lacking in self-discipline or clear orientation toward a goal.[4]

Also, in industrialized and technologically advanced countries like the United States, the period of adolescence is much longer than it is in underdeveloped countries mainly because of the need for increased training and specialization and less dependence on the family as a total unit. Education of the adolescent is extended beyond the secondary grades and even well into the college years, which means that the period of adolescence is often prolonged and the dependence on the family, at least financially, becomes even more accentuated and the transition from adolescence to adulthood is delayed. During the nineteenth century, education was not greatly emphasized in the United States, and the period of adolescence was not as extended as it is today.

In addition, in less-industrialized cultures and in primitive societies the treatment of adolescents and the transition from childhood to adulthood was much different.

> The younger teen-agers were sequestered from the community, starved for prolonged periods, then circumcised en masse. These ritualistic practices supervised and executed by the constituted authority of the gens or clan were probable assertions that the youth was not an independent entity, an island to itself, but belonged to his society (gens or clan). After the contemplation of these sadistic, humiliating, and impotenizing (castrating) rituals, the youngster was fully accepted into the fraternity of the males in his community. He had equal status with his elders in the men's house and participated on an equal basis with them in hunts and wars.[5]

In situations like the above where "rites of passage" from childhood to adulthood exist, the transition to adult status and delineation of role requirements are facilitated.[6]

[4] Ruth S. Cavan and Jordan T. Cavan, *Delinquency and Crime: Cross Cultural Perspectives* (Philadelphia: J. B. Lippincott Co., 1968), p. 8.
[5] S. L. Slavson, *Reclaiming the Delinquent* (New York: The Free Press of Glencoe, 1965), p. 7.
[6] Walter C. Reckless, *The Crime Problem* (New York: Appleton-Century-Crofts, 1967), p. 175.

Reckless cites Bloch and Niederhoffer on the adolescent gang in our society and its having rituals similar to rites of passage.

> The puberty rites of tribal societies not only prepared youth for adult status, but also satisfied the concealed needs of youth (such as the need to overcome anxiety and doubt). In the absence of such rites and ceremonies in modern society, spontaneous gang patterns develop which satisfy the needs and yearnings of youth. Hence, informal rituals of modern American gangs are quite similar to the puberty rites of tribes.[7]

Because of the extended period of adolescence, the youngster often looks to the group or the gang for the security and at least some definition of a role and expected behavior. This is even more accentuated if the family does not provide the needed structure and guidance.

The gang, which is often negatively oriented, provides the youngster with at least an orientation and often a role. This can be a substitute for his need for identification during the turbulent and nebulous adolescent period.

If the adolescent cannot obtain satisfaction from his home or from socially acceptable groups, he may be attracted to individuals who have similar problems and needs, and many times this takes the form of a gang. If the gang exerts a great deal of influence over him, he will begin to utilize their standards and value system. This value system is often in contrast to that of his parents and community. If the value systems greatly vary, serious delinquent behavior may result.

Research has shown that almost all youthful delinquent acts are committed by groups rather than by individuals. If a youngster is looking for some type of structure and guidance and support that he cannot find in his family, but can find in the group or gang, he will evidently take on the characteristics of the group, identify with it, and abide by its codes.

> Among the rites of contemporary gangs of modern America may be found: decoration which includes tattooing, scarification, wearing distinctive apparel; the acquisition of a nickname and gang jargon; the seclusion from women in hangouts "like the bachelor huts of some tribes," and the development of age gradations (the kids, the midgets, the juniors, the seniors); hazing and ordeal as tests of fitness to belong, etc. The ganging together in all levels of modern society alleviates the storm and stress of adolescence.[8]

Even though gang activity is not normative for most children, involvement with the group and the dynamic processes that take place are very much a part of the adolescent's adjustment phase and a very real exposure to his world.

> The freedom offered adolescents by the peer group does not come without a price. Often the peer group exercises a dictatorship over the attitudes

[7] *Ibid.*, p. 422.
[8] Reckless, *op. cit.*, p. 9.

and behavior of its members that is more tyrannical than anything ever devised by the adult world. Nevertheless a great many children evidently have to go through the process of submitting to group domination before they are ready to stand on their own feet and make their own decisions. It is hard for adults to understand the why's and the wherefore's of adolescent behavior. When we see an adolescent engaging in behavior which seems silly or illogical but which conforms to the standards or norms of his group, we forget that he may not be psychologically free to behave differently. He is in effect a prisoner of the norm.[9]

Many persons do not have the strength to resist the pressures of the gang or group, not only during the adolescent period but even in later years. The maturity level of these individuals is retarded, and they often have difficulty adjusting to the adult world of expectations, demands, and responsibilities.

The group, then, can exert a great deal of influence on the youngster, and group involvement can be normal and beneficial. The group experience can be devastating, however, if the group is negatively oriented and contributes to the youngster's becoming a delinquent.

Just as the majority of adolescents do not spend most of their time in negatively oriented groups, the period of adolescence is not a common phenomenon in all cultures. The state of the adolescent depends upon how he is perceived and what place there is in the society for him. Coleman states that

> adolescence is not a time of stress and turmoil in all cultures. Where the adolescent has a well-structured role, contributes to the social group and has assured status, he does not suffer the insecurities and fears of our adolescents or exhibit the extreme behavior many of our adolescents manifest in their attempt to feel important and worthwhile. In proportion then, as we encourage and plan for a useful part for our adolescents to play in their community, and insofar as we are able to solve our own uncertainties and provide a stable social and economic setting in which they can see a meaningful place as they reach adulthood, we shall be fostering mental health and preventing abnormal behavior.[10]

Like most technically advanced societies, ours keeps adolescents out of the labor market for as long as possible, thus extending and accentuating the adolescent period. As mentioned earlier, increased training and specialization are the main reason for this delay; however, an individual's job or vocational skill is one of the major factors in his achieving adult status and the rewards that go with it. If the youngster is kept out of the labor market because of the real or imagined need for educational diplomas and degrees, this has the effect of not only prolonging adolescence, but if the youngster quits school and cannot find a job, it can contribute to delinquent behavior.

[9] Henry Clay Lindgren, *Educational Psychology in the Classroom* (New York: John Wiley & Sons, Inc., 1967), p. 140.
[10] James C. Coleman, *Abnormal Psychology and Modern Life* (Glenwood, Ill.: Scott Foresman & Company, 1956), p. 596.

The Cavans point out that the traditional Eskimo society lacked both adolescence and delinquency.

> The child and youth was never physically separated from his family, either on a daily basis for education, employment or recreation, or on a yearly basis at college or for a prolonged journey. There were no hangouts or lighted street corners where youth might gather. As adult skills were learned, the child's status increased and in some groups special recognition was given as each new stage was reached. A special step toward adulthood was reached when a boy was given his own kayak, usually about the age of eight or nine, or when inland he brought down his first carabao at about age eleven or twelve. In some groups a killing of the first major meat animal called for a special celebration. As soon as the youth had killed at least one of each such animal he was considered ready for marriage. Thus, step-by-step the boy made his way from childhood to adulthood always living and participating in the activities of family and community.[11]

Even the Eskimo community, however, has been affected by technology and change, and at present, as the Cavans point out, there are increasing signs of youthful male delinquency. The delinquency occurs in the towns and not in the rural settings that once typified Eskimo life. Eskimos in towns have more difficulty conforming to the traditional Eskimo behavior, and the function of the family is changed. Because many of the Eskimo youngsters want steady jobs so that they can earn money and have the same luxuries as other local ethnic groups, there is an increased "breaking of the bonds" between the youth and their families. The result is that the extended family exerts less control and has less influence over the youngster's behavior and actions, which in turn affects the delinquency rates.

Adolescence has to be viewed both historically and culturally. We have seen that technological advancements and the resulting industrialization contribute to a prolongation of the adolescent period, which can have a great affect on delinquency rates. The following section will examine the normal adolescent in greater detail so that a more realistic and insightful picture can be obtained of the delinquent adolescent.

THE NORMAL ADOLESCENT

The combined physical and psychological changes that take place during the adolescent period affect the adolescent's conception of himself, the way he feels, and the way the environment often reacts to him. In the child's early development there is not the turmoil or negative behavioral manifestation that exists during adolescence. Even in the early stages of adolescence problems do not emerge. Josselyn describes the initial stages of adolescence as being generally

[11] Cavan and Cavan, *op. cit.,* p. 23.

free of anxiety and conflict. The youngster participates in his groups and associates with his peers in a very adaptable manner. His protests against his parents are minor and sporadic. The youngster handles problems with surprising facility and can even adequately adapt to tragedy, such as the loss of his parents. However, as Josselyn points out, this period does not last long, and the transition from the early period of adolescence to the next phase is anything but smooth. The transition takes place when physical maturity begins and when reproductive organs become developed.

> The youngster at this time may seem fatigued and often depressed—she may be sensitive, easily hurt and perhaps quarrelsome—teachers may observe the sensitivity and irritability. They may notice that she is not so reliable or conscientious as in the past. Concurrently she may make increased demands for greater independence and privileges. . . .[12]

In addition, there are often other expressions of erratic and hostile behavior.

> During adolescence, anxiety, emotional confusion, erratic social behavior, shifting concepts of self in the outer world, weakness of reality perception, vacillating moral standards, instability and irregularity of impulse control, and fickle ambivalent interpersonal relations may all be part of a normal transitional adaption. Transitory mild disturbances of these types may not constitute clinical pathology. Clinical diagnoses can in no way be based on intrinsic adolescent phenomena.[13]

Redl describes the different developmental clusters of behaviors that exist during adolescence and are part of the normal teen-ager's behavioral constellation:

> 1. Conflict of double standards: individual child still parent loyal, peer group code basically "anti-adult." Result: new waves of guilt and shame in both directions.
>
> 2. Embarrassment about open submission to adult politeness and good manner codes.
>
> 3. Shamelessness in language and behavior bravado through flaunting of health and safety rules, special joy in risk taking.
>
> 4. Avoidance of too open acceptance of adults in official roles even of those very much liked (teachers and parents, for example).
>
> 5. Loyalty to peers and risk taking in their favor even when they are personally despised or feared.
>
> 6. Openly displayed freshness against authority figures.
>
> 7. Deep-seated revulsion toward any form of praise or punishment which seems to be perceived as "infantilizing."

[12] Josselyn, *op. cit.,* p. 21.
[13] Nathan W. Ackerman, *The Psychodynamics of Family Life* (New York: Basic Books, Inc., 1958), p. 231.

8. Safety in homosexual groupings; view of the other sex as "hunter's trophy" rather than in terms of interpersonal relationships.

9. Negative loading of any form of official acceptance of help from adults; pride in "taking it bravely" at any price.

10. No prestige of verbal communication with a trusted adult; hesitation about communicating about feelings and emotions.

11. Apathy toward adult as partner in play life unless it is a group game situation.[14]

These comments about the normal adolescent are important for those persons working with the juvenile delinquent. It is often easy to forget that the youngster is an adolescent first and a delinquent second and that much of the behavior he manifests is normal for his particular age group. When working with delinquents, much of the behavior that is well within the range of "normal" limits for an adolescent may be interpreted as inappropriate and "abnormal." If the person working with the delinquent adolescent is too quick in shutting off the normal adolescent expression of verbalizations and behavior, this can compound the problems for the delinquent youngster. The delinquent youngster should have at least the same amount of leeway as his nondelinquent counterpart and should receive the same consideration. If the practitioner who is working with the delinquent does not understand the normal clusters of behavior typical of "normal" adolescents, he will have difficulty working effectively because he will often overreact to normal behavioral manifestations. This overreaction will affect his relationship with his client by constraining the youngster's normal actions and activities. This puts pressure on the youngster to act in a manner that is abnormal for teen-agers in general (quiet, sedentary, etc.). When the youngster is unable to handle this pressure, he often releases his energy in an exaggerated manner. The exaggerated behavior is often in the form of juvenile delinquency.

In many respects it is much more difficult for the practitioner today to work with the youngster who has been labeled delinquent than it was in the past. The styles of hair and dress and behavior of youngsters today are much different from those of even a few years ago. Therefore, it becomes much easier to stereotype and label youngsters, even when this is inappropriate and overgeneralized. Extensive overgeneralizations and labeling can hinder the helping process and create imaginary boundaries that do not have to be constructed.

There certainly is a general trend toward longer hair, sideburns, beards, mustaches and so on, among young men in our society just as there is a general trend toward fewer and more flimsy clothes, more casual clothes, longer, less constricted hair styles and so on, among young women. But today, none of this can be taken to be symbolic of growing youth rebellion or

[14] Fritz Redl, "Adolescents—Just How Do They React?" in *Adolescence: Psychosocial Perspectives,* Gerald Caplan and Serge Lebovici, Eds. (New York: Basic Books, Inc., 1969), p. 82.

any such thing. For the older members of our society these personal styles are still very much a subject of great concern—a symbol of revolt—because they have some effect on what the older members of our society think about the young and what they do. These personal styles are of significance, but they are not significant as symbols of a general youth culture. In general there are still far too many differences among young people in our society, especially class differences and so on, and these are still far too important to the young people themselves in many different specific ways, for a general youth culture in the sense of a distinct set of values, beliefs, commitments and everyday patterns of activity to have developed.[15]

The point is that although many adults feel that young people are a threat to the adult way of life, most youngsters are closely aligned with many adult values. Just as there is not the great schism of viewpoints between youngsters and adults that is often imagined, much of the behavior of the delinquent adolescent is well within the range of normal acceptance. It is not the purpose of the person working with the juvenile delinquent to change the youngster's entire personality and orientation, for much of his orientation, feelings, and expectations are the same as those of the normal adolescent. What does have to be altered are those aspects of his behavior that go beyond the limits of acceptability. This can best be accomplished by perceiving and treating him as an adolescent first and a delinquent second.

CHILDHOOD DEVELOPMENT

During the period of adolescence—especially in a highly industrialized culture like ours—not only are physical and psychological changes taking place, but the youngster is attempting to develop a self-concept. This is a difficult process; therefore, much of his behavior is contradictory and he often vacillates from one mood to another.

> Today he may idealize a certain philosophy of life only to express tomorrow slavelike devotion to a completely contrasting approach to the problems of living. At one time he follows too rigidly an idealized code of conduct, the demands of which if he really met, would deny him all human gratification. As if by a sudden metamorphosis of character he then violates—or more often talks of violating—even acceptable "behavior."[16]

The youngster's change in mood from day to day causes his parents much concern. The contradictions in his verbalizations or in his behavior or the contra-

---

[15] Jack D. Douglas, *Youth in Turmoil, America's Changing Youth Cultures and Student Protest Movements*, Crime and Delinquency Issues: A Monograph Series, National Institute of Mental Health Center for Studies of Crime and Delinquency, Public Health Services, Publication No. 2058, p. 30.

[16] Josselyn, *op. cit.*, p. 10.

dictions in both his verbalizations and in his behavior are, as Josselyn feels, the result of an attempt to find clear-cut answers to internal conflicts.

> He is attempting to avoid discord by choosing a variety of notes to play singularly. He does not know how to play several notes in harmony.[17]

This has important implications in working with the youngster. Adults often find it frustrating that the youngster fluctuates in moods and in behavior so readily and so easily. This frustration can be transmitted to the youngster and can contribute to his insecure feelings. If the adult merely takes much of the youngster's erratic behavior in stride, the "testing" he is doing on his environment and his parents will subside. With the guidance and support of the adult, more consistent orientations to problem solving can occur.

Coleman discusses the conflicts or problem areas that adolescent youngsters have to deal with during adolescence.[18] He points out the main areas of adaption that have to take place during this period if the youngster is going to handle his problems with some semblance of order and ultimately be a productive citizen. First, the youngster struggles with the phenomenon of dependence versus independence. Up to the point of adolescence, he has generally been dependent on his parents for the satisfying of both his emotional and his physical needs. As he proceeds through the adolescent period he becomes more independent, possibly by having a part-time job or by being able to spend his allowance with more flexibility. (Because the dependence-independence conflict is important, it will be elaborated upon later.)

Second, Coleman points out that the adolescent period is a transition also from pure pleasure to reality. Before the adolescent period and in the infant stages, the youngster did not usually have to be concerned about "basics" such as food, clothing, and shelter. As he progresses through adolescence, there is much pressure on him to start thinking about a vocation and a role in life. The reality of the future and how he is going to provide for himself becomes manifest.

Third, Coleman describes the problem the youngster has transcending from incompetence to competence. Before the adolescent period, the youngster did not have to have specific skills either educationally or vocationally to survive. With the onset of adolescence, however, he has to become competent so that he can support himself in the future. In addition to this, the adolescent youngster has to consider what Coleman identifies as extending beyond himself to "other-centered activity" rather than merely self-centered activities. As he goes through the adolescent period and starts thinking about an adult role and vocation, he has to extend beyond his own self-centeredness and egocentricity and learn to give as well as take. When he eventually prepares to raise his own family, this will

---

[17]*Ibid.*
[18]Coleman, *op cit.,* p. 65.

necessitate that he become involved in "other-centered" projects so that he can provide for their support.

Finally, Coleman mentions that the adolescent youngster develops from a nonproductive to a more productive orientation. Before adolescence and, ultimately, adulthood, the youngster did not have to be productive and contribute to the social group as a whole. His family made a major investment in him and provided for his physical and emotional needs. As he proceeds through the adolescent period and begins thinking about his adult obligations and responsibilities, however, he has to learn how to become productive. This is usually realized through a vocational or professional role which he attempts to prepare for. Obviously, not all these areas of adjustment that Coleman discusses are adequately handled by all adolescents.

> Although these pathways toward maturity characterize normal development, it is possible for development to be arrested or fixated at different points along the continuum from infancy to maturity. This might be the case with the middle-aged Don Juan whose sexual behavior resembles that of an adolescent or the developmental sequence may be reversed as in regression where the individual reverts to behavior which once brought satisfaction.[19]

Ackerman feels that one of the greatest struggles for the adolescent is to resolve his identification with his parents and to build an identification and self-concept that is uniquely his own.

> Adolescence is a groping, questioning stage, a phase in which the adolescent condenses the values that will guide his social perspective for the major part of his life. It is exactly here that he confronts the challenge of bringing into harmony his view of self and his view of the world. He must now link his life-striving with a personal philosophy. The adolescent asks: What is life? Who am I? What am I good for? Where do I fit? Who are my real friends? Who are my enemies? What must I fight, with whom, against whom, for what life goals? And finally: Is life really worth the struggle? The kind of feverish, anxious, searching for identity, values and social orientation is paralleled by an expanding interest in social and economic conflicts, in religion and philosophy. In the service of this search the adolescent mobilizes his intellect and exploits it as a defense against his anxiety. Such struggle deeply affects the adolescent's choice of group association, in the time of testing of parental images and temporary dissolution of self, the adolescent seeks to identify with something larger than himself. His urge is to ally with a cause greater than his own.[20]

There is a push-and-pull phenomenon which creates many difficulties and conflicts for the adolescent. On the one hand, his parents and their expectations

---

[19] *Ibid.*, p. 66.
[20] Ackerman, *op. cit.*, p. 215.

have been with him his entire life; on the other hand, the peer group begins to become much more important to him. The peer group often has a life-style and a value system that are much different from those of his family. Because in our society there is not the control of the extended family that existed in the past, the peer group takes on much more importance and therefore exerts much more influence. If the influence and the life-style of the peer group are greatly different from those of the family, problems can arise.

> The adolescent who loves his parents but who also wants to be accepted by his peers, may have a problem in deciding which standard will govern. Usually he makes some kind of compromise, letting parental standards govern some aspects of his behavior, and peer standards other aspects. But the peer group often has the edge in such contest partly because of the generally outward direction of social development, and partly because our culture places so much value on getting along with one's peers. This is less of a problem in other cultures. Young people in Germany, for example, are more concerned about maintaining good relations with their parents, whereas American youth tend to be more interested in getting others to like them—adolescents today, thanks to the general availability of part-time jobs and the generosity of their parents, are relatively free to do as they will, buy what they want and use time as they think best—all without being responsible to anyone.[21]

The increased freedom and material possessions, however, are often not much help when the youngster needs the guidance and assistance of mature adults and concerned parents. Wolfgang aptly points out that

> many youth feel forced into detachment and premature cynicism because society seems to offer youth today so little that is stable, relevant and meaningful. They often look in vain for values, goals, means and institutions to which they can be committed because their trust for commitment is strong. . . . The social isolation, social distance, alienation and retreat from the adult world are increased by many social and technological mechanisms operating to encourage a youth subculture. As the numbers and intensity of value sharing in the youth subculture increase, the process of intergenerational alienation also escalates. Parents have almost always been accused of not understanding their children. What may be new is that more parents either do not care that they do not understand or that it is increasingly impossible for them to understand. Perhaps then it is not that the parents are poor models for the kinds of lives that their youths will lead in their own mature years; parents may simply be increasingly irrelevant models for their children. So rapid is current social change that the youth of today have difficulty projecting a concept of themselves as adults.[22]

[21] Lindgren, *op. cit.*, p. 140.
[22] Marvin E. Wolfgang, "The Culture of Youth," *Task Force Report: Juvenile Delinquency and Youth Crime*, U.S. Department of Health, Education, and Welfare, p. 148.

Furthermore, the general status of the adolescent in our society is very tenuous, and in many respects he is the forgotten segment of the community.

> While young children occupy a special protected status and adults an authority status, adolescents have no defined position in current society.[23]

In effect, then, adolescents do not have the protection that is given to younger children, nor do they have the rights and privileges that accompany adult status. This is one of the main reasons that youngsters often retreat to the group or the gang. It has been suggested that the only way to rectify this lack of status is to involve adolescents in the decision-making processes of their community. The recent passing of voting rights bills and the granting of other privileges to youngsters are an attempt to involve the adolescent, at least the late adolescent, in these processes. This should resolve one of the problems of status affirmation which is often lacking in Western society and makes it difficult for the adolescent to find his rightful place as a contributing member of his community.[24] Much of the futility and frustration that exists among teen-agers can be reduced if they are involved in community problem solving and decision making. This not only will be a wise use of human resources but also will contribute to a more definite role definition for young people and possibly reduce many of the problems associated with the transition from adolescence to adulthood.

THE STRUGGLE OF DEPENDENCE VERSUS INDEPENDENCE

The prolongation of dependency relationships between parents and youngsters can have many negative ramifications. It is mandatory that parents understand the adolescent's conflict of wanting to be independent but becoming frightened when parental guidance and support are withdrawn too soon. (Chapter 3 discussed this aspect of child rearing.)

Parents often, either consciously or unconsciously, perpetuate the dependency relationship by never helping their child to become independent and self-sufficient through a mutual process of cooperation, communication, and assistance.

> Many parents while they consciously wish their child to grow up actually are resistant to this process. Perhaps they cannot face the vacuum that will exist when the child is no longer dependent on them. Sometimes they are jealous of the child entering early adulthood with all its apparent glamour when their own adulthood seems tarnished.[25]

Often parents live and relive their own childhood experiences and prob-

---

[23] Slavson, *op. cit.*, p. 8.
[24] *Ibid.*
[25] Josselyn, *op. cit.*, p. 29.

lems through their children. The child is not viewed as a unique individual but is used as a pawn to be manipulated for selfish parental interests.

If the child is forced into prolonged dependence or if his parents do not allow him to develop into an eventual productive citizen, he will often rebel through delinquent activity. Once delinquent behavior has become manifest and the child has come in contact with the juvenile justice system, it becomes much more difficult to bridge the communication gap between the youngster and his parents. When communication between them breaks down, the adolescent's perception of all adults can become negative.

> He perceives adults as agents bent on denying pleasures and frustrating consummation of sexual urges which are now at their height. He views adults as determined to restrict his awakening striving for self-direction and autonomy. While the adolescent attempts to defend himself against infantile strivings, he also feels with increasing anxiety, the strain of pressures of making his way into the wider world of which he knows he must become a part.[26]

In its extreme form, when problems snowball and when communication lines are broken between parents and the youngster, the situation becomes so severe that the youngster may completely disassociate himself from his family and make his own way in the community or in the delinquent group. Parents are then viewed as a necessary evil to provide the "basics" and material satisfaction.[27]

The precipitating factor that often directly contributes to faulty communication between the youngster and his parents is the youngster's attempt to achieve some independent status within his community and within the family constellation. Parents do not realize that the search for an independent identity is normal, as is the vacillation between dependency and independency. As Chapter 3 pointed out, when parents react in an extreme manner, such as overpermissiveness or authoritarianism, this does not solve the adolescent's struggle. It only accentuates it.

> As a result [of the struggle of dependence versus independence] he is apt to make demands for dependence which he has not made since he was a small child. At the time, he wants advice about what clothes to wear, what hours to keep, what food to eat, what political party to respect, or what ethical or moral formula to embrace.[28]

When the adolescent finds himself slipping ino dependency on his parents, he often overreacts by exerting his personality in a very independent manner. At this point his parents cannot be winners, only losers, and no matter what type of

---

[26] Slavson, *op. cit.,* p. 11.
[27] Lindgren, *op. cit.,* p. 141.
[28] Josselyn, *op. cit.,* p. 38.

advice they give the youngster it will not be satisfactory because he himself does not know what route to take. It is helpful if parents at least understand the dependent-independent dilemma. The mere understanding and awareness of this dynamic situation will prevent overreactions and will transmit to the youngster that his parents have the situation under control. When overreaction occurs, the youngster often retreats to his peer group for support and guidance.[29] The peer group may be negatively oriented and may therefore contribute to delinquent behavior.

THE DELINQUENT ADOLESCENT

The number of delinquent youngsters appearing before juvenile courts has become a serious problem.

> Youth crime seems to be predominantly a phenomenon of urban adolescents giving each other social support in the promotion of delinquency. Eighty to 90 per cent of offenses referred to juvenile courts involved two or more juveniles as associates in the offense. Similarly the proportion of inmates having co-defendants or rap partners in their offense is also regularly higher in youth prisons and reformatories than in penitentiaries for adult offenders. Each involvement in crime and each experience of arrest and correction or confinement increases a youth's estrangement from home and school, at the same time that it enhances his prestige and self-esteem in delinquent social circles.[30]

Again it should be emphasized that the delinquent adolescent is an adolescent first and a delinquent second. When this is forgotten, the practitioner in the juvenile justice system may have difficulty relating to the youngster as a teenager and be guilty of perpetuating the labeling process and viewing the delinquent as "extremely different." (See Chapter 2, "Theories of Delinquency Causation.")

WORKING WITH THE ADOLESCENT

Lubell points out that the existence of a youth subculture diametrically opposed to adult life styles, ideals, and values is probably exaggerated and that there are many more youngsters who share the viewpoints of their parents than those who do not.

> The dominant impression left by the term generation gap is that of a unified younger generation that is breaking drastically from both its elders

---

[29] Coleman, *op. cit.,* p. 595.
[30] Douglas, *op. cit.,* p. 21.

and society in almost every conceivable way. Actually through my inter-viewing over the last four years on how young people differ in their think-ing from their parents suggests that: (1) Much more continuity than gap exists between the two generations; (2) Parents have not been rendered obsolete but continue to exert an almost ineradicable influence on their children . . .[31]

Even though the differences between generations may not be as great as is popularly portrayed, there are at least some differences, especially between de-linquent youngsters and law-abiding adults. The practitioner in the juvenile justice system not only has to be aware of these differences but has to be willing to communicate honestly with these youngsters so that problem solving can be facilitated.

Adolescents in general are very difficult to work with, and delinquent adolescents present an even greater challenge. Slavson states that during the adolescent period

there is doubt about sexual and social adequacy and self-regard is at a low ebb. To a large extent the adolescent adopts as a defense against these self-doubts a stance of self-maximization and employs antiphobic attitudes of omnipotence so that he may maintain an image of strength. He thus wards off hopelessness and depression. To admit to doubts, vacillation, conflicts and especially inability to deal with problems on his own and to have to seek help, constitutes a source of severe narcissistic injury against which the adolescent defends himself. This complex of feelings constitutes one of the main sources of resistance to therapy, only second in intensity to the rise of awareness of inadequacy.[32]

The major purpose of this section has been to point out the dynamics and conflicts that exist in the developmental period called adolescence. Even if the youngster does not become involved in delinquent activity, there are still many problems and conflicts. It is necessary that the practitioner understand the dy-namic processes and conflicts of adolescence if he is to be successful in his delin-quency prevention and rehabilitation efforts. The practitioner should remember that he himself was an adolescent at one time and that during his teen-age years conflicts and frustrations (such as the struggle for independence) also existed. The conflicts and frustrations may take a different form of expression today, but the basic need to develop an adequate self-concept, feel worthwhile, and be accepted by the group is not much different from that of past generations. To be effective in working with young people, Anthony states that

adults need to recognize that adolescents are people, and particular people at that. It is important to remember that the stereotypes that have been

[31] Samuel Lubell, "That Generation Gap," in *Confrontation,* Daniel Bell and Irving Kristil, Eds. (New York: Basic Books, Inc., 1968), p. 58.
[32] Slavson, *op. cit.,* p. 11.

cultivated are not necessarily even true of a minority of adolescents and that adolescents are not all delinquent, irresponsible, hypersexual or simpleminded creatures in pursuit solely of a good time. As long as these stereotypes persist, adolescents will respond by setting up barriers to communication, excluding the adult by the conspiracy of silence or by a language and culture of their own. The adults are then narcissistically affronted that the youth want to act and look and talk differently from them and then interpret this as rebellion, overlooking the fact that the adolescents want to act and look and talk differently from the children and are deeply engaged in delineating their identities as in revolting against authority. The principle of secrecy and silence adopted by the adolescent culture toward the adult is a universal phenomenon appearing in all cultures and can be understood as a counterresponse to the secrets and silences that adults have preserved in the face of consistent childhood curiosities and interests.[33]

The concept that adolescents are people with feelings and problems, as well as with a unique status in life, must also be extended to the delinquent youngster, who in addition to having the normal problems of adolescence often has severe economic, social, and psychological problems.

What Socrates said about adolescents approximately twenty-five hundred years ago still applies today, even though the behavior of adolescents and the "symptoms" take a different form:

Our adolescents now seem to love luxury, they have bad manners and contempt for authority. They show disrespect for adults and spend their time hanging around and gossiping with one another—they are ready to contradict their parents, monopolize the conversation in company, eat gluttonously and tyrannize their teachers.

Caplan aptly points out that parents should look at their teen-agers in the context of total development:

If the adult remembers how much of himself has gone into the making of the adolescent he would be able to sympathize and empathize to an extent that should make for a partnership based on mutual respect and affection.[34]

The practitioner in the juvenile justice system dealing with the juvenile delinquent should also understand the problems and dynamics of the adolescent. This chapter will conclude with a discussion of a pertinent, contemporary adolescent problem—the use of drugs.

---

[33] James Anthony, "The Reactions of Adults to Adolescents and Their Behavior," in *Adolescence: Psychosocial Perspectives,* Gerald Caplan and Serge Lebovici, Eds. (New York: Basic Books, Inc., 1969), p. 82.
[34] *Ibid.,* p. 77.

ADOLESCENT DRUG ABUSE

The adolescent drug problem is so widespread that it can no longer be considered a phenomenon solely of urban centers. The adolescent drug user comes from all socioeconomic levels and all environments, and he cannot be associated with any particular racial, ethnic, or religious group. Not all drug users are dope fiends. Many respectable citizens and youngsters have been "hooked" on drugs, but regardless of socioeconomic class, the results of drug abuse are often devastating. Drug use has become so prevalent and drugs so widely available that the problem among adolescents has reached epidemic proportions. As pointed out previously, the youngster encounters many problems, both physical and psychological during the adolescent stage of development. Often, without proper guidance and support, deviant and delinquent behavioral adaption to the environment becomes commonplace. For the teen-ager who has difficulty in developing meaningful relationships with parents, adults, and peers and has problems adjusting to the environment, the use of drugs may become an expedient means of temporarily relieving frustration and strain.

The use of drugs has often been compared with the use of alcohol. Regardless of the similarities or dissimilarities, much more research needs to be done to determine the potential effects of both "hard" and "soft" drug use by teen-agers. The lack of scientific evidence and conflicting information regarding the effects of drugs should be reason enough to discourage its use. Excessive use of alcohol should also be considered drug abuse. This section will discuss the drug phenomenon because it is a contemporary problem and prevalent among adolescents. Reasons for drug abuse, the abuser, drug control, types of drugs, and methods of treatment will be examined.

Amount of Drug Abuse

The Drug Enforcement Administration reports that although no one really knows how many drug addicts there are in the country, at the close of June 1973 some 95,897 active narcotics addicts were recorded. Even though these statistics may not be totally reliable, they are the only ones available. There is approximately one narcotic addict for every 2,170 persons, and nearly 80 percent of the addicts are from seven states: California, Illinois, New Jersey, Pennsylvania, Florida, Michigan, and New York, which alone accounts for 51 percent. Nearly 70 percent of the addicts are between the ages of eighteen and thirty.

As opposed to the majority of the "hard" narcotic users who are reported by law enforcement agencies or private agencies, the users of marihuana, hallucinogens, stimulants and depressants are seldom discovered unless they are involved in a criminal action and arrested. Estimates of their numbers can be gained only through well-designed representative surveys of the populations. Therefore, there is no way at the present time to document the number of abusers of these drugs. There have, however, been estimates and controlled surveys which indicate that there may be as many as 20 million users of marihuana in the country, although this figure can be accepted only as an estimate. One thing is a fact—any individual who is dependent on a drug for any reason other than one established by the person's physician is an abuser of drugs.[35]

Recent statistics on the extent of illicit drug use among students indicate varying rates of usage. Surveys show that the proportions of high-school and college students who have ever used drugs ranges from 0 percent to 69 percent.[36]

In addition to the personal tragedy drug abuse causes for the user, there is also a great loss to the community. Not only are productive and potentially productive citizens affected because of the use of drugs, many crimes are committed by users so that they can support their habit.

The Drug Enforcement Administration reports that narcotic addicts drain millions of dollars from the economy because the cost of the drugs themselves on the illicit market is exorbitant.

The average addict spends approximately $58 each day for a narcotic drug. This means for several days a week, 52 weeks each year, he would require about $21,112—there are no weekends or holidays off from a drug habit. Based on the foregoing estimates, the cost of heroin for addicts in the United States is $36.3 million per day or $13.2 billion per year. Some of the hard narcotic addicts require almost $200 a day instead of $58. The habit produces the craving, and the addict must produce the money. Most of this money feeds directly into the organized criminal structure.

Because most addicts cannot legally obtain the cash to buy their drugs, they turn to crime. Most convert stolen merchandise into cash. It takes about $3-$5 in stolen goods to get $1 cash. So, to support a $58 a day habit, the addict has to steal $200 worth of property a day, or $73,000 a year.

Accepting the fact that some addicts are gainfully employed, some derive their income from selling drugs, while others are engaged in vice reduces considerably the number of addicts actually stealing property to support their habits.

If we assume that 60 percent of the estimated 626,114 heroin addicts steal property to support their habits, over 27 billion dollars worth of property is stolen each year to pay for heroin addiction.

The taxpayer also pays the bill to rehabilitate the addict. A research psychiatrist for one treatment program indicates it cost his State approximately $1,300 a year to rehabilitate just one addict. Doctors in another program estimate six weeks of in-patient treatment followed by aftercare

[35] *Fact Sheets,* Drug Enforcement Administration, U.S. Department of Justice (Washington, D.C.: U.S. Government Printing Office, 1975), pp. 15–16.
[36] *Fact Sheets* (1975), *op cit.,* p. 16.

programs totals $3,000. Just assuming the treatment programs were available to all addicts in the country, society would pick up a tab ranging from $828,000,000 to $1,680,000,000.

While these figures are alarming, they do not begin to reflect the total cost of the abuse of narcotics and dangerous drugs.[37]

The economic, social, and personal loss as a result of the use of drugs is therefore immeasurable. Furthermore, because of inadequate statistics and identification methods, only the tip of the drug iceberg is exposed. Many more persons who have developed a physical or a psychological dependence on drugs represent the submerged portion of the iceberg, which often does not emerge until tragedy, such as suicide, serious crime, or family disruption occurs.

Reasons for Drug Abuse

Some of the basic reasons why persons choose a deviant method of adaptation to the environment, delinquency, drug abuse—or both—have been discussed in earlier chapters. Contributing factors can include lack of opportunity, poor relationships with parents and peers, and inability to adjust satisfactorily in the community. Even though it is difficult to generalize the reasons for drug abuse, one of the most prevalent explanations is that youngsters use drugs because they feel alienated from their environment and the adult world. There is often a great deal of peer influence in the use of drugs; using them can be considered the "in" thing to do. Even though there are many deeper explanations for the use of drugs, many young people look for kicks and "this is one way to obtain kicks."[38]

Because many and various reasons exist for taking drugs, it is not particularly important to dwell on individual cases or rationalizations for the use of drugs. The point is that the totality of the problem must be understood, and it must be recognized that, unfortunately, the use of drugs is seen as a viable alternative by many youngsters.

The use of drugs or the motivation for using them does not suddenly emerge. Many experts feel that youngsters today are exposed to the drug culture long before actual usage. For example, youngsters often see their parents relying on barbiturates to help them go to sleep, stimulants and amphetamines to pep them up, and tranquilizers to calm them down. Many youngsters justify using drugs by rationalizing that their parents use them, although in different forms. Also television has transmitted advertisements and popular programming displaying the ready accessibility of legitimate drugs and the "magical" way that they can solve problems and contribute to happiness in our fast-paced world. The lack of a cohesive family structure can also be a contributing factor to increased drug

---

[37]*Fact Sheets* (1975), p. 16.
[38]Clifford Denton, "The Growing Drug Menace," *Pennsylvania Education*, 2, No. 1 (January–February 1970), p. 18.

use. Today the family no longer exerts as much influence on the child as it did in the past. The family has become restructured. The extended family, which consists of parents, children, grandparents, uncles, aunts, and cousins, no longer is a cohesive unit that can exert influence and on which the child can depend for support and guidance. Only the nuclear family, which consists of parents and their own children, is prevalent today.[39]

The family, however, still has a vital role to play today. It must help the youngster make the link between adolescence and adulthood in an orderly manner so that the youngster may become a productive citizen.[40] Through the family and the youngster's initial relationships with his parents, he learns how to effectively relate to his environment and handle its pressures and responsibilities. If parents relinquish their rightful roles of guiding, supporting, and teaching their youngsters, the peer group will become the primary source of influence. The peer group is usually not equipped to handle the youngster's problems or satisfy his needs in a socially acceptable manner.

It is unfortunate that some parents have—by accident or design—provided their children with material possessions but have failed to provide an emotional environment conducive to fostering future emotional stability and positive behavioral adaption in the community. When this emotional support is not provided, the youngster often sees drug abuse as an alternative.

Because many of today's parents were materially deprived in their youth, they overreact by providing their children with material possessions, often at the expense of providing emotional support and guidance as the youngster progresses toward adulthood.

> After listening to a tape recording on "Marcy," a drug addict and fugitive from home, one teenage boy commented, "It is beautiful. Why don't they explain the causes of what went wrong with Marcy. My father belonged to the depression generation, he suffered so much from lack of material things that he spent his whole life making sure we had the things that warm us outside, but he never had time to give us things that warm us inside."[41]

The Drug Abuser

There is much conjecture concerning the type of person who abuses drugs as well as his reasons for using them. Even though many persons are exposed to drugs, both legitimately and illegitimately, only a relatively few when compared with the total population become drug abusers.

Although much is known about the effects of drugs, with abuse potential, the user himself remains the enigma. Slum conditions, easy access to drugs,

[39]Urie Bronfenbrenner, "Parents Bring Up Your Children!" *Look* (January 26, 1971).
[40]The President's Commission, *Task Force Report: Juvenile Delinquency and Youth Crime* (Washington, D.C.: U.S. Government Printing Office, 1967), p. 41.
[41]"From a Hippie Soul," *Saturday Review* (December 16, 1967), p. 46.

peddlers and organized crime have all been blamed for the problem. While any of these factors may contribute, no single cause, nor single set of economic conditions clearly leads to drug dependency, for it occurs in all social and economic classes. The key to the riddle may well lay within the abuser in any one of many sets or conditions. True, drug dependency cannot develop without a chemical agent. Yet, while millions are exposed to drugs by reason of medical need, relatively few of these people turn to a life of drugs. It is true that in metropolitan areas there are invariably found groups of "hard-core" users and a large proportion of the young persons who use drugs in the ghetto areas. Even though drugs may be available on street corners, in metropolitan areas, only a small percentage of the individuals exposed join the ranks of abusers.[42]

Many assumptions have been made about the drug abuser. Some say he is emotionally unstable; others say the he has difficulty developing interpersonal relationships. His withdrawal from society seems to indicate that he cannot accept the responsibilities and pressures of society, and therefore he turns to a life of drugs as a way of avoiding reality. The teen-age years (when many addicts have their first drug experience) are very difficult, and the transition to adulthood is seldom smooth.

The early and middle teens bring a loosing of family ties, a diminution of parental authority, increasing responsibility and sexual maturing beset with anxiety, frustration, fear of failure, interconflicts and doubts. The adolescent may find that amphetamines and marihuana promote conversation and sociability, barbiturates relieve anxiety, hallucinogens heighten sensations and narcotics provide relief and escape. Drug abuse may provide the entree into an "in group" or be a way of affirming independence by defying authority and convention.[43]

The Drug Enforcement Administration typology divides drug abuse into four categories: situational, spree, hard-core, and hippie. The first type of abuser employs drugs for a specific or *situational* purpose. Users in this category could be students who use amphetamines to keep awake at examination time or housewives who use diet pills. The drug in these and similar cases provides an immediate function or "solution" for the user. This type of user does not usually become dependent on the drug, although he may manifest psychological difficulties and use drugs in particularly anxious situations.

The second type of drug user defined by the Administration is the *spree* user. Drugs are used usually by college or high school students for "kicks" or to be exposed to a new experience. Even though there may be little physical dependence, because of the sporadic nature of the involvement, psychological dependence can develop.

---

[42] *Fact Sheet,* Bureau of Narcotics and Dangerous Drugs, p. 4-1. Also *Fact Sheets* (1975), pp. 19-21.
[43] *Ibid.*

Some "spree" users may only try drugs once or twice and decide there are better things in life. Drug sprees constitute a defiance of convention, an adventurous daring experience or a means of having fun. Unlike "hardcore" abusers, who often pursue their habits alone or in pairs, spree users usually take drugs only in groups or at social functions.[44]

The third type of user is the *hard-core* addict. He often lives in a slum area of the city, and his life revolves around the use of hard drugs. He exhibits strong psychological dependence on the drug, often reinforced by physical dependence in the case of certain drugs. He feels he cannot function without the use of drugs and his drug abuse has often started on a spree basis. His drug abuse is more than a passing fancy.

The fourth type of drug user is the *hippie*. Hippies react to the system, or the "establishment." They believe the system is antiquated and wrong and that the use of drugs can provide a new experience and add new meaning to their lives. Even though drugs are an integral part of the hippie life-style and many hippies may be considered hard-core users at times, they are different from the typical hard-core type because most hippies do not come from slum areas. They come from middle- or upper-class families, and their educational level is much higher than that of the hard-core inner-city drug user.[45]

There can be much overlapping of the four types, and the spree user or the situational user may become a hard-core user if drug use is continued.

Slum sections of large metropolitan areas still account for the largest number of known heroin abusers. But frustration, immaturity and the emotional deprivation are not peculiar to depressed neighborhoods, and the misuse of drugs by middle and upper economic class individuals is being recognized with increasing frequency. Drug dependence is not discriminating. A drug, an individual, an environment which predisposes use, and a personality deficiency are the key factors in its development.[46]

Drug Control

Because the misuse of drugs is illegal in the United States, many persons feel that the drug control answer can be found in more stringent laws and that drug use can only be prevented through legal enforcement and penal sanctions. The result of this assumption in many cases has been mandatory prison terms and an increased punishment for repeated offenses. In many cases, however, severe punishment has not deterred drug use; hence, other methods are being considered.[47]

[44] *Ibid.*, pp. 4-1, 4-2.
[45] *Ibid.*, p. 4-2.
[46] *Ibid.*
[47] The President's Commission, *Task Force Report: Narcotics and Drug Abuse* (Washington, D.C.: Government Printing Office, 1967), p. 7.

In addition to rehabilitative efforts, numerous enforcement agencies have attempted to both detect persons using drugs and prevent the flow of drugs into the country. The Drug Enforcement Administration maintains units in various overseas districts to locate and seize illicit opium and heroin supplies before they appear in the United States. The Federal Bureau of Customs maintains a force at ports and along land borders to prevent the smuggling of contraband, which often includes drugs. The Customs Agency Service, which is composed of custom port investigators and enforcement officers, conducts vessel and aircraft searches and keeps airports, piers, and border-crossing points under surveillance. Customs Agency Service also investigates and disseminates intelligence information. Once the drug has been transported to the United States, the efforts of the Drug Enforcement Administration are coordinated with state and local law enforcement agencies to identify users and pushers and to prevent the dispersion of drugs.[48]

Even though there is a coordinated effort between federal, state, and local agencies to prevent drugs from coming into this country and to detect suppliers and users once they have arrived, many difficulties are involved in controlling illicit drugs, and enforcement in itself is not the answer.

Types of Drugs

The Drug Enforcement Administration aptly points out that even though opium poppies are not produced in the United States, heroin has taken its toll on the American population. Heroin begins in Asia where the poppy is grown. It is then sent to illegal laboratories in Europe and Asia, and then smuggled by various routes into the United States.

In 1973 there were four major supply complexes of illicit opium and its derivatives, morphine and heroin.

The primary complex involves Turkey, France, Western Europe, South America, Canada and the United States. The second complex is the "Golden Triangle Area" consisting of the remote border areas of Burma, Thailand and Laos through shipping points in Bangkok, Hong Kong, Malaysia, the Philippines, Canada and the west coast of the United States. The third complex is opium produced in India, Pakistan, Iran and Afghanistan. The fourth is Mexico, the supplier of a brown heroin that is seen with persistent frequency in the United States, particularly the west coast and boarder areas.

The heroin complex originating in Turkey has been the major supplier of Eastern United States cities where the heroin epidemic broke out in the late 1950's and early 60's. International trafficking groups purchase opium from Turkish farmers, convert it to morphine and smuggle it to clandestine laboratories in France via western Europe.

[48] *Ibid.*

Marseilles was and still is in 1973 a primary city where clandestine laboratories refine morphine into heroin. Within a one year period, French
narcotics officers aided by Drug Enforcement Administration agents uncovered five heroin laboratories in the Marseilles area.[49]

Thanks to extensive efforts by the Drug Enforcement Administration
in cooperation with foreign countries there has been progress in curtailing
illicit drug smuggling into the United States. The end of the Viet Nam War in
1973 also helped reduce the opportunity for illicit drug shipments. Recently
there has been an increasing problem with Mexican heroin and the Drug Enforcement Administration is working diligently to combat it.

To assist foreign narcotic control authorities in the suppression of the illicit narcotic traffic affecting the United States, the Drug Enforcement Administration has assigned 154 Special Agents and 109 clerical support
personnel to 51 officers in 35 countries throughout the world.[50]

In regard to other types of drugs, marihuana, although grown heavily in
the Near East and Middle East, is also produced in Mexico, the largest supplier to
the United States. A great majority of amphetamines and barbiturates that are
diverted to illicit use most often come from legal channels, although a small
proportion of illicit amphetamines and barbiturates are smuggled into the United
States from Mexico.

Other portions of the illegal supply originate through theft and by production in clandestine laboratories, operating illegally in garages, basements
and warehouses—even in trucks. Some registered manufacturers, under the
cloak of legality, make quantities of dangerous drugs unlawfully and dispose of them through the black market trade. The illegal "bulk peddler,"
who deals in hundreds of thousands of capsules and tablets, is an important link in the traffic in dangerous drugs. Since there is no legal production of hallucinogenic drugs in the United States, the illicit traffic depends
on production from illicit laboratories or smuggled drugs from Europe,
Mexico, Canada and Australia.[51]

Most of the narcotics and dangerous drugs (excluding heroin, marihuana, and
hallucinogens) are used for medicinal purposes and are dispensed by pharmacies
and prescribed by physicians. Because of the ready availability of legal drugs, the
drug abuser has much latitude in his methods for obtaining drugs, which may
range all the way from altering a legitimate prescription to stealing them. The
problems of control are obviously immense.

Drugs can be classified into five main types: (1) narcotics, (2) hallucino-

---

[49] *Fact Sheets* (1975), p. 8.
[50] *Ibid.*, p. 11.
[51] *Fact Sheet,* Bureau of Narcotics and Dangerous Drugs, p. 2.

gens, (3) stimulants, (4) depressants, and (5) marihuana. A description of each will follow (see accompanying chart, pp. 120–21).

Narcotics. The term *narcotic* refers to opium and to pain-relieving drugs made from opium, such as morphine, paregoric, and codeine.[52] Synthetic drugs such as demerol and methadone are also classified as narcotics. Narcotics are used in medicine mainly to relieve pain and induce sleep. The narcotic abuser develops a physical addiction to the drug, and as the body develops a tolerance, larger dosages are needed to satisfy the craving. When the narcotic is withheld or when use has ceased, there are withdrawal symptoms and physical trauma such as sweating, shaking, nausea, and even abdominal pains and leg cramps. In addition to the physical dependence, however, psychological dependence results, and the individual who uses narcotics and becomes addicted attempts to handle his problems by using the narcotic drug.

> Narcotic use can become even more of an escape than expected. Contaminated injections or unexpectedly high dosages caused over 900 deaths in New York City alone during 1969; over 200 of these were among teenagers.[53]

Heroin, the most prevalent narcotic taken by drug addicts, is usually adulterated and mixed with other substances, such as milk sugar or quinine. The drug makes the person believe that his problems have been eliminated or that he can deal with life more adequately. Once the drug has worn off, however, the reality of daily responsibilities and pressures becomes even more acute, and as a result increased dosage is usually needed to "feed the habit."

Because of the cost of the drug and the fact that it often reduces hunger and thirst, addicts often become malnourished and physically emaciated, and therefore more susceptible to diseases like tuberculosis and pneumonia. Negative side effects, such as hepatitis (from unsterile needles) and blood infections, are common. Even though narcotic addiction is still more prevalent among minority groups in the large inner-city areas, it has spread to persons of all backgrounds regardless of race, sex, or national origin. Professionals such as doctors and pharmacists have been cited to use drugs not only because of their ready accessibility but because they are a short-term method of dealing with pressure.

In addition to the stringent penalties established under the Narcotic Control Act of 1956 and revised under the Comprehensive Drug Abuse Prevention and Control Act of 1970, treatment for the narcotic addict is often complicated and is generally a long-term process. One of the greatest difficulties is that when the individual has been released from the hospital (after going through with-

---

[52] Most of the descriptive information relating to the different types of drugs has been taken from documents provided by the U.S. Department of Health, Education, and Welfare.

[53] *Narcotics, Some Questions and Answers,* U.S. Department of Health, Education, and Welfare, Public Health Service Publication, No. 1827 (Washington, D.C.: U.S. Government Printing Office, 1970).

	DRUGS	SCHEDULE	OFTEN PRESCRIBED BRAND NAMES	MEDICAL USES	DEPENDENCE PHYSICAL
NARCOTICS	Opium	II	Dover's Powder, Paregoric	Analgesic, antidiarrheal	High
	Morphine	II	Morphine	Analgesic	High
	Codeine	II, III, V	Codeine	Analgesic, antitussive	Moderate
	Heroin	I	None	None	High
	Meperidine (Pethidine)	II	Demerol, Pethadol	Analgesic	High
	Methadone	II	Dolophine, Methadone, Methadose	Analgesic, heroin substitute	High
	Other Narcotics	I, II, III, V	Dilaudid, Leritine, Numorphan, Percodan	Analgesic, antidiarrheal, antitussive	High
DEPRESSANTS	Chloral Hydrate	IV	Noctec, Somnos	Hypnotic	Moderate
	Barbiturates	II, III, IV	Amytal, Butisol, Nembutal, Phenobarbital, Seconal, Tuinal	Anesthetic, anti-convulsant, sedation, sleep	High
	Glutethimide	III	Doriden	Sedation, sleep	High
	Methaqualone	II	Optimil, Parest, Quaalude, Somnafac, Sopor	Sedation, sleep	High
	Meprobamate	IV	Equanil, Meprospan, Miltown, Kesso-Bamate, SK-Bamate	Anti-anxiety, muscle relaxant, sedation	Moderate
	Other Depressants	III, IV	Dormate, Noludar, Placidyl, Valmid	Anti-anxiety, sedation, sleep	Possible
STIMULANTS	Cocaine	II	Cocaine	Local anesthetic	Possible
	Amphetemines	II, III	Benzedrine, Biphetamine, Desoxyn, Dexedrine	Hyperkinesis, narcolepsy, weight control	Possible
	Phenmetrozine	II	Preludin	Weight control	Possible
	Methylphenidate	II	Ritalin	Hyperkenesis	Possible
	Other Stimulants	III, IV	Bacarate, Cylert, Didrex, Ionamin, Plegine, Pondimin, Pre-Sate, Sanorex, Voranil	Weight control	Possible
HALLUCINOGENS	LSD	I	None	None	None
	Mescaline	I	None	None	None
	Psilocybin-Psilocyn	I	None	None	None
	MDA	I	None	None	None
	PCP	III	Sernylan	Veterinary anesthetic	None
	Other Hallucinogens	I	None	None	None
CANNABIS	Marihuana Hashish Hashish Oil	I	None	None	Degree unknown

Controlled Substances: Uses and Effects

SOURCE: *Fact Sheets,* Drug Enforcement Administration, U.S. Department of Justice (Washington, D.C.: U.S. Government Printing Office, 1975).

POTENTIAL PSYCHOLOGICAL	TOLERANCE	DURATION OF EFFECTS (in hours)	USUAL METHODS OF ADMINISTRATION	POSSIBLE EFFECTS	EFFECTS OF OVERDOSE	WITHDRAWAL SYNDROME
High	Yes	3 to 6	Oral, smoked			
High	Yes	3 to 6	Injected, smoked			
Moderate	Yes	3 to 6	Oral, injected	Euphoria drowsiness, respiratory depression, constricted pupils, nausea	Slow and shallow breathing, clammy skin, convulsions, coma, possible death	Watery eyes, runny nose, yawning, loss of appetite, irritability, tremors, panic, chills and sweating, cramps, nausea
High	Yes	3 to 6	Injected, sniffed			
High	Yes	3 to 6	Oral, injected			
High	Yes	12 to 24	Oral, injected			
High	Yes	3 to 6	Oral, injected			
Moderate	Probable	5 to 8	Oral			
High	Yes	1 to 16	Oral, injected	Slurred speech, disorientation, drunken behavior without odor of alcohol	Shallow respiration, cold and clammy skin, dilated pupils, weak and rapid pulse, coma, possible death	Anxiety, insomnia, tremors, delirium, convulsions, possible death
High	Yes	4 to 8	Oral			
High	Yes	4 to 8	Oral			
Moderate	Yes	4 to 8	Oral			
Possible	Yes	4 to 8	Oral			
High	Yes	2	Injected, sniffed	Increased alertness, excitation, euphoria, dilated pupils, increased pulse rate and blood pressure insomnia, loss of appetite.	Agitation, increase in body temperature, hallucinations, convulsions, possible death.	Apathy, long periods of sleep, irritability, depression, disorientation.
High	Yes	2 to 4	Oral, injected			
High	Yes	2 to 4	Oral			
High	Yes	2 to 4	Oral			
Possible	Yes	2 to 4	Oral			
Degree unknown	Yes	Variable	Oral			
Degree unknown	Yes	Variable	Oral, injected	Illusions and hallucinations (with exception of MDA); poor perception of time and distance	Longer, more intense "trip" episodes, psychosis, possible death	Withdrawal syndrome not reported
Degree unknown	Yes	Variable	Oral			
Degree unknown	Yes	Variable	Oral, injected, sniffed			
Degree unknown	Yes	Variable	Oral, injected, smoked			
Degree unknown	Yes	Variable	Oral, injected, sniffed			
Moderate	Yes	2 to 4	Oral, smoked	Euphoria, relaxed inhibitions, increased appetite, disoriented behavior	Fatigue, paranoia, possible psychosis	Insomnia, hyperactivity, and decreased appetite reported in a limited number of individuals

drawal symptoms and the psychological problems associated with withdrawal), he often finds it impossible to remain off drugs and pursue a "conventional" existence in the community. Rehabilitation is complicated because not all addicts have the same problems, and therefore it is difficult to focus on specific methods of treatment. Also, many communities do not have facilities to help the addict once he has been released from the protection of the hospital.

The Narcotic Addict Rehabilitation Act of 1966 (NARA) gives certain addicts a choice of treatment instead of prosecution or imprisonment. If addicts are not charged with a crime, they have the right to ask for treatment on their own initiative or it may be requested by a relative. Federal legislation also provides for a complete range of rehabilitation services to be made available to addicts in their own communities. The act states the following:

1. An addict charged with a non-violent Federal offense who elects to be committed for treatment instead of prosecuted for his crime, can be committed to the Secretary of Health, Education and Welfare for examination, treatment and rehabilitation.

2. An addict after conviction of a Federal offense can be committed to the Attorney General for a treatment period of no more than ten years or for the maximum period of sentence that could be imposed for his conviction.

3. An addict not charged with an offense can be civilly committed to the Secretary of Health, Education and Welfare for treatment upon his own application or that of a relative or another "related individual."[54]

Care of the addict after his release from the hospital is a key aspect of his treatment. Aftercare programs can provide continuing treatment for up to three years in the addict's own community. These programs are individually designed to meet the user's special needs. NARA is administered by the National Institute of Mental Health, Department of Health, Education and Welfare and by the Department of Justice.

Hallucinogens. Hallucinogens are drugs that can have unpredictable effects on the mind. They include such drugs as peyote and mescaline, as well as lysergic acid diethylamide, or LSD, which is the best-known hallucinogen and will be the focus of our discussion. LSD is most known for the bizarre mental reactions it causes and the distortions in the physical senses of touch, smell, and hearing.

The reasons for experimenting with and using LSD vary with the individual's motivations. It may be taken because of curiosity, because of peer pressure, or because of claims that it can expand the mind and increase the physical sensitivities.

LSD can be taken in the form of a capsule or it can be placed in other substances. It can have both physical and psychological effects. Enlarged pupils,

[54] *Ibid.*

flushed face, and rise in temperature and heart beat are some of the common physical effects. Even though LSD is not a physically addictive drug, it can have psychological ramifications.

> Illusions and hallucinations can occur, and delusional thoughts are sometimes expressed. The sense of time and of self are strangely altered. Emotional variations are marked, ranging from bliss to horror, sometimes within a single experience. Because of the impaired time sense—a few minutes may seem like hours—such an experience can assume the proportions of a terrible nightmare from which one cannot easily awaken.[55]

The National Institute of Mental Health is attempting to determine the biological, psychological, and genetic effects of LSD on animals and humans. Research will continue until many of the questions about this drug have been answered. Many medical authorities believe that the chronic or continued use of LSD changes values and impairs the user's power of concentration and ability to think rationally. As of now, it has not been proven, as some proponents claim, that LSD can increase creativity. In fact, because of lack of research the actual workings of LSD in the body are not yet known.

> The strange sensations in clash of moods the drug causes can be frightening, even for a mature person. For young people who are still undergoing the process of emotional development, and who may lack the resilience to maintain the mental equilibrium under LSD, the effects can be even more frightening and confusing. The young, growing brain is more vulnerable to all mind-altering drugs than a brain in which metabolic activity is stabilized.[56]

Although LSD has not been used extensively for medical purposes, available evidence suggests that it may be useful, under controlled conditions, for neurotics and alcoholics. Although the drug may be a valuable tool in biomedical research, present indications are that its therapeutic value is limited. The penalty structure for illegal possession and distribution of LSD is delineated in the Comprehensive Drug Abuse Prevention and Control Act of 1970.

Stimulants. Stimulants are drugs, usually amphetamines, that stimulate the central nervous system. They can increase alterness and are often used to combat fatigue, reduce depression, and control appetite. In addition to amphetamines, stimulants include cocaine, dextroamphetamine, and methamphetamine ("speed"). Stimulants are also known as pep pills. Coffee, tea, and caffeine are considered mild stimulants.

Abuse of amphetamines and stimulants can begin in the doctor's office as

[55]*LSD, Some Questions and Answers*, U.S. Department of Health, Education, and Welfare, Public Health Service Publication, No. 1828 (Washington, D.C.: U.S. Government Printing Office, 1970).
[56]*Ibid.*

a result of a prescribed dosage which becomes abused and overextended. In some cases, over half of the legally manufactured supply of amphetamines finds its way into illegal channels for nonprescriptive use. In regard to the effects of amphetamine use:

> in ordinary amounts the amphetamines provide a transient sense of alertness, wakefulness, well-being and mental clarity. Hunger is diminished, and short term performance may be enhanced in the fatigued person. The drugs may increase the heart rate, raise the blood pressure, produce palpitation and rapid breathing, dilate the pupils, and cause dry mouth, sweating and headache—if use continues, however, a person can become psychologically dependent on the drug in a few weeks. The sense of power, self-confidence, and exhilaration artificially created by amphetamine use is so pleasant, and the fatigue and depression that follow discontinuance are so severe, that the user is heavily tempted to revert to the drug.[57]

Amphetamines can be taken intravenously to produce a quicker and more pronounced "high." Prolonged use of "speed" has many negative ramifications, including psychological disturbances and the impairment of physical health as a result of body abuse and poor nutrition. Because the use and abuse of amphetamines is fairly recent, especially intravenous injections, few specific rehabilitation and treatment services exist. Most formal drug treatment programs in the United States are designed primarily for narcotic addicts. Information services, however, are being developed daily to alert communities to the negative effects of the inappropriate use of stimulants, pointing out that housewives and businessmen can become dependent on these drugs even though they begin taking them for "legitimate" reasons. Research on stimulants such as amphetamines and cocaine is at present being undertaken by the National Institute of Mental Health. As is the case with other dangerous drugs, not enough is known about the effects of stimulants so that suitable treatment approaches can be initiated. A number of surveys supported by the institute are being undertaken to determine both the extent of the use of these drugs and the methods for combating their abuse.

Depressants. Depressants are sedative drugs that are manufactured for medical purposes to reduce tension and anxiety, as well as to treat epilepsy. Barbiturates are the largest group of sedatives, or depressants, and without medical supervision to avoid habituation, the ultimate effects can be very destructive.

Because barbiturates depress the brain function and the central nervous system, they create a very powerful depressant. Continued use can produce tolerance and create a desire for taking them on a long-term basis. When barbiturates are combined and used with amphetamines, a chemical imbalance can re-

---

[57]*Stimulants, Some Questions and Answers,* U.S. Department of Health, Education, and Welfare, Public Health Service Publication, No. 2097 (Washington, D.C.: U.S. Government Printing Office, 1970).

sult and can create a pleasant mood-elevating effect which entices a user to take increased amounts.

The majority of these drugs are used legally for tranquilizing purposes. Many of the drugs fall into illegal hands, however, and like the stimulant drugs, abuse can often start in the doctor's office as a result of a legitimate prescription.

Barbiturates can be dangerous when not taken under medical supervision, and death may result from an overdose. Withdrawal from the drug can cause many unpleasant physical symptoms—the withdrawal resembles delirium tremens. Like the stimulant drugs, sedative drugs are available only on prescription and are controlled by the Comprehensive Drug Abuse Prevention and Control Act of 1970.

> Tighter regulations and enforcement of law on the legitimate manufacture and distribution of barbiturates and tranquilizers are part of the answer. Because barbiturates and tranquilizers have sound medical usefulness, physicians must be wary of yielding to the demand of patients for increased amounts when, in fact, they may be manifesting tolerance. Widespread dissemination of information about the dangers of overusing these addictive drugs is essential.[58]

Like the other drugs mentioned, a great deal more has to be learned about the effects of sedatives on the body, brain, and nervous system. Consequently, research programs are under way to determine the entire scope of the use of sedatives, in both their positive and their negative aspects.

Marihuana. Marihuana is derived from the Indian hemp plant, *Cannabis sativa,* and grows wild in many parts of the world, including the United States. It can be used commercially in the production of fiber for ropes and birdseed. It can vary greatly in strength, depending upon where it is grown and whether it has been specifically cultivated for smoking or eating.

When smoked, marihuana enters the bloodstream and within a very short time can affect the mood and the thinking of the user. The specific reactions that the drug has on the mind are not completely understood, and therefore a great deal of research is being conducted to determine its many effects. Some of the specific physical effects, however, are reddening of the whites of the eyes, increased heart beat, and sometimes coughing due to the irritating effect of the smoke on the lungs. The psychological effects of the drug can vary markedly, depending upon the user and the strength and quality of the drug. Terms such as suspiciousness, exuberance, sleepiness, loss of recall, inability to make decisions that require logical thinking, and euphoria have all been used to describe the effects of marihuana.

As for comparing marihuana with alcohol:

[58]*Sedatives, Some Questions and Answers,* U.S. Department of Health, Education, and Welfare, Public Health Service Publication, No. 2098 (Washington, D.C.: U.S. Government Printing Office, 1970).

we know that alcohol is a dangerous drug physically, psychologically or socially for millions of people whose drinking is out of control. There is no firm evidence that marihuana would be less harmful if used consistently. American experience to date has largely been limited to marihuana of low potency, infrequently used over a relatively short period of time. In countries where the use of marihuana and related drugs has been widespread, "skid rows" based on marihuana use exist. At present the research evidence is insufficient to answer this question of certainty. It should, however, be remembered that it frequently requires extensive use over a long period of time by large numbers of people before the public health implications of a drug are clearly understood.[59]

Marihuana, which is not a narcotic, does not cause physical dependence as do heroin and other narcotics. Therefore, the body does not develop a tolerance to the drug, and withdrawal from marihuana does not usually produce physical sickness. Many scientists believe, however, that psychological dependence can develop. As to whether it leads to harder narcotics:

A 1967 study of narcotic addicts from city areas showed that more than 80 percent had previously used marihuana. Of the much larger number of persons who used marihuana, scientists agree that few go on to use morphine and heroin. No direct cause and effect link between the use of marihuana and narcotics has been found. Researchers point out, however, that a person predisposed to abuse a drug may be likely to abuse other, stronger drugs.[60]

The one general conclusion that can be drawn from the preceding discussion is that more research needs to be undertaken to determine the effects of all types of drugs so that a comprehensive program of education can be developed for the public, and especially for youngsters. The potential long-range problems will have to be identified. A knowledge of the different types of drugs and their effects, however, does not in itself solve the drug problem. It is only through effective prevention, rehabilitation, and education that the drug problem can be understood and adolescents can be saved the grief that predictably follows the abuse of drugs.

Drug Prevention and Rehabilitation Programs

According to the Drug Enforcement Administration:

Until recently, the public has regarded addicts as incurable. Once "hooked" there was no road back. This idea arose from the fact that so many opiate

[59] *Marihuana, Some Questions and Answers*, U.S. Department of Health, Education, and Welfare, Public Health Service Publication, No. 1829 (Washington, D.C.: U.S. Government Printing Office, 1970).
[60] *Ibid.*

addicts relapsed to drug use, even after long periods of hospitalization. Not long ago, treatment for addiction consisted of little more than withdrawal from the drug and detoxification. When more ambitious programs were attempted, they had only limited success in terms of "cured" addicts, but each contributed to knowledge about the addict, the drugs he uses and the ways to effect his rehabilitation.[61]

Drug rehabilitation and prevention programs today encompass much more than withdrawal and detoxification. With the support of the federal government, communities are attempting to develop services that can help the addict once he is released from the hospital. It is only through an intensive program that the drug addict can be "cured" and provided with new alternatives for functioning within the community. Such community services as mental health clinics, educational facilities, employment programs, and other methods of supporting the ex-addict will help solve the addiction problem.

Federal Efforts. In addition to the voluminous amount of drug education material it distributes, the federal government has two hospitals for drug addicts, one at Lexington, Kentucky, and the other at Forth Worth, Texas. Addicts can voluntarily commit themselves to treatment or be committed by the court. Many times the positive gains that were made at these hospitals could not be maintained because of a lack of viable community programs to assist the addict once he was released back to the community. When specific community services are not provided, the chance for the addict to become a productive citizen is very limited. The Narcotic Addict Rehabilitation Act of 1966 has been very effective in helping to combat addiction. It specifies that federal support can be given to states and communities for training programs and for the construction, staffing, and operation of new addiction treatment facilities on a joint federal-state basis. Because of the increased resources provided by the federal government, many states are now developing facilities that can more adequately deal with the addict. In addition, private facilities have been established in many communities. Private hospitals, halfway houses, service organizations, religious groups, and other community-based organizations have become more active in assisting the addict.

If drug addiction is to be conquered and drug use prevented, the community must become involved in programs of assistance, education, and prevention.

> If criminals are to change, they must be assimilated into groups which emphasize values conducive to law-abiding behavior and alienated from groups emphasizing values conducive to criminality—the community should restore a former addict to his proper place in society and help him avoid associations that will influence him to return to the use of drugs.[62]

[61] *Fact Sheets*, Drug Enforcement Administration, p. 12.
[62] Donald Cressey and Rita Volkman, "Differential Association and Rehabilitation of Drug Addicts," *American Journal of Sociology*, 69 (September 1963), pp. 129-31.

Synanon.   Synanon is a private organization which focuses on rehabilitating the narcotic addict. The Synanon program, initiated by Chuck Dederich, began in 1958 as an experimental project in response to the drug problem. The program is mainly funded by contributions from private citizens and businesses. The residents live, work, and interact in the "therapeutic community" of the Synanon program. The use of both individual and group counseling has proved successful in helping the addict adjust to his community without the use of drugs. The criticism has been made, however, that the Synanon program does not solve the problem because it makes the addict dependent on the program rather than on drugs. This is a minor criticism. Dependence on the program is a much more acceptable alternative than dependence on drugs. Synanon is one of the very few programs that has given some indication of success in treating and rehabilitating the drug addict.[63]

Methadone Maintenance Programs.   In 1963 Vincent P. Doyle, a physician at Rockefeller University, and Marie Nyswander initiated a treatment program for narcotic addicts which revolved around the drug methadone, a synthetic pain killer. Methadone blocks the euphoric high and the physical cravings for heroin. The exponents of the drug feel that when given under controlled conditions by a qualified person, the addict can live a normal life in the community. Even though methadone itself is a narcotic, it is felt that it can be a less harmful substitute for heroin and opium and a realistic partial solution to the hard addiction problem. Methadone programs, which can operate on both an in- and an out-patient basis, are felt to work best in the initial treatment stages of narcotic addiction. Methadone can best be used to help the addict through the withdrawal period rather than as a permanent substitute for heroin or opium use.[64]

There has been some controversy over the merits of a methadone program and its use in the community. A major criticism is that methadone only replaces one drug habit with another and that its use does not offer a cure, only a less expensive substitute. Some law enforcement personnel feel that if methadone is made too readily available, new addicts will be exposed to drug addiction and will become dependent on the methadone drug. Many questions still have to be answered about the use of methadone. Only through research can objective conclusions be drawn and the true merits of the treatment approach be evaluated.

Psychotherapy, Group Therapy, and Counseling.   Psychotherapy, group therapy, and counseling have been utilized in some cases to treat and rehabilitate the drug user (see Chapter 9). These methods are often used to supplement many methadone programs and other community programs such as Synanon. Like other approaches discussed, these methods are not the total answer. They are only supplemental resources which have to be coupled with client motivation and the use of total community resources.

[63] Alison Wyrley Birch, "Where Addicts Become Adults," *The Reader's Digest* (December 1970), pp. 92-96.
[64] "Methadone and Heroin Addiction: Rehabilitation without a Cure," *Science* (May 8, 1970), Reprint.

Drug Abuse Prevention Education. There is increased awareness that a primary method of preventing drug use is to provide a comprehensive education program for both youngsters and adults. Because the drug problem has become so immense in the last few years, it is difficult to change the attitudes of many present users. Therefore the education program has to be extensive and vigorous, and it has to reach young children.

In addition, adults have to be made aware of the contradictory picture that they present to youngsters. It is difficult to convince youngsters that drug use is harmful when they see their parents constantly using tobacco, alcohol, tranquilizers, and amphetamines.

Because the attitudes and values of youngsters will only be changed gradually, a total education program has to be initiated early in the youngster's training. Children are exposed at a very early age to drug abuse by not only their parents but also the mass media. "Television conditions the children from the age of two to wake up, slow down, be happy and relieve tension with pills."[65]

The schools can be an important vehicle for making children aware of the dangers of drug use. "It is the schools and the teachers that are capable of providing the best opportunity for instilling permanently an understanding of the dangers of drug abuse in our young people."[66]

The child spends more time in school than in any other institution except the family. Therefore, schools, as Denton points out, are the most logical choice for drug education. The presentation of drug education material should be honest and factual so that the teacher will gain credibility and the student will not feel that he is being "conned." Adult misuse of alcohol and other synthetic substances should not be condoned, and the dangers of misuse should be discussed. This transmits to the youngster that a double standard should not exist for adults and youngsters. The misuse of any synthetic substance, whether alcohol or drugs, is detrimental.

Denton gives the following criteria for coordinating and presenting a drug education program:

1. Organize an all-out drug prevention campaign promoted by radio, newspapers, and television.

2. Provide postgraduate seminar study for teachers so that they can review the range of the drug abuse program within their schools, check the quality of the program, and evaluate the need for expansion.

3. Encourage students to arrange "rap" sessions on their own for examining drug use.

4. Make stronger efforts to see that drug education, which is geared to the younger child whose attitudes are still being formulated, is in effect.

5. Encourage colleges to include drug education in their curriculum for

[65] "Does TV Make Drug Addicts?" *Listen,* 33, No. 10 (October 1970), p. 19.
[66] Clifford Denton, "Crusade in the Classroom," *Pennsylvania Education*, 2 (January–February 1970), p. 23.

student teachers, especially those in physical education. Provide work-shops for teachers already in the classrooms.

6. Encourage programs on drug abuse in schools providing training for the medical professions.

7. Arrange seminars for clergy and community leaders to gather support for community programs.

8. Establish "Dial-a-Junky" drug information centers, staffed by professionals and ex-addicts.

9. Tape dramatic one-spot television messages.

10. Mobilize ex-addicts to travel to schools to speak about their own first-hand experiences with drugs.

11. Increase the supply of literature on drugs available in school libraries and encourage students to read it.[67]

Even though the school will be the major vehicle for transmitting this educational information, the entire community should be involved in drug control, identification, prevention, and rehabilitation. Community agencies, both internal and external to the criminal justice system, must cooperate. Without total involvement and commitment by both the citizens and their service agencies, the problem will not be solved.

Education of youth is education for our nation's future. In the year 2000, today's kindergartner will be a mature adult. The parent and teacher of to-day must help our children to depend upon personal resources rather than chemicals for courage, insight, and a sense of purpose. Drug-taking during adolescence short-circuits biological clocks and the process of maturation that tempers young people into responsible adults. If too many of them are damaged and remain in perennial adolescence, our society inevitably will suffer.

Personal control of one's attitudes and values is the measure of maturity, according to many psychologists. Self-discipline, the ability to assess one's own moods, and the postponement of gratification is further evidence of proper development. Young people are not born with these abilities. Their education, training, environment, and circumstances are responsible in large measure for how they mature. Parents, teachers, and communities all share the responsibility for seeing that the young people in their care learn to cope with their personal and social conflicts. The quality of our future depends on how well we accomplish this. Recent statistics which verify the increase in drug abuse as an escape from responsibility are an ominous warning.

Researchers have found that many drug abusers have problems in setting life goals, are apathetic, disinterested, and tend to withdraw from society. Parents and educators must find ways of developing interests, values, atti-

[67]*Ibid.*

tudes, and life goals for children so that the "drug scene" is not more appealing to them than their daily lives.[68]

SUMMARY

This chapter has discussed the period of development termed *adolescence*. When the youngster does not adequately handle the pressures and areas of adjustment during the teen-age years, juvenile delinquency is often the symptomatic result and it can take the specific form of drug abuse. The constellation of factors surrounding adolescence, the delinquent adolescent, and the drug user were discussed.

QUESTIONS AND PROJECTS

Essay Questions

1. Is the adolescent period similar in all cultures?

2. Why is it important for the person working with delinquents to understant "normal" adolescent behavior?

3. Why is adolescence a difficult period of development?

4. Is adolescence more difficult for a youngster today than it was in the past?

5. Why is drug use so prevalent today?

Projects

1. Develop a realistic and workable drug education program for your community.

2. Establish guidelines to differentiate the delinquent adolescent from the "normal" adolescent.

3. Develop a process for involving teen-agers in community problem solving and community development activities.

[68]*Fact Sheets* (1975), p. 26.

chapter 5

Female Delinquency*

Research and literature in the field of juvenile delinquency have long been dominated by studies of male delinquents, as evidenced in the works of theorists like Cloward and Ohlin, Miller, Thrasher, and Cohen. Given society's tendency to respond to social problems, such as delinquency, when they become both highly visible and potentially threatening, this concentration on the delinquent behavior of boys is put in clearer perspective. Until recently, and particularly in the decades when delinquency theorists were doing a major portion of their work, female delinquency (and more generally female crime) had neither the characteristics nor the dimensions that transform a problem into an object of social concern and empirical study.

THE NATURE AND EXTENT OF FEMALE DELINQUENCY

Traditionally, women's involvement in the criminal justice system has been minimal. Although women make up 51 percent of the total population of the country, they account for only about fifteen percent of all arrests. In jail and prison populations, they are outnumbered by men twenty to one.[1]

The involvement of women in serious crimes and violent offenses has also been considerably less than their male counterparts. Similar patterns in the

---

*This chapter was written by Sydell M. Spinner, School of Criminal Justice, Michigan State University, East Lansing, Michigan.
[1] Virginia A. McArthur, *From Convict to Citizen: Programs for the Woman Offender* (Washington, D.C.: District of Columbia Commission on the Status of Women, 1974), p. 4.

total number of girls arrested, processed, and institutionalized, and the types of offenses in which they are involved, hold for the juvenile justice system as well.

In the past, researchers have tended to focus on the more overt, aggressive, and extensive nature of delinquent behavior among males, and have largely ignored the female delinquent. The current interest in the area of female delinquency and female crime is, to some extent, related to changes in the character and scope of the problem. Female involvement in all aspects of crime, including more serious offenses, has increased dramatically in the past decade, rising nearly three times faster than that of males.[2] Although youth crime in general has grown substantially in recent years, the figures for girls under 18 are even more revealing.

> Recent statistics indicate a dramatic increase in the rate of women's offenses. The FBI Uniform Crime Reports, released in August 1974, reveal that arrests for females under 18 years of age for violent crimes increased 393 percent and 334 percent for property crimes during the 1960-1973 period, while arrests for young males under 18 rose by 236 and 82 percent, respectively. . . .

> This increase in arrests for serious crimes is even more dramatic when notice is made of the arrest figures for murder committed by the young female, which show an increase of 296 percent - 252 percent for males; a robbery increase of 477 percent - 290 percent for males; an aggravated assault increase of 350 percent - 190 percent for males; and a burglary increase of 239 percent - 100 percent for males.[3]

There has also been a concurrent increase in the number of girls processed in juvenile court. Table 1 shows the comparative growth rate for male and female juvenile court dispositions. In 1957, males outnumbered females in juvenile court dispositions slightly more than four to one. By 1972, this ratio had been reduced to somewhat less than three to one. These increases in the visibility and seriousness of female offenses have served to focus attention and interest on the causes, characteristics, and problems of female delinquents.

FEMALE CRIME AND DELINQUENCY:
THEORETICAL EXPLANATIONS

Prior to the recent metamorphosis in the character of female offenses, the statistical differences in the amounts and kinds of criminal behavior among juvenile and adult males and females have often been thought to reflect a basic,

[2] Freda Adler, "The Rise of the Female Crook," *Psychology Today* (November, 1975), p. 46.
[3] Testimony by Mary K. Jolly before the National Congress for New Directions in Federal Correctional Programming, *Juvenile Justice Digest* (Washington, D.C.: Washington Crime News Service), Vol. 3, No. 14 (1975), p. 1.

TABLE 1. Number and Percent Distribution of Delinquency Cases
Disposed of by Juvenile Courts, By Sex, United States, 1957-1972

	Boys		*Girls*	
Year	*Number*	*Percent*	*Number*	*Percent*
1957	358,000	81	82,000	19
1958	383,000	81	87,000	19
1959	393,000	81	90,000	19
1960	415,000	81	99,000	19
1961	408,000	81	95,000	19
1962	450,000	81	104,500	19
1963	485,000	81	116,000	19
1964	555,000	81	131,000	19
1965	555,000	80	142,000	20
1966	593,000	80	152,000	20
1967	640,000	79	171,000	21
1968	708,000	79	191,000	21
1969	760,000	77	228,000	23
1970	799,500	76	252,000	24
1971	845,500	75	279,500	25
1972	827,500	74	285,000	26

SOURCE: Department of Health, Education, and Welfare, *Juvenile Court Statistics 1972*
(Washington, D.C.: U.S. Government Printing Office, 1974), p. 12.

perhaps even intrinsic, difference in the nature of criminality of the two sexes. The literature on female criminality, from Lombroso and Freud to more recent writers, is filled with assumptions about the "unique" psychological and physiological qualities of women that influence female crime.

Perhaps the most recurrent theme in these writings is that women turn to crime "as a *perversion of* or *rebellion against* their *natural feminine* roles."[4] This "natural feminine role" is defined in the worst stereotypical terms as dependent, narcissistic, emotional, underdeveloped in intelligence, morally deficient, and of course, anatomically inferior. Following such a definition any aggressive behavior, including by implication criminal behavior, is unfeminine and an attempt to achieve "inappropriate" masculine characteristics. The particular types of offenses women were typically involved in were also seen as a reflection of the female personality, since offenses such as shoplifting and petty larceny involve little aggressive behavior and physical danger, and are often directed towards the acquisition of material goods designed to enhance the traditional feminine role (i.e., clothes and jewelry).

Freudian theory and related works fail to take into consideration the powerful influence of other substantial factors on the formation of behavior, criminal or otherwise. The focus on criminality as the product of disturbance in the individual personality ignores the role of social, economic, and political forces. Both the types of offenses that females become involved in and the frequency of their involvement can be better explained by considering three

[4]Dorie Klein, "The Etiology of Female Crime: A Review of the Literature," *Issues in Criminology*, Vol. 8, No. 2 (Fall 1973), p. 5.

related factors: differences in socialization patterns, differences in opportunities, and differences in social control.

Socialization Patterns

The roles of male and female in this society have both general and specific behavioral expectations that affect the acceptability of delinquent or criminal behavior as an expression of deviance. Traditionally, women have been more law abiding than men—to a great extent as a result of role expectations emphasizing passivity, dependency, nonaggressiveness, noncompetitiveness and "femininity," which are not conducive to criminal behavior. Thus, offenses from armed robbery to disturbing the peace (which may involve the physical expression of anger) are less likely to be within the average woman's constellation of acceptable behavior and attitudes.

These characteristics, however, are far from intrinsic; rather they are conditioned responses reinforced and even encouraged by the socialization process which begins at a very early age. The socialization process also emphasizes a strong connection to the home and family which generally promotes a more protected environment for females. This may serve to discourage the participation of women in a wide range of activities outside the home, further reducing potential involvement in criminal behavior. The violation of these role expectations, particularly in regard to criminal behavior, may have severe repercussions. There is some indication, for example, that judges are turning to stiffer sentences for women offenders, possibly as a response to what they perceive as "unladylike" violence.

Differences in socialization patterns can also help to explain why many theories of male delinquency have limited applicability to female delinquency. Theories related to male delinquency have emphasized the frustration that lower-class males experience when they are unable to succeed in accordance with middle-class values (Cohen) or legitimately acquire symbols of success valued by society (Merton). Females who are socialized to a noncompetitive, nonaggressive role, and whose main "achievement" may involve becoming a wife and mother, may experience far less frustration at not making a place for themselves in larger society.

Martin Gold, in his study *Delinquent Behavior in an American City,* found "that (poor) performance in school is intimately associated with greater delinquency among boys, but not among girls."[5] He noted that "boys have objectively greater reason to achieve academically: much of what is important in their future development depends on it—and they know it."[6] The corollary to this conclusion is that girls do not view success in school as vital to their future, since achievement in the outside world will not necessarily be a measure

---

[5]Martin Gold, *Delinquent Behavior in an American City* (California: Brooks/Cole, 1970), p. 124.
[6]*Ibid.,* p. 73.

of their success. They are therefore less likely to turn to delinquent behavior as a form of compensation or as an alternate means of achieving status. Gold goes on to suggest that certain "kinds of delinquent behavior may, to a great extent, be a *male* response, particularly suited to the problems of male adolescents."[7]

Differences in Opportunities

Closely related to the socialization process for females is the number of opportunities available to them in both the legitimate and illegitimate spheres. Edwin Sutherland's theory of *Differential Association* provides an additional possibility for explaining variations in male and female delinquency. If as the theory suggests, a "person becomes delinquent because of an excess of definitions favorable to violation of law over definitions unfavorable to violation of law,"[8] it is likely that females who are more home-oriented and more protected would have fewer opportunities for exposure to this "excess of definitions" (unless they happen to be members of a family with a particularly strong "under the roof" criminal culture). In addition, females' exposure to attitudes, techniques, and "intimate personal groups" that encourage delinquent behavior does not have the same frequency, duration, intensity, and priority as that of males.

Studies of female delinquents and female adolescents have shown that girls are less involved in peer group activity than boys: "for boys, gang membership is not only more frequent but also involves more contact with delinquent conduct."[9] There is a stronger tradition of peer group association among males (e.g., Thrasher's normal play groups), which promotes a greater range of opportunities for potential delinquent influences.

Females are also less likely to have access to illegitimate means, such as guns or burglary tools, which facilitate the commission of certain crimes. If one considers Cloward and Ohlin's theory regarding differential access to illegitimate means, there are few "criminal apprenticeship" roles that apply to females and virtually no equivalent of a female "adult criminal subculture."

Social Control

Another variable that helps explain dissimilarities in male and female delinquency is the exercise of social control as it relates to females in this society. Generally, females are subject to more stringent regulation and more careful supervision than males, particularly during adolescence. This factor reduces some potential involvement of females in delinquent behavior, since

[7] *Ibid.*, p. 65.
[8] Robert C. Trojanowicz, *Juvenile Delinquency: Concepts and Control* (Englewood Cliffs, N.J.: Prentice-Hall, Inc., 1973), p. 38.
[9] William Wattenberg and Frank Saunders, "Sex Differences Among Juvenile Offenders," *Sociology and Social Research,* xxxix (September–October, 1954), pp. 24–51.

they are not as likely to be part of "street culture" and subject to negative peer influence. By the same token, however, this tighter control of female adolescents is often what provokes rebellious behavior, sometimes leading ultimately to involvement in the juvenile justice system.

Whereas a considerable amount of male delinquency is related to factors in the larger social system, the greatest proportion of female delinquency is typically explained as a result of *strains within the family*. This can be viewed as a combined effect of the socialization process which emphasizes females' attachment to the home, and the degree of social control to which they are subjected at home. The common view is "that girls get involved in delinquency because of tension-ridden homes in which they are on poor affectional terms with their parents."[10] The offenses for which girls are most frequently referred to the juvenile justice system—runaway, incorrigibility, and sexual misconduct—are closely associated with family strain.

Girls may be more likely to run away from home than boys if their primary source of emotional support and affection is disrupted. However, it is also probable that parents would report a runaway daughter more quickly than a runaway son. There may be comparatively less concern if a boy is gone overnight or for a few days than there would be if the child were a girl, since girls are rarely allowed the same degree of freedom.

Incorrigibility can also be viewed as a reflection of difficulties within the family. Parents who find that they cannot control the behavior of their daughters may, again, be more inclined to resort to official action, because of greater expectations for "proper" and cooperative behavior from their daughters. Boys may be allowed to "sow their wild oats" and have the run of the streets.

Sexual misconduct itself is usually interpreted as one means employed by female adolescents to compensate for a lack of affection and support at home.

> Unlike boys, girls do not have a network of rich same-sex peer group ties to fall back upon for emotional support, so that the affectional deprivation they experience at home becomes particularly difficult to handle. One response to this situation is to become heavily involved with boys so as to acquire substitute affectional gratification from that source.[11]

It is important to note, however, that parents, police, courtworkers, and judges are all apt to interpret *any* degree of sexual activity among female adolescents as *mis*conduct. This relates to role expectations for females and the "double standard" of sexual conduct. The sexual behavior of male adolescents is subject to far less control and rarely evokes as strong a response.

The combination of differential sex-role expectations; limited opportunities for access to criminal attitudes, techniques, and associates; and more severe

[10] Don Gibbons, *Delinquent Behavior* (Englewood Cliffs, N.J.: Prentice-Hall, Inc., 1970), p. 175.
[11] *Ibid.*, p. 182.

application of social control mechanisms act to produce substantially different patterns of delinquent behavior among girls and boys. As these factors are changed or modified, the resulting patterns of delinquent behavior also begin to change.

FEMALE DELINQUENTS IN THE JUVENILE JUSTICE SYSTEM

In its basic philosophy, capsulized in the concept *parens patriae,* the juvenile court has traditionally concerned itself with the care and protection of children. Its jurisdiction extends from illegal acts committed by children to behavior thought to be damaging to the child's moral development, such as associating with immoral persons, growing up in idleness and crime, and running away from home. In many ways, the juvenile justice system not only reflects, but actively reinforces the values and assumptions of society at large in regard to the behavior of females, so that standards for "protection and care" may be considerably different for girls than for boys.

Although it varies from state to state, juvenile court jurisdiction typically extends for children from the ages of nine through eighteen. Until recently, it was not unusual to find provisions in state juvenile codes which established a *longer term* of jurisdiction for girls than for boys. For example, New York State's "Persons In Need of Supervision" statute, under which juveniles are processed for noncriminal offenses such as runaway, incorrigibility, and sexual misconduct, extended until the age of sixteen for boys but until the age of *eighteen* for girls. The New York State Supreme Court ruled in favor of the female juvenile who claimed that the statute was discriminatory. The Court concluded that:

> Lurking behind the discrimination is the imputation that girls who engage in sexual misconduct ought more to be censured and their conduct subject to greater control and regulation than boys.[12]

Oklahoma, Texas, and Illinois are the only three states that still maintain such distinctions in their legal codes and those statutes have been held to be unconstitutional by state courts.[13]

The statutes themselves are not the only example of paternalistic concern for the behavior of female adolescents. The protective attitude of the juvenile justice system toward female delinquents produces a strange combination of differential treatment, which is sometimes more lenient and at other times more severe than that received by their male counterparts.

---

[12]*Ms.,* Vol. V (November 1972), p. 7.
[13]Mark Levin and Rosemary Sarri, *Juvenile Delinquency: A Comparative Analysis of Legal Codes in the United States* (Ann Arbor, Michigan: National Assessment of Juvenile Corrections, 1974), p. 13.

The Chivalry Factor

There is some evidence to support the contention that female delinquents receive some degree of preferential (in the sense of more lenient) treatment at various stages in the juvenile justice system. Beginning with police contact at the point of potential entry into the juvenile justice system, police have the option of either releasing a young female suspect with varying degrees of warning and reprimand, or arresting her with possible referral to juvenile court. A recent sudy in Philadelphia showed that:

> Officers tend to release a larger proportion of girls apprehended for law violations than boys. This research . . . suggests that police indeed have the paternalistic mind-set which says that girls should be treated chivalrously and released unless they need "protection."[14]

To some extent, this particular exercise of police discretion is based on the perceived dangerousness of female juvenile offenders. The statistics cited at the beginning of the chapter illustrate the considerably lower proportion of adult female offenders in the criminal justice system. Since males outnumber females approximately three to one in the juvenile justice system, but seven to one in the adult system, there is some reason to believe that females are less likely to *continue* into an adult criminal career than males. It is interesting to note, however, that the study cited here only revealed more lenient treatment for girls invovled in *law* violations. The same study found that "police are more likely to arrest a girl than a boy for a sexual offense . . . and more likely to refer to court girls accused of their first juvenile offense than girls accused of criminal offenses."[15]

This latter finding is perhaps more typical of the attitude that permeates the juvenile justice system. Official agents of control seem to perceive sexual misconduct and other "acting out" behavior of female adolescents as requiring definite intervention, either because this overt behavior by females is particularly threatening to community standards, or because they see the need to protect these girls from themselves.

Statistics on juvenile court referrals for females show a consistent bias towards processing girls for status offenses—those offenses such as truancy, runaway, and incorrigibility applicable to juveniles only. In 1967, the President's Commission on Law Enforcement and the Administration of Justice found that "more tha . one half of the girls referred to juvenile courts in 1965 were referred for conduct that would not be criminal if committed by adults; only one fifth of the boys were referred for such conduct."[16] These findings are not

[14] Meda Chesney-Lind, "Juvenile Delinquency: The Sexualization of Female Crime," *Psychology Today* (July 1974), p. 45.
[15] *Ibid.*
[16] President's Commission on Law Enforcement and the Administration of Justice, *The Challenge of Crime in a Free Society* (Washington, D.C.: U.S. Government Printing Office, 1967), p. 56.

atypical. A more recent study of the Honolulu Juvenile Court revealed that status offenses accounted for 70 percent of the female referrals but only 31 percent of the male referrals to court in 1972.[17]

It might be possible to interpret these figures as an indication that girls actually *are* involved in sexual misconduct, runaway, and similar offenses to a much greater degree than boys. However, recent studies of self-reported delinquency seem to indicate that official statistics, on which many of the assumptions about female delinquents are based, do not present an accurate picture of either the frequency of female involvement in delinquent behavior or of the types of delinquent behavior in which they engage.

In his extensive study of self-reported delinquency in Flint, Michigan, Martin Gold found that although girls were more involved in sexual offenses than boys (11 percent of all offenses versus 6 percent for boys), this did not constitute the major portion of their delinquent behavior:

> It seems unreasonable to characterize girl offenders by just 11 percent of their offenses. A more accurate picture of girls' delinquency shows it to be quite similar to boys', only smaller. . . . The mixture of girls' offenses was not very different from that of boys'.[18]

Studies such as Gold's seem to suggest that the police and juvenile courts choose to screen into the juvenile justice system those girls whose behavior is perceived as violating sex-role expectations and the double standard of sexual conduct in far greater proportion than those who are involved in minor law violations. This tendency to, in effect, exercise greater control over female delinquents who deviate from social sexual norms extends to other aspects of the juvenile justice process, as well.

Juvenile Detention

In most states, the use of secure detention for juveniles is limited to those children who are a threat to themselves or others, who may be victims of abusing or neglecting parents, who have runaway from home, or who need "observation, study and treatment." Juvenile detention facilities are the equivalent of county jails in the adult criminal justice system, and in practice are used primarily to provide *secure* custody for juveniles awaiting hearings or transfers to other placements. The use of detention in regard to female delinquents is particularly revealing of the inclination to overcontrol.

The recent study of the Honolulu Juvenile Court found that 43 percent of the detention home residents were girls, although only 30 percent of the juveniles arrested during the study period were females.[19] It appears that women

---

[17] Lind, *op. cit.,* p. 45.
[18] Gold, *op. cit.,* p. 118.
[19] Lind, *op. cit.,* p. 45.

are represented in the detention population in greater proportion than their arrest rates. Even within the single category of female offenders, "misbehavior offenses" are treated more severely than felonies.[20]

In comparing the types of offenses for which girls are held in detention to those for which boys are detained, a study of New York City detention facilities found that the percentage of girls held in detention for juvenile offenses was nearly three times the percentage of boys held for similar offenses (38 percent compared to 14 percent). The same study also revealed that only 6 percent of the female detention population was being held for offenses against persons or property, compared to 33 percent of the male population being held for those offenses.[21] Girls are not only detained more frequently for status offenses, but are also more likely to be held in detention for a longer period of time, often as much as three times longer than boys who are charged with law violations and released in a few days.[22]

All of these variations in detention practices as applied to female delinquents reflect the view that girls require closer supervision, even though they may not present a substantial threat to the community. Often, these practices are justified by citing the disturbed home situations of female delinquents and the need to provide alternate care and control. It is questionable whether the use of secure detention is an appropriate response to status offenses, or whether open, community-based, short-term care facilities would not provide a more suitable placement for these children.

Dispositions for Female Delinquents

Once enmeshed in the juvenile justice system, the female delinquent is again subject to the peculiar mix of lenient and harsh treatment. Girls may be more likely to appear before a juvenile court judge on their first offense and may be more likely to receive probation after only one offense. Overall, however, they have a better chance of receiving probation or some other form of supervision than boys.[23] Studies have also revealed that "probation officers are far more likely to recommend incarceration for girls than boys. While girls make up only 1/6 of the court population, they constitute one half of those recommended for institutionalization."[24] National data for 1965 showed that girls convicted of status offenses were more likely to be incarcerated than those convicted of criminal behavior.[25] These results can again be interpreted as

---

[20] An American Association of University Women study in Pennsylvania showed that 45 percent of the girls charged with juvenile or sex-role violations were detained prior to trial, compared to only 24 percent of those charged with misdemeanors, and 35 percent of those charged with felonies.

[21] Gertrude Samuels, "When Children Collide with the Law," *New York Times Magazine* (December 5, 1975), p. 138.

[22] Lind, *op. cit.,* p. 46.

[23] *Ibid.*

[24] *Ibid.*

[25] *Ibid.*

evidence that the sexual misconduct of girls, as well as other misbehavior, is seen as cause for protective intervention, which may in fact result in more severe treatment than the punishment of male law violators.

The data indicating that females are more likely to be incarcerated for juvenile offenses are confirmed by an analysis of the juvenile correctional institution population. Table 2 displays national figures for 1971 showing that the overwhelming majority of girls are institutionalized for status offenses, while boys are primarily incarcerated for felony offenses. It is also significant that the length of stay for females in juvenile institutions is generally longer than for males (10.7 months versus 8.2 months).[26]

This tendency to institutionalize female offenders for various behavior problems is again questionable in view of the lack of potential danger they present. Juvenile institutions are generally regarded as a last-resort placement within the juvenile justice system, and are designed to be used for juveniles who must be removed from the community. It is apparent that institutionalization of female delinquents goes far beyond protecting the community.

One of the possible explanations (although hardly a justification) for the extensive use of institutional placements for female delinquents is the relative absence of alternative and less restrictive placements. Female delinquents have not only been ignored in the literature and research, but also in preventive and correctional programming for juveniles.

The most common alternatives to institutional placements for juveniles who do not require the strict confinement of a training school are ranches, forestry camps, halfway houses, and group homes. Although there are more males in the system than females, alternative facilities for females are *extremely* limited; 90 percent of ranch and camp facilities and 72 percent of all halfway houses and group homes are for males only.[27] This is a particularly inappropriate distribution of resources given the less serious nature of female offenses and their amenability for treatment within the community.

Institutional Programs for Female Delinquents

The heavy reliance on institutional placements for delinquent girls is premised on the assumption that these facilities offer rehabilitative care that will facilitate the healthy growth, development, and readjustment of their inmate populations.[28] Often, however, this is not the case. Institutional programs for delinquent girls have been strongly oriented toward reinforcing so-called traditional roles and personality characteristics of women. It is questionable whether in a time of rapid social change, this emphasis on functions and behavior more appropriate to the past will adequately prepare young girls for survival. The problem of the appropriate philosophical orientation of institutions for

---

[26] Lind, *op. cit.*, p. 46.
[27] *Children in Custody, op. cit.*, p. 4.
[28] *Juvenile Justice Digest*, Vol. 3, No. 14 (1975), p. 2.

TABLE 2. Percent Distribution by Sex and Offense

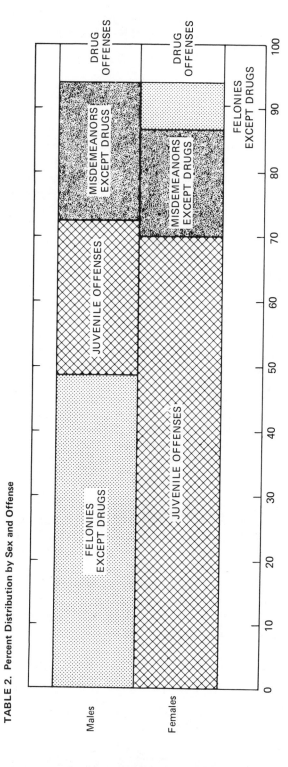

SOURCE: LEAA, *Children In Custody: A Report on the Juvenile Detention and Correctional Facility Census of 1971* (Washington, D.C.: National Criminal Justice Information and Statistics Service, 1973), p. 9.

female delinquents, however, is just one aspect of programming that bears reconsideration.

Family Contacts. Institutional programs for delinquent girls suffer from a number of deficiencies whose impact on the rehabilitative potential of the program may be substantial. Many programs fail to provide for ongoing and regular contact with the families of the incarcerated girls. If, according to some findings, "a greater proportion of girls' delinquency may be provoked by family conditions than is true among boys,"[29] it is particularly important that programs for delinquent girls involve the family in the treatment process. It is unlikely that girls will find successful adjustment easy if they return to a home situation that has remained virtually unchanged since the time of their commitment. In many cases, the isolated geographical location of the institution may interfere with continued family contact, but often no attempt is made to address this problem or initiate some program of regular contacts with families in closer proximity to the institution.

An interesting phenomenon occurs in some institutions, which can be interpreted as an effort to replace or provide a substitute for the affection and support of the family. Girls' informal groups frequently assume the structure of a "make-believe family." In this format, girls take on various family roles, such as father, mother, daughters, sons, and cousins, depending on the size of the group:

> The family structure is patriarchal in that it is always the girl who plays the role of the father who determines group content . . . The father has the right to "beat up" his wife and children, and assign tasks to the family members autocratically. The father expects gifts from the other members of the family and in return gives them protection from any phenomenon that might be construed as an attack.[30]

The strength and formality of these groups varies considerably. In some institutions the roles are more permanent in nature, while in others girls may interchange roles frequently. The groups may engage in some negative or destructive activities, depending on the leadership, and like most informal inmate subcultures, may be counterproductive to institutional program goals.

There has traditionally been some concern that the make-believe family is a manifestation of homosexual activities among female delinquents. Although this may occur from time to time, it is not considered a major characteristic of the make-believe family. Rather, it is more likely that:

> The make-believe family in girls' institutions is the female counterpart of informal groups in boys' institutions: that the form taken by the

[29] Gold, *op. cit.,* p. 128.
[30] "The Female Institutionalized Delinquent" in *Institutional Rehabilitation of Delinquent Youth* (Albany, N.Y.: Delmar Publishers, 1962), p. 164.

informal group represents a structure where basic . . . psychological needs can be met.[31]

The make-believe family can, however, create problems within the institution when staff try actively to fight against or break up the informal group, rather than redirect its activities toward more positive outlets.

Institutional Staff. The characteristics of the staff in institutions for girls often presents another problem that affects potential program success. As is true in many institutions for delinquents, cottage and supervisory staff share little in common with the inmate population. They are likely to be from a different social and economic class (particularly if the inmate population is primarily urban), and are often poorly trained to deal with the problems of delinquent girls. Frequently, they are older women, whose only experience with adolescents has been in raising their own children, and who are traditionally-oriented regarding the "proper" behavior of young girls.

These factors neither permit the staff to relate meaningfully to the girls, nor do they allow staff to serve as constructive role models for female delinquents. Although institutions are now making greater use of female counselors and professional staff, contact between the girls and these professionals may be minimal and attempts to provide continuous exposure to competent women in a variety of responsible roles are rare.

Institutional Programming. The emphasis on traditional behavior and characteristics is naturally reflected in the program activities and vocational training offered at most institutions for female delinquents. Activities such as sewing and home economics are common components of institutional programs for girls, but girls may have little opportunity to release any aggressive feelings through organized sports or other activities available to boys. Instead, it has been suggested that institutions substitute:

> Activities which cater more directly to the *narcissistic* make-up of the delinquent girl (such as) dramatics and interpretive dancing. . . . In fact, the dance in all forms should probably replace the typical gym and physical education program for girls.[32]

The vocational components of girls institutional programs, if they exist at all, are often a direct reinforcement of traditional women's roles. At one time, the vocational program offered at the girls' training school in Michigan consisted of laundry, cosmetology and cake-decorating; none of which provided any real job preparation. Other programs typically offer some token training in areas such as housekeeping, filing, typing, or nurse's aide. In many areas vocational training programs for girls are unavailable.

[31] *Ibid.*
[32] *Ibid.,* p. 167.

If a decision is made that placement in a vocational training center is the best alternative for a girl, she may well be required to leave her home state in order to receive the benefits of such training. While there are 48 Job Corps Centers for men, only 10 centers train women, even though young women have the highest rate of unemployment.[33]

There has been little consideration of and planning for the types of skills that may be required in the labor market in the near future, and little thought given to the fact that these young women may *have* to work to support themselves and/or their families. It should be noted that women currently comprise 40 percent of the civilian labor force, and that 6.6 million women in the labor force are the heads of households. By the end of the decade, projections indicate that there will be 39.2 million women in the labor force.[34] It is no longer sufficient to assume that girls do not really need vocational preparation.

Acknowledging that many institutionalized girls do indeed have marriage and a family as their main goals (and may in fact already have children), few institutions even provide adequate preparation in these areas. Program activities dealing with home management, budgeting, child care, and interpersonal relationships might be just a few of the potential offerings that could improve the girls' chances of success in their chosen roles. Since many of them do come from disrupted, and even abusing, families, it is particularly important for them to have access to the skills and knowledge that will allow them to respond to their own prospective families in more productive ways.

Although changes in staffing and programming are taking place at many institutions, progress is slow. If institutions are to qualify as even minimally viable programs for delinquent girls, they must recognize the changing needs and capabilities of the female delinquent.

Female Delinquents and Juvenile Parole

Little research has been done on the subject of female delinquents on parole. Although sufficient research in this area is lacking even for males, there are a few studies that analyze the characteristics and problems of male juvenile parolees. No comparable data exists for females.

The data that is available reveal that approximately 71 percent of female delinquents are discharged from institutions to aftercare or parole, the same as for male delinquents. A slightly higher percentage of females are discharged without supervision (11 percent) than are males (7 percent).[35] This is somewhat surprising, given the system's usual tendency to oversupervise females, but could be interpreted as a result of the longer length of stay for female delin-

[33] *Juvenile Justice Digest,* Vol. 3, No. 14 (1975), p. 2.
[34] U.S. Department of Labor, *1974 Manpower Report to the President* (Washington, D.C.: U.S. Government Printing Office, 1974), pp. 29–106.
[35] *Children In Custody, op. cit.,* p. 10.

quents in institutions, which might place them closer to the maximum age of jurisdiction at the time of discharge.

The other major category of releases for female delinquents is "transfer to other institutions." In this category, it appears that female delinquents are more likely to be referred to other programs operated by agencies outside of the juvenile justice system, indicating the need for extended supervision and services.[36] Females are just as likely to be returned from parole/aftercare status for violations of parole as males, but are far less likely to be *re*committed to institutions, after having been discharged initially from supervision.[37]

NEW DIRECTIONS

The philosophy and practices of the juvenile justice system as they relate to female delinquents are already undergoing modification and change, although to some extent this change is being imposed from the outside. Legal challenges have questioned the constitutionality of various statutes which appear to violate the rights of female delinquents, and steady progress is being made in this sphere.

Beyond specific court cases, there is a more general trend to modify the scope of the juvenile justice system, particularly as it relates to status offenders. Labeling theorists have long emphasized the potentially negative impact that official involvement in the juvenile justice system may have on a juvenile's self-concept, and on the production of further delinquent attitudes and behavior. Several states are considering, or have already passed, legislation that will eliminate status offenses from the juvenile code, or severely regulate the conditions under which court intervention is justified. Since the vast majority of status offenders processed in the juvenile justice system are females, this trend will have far-reaching implications.

In addition to new policy that will determine who enters the juvenile justice system, changes have already taken place affecting the dispositional alternatives for juveniles within the system. The 1974 Federal *Juvenile Delinquency Prevention and Control Act* makes funds available for program development only to those states that agree *not* to incarcerate status offenders in secure juvenile correctional institutions. This is a unique example of an attempt on the part of the federal government to promote change by providing monetary incentives for the development of alternative programs for status offenders. Again, since the majority of institutionalized females are confined for status offenses, the impact will be substantial.

Although new programs for status offenders are badly needed, an effort must be made to secure better and more appropriate programs for all female delinquents in the system. There is a particular need for more community-

[36] *Ibid.*
[37] *Ibid.*

based programs, for programs that work with the family, for programs which provide sound role models, and for programs which offer *viable options* for female adolescents, to train and prepare them adequately for the many alternative roles which are available to women in contemporary society.

Any discussion of female delinquency would be incomplete without some reference to the effect of the Feminist Movement. Although one could not with great confidence, attribute the rise of female crime and delinquency directly to the Feminist Movement, it would be equally inaccurate to deny its impact on the attitudes and behavior of women today. The Feminist Movement can be seen as affecting the *perceptions* of women in terms of their capabilities and aspirations:

> Today women believe they have more options, that they can do things that will change their lives, that they have the wherewithal to improve their economic status.[38]

It is unfortunate that within the context of the criminal justice system, this is often translated into the commission of more serious offenses, so that a woman may be more likely today to risk incarceration for the potentially high "payoff" of an armed robbery, rather than for lesser crimes such as petty larceny or shoplifting.

The Feminist Movement has also had its impact on the attitudes and behavior of those who work with female offenders in the system. The "chivalry factor" is quickly disappearing. Police, prosecutors, judges, and other professionals are beginning to give women equal treatment on the streets and in the courts. This partially accounts for the dramatic increase in arrest rates, which reflects not only an actual increase in the number of offenses committed by women, but also an increase that is the result of new enforcement policies.

In addition to changes in attitudes and awareness, the Feminist Movement has opened the door to greater opportunities for women, in both the legitimate and illegitimate worlds. Women's involvement in certain types of offenses, such as embezzlement, is likely to increase at least partially as the result of increased opportunities to commit these crimes. With increasing opportunities and aspirations, it would not be surprising if concurrent increases in strain and frustration produced additional deviant behavior, if many of the earlier theories (particularly Merton's "Social Structure and Anomie"), developed to explain similar behavior among males, hold true for females.

Female delinquency in the next decade will, no doubt, continue to mirror many of the changes taking place in society today. With more research and directed study, we will be better able to understand the problems and characteristics of the juvenile female offender, who is both similar and different from her adult female counterpart. Although efforts should be made to examine the unique factors which may contribute to delinquent behavior among females,

[38] Adler, *op. cit.,* p. 46.

we would also do well to consider explanations that stress *common* elements that may foster delinquency among both males and females. One such explanation is offered by Martin Gold, who suggests that:

> . . . delinquent behavior is a function of role inadequacy—of adolescents finding themselves unable to live up to expectations in school, at home and among friends. Faced with their failure to be adequate students, or sons and daughters, or teenagers, they are driven to find respectability in other ways. . . . If it is true that much delinquent behavior betokens youngsters' struggles to find a place among us, then we may justly ask why there is not enough room.[39]

In this respect, at least, the problems of both male and female delinquents may share a common origin and a common solution.

SUMMARY

This chapter has presented an overview of the female delinquent in the juvenile justice system. The less serious and extensive nature of female delinquency to date was noted as one reason for the relative absence of theoretical work in this area. Theories explaining male delinquency were reviewed for their applicability to females. Differences in socialization patterns, opportunities, and social control were suggested to explain dissimilarities between male and female delinquency. The changing role of women in society has already had an impact on the characteristics and extent of female crime and delinquency, and will no doubt continue to affect women's attitudes and behaviors. New programs and new approaches will be needed to deal with this rapidly changing phenomenon.

> The female delinquent of the 1970s has gravitated beyond the realm of status offenses. The time is long overdue that we focus adequate resources on the problems unique to female delinquents. Now is the time to understand why a girl becomes delinquent. Now is the time to assure that resources are available to prevent female delinquency. Now is the time to implement effective rehabilitation and treatment programs designed especially for the female offender.[40]

QUESTIONS AND PROJECTS

Essay Questions

1. Why are traditional theories of male delinquency inappropriate for explaining female delinquency?

[39] Gold, *op. cit.,* pp. 130–131.
[40] *Juvenile Justice Digest* (Washington, D.C.: Washington Crime News Service), Vol. 3, No. 14 (1975), p. 3.

2. In what ways have female offenses differed from male offenses, and why?

3. How does the juvenile justice system treat females differently from males?

4. What are some of the problems and deficiencies in institutional programs for girls?

5. What changes are taking place that will affect the juvenile justice system's response to female delinquents?

Projects

1. Develop a plan for surveying local enforcement agencies and courts to determine how many female delinquents are arrested and processed and for what offenses.

2. Develop a program that addresses some of the special needs and concerns of female delinquents.

3. Identify ways that the family could be involved in the ongoing treatment process for female delinquents.

4. Compare the treatment of female delinquents in this country to another country, such as Great Britain or Sweden.

chapter 6

Handling the Juvenile Delinquent within the Juvenile Justice System

This chapter will emphasize the major components of the juvenile justice system—the police department, the intake decision of the juvenile court, and the juvenile court. It will focus on the juvenile bureau of the police department, where the delinquent first comes in contact with the system and is either released or processed forward; the intake division of the juvenile court, where, again, the delinquent is either released or processed to the juvenile court; and the juvenile court, whose options range from outright release to incarceration. We will examine their philosophy, their duties, and the processes they use, individually and jointly, when handling the delinquent.

Other agencies can also be considered a part of the juvenile justice system, such as schools and related social work agencies. However, they do not usually deal with serious delinquent activity directly. They function mostly as a referral source to the police juvenile bureau or the juvenile court. In addition, we will examine the roles of the different professional groups that work with and handle the juvenile delinquent; namely the police, social workers (probation officers), and judges.

The police do not usually have the amount of formal education that judges and social workers have. The social workers are more behavioral science-oriented than either the police or judges and, many times, more transient because of job mobility. Many judges, because they are elected, often have political aspirations and, therefore, consider the juvenile court position only a stepping stone to higher office. Thus, the police in many respects are the most "stable" component of the juvenile justice system, whereas the judges, social workers, and lawyers come and go.

In terms of role definition for the three occupational groups, the police have the major role of maintaining public order and safety, as well as enforcing laws. They do this by collecting facts and processing those persons who have transgressed. Social workers, whether in the probation department, the court, or a mental health agency, have the major role of utilizing social science principles to develop treatment programs and to provide insight into human dynamics.

The judge makes a case determination by referring to the "facts" gathered by the police and the social science principles interpreted by social workers. The judge, then, with the assistance of police and social workers, has the major role of objective decision maker who supposedly weighs the facts, evaluates the situation and the circumstances, and decides what alternatives should be used in the particular case. The major components of the juvenile justice system must work with resource services and referral sources if a meaningful determination is to be made and the process of handling the juvenile is to be beneficial for both the community and the child. Each major component will be discussed separately.

ORIGIN AND DEVELOPMENT OF THE JUVENILE COURT[1]

The legal basis for the juvenile court can be traced back to the concept of *parens patriae,* mentioned in Chapter 1. This Latin phrase literally means "the parent of the country" and refers to the belief that the state, as the ultimate authority, has both the right and the obligation to direct and protect those of its citizens who, because of some impediment, demonstrate a need for such direction and protection. The impediment might be age, infirmity, mental incompetence, or, in the case of minors, immaturity. The nature of the intervention was conceived to be in the manner of parental guidance and admonition, with the strong emotional ingredient of familial concern. This attitude derived from the personal, individual manner of handling family disputes as opposed to the cold, legalistic justice of the criminal court.

A further legal basis of the juvenile court derived from the presumed innocence of children under seven years of age, which had long constituted an important feature of common law. Children were thought to be incapable of committing a criminal act since their immaturity precluded the presence of one of the most important prerequisites: guilt intent (*mens rea*). This principle of common law was later extended to older age groups and remains an integral component of the philosophy of the juvenile court.

Other developments heralded the advent of the juvenile court. As early as 1825, for example, special institutions were established for children. Probation, which from its inception was employed in the handling of both adult and

---

[1] Most of the research for this section on the origin and development of the juvenile court was accomplished by John M. Thomas in a graduate paper presented to Robert C. Trojanowicz, School of Criminal Justice, Michigan State University, East Lansing, Michigan.

juvenile offenders, was first used as an alternative to incarceration in Boston in 1841. Both of these reforms sprang from the work and experimentation of the pioneering Swiss educators Jean Jacques Rousseau (1712-1778) and Johann Heinrich Pestalozzi (1746-1827), who concluded that children, are distinct from adults, both physically and psychologically. Heretofore, children had been conceived of merely as "imperfect" adults or as "adults in miniature," who thus were expected to be able to adhere to adult standards of behavior. The humanitarian movement begun by these two giants culminated in the progressive educational reforms of John Dewey (1859-1952) in the United States at the turn of the nineteenth century. The movement spilled over into all areas concerned with children.

There is some disagreement concerning who actually established the first juvenile court. Some contend, for example, that the first children's courts were instituted in South Australia, by executive order in 1889 and by statute in 1895. Others credit the United States with the first juvenile court act. Since the controvery is limited to the English-speaking world, however, the authors suspect that a record search of the non-English-speaking world might produce some surprising findings.

Whoever passed the first act, the Colorado Legislature passed the "Compulsory School Act" on April 12, 1899. Chapter 136 reads as follows:

> Every child between the ages of 8 and 14 who absents himself habitually from school, or is incorrigible, vicious or immoral in conduct or who habitually wanders about the streets and public places during school hours, having no business or lawful occupation, shall be deemed a juvenile disorderly person subject to the provisions of this Act.[2]

Although this act contains some of the basic elements of a full-blown juvenile court act, especially in reference to status offenses, its primary concern is truancy. Therefore, the first comprehensive juvenile court act is considered to be the bill passed by the Illinois Legislature on July 1, 1899, called "An Act to Regulate the Treatment and Control of Dependent, Neglected and Delinquent Children." It mandated the institution of a juvenile court in all counties with a population of over 500,000. Only one such court was established since Cook County (Chicago and environs) was the only county populous enough to be required to comply. The act included the following features:

> jurisdiction over dependent, neglected, and delinquent children;
>
> emphasizing guidance, protection, and rehabilitation as opposed to punishment;
>
> elimination of the adversary tactics of formal criminal procedures, establishing a "summary" proceeding;
>
> the institution of a new vocabulary, i.e., a "petition," worded "State in

[2] Colorado Laws, Chapter 136, p. 342 (1899).

the Interests of Child" replaced the "complaint" of "State v. Child," "summons" was used instead of "warrant," "initial hearing" instead of "arraignment," "finding of involvement" instead of "conviction," and "disposition" instead of "sentence";

specially appointed judges in separate courtrooms with physical surroundings different from those of criminal courts;

ordered the separation of children from adults whenever both were confined in the same institution;

forbade committing a child under twelve to a jail or police station;

provided for probation officers, who would investigate cases and supervise children placed on probation.

The professed objective of the juvenile proceeding was not to contest a criminal charge but to determine what could be accomplished in the best interest of the child. The proceeding followed the character of a civil case, which virtually negated the child's basic constitutional rights of notice of the charges, the right to counsel, the right to a confrontation and cross-examination of the witnesses, the right to protection against self-incrimination and the observance of the rules of evidence.

An informal and flexible procedure of the nature described above was thought to be in the best interests of the child; it would cause less trauma to and labeling of the child and would therefore be more conducive to rapport, cooperation, and rehabilitation.

Following the Illinois example, a juvenile statute was passed in Colorado in 1903. By 1909 twenty states and the District of Columbia had passed similar bills. By 1920 all but three states had juvenile court acts on the books. Wyoming was the last to follow suit in 1945. (There are no federal juvenile courts. Children under eighteen who violate federal laws not punishable by death or life imprisonment may be sent to state juvenile courts or processed as delinquents in a federal district court.)

Initially, juvenile courts of various jurisdictions developed differently, especially as related to procedures and facilities. Nevertheless the Illinois act was copied more or less accurately in several of its major features:

1. the age at which a child could be declared a criminal was raised, usually from seven to approximately sixteen;

2. a child declared a delinquent, was subject to the jurisdiction of the juvenile court;

3. the juvenile court extended the doctrine of *parens patriae* to all children who were in need of state protection.

As the juvenile court movement spread, definitions of delinquency were broadened, the court's jurisdiction was expanded to include nondelinquency cases, such as illegitimacy and mental defectives. There also existed a tendency to raise the upper age limit of juveniles, subject to the court's authority, in some states to as high as twenty-one. The court was given authority over adults in certain cases involving juveniles, such as neglect, child abuse, and contributing to the delinquency of a minor. The juvenile court in the essential form established in 1899 remained operant and free of serious challenge until 1966.

The population explosion subsequent to World War II led in the sixties to a dramatic rise in juvenile crime. The overworked juvenile courts came under increasingly close scrutiny. Legal scholars and appellate courts especially began to doubt the wisdom of the flexible, informal procedures of the juvenile courts. Proponents of revision of the juvenile court found a voice in Joel F. Handler:

> The great humanitarian reform movement has led to an unbridled official discretion often resulting in capricious decisions. What is needed . . . is a return to clearer standards and orderly procedure which will facilitate the rendering of sound decisions and at the same time safeguard the rights of adolescents and their parents.[3]

More damaging in the long run than even the procedural questions was a questioning of the very motivation of the 1899 legislation. Platt and Fox, writing in the 1960s, for example, did not see the 1899 legislation as revolutionary or radically new but rather as a logical vehicle for serving middle-class interests by maintaining established institutions and value systems. To quote J. Lawrence Schultz:

> Paramount among these ideas (or biases) was *hostility*—hostility to the cities, to the new waves of East European immigrants, and even to their children, whom the reformers professedly wished to save from criminality and immorality.[4]

Schultz summarizes by quoting Platt:

> Child saving may be understood as a crusade which served symbolic and ceremonial functions for native, middle-class Americans. The movement was not so much a break with the past as an affirmation of faith in traditional institutions. Parental authority, home education, rural life, and the independence of the family as a social unit were emphasized because they seemed threatened at this time by urbanism and industrialism. The child savers elevated the nuclear family, especially women, as stalwarts of the family, and defended the family's right to supervise the socialization of youth.[5]

---

[3] Joel F. Handler, "The Juvenile Court and the Adversary System: Problems of Function and Form," 1965 *Wisconsin Law Review* 7, p. 10.
[4] J. Lawrence Schultz, "The Cycle of Juvenile Court History," *Crime and Delinquency,* Vol. 19, No. 4 (October 1973), p. 458.
[5] *Ibid.,* p. 46.

Another aspect of the juvenile court philosophy that came under fire in the sixties was the justification of different treatment based on rehabilitation. It had become patently apparent that rehabilitation was not achieving the desired results. This being the case, then, how could juvenile court procedures, which denied basic constitutional rights, continue to be justified?

The manifold rumblings against the juvenile court culminated in three U.S. Supreme Court decisions, which threaten to radically alter the nature of the handling of juveniles in the future.

In *Kent* v. *United States* in 1966, the Supreme Court reversed the conviction of a sixteen-year-old youth who had been tried as an adult for housebreaking, robbery, and rape. The high court held that the waiver to criminal court was procedurally invalid because the youth had been denied a hearing with the assistance of counsel and a statement of the juvenile court concerning its reasons for the waiver to criminal court. In its ruling, the Supreme Court demonstrated that the *parens patriae* philosophy of the juvenile court was "not an invitation to procedural arbitrariness,"[6] and further:

> There is evidence, in fact, that there may be grounds for concern that the child receives the worst of both worlds: that he gets neither the protection accorded to adults nor the solicitous care and regenerative treatment postulated for children.[7]

In re Gault, 387 U.S. 1 (1967), was the first juvenile court case in history to be decided on constitutional grounds; the commitment of fifteen-year-old Gerald Gault to a state industrial school for the duration of his minority for allegedly making an obscene telephone call was overturned. In light of the due process clause of the Fourteenth Amendment, the Supreme Court ruled that Gault had been denied the following basic rights:

1. notice of the charges;
2. right to counsel;
3. right to confrontation and cross-examination of the witnesses;
4. privilege against self-incrimination;
5. right to a transcript of the proceedings;
6. right to appellate review.

In reference to this case, Justice Fortas wrote "under our Constitution, the condition of being a boy does not justify a kangaroo court."[8]

The Supreme Court's decision in the Gault case had the effect of diluting the doctrine of *parens patriae* and the informal procedures of the juvenile court by suggesting that all the technical rules of evidence were to be adhered to.

[6] 383 U.S. 541, at 541 (1966).
[7] 383 U.S. 541, at 556 (1966).
[8] 387 U.S. 1, at 28 (1967).

This same general trend was continued in the 1970 decision *In re Winship,* 397 U.S. 358 (1970). The Supreme Court ruled that due process required the juvenile courts to follow the criminal court standard of "beyond a reasonable doubt" as opposed to the civil court standard of "preponderance of the evidence" in establishing guilt. Justice Brennan listed a number of reasons for the court's position, among which were:

1. the youth's interest in not losing his liberty;

2. society's concern for not convicting an accused when reasonable doubts concerning his guilt exist;

3. the need to insure the community of the fairness of the criminal law.[9]

In his dissenting opinion in the Winship case, Chief Justice Warren Burger could possibly have heralded a return swing of the pendulum to a greater adherence to the principle of *parens patriae:*

What the juvenile court needs is not more but less of the trappings of legal procedures and judicial formalism; the juvenile court system requires breathing room and flexibility in order to survive, if it can survive the repeated assaults from this court.[10]

Decisions in later cases seem to confirm a conservative renaissance. In *Mc-Keiver* v. *Pennsylvania* (1971), for example, the Supreme Court considered "whether the Due Process Clause of the Fourteenth Amendment assures the right to trial by jury in the adjudicative phase of a state juvenile delinquency proceeding."[11] Writing for the majority, Justice Blackmun upheld the state court decisions, holding that the concept of due process of law as applied to juvenile court proceedings does not include the right to trial by jury.

The controversy continues; the preponderance of literature presently supports a continuance of the trend of the sixties, which is critical of the principle of *parens patriae* and supportive of constitutional guarantees for minors. A related ramification of this trend has been the increasingly vocal and influential child advocacy movement, discussed in detail in the child neglect and abuse chapter of this volume.

Ultimately, it will be the Supreme Court of the United States that will determine whether the Illinois Juvenile Court Act of 1899 will remain the predominant model for handling juveniles in the juvenile justice system or whether, continuing the trend of lower voting and drinking ages, the juvenile justice system of the future will grant adult rights to juveniles. It seems to the authors that the latter course will only be acceptable if these newly acquired rights are balanced by a demand for increased responsiblity on the part of

---

[9] 397 U.S., at 361–364 (1970).
[10] 397 U.S. 358, at 376 (1970).
[11] 403 U.S. 528, at 530 (1971).

juveniles. Only thus can the trend of increasing disruptiveness in American life be halted.

Juvenile Court Legislation Today

The Illinois Juvenile Court Act remains to the present a model for emulation. Revised repeatedly, it reflects the state of the juvenile court today in its philosophy, jurisdiction, and procedures. Its statement of policy and purpose reads:

> The purpose of this act is to secure for each minor subject hereto such care and guidance, preferably in his own home, as will serve the moral, emotional, mental and physical welfare of the minor and the best interests of the community; to preserve and strengthen the minor's family ties whenever possible, removing him from the custody of his parents only when his welfare or safety or the protection of the public cannot be adequately safeguarded without removal; and, when the minor is removed from his own family, to secure for him custody, care and discipline as nearly as possible equivalent to that which should be given by his parents, and in cases where it should and can properly be done to place the minor in a family home so that he may become a member of the family by legal adoption or otherwise . . . This Act shall be administered in a spirit of humane concern, not only for the rights of the parties, but also for the fears and the limits of understanding of all who appear before the court.[12]

Jurisdiction of the act covers four categories of juveniles:

1. delinquent minors, defined as:

any minor who prior to his 17th birthday has violated or attempted to violate, regardless of where the act occurred, any federal or state law or municipal ordinance;[13]

2. minors otherwise in need of supervision, defined as:

(a) any minor under 18 years of age who is byond the control of his parents, guardian or other custodian;

(b) any minor subject to compulsory school attendance who is habitually truant from school;

(c) any minor who is an addict, as defined in the "Drug Addiction Act"; and

---

[12] *Illinois Criminial Law and Procedure for 1976,* Illinois Revised Statutes 1975 and Supplement. Brought to date through all laws enacted at the Regular Session of the 79th General Assembly, PA 79-1192 (St. Paul, Minn.) West Pub. Co. 1976, Chapter 37, "Juvenile Court Act," Section 701-2, p. 6.
[13] *Ibid.,* Section 702-2, p. 7, 8.

(d) on or after Jan. 1, 1974, any minor who violates a lawful court order made under this act.[14]

3. neglected minors, defined as:

any minor under 18 years of age

(a) who is neglected as to proper or necessary support, education as required by law, or as to medical or other remedial care recognized under state law or other care necessary for his well-being, or who is abandoned by his parents, guardian, custodian; or

(b) whose environment is injurious to his welfare or whose behavior is injurious to his own welfare or that of others;[15]

4. dependent minors, including:

any minor under 18 years of age;

(a) who is without a parent, guardian, or legal custodian;

(b) who is without proper care because of the physical or mental disability of his parent, guardian or custodian; or

(c) who has a parent, guardian, or legal custodian who with good cause, wishes to be relieved of all residual parental rights and responsibilities, guardianship or custody, and who desires the appointment of a guardian of the person with power to consent to the adoption of the minor.[16]

The civil court standard of a "preponderance of the evidence" is required in cases involving minors "otherwise in need of supervision, neglected or dependent." An adjudication finding that a minor is delinquent must maintain the criminal court standard of "proof beyond a reasonable doubt."

Any minor over 13 years of age who has committed a crime can be prosecuted under the criminal laws if a juvenile court judge, after the motion of a state's attorney, an investigation, and a hearing, rules that it is in the best interest of the minor or of the public to do so. Any minor may be prosecuted in criminal court for an offense committed on or after his 17th birthday. Any minor over 13 years of age may, with the consent of his counsel, file a motion with the court that criminal prosecution be ordered.

Other matters of jurisdiction include:

1. No minor under 16 years of age may be confined in a jail or place ordinarily used for the confinement of prisoners in a police station. Minors under 17 years of age must be kept separate from confined adults and may not at any time be kept in the same cell, room, or yard with adults confined pursuant to the criminal law.

2. No law enforcement officer or other person or agency may knowingly transmit to the Department of Corrections, Adult Division, or the Department of Law Enforcement or to the Federal Bureau of Investigation any

---

[14] *Ibid.,* Section 702–3, p. 8.
[15] *Ibid.,* Section 702–4, p. 8.
[16] *Ibid.,* Section 702–5, p. 8.

fingerprint or photograph relating to a minor who has been arrested or taken into custody before his 17th birthday, unless the court in proceedings under this Act authorizes the transmission or enters an order under Section 2–7 (concerning waiver to criminal court) permitting the institution of criminal proceedings.

3. The records of law enforcement officers concerning all minors under 17 years of age must be maintained separate from the records of arrests and may not be open to public inspection or their contents disclosed to the public except by order of the court or when the institution of criminal proceedings has been permitted under Section 2–7 or such a person has been convicted of a crime and is the subject of pre-sentence investigation or proceedings on an application for probation.[17]

Relative to constitutional rights regarding procedures, the minor, who is the subject of the proceeding and his parents, guardian, legal custodian or responsible relative, have the right:

1. to be present, to be heard, to present evidence material to the proceedings;

2. to cross-examine witnesses;

3. to examine pertinent court files and records;

4. to be represented by counsel;

5. to refuse to answer questions on grounds of possible self-incrimination;

6. to private proceedings, to which "only persons, including representatives of agencies and associations, who in the opinion of the court have a direct interest in the case or in the work of the court shall be admitted."[18]

The state's attorney (prosecuting attorney) represents the people at juvenile proceedings. The juvenile does *not* have the right to trial by jury.

It is clear from the above that the Illinois Juvenile Court Act, as amended in 1975, reflects the latest Supreme Court decisions and the most recent juvenile justice practice. It has the added advantage of relative simplicity, which facilitates its application, a virtue which is not at all a common feature of juvenile legislation.

Status Offenses

Although the National Advisory Commission on Criminal Justice Standards and Goals takes no position on status offenses, child care professionals are with increasing frequency recommending that status offenses be removed from the juvenile code. Status offenses are defined in the Illinois Juvenile Court Act as amended for 1975 in (2) (a) and (b) above. Michigan adds children who "idle

[17] *Ibid.,* Section 702–8, p. 9.
[18] *Ibid.,* Section 701–20, p. 7.

away their time," who repeatedly associate with "immoral persons," who frequent or patronize any place or tavern where alcoholic beverages are sold, and so on. The latter are termed status offenses because they derive from the status of being a minor, or offenses which would not accrue punishment, if they were committed by an adult.

Following the trend of weakening the principle of *parens patriae* affected by Supreme Court decisions in the Kent, Gault, and Winship cases, status offenses have been attacked as discriminatory against juveniles. It is felt by many that these offenses cause juveniles to be treated more severely than adults largely because of their powerlessness, and juveniles are thereby denied basic constitutional guarantees which are taken for granted in adult cases.

Professionals who support the removal of status offenses from the juvenile code contend that they are based on the extraneous factor of age. They maintain that society must recognize status offenses not as legal problems but rather as social problems that should be handled by appropriate social service agencies in the community rather than by the juvenile court. When handled by the juvenile court, they claim, the burden of guilt is not placed either on the parents or on society but always on the child, who is thereby stigmatized. Feminists have recently pointed out that girls are arrested more often and incarcerated for longer periods than boys for status offenses. Overall, an LEAA survey of juvenile detention and correctional facilities revealed that, in 1971 approximately one-third of all youths in institutions, including community-based facilities, were status offenders. Abolition of status offenses would, it is thus maintained, save the taxpayers great sums of money and simultaneously preclude the exposure of large numbers of children to correctional facilities that are recognized as being breeding grounds for crime more often than not. Proponents of removal claim that it will reduce the workload of the court to enable its staff, money, and other resources to be utilized in handling serious and repeat-offenders. Teachers, weary of disciplinary problems and unmotivated students, seek the abolition of the truancy offense to free themselves to work with the motivated children, which, it is hoped, will enable them to raise sinking average student standard scores, a problem that has been subjecting school personnel to sharp criticism.

Opponents of the removal of status offenses from the jurisdiction of the juvenile court claim that such action would produce a situation in which no agency would be empowered to detain a runaway child, for instance, against his or her will. No agency would be able to require treatment or behavioral change of any kind, which would remove an important source of protection for both the juvenile and for society as a whole. A significant number of status offenders are either unwilling or unable to seek help on their own initiative. If runaway, for example, is no longer an offense, to whom will a concerned parent turn for assistance in locating a runaway child? They further claim that there is no such thing as a juvenile who specializes in status offenses; juveniles who commit one kind of offense, status or otherwise, are considerably more likely to commit any of the other offenses. A study completed by Larry A. Theisen of the School of Criminal Justice, Michigan State University, in the Lansing, Michigan area, from June through December of 1974, showed that the number of persons charged with part one crimes, aged 17 and under, decreased 73 percent during the same month (August) that arrests of curfew violators peaked. In addition, with the exception of robbery and UDAAs, (Unlawful Driving Away of an Automobile), larcenies and all categories of assault were reduced during this same month. Moreover, the background factors associated with status offenses—poor parent-child relationships, poor scholastic achievement, and so on, are concomitants of all types of juvenile offenses.

The removal of status offenses would cause the prosecution of many more serious offenses, claim opponents; a status offense charge at present is often the result of plea bargaining, in which a more serious charge is reduced on the promise that the offender will seek help. Status offenses are also easier to prove, and a conviction enables the court to require treatment. With the removal of status offenses, the police, neighbors, teachers, and so on, will no longer need to be concerned about runaway, truant, or misbehaving youths until they have committed a serious offense, which action would thereby eliminate an important delinquency prevention strategy.

A current difficulty of the courts is the unwillingness of the community to provide alternatives to detention for their juvenile offenders. Opponents ask, Will these same communities be more willing to provide these and even additional services when status offenses are repealed?

The issue of status offenses is by far the most hotly debated aspect of juvenile court laws today. To date, approximately twenty-seven states have struggled with this problem. Often a possible solution has been seen in changing the designation of the offender from "truant," "curfew violator," "incorrigible," and so on, to "persons in need of supervision," "children in need of supervision," "minors in need of supervision," and so on. Subsequent studies have shown, however, that these efforts have merely changed the label rather than solved the problem; juveniles are still detained at rates equal to those before the change. Obviously, we are a long way from resolving the problem of status offenses and their manifold implications.

THE POLICE AND THE JUVENILE

The police is the first major component in the justice system to deal with the juvenile delinquent. Current statistics show that a large percentage of crime, including a significant number of serious offenses, is committed by juveniles.[19] The police also handle many nondelinquent juvenile matters, such as neglect, abuse, domestic problems, and so on. The specialized police unit for handling juvenile

[19] Richard W. Kobetz, *The Police Role and Juvenile Delinquency* (International Association of Chiefs of Police, Inc., 1971), pp. 33–34.

cases has come into increasingly widespread use. Of late, even special training programs for juvenile officers are coming into existence. The necessity for the specialized juvenile unit has derived from the increasing complexity of our communities and the impersonality of many of the organizations that serve community residents. In former times, the police officer lived in his district, knew its residents and, therefore, shared and could identify with their problems. Because of the intensity of his involvement with the inhabitants of his district, he could handle many problems informally and personally. Increased urbanization, however, soon brought with it increasing caseloads, leading to the routinization and impersonalization of his functions. Increased mobility, growing divorce rates, and many other factors disrupted family life significantly, resulting in an increased volume of youth crime and growing numbers of neglected and abused children. These and other practical matters led to the formation of the specialized juvenile unit.

The juvenile unit varies in size depending on the type of police department and the size and nature of the community. In those areas where there is a low volume of juvenile crime, certain officers may be assigned part time to work with juveniles. In other departments, the juvenile bureau can be a very large unit with the concomitant resources and personnel. Although the juvenile officer's responsibilities depend to a great extent on the size of the department, some features of his work are common to most departments. For example, he is usually charged with dealing with all offenses that involve juveniles, as well as family cases involving neglect and abuse. Routine duties will include contacting and interviewing juveniles, their friends, their parents, teachers, employers, the complainant, and so on, determining the circumstances surrounding an offense, maintaining juvenile records, and appearing in juvenile court. In more sophisticated departments, the juvenile officer is also involved in preventive-type activities, such as giving speeches to schools and coordinating programs with other agencies in the community. The juvenile officer may also attempt to influence the members of his department by making them aware of the special problems that exist when dealing with juveniles and the appropriate methods for processing them.

The police have a great deal of discretionary power, ranging all the way from the option of releasing the juvenile at initial contact in an unofficial manner to referring him to the juvenile court, which may result in detention. The officer can also refer the youngster to a community agency, such as a big brother organization or a mental health clinic. He can also apprehend the youngster and take him to the police department. In almost all cases, the officer will contact the parents. The only exception to this would be when the incident is minor and a verbal warning is considered sufficient.

In sum, the range of police dispositions is considerable, and the criteria for selection of a disposition are seldom set forth explicitly, ordered in priority, or regularly reviewed for administrative purposes. Inservice training designed to assist police in exercising their discretionary functions

is unusual; . . . further investigation for improvement of the police discretionary process holds promise of more discriminating judgements between offenders who should be retained in the system and those who
need, if anything, service rather than adjudication.[20]

Figure 1 illustrates the steps followed when a police officer comes upon
an "event" or receives a complaint. This is the beginning of the process that
ultimately determines whether the youngster will come into contact with the
court or whether he will be released. At the time of the event or the complaint,
the officer may decide that the offense is minor and does not necessitate further
investigation; he may therefore release the child on the spot. If he feels that
additional information is necessary, he can briefly interview the youngster and
then perhaps decide that the situation does not warrant further discussion and
release him to his parents. If the officer considers the offense or complaint
serious enough to warrant further investigation and discussion, he can refer the
case to the police department's juvenile bureau. The options of the juvenile
bureau are illustrated in Figure 1. A juvenile bureau officer can interview the
child and then release him with an informal reprimand. An official or recorded
reprimand may be the officer's choice. Another option, although used infrequently, is to release the youngster with police supervision. In all these cases,
the child is released to the community, which usually means to his parents.
The process in these cases would end with the juvenile bureau of the police
department. If, however, the juvenile officer feels that the situation warrants
further attention, the child can be referred to the juvenile court for a determination. Before a determination, however, the youngster can be delivered to a
juvenile home or a detention facility. The *intake* unit, usually a division of the
probate court, will then make a determination as to whether the process should
end at intake or continue further in the juvenile court.

Because of the great number of delinquent offenses, as well as the wide
range of discretionary powers held by the police, procedures vary considerably
from community to community. Other factors also enter into the decision-
making process:

Decisions are generally based on the nature of the offense, the appraised
character of the youth, which in turn is based on such facts as his prior
police record, age, associations, attitude, family situation, the conduct of
his parents, and the attitude of other community institutions such as his
school. The external community may exert pressure on the police department which may affect the disposition of any case. Here attitudes of the
press and the public, the status of the complainant or victim, the status of

[20] *Task Force Report: Juvenile Delinquency and Youth Crime,* The President's Commission
on Law Enforcement and Administration of Justice (Washington, D.C.: U.S. Government
Printing Office, 1967), p. 14.

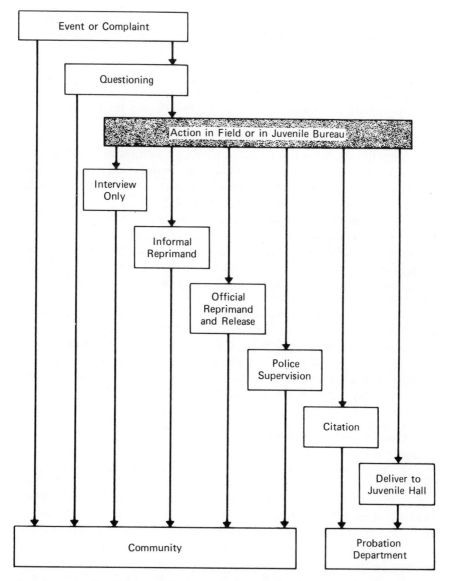

FIGURE 1. Decision Points in Police Handling of Juveniles

From James T. Carey, Joel Goldfarb, Michael J. Rowe, and Joseph D. Lohman, *The Handling of Juveniles from Offense to Disposition,* U.S. Department of Health, Education, and Welfare (Washington, D.C.: Government Printing Office, 1967), p. 26.

the offender, and the conditions which prevail in the available referral agencies (the length of the waiting list, the willingness of the social agencies to accept police referrals) are all of consequence. Internal police department pressure such as attitudes of co-workers and supervisors and the personal experience of the officer may also play an important part in determining the outcome of any officially detected delinquent offense. These factors also indirectly determine the officially recorded police and court delinquency rates.[21]

Many factors, therefore, determine whether a youth is to be processed or not and whether he may eventually end up in the formal juvenile justice system. The police procedure for handling juveniles from initial contact to disposition involves many important elements.

The processing and handling of juveniles has become much more legalistic in the last few years, and the juvenile court is taking on many of the same characteristics as the adult court. Juveniles, like adults, for example, must be advised of their rights, evidence cannot be unlawfully served, nor can the juvenile's rights in any other area be infringed upon. In other words, all the legal safeguards given to adults must likewise be afforded to juveniles.

To make the police officer's job even more complex, not only must he deal with delinquent youngsters, but he must also be astute in determining child abuse and neglect. (Because the problem of child abuse and neglect is so prevalent today and offers one of the greatest challenges for juvenile justice professionals, the next chapter will specifically focus on this topic.) The following procedures are of special importance to police officers when handling juveniles.

Detaining and Taking Custody

If the police officer determines that the circumstances are such (a serious offense, lack of parental supervision, and so on) that the child should be detained and/or taken into custody, then procedural safeguards should be followed. Different jurisdictions have varying guidelines for this process. Michigan's statute in this regard is typical of most jurisdictions. Section 712-A.14 of the compiled laws of Michigan of 1948, as amended by Act 133 of the public laws of 1952, states:

> Any municipal police officer, sheriff, or deputy sheriff, state police officer, county agent, or probationary officer of any court of record may without the order of the court immediately take into custody any child violating any law or ordinance, or whose surroundings are such as to endanger his health, morals, or welfare. Whenever any such officer or

---

[21] *Ibid.,* p. 419.

county agent takes a child coming within the provisions of this statute into custody he shall forthwith notify the parent or parents, guardian or custodian, if they can be found within the county. Unless the child requires immediate detention as here and after provided, the arresting officer shall accept the written promise of said parent or parents, guardian or custodian, to bring the child to the court at the time fixed therein. Thereupon such child shall be released to the custody of said parent, parents, guardian or custodian. If not so released, such child and his parent, parents, guardian, or custodian, if they can be located, shall forthwith be brought before the court for preliminary hearing on his status and an order signed by the judge of probate authorizing the filing of a complaint shall be entered or the child shall be released to his parent, parents, guardian, or custodian.

After the juvenile has been taken into custody, certain procedural rights and safeguards must be considered before his parents are notified. As mentioned earlier the same rights given to adults must be afforded to juveniles. As a result of the 1964 *Escobedo* v. *Illinois* decision, police officers are required to notify suspects of their right to legal counsel at the time of arrest.[22] This also applies to juveniles. The 1966 *Miranda* v. *Arizona* decision requires that suspects be advised of their rights before interrogation, otherwise their confessions cannot be used in court.[23] The officer must advise the suspect of his right to remain silent and his right to speak to an attorney and must inform him that if he wishes an attorney but cannot afford one, the state will provide him with one. Finally, he must be told that anything he says may be used against him. The court has the responsibility to determine whether the youth, if he waived these rights, understood what he was doing. If the youth is processed further and comes into contact with an intake probation officer, this officer should also read the Miranda warnings to him, thereby providing added assurance that the child's legal rights have been protected.

Notification of Parents

The officer who takes the child into custody is also responsible for notifying the child's parents. For example, Michigan Juvenile Court Rules of 1969 not only require notification of parents or guardians, but also specify that a written record must be prepared and filed with the court indicating the names of persons notified, the time of notification or what attempts were made to notify. Rule 2, Section 2, of these rules defines the conditions under which an officer may take a juvenile into custody without a court order; they are as follows:

[22] *Escobedo* v. *Illinois,* 378 U.S. 478 (1964).
[23] *Miranda* v. *Arizona,* 384 U.S. 436 (1966).

1. When a child is found violating any law or ordinance.

2. Conditions exist which make an arrest lawful, if the child were an adult.

3. The officer reasonably believes the child is evading the person or proper authority having legal custody.

4. Conditions or surroundings under which the child is found are such as to endanger his health, morals, or welfare.

5. The officer continues a lawful arrest made by a private citizen.

After parents have been notified, the juvenile still has the same constitutional right as an adult—he has the right to contact an attorney or have anyone of his choosing present during an interview. The basis for this is the 1963 Supreme Court decision which ruled, on an appeal case of *Gideon* v. *Wainright,* that new trials could be demanded by anyone convicted of a crime without legal counsel.[24] The *Gideon* decision, the *Escobedo*[25] decision, and the *Miranda*[26] decision all apply to both adults and juveniles.

Interviewing the Juvenile Offender

Because the officer can have a great deal of influence on the youngster, both positive and negative, he should be concerned about his behavior and demeanor. Many favorable, as well as unfavorable, impressions have been transmitted as a result of this first contact.

Because the police officer makes the first contact with the juvenile and because he has wide discretionary powers, he can have a great influence on the child's future behavior. Many times, the first contact that a child has with the juvenile justice system is with a police officer. Many young people, delinquents in particular, have problems with authority because of poor authority relationships in their past. If a child's first contact with a police officer is negative and the officer exerts his authority in an arrogant manner, this can support the child's already negative concept of authority and contribute to his further acting out against authority. However, an officer who impresses the child as being an understanding but firm adult, who will treat him fairly, can have a positive impact and can be one of the major factors in influencing the child to alter his behavior and divert his energy into socially acceptable channels. Physical abuse, profanity, and other such behavior are not appropriate during the interviewing of youngsters about their involvement in the devious events. A thorough investigation of the circumstances, as well as a determination of the youngster's family situation and environmental conditions, will be of immeasurable importance in assisting the child and protecting the community.

[24] *Gildeon* v. *Wainright,* 372 U.S. 335 (1963).
[25] *Escobedo, idem.*
[26] *Miranda, idem.*

Fingerprinting and Photographing

Fingerprinting and photographing juveniles, as well as keeping records, are sources of controversy. Even though these may be important tools for the police in detecting crime and preventing delinquency, they nevertheless must be used with discretion. Records can be helpful for both the community and the juvenile when they are used properly. They are useful for providing background information on offenders so that the agencies in the juvenile justice system can best protect the community and provide treatment and rehabilitation for the youngster.

The controversy about records revolves around the question of who is to see them and what data should be recorded. Professionals in the juvenile justice system have to use good judgment, but, in general, records of any client in which a formal disposition is necessary should be kept and preserved. In regard to the fingerprinting and the photographing of juveniles, some states prohibit either, except when a special court order is issued. Different policies exist in different jurisdictions; the police officer must be familiar with the policy of his area. (See the Illinois Juvenile Court law referred to earlier.)

If a juvenile is requested to appear in a lineup, his counsel is entitled to be present as a result of the decision of *U.S.* v. *Wade,* which requires the presence of counsel at a lineup for adult prisoners.[27]

Many persons object to photographing, fingerprinting, and keeping records on juveniles because it is too akin to adult criminal proceedings. As pointed out earlier, however, juvenile procedures are becoming more and more closely aligned with adult procedures. This is just one of the many dilemmas facing the professionals who work with juveniles.

Disposition of Offenders Taken Into Custody

After taking a juvenile into custody and abiding by the legal safeguards and procedures outlined above, it must be determined whether the child should return to his parents without a court referral or whether court action is necessary. The decision will be based on the police officer's investigation, which will include the circumstances surrounding the offense, the offense itself, and an assessment of the youngster's family situation (as well as available alternatives within the community). The juvenile will generally be released to his parents, if the offense is minor, there is no habitual delinquency pattern, and if the parents are deemed capable of providing a positive influence in the situation.

The juvenile court judge is the final authority in determining whether the juvenile will be held in custody and when the hearing will take place. In regard to detention, Section 712A.15 of the compiled laws of Michigan, 1948, states:

[27]*U.S.* v. *Wade,* 338 U.S. 218.

Detention pending hearing shall be limited to the following children:

A. Those whose home conditions make immediate removal necessary.

B. Those who have run away from home.

C. Those whose offenses are so serious that release would endanger public safety.

The judge will render the detention determination upon the request of the arresting or juvenile officer, if the latter considers detention warranted. Otherwise, the child will be released to his parents on their written promise to produce the child in court.

If a referral to the court is made, all relevant information should be provided by the officer because even though the juvenile court conducts it own investigation, it is most concerned with social and psychological factors. The police report provides such material as the name, address, birthdate, race, religion, school, and grade of the offender, as well as the names and addresses of the parents or guardian. Most important, however, is the investigative report which details the events surrounding the offense, as well as information related to the youngster's attitude, his family situation, and a determination as to whether the behavior is situational, accidental, or repeated behavior which has to be temporarily interrupted. Names and statements of the complainant will also be an important part of the report.

Waiver of the Juvenile to Adult Court

Some youngsters have been involved in repeated difficulties and have been through the juvenile justice system several times and come into contact with all available community services. In addition, they are close to adult by statutory age. The youngster may have reached the point at which he is a danger to himself and to the community and may contaminate other youngsters incarcerated with him in juvenile facilities. The investigating officer in such a case provides the prosecuting attorney and the juvenile court judge with the information illustrating the severity of the offense so that a decision can be made as to whether or not the offender should be prosecuted in adult court. The prosecuting attorney will make the determination.

THE JUVENILE COURT—INTAKE AND PROCESSING

As mentioned earlier, there is a juvenile court in every state of the union. It is usually a specialized unit of the state judicial system and is based in the local community. It can receive funding from both the state and local jurisdiction. Financing depends on the particular jurisdiction. Depending on the particular state, there are various appeal procedures available to a disgruntled juvenile client. The judge is elected, and the police, the schools, and other agencies make referrals to the juvenile court.

There are considerable variations in the philosophy, structure, and procedures of juvenile courts across the country,[28] and because the court is dependent on local resources and because it does not always enjoy high status either within the community or among other courts, organizational difficulties may also exist. The court often operates under unsatisfactory fiscal conditions, which is neither conducive to an orderly operation nor to the provision of services to the client and the community:

> The court's dilemma in coping with such critical pressures is sharpened by its dependence on local agencies or publics for support and cooperation. Many local units must be relied upon to provide assistance in case handling and service. The resources of police departments, schools, social agencies, welfare bureaus, the bar association, and the medical societies are needed to supplement those of the court. The dilemma also has more general terms of reference. The election of the judge and the basic operating budget necessitate maintenance and good will from a broad range of local units and interest groups. Certain organizations, furthermore, play crucial roles in validating court performance among the general public. Police judgements, in particular, but also those of schools, welfare agencies, and professional associations are taken as more or less authoritative evaluations of juvenile court activity and the risk of public challenge from these units must be taken into account as the court deals with individual cases.[29]

The organizational pattern of the juvenile court varies from state to state, and few juvenile courts are independent. Most of them are part of the circuit, district, superior, county, common pleas, probate, or municipal courts. Regardless of the administrative and organizational pattern of the court, its jurisdiction generally includes delinquency, neglect, and dependency cases; however, adoption, appointment of guardians for minors, determination of custody and termination of parental rights are also included in juvenile court jurisdiction. The age of the juvenile processed by the court also varies. The upper limit is usually eighteen, even though jurisdiction can extend all the way to age twenty-one under specific statutes.

The juvenile court is greatly misunderstood not only by the general public but also by the various components of the juvenile justice system, including the police. Because of this misunderstanding often resulting from a lack of knowledge of court procedures, the child often receives the worst of two worlds: he does not receive the procedural safeguards guaranteed in adult criminal

[28]*Special Study Commission on Juvenile Justice,* State of California, February 2, 1959.
[29]Robert D. Vinter, "The Juvenile Court as an Institution," *Task Force Report, op. cit.,* pp. 86–87.

courts, nor is he given the individualized treatment that was the original intent of the juvenile court movement.[30]

Because the court is generally part of a larger court system, such as probate court, the amount of time that the judge spends on juvenile matters will be determined by the caseload of his court and his other duties and priorities.

The juvenile court, beside having a judge, usually has at least one probation officer, who may work either part time or full time, depending on the resources of the community. In large cities, the court employs many probation officers;

> Regardless of their organizational niche, juvenile court probation officers serve two major functions: making social studies of cases referred to the court and supervising juveniles placed on probation. Their duties may, in addition, entail intake functions such as screening cases referred to the court and determining the necessity for detention, administering the juvenile detention facility, and managing the court's probation department and court attached diagnostic and treatment services (clinics, camps, halfway houses, community residential facilities).[31]

Qualifications of court personnel, including both the judge and the probation officers, vary from jurisdiction to jurisdiction. Some judges have few qualifications for handling juvenile delinquents. The judge should be a lawyer so he can understand judicial process. Ideally, he should also have training in the behavioral sciences. The qualifications and training of probation officers are equally uneven; some jurisdictions do not have a single probation officer with a college degree.

Even though the juvenile court's original intent was to rehabilitate rather than punish, a lack of resources, lack of cooperation, and lack of insight have often turned it into a second-rate agency for processing juveniles. Ideally, the court should be able to guarantee the child's legal rights through procedural safeguards without losing sight of the individualized treatment approach, which is the avowed purpose of juvenile court philosophy.

THE INTAKE DIVISION OF THE JUVENILE COURT

The procedure of the juvenile court begins with a *petition* against the child, which usually originates with a law enforcement agency, although it can be initiated by other sources. School authorities, for example, can refer truancy and vandalism cases. Other agencies may also make referrals, but most referrals come from the police.

---

[30] *Kent v. U.S.* 541 (1966).
[31] *Task Force Report, op. cit.,* p. 6.

Most juvenile courts employ a well-defined routine in processing juveniles who are brought before the court on a petition alleging delinquency, dependency, or neglect. The *intake* or initial screening is usually performed by an intake unit, controlled and supervised by the juvenile court, which consists of one or more probation officers (caseworkers). Often the intake unit performs court functions other than those of initial screening only. The modern thrust to divert youths before adjudication has created a new responsibility and a new challenge for many intake units. Thus the initial screening might result in a diversion of the child from the court into programs run by expert child-serving institutions, such as "youth service bureaus" or "child advocacy centers." To quote the President's Commission on Law Enforcement:

> intake is essentially a screening process to determine whether the court should take action and, if so, what action or whether the matter should be referred elsewhere. Intake is set apart from the screening process used in adult criminal courts by the pervasive attempt to individualize each case and the nature of the personnel administering the discretionary process. In adult criminal proceedings at the post-arrest stage, decisions to screen out are entrusted to the grand jury, the judge or usually to the prosecutor. The objective is screening as an end in itself: attempts to deliver service to those screened out are rare . . . At intake in the juvenile courts, screening is an important objective, but referral is an additional goal. Thus, the expressed function of intake is likely to be more ambitious than that of its criminal law counterpart and the function is performed chiefly by persons who are neither legally trained or significantly restricted in the exercise of their discretionary authority by procedure requirements comparable to those of the criminal law.[32]

The National Advisory Commission on Criminal Justice Standards and Goals recommends that an intake unit should:

> 1. make the initial decision whether to place a juvenile referred to the court in detention or shelter care;
>
> 2. make the decision whether to offer a juvenile referred to the court the opportunity to participate in diversion programs; and
>
> 3. make, in consultation with the prosecutor, the decision whether to file a formal petition in the court alleging that the juvenile is delinquent and ask that the family court assume jurisdiction over him.[33]

Figure 2 illustrates the process of alternatives that exist at the intake phase. The intake unit, if it is part of a large organization, assigns an intake worker to screen the incoming cases. The intake worker reviews the case and

[32] *Task Force Report, op. cit.,* p. 14.
[33] *National Advisory Commission on Criminal Justice Standards and Goals, Task Force on Courts* (Washington, D.C.: U.S. Government Printing Office, 1973), p. 296.

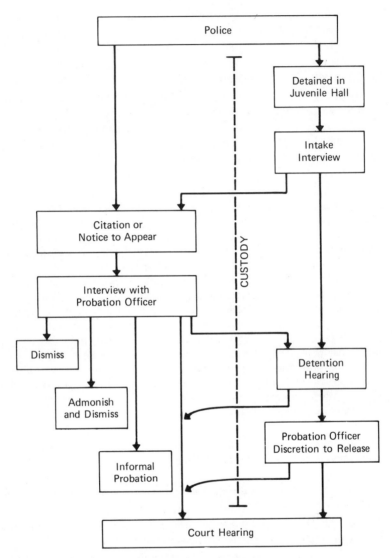

FIGURE 2. Decision Points in Probation Handling of Juveniles

From James T. Carey, Joel Goldfarb, Michael J. Rowe, and Joseph D. Lohman, *The Handling of Juveniles from Offense to Disposition,* U.S. Department of Health, Education, and Welfare (Washington, D.C.: Government Printing Office, 1967), p. 26.

the circumstances, verifies the facts and usually prepares a brief social history for the court. The case often goes no further than this, and the determination is made to dismiss and release the child to his home, to admonish and dismiss or possibly to put him under informal probation supervision by one of the probation officers or perhaps by a court volunteer, who will agree to spend a certain number of hours with the child per week for a specified period of time. Informal probation, however, is often not used because of increased legalism of juvenile justice procedures.

In summary, after the intake process then, there can be outright dismissal, admonishment and dismissal, informal supervision by the probation staff, referral to a community agency for mental health services, or other types of nonjudicial sources. Many courts promote the philosophy that it is far better to handle the youngster, if he needs supervision, in an informal manner, or by a nonjudicial community agency, so that he does not have to come into contact with the formal juvenile justice court processes. The research, especially regarding the use of volunteers, confirms the wisdom of this philosophy. (See Chapter 10 on research.) The further the child proceeds through the juvenile justice system, the greater are the chances that he will be labeled delinquent, which has negative ramifications for him both in the immediate situation and in the future. To quote D. F. Duncan:

> The delinquent label accomplishes four major changes in the life of the child to whom it is attached. First, as a self-fulfilling prophecy, it encourages the child to identify himself as a delinquent and bad. He organizes his behavior, attitudes, and ambitions accordingly.
>
> Secondly, the label acts to strip the youth's community of the positive means of control it normally employs to hold the behavior of its youth in line with its values. By rejecting the child who has acquired a delinquent label, society withdraws its recognition and affirmation.
>
> Third, the label serves effectively to cut off legitimate opportunities for success and recognition. The most significant people in a child's life—his peers, family, neighbors and authority figures react to the child labeled delinquent with mistrust, suspicion and caution.
>
> The fourth and most critical result of the delinquent label is that it opens the door to illegitimate opportunities to the child. If a youth accepts its delinquent label and seeks out friends who have also been labeled, his behavior will tend to conform to the standards of those friends from whom he is forced to seek recognition and approval.[34]

The intake and screening process is an important aspect of the juvenile justice system. When used properly, it can effectively curtail or interrupt much delinquent behavior before it becomes serious. The intake process can also

[34] D. F. Duncan, "Stigma and Delinquency," *Cornell Journal of Social Relations,* Vol. 4 (1969), pp. 41–45.

stimulate community agencies to help parents to better understand their children's behavior and the measures needed to prevent future delinquent acts.

If the child is released at intake and no further processing takes place, there should still be a follow-up after any referral to a community agency by either the police or the intake unit. Follow-up facilitates not only the rendering of services to the child, but also promotes closer cooperation between the agencies involved.

JUVENILE COURT PROCESSING BEYOND INTAKE

If the intake unit has placed the child on informal probation, but the child is having difficulty and it is deemed necessary that further action be taken, the probation officer can initiate the *petition*. For those cases that the intake unit feels further action is deemed immediately necessary after a police referral, a petition will be originated without first putting the child on informal probation. The petition, which states the circumstances of the child's situation, precedes the *preliminary* hearing, which takes place in the presence of a judge. The reason for the preliminary hearing is to decide if there are enough facts to warrant court action. The petition that originates this action can request a declaration of delinquency, dependency, neglect, or any other type of juvenile disposition. The petition can be signed by any authorized person: a police officer, the probation officer, who was supervising the child if he was on informal probation, or a citizen. The parents are notified of the action. If the youngster is to be waived to criminal court, he must be provided with the legal safeguards stated in the *Kent* case: a hearing, the right to counsel, the right to see the court reports, and a statement by the judge in writing covering his reasons for the waiver.

The *Gault* decision states that there must be adequate notice in writing of the charge, and verification of the child's right to counsel at the hearing must be made unless it was intelligently waived. There is also a privilege against self-incrimination unless intelligently waived, and in the absence of a valid admission, determination of delinquency rests upon sworn testimony in open court. If at the preliminary hearing the judge decides that the facts warrant court action, the case will be scheduled for an adjudication hearing.

Adjudication Hearing

At the adjudication hearing, which is considered a part of the preliminary hearing, the youth is questioned about the offense, the circumstances, and the facts that have been presented. The petition may be dismissed at this hearing if there is not enough evidence. If there is a finding of delinquency (or neglect, and so on), a new court date is set for the *disposition hearing*.

The National Advisory Commisson on Criminal Justice Standards and Goals recommends that the following procedures be employed at the adjudicatory hearing:

> At the adjudicatory hearing, the juvenile alleged to be delinquent should be afforded all of the rights given a defendant in adult criminal prosecution, except that trial by jury should not be available in delinquency cases.
>
> In all delinquency cases, a legal officer representing the State should be present in court to present evidence supporting the allegation of delinquency.
>
> If requested by the juvenile, defense counsel should use all methods permissable in a criminal prosecution to prevent determination that the juvenile is delinquent. He should function as the advocate for the juvenile, and his performance should be unaffected by any belief he might have that a finding of delinquency might be in the best interests of the juvenile. As advocate for the juvenile alleged to be delinquent, counsel's actions should not be affected by the wishes of the juvenile's parents or guardian if those differ from the wishes of the juvenile.[35]

Disposition Hearing

There is supposed to be enough time between the adjudication hearing and the disposition hearing to allow the probation officer to make a social investigation. At the disposition hearing the judge uses this investigation to decide what alternatives will be most appropriate for the child. The social investigation includes an evaluation of the child's environment, the interrelationships of the child and his family, the child's attitude and behavior in his neighborhood, his community and his school, the amount of supervision he gets at home, the circumstances regarding his difficulty, and the ability of the parents to provide supervision and guidance at home. The probation officer can consult neighbors, school counselors, teachers, and any other persons who may know the youngster. After the judge has studied the social investigation, he may also question the parents or the probation officer to acquire additional material that may not be a part of the social investigation. After considering all the relevant facts in the case, the judge makes a disposition. He can:

1. Release the child to his parents (with possible referral to a community social agency).
2. Place the child on probation.
3. Commit the child to an institution.

---

[35] *National Advisory Commission, op. cit.,* pp. 302, 474.

4. Utilize a foster home placement.

5. Makes the child a ward of the court so that he can receive necessary medical services or other supervision, especially in cases of neglect.

In severe cases of neglect, the court can also terminate some parental rights. This option is not often used: the removal of children from their natural parents is a very difficult decision to make.

The National Advisory Commission on Criminal Justice Standards and Goals recommends that the procedures followed at the disposition hearing be identical to those followed in the sentencing procedure for adult offenders.

Probation, the most commonly employed dispositional alternative, is a service provided by the court which compels the child to meet certain requirements established by the court and carried out under the supervision of a probation officer. The major requirement is that the youngster meet with the probation officer regularly for a specified period of time. Probation is a trial period during which the youngster attempts to mobilize his own resources as well as those of the community, and, under the supervision of the probation officer, become rehabilitated. The length of probation can range from a few months to a few years. While the younster is on probation, it is expected that the resources made accessible to him be utilized and that the supervision and guidance that he did not get in his home will help him to succeed not only on probation but also in the community after he has been released from probation.

If the probationer abides by the rules set by the court and satisfactorily completes the requirements, he is then released from probation and expected to make a successful adjustment in the community. If he is not successful on probation and becomes involved in recurring difficulties, another plan may be made for him. This plan could include incarceration in an institution or placement in a setting that would provide more stringent supervision and guidance, for example, a halfway house.

Chapter 8, "Prevention Programs," will discuss institutional facilities. Chapter 11, "An Example: Community-Based Treatment Programs," will discuss services such as halfway houses. Upon release from an institution or another residential facility, the child is often supervised by an aftercare worker, a parole officer, or some person with a similar title. The supervision is equivalent to what the child would have received had he been placed on probation and not incarcerated.

In some states the court has jurisdiction over aftercare services, while in other states they are the responsibility of such organizations as the Department of Social Welfare or Social Services. Regardless of the administrative structure, the basic purpose is to provide supervision and guidance on the assumption the youngster is not ready to experience total freedom in his community.

CONCLUSION

Taking a long look at the origin, development, present state, and the tenor of a movement to reform the juvenile court, J. Lawrence Schultz finds that "the more things change, the more they remain the same":

> Until recently, not only the indictment but also the agenda for reform was the same as it was in Jane Addams' Chicago: (1) keep kids out of big, coercive institutions and put them into small, community-based facilities (a variation of the idea behind probation); (2) replace the juvenile courts with "radical alternatives" like community councils on the "Scandinavian model," for kids who need help (that was the idea behind an "informal procedure" in Cook County); (3) "divert" kids from juvenile courts into programs run by expert child-serving institutions called "youth service bureaus" or "child advocacy centers" (i.e., develop individualized treatment programs"). Even procedural reform . . . is consistent with the main current of turn-of-the-century thinking.

Schultz continues by describing further developments in the juvenile court reform movement:

> One trend today seems to be to respond to many of the problems of children and adolescents by doing little or nothing unless severely provoked: eliminate altogether the jurisdiction of juvenile courts over misbehavior of children that either defines a vague status ("incorrigible" and the like) or is peculiarly defined as misbehavior only for children (such as truancy); (2) bring only the most serious lawbreakers before the juvenile courts, referring others to entirely voluntary agencies and counseling, job placement, and "peer group activities;" (3) commit juveniles to brief, determinate terms in coercive programs, instead of indeterminate terms that may stretch on for many years, sometimes longer than an adult could receive for the same offense.[36]

To say the least, there are many and varied philosophies on how the juvenile court should operate. Perhaps the following case study will provide the reader with some guidelines and structure.

A CASE STUDY*

The case involves a youngster whom we will call John Smith. John is fifteen years of age and lives in Marquette, Michigan. The contact John has with the Lansing, Michigan police is the result of his being stopped for a traffic infrac-

*Developed and coordinated by Lt. Ray C. Valley, Michigan State Police, East Lansing, Michigan.

[36] J. Lawrence Schultz, *op. cit.*, p. 474.

tion. John is unable to produce a driver's license or a registration for his vehicle. The officers, because they are suspicious, make a quick radio check with their headquarters and determine that the car was stolen in John's hometown. John is apprehended for unlawfully driving away an automobile (felony), for failing to stop at a red light, and for not having an operator's license or a vehicle registration on his person.

After a short conversation John tells the officers that he stole the car in Marquette and that he would like to talk about the incident.[37] At this point the officers are obliged to (1) advise John of his constitutional rights, (2) determine his age, which in this case is easily learned through other identification that John has on him, (3) obtain the address of John's mother and father because it is necessary to contact them immediately and notify them of the detention of their child, who is four hundred miles away from home. A record of the notification is also made.[38]

The officers make contact with John's parents, and the parents give a verbal waiver which allows the officers to interview John. The local probate court is contacted, and the judge gives his verbal agreement that custody and detainment is advisable in this case and that a petition will be signed later in the morning.[39]

The vehicle John is driving has the original license plates on it, as determined by a check of the owner, who lives in Marquette. The owner is advised that the vehicle is being held in Lansing. The owner states that John has taken the automobile without permission, hence verifying that the vehicle was stolen.

The officers take John to the juvenile home where he is lodged, and a custody statement is filed.[40]

John, acting somewhat remorseful, states again that he would like to talk about the circumstances under which he stole the automobile. The officers again advise him of his constitutional rights before interviewing him and request that he sign a waiver. The officers make the determination that he is sophisticated and intelligent enough to make this waiver.[41]

The next morning a probation officer is assigned by the local judge to act as John's guardian until he is returned to his home community.[42] The probation officer decides to advise John against further interviews by the police officers, and all interviews are terminated.[43]

[37] *Gallegos, idem.* (limitation re interrogation of minors); *Miranda, idem.* (interrogation of suspects).
[38] Officer's custody statement and record of notification to parent, guardian, or custodian (the specific form used in this case and following examples will depend on the state).
[39] *People* v. *Roberts,* 364 Mich. 60 (duty to take before court, 1961); *In re Mathers,* 371 Mich. 516 (adequacy of petition, 1964).
[40] *Obinetz* v. *Buddo,* 315 Mich. 512 (statement of custody).
[41] *Hailing* v. *U.S.,* 295 Fed. 161 (use of admissions following waiver, 1961); *Reddick* v. *U.S.,* 326 Fed. 650 (admissibility of conversations with police, 1964); *Gault, idem.*
[42] Michigan juvenile code, 12A, 14 (juvenile in custody; detention areas:" . . . child to be completely isolated so as to prevent any verbal, visual or physical contact with any adult prisoner.").
[43] *Kent, idem.; Gallegos, idem.*

Arrangements are made for John to meet with the probate judge that morning at 10:00 A.M., at which time the officers request an authorization for a petition. The petition is authorized, it is signed by the officers, and the following charges are made before the judge: (1) unlawful driving away of an automobile, (2) no operator's license, (3) no vehicle registration, (4) failure to stop for a red light. The petition must allege the facts with particularity.[44]

The preliminary inquiry is held before the judge. John, the officers, the probation officer, and John's parents are present. At this time the judge decides that since the automobile was stolen in another community, John should be tried and a disposition should be made in that community. John is then returned to Marquette by juvenile authorities of that community.[45]

If the judge had determined that John could return with his parents, a bond might have been required to assure that John would appear before his home court.[46]

It is determined before John's leaving for home that fingerprints and a photograph will be helpful, and permission is granted by the court.[47]

Summary of procedures thus far:

1. Custody was taken when subject was apprehended for a felony and misdemeanors.

2. Juvenile was advised of his constitutional rights.

3. Parents were contacted and notified of apprehension, and the time was recorded.

4. Probate court was contacted: detention was requested and was granted by the court.

5. Waiver was obtained before interviewing the juvenile.

6. Request for a petition was made and granted.

7. Petition was signed, and alleged facts were set forth with particularity.

8. After the judge has considered all the facts, John was transferred to his home community.

9. Petitions for fingerprinting and photographing were approved by the court.

10. John was returned to his home community.

In Marquette the juvenile authorities are presented with the information that has been compiled thus far by the Ingham County Probate Court. After reviewing the information and again being advised of his constitutional rights, John is

---

[44] *Gault, idem.*
[45] State statutes relating to the transfer of juveniles.
[46] State statutes relating to the right to bond.
[47] State statutes relating to fingerprinting and photographing juveniles.

released to his parents. The parents sign a written release assuring the court that John will be present when a time is designated.[48]

The preceding steps taken in court are part of the preliminary hearing, which must be held forty-eight hours from the time the juvenile is taken into custody. Since the purpose of the hearing is to determine if there are enough facts to support court action and if protection or supervision of the court is necessary, in most cases the hearing is informal and a lawyer is not required. Where a felony has been committed, however, such as in the present case, an attorney can and probably will be called.[49] There are two more phases of court hearings, an adjudication hearing and a disposition hearing.[50]

The adjudication hearing is considered a part of the preliminary hearing, and both this hearing and the disposition hearing usually have stenographic equipment to record what takes place. States differ in their requirements, but if no specific law exists, there is usually a probate rule or a written memorandum referring to the use of stenographic or mechanical equipment.

The adjudication hearing determines whether the child will come under the jurisdiction of the court. The child and his parents or a guardian ad litem are present. All witnesses and evidence or facts are now brought before the court. The juvenile has the right to waive his right to counsel or to retain counsel at this time. If the juvenile does not understand his constitutional rights, the judge appoints counsel for him. The judge does this if he feels that the child will not adequately be represented by the parents. The request for an attorney is made in writing, stating the names of the parties represented. The attorney is furnished copies of all pleadings.[51]

In regard to the hearing being held before a jury, there is some confusion over this matter and most states do not allow jury trial for juveniles.

At the adjudication hearing for John, the facts presented are sufficient and a disposition hearing date is set. The probation department is requested to do a social investigation of John to provide the judge with adequate information so that a meaningful disposition can be made. If a youngster pleads guilty to an offense and if his parents and his attorney consent, the disposition phase can sometimes be held immediately.

The plea of guilty has much more significance in adult court. In juvenile cases the emphasis is not on guilt or innocence, but on individualized justice. There is concern not only with the incident but with the future welfare of the child as well. The social investigation is important in contributing to this end.

---

[48] State statutes relating to duty to release the juvenile upon assurance of parents that he will appear before court when requested.

[49] *Escobedo, idem.* (right to counsel); *Gault, idem.* (right of child and parent to be notified).

[50] *Gault, idem; In re Mathers,* 371 Mich. 516 (1964).

[51] *Gault, idem.*

In the case of John, a probation officer conducts a social investigation including the factors that were mentioned earlier in the chapter.

The dispositional hearing determines what measures the court will take in selecting an alternative that will be most beneficial to John. The allegations are read and presented, and John and his parents are again advised of their right to counsel. John is also advised of his right to remain silent and his right to cross-examination. A record of the proceedings is also made.[52]

After all the facts are considered, the judge makes a determination as to the disposition of the case. The alternatives open to the judge were mentioned earlier.

Probation is usually the alternative selected, and in the present case, John is placed on probation. It is determined that his offense is not an indication of a pattern of delinquent or criminal behavior and that he can be helped at home and can be guided and supervised by a probation officer. In John's case, it is concluded that he stole the car upon a dare from friends after they had been involved in "drinking." John and his friends were only going to take the car for a short ride, but they were having so much fun driving the automobile that they impulsively decided to take it out of town. John is to report to a probation officer for two years, and he cannot apply for a driver's license until he is released from probation.

SUMMARY

This chapter has focused on the processing and handling of juveniles through the various components of the juvenile justice system. The three major components discussed were the police, the intake division of the juvenile court, and the juvenile court. A case study was utilized to illustrate the procedure involved.

It cannot be assumed that merely because an agency has a part of its function the prevention, control, and treatment of delinquency, the goal will necessarily follow the good intentions of the initiators of the particular program. All agencies that deal, either directly or indirectly, with delinquents have the potential for perpetuating and, in fact, sometimes producing the delinquency, as well as reducing it.[53]

The School. Dinitz, Reckless, and Murray and others have shown that in addition to being a vehicle for directing the student's energy into positive

---

[52] *Gault, idem.*
[53] Walter Miller, "Inter-Institutional Conflict as a Major Impediment to Delinquency Prevention," *Human Organization* 17 (Fall 1958).

channels, the school can also contribute to the student's developing a negative self-concept, which can have implications for his future behavior both in the school and in the community.[54] Many students, particularly those from disadvantaged groups, have difficulty competing in the classroom in accordance with the criteria that have been established by the particular school system. As a result, some students are handicapped because of a lack of competitive and social skills. They retreat from the academic competition, which is subsequently interpreted as their not being interested or capable of producing within that system. When a child retreats in this manner and is labeled as a failure or a potential failure by his teachers, this can affect his self-concept not only in the school, but outside the school, and help create and perpetuate the child's feeling that he is less than capable when compared with his peers. Albert Cohen pointed out the negative ramifications of an unequal competitive system and its relation to the delinquent phenomenon.[55] When children are unable to compete in the "system" and do not learn to sublimate their energies in a socially acceptable manner, a delinquent solution to problem solving is often the result. School programs and teachers have to be responsive to the needs and abilities of all students. Flexible and innovative programming and curriculum development accompanied by sensitive classroom behavior by teachers is mandatory.

The Juvenile Court. The juvenile court also has the potential for producing and perpetuating delinquency. If the court is not responsive to the needs of the total community and, in fact, indiscriminately prosecutes and processes children from limited segments of the community, the indiscriminate labeling can affect both the child's attitude toward himself and the community's attitude toward him. The social ostracism and the negative self-concept can contribute to his antisocial behavior in the community. Court procedures should be equitable and sensitive to the possible negative ramifications of hasty labeling. Realistic, humane, and appropriate methods of processing and treating juveniles are necessary, if the court is to be an effective component in the criminal justice system.

The Police. Police agencies can also contribute to the perpetuation of delinquent behavior. Many times, as pointed out earlier, the first contact that a child has with the criminal justice system is with a police officer. Many young people, delinquents in particular, have problems with authority because of poor authority relationships in their past. If a child's first contact with a police officer is negative and the police officer exerts his authority in an arrogant manner, this can support the child's already negative concept of authority and contribute to his further acting out against authority within the community. However, an officer who impresses the child as being an understanding, but firm adult who

---

[54] Simon Dinitz, Walter Reckless, and Ellen Murray, "Self-Concept as an Insulator against Delinquency," *American Sociological Review*, 21 (December 1956).
[55] Albert Cohen, *Delinquent Boys* (Glencoe, Ill.: The Free Press, 1955).

will treat him fairly, can have a positive impact and can be one of the major factors in influencing the child to alter his behavior and divert his energy into socially-acceptable channels.

Social Work Agencies. Social work agencies can also contribute to delinquent behavior by perpetuating the delinquent's irresponsible behavior. Too often, social workers, in an attempt to help the delinquent or the predelinquent, readily give him excuses for his behavior and transmit to him either overtly or covertly that because of his past and present circumstances, he does have an excuse for committing delinquent acts. Social workers should remember that it is possible to accept the delinquent's negative feelings toward authority and the community, but at the same time, not transmit to him that he has a "right" to act out against the community. It is possible to accept the child's feelings, but not his negative behavior. A more responsible attitude on the part of some social workers can help in reducing the acting out of negative impulses within the community.

All agencies that deal with the juvenile delinquent have to be constantly aware of their presence in his life and not take for granted that merely because they were established to prevent and treat juvenile delinquency, their programs and policies always foster this end. Many times, these same "helping" agencies produce, foster, and perpetuate the very phenomenon that they are trying to eliminate.

Because there is need for the police officer and the social worker to have greater insight into each other's profession, new models for training may have to be developed for both professions. Joint training efforts could produce a more effective and coordinated treatment and prevention process.

It would be helpful if the police were to absorb some of the social workers' general theories and concepts which would aid them in understanding social problems and people who are afflicted. On the other hand, it would be helpful if the social worker were to absorb some of the police officer's "reality therapy" and appreciate some of the problems he encounters in his face-to-face confrontation with the social deviant.

QUESTIONS AND PROJECTS

Essay Questions

1. Should the police be given more discretion or less discretion in their handling of juveniles?

2. With all the recent Supreme Court rulings, has the handling of juveniles become too legalistic?

3. How can a community guard against "assembly line" justice within its juvenile justice system?

4. *Why do some communities have much more effective procedures for handling youngsters than other communities?*

5. *Why are some juvenile cases handled informally by the court while others are processed through formal channels?*

Projects

1. *Develop the ideal criteria that should be applied when selecting a juvenile court judge.*

2. *Develop a list of alternatives that the community can use in place of formally exposing the youngster to the juvenile court.*

3. *Develop an information services program that alerts the community to the needs of its youngsters and keeps the community abreast of new developments.*

chapter 7

Child Abuse and Neglect

THE PROBLEM

Although it is difficult to maintain accurate statistics on child abuse and neglect because of the American attitude toward the inviolability of the home and family, some experts claim that it is the primary cause of childhood death in America. What is certain is that reported cases of severe physical abuse and neglect are increasing annually at an alarming rate. The United States Children's Bureau estimates that from 50,000 to 75,000 incidents of child abuse occur in the U.S. every year. Dr. Vincent De Francis, of the Children's Division of the American Humane Association, estimates that 10,000 children are severely battered every year, at least 50,000 to 75,000 are sexually abused, 100,000 are emotionally neglected, and another 100,000 are physically, morally, and educationally neglected. Dr. David G. Gil of Brandeis University conducted a nationwide study of reported child abuse cases by studying registry reports and interpreting questionnaires. He uncovered a total of 5,993 cases of physically abused children in the states and territories of the U.S. in 1967 and 6,617 in 1968. Gil is of the opinion that if a survey were to include the number of abuse cases personally known to those sampled by questionnaire, extrapolated figures would indicate an incidence of approximately 2,500,000 cases of physically abused children in the U.S. annually.

Experts have shown a clear relationship between child abuse and neglect and adolescent and adult criminality. Karl Menninger believed that every criminal was unloved and maltreated as a child. At a hearing of the New York State Legislature's Select Committee on Child Abuse and Neglect in December of

1971, Dr. Shervert H. Frazier, Jr., reported that his study of ninety murderers revealed that as children they had been "victims of remorseless brutality." Dr. Arthur H. Green, in his child-oriented study of the Brooklyn area, discovered strong indications that child abuse results in adolescent and adult criminality. Family Court Judge Nanette Dembitz made the following observation before the Committee of the New York State Legislature on Child Abuse and Neglect on December 7, 1971:

> A child growing up in a situation of indifference to his well-being and of violence, cannot respect himself or others. It is as natural for a maltreated child to grow up to carry a knife as it is for a loved and cared-for child to carry a pen or pencil.[1]

And, regarding the types of physical abuse inflicted on children,

> The forms or types of abuse inflicted on these children is a negative testimony to the ingenuity and inventiveness of man. By far the greater number of injuries resulted from beatings with various kinds of implements and instruments. The hairbrush was a common implement used to beat children. However, the same purpose was accomplished with deadlier impact by the use of bare fists, straps, electric cords, T.V. aerials, ropes, rubber hose, fan belts, sticks, wooden spoons, pool cues, bottles, broom handles, baseball bats, chair legs and, in one case, a sculling oar. Less imaginative, but equally effective, was plain kicking with heavy work shoes.
>
> Children had their extremities—hands, arms and feet—burned in open flames as from gas burners or cigarette lighters. Others bore burn wounds inflicted on their bodies with lighted cigarettes, electric irons or hot pokers. Still others were scalded by hot liquids thrown over them or from being dipped into containers of hot liquids.
>
> Some children were strangled or suffocated by pillows held over their mouths or plastic bags thrown over their heads. A number were drowned in bathtubs and one child was buried alive.
>
> To complete the list—children were stabbed, bitten, shot, subjected to electric shock, were thrown violently to the floor or against a wall, were stomped on and one child had pepper forced down its throat.[2]

This kind of treatment resulted in bruises; contusions; welts; swollen limbs; split lips; black eyes; lost teeth; simple, compound, and often multiple fractures of arms, legs, and ribs; in brain concussions; skull fractures; ruptured livers, ruptured spleens, and ruptured lungs, often resulting in death.

Neither as bizarre nor as revolting as physical abuse but equally disastrous in its effects is the emotional neglect of children. The Child Welfare League of

[1]Vincent J. Fontana, *Somewhere a Child is Crying* (New York: New American Library, 1976), p. 101.
[2]Vincent De Francis, *Child Abuse—Preview of a Nationwide Survey* (Denver: Children's Division, American Humane Association, 1963), pp. 5–6.

America defines emotionally neglected children as those children, who are "denied normal experiences that produce feelings of being loved, wanted, secure and worthy, or are emotionally disturbed due to continuous friction in the home, marital discord, or mentally ill parents."[3]

One manifestation of the neglected child's emotional disturbance is his feeling of rejection, which "generates a vicious cycle in the parent-child relationship. The child becomes anxious and insecure—do the parents really love him? He tests them, retaliates or rebels, or withdraws. The parents, therefore, feel unappreciated, rejected, and their negative, hostile, and rejecting feelings are further stirred up, aggravated and intensified."[4]

Parad and Caplan differentiate between a "passive" type of emotional neglect, in which families overlook or forget the needs of a child and an "active" type, in which a child is "emotionally exploited through investing him with a role which does violence to his needs as an individual."[5] According to Max Wald, "A child might, for example, be used as a pawn or as a scapegoat by the parents."[6]

Emotional neglect results in conduct disorders such as defiance, rebellion, tantrums, destructiveness, cruelty, overactivity, negativism, lying, stealing, withdrawal, asocial behavior, deviant sex activity, neurotic traits including jealousy, inhibition of play, imagination, curiosity, inhibition of aggression, sleep disorders, night terrors, sleepwalking, enuresis, masturbation, disturbances of body attitudes, speech disorders, fear of animals, darkness, thunder and hysterical, phobic, obsessive, compulsive, and hypochondriacal disorders.[7]

In cases of physical abuse, the parents are the offending agents in 75% of the cases. Stepfathers are responsible in roughly 15% of the cases, the stepmother, contrary to popular myth, is the offending party in only 3% of the incidents, followed by the mother's boyfriend, aunts, uncles, grandparents, and older siblings. In the case of neglect, blame must be placed on the family as a whole, not only on the mother and the father, but on other family members, including siblings, as well.

Causes

Abusing and neglecting parents have many similar characteristics:

[3] *Child Welfare League of America Standards for Child Protective Services* (New York: Child Welfare League of America, 1960), p. 10.
[4] David Hollowitz and Burton Stulberg, "The Vicious Cycle in Parent-Child Relationship Breakdown," *Social Casework* (May 1959), p. 268.
[5] Howard Parad and Gerald Caplan, "A Framework for Studying Families in Crisis," *Social Work* (July 1960), p. 7.
[6] Max Wald, *Protective Services and Emotional Neglect* (Denver: Children's Division, American Humane Association, 1963), p. 4.
[7] N. W. Ackerman, *The Psychodynamics of Family Life* (New York: Basic Books, Inc., 1958), pp. 201–204.

Both need and demand a great deal from their infants, and are distressed when met by inadequate response, so it is not surprising that we occasionally see an infant or child who is both neglected and abused. Yet there is a striking difference in these two forms of caretaker-infant interaction. The neglecting parent responds to distressing disappointment by giving up and abandoning efforts to even mechanically care for the child. The abusing parent seems to have more investment in the active life of the child and moves in to punish it for its failure and to make it "shape up" and perform better.[8]

Abusive families represent the entire socioeconomic spectrum, whereas neglectful families demonstrate inordinately high rates of financial insufficiency, broken homes, less education, substandard housing and neighborhood, excessive family size, alcoholism, and problems of mental health.[9] Elizabeth Philbrick describes neglectful parents as pleasure-seeking, irresponsible, and impulsive, placing their needs before those of their children. She writes:

We were struck by the misery and all-pervading failure which surrounded the total life experience of these impulse-ridden persons. They are at odds with the whole world. All their relationships, within and outside the family, operate in an atmosphere that at various times includes hostility, suspicion, aloneness, futility, frustration and rage. But under the bravado of "leave me alone" we found an abysmal sense of unlovability and low self-esteem. Their histories almost universally indicate lifelong deprivation in all areas of their experience. Nobody ever cared enough for them, and now they don't believe anybody can.[10]

Robert M. Mulford and Morton I. Cohen find that neglecting parents' "participation in organizational activities of their surrounding social world is at a minimal level and even possibilities of such participation is limited by the high degree of residential mobility."[11] They also found a high level of interaction with the extended family. In their human relationships, neglecting parents tend to be isolative or destructive and not supporting, controlling of others, poor in the role of spouse, and poor disciplinarians as parents. They rate low in social problem-solving skills and think of themselves as failures. They feel isolated, alienated, frustrated, powerless, and incompetent.

Since abusive parents come from every segment of the socioeconomic spectrum, the causes for their behavior must be sought in areas other than pure

[8] B. F. Steele and C. B. Pollock, "A Psychiatric Study of Parents Who Abuse Infants and Small Children," in *The Battered Child,* Ray E. Helfer and C. Henry Kempe, Eds. (Chicago: Univ. of Chicago Press, 1974), p. 99.

[9] Hans W. Hoel, "Child Protective Services—A Public Responsibility," in *Second National Symposium on Child Abuse* (Denver: Children's Division, American Humane Association, 1973), p. 36.

[10] Elizabeth Philbrick, *Treating Parental Pathology Through Child Protective Services* (Denver: Children's Division, American Humane Association, 1960), pp. 7–8.

[11] Robert M. Mulford and Morton I. Cohen, *Psychosocial Characteristics of Neglecting Parents. Implications for Treatment* (Denver: Children's Division, American Humane Association, 1967), pp. 7-12.

deprivation. Steele and Pollock, for example, suggest that some of the roots of child abuse are to be found in child-rearing patterns which are acceptable manifestations of American culture. In popular parlance "sparing the rod" has always been equated with "spoiling the child." Quiet, conforming, passive behavior remains the norm in our schools, which is believed to be a contributing factor to the generally better performance of girls in the schools. Deviance from this pattern, be it ever so minor, results in punishment. Since the nonconformists are more often than not boys, the punishment is also often corporal, meted out by teachers or parents in the name of discipline.

Whether or not one agrees with this type of discipline, it does often lead to abuse, especially if applied in anger. Discipline becomes abuse when the child suffers actual physical harm, most especially, however, when the person applying the punishment actually enjoys what he or she is doing. Dr. Vincent Fontana marks a clear-cut difference between discipline and abuse: "the parent who disciplines has in mind the welfare and best interests of the child; the one who abuses is indulging himself."[12]

Fontana continues by discussing the nature of the abusing parent:

> I do not believe we will ever produce a composite picture of the abusing parent. He is not one type of person; he is many. His motives cannot be simply traced to poverty, to cruelty, to rage, to a mistaken concept of discipline, to our child-rearing philosophy, or to the violence in our society. They are rooted in the sociological, psychological, and even biological characteristics of the offender.[13]

Fontana classifies abusing parents into the emotionally immature, neurotic or psychotic, mentally deficient or uninformed, disciplinarians, criminal-sadistic, and addictive.

He defines emotionally immature parents as those who continue to place their own needs before those of their children. The child often gets in the way of the quest for fulfillment of their childish needs. Others seek to bolster faltering egos by dominating the child or expecting him to meet unrealistic expectations, abusing and rejecting him when he cannot. Still others expect the child to fill an emotional void in the parents' life, turning upon the child when he is unable to do so. Also in this group are untrusting, alienated people who have difficulty establishing meaningful relationships with anyone.

Fontana defines neurotic or psychotic abusers as those whose own upbringing and experiences have disturbed their personalities, attitudes, and values to the extent that they are unable to care about others and incapable of sharing of themselves. Their distorted spirits cause them to feel an unreal persecution at the hands of their children. They attribute to the child an adult capacity for organized, purposeful, and malevolent behavior, striking out at him in an attempt to salvage what they can of themselves.

[12] Vincent J. Fontana, *op. cit.,* p. 57.
[13] *Ibid.,* p. 58.

Then there are the hopelessly retarded who cannot learn to be effective parents, whose inability to handle even the most minor stresses of parenting causes them to strike out and injure their helpless offspring. Fontana expands:

> In all categories of maltreating parents we find that a "special kind of child" often triggers the maltreatment. He may be unlovable (because he is not cute), or difficult, or irritating, or finicky of appetite, or have a birth defect, or be a boy instead of a girl, or scowl instead of smile, or cry all the time, or have a particularly grating quality to his cry that drives his parents, or one of them, to distraction. But among the abusers of borderline intelligence, we are far more likely to hear the excuses that "there is something wrong with this child," "he doesn't belong to us," "I don't know where he came from: he isn't one of us, he's different."[14]

In addition, there are parents of normal intelligence who simply have no notion of child development, who expect behavior from a child that he is not capable of producing and who therefore strike out when their unrealistic expectations are disappointed.

The "disciplinarian" abuses his child in the puritanical tradition of American culture—always inordinately violent—which holds that children are merely imperfect adults who must learn to conform to adult behavior and standards by whatever means that seem necessary. Normal childish exuberance, joy, and especially sensuality of any kind have no place in this puritanical attitude, which posits that life is a result of the fall of Adam, a punishment, and thus any joy derived from it a manifestation of evil, a threat to eternal salvation, which must be stamped out. Vestiges of this grim philosophy remain extant in American culture to an extent that we are seldom if ever willing to admit.

Criminally sadistic child abusers, those who kill and maim for the sheer joy of it, are in exceedingly small number, even though they are the ones who appear in the headlines and lead the public into believing that anyone who would abuse and kill a child in such callous fashion is a monster. They serve the purpose of drawing public attention to child abuse; their excesses often spur legislation concerning child abuse and neglect. Society must be protected from them, but fortunately, their numbers are small; any action aimed at the prevention and treatment of child abuse and neglect must be designed for those more common abusers, who are discussed in other parts of this section.

The addict child abuser is a manifestation of modern, industrial, technological society; his numbers are increasing. In this category we find not only those parents addicted to drugs, but also those dependent on alcohol. The incidence of delinquency among the children of addicts is very high.

Babies born to addicted mothers can suffer permanent damage. The addict will steal, mug, kill, pimp, prostitute—anything to secure money, which is spent primarily on drugs to the neglect of other familial necessities. The best that can

---

[14] *Ibid.,* p. 62.

happen to a child in this situation is that he is neglected. He can also become addicted himself. He can even be badly beaten or killed during a parent's drunken rage or the depression that accompanies withdrawal.

Fontana finds that there are but a few factors that are more or less constant in the characteristics of abusive parents: as children, nearly all of them were brutalized and neglected themselves; they are unable to identify with or relate to other people and they are unable to cope with stress. Further common characteristics identified by Steele and Pollock were: oral conflicts, underlying feelings of depression and worthlessness, and the failure to establish age-appropriate ego identities.[15]

Maltreatment occurs most frequently in broken or disintegrating homes. A potentially abusive parent is attracted to a mate with similar tendencies or to one who is so passive as to be unable to modify the abusive behavior of the maltreating spouse. De Francis makes some observations on the basis of a study reported on in 1963 regarding family characteristics in which child abuse occurs. He reports that four out of five abusive homes had both parent figures in them, although in a little over 16 percent of the situations, one of the parents was a step-parent. Roughly one of twelve homes were one-parent homes. In six percent of the cases, the child was living in the home of another relative albeit in the presence of the mother. Battering families live in the poorest slum areas to country club districts; they originated from culturally deprived families to those of high business and professional status. About one-third of the mothers were employed outside of the home for a considerable portion of the day. A majority of these worked as waitresses. The average age for mothers was twenty-six, for fathers slightly over thirty. In many cases there existed a history of marital problems, alcoholism, adult crime, and delinquency by older siblings. Many had received either in-patient or out-patient psychological counseling.[16] Edgar J. Merrill found that the majority of abusive families had lived in their communities for years and had not moved extensively within their communities, were self-supporting, did not show great integration in their communities, were not fully accepted within their communities, and demonstrated serious social problems, which were, in the order of their prevalence: marital discord, financial difficulty, other family conflicts, and family community relationship problems. In slightly less than 50 percent of the sample families in his study, premarital conception had occurred. Abusers are also usually young at the time of marriage. Normally only one child in the family was selected for abuse and this treatment became repetitive. Half of the abused children were under the age of seven and three-quarters of them under thirteen.[17]

De Francis describes several situations which have resulted in child abuse. A frequent pattern is an emotional explosion by the father in reaction to a particularly irritating occurrence or as an attempt at discipline, in which he loses

[15] Vincent De Francis, *Child Abuse, Preview of a Nationwide Survey, op. cit.,* pp. 7–8.
[16] *Ibid.,* pp. 7–9.
[17] Edgar J. Merrill, "Physical Abuse of Children—An Agency Study," in *Protecting the Battered Child* (Denver: Children's Division, American Humane Association, 1962), p. 3–6.

control. In the case of mothers, the abusive behavior often results from feelings of hopelessness and despair. In some cases in which children are killed by their mothers, mercy seems to be the motivation: either the children are suffering from severe handicaps or the mothers fear that they will become victims of such handicaps. Some mothers seriously abuse their children as a result of having been discharged from mental hospitals before they were ready to tolerate the stress that this adjustment entails. Duane W. Christy adds the modern phenomenon of tolerance for unwed motherhood as a precipitator of child abuse. Many more unwed mothers are keeping their babies. Unfortunately, it is usually the most unstable who keep their children, either out of rebellion against their parents or as an attempt to punish the father or to force him into marriage. These emotionally troubled girls are frequently driven by frustration to abuse their babies.[18] Elizabeth Elmer found that abusive people have much more medical stress than others. Moreover, abusive mothers perceive far more social and pregnancy stress than do nonabusive mothers. Abusive parents have very little support from religion, income, neighbors, and relatives. The rate of prematurity among abused children is considerably above the norm.[19]

Dr. Irving Kaufman discusses some of the psychiatric implications of the physical abuse of children:

> Severe physical abuse of a child in some way implies a lack or distortion of reality. The human infant and child, of all living creatures, is the most dependent and least able to care for itself for the longest period of time. For a full-grown adult to perceive the child or infant as a suitable target for its rage, anger and abuse to the extent of injuring, sexually assaulting or killing the child, implies that the child is not perceived as a child but some symbolic or delusional figure. The child, for example, may be perceived as the psychotic portion of the parent which the parent wishes to control or destroy. Other parents, who are extremely infantile and wish to be babied themselves, resent the dependency and needs of their child and express this resentment in hostile ways. This is in contrast to the many parents who semi-jokingly say that their lives are run by their children and feel threatened, fatigued and frustrated by their children's demands. . . . attacking a child is a crime of violence, and some of the persons who get so violently out of control may fall into the category of the antisocial schizophrenic . . . These people attempt to handle the overwhelming anxiety they feel within themselves, which they fear will overwhelm and destroy them, by externalizing this destructive force and attacking or killing. . . . These violent outbursts of rage express a sense of inner dissatisfaction and frustration, and the child is used as a means of expressing it. . . . They project much of their difficulty onto their child and feel that the child is

[18] Duane W. Christy, "Marshaling Community Resources for Prevention of Child Neglect and Abuse," in *Fourth National Symposium on Child Abuse* (Denver: Children's Division, American Humane Association, 1975), pp. 88–90.
[19] Elizabeth Elmer, "A Social Worker's Assessment of Medico-Social Stress in Child Abuse Cases," *ibid.* pp. 88–90.

the cause of their troubles. In this way they attempt to relieve their anxieties by attacking the child instead of facing their own problems.[20]

Sexual Abuse

Vincent De Francis estimates the occurrence of at least 50,000 to 75,000 incidences of sexual abuse annually. In a three-year study of the sexual abuse of children in New York City, he showed that 27 percent of the offenders were members of the child's own household. Another 11 percent did not live in the same house but were closely related to the child by blood or marriage. An additional 37 percent of the offenders were friends or acquaintances. The remaining 25 percent were allegedly strangers. A large proportion of the incidents occurred in or near the child's own home or in the home of the offender. Very few of the offenses happened in public areas. On the basis of these facts, Fontana is compelled to assume that the parents must share at least partial responsibility in most cases. Either they themselves were the perpetrators or they contributed to the act through apathy, negligence, or even cooperation with the offender.

In incest cases, the father was most often the offender, sometimes having relations with more than one child; the mother was frequently at least aware of the situation and often cooperative. In 79 percent of the cases in the De Francis study, the family was suffering from physical, moral, medical, emotional, and educational neglect. Physical abuse occurred in 11 percent of the families. Two-thirds of the sexually exploited children showed signs of emotional disturbance. The median age of the victims was eleven-and-a-half years. The oldest children were just under sixteen and the youngest were infants.[21]

According to Yvonne M. Tormes

the failure of the mother to protect the child against the contingency of incestuous victimization is a crucial and fruitful area of study pertinent to the general problem of control of father-daughter incest behavior . . . the mother . . . is the sole restraining agent available when the father deviates from his protective role. . . . The daughter victim, especially in the restrictive environment under which she is brought up, can be expected to derive the ego strength necessary to resist the father's overtures only from the mother image, or through actual support by the mother, which, somehow, she fails to get. . . . However, she is not a good prospect in this role. She appears, even before her marriage, to be a passive character, more willing than in the non-incest case to accept premarital pregnancy and unwed mother status. She marries younger, presumably exercising less choice in the decision. She has less education than her husband and less education than the mother represented in the non-incest group. She comes more

---

[20] Irving Kaufman, M.D., "Psychiatric Implications of Physical Abuse of Children," in *Protecting the Battered Child* (Denver: Children's Division, American Humane Association, 1962), pp. 17–20.

[21] Vincent De Francis, *Protecting the Child Victims of Sex Crimes Committed by Adults* (Denver: Children's Division, American Humane Association, 1970).

often from a foreign background and has had less exposure to any milieu other than her own. She has had no previous experience in marital relationships and she remains faithful to her marriage vows. . . . (she has) more children and less extensive histories of employment outside the home.[22]

In a study conducted in a psychiatric clinic in California in 1955 and reported by Vincent De Francis, child victims of adult sex crimes were shown to be of two different types: accidental victims, violated by strangers, the act occurring only once—with no reward to the victim—and reported immediately after its occurrence; and the participant victim, who received a reward, had repeated sexual experiences with the same or different adults, knew the offender, who was frequently a friend or relative.

The participant group outnumbered the other slightly more than two to one. Personality factors in some children cause them to initiate and maintain a sexual relationship with adults. . . . All the participant victims had guilt about their sexual activities, guilt which, if not expressed directly, was manifest in phobias, nightmares, anxieties, etc.[23]

Another study, reported in 1954, showed that incest victims suffered depression and guilt, some had learning difficulties, some were sexually promiscuous, some ran away from home, and some had somatic complaints—most frequently loss of appetite and abdominal stress. All of the girls tended to perform below their ability, performance scores generally higher than verbal scores.

The main trends which showed up in the Rorschach were depression, confusion over sexual identification, fear of sexuality, oral deprivation, and oral sadism. The chief mechanisms of defense were denial, repression, and sometimes projection.[24]

Child Abuse and Law Enforcement

Three out of four complaints of child abuse are reported to law enforcement authorities; this statistic reflects the community attitude that child abuse is a law enforcement problem. The first laws seeking reports of injuries inflicted on children were introduced and passed in 1963. By 1965 all fifty states had such laws. Currently, all of them are mandatory, meaning that all suspected cases of child abuse must be reported by those to whose attention they have come, otherwise the latter may themselves be prosecuted. The law enforcement function in child protection is thus of major importance. The police department is

---

[22] Yvonne M. Tormes, *Child Victims of Incest* (Denver: Children's Division, American Humane Association, 1966), pp. 32–35.
[23] Joseph Weiss, M.D., Estelle Rogers, M.D., Miriam R. Darwin, and Charles F. Dutton, Ph.D., *Psychiatric Quarterly* (January 1955), pp. 1–27.
[24] Irving Kaufman, M.D., *et al.*, *The American Journal of Orthopsychiatry*, XXIV, 2, (April 1954), pp. 226–68.

the only agency that is always available on a twenty-four-hour basis. It is safe to assume that not all child abuse occurs between 9 A.M. and 5 P.M. Mondays through Fridays. Moreover, the public is accustomed to reporting cases of physical violence to the police. Also, child protective services in many communities are either nonexistent or inadequate, leaving only the police to perform them. The police are also the only public agency with legal authority to enter homes to protect victims of violence.

The time factor is decisive in the police response to child abuse complaints. Often the complaint is lodged during the actual battering of the child or shortly thereafter. After evaluating the validity of the complaint, the primary duty of the police officer is the immediate protection of the child. Thus his first official act will be to secure medical attention for the child. Most state laws require that an attempt be made to resolve the situation without removing the child from his home. It is, however, sometimes absolutely necessary to take the child into protective custody, especially if there is no reasonable assurance that the abuse will cease. There can exist no such assurance if there is not someone in the home who can prevent the abuser from indulging in violence in the future.

Second, as a law enforcement officer charged with upholding public standards and maintaining public order, the officer must determine whether or not the law has been violated, and, if so, whether there exists sufficient evidence to initiate a criminal action against the abuser. He must, therefore, conduct an investigation as he would in any criminal case. If his investigation reveals sufficient evidence of a grave nature, he will take the suspect into physical custody.

The arrest of abusive parents is a controversial issue among child welfare professionals. Some claim that abuse cases are too difficult to prove, and that the exculpated parents leave a court proceeding with increased bitterness, which subjects the victim to added danger. Moreover, an unsuccessful prosecution may be viewed by the abuser as a vindication of his behavior and an encouragement to continue it. Furthermore, the risk of prosecution may prevent abusive parents from seeking medical help for the injured child until it is too late. Also, doctors are notoriously reluctant to become involved in any kind of litigation. Some social workers contend that arrest and prosecution are traditionally viewed as punishment and that punishment inhibits rehabilitation.

From a law enforcement perspective, child abuse represents a felonious act of grave proportions, a form of violence that threatens the very fabric of society; it thus cannot be treated casually. Moreover, it is not the function of the police to punish, but merely to bring criminal suspects to the attention of the courts, where a disposition will be prescribed. Arrest and prosecution may be the only means to assure that a program of rehabilitation will be initiated and adhered to. In the words of Jack Collins of the Los Angeles Police Department:

> Police action obligates agencies concerned with rehabilitative programs to become involved. When the police take juvenile victims into protective custody and/or arrest adults suspected of inflicting traumatic injuries on children, the attention of other agencies is automatically focused on the

problem. Prosecuting attorneys, criminal and juvenile courts, probation departments and other concerned social agencies must necessarily perform their assigned duties. This results in an official review and consideration of childbeating cases by community agencies charged with the responsibility of developing and implementing rehabilitative programs.[25]

Vincent De Francis and Carroll Lucht, themselves lawyers, add:

An additional consideration is the fact that punishment of abusing parents through criminal prosecution does not correct the fundamental cause of their behavior. If we recognize the mental, physical and emotional inadequacies of these people then we must recognize that prosecution and punishment will not produce true change in their behavior. At best it can only produce surface compliance, with deeper motivational forces remaining untreated and emotional damage to their personality becoming greater as a result of the punitive experience.

The decision of whether or not to prosecute in a given case should rest with the county prosecutor. In making this decision he must also consider what happens to children. No decision to prosecute parents can afford to overlook the necessity for adequate planning for the abused child and other children in the family.[26]

In its early stages child abuse legislation encouraged the reporting of cases of child abuse to law enforcement authorities. Present trends, however, encourage that reports of child abuse and neglect be made to social service agencies so that corrective steps can be taken to help the parents as well as the child and to salvage the family, which is still the best milieu in which to raise and nurture a child.

Child Protective Services

The most logical agents to assume this burden are the various child protective services, defined by Vincent De Francis as follows:

Protective services means specialized social service in behalf of children whose health and welfare is impaired or under immediate threat of impairment as the result of a violation or non-compliance with a law or legal responsibility for the protection of children, their education, employment, physical or emotional health or welfare.[27]

[25] Jack G. Collins, "The Role of the Law Enforcement Agency," in *The Battered Child,* Helfer and Kempe, *op. cit.,* pp. 184–86.

[26] Vincent De Francis, J.D., and Carroll Lucht, J.D., *Child Abuse Legislation in the 1970s* (Denver: Children's Division, American Humane Association, 1974), p. 4.

[27] Vincent De Francis, *Protective Services and Community Expectations* (Denver: Children's Division, American Humane Association, 1961), p. 15.

De Francis continues in another publication:

> The focus of the service is preventive and non-punitive and is geared toward a rehabilitation of the home and a treatment of the motivating factors which underlie neglect. This implies that parents and children are given help with those problems which have directly affected the parents' ability to provide proper care and guidance.
>
> The service is usually initiated on a "complaint" or referral from sources outside the family. The agency providing protective services has authority granted it by law or charter which imposes an obligation to provide the service when needed and which grants the right to explore, study and evaluate the facts of neglect and their effect on children. The agency has responsibility for invoking the authority of the Juvenile Court when such action is necessary to secure adequate protection, care and treatment of children whose parents are unable or unwilling to use the help offered by the agency.[28]

In a 1967 survey, De Francis found that protective services under voluntary agency auspices exist in ten states; those under public welfare auspices exist in forty-seven states, the District of Columbia, Puerto Rico, the Virgin Islands, and Guam; no state or community, however, "has developed a child protective service program adequate in size to meet the service needs of all reported cases of child neglect, abuse and exploitation."[29]

History of Child Protection

Although the ideal in child protective services will probably never be reached, monumental progress has been made since that day in 1874, when nurse Etta Wheeler, while making her rounds, stumbled upon a nine-year-old child named Mary Ellen. At the insistence of neighbors, nurse Wheeler entered the apartment of Mary Ellen's parents to find the child chained to a bedpost. She had obviously been beaten often and was dangerously undernourished. Wishing to take legal action, nurse Wheeler and other interested parties discovered that there was neither legislation nor a public agency which might empower them to move in such a case.

In desperation, the nurse and her friends appealed to the Society for the Prevention of Cruelty to Animals on the basis that Mary Ellen, as a member of the animal kingdom, qualified for their aid. The society perceived its legal jurisdiction immediately and had Mary Ellen removed from her home.

Although weak, ill, stunted in growth, battered, and bruised, Mary Ellen was redeemed for a useful life. It was her case which dramatized the fact that, up

---

[28] Vincent De Francis, *Community Cooperation for Better Child Protection* (Denver: Children's Division, American Humane Association, 1959), pp. 2–3.

[29] Vincent De Francis, *et al.*, *Child Protective Services, A Nationwide Survey* (Denver: Children's Division, American Humane Association, 1967), p. VII.

to that time, the welfare of animals had been considered of more importance than that of human children. As a consequence of this sobering realization, the first Society for the Prevention of Cruelty to Children was organized in New York in 1875. Many similar organizations sprang up in various parts of the country thereafter. For decades, only the private sector concerned itself with child abuse and neglect.

In 1946, radiologist John Caffey reported on six infant patients with subdural hematoma and a combination of twenty-three fractures and four contusions of the long bones. As a possible cause of this combination of symptoms, he cautiously suggested the possibility of parental abuse and neglect.

As a result of treating four infants in a single day who had been badly battered, Dr. C. Henry Kempe undertook, with his colleagues, a nationwide survey in an attempt to determine the frequency of cases of physical abuse in a given year. In discussing the results in the *Journal of the American Medical Association*, he coined the new term: the *battered child syndrome*. The survey uncovered a social malady of overwhelming dimensions. The publication and dissemination of the survey was largely responsible for the aforementioned child protective legislation and for the corrective programs we shall now discuss.

Child Protective Methods and Programs

Child protective work is not viewed solely as a method for rescuing children from neglect and maltreatment but additionally as a means of helping the family cope with life in a more acceptable manner. It has evolved into a unique branch of social work because of its peculiar characteristics. In the normal social work situation, the client seeks the aid of the agency. The neglected child is in no position to request aid, thus, the child protective worker must seek his child clients. Moreover, although the primary client is the child, there can be no hope for improvement if the parents are not somehow involved in the healing process.

Child protective services represent that arm of the community that reaches out to take up the slack left when one or more of its members is either unable or unwilling to "pull his weight." Therefore child protective services carry the force of legal authority. They may invoke this authority if other alternatives seem inappropriate. The force of law, however, also requires of child protective services that they remain with a case until it is somehow resolved, an obligation which far exceeds that of the private agency, whose responsibility is to the client alone and not to the community as a whole.

Child protective services work in conjunction with any number of agencies, depending upon their availability in a given community. Their task, after having identified and diagnosed a case, consists largely in attempting to convert involuntary clients into voluntary ones who will actively participate in the healing process. This process will often be the function of another agency, to whom the problem family is referred.

The nature of the healing process is based primarily on the needs and the rights of the child. Probably the best description of these was proposed by the New York State Youth Commission. It is called "The Children's Bill of Rights."

Children's Bill of Rights

For Each Child, Regardless of Race, Color or Creed:

1. The right to the affection and intelligent guidance of understanding parents.

2. The right to be raised in a decent home in which he or she is adequately fed, clothed and sheltered.

3. The right to the benefits of religious guidance and training.

4. The right to a school program which, in addition to sound academic training, offers maximum opportunity for individual development and preparation for living.

5. The right to receive constructive discipline for the proper development of good character, conduct and habits.

6. The right to be secure in his or her community against all influences detrimental to proper and wholesome development.

7. The right to individual selection of free and wholesome recreation.

8. The right to live in a community in which adults practice the belief that the welfare of their children is of primary importance.

9. The right to receive good adult example.

10. The right to a job commensurate to his or her ability, training, and experience, and protection against physical or moral employment hazards which adversely affect wholesome development.

11. The right to early diagnosis and treatment of physical handicaps and mental and social maladjustments, at public expense, whenever necessary.

The Hawaii State Legislature appropriated funds to expand the public welfare agency's protective services program and to establish the *Children's Protective Services Center* in fiscal 1969. This program has since become a model to be emulated worldwide. It consists of a team, whose members are the public welfare social work supervisor, a pediatrician, a psychiatrist, and a psychologist. The team meets weekly for two hours to provide diagnostic consultation on cases considered by social workers to be their most difficult. The social worker prepares a written social study. The social work supervisor acts as conference chairman; he introduces the case and surrounding circumstances. Other team members present their findings and preliminary diagnoses. As needed, lawyers, public health officials, vocational rehabilitation officials, and so on participate as team members. All members made suggestions concerning the most appropriate treatment plan. The social work supervisor then summarizes the collective recommendations. The ultimate choice of treatment plan and its implementation, however, is made by the social worker who submitted the case.

In Denver, a pioneer city in the field of child protection, *lay therapists*, who act as surrogate parents to maltreating parents, have long been active and successful. In more recent times, another dimension has been added. *Foster grandparents* over the age of sixty-five are assigned to hospitalized children. The grandparent acts in every way possible like a normal grandparent. In many instances the parents respond as well to this treatment as the children, if not better. In some cases, such relationships continue beyond the hospital stay to the lasting benefit of all concerned.

Another aspect of the Denver program uses *parent aides* from the ages of twenty-four to sixty. The parent aide concentrates not on the child but on the unfulfilled parent, who is mothered, supported, and generally administered to emotionally.

Dr. Vincent Fontana initiated the establishment of a *temporary shelter-home* program for the treatment of abusing and neglectful mothers at Foundling Hospital in New York. It employs a multidisciplinary, medical-social approach and provides the therapeutic and preventive services necessary in a comfortable and homelike family atmosphere. The facility supports eight to ten mothers and up to fifteen children at any one time. A typical program lasts three months with a year of follow-up. Fathers, boyfriends, and so on are included. The objectives of the program as stated by Dr. Fontana are to:

> (1) prevent separation of parents and children; (2) prevent the placement of children in institutions; (3) encourage the attainment of self-care status on the part of the mothers; and (4) stimulate the attainment of self-sufficiency for the family unit.[30]

Mothers, together with their children, are given psychiatric and medical treatment, attend group therapy sessions twice a week, and are taught the basics of child care. Pediatric services are provided for the children. Twenty-four-hour crisis support is readily accessible. If pressures become too great, there exists the possibility of a temporary home-away-from-home which enables mothers to gain some distance and perspective. Each mother has her own parent surrogate in the form of a social worker assistant, a mature woman who has been a successful mother. The educational program includes courses on child rearing, nursing, children's medical problems, homemaking, shopping, consumerism, venereal diseases, alcoholism, and drug addiction.

Odyssey House, founded in 1971 in New York City by Dr. Judianne Densen-Gerber for drug-addicted parents and expectant mothers, attempts to deal with mothers and sometimes fathers as a family unit. The objective of the program is to salvage present and successive generations and to determine whether mothering can be taught. Dr. Densen-Gerber made the following statement to the *New York Times* on December 18, 1972:

> I wonder if the entire concept of mothering as a natural instinct is off the wall, and the supposition that it can be taught is in question. We want to

[30] Vincent J. Fontana, *op. cit.,* p. 165.

see if, with proper input, it can . . . If I had to flip a coin now, I would say that it can't. This has profound ramifications for the entire country. If mothering can't be taught, you've got to get many children away from their mothers.[31]

The National Center for the Prevention and Treatment of Child Abuse and Neglect maintains a *crisis nursery*, where potentially abusive parents may leave their children for periods from a few hours up to a maximum of three days. Children between the ages of two weeks and seven years are accepted at any time of the day or night with no questions asked. It is hoped that the respite provided will allow the crisis to defuse so that normal functioning can resume.

The Bowen Center in Chicago provides comprehensive family support services for families who are unable to cope. Sponsored by the U.S. Children's Bureau and three Chicago foundations, the core of the center is an interdisciplinary team, under a common administration, which delivers an integrated program of services; casework with parents, group services to parents and school children, a day-care center for preschool children, homemaking therapists, a shelter care for use in emergencies, temporary foster care facilities, tutoring for children with learning problems, pediatric attention to health needs, and financial aid for special rehabilitative needs. The primary method of treatment is social casework.[32]

The Children's Aid Society of Buffalo, New York, sponsors a number of innovative child protective programs. Public relations efforts include conferences on neglect for social service workers, conferences with family court judges, state and county officials, representatives of Legal Aid, the Medical Society, the hospitals, the District Attorney, the schools, and the police, and public service spot announcements by radio and television stations. Actual agency programs include twenty-four-hour emergency casework services, an emergency parent service, emergency homemakers (homemakers aid the natural parents while emergency parents supplant them temporarily), and emergency foster homes. The team approach is employed in all of these services: emergency, intake, diagnostic, and treatment. Other teams are organized around specific problems (the multiple-problem family, child abuse, and so on). The agency also operates a family day camp, provides parent education, trains and assigns volunteers to special projects, and maintains a rehabilitation fund to assist a family in healing its immediate wounds; in one case funds were used to pay for a permanent (hairdo) for a mother of six, who had never had a permanent, as a means of enhancing her self-esteem.[33]

Parents Anonymous (P.A.) is a self-help, help-each-other organization which employs the same basic techniques as Alcoholics Anonymous. It was founded in 1970 in Los Angeles. Its basic philosophy holds that people with

---

[31] *Ibid.*, p. 173.

[32] G. Lewis Penner, *The Protective Services Center* (Denver: Children's Division, American Humane Association (1967), p. 5.

[33] Norman W. Paget, "Areas of Innovative Practices," in *Innovative Approaches in Child Protective Services* (Denver: Children's Division, American Humane Association 1969), pp. 14–24.

common problems can work together to help themselves, each other, and their children. Older members take newcomers under their wing. Newcomers later become old-timers who extend the helping chain to successive generations of problem-plagued parents. Members are able to express their thoughts, feelings, and problems openly with others of similar experience without fear of condemnation. They also learn where to turn when they feel the stresses building beyond the point at which they are able to tolerate them; a twenty-four-hour-a-day crisis intervention system, manned by members, is only as far away as the telephone. In addition, P.A. organizes group therapy sessions and ego-building. Occasionally mothers can exchange children, since an abusive mother is less likely to vent her anger on a strange child than on her own. The primary objective of P.A. is to achieve behavior modification: abusing parents must learn to seek out help, to deal with their negative feelings, and to direct their destructive actions into acceptable channels.

Child Abuse Listening Mediation (C.A.L.M.) was founded in 1970 on the private initiative of nurse Claire W. Miles. Based in Santa Barbara, California, it has grown into an organization of twenty-one volunteer workers with ready access to psychiatric and psychological services. C.A.L.M. advertises a telephone number in the newspaper which is to be called by anyone who knows of an abused or neglected child. When a call is received, a volunteer visits the home, evaluates the situation, and takes whatever action seems appropriate. This might range from simple, sympathetic listening to referral to a social or judicial agency. No call goes unanswered.

Prevention

Obviously, if any real progress in the problem of child abuse is to be made, the thrust in the future must be in the area of prevention. Eli H. Newberger, M.D., outlines the "Attributes of Model Systems for the Prevention and Control of Child Abuse and Neglect" as follows:

1. Child abuse seen as a symptom of family crisis, with professional services oriented to making families stronger.

2. Recognition of the community context in which child abuse occurs: attention to the values of the community, its indigenous techniques of problem solving, its traditions of child rearing, its resources and its leadership, in both the development of programs to help families, and in the approach to preventing child abuse on a larger scale.

3. Systematic attention to the development of public policies which strengthen family life, based on what is already known about family strength and stress.

4. Protection of information about people; consistent and rigorous identification of the rights of children and their parents; and advocacy at all levels of intervention action to assure that fundamental civil liberties are not violated.

5. Citizen supervision of professional policies and practices through community-based Councils for Children.

6. Regular evaluation of the effectiveness of intervention on several levels: around the individual case, both to assure continued physical protection and the promotion of health and psychological growth; and, for the program in general, to assure the adherence to the highest principles of human service.

7. The program should be population based: all people should be eligible for service. Neither a small-scale pilot program nor a major undertaking focusing only on the protection of children whose cases happen to be reported, it should identify the dimensions of the problem, all possible avenues of individual and larger-scale intervention, and recruit and sustain the interest and participation of competent and varied providers of service. Emphatically, it should not be identified as a poor people's program, although it is certain that many children of the poor will be reported, partly but not exclusively because of the circumstances of poverty which may lead their families to fail. It should be a program to which private medical practitioners and voluntary family service agencies, as well as suburban school systems, would feel comfortable in reporting cases, because its services would be helpful and its orientation toward keeping families together and toward preventing child abuse.

8. Administrative organization allowing both flexibility in staff development, supervision, and assignment and, at the same time high-level access to the human services leadership, in order most effectively to promote collaboration, constructive and mutual program planning, and, ultimately, the evolution of a human service system which would identify the *family* as the unit of practice, rather than, as at present, to fragment health, social, and psychological problems into discrete program units.

9. It would incorporate child advocacy (as defined in the Report of the Joint Commission on the Mental Health of Children) and child development education.

10. It would identify who is responsible to whom for what; minimize to the extent possible uninformed, reflexive and precipitous action on the part of intervention personnel; maximize the career development possibilities for these personnel in the context of the program structure; integrate into the career development program a systematic method for recruiting and training professional personnel from minority groups; and allow for the acknowledgement and reward of successful work.

11. Services would be provided 24 hours a day.

12. It would assure adequate legal representation for all parties in any court proceeding relating to child abuse; and active and high-level advocacy to assure judicial determinations consonant with the high standards of modern family law. Its goal would be to integrate families rather than to punish parents; to use the authority of the court, when necessary, to force family change; and, as a last resort, when families utterly and completely fail, to allow children who are dependent on the state maximal opportunities for growth in homes they can identify as their own.

13. There would be an adequate commitment of resources to assure that a successful program would be able to continue.

14. The system should be able to respond creatively to individual families' problems with services suited to their needs, to include:

    a. social work counseling, liaison with other services and structures;

    b. medical and psychiatric consultation, and, where necessary, treatment;

    c. advocacy;

    d. child development services, including education, child care, and psychological intervention;

    e. legal services;

    f. temporary foster home care; and

    g. round-the-clock emergency services, such as homemaker services, to prevent family breakup and continued child abuse or neglect.[34]

As a final note it might be well to review Vincent De Francis' statement to the House Subcommittee on Juvenile Delinquency on May 29, 1957:

> Current thinking with respect to the preventive aspects of "control and diminution" of juvenile delinquency has given great support to group work and recreation activities. The emphasis on diverting the interests of children into controlled activities and constructive channels is sound and necessary.
>
> Of greater generic value, however, is the service which "reaches out" to the child's own home and brings stability to insecure, deteriorating, neglectful or disintegrating homes and repairs the damage BEFORE the child is seriously affected by the physical and emotional traumas and stresses in such homes.
>
> Protective services for children do just that!
>
> Let me initially make clear that we recognize that no single service alone can provide a "cure all" which will eliminate all delinquency. We do say, however, that no other service is geared to reach the heart of a major factor in delinquency causation to the same extent and with the same force as does "Child Protection." Perhaps our thinking can best be epitomized by such catch-all phrases as "the neglected child of today is the delinquent of tomorrow" or "Scratch a delinquent and you will find a neglected child underneath," or again, "Stop neglect—Prevent delinquency."
>
> Those of us who work in the field of child protection recognize that delinquency has many roots and causes. We know that children react to influences both within the home and outside it. We believe, however, that no child is born delinquent and if he displays a pattern of abnormal behavior it is the product of adverse influences and pressures. The stronger the pres-

---

[34] Eli H. Newberger, "Interdisciplinary Management of Child Abuse: Problems and Progress," in *Fourth National Symposium on Child Abuse* (Denver: Children's Division, American Humane Assoc., 1975) pp. 24–26.

sures, whether physical or emotional, the deeper the maladjustment and perhaps the more abnormal the behavior.

We believe, too, that the child who is brought up in a happy, normal home with adequate, considerate and loving parents, is less apt to succumb to influences which may lead him to delinquent behavior. To begin with, his exposure to such harmful influences would have been reduced by the very fact of the normal home environment.

On the more positive side, he will have received a solid foundation for adequate personality and emotional development. He will have received affectional security for he is both loved and wanted. His physical and health needs are of concern to his parents. They want him to receive the benefits of a good education. By their example they have given him sound moral and spiritual guidance and he will have learned to respect the property rights of others. These, then, are the stabilizing influences which a normal homelife will provide as a shield against adverse influences to which the child may be subjected outside the home.

Conversely, a child who is brought up in a less adequate home, or one which is grossly inadequate because of neglect, fails to receive the warmth of affection, the sense of being wanted, and the physical, emotional or spiritual care which are so necessary for the building up of a secure and emotionally stable personality. Such a child is so much more likely to respond to stimuli and influences which more easily and readily will lead him to antisocial, aggressive and delinquent behavior.

We firmly believe, therefore, that if we can reduce the number of neglected, inadequate, subnormal homes, we will also reduce the number of children who will need to satisfy their emotional needs through behavior which society has classed as delinquent.

Quite obviously, then, the child protective agency plays a major role in the prevention and diminution of delinquency. It is a role which it has never before seriously interpreted to the community. It is a responsibility which is inherent to its function and which, because of the preventive approach, will permit the community to "lock the stable *before* the horses are stolen."[35]

SUMMARY

Cases of severe physical abuse and neglect are increasing annually at an alarming rate. Experts have shown a clear relationship between child abuse and neglect, and adolescent and adult criminality. Abusing and neglecting parents have many similar characteristics: an inordinate need for love and warm response, which they seek from their children, a sense of unlovability and low self-esteem. Abusive families represent the entire socioeconomic spectrum, whereas neglect-

---

[35] Vincent De Francis, *Accent on Prevention* (Denver: Children's Division, American Humane Assoc., 1957) pp. 1–2.

ful families demonstrate inordinately high rates of financial insufficiency, broken homes, less education, substandard housing and neighborhood, excessive family size, alcoholism, and problems of mental health. Fontana classifies abusing parents into the emotionally immature, neurotic or psychotic, mentally deficient, uninformed, disciplinarian, criminal sadistic, and addictive.

Maltreatment occurs most frequently in broken or disintegrating homes. A potentially abusive parent is attracted to a mate with similar characteristics or one who is so passive as to be unable to modify the abusive behavior of the maltreating spouse. Situations resulting in child abuse are: attempts at discipline, hopelessness and despair, mercy in the face of physical or mental handicaps, the mental illness of the parent, unwed motherhood, medical and social stress, and premature births. In instances of sexual abuse the parents share at least partial responsibility; when not the perpetrators themselves, they often contribute to the act through apathy, negligence, or even cooperation with the offender.

The community in general perceives child abuse as a law enforcement problem. All fifty states currently have mandatory reporting laws. In its early stages, child abuse legislation encouraged the reporting of cases of child abuse to law enforcement authorities. Present trends, however, encourage that reports of child abuse and neglect be made to social service agencies so that corrective steps can be taken to help the parents as well as the child and to salvage the family.

Child protective services exist in all states as a result of the famous "Mary Ellen case" of 1874, when a severely maltreated child had to be represented by a society for the prevention of cruelty to animals because no such protection existed for human children.

Social casework is the primary method of treatment of child protective services. The nature of the healing process is based on the needs and the rights of the child. There exist many imaginative and innovative programs designed to accomplish this goal. If any real progress in the problem of child abuse is to be made, the thrust in the future must be in the area of prevention, which is currently receiving a great deal of attention. Child protective services are, by their very nature, primarily preventive.

QUESTIONS AND PROJECTS

Essay Questions

1. Why are cases of physical abuse and neglect increasing annually?

2. How can a child be used as a pawn or a scapegoat by the parents?

3. What is the difference between discipline and abuse? Explain your answer in detail.

4. Why is a child who is "different" often the object of abuse? Can you find examples of this same basic dynamic in society at large? Discuss them.

5. Why must parents share at least partial responsibility in cases of sexual abuse?

6. What is the proper role of the law enforcement agency in cases of child abuse?

7. Should child abusers be prosecuted? Give reasons for your answer.

Projects

1. Develop a therapeutic model for a young, working-class couple who have abused one of their children.

2. Do the same for a successful, upper-middle class, professional couple.

3. Devise a list of procedures to be followed by police officers in abuse and neglect cases.

chapter 8

Delinquency Prevention Programs

Every society requires a greater or lesser degree of conformity to its behavioral norms or laws. It invariably responds in some fashion when these are violated. The nature of the response varies widely according to the act and from society to society. Moreover, it is subject to a development which parallels the state of a society at a given period. One act might be considered gravely serious at one point in time and relatively harmless at another. A society threatened by an external enemy, for example, is likely to react to behavioral deviations differently than it would in a time of peace and prosperity. In addition to fluctuations in response due to alternating periods of stress and calm, societal responses to illegal behavior evolve historically in roughly the same manner as do societies themselves.

In preliterate societies, a high degree of cooperation was required if the group was to survive. Every group member had his or her function to perform according to ability and status. Some members hunted while others fashioned weapons. Some prepared the food and tended the fire, others sewed clothing, and so on. In these primitive organizations, there existed a high degree of immediate, mutual dependence. If one member failed to perform his task satisfactorily or in any way disrupted the equilibrium of the group, the survival of all was threatened. Since a very high degree of conformity was necessary under such conditions, practically every aspect of life became ritualized. Violations of the rituals, which included witchcraft and sacrilege as well as treason and poisoning, were responded to either by the annihilation or the banishment of the offending member. The offender was considered unclean; he had to be removed as a social hygiene measure. Offenses against private individuals of different families such as assault, murder, and theft were avenged by the relatives of the victim in blood feuds and were not considered sufficiently grave to require societal response. Injuries to other members of the same family were dealt with totally within the family. Thus, the responses to deviant and what would now be termed criminal or delinquent behavior were not punitive in the modern sense but rather arose from a desire to annihilate an enemy of the group, to offer sacrifice to appease or otherwise avert the wrath of the gods, to cleanse the community of pollution, to avenge cases of private injury, and to show surprise and disgust at one who would offend a family member.

As societies became larger, more complex and subject to a central authority in the person of a king, reaction to wrongs came to be viewed as collective or social, as offenses against the group as well as against the victim. If an offender was executed, it was to remove him as a potential danger to other members of the group. If his hand was cut off or he was branded on the forehead, it was not done with the intention of inflicting pain or deterring others with similar inclination by example, but rather to inhibit the offender's ability to repeat his offense by either incapacitating him or labeling him untrustworthy so that other group members could take precautionary measures against potential loss. Fines were levied with a view toward restitution of the victim, rather than as a method of punishing the offender.

It was not until the modern period, beginning roughly in the second half of the seventeenth century, that the inflicting of pain on an offender came to be regarded as having value in the deterrence of crime. The classical school (mentioned earlier), which included such noteworthy adherents as Rousseau, Montesquieu, Voltaire, and Beccaria, maintained that the individual calculates pleasures and pains in advance of action and regulates his behavior accordingly. Thus, society's response to crime should be calculated in a fashion that would render the punishment of an illegal act more painful than the pleasure accruing from it. The potential offender could then calculate the results of his act in advance. It was hoped that the fear of pain would exceed the anticipated pleasure of the act and the individual would therefore opt for socially acceptable behavior. If he chose the criminal act, the pain of punishment inflicted on him would help enable him to better order his priorities in the future. Also, pain served to repay society for his deviant acts, considered an offense against the group. Pain, thus, served the twofold purpose of pacifying a community that had felt its equilibrium threatened by an offensive act and of reforming the offender. The inflicting of pain as a societal response to illegal acts has remained up to the present the most prevalent of the several alternatives. Present-day offenders still refer to their sentences as "repaying their debt to society." Repayment takes the form of pain in most correctional measures, although it is more psychological than physical at present. The nature of the pain inflicted varies considerably according to time and place, but generally it includes death, exile, imprisonment, physical torture, social degradation, and financial loss. In modern, industrial societies, fines and removal from the group by imprisonment are the most frequently employed methods.

In the late eighteenth and early nineteenth centuries, the prison, which up to that time had been used primarily for debtors, political prisoners, and criminals awaiting other dispositions, became the major correctional vehicle. Imprisonment is ideally suited to the retribution-pleasure-pain deterrent theories since its length can be varied with the crime. Parole and probation can be viewed as modified extensions of imprisonment.

Chapter 2 pointed out that the positivist school of criminology advocated by Lombroso, Ferri, Garofalo, and others, held that criminality arises from a multiplicity of factors, including heredity and environment. This position denied individual responsibility for criminal acts, thereby eliminating the justification of punishment as a response. According to this school of thought, criminals should be treated with a view toward reform. Society, however, must be protected from those who cannot be salvaged; they must be maintained in segregation. Segregation, however, should be the last resort. Prevention, as it is known today, is a relatively new concept. Preventing the problem before it occurs is the ideal solution.

Delinquency Prevention

Juvenile delinquency prevention is one of the most elusive concepts now existing in criminological theory, thought, and literature. Many contemporary prevention programs and treatment approaches make assumptions about human behavior which often do not have a firm basis in either science or causal relationships. Furthermore, there is not a great deal of evidence that either proves or disproves the effectiveness of the many treatment approaches, programs and strategies.

Early efforts at delinquency prevention and the establishment of programs and strategies were usually local endeavors initiated by privately-supported family-centered agencies and groups. Urbanization necessitated that both private and public agencies become involved in delinquency prevention because of the immensity of the problem and the complexities of the urban society.

In recent years, a wide variety of community, state, and national agencies have become involved in delinquency prevention, control, and treatment. Most of these efforts, however, have been independent and uncoordinated.

By the mid-1950's, the delinquency prevention effort in virtually every large city was like a jigsaw puzzle of services involving important government departments which had theretofore operated with relative independence. The agencies concerned with delinquency prevention included the schools, recreation departments, public housing authorities, public welfare departments giving family service and administering child welfare, private social agencies and health departments and other medical facilities (including psychiatric hospitals and clinics). The size, shape, and strength and position (role in the community) of the various pieces of the delinquency prevention picture varied greatly from one city to another—the format for delinquency prevention services varied from city to city partly because the coordinating agency in each city is the one which happened to be the strongest.[1]

Many other problems also hinder delinquency prevention efforts, and often a coordinated endeavor by the community does not exist.

A general lack of communication between agencies and between disciplines was increasingly evident and variations in policies between agencies often made it impossible for them to function effectively together for the benefit of the child.[2]

The absence of rigorous evaluation, as Chapter 10 will emphasize, has been criticized in relation to most delinquency prevention and treatment programs, and the importance of proper evaluation cannot be overstressed. Evaluation is absolutely essential when making judgments about alternative strategies for delinquency prevention, control, and treatment. The social policy implications are obvious.

Wilkins points out that

the best research in the fields of criminology and penology seldom seems to do more than clarify the unknown. It is doubtful whether even the most enthusiastic research worker in these fields could sustain a claim to having added significantly to knowledge. Myths and beliefs of the past have little or no support when subjected to rigorous examination, but in their place only the most tentative suggestions can be brought forward. This is perhaps to be expected and hardly to be regretted. More regrettable is the fact that all too often research ends by noting nothing more significant than that the questions with which the project began were inappropriate. But these types of research are in the main the most satisfactory studies. Most research projects make larger or more practical claims and usually lack validity when subjected to critical assessment.[3]

Two types of delinquency prevention will be discussed in this chapter: *pure prevention,* or primary prevention, which attempts to inhibit delinquency before it takes place; and *rehabilitative prevention,* or secondary prevention, which treats the youngster once he has come in contact with the formal juvenile justice system. Rehabilitative prevention, if effective, can also be considered a

---

[1] *Juvenile Delinquency Prevention in the United States,* U.S. Department of Health, Education, and Welfare, Children's Bureau (1965) p. 12.

[2] *Ibid.,* p. 17.

[3] Leslie T. Wilkins, *Evaluation of Penal Measures* (New York: Random House, Inc., 1969), p. 28.

preventive mechanism if the treatment provided deters future delinquent behavior. Pure prevention therefore deals primarily with youngsters who have not
been adjudicated delinquent, whereas rehabilitative prevention deals with
youngsters who have been adjudicated delinquent.

Other typologies have been used to classify programs that attempt to
prevent, control, and treat delinquency. Lejins describes the following typology:

> The ambiguity of the concept of prevention is one of the main obstacles
> to discussing prevention meaningfully to obtain generally significant
> research data and even to describing existing preventive programs. The
> term prevention refers to several different types of societal action, so dif-
> ferent in fact that in most cases a clarification of the particular type of
> prevention in question is indispensable to making communication mean-
> ingful. Three types of prevention or three distinct meanings of the concept
> can be differentiated: punitive prevention, corrective prevention, and
> mechanical prevention.[4]

Punitive prevention is the threat of punishment under the hypothesis that
punishment will presumably forestall the criminal act. *Corrective prevention*
refers to the attempt to eliminate potential causes, factors, or motivations
before the criminal behavior actually takes place. *Mechanical prevention* emphasizes placing obstacles in the way of the potential criminal so that he will
find it difficult or impossible to commit an offense. Increased security measures
and increased police protection are mechanical efforts at prevention.

Sullivan and Bash use a different type of classification for prevention
programs. Like Lejins's classification, theirs includes a three-phase typology:

> 1. Programs that have explicit primary functions and goals involving
> deliberate intervention in the lives of specifically identified individuals
> for the expressed purpose of preventing the occurrence of behavior that
> would label them as antisocial or as delinquent by the laws and rules of
> general society.
>
> 2. Programs that have explicit primary goals of planned intervention and
> participation in the development, employment and organization of inter-
> relationships of various social institutions, groups, and agencies within the
> community with the intention of preventing formation of patterns of
> delinquent behavior in specific individuals or groups.
>
> 3. Programs that have explicit primary goals of deliberate participation in
> the special processes of reviewing laws, social policies, and public attitudes
> that have a specific and direct relevance to activities designed to prevent
> delinquency.[5]

---

[4] Peter Lejins, "The Field of Prevention," in *Delinquency Prevention: Theory and Practice,*
William Amos and Charles Wellford, Eds. (Englewood Cliffs, N.J.: Prentice-Hall, Inc.,
1967), p. 3.
[5] Clyde Sullivan and Carrie Bash, "Current Programs for Delinquency Prevention," in Amos
and Wellford, *op. cit.,* pp. 61–62.

Lejins's typology differentiates prevention programs by their goals and the means utilized to obtain goal achievement. Sullivan and Bash differentiate programs by their service orientation.

Although the pure prevention and rehabilitation prevention dichotomy was selected to facilitate discussion, it is difficult to pigeonhole prevention efforts into such neat categories because many programs include both adjudicated and nonadjudicated youngsters. Most programs range in the continuum from pure prevention to rehabilitative prevention.

An overview of both pure prevention and rehabilitative prevention programs follows.[6] Many of the programs, however, will be middle-range-type efforts which extend services both to youngsters who have been adjudicated and to those who have not come in contact with the formal juvenile justice system. An example of a middle-range program is the Youth Services Bureau concept in the state of Massachusetts:

> The Governor's Public Safety Committee in Massachusetts has developed a Youth Services Bureau emphasizing mental health and special services for referred youth. The Bureau, which serves two communities, has a mental health orientated staff and involves young people in policy decisions and program development. Youth are referred to the Center by schools, police, courts and parents. . . . For each young person referred, the Bureau does a complete diagnostic examination, after which the youth is usually referred to a particular program or agency in the community for specialized treatment. Each young person referred from the Bureau is followed by the community specialists to insure that he or she has received the treatment or services recommended.[7]

The Youth Services Bureau often serves as an alternative to exposing the youngster to the formal court procedures and the stigmatization that often ensues. It can assist almost all children except those who are involved in the serious types of difficulty that endanger both themselves and the community.

> The Youth Services Bureau would provide services ranging from remedial education to psychiatric diagnosis and treatment, either directly through its staff of professional workers and volunteers or by referral to other community agencies whose services should be purchased by the bureau. The Bureau would develop those services lacking in the community, thereby insuring comprehensive services for children rather than becoming a coordinator of existing services. For if the Bureau is viewed as the coordinator of existing services, those services presently lacking in the community will not be provided, and the cooperation of the existing agencies, which seems resistant to the organization of a community "coordinator"

[6]*Annual Report of Federal Activities in Juvenile Delinquency, Youth Development and Related Fields,* U.S. Department of Health, Education, and Welfare, Social and Rehabilitation Service (1971), pp. 130-32.
[7]*Ibid.,* p. 19-20.

will be more difficult to obtain. The Bureau must be able to offer short-term crisis oriented case work through its full-time professional staff who should have ready access to the services of a psychologist and psychiatrist for assistance in diagnosis and for consultation.[8]

The Youth Services Bureau concept is valuable because it can provide services to both adjudicated and nonadjudicated youngsters.

Regardless of the particular type of prevention or treatment program attempted by the community, however, the effort will be meaningless unless the community understands the program, accepts is concepts, and is willing to support it.[9] The efforts of program innovators and initiators will be futile if the community does not understand the seriousness of the problem.

For example, a community may fail to support and use psychiatric services in a child guidance clinic but may grab at simple solutions such as curfews, banning comics or restricting movie attendance.[10]

There are no simple solutions to delinquency prevention, control, and treatment. Community support is needed so that resources can be provided and well-organized programs based on solid theory and investigation can be initiated. If such programs have community support and built-in methods of evaluation, they will have greater chance of success than piecemeal efforts that do not incorporate these ingredients.

If the available youth servicing agencies and organizations are to be improved, if needed services not presently available are to be procured, if all resources are to be so articulated that the specialized needs of pre-delinquent and delinquent children are to be met at the strategic time and with the most promising prescription of service, two conditions must prevail: (1) there must be a continuous study of local youth problems and local youth servicing agencies and (2) there must be some community system or body established that will ensure overall organization, planning and coordination of services to all youth.[11]

PURE PREVENTION PROGRAMS

Most pure prevention programs are community endeavors that attempt to identify the conditions and problems that contribute to crime and delinquency and prevent the problem before it occurs. In general, there has been little evalua-

---

[8] G. David Schiering, "A Proposal for the More Effective Treatment of the 'Unruly' Child in Ohio," in *Diverting Youth from the Correctional System*, U.S. Department of Health, Education, and Welfare, Youth Service Bureau (1971), p. 77.

[9] William Kvaraceus, *The Community and the Delinquent* (New York: The World Book Company, 1954), p. 162.

[10] *Ibid.*, p. 162.

[11] *Ibid.*, p. 163.

tion of prevention programs (see Chapter 10). Many of the programs that will be discussed in this section are fairly new, which precludes intensive evaluative comments. Other programs were established under less than optimal conditions, and their planning and implementation did not facilitate meaningful research and evaluation. Wooton mentions that it is difficult to evaluate many delinquency programs because

> they produced insignificant material, because their statistical findings could not be divorced from the tests or were presented in a form which defied comparative use or because the samples used were inadequate. Thus, Shaw and McKay's famous ecological study and Lander's Baltimore investigation were excluded on the first grounds, while other studies are excluded because of the latter reason.[12]

The federal government has made vigorous attempts to prevent delinquency and has provided financial support through its various departments. It has also focused on many of the contributing factors to determine methods for successful prevention, control, and treatment. The cross sections of federal government programs that follow are not comprehensive, nor are all government efforts mentioned, but they do present a realistic overview.

Federal Government Efforts

The Juvenile Justice and Delinquency Prevention Act of 1974 (P.L. 93-415) provides for the coordination of federal delinquency programs. The act established an Office of Juvenile Justice and Delinquency Prevention (OJJDP) and, within that office, a National Institute for Juvenile Justice and Delinquency Prevention (NISSDP) as its research, evaluation, and information center. There are several provisions in the act that insure a coordinated interagency and interdisciplinary approach to the delinquency problem. It establishes overall objectives and priorities and creates a coordinating council on juvenile justice and delinquency prevention and the National Advisory Committee on Juvenile Justice and Delinquency Prevention. The coordinating council has representatives of Federal agencies and is chaired by the Attorney General. The advisory committee is composed of private citizens appointed by the President, four members being under the age of 26 at the time of the appointment.[13]

Department of Health, Education, and Welfare. The activities of the Department of Health, Education, and Welfare range from mental health services to educational research and training programs. One of the programs related to

---

[12] B. Wooton, *Social Science and Social Pathology* (London: George Allen and Unwin, Ltd., 1957).

[13] *First Comprehensive Plan for Federal Juvenile Delinquency Programs,* Office of Juvenile Justice and Delinquency Prevention, LEAA, U.S. Dept. of Justice (Washington, D.C., 1976), pp. 1–70.

delinquency prevention is the Upward Bound Program, which is directly administered by the Office of Education and provides services to the young.

Upward Bound is a precollege preparatory program designed to generate the skills and motivation necessary for success in education among young people from low-income families who do not have the adequate secondary school preparation.

> Students must meet income criteria established by the commissioner. Upward Bound consists of a summer program lasting from six to eight weeks and continues through the academic year with programs on Saturdays, tutorial sessions during the week, and periodic cultural enhancement programs.[14]

Youngsters involved in this program are encouraged to complete secondary school training and, if advisable, to pursue a college education. Schools that are involved in the program are given financial support by the federal government.

Because the program focuses on disadvantaged youth and provides them with skills necessary to adapt in their environment and achieve satisfying rewards, many youngsters are given an opportunity to fulfill these goals who would not have been able to do so through conventional community services. This program is focused not only on preventing delinquency but also on reducing delinquency. It helps those youngsters who, without the program, often become exposed to the juvenile justice system.

Department of Justice. The Law Enforcement Assistance Administration (LEAA) under the Department of Justice created by Title I of the Omnibus Crime Control and Safe Streets Act, has three basic objectives: (1) to encourage state and local governments to prepare plans for comprehensive law enforcement, (2) to improve and strengthen law enforcement through grants to state and local governments, and (3) to encourage research in crime control and prevention.

> Police, courts and corrections are the major concerns of LEAA. The approaches to these areas vary because the states set their own priorities; however, every aspect to the nation's crime problem is being reviewed including the serious juvenile crime problem.[15]

Grants provided by LEAA have been used to facilitate these objectives. Not only are problem areas identified, but youngsters are actively involved in program development and problem solving. Programs such as the control and prevention of gang violence, which was initiated in Philadelphia, have been developed. In this particular project, resources were utilized and the ideas from many academic disciplines incorporated to prevent gang violence and reduce

---

[14] *Annual Report of Federal Activities,* p. 79.
[15] *Ibid.,* p. 89.

the potential of youngsters' becoming involved in civil disorders. A project in San Antonio, Texas, has as its objective the reducing of juvenile delinquency by offering an educational program for parents and offenders, which includes counseling and job placement services.[16]

The major thrust of the projects developed to reduce juvenile delinquency has been to identify causal factors so that solutions to the problems can be given.

Department of Agriculture. Federal extension services under the Department of Agriculture provide programs for youngsters which can often indirectly contribute to reducing juvenile delinquent activities. The 4-H program operated under the Federal Extension Services branch of the Department of Agriculture has become even more involved in preventing delinquency in urban areas:

> Cooperative Extension Service agents work through schools, churches, service clubs, public housing directors, juvenile correctional institutions, neighborhood councils and centers, community action panels, etc., to introduce 4-H programs and methods. Professional Extension staff are assisting in the program through the use of paid program assistance and by volunteer adult and teen-age leaders.[17]

For example, in Providence, Rhode Island, Cooperative Extension Service attempts to reach troubled youngsters in deprived areas through such means as the establishment of storefront offices within the inner city. VISTA workers and volunteers become involved with community residents in problem solving. Hartford, Connecticut, has initiated a program that helps Puerto Rican youths, as well as other community youngsters. An urban 4-H agent is employed and is assigned to the inner city to help youngsters develop socially acceptable behavioral alternatives. In Wilmington, Delaware, Cooperative Extension Service is working with the city to establish and maintain various youth centers. These facilities provide recreational activities for city youngsters who do not have the money or the opportunity to satisfy their needs in a socially acceptable manner.

Federal extension programs under the Department of Agriculture have mainly served rural youths, but because of an increased awareness of the many problems that exist in urban areas an attempt is being made to provide resources to the cities so that many of these problems can be eliminated or alleviated. The resources provided by the government to these communities can be helpful in identifying problems and initiating programs for their solution.

Department of Labor. The United States Department of Labor Manpower Administration operates three types of youth serving activities under the Neighborhood Youth Corps program authorized by the Economic Opportunity Act of 1964.

[16]*Ibid.,* p. 90.
[17]*Ibid.,* p. 107.

The in-school program provides part-time employment, on-the-job training and useful work experience for youths still in school or in need of money to remain in school. The out-of-school program provides work and training and sufficient supportive services to obtain meaningful employment for unemployed or underemployed low-income persons. The summer program is designed to offer training, work experience and income to help disadvantaged students to return to school in the fall.[18]

One of the main programs of the Neighborhood Youth Corps, which was inaugurated in 1965, involves working in the poorest and most disadvantaged areas within inner-city limits. It focuses resources in these areas to help alleviate problems which have often resulted from extreme poverty conditions. In 1968 more than 620,000 youths from disadvantaged areas of the city were enrolled under the auspices of the Neighborhood Youth Corps. Of this number, the Manpower Administration reports that 70 percent have improved themselves after termination of their youth corps projects.[19]

Office of Economic Opportunity. The Office of Economic Opportunity also provides services that either directly or indirectly relate to delinquency prevention. Its Office of Program Development has become involved in several attempts at programs that affect both delinquent juveniles and predelinquent juveniles.

Through 409 Community Action Agencies, the office administers a youth development program. Despite its emphasis in 1969 on summer recreation, the program is moving toward a year-round project . . . The OEO Office of Health Affairs also funded nine projects dealing with rehabilitation of young addicts in the fiscal year of 1970 . . . These comprehensive drug rehabilitation programs are operated through Community Action Agencies or their delegate organizations.[20]

The programs under OEO, as well as other federal programs previously discussed, are an effort by the government to funnel resources into areas with high rates of crime and delinquency in an attempt at social problem solving. Many of these efforts are relatively new, and therefore it is difficult to generalize about their successes or failures until more meaningful and valid research and program evaluation is available. It should be pointed out, however, that programs of this type can be effective in reducing delinquency and preventing many youngsters from becoming involved in delinquent activities. Resources funneled into areas of high rates of crime and delinquency can be effectively utilized to develop favorable alternatives in behavioral adjustment for youngsters who are not exposed to an adequate opportunity structure. Cooperative endeavors by the federal government and local communities can facilitate the development of

[18] *Ibid.,* p. 109.
[19] *The Neighborhood Youth Corps: Hope and Help for Youth,* U.S. Department of Health, Education, and Welfare, Manpower Administration (1969), p. 6.
[20] *Annual Report of Federal Activities,* p. 111.

pure prevention programs which will improve community conditions and help reduce delinquency and crime.

The next section of the chapter will discuss further efforts at community problem solving. Many of these programs are funded at least partially by the federal government, but like many of the federal activities and programs already mentioned, they have not been subjected to appropriate testing and therefore it is difficult to evaluate them objectively.

Community-Based Programs

The Chicago Area Project. One of the earliest projects to deal with the problem of juvenile delinquency as well as other social problems was the Chicago Area Project. The project operated on the assumption that

> much of the delinquency in the slum areas is to be attributed to lack of neighborhood cohesiveness and to the consequent lack of concern on the part of many residents about the welfare of children. The project strives to counteract this situation through encouraging local self-help enterprises through which a sense of neighborliness and mutual responsibility will develop. It is expected that delinquency will decline as youngsters become better integrated into community life and therefore influenced by the values of conventional society rather than by those of the underworld.[21]

The project concentrated its efforts in areas of high delinquency and crime in an attempt to mobilize the support of the community so that delinquency could be prevented and new opportunity structures provided for area residents. Such programs as the sponsorship of recreation projects, a campaign for community improvement, and other efforts directed at helping youngsters were initiated. Both professional and volunteer workers in the community made contact with those youngsters who were identified as needing assistance. The personalized service and the concentration of resources in the area was felt to contribute to more effective problem solving in the Chicago area. Even though objective research of the success of the program is minimal, this was a very early attempt to mobilize community resources in high crime areas to ensure that the youngsters of the area would be provided with the opportunity to adjust to their environment satisfactorily. It was felt that if legitimate opportunities were provided for youngsters, much of the frustration and strain that exist in the disadvantaged areas of large cities could be reduced and this could have a direct impact on reducing crime and delinquency.

The Midcity Project. The Midcity Project was initiated in a lower-socio-economic class district of Boston in 1954 to reduce the amount of illegal activity

---

[21] Rose Giallombardo, "The Chicago Area Project," in *Juvenile Delinquency: A Book of Readings* (New York: John Wiley & Sons, Inc., 1966).

engaged in by local adolescents.[22] The focus was somewhat similar to that of the Chicago Area Project because of its thrust in a large inner-city area to reduce and prevent crime and delinquency. This multifaceted program had as one of its major goals the improving of coordination and cooperation between the existing social agencies of the community. In addition, the project attempted to identify and work with chronic problem families within the area who had histories of long use of public welfare services and other governmental programs. Workers were assigned to the area to develop positive relations with juveniles so that solutions to problem solving could be facilitated. Between June 1954 and May 1957 seven project field workers maintained contact with approximately four hundred youngsters between the ages of twelve and twenty-one.

A summary of the findings and an evaluation of the project indicate that there was no significant measurable inhibition of either law violation or unethical behavior as a consequence of project efforts. Even though the statistics and the evaluation of the project were not particularly encouraging, it was felt that the cooperation and communication between residents and agencies had been improved.

South Central Youth Project. The South Central Youth Project was established by the Community Welfare Council of Hennepin County (Minneapolis).[23] The project was directed by a planning committee which included executives of both public and private agencies. Like the Midcity Project, one of its major objectives was to make community agencies more responsive to community residents' needs. In addition, because of many interagency problems, services were not being adequately provided to youngsters and families within this area. The goal of the project was to detect the beginning stages of delinquency and to improve interagency communication and agency cooperation with community residents. Although it was felt tht some of the existing agencies within the community were effective, many residents were not receiving the benefit of community resources. These residents lived in the south central area of Hennepin County.

Most of these residents were socially and economically disadvantaged and did not know how to utilize community resources or operate within large bureaucratic structures. Because of these and other factors, they often did not seek the services of their community agencies. Consequently, the project focused on identifying those families that needed help but were not getting it so that resources could be provided. This project, like other programs mentioned, has not undergone rigorous evaluation. One of the conclusions reached as a result of the South Central Youth Project was that agencies established to service community residents are often ineffective. There is a lack of cooperation be-

[22] Walter Miller, "The Impact of a 'Total Community' Delinquency Control Project," in Giallombardo, *op. cit.,* p. 493.
[23] Gisele Konopka, "South Central Youth Project: A Delinquency Control Program (1955–57)," *Annals, American Academy of Political and Social Science,* 322 (1959), pp. 30–37.

tween the agencies themselves as well as a lack of communication between the agencies and the community residents. New insights were gained as a result of this project in regard to the process of developing linkage between the agencies and the community residents.

The Quincy Community Youth Development Project. The Quincy Community Youth Development Project also attempted to help youngsters in areas with high rates of delinquency.[24] After identification of these youngsters, an experimental and a control group were used in an attempt to evaluate the efforts of the project. The first efforts were directed toward placing children in foster homes as well as utilizing casework and recreation as alternatives for problem solving. The local school system was also involved in the project and two experimental classrooms were established, but the control group was given no special treatment. All the children involved in the project were ninth graders and were below the class average, and they had also done poorly in the eighth grade. The school experiences of these children varied greatly from those of normal ninth graders. Films, tapes, and articles from newspapers and magazines were used as text material. The students in the experimental group did not compete with other ninth grade students. The purpose of this approach was to make the learning process more interesting so that the students would become involved in a learning process and acquire useful skills.

Even though there was apparently only slight improvement in academic skills, personal adjustment, and dropout rates in the experimental group as compared with the control group, the youngsters in the experimental group did have a better job success rate as measured by the number of boys employed and their length of employment. The attendance records also indicated that they had developed a greater interest in school. There was also an indication that the rate of delinquency had dropped in the experimental group while it had increased in the control group.

Although the project attempted to reduce delinquent activity in the area, findings were inconclusive.

The Los Angeles Youth Project. The Los Angeles Youth Project was initiated in 1955 and focused its efforts on youngsters who were difficult to reach and influence.[25] The downtown south end of Los Angeles was used as the target area because of its high rates of delinquency, many health problems, low incomes, and poor housing. Youngsters in the community were contacted, and attempts at communication were initiated. The workers assigned to this area developed a relationship with the members of gangs as well as with other individuals so that the youngsters' needs could be identified and referral to appro-

---

[24] Paul H. Bowman, "The Quincy Community Youth Development Project," *Annals, American Academy of Political and Social Science,* 322 (1959), pp. 53–62.

[25] Estelle Aeston, "The Social Welfare Forum Proceedings of the National Conference of Social Work, Atlantic City" (New York: Columbia University Press, 1951), pp. 281–94.

priate community agencies could be made. It was difficult for the workers to communicate effectively with the youngsters and develop a positive relationship. Many families in the area were disorganized, and the social control processes both within the family and in the community were ineffective. Many youngsters in these families were hostile and resentful and joined groups within the community in an effort to escape unhealthy family situations. The concentrated effort of the Los Angeles project to identify youngsters and problems attempted, like other programs mentioned, to focus resources in areas of high rates of delinquency. Projects were then started to help the youngsters develop more socially adaptable patterns of adjustment. By focusing resources on families and youngsters who had multiproblems, it was also hoped that the number of unsatisfactory conditions contributing to crime and delinquency could be reduced.

The Central Harlem Street Club Project. The Central Harlem Street Club Project was operated under the guidance of the Welfare Council of New York City.[26] The council, a volunteer organization, was created in 1925 to act as a coordinating and planning center for welfare and health services in the boroughs of New York City. Financial support for the project was obtained from such varied sources as individual contributions and foundations. The project began in 1947 and ended in 1950. The target population was four gangs, whose membership ranged from thirty-five to over one hundred. Workers involved in the project contacted about three hundred members and frequent contact was made with about half of this number. The gangs selected were the most anti-social in the area, and they were involved in many delinquent activities within their communities. There was also much intergang conflict and fighting. Many boys joined gangs because of their need for the protection provided by the gang.

Much of the activity in a gang included loitering and was conducive to the development of unproductive and negative personal habits. The workers in the project attempted to influence gang members so that their activities would be more socially acceptable. Developing a relationship with the youngsters was often difficult because of the conditions that existed in Harlem and the resentment of the youngsters in the area.

This program was limited because of a lack of funds. Lack of resources hindered an intensive evaluation of the program, although the accomplishments listed showed that at least some negative behavior was altered because of the youngsters' relationship with the workers. Also, in some cases, more appropriate alternative modes of environmental adaption were presented to the boys.

The community-based programs that have been presented thus far have some characteristics in common. They were all initiated in areas of high crime and delinquency, and attempts were made to link community resources to area

[26] D. Molamun and J. R. Dumpson, "Working with Teenage Gangs," Welfare Council of New York City (New York, 1950).

residents. Many variations of programs and alternatives were developed as a result of these projects. More important, however, the focus and emphasis on providing resources in high delinquency and crime areas was seen as the major purpose of these programs. Because these efforts and similar efforts did not run the test of rigorous evaluation, it is difficult to gauge their merits. This is not to belittle the efforts of the communities that were involved in these projects, however. Often projects are not adequately evaluated and researched because of a lack of funds and long-range planning. Future efforts will have to be concerned with sound planning and have methods of evaluation built into the programs so that short- and long-term goals and effectiveness can be determined and the most successful aspects of the programs can be replicated.

The following programs are less ambitious efforts than those community programs already discussed, and their methods of problem solving are more specific.

Louisville Red Shield Boys Club. The Louisville Red Shield Boys Club was established to reduce rates of delinquency in the neighborhood. The club operated in an area where the socioeconomic status was low and the housing was substandard. The delinquency rate was high, and the club was the only major youth-serving agency operating within the area.[27]

The program was evaluated by utilizing census data in the area and determining the delinquency rate of youngsters between the ages of five and sixteen. The findings of the research indicated that the delinquency rate decreased rather steadily—from one out of nineteen boys in 1946, when the club opened, to one out of thirty-nine in 1954. The decrease in the delinquency rate in the area served by the club was in contrast to an increase in delinquency for the city overall where delinquency increased from one out of twenty-nine boys in 1946 to one out of eighteen in 1954. The decrease in delinquency in the study area was felt to be at least partly attributable to the activities of the boys' club. There was some skepticism regarding the direct amount of influence the club had had in reducing delinquency, because of some uncontrolled variables. Because the club was the major youth-serving agency in the area and the rates of delinquency were less for that area, it was concluded by the researchers that the club did in fact have an effect on rates of delinquency.

Carson Pirie Scott EE Program. The Carson Pirie Scott EE Program was developed in 1961 in cooperation with the Chicago Board of Education and the Ford Foundation.[28] The EE (Employment Education) program was established by Carson Pirie Scott, a large department store which employs ten thousand persons, after an effort to recruit young men and women for a variety of jobs pointed up a shortage of qualified personnel.

[27]"The Effectiveness of a Boys Club in Reducing Delinquency," Louisville Red Shield Boys Club, *Annals, American Academy of Political and Social Science,* 322 (1959), pp. 47–52.
[28]William Amos, Raymond Southwell, and Marilyn A. Southwell, "Carson Pirie Scott E.E. Program," in *Action Programs for Delinquency Prevention* (Chicago, 1965).

Company officials contacted the local superintendent of schools and were advised that one source of employment might be the large number of youngsters who either had already dropped out of school or had been identified as potential dropouts.

In the spring of 1961 the store began a pilot project in conjunction with the Board of Education and a grant to the school board of sixty thousand dollars from the Ford Foundation. The two major objectives were (1) the training of disadvantaged boys and girls in skills that would ensure their employment in the future and (2) education or study to complement the employment skills that were acquired. A training company was developed, and the trainees spent about forty-eight hours per week in the program, with three days on the job and two days attending classes. Two trainees were assigned to each job to ensure that the position would be filled for the normal work week. They were compensated at an hourly rate and also received raises for satisfactory performance.

The students were also involved in a training program to improve their personal hygiene and grooming and thus increase their employability after the program was completed. They were also given actual experience in retail merchandising by operating their own company, the "Gift Shop," for one month.

The pilot program ended in 1962; the regular program started in the fall of that same year. One hundred twenty-five boys and girls participated in the regular program, and since an evaluation indicated that the program was successful, the project was established on a permanent basis.

The Henry Street Settlement House. An attempt was made at the Henry Street Settlement House in New York City to prevent and treat delinquency through early identification of antisocial behavior. A predelinquent gang project was designed to prevent the development of new gangs in the area. One of the main purposes of the project was to involve parents and youngsters in joint problem solving in the community. It was felt that if children and parents would cooperate and work toward solving both family and community problems, delinquency rates would be reduced—a closer relationship would give parents more control over their children and more influence over their children's activities. The settlement house sponsored, in cooperation with the children and their parents, many activities and programs that could be carried out jointly. Clubs were formed with the guidance of the settlement house and the supervision and interest of the parents. The operation of the club was felt to have influenced delinquency rates in the neighborhood and to have reduced the incidence of negative behavior. As a result of the project, parents seemed to exert more influence over their children and take more interest in their activity.

It would seem then that when adults, particularly the parents, close ranks and stand together, the very ground that these children travel from home to various parts of the neighborhood becomes more solid.[29]

[29] Ruth S. Tefferteller, "Delinquency Prevention through Revitalizing Parent-Child Relations," *Annals, American Academy of Political and Social Science*, 322 (1959), pp. 69–78.

The Fuld Neighborhood House. The Fuld Neighborhood House of Newark, New Jersey, attempted to identify a target population of boys fourteen to seventeen years of age who had social and emotional problems and had also been involved with the police because of minor offenses.[30] A trained group worker made contact with the neighborhood boys to try to develop a positive relationship with the boys and influence their behavior. The program operated on the premise that the boys viewed their environment as hostile, negative, and manipulative; consequently, they attempted to achieve power and status through negative and devious methods. In the six-week summer program conducted in 1957, the boys became involved in work programs under the supervision of a park commission foreman and a group worker. The organization of the program in its initial stages had some difficulty in that there was not enough structure and coordination within the work program, and many of the boys rebelled and became involved in disruptive behavior. This created additional problems and made it more difficult for the group worker and the staff to communicate satisfactorily with the boys and influence their behavior into positive channels.

Even though the program did not always operate smoothly, it was felt that some positive gains were made and new insights developed. A program of this type, combining work experience and counseling, could undoubtedly be effective if the goals were identified, with sound planning and coordination between the different facets of the program. Sound guidelines and limits would have to be established so that the boys could operate within some structure. In addition, more aggressive leadership by both the group worker and the work foreman was necessary. The boys should also have realistic expectations in regard to the type of work they were expected to do and the quality of their output. Recreation could be a valuable complementary activity, but the boys should be able to choose the form and type of activity. In sum, although the work environment should be structured, the recreational activities should not be. The complementary relationship between recreation and an efficient work program could produce positive results and could have a positive effect on juvenile delinquency if the program was well planned and coordinated.

The preceding four programs described localized neighborhood efforts which attempted to work with socially and economically disadvantaged area residents. Different types of activities and alternatives were initiated, all revolving around the community-based house or center. Upon evaluation it was felt that most of these programs did positively influence the youngsters in the area and did help to reduce rates of delinquency. However, like other programs discussed, the evaluation was not rigorous and many of the variables were not controlled. Therefore it is difficult to realistically evaluate their success and definitely state they they did have a major impact on reducing crime and delinquency.

[30] A. Fried, "The Fuld Neighborhood House of Newark, New Jersey, A Work Program for Potential Delinquents," *Annals, American Academy of Political and Social Science*, 322 (1959), pp. 38–46.

The next six programs to be described are in some respects contemporary counterparts of the Chicago Area Project in that they attempted to mobilize the efforts of community residents in community problem solving. These six programs received support from the Office of Juvenile Delinquency and Youth Development of the Department of Health, Education, and Welfare. They were all based on the assumption that social, structural, and environmental pathology were major causes of youthful deviance.

> The projects varied greatly in size, geography and program—efforts were directed to the evaluating and examining a variety of issues relevant to community organizations represented within the six projects.[31]

Mobilization for Youth. One of the main objectives of the Mobilization for Youth project was to overcome the apathy and defeatism of the slum dweller through a system of self-help programs which attempted to organize the unaffiliated residents of the target area.

> The rationale was that youth could not be successfully integrated into socially constructive community life unless their adult role models (parents, etc.) themselves were a part of the community.[32]

The target selected was a sixty-seven-square-block area on the east side of New York, with a population of one hundred thousand persons. The goal of the project was to organize the various groups in this area into an effective source of power. It was felt that the individual in the community was unable to deal with poor housing, poor schools, inadequate police protection, and other issues himself and that in a coordinated group effort many of these problems could be dealt with and solved through pressure exerted by the "people's" organizations. This project met with resistance from one of the city's largest newspapers, as well as from many government officials. There was little cooperation or open acceptance by many governmental units and public officials within the community, and an investigation of the program did turn up irregularities, such as administrative difficulties.

Syracuse Crusade for Opportunity. The Syracuse Crusade for Opportunity was similar to the Mobilization for Youth project in that it attempted to coordinate community resource groups so that action programs could be initiated. The target areas were designated within the Syracuse, New York, area according to the number of problems that existed in various Syracuse neighborhoods. Problems characteristic of the neighborhoods included poverty, transience, and chronic dependency on such governmental services as the welfare system. The particular

---

[31] These six programs are described in Charles Grosser, *Helping Youth, A Study of Six Community Organization Programs,* U.S. Department of Health, Education, and Welfare, Office of Juvenile Delinquency and Youth Development.
[32] *Ibid.,* p. 7.

target area was chosen because of the many pathological conditions that existed. The project's major emphasis was on a community development approach, with the residents themselves becoming responsible for changing the character of their neighborhood.[33]

The crusade began by involving residents in elections to establish neighborhood boards. The boards constituted representation from the various target areas. From time to time these boards would have joint meetings to discuss certain issues and common problems and possible solutions to the problems. Friction did develop between the professional staff and the nonprofessional persons. Because of this conflict there were problems in decision making, with both groups wanting the major voice. Lack of administrative direction and sound decision making did affect the operation of the project, although some of the programs which were established to focus on teen-agers and develop teen-age activities did appear to have a positive impact.

United Planning Organization. The United Planning Organization project focused on a high delinquency area of Washington, D.C. A strong relationship between juvenile delinquent activity and socioeconomic conditions was thought to exist in this area, which contained many youngsters who had come in contact with the juvenile justice system. Because the opportunity structure within this area was obviously not conducive to the youngsters' achieving their goals and satisfying their needs in a socially acceptable manner, it was felt that better community coordination and more efficient delivery of services from community agencies would solve many of the problems.

The development of self-help organizations and the involvement of citizens in community decision making were encouraged. Citizen involvement in problem solving was felt to be one of the answers to developing awareness of the problems and fostering community participation.

Neighborhood centers were developed to filter information about the problems of the community to residents and serve as headquarters for disseminating information. One of the strategies of the project was to change the attitudes of both the residents and the institutions established to serve them. It was estimated that at the peak of the project there were twenty-five block clubs as well as many other organizations working to solve the problems of the area. Better leadership and more active citizen involvement resulted in some projects being more successful than others.

The decentralized approach to decision making and administration was felt to be more conducive to citizen involvement than a centralized orientation. One of the shortcomings of the decentralized approach, however, was that communication channels were often garbled and therefore coordination between different projects and citizen groups was difficult. One of the most interesting aspects of the program was the wide acceptance and use of credit unions owned and operated by community citizens who lived within the target

[33] *Ibid.,* p. 21.

area. Before the United Planning Organization, there was only one credit union for the poor. After the success of the community-operated credit union, similar credit unions emerged in the community and were supported by the residents.

This project also emphasized the solving of practical problems such as housing and unemployment. One of the major efforts was the development of a housing project. United Planning Organization did encounter some administrative difficulties, as did the Syracuse Crusade for Opportunity and the Mobilization for Youth programs.

Houston Action for Youth. The Houston Action for Youth program was similar to the United Planning Organization program in that it was a self-help neighborhood effort that focused on a densely populated target area. The program depended on citizens who had the time and the motivation to devote to community problem solving. Most of those persons involved in the project were from the stable working class in the densely populated areas of Houston, Texas. Self-determination and self-expression were seen as the major goals of the program.[34]

Because of the size of the target population and its density, there was a proliferation of community organizations. To combat this problem, many small neighborhood groups were brought together in three area councils. Members from the various groups comprised the board of directors. The thrust of the project was to use low-pressure tactics in solving area problems rather than confront the local government directly. It was felt that confrontation would only create ill will and hinder cooperation. The organization took the position that only through cooperative effort between the community citizens and the community agencies could power be used effectively. Many different types of projects were developed. The success of a project depended on the amount of involvement of the community residents and the degree of cooperation between the agencies and the residents.

Action for Appalachian Youth. The Action for Appalachian Youth program focused on an area near Charleston, West Virginia. The basic premise was that value conflicts between urban and rural society were a source of much tension, strain, and frustration. This supposedly creates a system where there is a lack of "meshing" between persons within the same environment, and this lack of meshing creates conflicts which in turn contribute to social problems like delinquent behavior.[35]

The residents of the target areas were difficult to reach because of such geographical factors as mountains, ridges, and creeks. It took a great deal of physical endurance even to make contact with the residents. Furthermore, because of long years of isolation, the people had developed a life-style much different from that of "conventional persons," which made communication

---

[34] *Ibid.,* p. 30.
[35] *Ibid.,* p. 37.

very difficult. Each target "hollow" was assigned a neighborhood worker. The worker's presence was difficult to explain because there was no precedent for such a program. It took a long time to become acquainted with the residents.

Some of the main concerns of the residents were the need for better roads and increased recreational facilities. As a result of assistance provided by the worker, various improvement associations evolved with elected officers, committees, and regular meetings.

Numerous problem issues were raised and discussed at these meetings, and petitions were circulated to elicit public opinion and support.

Each neighborhood improvement association sent delegates to a general council which functioned on a countywide basis. A technique of the neighborhood staff worker was one of nonintervention—a nondirective approach was used with the community. Some workers questioned this role because they felt that a more active, aggressive approach was needed to help solve problems in these isolated backward areas. The project and the contact of the worker with the community facilitated communication, problem delineation, and in some cases problem solving.

The HARYOU ACT. The HARYOU ACT (Harlem Youth Opportunities, Unlimited, Associated Community Teams) was initiated in Harlem, New York, a target area of a quarter million people, 94 percent black, living in a three-and-a-half-square-mile urban area. The program attempted to increase the chances for the youth in the community to lead productive lives and develop socially acceptable types of behavior.[36]

Even though the goal of the program was commendable, it did encounter difficulties in administration and pressures were exerted by various interest groups. There was also competition within the program itself, and "too much was expected too fast."

The massive problems that existed in the Harlem area, along with the administrative and pressure group difficulties, hindered the effective operation of the program.

Unfortunately, many of the potential positive results of the last six programs described were neutralized by inefficient administration, internal problems, and conflict between community interest groups. The actual positive results are also difficult to determine because the areas in which the programs were focused had many massive problems.

Ideally, programs of this kind could do much to solve community ills and help reduce crime and delinquency; however, many of the goals initially established are not achieved. If methods of research and project evaluation were built into all projects dealing with community improvement and crime and delinquency problem solving, the positive and negative aspects could be clearly identified. When program results are not identified, it is difficult to induce community involvement and obtain financial support from the governmental

[36] *Ibid.,* p. 44.

structure. When there are not sound methods of administrative control and a clearly defined goal orientation, many internal difficulties arise and overall sponsorship of the necessary governmental and private units is difficult to obtain. Although one should be skeptical of the operation of some of these projects, this should not detract from the major impetus and idealistic focus of the programs. The goal orientation, and the enthusiasm and motivation, are often commendable.

All the programs discussed thus far can be considered mainly pure prevention efforts, in that their major focus is an attempt to alleviate conditions that breed crime and delinquency by involving community residents in problem solving and decision making. The youngster is assisted before he comes in contact with the formal juvenile justice system. The final discussion of pure prevention will identify a few additional efforts at delinquency prevention. These efforts are different from those already examined in that their focus is not as rigorous, nor is the target population as massive and disadvantaged by poverty conditions. The following programs, although they are believed to contribute to delinquency prevention and control, have in many cases not been thoroughly evaluated and researched.

Additional Pure Prevention Programs.

Police-School Liaison Programs. The police-school liaison concept is relatively new and has been introduced into various schools throughout the country. Two of the earliest programs originated in Michigan—one in the Flint Police Department and the other in the Michigan Department of State Police. Both departments were concerned with the alienation and hostility that existed between police and youngsters. It was felt that a police-school liaison program could improve communication between the two groups.

A police-school liaison program is initiated when an officer is assigned to a school to act as both a law enforcement officer and a resource person who can also be a counselor. He can listen to student problems, help coordinate efforts to reduce delinquent activities, and foster better understanding between the police and adolescents. The specific duties of the officer will depend on the police department and the school system to which he is assigned.

> The generally stated purpose of such a program is to instill in the pupils a greater appreciation and a better and more positive understanding of the nature of policemen and their work. It is intended that this appreciation of law enforcement and its necessity will help to decrease the number of juvenile delinquencies. It is reportedly a format for building positive police/community relations with that segment of the population just entering an age where attitudes are beginning to crystalize and where a negative attitude toward law enforcement can be most dangerous.[37]

---

[37]Charles L. Weirman, "A Critical Analysis of a Police-School Liaison Program to Implement Attitudinal Changes in Junior High Students" (Master's thesis, Michigan State University), p. 9.

Shepard and James list five objectives of a police-school liaison program: (1) to establish collaboration between the police and the school in preventing crime and delinquency, (2) to encourage understanding between police and young people, (3) to improve police teamwork with teachers in handling problem youth, (4) to improve the attitudes of students toward the police, and (5) to build better police and community relations by improving the police image.[38]

The program in Flint, Michigan, can be considered the forerunner of police-school liaison programs, although the city of Atlanta reports that it had officers assigned to the school more than thirty-six years ago; the duties of these officers, however, were not typical of the duties of present-day school liaison officers.

The Flint program was sponsored by the Mott Foundation, which subsidized the program in its initial stages. Even today the Mott Foundation supports the Flint program, and there is now a liaison officer in each junior and senior high school in the city. Under the Flint concept, the officer is part of what is called a regional counseling team. This team is comprised of the dean of students, the principals of the elementary schools, and the principal of the high school, as well as the liaison officer. This combined approach is felt to be conducive to solving problems in a coordinated manner and keeping all agency personnel involved in the planning and implementation of programs that serve juveniles within the Flint area. The following quotation describes the Flint approach to police-school liaison:

> Let us use the example of the child who steals a lunch. The theft is reported; the accusation is made. The child confesses to the deed. In reviewing the child's background from files kept by each member of the team, the school nurse may discover the child has a history of illness; the dean may discover the fact that the child's grades had been declining. The community school director may be aware of the fact that he is not seeing the child participating in after-school activities as he used to; the principal may recall that the child's family has had minor disturbances in the past. The presence of a police officer with punitive power, although he may not use it in this instance, impresses the child with the seriousness of the wrongdoing. By coordinating their efforts and combining their knowledge of the case, the team can guide the child into safer channels.[39]

Many other programs have been patterned after the Flint program. Police-school liaison programs have been considered effective in preventing juvenile delinquency because of the following reasons:

1. An increase in information and improvement of communication between students and their families.

[38] George H. Shepard and Jessie James, "Police—Do They Belong in the Schools?" *American Education* (September 1967), p. 2.
[39] The Mott Foundation, "The Police-School Liaison Program," brochure prepared for distribution to interested agencies (Flint, Michigan).

2. An increase in information and improved communication between the schools and all other groups within the community.

3. Earlier identification of predelinquent children and earlier referrals of such types.

4. Improved communication between the police and the school personnel.[40]

Even though most comments about police-school liaison programs have been positive, there have been some negative reactions. Some of the criticisms have revolved around using students as informers for police, using police as disciplinarians, allowing police to carry weapons on school property, and indiscriminately questioning juveniles even though they have not been charged with an offense. Some persons just generally feel that the school and the police are incompatible.

It appears that fear of the police, which is one of the targets of change in the police-school liaison programs, is a primary reason for criticism of the concept. The detractors do not base their opposition upon actual transgressions but rather upon their perceptions of supposed police oppression. That is not to say that their fears could not be based on valid reasons of proven turpitude on the part of the police. There are too many obvious examples of law enforcement's ineptitude in working with juveniles in the past to hold that such views are completely groundless. The fact remains that the literature does not reflect actual reported malfeasance on the part of police-school liaison officers.[41]

There are other approaches that are similar to police-school liaison programs, but they have different names or somewhat different orientations. The "officer friendly" concept in the Chicago Police Department is one example. These programs are aimed at the primary grades and attempt to involve the students in a better understanding of police work and encourage them to be "community helpers."

Various studies have evaluated the police-school liaison concept. Weirman concluded that a police-school liaison program was effective. As a result of comparing a control group (without a liaison officer) with an experimental group (with a liaison officer), he found that whereas negative attitudes of children toward police increased markedly in the control school, negative attitudes of children in the experimental school, with few exceptions, remained relatively constant. Although the attitudes did not show a marked improvement in the experimental school, the officer nevertheless held his ground. As Weirman states:

[40] Minneapolis Police Department, "The Police-School Liaison Program," Final Report submitted to the Office of Law Enforcement Assistance regarding their grant 31, mimeographed, November 1968, p. 11.

[41] Weirman, *op. cit.,* p. 45.

Finding that the control school became more negative toward the police while the experimental school remained fairly constant does not indicate that the liaison officer was not successful and positively effective in changing the attitudes of the students of the school he was in. It might rather be interpreted to mean that had the liaison officer not been present attitudes would have become more negative toward the police during that same period of time.[42]

Weirman's study pointed out that negativism toward the police exists in even junior high school students. One method of combating this growing antagonism toward law enforcement and its representatives is the use of a police-school liaison officer. When police-school liaison programs are properly constructed and adequately supervised, they can be effective in changing youthful attitudes toward the police and indirectly influencing the rates of crime and delinquency in the particular school district.

Educational Programs. In communities throughout the United States, programs have been initiated that attempt not only to influence and change youngsters' attitudes toward the police but also to educate youngsters regarding the detrimental effects of using drugs and becoming involved in devious social behavior. Programs developed by some communities are staffed by young persons who attempt to prevent drug abuse by providing counseling services for youngsters who are experimenting with drugs. Educational information and counseling services are also provided for youngsters who may be considering experimenting with drugs, and both professionals and paraprofessionals are used. Psychiatrists, psychologists, social workers, counselors, teachers, parents, and both high school and college students are often participants in these programs. Assistance is also available from medical doctors, attorneys, and ministers, and funding is provided by governmental, private, and business organizations. The use of drug education centers indicates an awareness by the community that the most effective means of combating illicit nonmedical drug use—and saving youngsters the discomfort and agony related to drug abuse—is having the entire community become involved in drug education.

Communities throughout the United States are also placing an increased emphasis on programs for youngsters who are runaways. The runaway problem has become serious in many communities and specific programs have been established, often operated by youngsters themselves to help the runaway solve his problems. Homes for runaways give the youngster a chance to reflect upon his own situation and with the assistance and guidance of staff members, both professional and paraprofessional, develop new alternatives to problem solving other than flight. In most of the programs youngsters are encouraged to communicate with their parents or legal guardians to help promote more positive communication. With the assistance, guidance, and counseling of the staff, in

---

[42] *Ibid.,* p. 195.

conjunction with the cooperation of the parents, problems can often be resolved before they become serious.

Provisions are also made at these houses to allow youngsters to stay overnight if they have permission from parents, legal guardians, or the local detention home. Permission can usually be obtained by telephone. If the youngster stays longer than one night, local laws specify the procedure to be followed and the legal ramifications of extended residence. The administration of such programs will vary depending on the community, the legal limits of the particular jurisdiction, and the orientation of the house staff members. The important concept, however, is that innovative approaches such as homes for runaways can be helpful in reducing delinquency. The youngster can be helped with his problems before they become so severe that formal intervention is necessary.

Many communities have also attempted other educational approaches as well as residential and semiresidential programs to prevent delinquency and assist youngsters in problem solving. Some schools have developed programs that teach youngsters skills through innovative educational approaches while at the same time linking the school experience to the employment world. This provides the youngster with a practical approach to problem solving and increases his chances of being successful in his community.

In Flint, Michigan, a Personality Improvement Program has been initiated. It is sponsored by the Mott Foundation, the Genesee County Board of Education, the Probate Court of Genesee County, and citizen interest groups. The program is designed to help students eleven to fifteen years of age who are having school problems. The goals of the program are as follows :

1. To provide school activity during periods of public school suspension for disruptive students.

2. To remove disruptive students from public school classrooms.

3. To apprise the disruptive student of his potential service to society.

4. To place as many of the students back into the school setting from which they came with as positive an attitude as possible.

5. To provide support services from the Genesee County Probate Court to Flint community schools with incorrigible students.[43]

Some of the problems that the children who are admitted to this program may be encountering in school are generally disruptive-type activities, such as being unable to keep quiet during classroom presentations, not staying in their seats, talking out of turn, not doing homework, or manifesting other aggressive behavioral problems toward their fellow students and teachers.

If it is deemed necessary that the child be referred to the Personality Improvement Program, his school files for written permission to the probate

---

[43]"Personality Improvement Program of Genesee County" (pamphlet, Genesee County Probate Court), p. 1.

court, requesting that the student be placed in the program. The school then agrees to take the youngster back at the end of a six-week period. If the youngster meets the legal criteria, the court commits him to the Genesee County Children's Facility for a twelve-week period with the recommendation that he be placed in the Personality Improvement Program. The program emphasis is on helping the youngster develop more positive modes of behavioral adaption. The first six weeks involve a day-care program where the child is involved in behavioral modification classes. In the second six weeks the youngster is reintegrated into the public school. A counselor works with him by providing help and guidance to facilitate readjustment to the school situation.

The youngster returns to his home in the evening and commutes during the day. If the youngster happens to be truant, he can be detained in the Children's Facility to assure attendance at class.

Staffing of the Personality Improvement Program consists of a program coordinator and an assistant coordinator, a counseling service supervisor, two instructors certified as public school teachers, two counselors, and a secretary. This type of program is helpful in preventing delinquency by keeping the youngster constructively busy and acquainting him with new skills. It is unlike a detention program where the youngsters are often only held inactive for a period of time. In the Personality Improvement Program the youngster can improve such basic academic skills as reading, English, and mathematics. In addition, an experienced caseworker or counselor works with him on a follow-up basis after the initial six-week day-care program. The immediate goal of the program is to reintegrate the youngster into his public school classroom on a nondisruptive basis. The long-range effects of this program can contribute to the youngster's acquiring new skills so that his behavioral energy will be directed in more socially acceptable channels. The prevention of delinquency is often the result of this program.

The Lansing Police Department has an instructional program, the Community Youth Citizen Project, which attempts to help youngsters formulate new values that will alter negative attitudes and behavior toward authority. Because data reflect that much crime and disruption is caused by youngsters, it was felt that an education program that emphasizes the law, its history and definition, the role and duties of law enforcement, and the citizen's responsibility to his community would be helpful in reducing delinquency. The Community Youth Citizen Project is a joint effort between the Lansing Police Department and the Lansing Board of Education. The objectives of the program are as follows:

1. Prevention of crimes through understanding and communication between law enforcement agencies and the youths of the community.

2. To improve the image and stereotype of the police, family, school personnel and youth by promoting a better understanding of the role each plays in society.

3. To aid in the betterment of society through the understanding of the rights and responsibilities of citizenship.

4. To aid the student in identifying his role and responsibility in the community.

5. To aid the student in making moral decisions.

6. To reveal the intent and purpose of law and interpret its meaning.

7. To clarify the role of the citizen in the procedure and performance of law.

8. To advise the youngster in all phases of law.

9. To present the role and the procedure of law enforcement, encompassing all law enforcement agencies.

10. To clarify the functions of law enforcement in a democratic society.[44]

Five Lansing police officers are involved in the program. The officers are selected from a variety of units so that the department will have a well-rounded representation. Many types of educational aids are utilized, such as books, pamphlets, and audiovisual materials. The method of classroom presentation is flexible, depending on the officer and the method he is most comfortable with. Even games are sometimes used to get a particular point across to youngsters. The officer's presentation is made as interesting as possible to insure that the youngsters will pay attention to the speakers.

The topics that the officers discuss in the classroom include the reasons for laws, the way laws pertain to citizens, and the definition of law. There is a discussion of criminal and civil law, as well as a delineation of the consequences of a criminal record. The officer also describes the rights every citizen is guaranteed by the United States Constitution, the various branches of government, and the way they work to protect the citizen and make government an orderly process. Field trips are made to the various court facilities in the community so that the students can observe the different aspects of court administration and processing. Throughout the entire program the youngsters ask questions about the criminal justice and juvenile justice processes so that many of their misconceptions can be corrected.

One of the secondary benefits of the program is that the participating youngsters learn to relate to the police officer in a much more realistic manner. They learn to look beyond the uniform and to identify with the person who has been their instructor for many weeks. As a result of this closer identification with the officer and the instructional material that has been presented, youngsters have a much better understanding of the law, its function, and the criminal and juvenile justice processes. Programs of this kind can help alter the negative attitudes youngsters have toward police officers. An increased awareness of the

---

[44]"Community Youth Citizenship Project" (pamphlet, Lansing School District and Lansing Police Department), p. 2.

processes of law and a more positive concept of authority can indirectly relate to the reduction of juvenile delinquent behavior.

Programs like the Community Youth Citizen Project also give youngsters the opportunity to voice their opinions and make suggestions for improving the process of justice in their community. Such programs have a commendable orientation to problem solving, although there is usually little evaluation or feedback regarding the success of these endeavors.

Many other community programs could either directly or indirectly be considered pure prevention-type efforts. Even when the focus of a program is not on delinquency prevention, one of the secondary results is often the reduction of delinquency. Police athletic leagues, Boy Scouts, youth opportunity centers, youth assistance programs, recreational programs, vocational guidance programs, Alateen (a subsidiary of Alcoholics Anonymous), vocational rehabilitation, and YMCA and YWCA programs can also play a role in preventing and reducing juvenile misbehavior in the community.

The increased emphasis on involving youth in community problem solving and on developing closer relationships between youth and juvenile justice agencies, especially police departments, together with a total community effort at delinquency problem solving and a more effective evaluation of programs, will contribute to a more successful delinquency prevention.

All the programs discussed in this section are mainly pure prevention efforts—in other words, they attempt to prevent delinquency before it starts. The next section will emphasize rehabilitative prevention—working with the youngster after he has been exposed to the formal processes of the juvenile justice system.

REHABILITATIVE PREVENTION PROGRAMS

Most community and governmental efforts at delinquency and crime prevention emphasize rehabilitative prevention. The reason for the greater emphasis on rehabilitative prevention is not only because of the lack of commitment to, and the lack of resources for, pure prevention programs but also because many of the pure prevention programs have not had adequate evaluations, nor have they been objectively researched to determine their effectiveness. It is often difficult to convince the community legislators and the funding agencies that pure prevention programs should be initiated and developed, and therefore rehabilitative prevention programs receive most of the attention. Rehabilitative prevention, although at present necessary, would not be needed on a large scale if pure prevention efforts were prevalent and successful. Rehabilitative prevention also suffers from a lack of resources, and community programs are often merely sporadic attempts to deal with the problem once it has occurred. Because the problem has progressed to a very serious point by the time rehabilitative prevention is initiated, it is often difficult to successfully help the youngster.

All the following programs are rehabilitative programs. Some have been evaluated and researched and definite conclusions can be drawn. Others have not been rigorously evaluated, and therefore it is difficult to measure their successes and failures.

Institutional Rehabilitative Prevention

Institutions which house thousands of juveniles have become considerably more humane over the years. The lock-step, rules of silence, physical punishments, lengthy banishment to solitary confinement, and so on, have either been abolished or considerably modified. In modern institutions, residents are permitted to have radios, see movies regularly, are fed well, and receive good medical and dental care. Visitation policies have been liberalized and, in general, the resident is less isolated from his family and his community.

The nature of incarceration varies considerably from one jurisdiction to another in terms of the size, the architecture of the institution, the resources available for programs and facilities, and the nature of the resident population. Institutional populations range from several hundred to several thousand residents. The most common American prison for adults is surrounded by high walls and topped by gun towers at strategic intervals; it houses its inmates in tiered cell blocks and provides dining halls, work and recreation areas where prisoners are handled in mass fashion. A large percentage of the inmates in prisons are under 18 years of age. Camps and prison farms represent a less restrictive form of incarceration. County and municipal jails show the greatest variety in facilities, programs, and populations. Reformatories usually handle prisoners under twenty-five years of age and prisons and penitentiaries house more "mature" individuals, although some "juveniles" are still housed in prisons. Training schools are designed solely for juvenile offenders.

Institutional operations are subject to considerable outside pressure which waxes and wanes with the condition of society in general. In times of economic stress, for example, pressures for punitive measures are greater, institutional industries are curtailed because of the competition they pose for community industries, and expensive rehabilitative programs are cut back. At other times, various community organizations apply pressure for more therapy programs. The former result is the increased idleness of residents, which is characteristic of many American institutions, while the latter produces an upsurge in resident activity.

The largest number of institutional employees are employed in custodial activities. Business, clerical, and bookkeeping personnel manage the flow of goods and supplies into and out of the prison. Usually a small group of workers are designated as treatment personnel. Of these, an even smaller number are actually assigned to activities that might be termed rehabilitative in nature. These include psychiatrists, psychologists, social workers, chaplains, and teachers.

Subsequent to incarceration, an offender, either juvenile or adult, is usually assigned to a diagnostic center or classification unit where he is interviewed and tested and where his record is reviewed so that the appropriate decision regarding custodial and program assignments can be made. Educational and vocational programs are available in many institutions. The vast majority of residents, however, are assigned to jobs maintaining the institution or in the manufacturing of clothing or shoes for other state agencies, road signs, license plates, and so on. Younger residents usually attend school at least part of the time.

Although the custodial function is still primary in the many American institutions, an ever greater number are becoming treatment oriented. These are characterized by a more relaxed, less coercive social climate than the more traditional facilities. Staff is encouraged to be receptive, passive, tolerant, and relaxed. Treatment workers are more or less influential, depending upon the purposes for which they were hired by the top-level administration. They can be integral components of the institution or mere "window dressing" to pacify some pressure group or other. Often staff and treatment workers work at cross-purposes with one another, the former primarily concerned with security and considering the latter a threat to it. Treatment workers consider a preoccupation with security measures detrimental to rehabilitation. Because of the relative newness of the treatment orientation, relations between staff and treatment workers are confusing at best and are often actually hostile.

The "code" generally requires residents to cooperate with one another in defiance of institution authority, thus resistance to treatment exists to a greater or lesser degree according to the nature of the population and the climate of the institution.

The institutionalization of most juveniles is usually effected by remanding them to training schools. However, as mentioned earlier, "juveniles" in large numbers are residents in adult prisons. Training schools are ordinarily considerably smaller than adult prisons and are organized along different lines. They normally have no walls and a dozen or more juveniles are housed in a number of smaller dormitory-like buildings called "cottages." These are complemented by a variety of additional structures, such as a school building, vocational shops, and other structures to lend the institution the appearance of a boarding school. Most residents are placed in an academic or vocational program, some work in the maintenance of the institution. The primary emphasis in many juvenile institutions is, as in adult institutions, custodial, rather than rehabilitative. Here, also, relationships between custodial and treatment personnel tend to be tense, with the treatment-oriented schools more conflict-prone than the strictly custodial facilities. A code of resident conduct, similar to that of adult prisons, inhibits relations between the juveniles and their keepers and treaters. Since the peer group is the most significant determinant of juvenile behavior, its nature influences both the form and the results of treatment.

In regard to the function of training schools or juvenile institutions, the Children's Bureau of the Department of Health, Education, and Welfare states that

The prime function of a training school is to re-educate and train the child to become a responsible, well-adjusted citizen—leading figures in the field believe that the main purpose of institutional placement today is treatment and the training schools must be essentially treatment institutions with an integrated professional service wherein the disciplines of education, casework, group work, psychology, psychiatry, medicine, nursing, vocational rehabilitation and religion all play an important role. Through such an integrated program the child is expected to learn self-discipline, to accept more responsibility and act and react in a more socially acceptable manner.[45]

All states have at least one facility for the treatment of youngsters within an institutional setting. Michigan, for example, has a complex of institutional arrangements which are a division of the Department of Social Services. Institutions are located at various sites in the state, and there are varying degrees of custodial supervision, depending upon the needs of the youngster and the seriousness of the behavior problem. For example, there is a closed facility at Whitmore Lake, Michigan, where youngsters who have severe behavior problems are housed. There are also more open facilities for youngsters who do not need the intense supervision necessary under the Whitmore Lake program. In addition to these facilities, there are camp programs, as well as halfway houses and group homes, for those youngsters who do not have to be removed completely from the community but cannot be permitted to stay in the community on probation or some other minimal supervision program. All these facilities attempt to provide the youngster with training and education he can utilize on his release. He also receives counseling to help him conform to the demands of the community and adjust more satisfactorily to his environment.

As for juvenile institutions, it is far better to find alternatives for the youngster rather than place him in a closed setting. The less the youngster is exposed to the formal processes of the juvenile justice system, the greater are his chances of satisfactory adjustment in the community, and the less stigmatization will be a factor in future delinquent behavior. Some youngsters cannot tolerate the freedom of the community and need the closed setting of an institution. Institutions, however, often suffer from a lack of resources and trained personnel and should be used only sparingly and when other alternatives are not available.

In view of the above realities concerning institutions, plus the statistics on recidivism, which show that incarceration tends to promote and harden offender attitudes and behavior rather than rehabilitate, thinking has evolved more and more to the position that institutions, as they are now constituted, are hardly appropriate settings for therapeutic endeavors. According to some experts, the best that can be expected of institutions is that they successfully implement programs which are valuable adjuncts to treatment, such as humani-

---

[45] *Institutions Serving Delinquent Children: Guides and Goals,* U.S. Department of Health, Education, and Welfare, Children's Bureau (1975), p. 3.

tarian handling of inmates, vocational and educational training, religious activities, recreational participation, and prerelease planning. The actual treatment, which constitutes a basic modification of behavior and attitudes, is probably best effected outside institutional walls. Whenever possible, alternatives to incarceration are recommended. The National Advisory Commission on Criminal Justice Standards and Goals, for example, recommends the following:

> Each local jurisdiction, in cooperation with related state agencies, should develop and implement by 1975 formally organized programs of diversion that can be applied in the criminal justice process from the time an illegal act occurs to adjudication.[46]

At present, more than two-thirds of all convicted offenders under correctional control are in the community. The "treatment" afforded them, however, is often more illusion than reality.

Needless to say, not all offenders can remain in the community subsequent to conviction. There are those who represent a real threat to community security. In other cases, public opinion demands retribution even though the offender is relatively harmless to others. In any case, there will probably always be a need to incarcerate a certain number of persons. Institutional reforms need to be implemented so that these individuals are not further alienated from society since approximately 98 percent of them will return to the community. Society, thus, has a large stake in the outcome of their exposure to incarceration. The more or less frequent institution riots of the last twenty years have drawn public attention to American penal institutions. Often penal reform has been the result. The most noteworthy disturbance, the Attica, N.Y., riot of September 1971, which claimed forty-three lives, resulted in a plethora of reforms in that institution. These can perhaps be best noted in the prison's budget appropriation, which was increased from $94 million in 1971 to $169 million in 1974.

The institutions of the future, as envisioned by the President's Task Force on Corrections, should remove some of the current isolating effects of incarceration thereby facilitating the difficult transition back into the community for those who have been imprisoned. The Task Force envisions a completely new kind of correctional institution:

> This would be architecturally and methodologically the antithesis of the traditional fortress-like prison, physically and psychologically isolated from the larger society and serving primarily as a place of banishment. It would be small and fairly informal in structure. Located in or near the population center from which its inmates came, it would permit flexible use of community resources, both in the institution and for inmates released to work or study or spend short periods of time at home . . . It

[46]National Advisory Commission on Criminal Justice Standards and Goals, *Corrections,* (Washington, D.C., 1973), p. 95.

would receive newly committed inmates and carry out extensive screening and classification with them. For those who are not returned quickly to community treatment, the new institutions would provide short-term, intensive treatment before placing them in the community under appropriate supervision. Still other offenders, after careful diagnosis, would be sent to higher custody facilities required for long term confinement of more difficult and dangerous inmates. But they might eventually be returned to the small facility as a port of reentry to the community.[47]

In order to maximize inmate participation in treatment programs, the report further recommends that inmates be handled in a more individual and humanitarian fashion and be permitted to cooperate in making the decisions which affect their destiny. This increases communication between the inmates and the custodial staff and breaks down the adversary type relationship between the keepers and the kept, which is presently the rule. Collaboration has, for example, been particularly effective in group counseling sessions in which inmates can help each other by hard and insistent demands for honesty in self-examination.

Stimulated by federal government and increased citizen involvement, American institutions are presently in a state of ferment. Experimentation in the handling and treatment of both adult and juvenile inmates is taking place with increasing frequency and intensity. Following are descriptions of a few of the more interesting and progressive institutional programs that have been started in recent years. Not all the programs described can be considered treatment in the strict sense. Some are merely adjuncts to treatment, but they illustrate nevertheless the direction that American corrections is taking.

The *Behavior Management Program of the Shelby County, Tennessee, Penal Farm* was instituted in 1972 with a grant from the Law Enforcement Assistance Administration. It attempts to identify and positively reinforce those behaviors which are deemed appropriate for successful functioning in society. Appropriate behaviors are reinforced by awarding a number of points commensurate to the behavior. In addition to learning what behavior society expects in this manner, educational opportunities, counseling, and employment are provided for participating inmates.

The individuals in the program also earn points for appropriate behaviors in educational activities, group discussion, institutional work assignments, athletic activities, dormitory and personal hygiene, and social behaviors with peers and staff. The points earned may be exchanged for telephone calls, movies, television time, stereo music, magazines, football games, special trips into the community, and so on. Careful records are maintained to evaluate the progress of each individual. An employment and placement service constitutes the final phase of the program.

---

[47] The President's Commission on Law Enforcement and Administration of Justice, Task Force on Corrections, *Task Force Report* (Washington, D.C., 1967), p. 11.

The focus of the Behavioral Management Program as stated by H. D. Harrison, Senior Counselor, is as follows:

> If a man is to change his antisocial or asocial attitude and behavior, he must know and understand the impact that his actions may have in a social setting. If these behaviors are to be followed by positive consequences, the individual must be able to recognize and to act out what is expected of him in that social setting. This becomes possible as the individual learns to make decisions and act in ways that are "best" for him.[48]

The *Feminine Development Program* for incarcerated female offenders is now offered to women in sixty-five prisons, jails, and juvenile detention centers. The program includes three courses: charm and job preparation, designed to enhance a woman's appearance and self-esteem to facilitate employment and job retention; guides for better living, which teaches the principles of motivation; and body dynamics, which teaches coordination, rhythm, and the art of relaxation. Follow-up studies show that the recidivism rate of women completing the program is less than half the normal rate.[49]

A highly successful vocational program for *keypunch* operators has been functional at the *Kentucky Correctional Institution for Women.* Sixteen keypunch and eight magnetic disc machines process state business daily in a bright, cheerful structure built by male inmates from the nearby state reformatory at LaGrange. According to Sue Ann Salmon:

> The working atmosphere is friendly and relaxed. Each inmate may wear ordinary street clothes. And like women in most business offices, some sport fancy hairdos and makeup while others opt for the more natural look . . . During fifteen-minute breaks in the morning and afternoon inmates enjoy a lounge area with free coffee and comfortable chairs.

In its first year of operation, the program was able to place ten out of twelve women trained in the program in jobs outside.[50]

The *Kentucky Department of Corrections* has established a novel incentive program to promote good behavior in state correctional institutions. Inmates on good behavior are permitted to make collect *long-distance calls* each month to friends or relatives whose names have been submitted in advance for approval. The program is still too new to provide accurate statistical data concerning its effectiveness but indications are that it raises morale and deters disruptive behavior. More importantly, it enables the inmate to maintain familial and

---

[48] H. D. Harrison, "Behavioral Rehabilitation," *Criminal Justice Digest*, Vol. 2, No. 3 (March 1974), pp. 4–6.

[49] Davida L. Epton, "Outer Appearance Can Change Attitudes," *Criminal Justice Digest,* Vol. 2, No. 6 (June 1974), pp. 11, 12.

[50] Sue Anne Salmon, "Punch, Not Clout is the Key to High Earnings in Prison," *Criminal Justice Digest,* Vol. 2, No. 2 (February 1974), pp. 2, 3.

community ties, reducing his isolation and, and it hoped, easing his transition from life in the institution to life in the community.

The *Massachusetts Correction Institution in Framingham* was one of the first in the country to *mix men and women residents.* It is a minimum security institution with a swimming pool and a full range of sports facilities. Males and females live in separate dormitories and romances are discouraged. The inmates are called "residents," wear their own clothes, live in cottages, and can decorate their cells as they please. Some even have their own color television sets. Most of the residents are serving short terms; they work outside during the day and return to the institution at night.

A program at the *Kalamazoo County Law Enforcement Facility* under the direction of Joseph P. Devine seems to have reversed the normal outcome of incarceration. Mr. Devine relates the abnormally low recidivism rate of the program participants (15 percent) to the length of stay in the institution: "The longer they stay, the better they get." The program puts emphasis on physical, intellectual, and emotional growth in a highly structured, disciplined, secure environment. Physical skills are important because of their relationship to energy levels and productivity. Reading, writing, and mathematics skills develop an inmate's intellectual ability. In addition, he is sensitized to interpersonal relationships so that he may learn to explore how he feels about where he is in relation to his world, to understand where he is in relation to where he wants and needs to be, and to learn how to get there.

> Each inmate is tested before placement in the program. From the analysis of test results, inmates are placed into individualized programs predicated on their specific physical, intellectual and emotional needs. As the inmate enlarges his repertoire of skills and advances to a higher level of functioning, he is rewarded with more privileges and given greater responsibilities. The inmate is never given more than he is able to do to preclude failure, but he is always challenged to do no less than he can do.

Besides training, the program helps the inmates find jobs, acquire vocational training after release and makes them aware of outside referral services.[51]

The *Federal Youth Center at Pleasanton, California,* will provide correctional programs for two-hundred-fifty male and female offenders between eighteen and twenty-five years of age. It has neither gun towers nor cellblocks. Inmates have individual rooms. Male and female offenders live in separate quarters housing one hundred or fewer inmates. They do, however, participate jointly in a wide range of educational, counseling, and training porgrams. Pleasanton is built on the premise that individuals can change, that they can learn and mature, that their individuality and human dignity can be kept intact and actually enhanced.

Achievement Place is a residential treatment program in Lawrence, Kansas, which is designed to rehabilitate delinquent and neglected youths. It operates

[51] "In Kalamazoo Rehab Equals Training," *Frontline*, Vol. 2, No. 9 (April 1974), pp. 4, 5.

on the premise that youthful deviant behavior is based on a lack of social, academic, self-help, and vocational skills rather than psychopathology. After being placed in the program by the courts, youths learn needed skills with the help of specially trained married couples who are "teaching parents." Six to eight youths live with the teaching parents in a family-sized home located in their own community which permits them to maintain contact with their own families and to attend classes in local schools. The teaching parents are trained to work closely with the parents, teachers and other members of the community.[52]

The *Georgia Prison System* is searching for seven thousand volunteers in an effort to involve private citizens and local communities in the state's corrections and post-release rehabilitation programs. The volunteers will act in various capacities but their main function is to be a friend to someone who really needs a friend, to provide moral leadership and good examples to offenders. The unpaid citizen volunteers, housewives, business people, factory workers, senior citizens, clergymen, students, and so on, bring distinct advantages into a relationship with an offender: they can draw on contacts and experience from outside the criminal and juvenile justice systems; they cannot be identified by the offender as representatives of the authorities that have judged and jailed him; they can operate with a vitality of conviction that is convincing and contagious because they are contributing their services not for money but because they feel they must.

One state utilizes prison inmates who work with retarded children in a program which has proved to be mutually beneficial.

Another innovative effort involves women from the Junior League who counsel male sex offenders.

The inventory of innovations could be continued almost *ad infinitum,* a fact which should suffice to illustrate that large segments of American society are making significant efforts to heal the gaping wounds of delinquency in our midst by developing programs for both youthful and young adult offenders.

Alternatives To Institutionalization

The most common alternatives to institutionalization, *parole* and *probation,* derive from the positivist school of crime causation. The positivists maintain that an offender has social, intellectual, or emotional deficiencies that can and should be corrected so that he may assume a productive role in his community.

Probation. Probation is a tool of rehabilitative prevention. According to Haskell and Yablonsky:

> The correctional system provides for the treatment and supervision of offenders in the community by placing them on probation in lieu of confinement in a custodial institution. In most cases probationers serve the

---

[52]"Youth Program Expansion Funded by Federal Government," *Juvenile Justice Digest,* Vol. 2, No. 10 (October 1974), pp. 5, 6.

sentence of the court under the supervision of the probation officer assigned by the court. The judge has broad powers in this situation and can
set the conditions of probation and the length of supervision. He maintains
the power to order revocation of probation, usually for a violation of one
of the conditions set by him or his agent or for the commission of another
offense. The effect of revocation is to send the prisoner to a custodial
institution.[53]

The specific administration of the probation program depends upon the
state and the jurisdiction. Although in many states probation is a part of the
court—a juvenile court, probate court, or some other court jurisdiction, one probation department may be quite different from another, depending upon the
jurisdiction. In thirty-two states juvenile courts administer probation services,
while in the other states there is a variation.

More than half the offenders sentenced to correctional treatment in 1965
(684,088 individuals) were placed on probation. It was estimated that by
1975 the number will be over a million. The average caseload assigned a
probation officer is usually around 75. The typical probation caseload is
usually a random mixture of cases requiring varying amounts of service
and surveillance.[54]

The probation officer can use a variety of techniques in counseling the
youngster assigned to him—vocational guidance, personal counseling, and in
some situations psychotherapy, depending upon the skill of the probation officer (see Chapter 9). It is obviously difficult for the probation officer to adequately serve a case load of seventy-five or more individuals. Much of the time
he has to establish a priority list to determine which youngsters are in greatest
need of assistance and must be taken care of first. In many jurisdictions the probation officer's major problem is "putting out fires." He has little time for counseling other than on a superficial level. It is, unfortunately, unusual for the
probation officer to have sufficient time and resources to adequately serve his
case load.

Pilot programs have been initiated which have attempted to provide sufficient resources so that the probation officer can be more effective as a result of a
reduced case load. For example, in Genesee County (Flint, Michigan) two different programs attempt to provide more effective and comprehensive services to
probationers. The first program, the Citizens Probation Authority, is a community probation program in which volunteers assist in providing services to the
probationer. Probation is used in lieu of full prosecution in the criminal court.
Even though this program is mainly for adult law violators, it can also be used
with juveniles. The program offers counseling and supportive services for a peri-

[53] Martin R. Haskell and Lewis Yablonsky, *Crime and Delinquency* (Chicago: Rand McNally
& Co., 1970), p. 432.
[54] *Ibid.*, p. 432.

od of up to one year. Volunteers provide most of the supervision. If the probationer successfully completes the program, the pending prosecution is dismissed and the offender can apply for the removal of the offense from his record. The major purpose of the program is threefold: first, crime prevention; second, volunteer participation in the processes of criminal and juvenile justice; and third, rehabilitation of first or early stage offenders without the stigma of conviction. Referrals can be made from many sources, but they generally originate from the prosecuting attorney's office or the municipal court.[55]

The second program that assists probationers in the Flint community, Positive Action for Youth, is financed by the Mott Foundation and operated by the board of education and the probate court. This program provides individualized counseling for in-school juvenile probationers on a more intensive basis than could be provided by just the probate court's probation department. The youngster is helped to utilize community resources and mobilize inner strengths and is made aware of the consequences of his behavior and the self-destructiveness of his delinquent orientation.[56]

The Citizens Probation Authority and the Positive Action for Youth programs are examples of how one community is attempting to better serve probationers by providing the necessary resources to deal with the problem. In the Flint programs the use of volunteers is very prevalent. The use of volunteers is also becoming acceptable in other communities throughout the country. This is one method of reducing the pressure on probation officers and involving citizens in the criminal and juvenile justice systems processes. Volunteer programs have been successful in many communities and can be a valuable resource for assisting the youngster, preventing delinquency in the community, and making citizens more aware of the criminal justice system process and their responsibility for helping it operate effectively.

In 1920 to 1940 court volunteer programs went thoroughly in eclipse; their return in about 1940 was hailed as a fresh discovery of a near-miraculous new problem cureall.[57]

The National Information Center on Volunteers in Courts has provided extensive information relating to the use of volunteers and the methods for proper administration. As the center emphasizes, only skilled leadership can insure the success of volunteer programs.

Parole is similar to probation in that they both handle offenders in the community and are generally organized along the same lines although the populations of offenders are quite different. Parolees tend to be more serious offenders with more hardened offender attitudes. They have been incarcerated in either a juvenile or adult institution and subjected to the institution "code" and

[55] Citizens Probation Authority (Flint, Michigan).
[56] The Mott Foundation, "Positive Action for Youth" (Flint, Michigan).
[57] Ivan Scheirer, *Catalog of Volunteer Program Leadership Publications* (National Information Center on Volunteers in Courts, P.O. Box 2150, Boulder, Colo.).

all that that implies. Probationers, on the other hand, are more often juveniles and first offenders convicted of less serious offenses and who, because of their offenses and past records, were not deemed an immediate threat to the security of the community at the time of their sentencing. As might be expected, given these realities, success rates of probationers are considerably better than those of parolees.

Although the decision to grant a parole is in theory based on an inmate's improved attitudes and behavior and his potential for success in the community, the paroling authority is seldom in a position, either by training or knowledge, to make an informed, individual evaluation of him. More importantly, statutes often limit the discretion of the paroling authority so that an offender must serve a certain minimum sentence before he is eligible for parole regardless of his attitudes and behavior. Moreover, community pressure is exerted on the parole board which prevents it from acting solely in the interests of the offender.

The use of parole varies considerably from one jurisdiction to another; some employ it extensively and others hardly at all.[58]

The use of probation is subject to the same vagaries as that of parole. Juvenile probation service is authorized by statute in all fifty states and Puerto Rico. However, in many states probation service is not uniformly available in all counties and localities.

Generally both parole and probation have three major functions to perform. The primary function is that of *surveillance*. The officer must maintain contact with the offender, his family, his school, and or place of employment to determine his adherence to the correction plan, to gauge his progress and generally to show interest and concern. Supervision of this nature should constitute more than a mere threat. Properly applied, it can aid the offender in determining his responsibilities and the expectations that society places upon its functioning members so that he will not repeat the mistakes of the past. Second, the officer must make the offender aware of those *community services* that are available to help him solve his individual problems. Third, the officer must *counsel* the offender and his family and other persons important to him to help them understand the conditions that led to the original deviant behavior with a view toward eliminating its underlying causes.

The current trend is toward increased use of parole and probation since they seem to offer greater promise for rehabilitation. Theoretically, the more intact community ties remain, the quicker and more complete the integration of the offender will be. Correctional treatment in the community permits an offender to confront his problems in the environment in which he eventually must succeed or fail. The National Advisory Commission on Criminal Justice Standards and Goals, cited earlier in this chapter, recommends the use of alternatives to incarceration whenever possible. That this practice is already fairly common is attested to by the fact that more than two-thirds of all convicted offenders are

[58] U.S. Department of Justice, Federal Bureau of Prisons, "National Prisoner Statistics: Prisoners in State and Federal Institutions for Adult Felons, 1964," *National Prisoner Statistics Bulletin,* Vol. 38, No. 11 (November 1965).

currently handled in the community. The treatment afforded them, however, is still more illusion than reality. The United States spends only 20 percent of its corrections budget and allocates only 15 percent of its total staff to service the 67 percent of offenders in the corrections workload who are under community supervision:

> Probation and parole officers have too much to do and too little time in which to do it. Over 76 percent of all misdemeanants and 67 percent of all felons on probation are in caseloads of 100 or over, though experience and available research data indicate an average of 35 is about the highest likely to permit effective supervision and assistance. At best, they receive cursory treatment from overworked probation officers who must also spend typically half of their time preparing presentence investigations for the court. In addition, their efforts are held suspect by employers, police, school officials and other community figures whose help is essential if the offender is to be fitted into legitimate activities.[59]

Despite these sobering realities, the following experiments are being implemented with varying degrees of success in an effort to increase the success rate of individuals who have come under the jurisdiction of the juvenile justice system.

Foster Homes and Group Homes. Foster home placement has long been utilized as an alternative to incarceration as well as a routine aspect of juvenile after-care. Increasing dissatisfaction with foster homes over the years as well as their unavailability has led to the development of group homes in a number of states. *Achievement Place* in Lawrence, Kansas, is one of the more successful of these. Its program was described earlier in this chapter.

The Halfway House. The "halfway house," an increasingly popular alternative to incarceration, was originally conceived of as an institution "halfway out" to help incarcerated offenders make the difficult transition from the rigid control of the penal institution to the freedom of the community. Recently it has come to be viewed as a potential alternative to imprisonment, an intermediate solution between probation and institutional control. A number of cities are experimenting with halfway houses as programs for misdemeanants both on probation and prior to parole in urban as well as rural settings.

Some halfway houses are large, single-family dwellings while others are located, for example, in a YMCA hotel. Most are in neighborhoods with mixed land usage, racial integration, and nearby transportation. Residents wear civilian clothes, secure work in the community, and gradually earn more freedom in the form of leaves and excursions until they are finally permitted to move out—although they might still be required to return for conferences with greater or

[59] The President's Commission on Law Enforcement and Administration of Justice, *op. cit.*, pp. 4, 5.

lesser frequency, depending upon individual progress and court order. Regular individual counseling and group sessions form an integral part of the treatment program. (Chapter 11 expands on the halfway house concept.)

College Student Advocates. When the state of Massachusetts summarily closed its correctional institutions for juveniles in 1972, a selected group of delinquents were placed on the Amherst Campus of the University of Massachusetts. The program was successful and has been continued. Participants are referred by corrections officials around the state. Only those involved in serious crimes such as rape, murder, or arson are not considered for the program.[60]

Youths are placed in a dormitory room with a student, who is called an "advocate." There is a two-week trial period to determine whether the youth and the advocate are compatible. The final step in acceptance into the program is a performance contract drawn up by the advocate and the youth. Included in the contract are rules for the youth and a description of the kinds of experiences and job learning situations in which the youth will be involved.

Student advocates take only two classes during the period of involvement with the youth and receive twelve additional credits for their participation in the program, which entails sharing their daily lives with the youth, including academic, social, cultural, and recreational activities. In addition, there are special programs for the youth comprised of an alternative school and special tutoring.

Only four of the first twenty participants in the program were involved with the police while living on campus. Two graduates of the program have entered the University as bona fide students.[61]

Counseling and Referral. Predelinquents of Santa Clara County, California, were traditionally remanded to juvenile hall and assigned to the custody of the probation department. Since 1972, however, a new approach in dealing with these youths has reduced lockups by 66 percent and recidivism by 24.2 percent. The probation department works closely with the police to familiarize them with existing community agencies and facilities. Officers are also given training in family counseling, psychology, crisis intervention, and techniques in working with juveniles. Most of the police departments involved in the program have one full-time diversion officer who visits the family after the incident to determine their specific needs. He attempts to resolve the problem in the home or school and if that fails, he recommends the services of nearby community agencies and facilities.

Learning Centers. The state of Washington has established five "learning centers" as an alternative to institutionalization for some 800 problem youths. The basic objectives of the centers are to maintain the offender in his community, thereby reducing the possibility of further alienation and to enhance

---

[60]"College Life Aids Juvenile Delinquents," *Target*, Vol. 3, Issue 5 (August 1974), p. 2.
[61]*Ibid.*

treatment by integrating the attitudes of parole counselors, who are primarily concerned with treatment, protection of the parolee's rights, and crisis intervention, and educators, whose primary interests are attendance, task completion, and appropriate behavior. The centers should permit concentration on the common goal of teaching new skills. Clients enroll in one of six basic programs:

1. Improvement of basic skills in mathematics and reading.

2. Education for reentry into school.

3. General educational development for students unable to acquire a high-school diploma.

4. Vocational development.

5. Employment placement.

6. Improvement of social as opposed to academic skills.[62]

St. Louis Home Detention. The St. Louis home detention program was designed as a rehabilitative alternative to institutionalization. It places youths, who would otherwise be incarcerated, under the supervision of a community worker. The youthful offenders are either returned to their families or placed in surrogate homes. No more than five youths are assigned to a community youth worker, who comes from the offender's community. Delinquents are placed in the program sometime between their arrest and the formal disposition of their cases. The objectives of the youth workers are to keep their charges available for appearance in court and to prevent the commission of further criminal offenses. Youth workers are free to structure individual programs as they see fit. They work under the direction and supervision of the Assistant Superintendent of Detention and are required to develop close working relationships with the probation staff.

The youth workers function in two-person teams; this permits them to relieve each other in individual cases; and they are assigned to specific areas of the city. They are required to maintain daily contact with each youth as well as with other persons with whom the youth has frequent contact. In addition, they are responsible for involving and supervising their assignees in various kinds of activities such as attendance at sports events, movies, bowling, and so on. A telephone answering service keeps the workers on call twelve hours per day.

During the course of the demonstration project, which ran from September 30, 1971, to July 1, 1972, there was not one instance of a youth not being available to the court. Only 5.15 percent of the youths committed new offenses, none of which was violent, 21 percent had to be returned to detention because their programs were not working, even though they did not commit new offenses. The estimated cost per child-care day of the home detention program was

---

[62] "Learning Centers Help Parolees," *Criminal Justice Newsletter*, Vol. 5, No. 17 (September 23, 1974), pp. 4, 5.

$4.85 as opposed to $17.54 in the detention facility. Moreover, the program was well received by the community.[63]

Court Referral. In order to better coordinate the efforts of the large number of competing programs for drug addicts in New York City, a Court Referral Project has been established as a central intake and referral system. Primary program objectives are to provide selected addicts with treatment instead of incarceration, to reduce the time spent by addicts in detention, and to create a central point of contact between the court and various treatment programs.[64]

Only persons charged with drug-related offenses are selected for the program. Those accused of grave crimes such as homicide, serious robbery, serious assault, residential burglary, and most sex crimes are excluded. Prospects are referred by the court or are approached in prisons and jails and interviewed so that their readiness for rehabilitation may be determined and a decision made as to which program is best suited to their needs. Approximately one-third of those interviewed are recommended for treatment. If the client is accepted in the program, his lawyer is notified. The latter then makes the necessary arrangements with the court and the client is referred to a treatment program which might comprise methadone maintenance, a halfway house, family therapy, and so on. Although recidivism rates have not yet been established, an average of 270 drug abusers are diverted from the criminal justice system in an average month.[65]

Family-Oriented Drug Counseling. In recent years a large number and variety of programs have been initiated to counteract the increasing frequency of drug abuse among American youth. The Youth and Family Alternative Program in Montgomery County, Maryland, differs from most in its emphasis on conjoint family counseling:

> The program incorporates two basic principles in its efforts to help youths with drug related problems. The first is that by involving all members of the youth's immediate family in a routine manner, changes can be made in his living environment which will enable him to better resolve his own problems, while also working to prevent the development of self-destructive or antisocial behavior among his siblings. The second is that involvement in the planning and programming of alternative activities provide a young person with satisfying and constructive experiences to replace the adventure and excitement of drug abuse.[66]

After a family volunteers to participate in the program, they are assigned to a team of two counselors who help them define their problems and establish

[63] Paul W. Kene and Casimir S. Zantek, "The Home Detention Program of St. Louis, Missouri," *Delinquency Prevention Reporter,* U.S. Department of Health, Education and Welfare (September–October 1972), pp. 3-6.
[64] "Court Referral Project Diverts Addicts," *Target,* Vol. 3, Issue 2 (May/June 1974), p. 7.
[65] *Ibid.*
[66] "Family Oriented Drug Counseling," *Target,* Vol. 3, Issue 5 (August 1974), pp. 5, 6.

goals for resolving them. This completed, the family as a whole is placed in their team's multiple family group. The youth is placed, in addition, in a youth group.

The family groups meet once a week for six months in an effort to facilitate communication among the members. The youth groups also meet once a week for six months. Here the counseling is focused on personal problems. The youth group also engages in recreational activities such as backpacking, rock climbing, cave exploration, camping and white-water rafting. Tutoring, and vocational and career counseling are also available to the participants.

Law enforcement officials attribute decreased recidivism rates and a 13 percent decrease in drug arrests in 1973 largely to the family-oriented drug counseling program.

Neighborhood Probation Service. The Neighborhood Probation Service in Minneapolis is based on the principle of providing probation programs for the client in his own neighborhood. It is located in a former bakery building in a minority neighborhood and employs four professional probation officers, six paraprofessionals, and twenty-five volunteers. The paraprofessionals and the volunteers are minority members who were recruited and trained specifically for the project. Each volunteer is assigned to one probationer. In addition the program provides referral service in job placement and training, housing, legal assistance, public assistance, drug dependency, and medical assistance. Alcoholics Anonymous meetings are held weekly at the center and a driver's license service for those charged with driving without a license has been established. The overall recidivism rate for probationers referred to the service is a very low 9.1 percent.[67]

Community Treatment for Parole Violators. The large number of parole violators routinely returned to institutions for an average of two years once cost the state of Ohio $5,000 per year each. In addition to the cost, recidivism rates were high. Seeking alternatives, three residential parole reintegration centers were established in 1972. They were designed to treat nonviolent parole violators within their own communities. Located in Cleveland, Columbus, and Cincinnati, each center is based on a distinct treatment model with the general objectives of improving the self-esteem of the violators, changing their negative attitudes, and raising their levels of aspiration. All three centers provide some variant of a structured environment. One maintains rigid control, another minimal custody and control, the third employs a medical approach. Treatment ranges from group interaction and motivational and achievement training to treatment for alcoholism and training in budget management. Community psychiatric and medical services as well as recreational facilities are used as needed. The average stay at a center is twelve weeks. Fifty-five percent of the residents are employed while in the reintegration program. As of July 1,

[67]"The Bakery Takes Probation Services to the Community," *Target,* Vol. 3, Issue 5 (August 1974), pp. 6, 7.

1973, of the sixty-three parole violators who participated in the program, only six had to be returned to prison.[68]

Other Alternatives to Institutionalization

In Salem, Massachusetts, District Judge Samuel E. Zoll has established the following penalties for juvenile offenses: for turning in a false fire alarm, 80 hours of polishing fire engines; for slashing trees, 40 hours of planting seedlings in town parks; for vandalizing a school, washing down school walls and writing an essay on citizenship.[69]

Although the employment of alternatives to incarceration is a relatively new development as a response to crime and delinquency, data on certain programs which show its effectiveness have been produced.[70] California's Community Treatment Project for Youthful Offenders, for example, was begun in 1961. Early in 1974 it was phased out. Data show that the arrest rate during parole for participants in the program was 63 percent lower than that of a similar group which subjected to the traditional institution-parole cycle.[71] A research study by Dr. Ted Palmer shows, however, that not all types of offenders did well; this finding underscores the need for a flexible approach somewhere between the extremes of total commitment to community corrections and total commitment to incarceration. Neurotic offenders seem to perform best in community-corrections programs whereas those who are power-oriented perform worst. The large number of passive-conformists show mixed results. Interpretation of the data show clearly that youthful offenders must be placed on a strictly individual basis.[72]

The Los Angeles Venture in Treatment. In addition to comprehensive probation and detention services within the Los Angeles County probation department, two special programs have been initiated. The first one is the Family Treatment Program.

> The Family Treatment Program is groups of boys and girls living together at the Juvenile Hall in special units, separate from the other children; like family units sitting down together perhaps for the first time talking about their feelings and thoughts in an attempt to change attitudes and behavior with the probation officer acting as the family therapist.[73]

---

[68] Community Treatment for Parole Violators," *Target*, Vol. 2, Issue 6 (November–December 1973), pp. 1, 2.

[69] *Newsweek* (December 23, 1974), p. 70.

[70] *Ibid.*

[71] "Community Treatment Was Success," *Criminal Justice Newsletter*, Vol. 5, No. 16 (August 1974), p. 4–5.

[72] *Ibid.*

[73] "National Strategy to Prevent Delinquency," U.S. Department of Health, Education, and Welfare, Social and Rehabilitation Service, Youth Development and Delinquency Administration, p. 4.

The Family Treatment Program was developed to cope with the chronic over-crowding in the juvenile halls and to take advantage of a negative situation. Sub-sidized by the California State Aid to Probation Services Program, the family treatment concept now operates in all three juvenile halls in Los Angeles County. The probation officer acts as the group leader and the catalytic agent to produce change and discussion "within the family." He is not only an authority figure but a parental substitute.

> In family treatment the family is seen as the dysfunctional unit. The goals during the six weeks of intensive counseling are to bring awareness, self-respect, identity, respect of peers, and to help the youth prepare for life as a mature and useful citizen. At the same time by opening up communication within the family and placing emphasis on relationships of all family members, the family as a whole and the therapist can explore and support the positive aspects within the family. The parents of the young-sters also meet in parent group sessions. This enables them to realize that they are not alone in coping with the problems of raising an adolescent in today's society. By interacting they learn of each other's solutions and this often helps them solve their own problems.[74]

The youngsters are allowed to go home on weekends, and after they are re-leased from the program, they can still receive outpatient counseling for a period of up to six weeks. The environment of the Family Treatment Program is con-structed to be as similar to the actual family situation as possible. This means that there are many aspects of the program—for example, reaction and educa-tional activities supplement the counseling. All facets of the Family Treatment Program are appropriately coordinated to provide the youngster with a well-rounded experience.

This innovative program utilizes both the internal resources associated with detention and community volunteers to increase programming effectiveness. Los Angeles County reports that 85 to 90 percent of all youngsters sent home following completion of the program are still living at home after six months.[75]

Los Angeles County uses volunteers extensively, and the second program it has initiated is called VISTO (Volunteers In Service To Offenders). The volun-teers learn firsthand about the problems of probationers. Many types of workers are involved in the program, including housewives, teachers, college students, businessmen, professionals, and senior citizens.

> VISTO seeks to aid the offender who is on probation without removing him from the community. To accomplish this, neighborhood volunteers are trained to work with probationers—both adult and juvenile. Commu-nity awareness and concern is created by the use of these volunteers. VIS-TO volunteers contributed an average of 10,071 hours a month. Out of

[74] *Ibid.*, pp. 4–5.
[75] *Ibid.*, p. 5.

the total time, 6,646 hours or 66% are utilized to work with probationers on a one-to-one basis and 1,875 hours or 18.6% are spent in working with the probationers in groups. An additional 1,550 hours are contributed to such activities as orientation and training, advisory board meetings, community meetings, and other tasks.[76]

Evidently volunteers have been effectively utilized in the Los Angeles programs and preliminary indications are that the programs have been successful.

The Provo Experiment. The Provo Experiment in delinquency rehabilitation was begun in 1956 in Provo, Utah, by a volunteer group of professional and lay people known as the Citizen Advisory Council to the juvenile court.[77] The program was funded by the court, and the research was financed by the Ford Foundation. The program accepted boys from all the major communities around Provo. Only habitual offenders fifteen to seventeen years of age were assigned to the program, and not more than twenty boys were admitted at any one time. The length of stay was specified by the court, and release usually came some time between four and seven months. The boys lived at home and spent only part of each day at Pine Hills, the program center. Otherwise they were free to interact in the community and participate in community activities. The program did not utilize any testing, gathering of case histories, or clinical information. The experiment was initiated because it was concluded that

1. The greatest part of delinquent activity takes place in a group—a shared deviation which is a product of differential group experience in a particular subculture.
2. That because most delinquents tend to be concentrated in slums or to be the children of lower-class parents their lives are characterized by living situations which limit their access to success goals.[78]

The treatment system of the Provo Experiment consisted of two phases. Phase one, the "intensive treatment phase," was an effort to create a social system oriented to the task of producing change. Phase two, "the community adjustment phase," was an effort to maintain reference group support for a boy after the intensive treatment of phase one. The boy continued to meet with his group periodically for discussions. Treatment was continued on an intensive basis, unlike traditional methods such as probation or parole where only periodic visits take place.

The Provo Experiment was an attempt to treat the youngster in an intensive manner while allowing him the freedom of the community. It was different

---

[76] *Ibid.*, p. 6. (For further information regarding these programs write Mrs. Patricia Hunsicker, L.A. County Probation Department, Public Information Office, 320 West Temple, Los Angeles, Calif.)

[77] Lamar T. Empey and Jerome Rabow. "The Provo Experiment in Delinquency Rehabilitation," *American Sociological Review*, 26 (October 1961), pp. 679–95.

[78] *Ibid.*

from probation in that the treatment orientation was mainly group counseling and group interaction. The youngsters assisted each other in problem solving, and they learned that the gang or group had a great deal of influence on their behavior. When they formally completed the program, they were aware of the negative influences that could be exerted by peer pressure. This awareness, it was felt, would help the boys avoid negative peer group situations. Also, because many of the youngsters who participated in the Provo program belonged to the same gangs, much of the delinquent activity of these groups would be neutralized. The boys began to use positive peer pressure to influence each other to become involved in more socially acceptable activities. An evaluation of the program indicated that recidivism rates for boys in this program appeared to be significantly lower than those for comparable boys who had been committed to training schools.[79]

The Highfields Project. The Highfields Project was started in New Jersey in 1950 because there was no adequate facility for youngsters on a short-term basis. It was believed that short-term treatment (not to exceed three months) would be more appropriate than long-term institutionalization for many juveniles. Guided group interaction was the major treatment method and was supplemented with a work and recreation program. The program of guided group interaction and exposure to work experience was directed toward providing the boys with increased work skills and broadening their perspective and alternatives to problem solving.[80]

Two evaluations have been made of the Highfields Project. In the first evaluation, which was made by McCorkle and others, it was determined that although 18 percent of the Highfield boys violated parole, 33 percent of the control group violated parole. The Highfields boys adjusted better over extended periods of time up to five years after release.[81]

In the second evaluation, which was made by H. Ashley Weeks, the Highfields boys were also compared with boys who had been sent to the Annandale Reformatory. Whereas 63 percent of the Highfields boys made a good adjustment in the community, only 47 percent of the control groups succeeded on parole.

The whole Highfields experience is directed toward piercing through the strong defenses against rehabilitation, toward undermining delinquent attitudes and toward developing a self-conception favorable to reformation. The sessions on guided group interaction are especially directed to achieve this directive. Guided group interaction has the merit of combining

---

[79] *Task Force Report: Corrections,* The President's Commission on Law Enforcement and the Administration of Justice (Washington, D.C.: U.S. Government Printing Office, 1967), p. 39.

[80] Lloyd W. McCorkle, Albert Elias, and F. Lovell Bixby, *The Highfields Story* (New York: Holt, Rinehart and Winston, Inc., 1958).

[81] *Ibid.,* p. 143.

the psychological and the sociological approaches to the control of human behavior. The psychological approach aims to change the self-concept of the boy from a delinquent to a non-delinquent. This process involves changing the mood of the boy from impulses of lawbreaking to impulses to be law-abiding.[82]

The success of the Highfields Project was one of the major reasons the Provo Experiment was started. An evaluation of the Provo Experiment indicated that 29 percent of the experimental group violated parole after fifteen months, while 48 percent of the control group which did not have the benefit of the treatment were parole violators.

The Youth Advocacy Program. The Youth Advocacy program of the Urban Coalition of St. Joseph County (South Bend, Indiana) attempts to divert youths from the juvenile justice system into alternative programs, reduce youth-adult alienation, provide more socially acceptable and meaningful roles for youths and eliminate the labeling of youths that creates negative consequences. The program offers a street academy as an alternative to traditional classroom education with emphasis on preparation for life and on work skills, a counseling center which provides individual, group or family counseling for walk-ins or referrals from community agencies, community service workers who attend youth functions and ride school buses to prevent disturbances and vandalism, and a lawyer and two legal interns who provide legal counseling for youths and defend youth interests through class action suits. The program is funded by the Youth Development and Delinquency Prevention Administration. Technical assistance is provided by the University of Notre Dame.[83]

The Focus Program. Runaway children have become an increasingly serious problem since the heyday of the youth movement in the late sixties and early seventies. More often than not these wayward youths come into contact with the juvenile justice system. The Focus program, housed in a rambling mansion on the outskirts of Las Vegas, Nevada, attempts to jolt runaway youths back to reality by employing methods adopted from the renowned Synanon drug rehabilitation approach. Focus tries to help build individual responsibility by teaching youths to come to grips with their problems. Every young runaway who comes to stay at Focus must contact his parents within twenty-four hours. A three-way telephone conversation involving parent, child, and counselor is arranged. The resident is also required to participate in group encounter therapy three days a week and to share in a variety of housekeeping chores. The youths themselves run the house, their individual responsibilities being gradually increased as they show the ability to handle them. A youth is required to leave the facility for any breach of the regulations. The average stay at Focus is short,

---

[82]*Ibid.*, p. v; also H. Ashley Weeks, *Offenders at Highfields* (Ann Arbor: University of Michigan Press, 1963).
[83]"Youth Advocacy," *Delinquency Prevention Reporter* (May–June 1972), p. 5.

just under three and a half days. In 1972, the program served 803 runaway youths of both sexes. Of these, 672 returned home, 99 others were placed in foster homes, with relatives or in temporary therapeutic live-in facilities. Eighty-two percent of the young people served by Focus have remained at home.[84]

Crime Prevention Measures

Although not the primary purview of this chapter, it might be informative to note in conclusion some *purely technical crime prevention measures*. The Public Safety Dept. of Dade County, Florida, for example, supplies speakers to groups interested in structure security and the philosophy of crime prevention from a physical standpoint. "Operation Identification" in St. Louis, Missouri, has reduced burglaries among participants by 88 percent. Residents obtain engraving tools and materials from the police department, engrave their license numbers on valuable property, and display the program decal on doors and windows. An Auto Guardian Computer, the size of a cigarette pack and mounted on the dashboard of a motor vehicle, prevents it from either being started normally or hotwired until the proper combination has been selected. The odds of anyone guessing the combination are approximately 8,000 to 1. At Indiana University, a small computer that monitors access to sensitive campus facilities creates a climate for honesty. People authorized to enter specific doors are issued badges for those entrances. The IBM computer "reads" information on a thin, magnetic strip on the badge, unlocks the door if the person has authorized entry, and records entry times along with the badge number that identifies the individual.

The use of mechanical devices like that mentioned above or newer and better locks and lights, although not a panacea or long-range solution, is a necessary element in any crime prevention effort.

The first priority in crime prevention should be primary or pure prevention, attempting to deal with the causes of crime and delinquency. The second priority should be rehabilitative prevention dealing with the youngster after he has had contact with the juvenile justice system. Mechanical prevention can be seen as the third priority. In many circles, mechanical prevention is viewed as the total prevention approach. Ideally, there should be a blending of the three approaches—pure, rehabilitative, and mechanical.

SUMMARY

This chapter has presented a sampling of the various prevention efforts that have been tried and are being used to prevent, control, and treat juvenile delinquency. Many of the programs discussed were *pure* prevention efforts—preventing delinquency before it occurs. Other programs were a combination of pure prevention

[84] "Focus Project Helps Runaways Understand Their Problems," *Youth Reporter* (December 1973), pp. 1, 3-6.

and rehabilitative prevention—treating both youngsters who have come in contact with the juvenile justice system and those who have not. The last programs
described were those established mainly for youngsters who have come in contact with the juvenile justice system and who need rehabilitation and treatment
so that future delinquent behavior will not be manifested in the community.

The next chapter, "Methods of Treatment," will discuss treatment approaches, counseling methods, and other therapeutic strategies. Just as it was
pointed out in this chapter that there are many prevention-type programs, the
next chapter will examine a variety of approaches and techniques of treatment
that have been tried and are being used with youngsters.

QUESTIONS AND PROJECTS

Essay Questions

1. Differentiate between pure *and* rehabilitative *prevention.*

*2. It is recognized that pure prevention is more effective in dealing with
delinquency than rehabilitative prevention. Why, then, are there not more
pure prevention programs?*

*3. Compare the advantages and the disadvantages of probation versus in-
stitutionalization.*

4. What is the difference between punishment and incarceration?

*5. Should police officers be placed in schools through police-school
liaison programs?*

Projects

*1. Develop a network of community-based programs for youthful offen-
ders for your community.*

*2. The child spends more time in school than in any other community in-
stitution. Develop a school program that specifically attempts to prevent
delinquency.*

*3. Identify duties and functions within the juvenile justice system that
can be effectively performed by volunteers.*

chapter 9

Methods of Treatment

Specific methods of treatment in handling the juvenile are used both in formal prevention, control, and treatment programs and in the agencies that deal with him while he is in the community. Many approaches and methods can be used in treating the delinquent. Most of the methods have a theoretical orientation, and they relate to the theories and assumptions about human behavior that were discussed in previous chapters. For example, the psychoanalytic and psychiatric method of treating the youngster is the outgrowth of research that emphasized the intrapsychic interplay of the dynamics of the individual and the forces that determine his behavior.

The various treatment methods to be described are strategies that attempt to change those conditions thought to be causative factors in juvenile delinquency.[1] Even though an approach can take many forms, it can usually be classified as either an individual approach to treating the offender or a group approach where the offender is treated within the constellation of the group and among his peers. A third category of treatment, punishment, is not as prevalent today as in the past. Although those who prescribe punishment as a method of treatment in itself feel they can justify their position, it will not be considered in this chapter as a viable technique of treatment. The rationale underlying the use of punishment is that pain serves as a deterrent to further criminal action. Punishment, as an end in itself, is often used when staff are untrained and when more appropriate methods of treatment are unknown. In the context used in the present discussion, punishment is not to be equated

[1] Paul Lerman, *Delinquency and Social Policy* (New York: Frederick A. Praeger, Inc., 1970), p. 37.

with the setting of limits or the transmission of expectations with resulting enforcement of restrictions or reprimands if reasonable expectations are not adhered to. The setting of limits and restrictions and reprimands are a necessary element in any method of treating and handling the youngster. They can be effective supplements to the major treatment approach utilized. It is when punishment or restriction becomes an end in itself that it cannot be justified or regarded as effective "treatment."

The two basic approaches, then, when dealing with youngsters, are the individual and the group method of treatment. The individual method is generally used by psychiatrists, psychologists, and social workers, while the group method involves school teachers, recreation specialists, and social workers. It is difficult, however, to classify professions by method because psychologists often use the group method, while social workers and even some sociologists use the individual method. There is also a blending of the individual and the group work approach, with the possibility that the same person will be using both the individual and the group method. The method that the therapist or the counselor selects usually fits his professional training, his personality, and his clientele. Even though a combination of approaches will generally be used, one major orientation will be taken, with specific assumptions about human behavior.

Knowledge of the various approaches for treating and rehabilitating the lelinquent or the predelinquent is important for the professional within the juvenile justice system. Regardless of the phase of juvenile justice that he is involved in (police work, social work, courts, probation, parole, corrections, research), an awareness of treatment methods and strategies will familiarize him with the many approaches, the current terminology, and the assumptions about human behavior made by other professionals in the juvenile justice system.

Although the police officer, for example, may not use or be trained to use many of these methods and may not even agree with their orientation, knowledge of them will give him greater insight into the reasons why his professional counterparts in other agencies take their particular orientation to delinquent behavior problem solving. Furthermore, exposing all the different professionals within the juvenile justice system to the various treatment approaches and strategies may be instrumental in the development of an orientation that will be generally normative and acceptable to all the various professions. A more coordinated and normative orientation to treating the delinquent would be conducive to providing a consistent approach to delinquency problem solving.

Because of the many treatment methods, the professional soon learns that there is no "right way" to treat the youngster and that many approaches have merit. This allows him to select the approach or the parts of many approaches that he feels will be most effective and beneficial for his client.

As pointed out earlier, it is difficult to correlate specific approaches with a particular academic orientation—sociologists usually take a "social engineering" approach to delinquency prevention and treatment, while psychologists treat the individual. In other words, sociologists attempt to determine the conditions of the social structure that breed delinquency, while psychologists emphasize the individual and his interpersonal dynamics. Sociology has typically been regarded as a theoretical discipline researching the causes, rates, and effects of crime and delinquency. The profession of social work is the "practical arm" of the sociologist. The social worker attempts to put into practice the assumptions that have been posited by sociologists. However, social workers base much of their actual treatment of clients on psychological and psychiatric theories and principles. A sociologist, psychologist, or any other professional who specializes in crime and delinquency causation, prevention, control and treatment is a *criminologist.*

The social worker, then, translates the theories and assumptions of both psychological and sociological theory into action. This is one of the main reasons why individual and group approaches to treatment are often blended.

In addition to his theorizing about causes of delinquency, the psychologist, like the social worker, often becomes involved in the specific use of treatment methods. The sociologist usually orients himself to the more massive problem of "social engineering."

The discussion of the functions and orientation of sociologists, psychologists, and social workers can be quite confusing, and because of the blending of approaches, a professional differentiation is often difficult to make because some sociologists are more psychological than some psychologists, and vice versa.

The terminology used for the particular treatment method and the label used for the treater can also be confusing. Some treatment approaches are similar but have different names. Also, the function and the role of the treater can be similar for the various methods, but he may be called a counselor, caseworker, therapist, or psychotherapist.

A discussion of the individual and group methods of treatment follows. Although it is difficult to assign a particular academic discipline or profession to the many approaches, the professionals who utilize the following methods are generally psychologists, psychiatrists, and social workers. There are approaches, however, that such professionals as the police and school counselors can use, and these approaches will also be emphasized.

PSYCHOTHERAPY

Both Kolb[2] and Wolberg[3] define *psychotherapy* as a method of treatment of emotional and personality problems by psychological means. The aim of this method is to remove or retard symptoms or behavior patterns that are con-

[2] Lawrence C. Kolb, *Noyes' Modern Clinical Psychiatry* (Philadelphia: W. B. Saunders Co., 1968), p. 346.
[3] Lewis R. Wolberg, *The Techniques of Psychotherapy* (New York: Grune and Stratton, Inc., 1967), p. 3.

tributing to dysfunctional behavior. The promotion of personal growth is the end product. Nikelly states that

> any form of psychotherapy involves change in the client's attitude as well as his feelings and such change will ultimately be reflected in the client's value system. The therapist should not hesitate to disclose that he too has values and that his and the client's values may occasionally clash. Such a conflict can actually form a landmark during the process of psychotherapy because the client must examine his own values carefully in order to understand why they fail to help him function effectively as an emotionally healthy and adjusted person.[4]

Psychotherapy is an outgrowth of psychoanalytic and psychiatric assumptions. One of the basic concepts of psychotherapy is the phenomenon of *transference,* the redirecting of feelings from the client to the therapist, which in turn enables the therapist to probe the attitudes, thoughts, and feelings about significant persons in the client's past through his own relationship with the client. Many times the therapist will represent an authoritative figure of the client's early past, and in the case of a delinquent, the therapist often represents a parental figure. Aichhorn felt that transference was one of the most important elements in treating the juvenile delinquent.[5] Through his research, he concluded that all the extremely aggressive boys in his institution had had similar life experiences with their parents, that is, constant quarrels between parents or parental figures. There is much hate between the youngster and his parents because of these early relationships. Since the early relationship of the youngster with his parents was not satisfactory, his emotional development was often retarded, with the effect that a delinquent boy was often impulsive in an attempt to satisfy infantile urges not satisfied in the normal manner within his family. Satisfying these urges and impulses can take the form of antisocial behavior within the community.

One of Aichhorn's methods of handling boys who had grown up in such a situation was to utilize the method of transference and allow the boys to satisfy their impulses while under the guidance of a sympathetic adult (or parental substitute) whom the youngster could trust and rely on.

> If delinquency is to be cured and the asocial youth made fit again for life in society, the training school must provide him with new ties and induce him to attach himself to persons of his environment. We try to bring about such attachments by the kindly manner in which we treat our pupils.[6]

[4] Arthur G. Nikelly, "Basic Processes in Psychotherapy," *Techniques for Behavior Change* (Springfield, Ill.: Charles C Thomas, Publisher, 1971), p. 31.
[5] August Aichhorn, *Wayward Youth* (New York: The Viking Press, Inc., 1963).
[6] August Aichhorn, *Delinquency and Child Guidance* (New York: International Universities Press, Inc., 1964), p. 29.

Aichhorn was explaining that the institutionalized child under his direction was allowed to operate in an atmosphere of love and acceptance and therefore did not have to fear severe rejection or physical punishment. The child, under these conditions, would learn to develop a satisfactory relationship, trust the adult figure, and satisfy his needs. Aichhorn felt that this trust, as a result of the warm friendly relationship, could be generalized to other adults and institutions in the community. Just as the youngster had generalized his negative experiences from his parents to the community, acquainting him with positive identification models within his treatment environment could effectively help him generalize the positive associations to the community. This would eliminate much of his impulsive necessity to act out against authority substitutes.

Friedlander, whose orientation to human behavior is similar to that of Aichhorn, discovered that there were changes in behavior due to the transference established between boys and the counselor.

> The aggressiveness was not just acted out; the person of the educator [therapist] became an important factor in it. The boys clearly wanted to provoke him to punish them and were therefore specially destructive when in his presence. This punishment would have provided them with an instinctive gratification on the sado-masochistic level which they had been able to obtain in all their former environments. When the punishment did not come, the boys grew dissatisfied. Not only did they not derive sufficient gratification when destroying inanimate things but the unforeseen reaction of their educators put them in a difficult position; there was no longer any justification for their hatred. They still tried to get what they wanted by being more and more aggressive but in the end they had to give in: they began to feel guilty (the first stage of superego development) and they broke down. Behind their aggressiveness and their wish to be punished, which had been transformed to the educators, there now appeared a fierce longing to be loved. This was still very untamed. Their demands for the affection of the leader being insatiable but they now had an emotional relationship to an adult which made education possible.[7]

The above quotation illustrates the transference phenomenon in operation. The boys generalized to the educator or the therapist their early attitudes and feelings toward adults. They expected the therapist to react the way their parents would have reacted. When they found that not all adults reacted the same as their parents, they began to evaluate their attitudes and their behavior and concluded that not all adults were the same and that a discriminating approach to evaluating adults and the environment was most effective. When the youngsters began to evaluate adults on an individual basis, they did not have the generalized hatred to all adults or all adult institutions, and their acting out behavior began to diminish greatly.

[7]Kate Friedlander, *The Psycho-Analytical Approach to Juvenile Delinquency* (London: Routledge & Kegan Paul Ltd., 1947), p. 243.

Long and Kamada believe that in the initial therapeutic stages, it is essential to develop a basis of trust between the therapist and the youngster.[8] All youngsters, whether in a therapeutic situation or in the family constellation, constantly test to determine the limits of acceptable behavior and the reaction of the adult. Most delinquents come from family situations where there was very little trust in the family and very little predictable emotional security. Sometimes even such basic necessities as food and clothing were not provided. Therefore, they are very skeptical in treatment situations, and it is difficult to build up a trust relationship. If the therapist cannot establish himself as a trusting person who will be unlike the youngster's brutal and insensitive parents, it will be difficult for the youngster to benefit from the treatment.

Szurek stresses the importance of recognizing that the impulsive child needs to receive the experience of love previously denied him and that he needs to receive this love as a person, not merely as a reward for conformity.

> He needs this love for the prolonged period necessary for him to develop an essential sense of security. He also needs frank unyielding firmness coupled with uncompromising fairness and justice. The therapist needs to be able to recognize the many forms which the patient's distressful unmodified egocentricity and revengefulness may take and yet not be swayed from this therapeutic goal. . . . At least an approximation of these conditions may offer a chance that the child will become attached to the adult; if the relationship is continued long enough he will begin to identify with the adult's ideals, to understand the adult wishes for his own welfare and to acquire a new sense of his own worth as a person.[9]

It is important for the therapist to be well adjusted and not have an extensive amount of "hangups" or difficulties with authority himself. Unfortunately, too often the therapist or the counselor does have psychological problems of his own, and these are transferred to his work with youngsters. If the therapist is emotionally unhealthy himself, the therapeutic situation can do more harm than good, and the transference created may perpetuate and even foster negative behavior within the community. Chapter 4 pointed out that the unhealthy and dishonest professional can often perpetuate negative behavior, and it is precisely within the therapeutic situation and often through the transference phenomenon that it is fostered.

Holmes points out that many delinquent youngsters, even though they may be in their late teens, fantasize a great deal and have feelings of omnipotence. Everyone is aware that a very young child, as a result of his fantasizing, can pretend he is anybody he likes, including strong and powerful individuals. Because delinquent youngsters have not had satisfying or emotionally secure

[8] Anna Marie Long and Samuel I. Kamada, "Psychiatric Treatment of Adolescent Girls," *California Youth Authority Quarterly*, 17 (Summer 1964), pp. 23–24.
[9] S. A. Szurek, "Some Impressions from Clinical Experience with Delinquents," in *The Antisocial Child: His Family and His Community*, S. A. Szurek and I. N. Berlin, Eds. (Palo Alto, Calif.: Science and Behavior Books, Inc., 1969), pp. 80–81.

environments, they utilize fantasy to increase their feelings of worthfulness, deny unpleasant circumstances, and avoid facing the reality of their environment and its demands and requirements. When the youngster's behavior is dealt with thoroughly and objectively by the therapist, this can be surprising to the youngster and can neutralize many of his fantasies about adult authority figures. Being treated fairly and objectively is often a new experience for a youngster, and when this does occur it is both unexpected and incongruent with his earlier life experiences.

> Although it is often necessary to outsmart the delinquent youngster, it is not necessary to withhold a reasonable expression of critical appreciation for his manipulative virtuosity. Even as he frustrates an attempted swindle, the therapist may use the incident to demonstrate some of the advantages of a direct as opposed to a devious approach to people.[10]

Holmes is emphasizing the importance of directness with the youngster. When the delinquent youngster manipulates and uses devious means to satisfy his needs, he is usually accustomed to the same type of reaction from adults within his environment. When this negative, manipulative, devious cycle is interrupted by the efficient therapist, the youngster becomes aware of his negative cycle of behavior and realizes that some adults do react differently and do not always play dishonest games of manipulation. Holmes is also careful to point out the importance of going beyond merely making interpretations of behavior in psychotherapy. Interpretation in itself does not always alter behavior.

> If an adolescent boy prefers stealing cars to suffering the anxiety he would experience if he did not steal cars, he would probably not be helped by interpretation alone. The general principle is the same as in the treatment of addictions of perversions. It is virtually impossible to treat a chronic alcoholic successfully in a tavern.[11]

The therapist, then, interprets behavior to point out the negative dynamics, and he must also point out the reality of the situation and of the behavior itself. For example, to merely explain to a youngster that he is stealing cars because of an unresolved oedipal conflict will not usually in itself contribute to diminished car stealing. This interpretation, however, along with pointing out the reality of the negative ramifications of car stealing and the long-range problems that will be created by it, can be helpful. The youngster will learn that the negative consequences of stealing cars and possible incarceration are not very pleasurable and that other modes of behavior or other alternatives can be developed to satisfy his desires and impulses. The therapist as the authority person can, in addition to making an interpretation, provide healthy alternatives

[10] Donald J. Holmes, *The Adolescent in Psychotherapy* (Boston: Little, Brown and Company, 1964), p. 158.
[11] *Ibid.,* p. 185.

and guidelines for the youngster. The inefficient therapist may be able to interpret, but he will be unable to provide feasible and positive alternatives that will
be compatible with the expectations of the youngster's environment.

In addition to being honest and direct, the therapist must avoid empty
threats of punishment not only because they do not work in most cases but
because they may also transmit failure to the youngster and indicate that he is
incapable of handling his problems without them. The therapist must be realistic
and point out that if the youngster is involved in uncontrolled deviousness within the community, he cannot expect the same warm humanistic treatment by
community agencies whose duty it is to control and interrupt negative behavior.
For example:

> when a boy runs away from the hospital and steals a car which is a felony
> we would be doing him a serious disservice to withhold the explanation
> that although we are willing to view this as symptomatic it can be ex-
> amined in quite another light under the law and can possibly result in his
> being removed from our relatively benevolent sphere of influence. He has a
> right to know this and we have the obligation to tell him. In some psychi-
> atric settings it is too easy for the antisocial adolescent to nourish the
> delusion that his status as a patient automatically exempts him from all
> other legal, moral and religious responsibility.[12]

Jurjevich also believes that the delinquent youngster must be responsible
for his own behavior even when he is in an institution, or on probation, or in
another facility where an attempt is made to provide a benevolent and warm
atmosphere.[13] From the many case histories that Jurjevich reviewed and the
clients he worked with he found that there were many difficulties in the youngsters' backgrounds, but he felt that these unfortunate circumstances could not
be used by the clients as excuses to act irresponsibly because they would still
be evaluated according to the normative criteria established by society, which
its institutions of control would enforce. Thus his main direction was not
focused on past traumas or injuries or on personal handicaps, but in the direction of providing new alternatives for the youngster so he could avoid future
problems in the community. He assisted his clients in developing a life process
so that they could achieve their goals yet avoid the deviant behavior that was
so much a part of their past.

> The main method of achieving changes in the girls was considered to be
> helping them comply with the reasonable demands of training and disci-
> pline and accept the stresses of their situation without overreacting—the
> main facilitating factor in changing them appeared to be a warm respect-
> ful and when necessary frank but not a bluntly disapproving relationship
> between them and the therapist.[14]

[12] *Ibid.*, p. 262.
[13] Ratibor-Ray M. Jurjevich, *No Water in My Cup: Experiences and a Controlled Study of
Psychotherapy of Delinquent Girls* (New York: Libra Publishers, 1968).
[14] *Ibid.*, p. 107.

Jurjevich never openly forced the girls to change or comply to normative behavior, but he was always quick to point out what would be more acceptable and more rewarded in the community and what would be most disapproved of and sanctioned.

The psychotherapeutic method is often ascribed an aura of mysticism. In very simple terms, psychotherapy is merely a method of conversation between the client and the therapist to allow them to get to know each other so that they can be comfortable in exchanging communication. The communication allows the client to begin to relate personal experiences, perceptions, ideas, and reasons for negative as well as positive behavior so that solutions will be forthcoming. The effective therapist will create an atmosphere where the youngster can be comfortable and can relate his feelings and attitudes but will always be provided a base or reference to reality. The emotionally secure and able therapist or counselor will provide these reference points even when they are not popular with his client but in the long run will be most effective for positive behavior.

In conclusion, psychotherapy is the technique utilized by individuals who call themselves therapists, and it emanates from the framework of psychoanalysis and psychiatric theory. The therapist or, in layman's terms, the counselor evaluates the client's feelings, experiences, and inner dynamics. He attempts to point out faulty perceptions and provide positive alternatives to behavior adaption. He facilitates the solving of conflicts and helps the client make a positive adjustment to his environment. The therapist usually represents many adults in the youngster's past. An effective therapist can influence the youngster in a positive manner, facilitating the generalization of the results of this relationship to other adults in the community. The new positive attitude of the youngster which results from his relationship with the therapist can effectively alter his negative behavior in the community and contribute to his satisfactory adjustment.

SOCIAL CASEWORK

Social casework, according to Tappan, is that phase of social work dealing directly with the maladjusted individual to determine the kind of help he needs and to assist him in coping with his problems.[15] Ferguson feels that "when social work is primarily concerned with the fullest possible degree of personality development we call it social casework."[16]

Although similar in many respects, technically social casework should be considered different from psychotherapy, and professionals working in the community are not often able to distinguish between them. In fact, those social

[15] Paul W. Tappan, *Juvenile Delinquency* (New York: McGraw-Hill Book Company, 1949), p. 362.

[16] Elizabeth A. Ferguson, *Social Work: An Introduction* (Philadelphia: J. B. Lippincott Co., 1963), p. 9.

workers utilizing social casework often see themselves as therapists and feel that even though they have been trained in social casework, the specific focus of their social casework training has been in the psychotherapeutic area. Regardless of the technical difference between the two, they both rely on developing a positive relationship with the client so that he can be assisted in problem solving. In casework, as in psychotherapy, the client relates on a one-to-one basis with the caseworker (or therapist, counselor, etc.). This type of interaction can result in a joint effort at problem solving and the development of socially acceptable alternatives to community adjustment. The American Correctional Association states that the casework method is very helpful in altering deviant behavior.[17] The casework method is conducive to determining the conditions that contribute to deviant behavior and pinpointing the resources necessary to support the client in his efforts to become a contributing member of society. The caseworker utilizes the social history to explore the client's background, environment, and relationship with his family, friends, and peers. The social history, or case history, affords the caseworker who may be a probation officer, parole officer, prison counselor, mental health worker, or school social worker the opportunity to evaluate the personal strengths and weaknesses of the client as well as his environment so that a treatment plan can be devised and carried out. The youngster will be counseled or "treated," and if possible his environment will be altered. In terms of environmental manipulation, the youngster may be removed from his environment and placed in a rehabilitative agency or treatment program so that he does not have to experience the severe pressures of his family or peer group who are contributing to his negative behavior.

When working with delinquents it is often difficult to obtain their cooperation because they are unwilling to trust the caseworker. The delinquent's family may also be resistant and may become defensive and feel threatened by the caseworker's "probing." Parents often fear that the negative dynamics of their family and their relationship with their youngster will become known and that they will be blamed for their youngster's predicament. Even though social casework, like many other methods, has been successful with neurotics, it has often not been successful with delinquents. Neurotics are usually motivated in the helping relationship, while delinquents are not. The intensity of the one-to-one relationship with the caseworker is also threatening. Some of the assumptions of social casework are not applicable when treating the delinquent. For example, the caseworker often takes a passive approach to treatment under the guise of client self-determination and the need for client involvement and commitment. Delinquents need a more direct and aggressive approach, which accelerates client involvement and joint problem solving. Because passive techniques have generally been unsuccessful with delinquents, the present trend is to use a more aggressive approach.

The word aggressive . . . describes nothing new in casework. It is used to characterize the kinds of adaptions in practice which are necessary when, because children are in trouble, a caseworker goes out to serve families who do not want her.[18]

The caseworker often meets with much resentment and hostility not only from the delinquent who did not ask for help but also from the youngster's parents who are perpetuating the delinquent behavior. Nevertheless, the caseworker, if he is going to be successful, must convince the family that casework intervention and counseling are needed to assist them in problem solving. It is often difficult to convince the parents that they need assistance, and this necessitates a great deal of effort and perseverance by the caseworker. He can explain that it is to the family's advantage to accept assistance and solve the problem before it becomes so unmanageable that the youngster will seriously harm himself or the community.

In some cases the family refuses to become involved in the helping process even when the *aggressive casework* method is utilized; consequently, the caseworker may have to call upon an authoritative agency like the juvenile court to intervene in the problem situation.

Steps toward the use of aggressive casework arise from the acceptance of a social philosophy that assigns to the community not only the right to protect children but the responsibility of taking vigorous action on their behalf when their behavior reflects a destructive process that the family itself cannot or will not control.[19]

Casework with delinquents can be viewed as a three-phased process. Initially and in less-severe cases, the typical method of passive involvement with the clients can often be utilized. If, however, the youngster is a chronic offender, he has usually been through the passive processes of self-determination and cathartic verbalization. He may be resentful and cynical of not only the process itself but also the adult who is using it. Furthermore, if the parents are contributing to and fostering his delinquent activity, the caseworker's passive methods will not be successful because of their hostility and unresponsiveness. Therefore, the second phase involves the use of aggressive casework in which the worker must be persistent and direct in his approach to the problem. He confronts the parents and defines the problem, the consequences if the problem is not handled, and the alternatives he sees for its solution. The worker must provide a great deal of support in the early stages of treatment so that the family will become involved in the problem-solving process and will be able to make realistic decisions and accept responsibility.[20] Finally, if the first phase of passive casework and the second phase of aggressive casework are not success-

[18] Alice Overton, "Aggressive Casework," in *Reaching the Unreached*, Sylvan S. Furman, Ed. (New York: New York City Youth Board, 1952), p. 51.

[19] Harry Manuel Shulman, *Juvenile Delinquency in American Society* (New York: Harper & Row, 1961), p. 642.

[20] Overton, *op. cit.*, p. 54.

ful, an authoritative agency such as the juvenile court may have to be presented to the family as the only alternative and may have to intervene to insure that the parents and the youngster will begin to look at their problem realistically and attempt to seek solutions.

Frequently, regardless of whether the technique utilized is the passive approach or the aggressive approach, it is still difficult to work with youngsters and their families because the atmosphere is usually tense and pervaded with hostility and resentment toward the criminal justice system. A new form of casework called "directed friendship" is becoming popular. This approach actively seeks out clients and is described by Powers and Witmer.[21] They point out how paid nonprofessionals can visit homes and schools for the express purpose of giving personal advice and guidance. A relationship with the youngsters is developed so that the "friendship person" can be a readily available source of advice, guidance, and support to the youngster before he becomes involved in more difficulty with the law. This is a much different approach than waiting until the youngster becomes chronically involved in serious difficulty.

After the onset of chronic delinquency, the youngster and his family are often hostile and resentful. The directed friendship technique in seeking out youngsters who may be borderline delinquents, or at least less than chronic, can be effective in not only pinpointing delinquents but in utilizing casework or other techniques before the problem becomes extremely serious for the youngster and the community. Once a serious problem occurs, it is twice as difficult to deal with the problem and develop a positive relationship with the youngster and his family.

REALITY THERAPY

The major basis of the *reality therapy* approach is that all persons have certain basic needs. When they are unable to fulfill these needs, they act in an irresponsible manner. The object of reality therapy is to help the person act in a responsible manner—in the case of a delinquent, to help him refrain from antisocial activity. A premise of this approach is that regardless of what the delinquent youngster has done and the extenuating circumstances—for example, inadequate parents or negative environmental conditions, the youngster is still responsible for his behavior. There are no acceptable excuses, and the irresponsibility that is manifested through delinquent activity and law breaking is not condoned. The reality therapy method is an understandable, commonsense approach which its originator, Dr. William Glasser, holds can be utilized by all members of the criminal justice system ranging from the arresting officer to the counselor in

---

[21] Edwin Powers and Helen Witmer, "The Cambridge-Somerville Study," in *The Sociology of Punishment and Correction,* Norman Johnston, Leonard Savitz, and Marvin E. Wolfgang, Eds. (New York: John Wiley & Sons, Inc., 1970), p. 588.

the training school. Anyone who comes in contact with the delinquent can utilize this approach because it does not emphasize nebulous psychiatric terms, extensive testing, or time-consuming case conferences.

> The only case records needed are occasional notes about what has occurred that shows increased responsibility. If the boy fails, the reason is that we were not able to help him become responsible enough to live in society. We need no detailed record of this failure to explain why.[22]

In sharp contrast to the psychotherapeutic methods, reality therapy emphasizes the present behavior of the youngster and considers it the most important event. What happened in the past is insignificant because regardless of how much is known about the past extenuating circumstances and the relationship of the youngster with his parents, the past cannot be changed. The basis of psychotherapy is that a person cannot change his present behavior unless he can clearly tie it to events in the past. Glasser states that delving into the past is "a fruitless historical journey—which leads to excusing the offender's present actions as an unfortunate culmination of his history."[23] The premise is that since a person's past history cannot be changed or objectively reconstructed, he can never fully understand the reasons why he committed a certain act, and interpretations are often merely guesses as to causative relationships. Furthermore, if present behavior is merely a reflection and the sum total of all past experiences (as traditional psychotherapies propose), then when the present behavior is modified and changed this nullifies all past experiences. In other words, if the child learns to refrain from delinquent activity, the drives, urges, impulses, and experiences that caused the symptomatic delinquent manifestation will be nullified as a result of the new socially acceptable life-style.

If there is too much emphasis on the past and on extenuating circumstances, this can excuse the client's transgressions, contribute to his feeling that he is sick, and thus excuse his present and future delinquent activity within the community.

Glasser believes that many therapists, caseworkers, and counselors feel that the youngster is unhappy because of his past circumstances, and therefore he acts out within the community because of his unhappiness. Efforts to make the youngster happy invariably fail because the unhappiness is the result of irresponsible behavior (delinquent activity) and not the result of past personal and environmental circumstances. Since everyone wants to feel worthwhile and be evaluated positively by his peers, irresponsible delinquent behavior causes negative self-evaluations and hence feelings of worthlessness or unhappiness. The only way a person can be made to feel worthwhile and fulfill his

[22]William Glasser, "Reality Therapy: A Realistic Approach to the Young Offender," in *Readings in Delinquency and Treatment,* Robert Schasre and Jo Wallach, Eds. (Los Angeles: The Delinquency Prevention Training Project, Youth Studies Center, University of Southern California, 1965), p. 65.
[23] *Ibid.,* p. 57.

basic needs is by acting in a responsible manner, which means avoiding delinquent behavior.

The main objective of reality therapy is to make the individual a responsible person within the community, and this starts with a positive relationship and interaction between him and the therapist. If the therapist treats the youngster as a responsible person and expects him to respond in a positive manner, this transmission will give the child confidence and will be the catalytic agent in his acting positively. If the child is treated as a responsible person and not as an unfortunate youngster, this will transmit strength to the youngster. The therapist should be a warm and honest person who emphasizes the positive rather than the negative and strength rather than weakness, and he should have confidence that the youngster will act responsibly. The youngster is expected to obey rules, but he is not rejected when he breaks one. The reality of the situation and the possible negative consequences of his unlawful activity are, however, pointed out to him. The therapist never asks why the youngster became involved in the activity. Only present events are considered. Questions by the therapist concern only the circumstances of the youngster's problems, not their underlying causes.

> Open ended questions such as "Why did you do it?" should be avoided. Too much questioning, too much initial conversation gives him the opportunity to make excuses, to feel antagonistic toward authority, to justify in his mind that what he did was not very wrong or if wrong not really his fault.[24]

In reality therapy, the therapist always gives the client a great deal of support when he acts in a responsible manner. He always transmits to the youngster a certain set of expectations or rules, defines the limits of acceptable behavior, and follows through with any consequences that have been laid down in the "contract."

Reality therapy has been criticized because many feel that it is an oversimplification of human behavior and that in some cases the transmitting of expectations to the youngster can have negative effects if the youngster came from a situation in which there were a great many expectations transmitted to him which he could not live up to and follow. Regardless of the criticism, however, Glasser has proved through research that his method can be effective not only in juvenile courts and in probation settings but also in institutions.

Reality therapy, like other therapies, is only as good as the individual counselor or therapist who is using it. Reality therapy is a logical, down-to-earth, and commonsense approach, but if it is not used correctly it can be a punitive technique when treating youngsters. For example, a therapist, in a coldhearted manner after a youngster has been apprehended, can say to him, "I don't want to know why you are involved in a difficulty. You are irrespon-

---

[24] *Ibid.,* p. 53.

sible and I will not become involved with you as your counselor until you react in a more responsible manner." This, of course, can be a very hostile attitude transmitted to the youngster under the guise of reality therapy. Any therapy, regardless of its techniques, can be used as a hostile, punitive mechanism by an inefficient therapist.

As stated earlier, reality therapy can make an important contribution to the juvenile justice system process. One of the major problems in handling and treating juveniles is *consistency*. Because the juvenile justice system is composed of professionals from various backgrounds, training, and orientation, consistency is often lacking within the system.

In Chapter 3 we saw how inconsistency in the family can contribute to "acting out" behavior by the youngster. Inconsistent handling of the juvenile in the juvenile justice system can also have negative consequences. Reality therapy can be effective in combating inconsistencies in treatment and handling and can provide the base for a more coordinated approach to treating the delinquent. All professionals within the system can use this approach with a minimal amount of training.

TRANSACTIONAL ANALYSIS

Transactional analysis, which can be utilized both individually and in groups, is mainly concerned with evaluating and interpreting interpersonal relationships and dynamic transactions between the client and his environment. According to Berne, transactions between individuals can be viewed as "pastimes and games."[25] In other words, much of the interaction that takes place with individuals can be viewed as games or game playing.

Transactional analysis is based on the following assumptions.

1. Human relationships consist of competitive acts of social maneuvers which serve a defensive function and yield important gratification which can be labeled "games."

2. All persons manifest three different "ego states": the *child,* a relic of the individual's past; the *parent,* whom he has incorporated through identification with his parents; and the *adult,* who is the mature and responsible self.

3. Each of these "ego states" perceives reality differently: the child prelogically, the parent judgmentally, and the adult comprehensively on the basis of past experience.

4. The three states operate constantly in response to the person's needs and the "games" in which he indulges at a given time.[26]

[25] Eric Berne, *Transactional Analysis in Psychotherapy* (New York: Grove Press, 1961).
[26] Wolberg, *op. cit.,* p. 257.

The major purpose of therapy is to point out the various games that the client plays and attempt to strengthen the adult component of the personality, displace the immaturities of the child component, and reduce the subjective judgment of the parental component. Before using transactional analysis, the therapist, through diagnosis of the patient's demeanor, gestures, vocabulary, and voice, attempts to determine the ego state responsible for the patient's symptoms and disturbances. For example, it may be pinpointed that even though the delinquent youngster is an adolescent, much of his behavior is manifested like an impulsive, immature child and this is the reason he gets involved in difficulty. In other words, the game playing that he is involved in is through the dynamic child component, and the major portion of his time is spent in these childish activities which ultimately result in hedonistic, impulsive behavior within the community. After the initial diagnosis and interpretation, the individual may have sessions with the therapist to further pinpoint his game playing and those components that are most manifest. He may also be placed in a group where his transactions and game playing become more revealing in interaction with others.

Even though this method has primarily been used with adults, Berne feels that it has a special value for adolescents because of their typical resistance to psychotherapy. Not only are adolescents resistant to psychotherapy, delinquent adolescents are even more so :

> Since the majority of teenage patients are sent or brought to treatment, the relationship to the therapist is not an autonomous one so that there is a strong temptation to rebellion, withdrawal, or sabotage. In effect, the therapist becomes a delegate of their parents which under the usual contract puts him in a great disadvantage from the beginning. The sought for "cure" too often resembles a prescription written by the parents, who visualize the therapeutic relationship as a *Parent-Child* one, and the patient tends to do the same. The situation can be decisively altered at the social level by explicitly setting up an *Adult-Adult* contract, whereby the therapist offers to teach the patient transactional analysis, with the provision that the patient can do as he pleases with what he learns.[27]

In this situation the adolescent or the delinquent adolescent does not necessarily take a subservient role but is taught the method of transactional analysis. The major principle learned is how to identify the three dynamic components of the personality. The therapist can point out that he too has components of the *parent* and the *child* as well as of the *adult*. He can also illustrate to the youngster in what cases his own *child* component, or childishness, is manifested. The child then does not have to operate as a subservient, he can learn the method and apply it to his own situation when he is ready and feels it will be helpful. Transactional analysis can be effective by teaching the youngster a method of evaluating his own behavior and categorizing it as adult ori-

[27] Berne, *op. cit.,* p. 355.

ented, parent oriented, or child oriented. In most cases the youngster can make the final determination as to the appropriateness of his behavior and the category into which it falls. If he constantly evaluates his behavior and actions as childish, through his own awareness of the method and "diagnosis," he can alter the impulsive childish component of his personality and emphasize the more acceptable adult characterization.

VOCATIONAL COUNSELING

Vocational counseling is different from the preceding therapeutic methods and does not necessarily attempt to understand the interpersonal dynamics of human behavior or spend a great deal of time on diagnosis. The main purpose of vocational counseling is to increase the client's knowledge of career choices, job specifications, and qualifications and training needed for successful employment. The vocational counselor can help the young person identify his interests by questioning him about his attitude toward work in general and the specific types of employment that appeal to him. Aptitude and interest testing may also be used. This experience is often a whole new area for the delinquent adolescent because he has never held a job and hence has never experienced the problems that exist or the positive rewards that can result. The positive attitudes, skills, and habits that the youngster develops and refines in the work situation can be carried over to the community and can positively affect his relationships with others.

> Perhaps the most crucial problem to tackle in helping young people prepare for the adult world of work is in positively influencing their attitudes toward work. Many characteristics typical of the delinquent youth militate against a ready adjustment to employment. Typically the delinquent lacks self-confidence. He knows that he will make serious mistakes on the job. He goes forth expecting not to be liked, looking for slights and unfairness. He seeks immediate gratification of his impulses and has difficulty in working toward goals which are as remote as a pay check which comes only once a week. Basic skills are important primarily because they influence a child's attitude toward work and self-confidence. It is upon the development of constructive attitudes toward and reactions to work that emphasis should be placed. This means that an analysis of each child's interest, aptitudes, and capacity to tolerate the demands of the assignment should be made before work and shop assignments are made. His initial experience should be carefully structured to assure some sense of achievement and to avoid too much frustration.[28]

The work situation can provide a realistic environment where behavior can be evaluated and many of the youngster's problems can be resolved. The astute

[28] National Conference of Superintendents of Training Schools and Reformatories, *Institutional Rehabilitation of Delinquent Youth: Manual for Training School Personnel* (Albany, N.Y.: Delmar Publishers, Inc., 1962), pp. 106-7.

counselor can utilize problem situations that occur in the work environment to point out interpersonal difficulties that the youngster has, which usually also exist outside the work environment. The personal relationships that exist between youngsters and their work supervisors or work peers can be critical in altering attitudes and behavior and in facilitating solution to problems.

> Whether or not a boy or girl becomes particularly skilled on the work assignment is one factor but more important is the satisfaction he realizes from a working relationship. If he can gain confidence in his supervisor he has made the first step toward placing confidence and trust in other individuals—If the training can reconcile the child's aptitudes and personality needs with the basic rules of society then it has accomplished this rehabilitation and has indeed trained and educated him for life in the community.[29]

A positive identification model can frequently be the most effective means of influencing the youngster to develop positive alternatives to problem solving.

The astute counselor (therapist, caseworker, and so on) is also aware of the resources in his community and the programs available to help train and retrain youngsters so that they can become more effective citizens and successful workers. Helping the youngster adjust to his work environment is as much a part of therapy or counseling as the communication and interpretation of interpersonal dynamics that take place within the context of therapeutic interview.

Vocational Guidance

Vocational guidance programs that involve vocational counseling have often been effective in redirecting the engery of delinquent youngsters into positive channels. Experimental projects have been developed to encourage youngsters to stay in school so that they can acquire a vocational goal and increased skills which will contribute to a more positive self-image and success in the community. Various attempts have been made both with individuals and with groups to encourage youngsters to develop needed skills and discuss their attitudes about work and the problems that they perceive or encounter in the work world. One such project attempted to encourage boys to discuss their perceptions of work. This was accomplished through the group process of discussion meetings.

> The only regulations voiced at the very onset were that the participants must not damage or destroy any of the office property and not do bodily violence to any member of the group. These regulations were accepted and respected throughout the group sessions.[30]

[29] *Ibid.*, p. 108.
[30] Frederick Weiner, "Vocational Guidance for Delinquent Boys," *Crime and Delinquency,* 11 (October 1964), p. 368.

The meetings were set up to discuss various situations that the boys encountered at work and the relationships they had with work supervisors, work peers, and other persons within the environment. In other words, the entire constellation of factors that related to work assignments, work skills, and activities and duties were covered. The open discussions were

> not merely an outpouring of hostility because as the meetings progressed some of the boys interpreted the behavior of others in the group. They began to be critical of themselves. At first their hostility was directed towards school authorities and then to their parents, representatives of the law, and peers. Finally they began to realize that they were also involved.[31]

The main point is that the effective counselor can utilize the group itself to solve problems and increase the awareness of individual members in the group of their involvement in the interpersonal work processes. In addition, new alternatives for behavioral adaption can be developed for the work environment and the community in general.

Programs like the Neighborhood Youth Corps (see Chapter 8) have been effective in combining work training with vocational and interpersonal counseling.

> It is work focused so that all aspects of the youth's life are dealt with in terms of their relevance for his career. Counseling is concerned primarily with helping the youth examine his desires, feelings, and attitudes, his day-to-day problems and his behavior in the counseling situation itself. The group is used as a reference group and all are expected to help each other.[32]

The New Careers Program concentrates on creating new technical-level jobs by providing counseling, education, skill training, and supervised on-the-job training and experience. Programs such as these have been successful in realistically helping the youngster develop work skills in addition to providing counseling for interpersonal problems. Vocational counseling and vocational guidance programs can play an important part in preventing delinquency and rehabilitating a youngster who has been labeled delinquent.

BEHAVIOR THERAPY

Behavior therapy, or behavior modification, is based on the assumption that delinquent behavior is learned. Maladaptive behavior usually has to be modified through the development of new learning processes. Generally, behavior therapy

---

[31] *Ibid.,* p. 369.
[32] Beryce W. MacLennon and Naomi Felsenfeld, *Group Counseling and Psychotherapy with Adolescents* (New York: Columbia University Press, 1968), p. 148.

assumes that behavior will change in direct proportion to the amount of rewards or punishments that exist as reinforcement—negative or unpleasant reinforcement will reduce or eliminate much negative behavior, whereas positive or pleasant reinforcement will tend to maintain or even increase positive behavior. If positive behavior is adequately rewarded, it will be perpetuated. Conversely, if negative behavior is not rewarded, it will eventually subside.

Shah states that according to the behavioral approach the therapist must deal with clear and observable aspects of behavior so that objective conclusions and evaluations can be made.[33] Thorp and Wetzel point out that observable behavior, whether positive or negative, can be reinforced or punished accordingly.[34] The client can be made aware of the sequence of events that culminate in particular types of behavior. Negative behavior like delinquent activity can be pinpointed, and negative reinforcements like restrictions can be implemented. Positive behavior, like success on the job and in school, can be positively reinforced and rewarded.

Dressler points out that if the therapist is going to be effective in accomplishing behavior modification, he must first determine each individual's "reinforcers."

> A youngster's reinforcers may be determined by carefully observing his behavior, since each child has his own list of reinforcers which can be ranked for importance. Candy for the quite young and money for those who are older are generally in the category of reinforcers but, aside from these, reinforcers usually cannot be accurately determined without observation of the child and inquiry of him and significant others, such as family, peers, and teachers. The investigator wants to know what people, things, and events motivate the particular individual. What does he want to get out of them?[35]

Reinforcers, then, are those aspects that are deemed important by the youngster, which he will strive to achieve so that he will gain personal satisfaction. Praise, attention, money, food, and privileges can be considered positive reinforcers. Threats, punishment, confinement, and ridicule are negative reinforcers. Even though both types can be employed in modifying behavior, research has shown that positive reinforcements tend to produce more effective and enduring behavioral changes.[36]

The therapist, in an attempt to achieve a desired goal, tries to shape the behavior of the youngster by employing slow and gradual changes beginning with the individual's existing level of performance—the therapist determines

[33] Saleem A. Shah, "Treatment of Offenders: Some Behavioral Concepts, Principles and Approaches," *Federal Probation*, 23 (September 1959), p. 29.
[34] Ronald G. Thorp and Ralph J. Wetzel, *Behavior Modification in the Natural Environment* (New York: Academic Press Inc., 1969), p. 186.
[35] David Dressler, *Practice and Theory of Probation and Parole* (New York: Columbia University Press, 1959), pp. 229-30.
[36] *Ibid.*, p. 230.

the behavioral level of his client. For example, the youngster may be a chronic delinquent who has been involved in much delinquent activity. The "treatment" has to begin at this point. Because the therapist proceeds at a very slow pace and behavior modification is attempted in only small doses, success is a gradual process and the little successes become stepping-stones to larger achievements.

> Each appropriate or correct move toward the goal is provided external or extrinsic reinforcements (praise, approval, prizes, candy, good grades, etc.). Such progress may also generate internal or intrinsic reinforcements for the individual.[37]

In other words, as the behavior is modified and as rewards are provided, the delinquent activity is reduced, allowing the individual to develop a self-image of being able to achieve personal satisfaction in a socially acceptable manner. If the youngster is able to stay on the job and receive gratification through the paycheck he receives, this may be a new experience for him, and the satisfaction and the positive reinforcements can affect his internal self-concept and alter his behavior in the community.

Schwitzgebel utilized behavior modification in his research and work in communities with high rates of delinquency. He told youngsters that he was an experimenter who was studying delinquency and needed subjects whom he would pay to help him. Each subject came to Schwitzgebel's office to talk about anything he wanted to related to juvenile delinquency. The sessions were recorded. At the end of the session Schwitzgebel paid the youngster for the information provided and set up another appointment. Because each subject obviously spoke of delinquency partly in terms of his own involvement, Schwitzgebel hoped that the result would be an extensive self-examination leading to development of insights and, ultimately, the desire to change. Important in his experiment was the aspect of the experimenter being the employer by giving cash or rewards to the youngster *and* the youngster being the employee or the recipient of the cash or rewards. The arrangement was a business relationship, and the youngster was encouraged to believe that he was coming to collect his pay for providing a service and that he was not coming to receive counseling. The payment was used to effect behavioral change. Schwitzgebel discovered that delinquents seemed to be deficient in time sense and attempted to modify their behavior:

> They [delinquents] treated appointments casually, they arrived at the office almost any time except when scheduled. It was not uncommon for them to arrive even on a wrong day. At first Schwitzgebel did not reprimand them, making use of their services no matter when they arrived. Little extra rewards were paid for arriving at all—candy or fruit, for instance. When the youth's adherence to schedule improved even slightly,

---

[37]Shah, *op. cit.,* p. 32.

he was rewarded with praise. If he produced especially good material in the session, he might receive a $.50 or $1.00 bonus on top of his regular pay. With these positive devices, Schwitzgebel was teaching the boys to appreciate and adhere to time schedules.[38]

Thus, in the slow process of paying the boys or rewarding them for the information they were providing as well as rewarding other behaviors, like being on time for appointments, the boys unknowingly began to develop certain positive habits which could be carried over to the work world or to other situations in their community. For example, their new time sense would be helpful in attending school or getting to work on time. The slow process of change through the reward or positive reinforcement system established by Schwitzgebel could have both immediate and long-range positive results, especially if positive behavior continued to be rewarded. If the youngster, however, did not receive encouragement from his family or his reference groups he might relapse into old habits and become further involved in delinquent activity.

The National Training School Project also used behavior modification techniques. Successful performance was reinforced by a point system. Points earned could be used to purchase a variety of items, such as cokes, food, clothing, and access to a comfortable lounge. The boys were not compelled to study, but their performance and motivation did show marked improvement.

The points could only be *earned* by the individual's satisfactory performance in educational work and a careful record of the points earned by each person was kept by the project staff. Thus, points could *not* be given away, loaned, borrowed, begged, or stolen—they could only be earned and used by the person working for them. Since behavior upon which the points were continued was rather concise, it could objectively be measured . . . only the desired educational behaviors were reinforced.[39]

Behavioral modification has been used successfully to alter negative behavior and encourage positive achievements. The family is the first "institution" that either directly or indirectly uses the behavior modification approach. The juvenile soon learns how to respond to his environment. Parents who have been consistent in their reward and punishment system can influence their children to act in a socially acceptable manner. If parents are inconsistent or perverted in their approach to child rearing, they will not be successful in positively influencing their children. Ineffective role modeling by parents will often result in their youngsters' becoming involved in delinquent behavior.

Behavior modification is simply a method of establishing or reestablishing an effective reward and punishment system to help the youngster become more compatible with the expectations and demands of his environment.

[38] Shah, *op. cit.,* p. 34. (Ralph Schwitzgebel, *Streetcorner Research,* Cambridge: Harvard University Press, 1964.)
[39] *Ibid.,* p. 36.

BEHAVIORAL CONTRACTS

Behavioral contracting has become a very popular and useful method of working with delinquent adolescents. The assumptions of behavior modification contracting have proven useful in graphically illustrating to the client the expectations of the counselor and the consequences of client behavior. The client is actively involved in developing the contract and, in effect, it is a partnership between counselor and client.

Rutherford explains that:

> Behavioral contracting involves the systematic negotiation between mediator (parent, teacher, probation officer, social worker, unit counselor, or supervisor) and a target (delinquent adolescent) of the behaviors to be performed within a given environment, and the specific reinforcing consequences or "payoffs" to be provided when performance requirements are met. Behavioral contracting is based upon an applied behavior analysis model whereby the environmental dynamics which maintain behavior are assessed. In behavioral contracting, a behavioral analysis involves specifying: (A) the antecedents which will cue the contract behavior, (B) the contract behavior to be developed, and (C) the consequences which will maintain the contract behavior (see figure below).

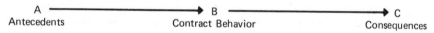

A —————————————→ B —————————————→ C
Antecedents   Contract Behavior   Consequences

FIGURE 1. Behavioral Analysis of Contract Behavior

> The "antecedents" are events which are present in the environment to cue behaviors. They include those stimuli, cues, directions, or prompts that set the occasion for a given behavior and a specific, predictable consequence. The antecedent cues for doing 20 arithmetic word problems at home may be a math book, a sharp pencil, 3 sheets of paper, directions at the top of the page, and a quiet, well lighted room. These cues may signal that the "consequences" of completing the "contract behavior," e.g., math problems done correctly by 9:00 a.m. the following morning, will be positive. The positive consequences may be a higher letter grade, praise from teacher and parents, and/or a specifically contracted item or event such as a coke or 20 minutes of free time at midday. Behavioral analysis makes the assumption that consequences which are positive will result in an increase in the frequency of the desired behavior.

> In summary, behavioral analysis involves planning before the fact and behavioral programming after the fact of a given behavior. Sound behavioral contracts specify systematically each of the three steps of the behavioral analysis mode.[40]

---

[40] Robert B. Rutherford, "Establishing Behavioral Contracts with Delinquent Adolescents," *Federal Probation*, Vol. 39, No. 1 (March 1975), p. 29.

In addition, Rutherford has developed several steps that must be followed to insure success of behavior contracting. Most noteworthy are the following. There must be an analysis of the client's behavior to determine the antecedents and consequences of behavior. The behavioral contract must not only be fair and formal, but it must precisely state the conditions of the agreement. In addition, the contract should be stated in positive terms and implemented with positive rewards for positive behavior.

CRISIS INTERVENTION

Even though *crisis intervention* has not been utilized extensively with youngsters in the past. Villeponteaux believes that it can have great therapeutic value in dealing with acting out adolescents.[41] The basis of the theory is that when a person experiences a crisis, his psychological resources may become overtaxed, making him vulnerable to further breakdown. The resolution of the current crisis may lead to the solution of older problems, as well, because of the reawakening of fears and repressed problems that recur during time of crisis. Redl and Wineman describe it as "emotional first aid on the spot." They go on to say that

> problem situations in the child's day-to-day life have strategic and therapeutic importance when they can be dealt with immediately before or immediately after they occur and even more when the person who deals with them has witnessed the incident.[42]

The delinquent, unlike most typical middle-class persons who use verbalizations to express aggression, usually expresses his aggression by acting out in the community and coming in conflict with the law. If the therapist witnesses or is told how the youngster handles and expresses his aggression and how he reacts to frustration and strain, he can use the immediate situation to help the youngster develop new methods of adaption. Villeponteaux provides an example of the techniques used at Horizon House:

> A minor infraction of a rule could be handled in one of several ways. For example, a boy might (and in fact, often did) come late to the program. If he was three or four minutes late, the worker could simply overlook this tardiness, or could reprimand, or warn him, or "make an issue" of it.[43]

If the therapist wanted to "make an issue" of the boy's behavior, he could emphasize the problem by pointing out in an actual and objective manner how the

[41] Lorenz Villeponteaux, Jr., "Crisis Intervention in a Day School of Delinquents," *Crime and Delinquency,* 16 (July 1970), pp. 318–19.
[42] *Ibid.,* p. 319.
[43] *Ibid.,* p. 320.

boy was functioning. The immediate problem could then be related to the way the boy functioned in other situations in the past. The present situation or crisis can be used for problem solving because it is probably part of a pattern of behavior that the youngster uses in relating to the environment. This pattern often contributes to a delinquent behavioral adaption. The successful resolution of the crisis in the immediate situation can be generalized to similar situations in the future and can be helpful in acquainting the boy with a new prob-lem-solving process that will contribute to more appropriate behavior in the community.

Handling problems when they are at the crisis stage and when there is a great deal of anxiety can contribute to problem solving. Because youngsters who are involved in chronic delinquent behavior often do not experience anxiety and guilt, it is difficult to rehabilitate them or motivate them enough so that they want to get involved in the change process. The anxiety that exists in the crisis situation can be used as a motivating force for change. Crisis intervention, as a technique for dealing with problems on the spot, can be effective in producing change and helping the delinquent develop new methods for handling strain, frustration, and aggression in crisis situations.

INDIVIDUAL AND GROUP COUNSELING

Counseling can be used with both groups and individuals. Usually, the major goals of counseling are support and reeducation.

> The counseling procedure involves the client's understanding of his im-mediate situation and the solving of a problem which affects him and others. No attempt is made to affect a fundamental change of the client's personality—when a person needs reorientation to a particular situation, counseling is indicated. If the problem is of a long-standing duration, psychotherapy is recommended.[44]

The American Correctional Association defines the technique as follows:

> Counseling is a relationship in which one endeavors to help another understand and solve his problems of adjustment. It is distinguished from service or admonition in that it implies *mutual* consent.[45]

These quotations illustrate an important principle. Methods of treatment can be viewed on a continuum. Vocational counseling and individual and group counseling are sometimes considered superficial approaches to interpersonal problem solving. Their main objective is usually to help the client handle im-mediate practical problems. No major attempt is made to restructure the person-

[44] Nikelly, *op. cit.,* p. 28.
[45] The American Correctional Association, *op. cit.,* p. 422.

ality or make extensive diagnostic evaluations. More sophisticated methods, such as social casework and psychotherapy, are needed for intensive personality evaluation and treatment. Approaches like transactional analysis and reality therapy fit somewhere between the more superficial counseling methods and the more intensive psychotherapeutic methods. A youngster could conceivably be receiving assistance simultaneously from professionals using the various methods mentioned. For example, his school counselor or vocational counselor could be helping him handle the day-to-day problems that occur in school and on the job, while his probation officer could be helping him through the use of principles extracted from reality therapy, behavior therapy, or transactional analysis. At the same time the youngster could also be evaluated and even treated by a psychiatrist who used psychotherapeutic techniques. Although this example would not be typical, it would be possible.

The most prevalent group treatment approach in institutional settings and juvenile court programs is called group counseling, which involves the sharing of personal concerns, problems, and day-to-day experiences within the group.[46]

Sharp notes that the group approach often is successful in teaming up with individualized services.[47] Together they provide a complementary orientation to individual and group problem solving.

In the counseling situation, the

> counselor establishes and operates within an atmosphere which is open and accepting. It is only when the child is free from the feeling that he must defend himself that he is also free to explore himself openly with a degree of candor. . . . The counselor is an "enabler"—not a judge or an instrument of retribution.[48]

In group counseling, it is important to select those youngsters who can benefit from the group but who will not be scapegoated. Some youngsters, for personality reasons or for other factors such as extreme passiveness and dependency, can be harmed by the group because of the hostility that will be directed toward them and the scapegoat role that they may be forced into.

Role playing may be a highly effective component of group counseling because it enables youngsters to view situations as others do. The participants in the group have to be comfortable enough with one another so that the role playing will come naturally and so that they will not feel self-conscious or inhibited by the role-playing process. The basic concept of role playing is that because behavior of an individual is mainly the result of a reaction to what other people think of him or what he believes they think of him, the assuming of different roles will allow the youngster to test out his perceptions in a non-

---

[46] Rosemary C. Sarri and Robert D. Vinter, "Group Treatment Strategies in Juvenile Correctional Programs," *Crime and Delinquency*, 11 (October 1965), p. 330.

[47] E. Preston Sharp, "Group Counseling in a Short-Term Institution," *Federal Probation*, 23 (September 1959), p. 8.

[48] *Ibid.*, pp. 8–9.

threatening situation. The counselor or the group leader can objectively evaluate the role-playing behavior and the responses of the group to it. New insights which can be carried over to real-life situations can then be fostered.

In these processes, the group members are given an opportunity to try on the psychological shoes of others. They are exposed to processes which may give them some idea about how others may feel or think. A lack of awareness or caring about how others think or feel may be one of the major causal factors of delinquent behavior. It has been found that many delinquent children cannot realistically appraise or react to the feelings and thoughts of others.[49]

Many formats can be followed when utilizing the role-playing method. An actual skit can be developed, with participants placed in various roles. The role playing can also be spontaneous as a result of suggestions by either the members of the group or the leader. Sharp relates a case study in which boys were constantly complaining about the staff and their mistreatment of the boys.[50] The boys were asked to reverse roles and play the parts of the supervisors. As a result of this reverse role playing, the boys soon learned how to look at problems through the supervisors' eyes and were able to understand their roles. Likewise, the supervisors were able to understand the boys' position and this mutual understanding contributed a great deal to the formation of increased positive relationships between the boys and the staff.

It often becomes difficult to manage these group sessions because of the very nature of the boys' personalities and the hostility that is often directed at the group leader.

A leader needs to have some concept of what is the therapeutically effective activity on the part of the group and when it is utilizing the time efficiently toward moving in that direction. (This is determined by the degree of expression of feeling, the group interaction, sincere interest in helping each other, the feeling of group intensity, evidence of insight being developed, attitude changes, etc.)[51]

There does have to be some initial structure from the group leader. He should point out that the major purpose of the group is to solve problems through the understanding of each other's viewpoints and the expression of ideas, feelings, and alternatives. The group leader is mainly an objective observer who can give the group direction. He should not be an authoritarian and should be open to a variety of topics within a broad framework. It is the group's responsibility to initiate subjects that will be worth listening to and of interest to other group members. Even though the group leader will manage the discussion to provide

[49] *Ibid.,* p. 10.
[50] *Ibid.,* p. 11.
[51] Glen J. Walker, "Group Counseling in Juvenile Probation," *Federal Probation,* 22 (December 1959), p. 34.

some direction, it is up to the group to keep the discussion going. The two major results of the group discussions will be the expression of feelings and ultimately a concerted effort at problem solving by the entire group.[52]

GROUP THERAPY

Differentiating between *group therapy, group counseling, group psychotherapy, guided group interaction,* and *social group work* can be confusing. Sarri and Vinter, in summarizing juvenile group treatment strategies, include group psychotherapy, guided group interaction, and social group work under *group therapy*.[53] They maintain that these various methods are distinguished only by the type of worker who performs the service. Gazda feels that the terms *group therapy* and *group psychotherapy* are generally used synonymously.[54]

> Parole and probation agencies have been experimenting with group methods in recent years. Rather loose and ambiguous terminology has resulted. The terms group therapy, group counseling, group guidance, and guided group interaction are employed variously and often interchangeably. Almost anything undertaken with more than one individual at a time is likely to be termed group work or group therapy.[55]

Some writers feel that group therapy is a more intense process than social group work and that the emphasis is still on the individual while utilizing the group as a mechanism to better understand the individual and his behavior. Because the delinquent often manifests his behavior as a part of a group or a gang, it is felt that the group therapy situation is the natural vehicle in which to view the way he reacts to the group and the pressures it produces to influence his behavior. Furthermore, the one-to-one relationship with a therapist in social casework or individual psychotherapy can be very threatening to adolescents, since they are more comfortable interacting with their peers and being a part of a group. The adolescent often acts much differently outside the natural environment of the group. In addition, in individual counseling there is a more obvious superior-subordinate relationship. This situation is neutralized in the group where the youngster can receive a great deal of support from his peers. The "naturalness" of the group and the interaction are often conducive to the leader's making more valid judgments about the youngster, his patterns of interaction, and his method of problem solving.

> The mere fact that the group therapist is outnumbered by the adolescent and his peers frequently has a dramatic impact on the over-all attitudes

[52] *Ibid.,* p. 35.
[53] Sarri and Vinter, *op. cit.,* p. 332.
[54] George M. Gazda, *Basic Approaches to Group Psychotherapy and Group Counseling* (Springfield, Ill.: Charles C Thomas, Publisher, 1968), p. 4.
[55] Dressler, *op. cit.,* p. 183.

of the client toward the therapist and vice versa. There is a freedom about openly acknowledging and sometimes overtly expressing feelings in the group situation which often appears only during the later phases of individual treatment.[56]

The group can either support or not support the individual in his reactions both positive and negative in the group. The individual group member can find a great deal of reassurance from his peers, thus facilitating the expression of feelings. Even though the group can facilitate problem solving, not all youngsters should be placed in a group. Placement in a group has to be on a voluntary basis, and the group member should be allowed to quit whenever he feels that the situation is too threatening or that he would prefer to continue his counseling or therapy on a one-to-one basis. If the group member cannot be encouraged to talk freely, and if he is extremely threatened by the group, keeping him in the group can do more harm than good.

The group process does not in itself solve all the problems of resistance to treatment. Just as there is resistance to the individual method, there is resistance to the group method. The groups generally pass through various phases with distinguishable characteristics and processes. In the initial stages of the group meetings, some boys will not talk at all, while the more verbal boys will try to monopolize the conversation with trivia. The group manipulators attempt to justify their involvement by making the leader and the group members believe that the group cannot function without them and that they are the leaders. Many times these pseudotherapists attempt to manipulate the group to the point where meaningful and relevant problem situations are never discussed.

The therapist has to recognize the mood of the group and the corollary role that the con man is playing. He tries to elicit general feelings and tries to open up the hitherto silent members of the group. These sleepers often provide the therapist with a clue as to what is going on at the moment.[57]

Once the "con man," or manipulator can be controlled to the point where more significant group verbalization and discussion can take place and where the other group members are finally able to express their feelings, the group begins to open up and their ideas and gripes begin to be manifested. The youngsters soon find that they can make their ideas known and can express their feelings without the threat of retaliation by other group members or by the group leader. Manipulators in the group constantly try to test the group leader's authority and position. In the early stages of the group meetings, the group

[56] Harris B. Peck and Virginia Bellsmith, *Treatment of the Delinquent Adolescent* (New York: Family Service Association of America, 1954), pp. 25-26.
[57] Robert S. Shellow, Jack L. Ward, and Seymour Rubenfeld, "Group Therapy and the Institutional Delinquent," *International Journal of Group Psychotherapy*, 8 (1958), 267.

members do not want the spotlight focused on them. Hence the reason for the expression of hostility toward the leader and the attempt to divert the group processes into unproductive channels. The astute group leader, however, is not easily manipulated and understands the group process and the phases that the youngsters have to go through before meaningful dialogue, discussion, and problem solving can take place.

Throughout the group sessions and especially in the initial and middle stages, there is also considerable ambivalence toward the authority figure who is the group leader. Although the boys often want to receive the guidance of the leader in problem solving, they are not sure whether the leader can be trusted because of their past negative experiences with adults. The group leader has to recognize this and allow the youngsters to go at their own pace.

Ideally, the group will advance to the point where the expression of honest feelings will become commonplace. Once positive feelings begin to be expressed about the group leader, it is an indication that the group is progressing to the point where they will begin to look at their problems in a realistic manner and assist one another, with the help of the leader, in arriving at successful alternatives and solutions to common problems.

The group method does not always follow the sequence that has been described—the discussion of trivia, the expression of hostility toward the adult authority figure, the phase of acceptance of the authority figure, and then problem solving. There are peaks and valleys, and often when the group seems to be progressing well, there are backward trends or regression to earlier phases. However, the regression does not last long, and if the leader can ride out the storm, the group begins to progress again and can attain new levels of interaction and understanding.

Of the many variations of the group method, Allen describes an approach in which the professional group leader is a "silent observer." Allen feels that this facilitates problem solving.

> The silent observer method is a variation on traditional dual therapy techniques. It is hypothesized that group interaction might be improved by the adoption of a dual therapy technique in which the role of the second therapist was modified to that of a silent observer. Among the potential advantages of the new method was the fact that the observer being less involved with the group than the therapist himself would be in an excellent position to make objective observations about the group.[58]

Even though the observer does not react directly, he can evaluate the dynamic interplay taking place in the group. He is also not placed "on the defense" or "on the spot" like the primary group leader. After the group meeting, he can provide the primary therapist or the leader with new insights regarding the dynamics of interaction and alternatives for problem solving. Allen feels

[58] James E. Allen, "The Silent Observer: A New Approach to Group Therapy for Delinquents," *Crime and Delinquency,* 16 (July 1970), p. 325.

that the use of the silent observer not only accelerates and enhances the treatment process in the group but also provides a training laboratory for new group leaders. The training aspect of the silent observer role may well be the most important benefit of the method.

Like most other methods discussed, the specific orientation (within a general structure) that the group leader takes and the path he pursues toward his goal of helping youngsters will vary depending on his training, his personality, and his client group. The various group methods, just like the individual methods, do allow for individual variation and experimentation.

SOCIAL GROUP WORK

Ferguson defines *social group work* as social work "focused on the individual in a group setting" which attempts to help him function more effectively in groups and derive greater satisfaction from this participation.[59] According to Dressler, social group work is differentiated from social casework by its additional goal of furthering the group's accomplishment of a social purpose as a group;[60] its similarity to social casework is evident in its goals of improving the individual's relationships and subjective responses to the social environment.[61]

The social group work method operates under many of the same assumptions as social casework, although it is more complex because of the number of group members and the increased interpersonal dynamics. It is possible for an individual to be involved in both social casework and social group work at the same time, but not all clients are capable of this dual involvement. Konopka lists some of the principles of social group work:

1. The worker's main function is helping and this helping is perpetuated to establish purposeful relationships with group members.

2. The worker must be warm, understanding, and spontaneous, but yet be able to maintain and enhance group direction.

3. The worker has to accept group members without accepting their behavior and often "limits" have to be utilized but in a constructive manner.

4. The worker has to manage the group while at the same time not forgetting the uniqueness of the individual.[62]

In summary, the worker has to be able to not only empathize and understand individual problems but also visualize and conceptualize how the group processes can contribute to problem solving. He must also be both sympathetic and

[59] Ferguson, *op. cit.*, p. 13.
[60] Dressler, *op. cit.*, p. 162.
[61] Tappan, *op. cit.*, p. 366.
[62] Gisela Konopka, "The Social Group Work Method: Its Use in the Correctional Field," *Federal Probation,* 20 (July 1956), pp. 26–27.

consistent in the way he manages the group so that there will be a structural framework that will facilitate goal achievement.

Pierce visualizes the group as a "social laboratory" in which the individual group member experiments with new patterns of social functioning.[63] The individual can then evaluate his new patterns of behavior by the reactions of the group members. If there is a satisfactory response, he may try them in his relationships with peers outside the groups or in institutions in the community.

> As group members develop a sense of the group as something more than a collection of individuals interacting, they are able to use this identification with the group as a force for modifying their own behavior and attitudes. Often one is able to risk change or growth because "the group is behind me."[64]

Of the many different types of group work and group therapy, one particular variation that has been effective with gang members in large cities is what is called the "detached" group work method. Some youngsters do not have the desire to come to an agency to participate in formal group meetings; therefore, the group worker has to extend beyond the confines of his agency and develop relationships with youngsters "on the street."

> Group workers act on a tolerant basis and accept the gang members as individuals while making clear that they do not go along with their delinquent behavior. This gain and acceptance requires time. In time, the group worker hopes to get the gang to modify its role in the community and the priority of the individual's role. The aim is to reduce the individual gang member's role as a delinquent.[65]

The role of a detached group worker is difficult, and McCarthy and Barbaro have summarized his objectives. Basically, he attempts to reduce antisocial behavior within the community, broaden the gang members' social horizons, provide the individual gang member with new alternatives to social behavior both with his peers and with community institutions, and generally improve his personal and social adjustment which, in turn, will improve his relations with the community. It is difficult, however, to achieve these ends if the group worker is not able to interact meaningfully with the gang members, gain their acceptance and trust, and influence their behavior.

The personality of the gang group worker has to be such that he is comfortable interacting in the community and associating with youngsters who frequently typify a life-style and personal orientation much different from his own. The youngsters will only develop trust and confidence in the worker if he is able

[63] F. J. Pierce, "Social Group Work in a Women's Prison," *Federal Probation*, 27 (December 1963), pp. 37–38.
[64] *Ibid.*, pp. 33–38.
[65] Mabel A. Elliott, "Group Therapy in Dealing with Juvenile and Adult Offenders," *Federal Probation*, 27 (September 1963), p. 54.

to understand their life-style and empathize with them. Youngsters quite naturally in these situations wonder what the worker has in mind and how he is going to benefit from helping them. Gang workers are often considered intelligence agents for the police, thus making it difficult to gain youngsters' trust and confidence. Once the gang worker demonstrates that he is there to help— to look at their situation and help them solve their problems—trust and positive results will be forthcoming. Many of the youngsters whom the gang worker comes in contact with have had few positive life experiences. Once their trust is gained, the gang worker can begin to redirect the gang members' energy into socially acceptable channels through many different means, such as organizing athletic teams or dances.[66] "Inasmuch as many of the intergang conflicts stemmed from a need for status or 'rep' for being the 'baddest gang' [sic], it was assumed that if the gang gained a sufficient status through socially acceptable activities it would not need to maintain their 'rep' through fighting."[67]

Not all social group work takes place within a gang setting, but many of the positive results that have taken place in social group work with delinquent youngsters is the result of gang workers' interacting with youth in their "natural setting."

> The essence of working with street clubs involves the establishment of meaningful relationships between the worker and gang members, so that these relationships can be utilized for the redirection of the anti-social activities of gangs and their members.[68]

The social group work method can be effective, especially in helping delinquent youngsters to understand their deficiencies and developing new and more productive patterns of interaction in the community.

GROUP PSYCHOTHERAPY

Even though there is a blending of the various therapeutic approaches and it is often difficult to differentiate between them, a separate discussion of each is helpful because it illustrates, at least numerically, the descriptive approaches that exist. *Group psychotherapy,* when compared with other group methods, is usually thought of as having more ambitious goals, such as deep insight development and personality restructuring. Many of the techniques utilized, however, are similar to other group methods, and the major difference is in the *degree* of "probing" and the intensity of the relationship.

When working with adolescents, it is often difficult to develop group

---

[66] James E. McCarthy and Joseph S. Barbaro, "Redirecting Teenage Gangs," in *Reaching the Unreached,* Sylvan S. Furman, Ed. (New York: New York City Youth Board, 1952), p. 108.

[67] *Ibid.,* pp. 110-11.

[68] *Ibid.,* p. 111.

exists between group members, although this can be somewhat controlled with adequate selection procedures. Even in groups that have many similar characteristics, it is difficult for group members to empathize with one another.

> This may be particularly true of delinquents who are notoriously self-centered. They form groups not out of friendship, but for mutual security against the adult world which is perceived as hostile.[69]

Schulman states that the components necessary for an effective group psychotherapy situation, such as personal interaction, cooperation, and tolerance, are in direct conflict with the dissocial, antagonistic, and exploitive orientation of delinquents.[70] He feels that traditional therapeutic techniques must be modified when working with the delinquent, who is not motivated for psychotherapy and lacks the qualities of group identification and empathy which are necessary for positive group results. To facilitate group identification, it is important to point out the common benefits that can be gained by all group members by their participating in the group. Even though group members will initially be skeptical of the benefits they can receive, once the group is in progress, the secondary benefits of associating with the group and socializing with their peers will contribute to greater cooperation and goal achievement.

One of the major problems that delinquents have in their communities is that their behavior and demands are not realistic. In other words, they are not very effective at "reality testing." Their personalities, in many cases, have been retarded at early impulsive levels of functioning, and they often do not have adequate reality reference points. Group psychotherapy, as well as some other group methods discussed helps the delinquent to test reality and the attitudes and reactions of the leader and the other group members before extending into the "uncertain waters" of the community.

For increased effectiveness with delinquent youngsters, it is helpful if the parents also receive some type of treatment. It is discouraging to treat the youngster and then release him to a family that will contribute to further delinquent behavior. Parents who tend to subvert the efforts of the therapist with their youngster and who contribute to his acting out behavior in the community often have to be confronted and dealt with on the same therapeutic basis as their youngster. Many examples can be given of how parents can destroy all the positive efforts of the therapist. If the family is not treated along with the youngster, results will be minimal and the youngster will fall back into the same trap that existed before his exposure to treatment.

Through *family therapy*, parents are made aware of the often hidden and distorted negative aspects of their relationship with their youngsters. The therapist can point out these negative dynamics and patterns of behavior so that they will be recognized and altered.

[69] Marvin Hersko, "Group Psychotherapy with Delinquent Adolescent Girls," *American Journal of Orthopsychiatry,* 32 (January 1962), pp. 170–71.
[70] Irving Schulman, "Modifications in Group Psychotherapy with Antisocial Adolescents," *International Journal of Group Psychotherapy,* 7 (1957), p. 310.

Regardless of whether the therapy involves a group of family members or a group of delinquent youngsters, the techniques are similar in that the group is used as a vehicle to foster expression of feelings, to involve the members in problem solving, and to observe the interaction and interplay of group participants. The positive insights and the behavioral modification that take place in the group can then be transferred on a more permanent basis outside the group to the community.

ACTIVITY THERAPY

Many clients do not have the verbal ability necessary to communicate effectively in a conventional individual or group therapeutic situation. Very young children and resistant subjects such as delinquents and predelinquents are especially suited to the *activity therapy* method. A group of six to eight children are gathered or invited to meet at a specific time and place to engage in play, such as group games or some artistic endeavor like modeling clay. The atmosphere is permissive, and the youngsters can use their time as they wish.

> A moderately neurotic child finds great release in a permissive environment where he can act out his repressed hostility and aggression in creative work, play, mischief, and hilarity. Because his behavior does not call for retaliation, punishment, or disapproval, pent-up emotions find appropriate discharge. Perhaps of even greater value is the fact that he sees other children act freely without dire or destructive consequences. This has the effect of reducing guilt about hidden impulses of hate and feelings of being bad or worthless. Not only are the blockings to free expression through unrestricted acting out removed by *activity catharsis,* but the individual psychotherapy with these patients is facilitated as a result. The child communicates more freely and is less protective and less suspicious of the caseworker or psychiatrist.[71]

Slavson points out that only certain types of children can effectively utilize activity therapy as a substitute for the more verbal orientation of conventional group therapy or individual psychotherapy.[72] The open aggression and hostility that is permitted within a permissive situation can create anxiety in some neurotic children and overwhelm them to the point where the activity group experience can become devastating. Typologies can range all the way from the accidental or situational offender to the chronic character disorder offender. Each of these diagnostic classifications often necessitates special consideration and specific therapeutic techniques. For example, because the neurotic offender suffers from anxiety and guilt, his delinquent behavior is merely a symptom of his attempt to resolve this inner conflict; whereas the character disorder offender has a minimum amount of anxiety and guilt, and his acting out is a result of a

[71] S. R. Slavson, quoted in Tappan, *op. cit.,* p. 368.
[72] *Ibid.*

lack of conscience structure, or superego. Thus, methods of treatment will have to vary considerably between the two diagnostic categories. Anxiety and guilt should not be clinically induced in those neurotic children who already suffer from them, but methods that use even the minimal amounts of anxiety felt by the character disorder client can be the motivating force for his seeking inner change and new modes of adaption.

Even though the pure categories of *neurotic* offender or *character disorder* offender may not actually exist, those youngsters whose personality structure can be evaluated as predominantly neurotic can benefit most from such insight-type methods of treatment as psychotherapy and casework. The character disorder offender can benefit most from such methods as reality therapy and behavior modification because he does not have as much motivation, anxiety, or desire to develop deep insight into his problems—the main goal is to interrupt his negative cycle so that he ceases to come in contact with the law. Any insight that he gains into his problem and the reasons for its manifestations is a bonus.

Activity therapy can therefore be useful for some youngsters. But the neurotic child who has difficulty handling his hostile impulses may be extremely threatened by a technique like activity therapy with its permissive open atmosphere where impulses can be easily manifested. It is often difficult for him to control the expression of these impulses once he leaves the confines of the activity therapy room and returns to his home and community. Regardless of the therapeutic technique utilized, a careful evaluation has to be made regarding its appropriateness for the particular client. Not all clients can benefit from the same technique, and in fact a combination of techniques is often required.

GUIDED GROUP INTERACTION

Guided group interaction is basically similar to group therapy or group psychotherapy in that it is also based on the assumption that through the group and its processes the delinquent can solve his problems. The group is the major vehicle for change.

According to McCorkle, guided group interaction assumes that delinquents will benefit from the freedom to discuss and analyze problems and their own roles and relationships within the group.[73] McCorkle feels that guided group interaction operates most effectively in an informal atmosphere where most of the social controls evolve from the group itself and where meaningful interaction of group members can ultimately produce insight and new patterns of adaption to the community.

> The object is to develop a group culture in which those involved will make themselves responsible for helping and controlling each other. The assumption is that a delinquent is more likely to be influenced by his peers than

[73] Lloyd W. McCorkle, "Group Therapy with Offenders," in Johnston, Savitz, and Wolfgang, *op. cit.,* p. 518.

by professional staff. The individual member is not likely to manipulate others nor will he be able to lie or alibi himself out of uncomfortable situations in front of his peers. They have all been down the same road and they are not easily hoodwinked.[74]

This description of guided group interaction is not much different from the description of group psychotherapy and group therapy. The group can exert a great deal of pressure on its individual members after the group has been stabilized and the leader trusted, and meaningful dialogue has taken place. The peer group has extensive power over the individual members and can impose sanctions if one of the members does not become meaningfully involved. Empey and Rabow relate that at Pine Hills, a facility for delinquent youngsters, the group is permitted to use sanctions, within the confines of the treatment system, on members who do not cooperate. The ultimate sanction is refusal to release a boy from the program.[75]

The process described for guided group interaction in regard to the structure of the group and the means it takes to achieve meaningful dialogue, communication, and expression of feelings is similar to the group processes discussed earlier. The group leader plays an important role in directing and managing significant aspects of the interaction, although he attempts to do this according to a democratic model of group participation, discussion, and ventilation of feelings. The initial stages of the group are used to vent hostility and aggression. Initially the group members are self-centered and unable to realistically or meaningfully involve themselves or their peers in the problem-solving process. Later, as the group progresses and the group members see that their group peers have similar problems and backgrounds, empathy and group identification is facilitated.

Simultaneously, the behavior of the group becomes more orderly and the leader finds increased support for its earlier definitions. If the initial anxieties and resistances have been adequately handled, warmer, friendlier relations replace the earlier aggressive, destructive, hostile responses. With the release of hostile, aggressive feelings and some understanding of the origin of these feelings, deeper levels may be reached.[76]

McCorkle gives the following criteria for selecting a boy for a group and for using when the group is in actual operation: The boy should be able to contribute to group maintenance, and members should be suited to each other. Generally, group members should be of the same age, educational level, and intelligence, and participation should be on a voluntary basis. The group should

[74] Dressler, *op. cit.,* p. 202.
[75] Lamar T. Empey and Jerome Rabow, "The Provo Experiment on Delinquency Rehabilitation," in *Juvenile Delinquency: A Book of Readings,* Rose Giallombardo, Ed. (New York: John Wiley & Sons, Inc., 1966), p. 541.
[76] McCorkle, *op. cit.,* p. 522.

meet at regular intervals and at specified times and should not exceed twenty in number.[77]

MILIEU THERAPY

Whether the youngster is in an institution, a halfway house, or some other controlled or semicontrolled setting, *milieu therapy* attempts to produce an environment that will facilitate meaningful change, increased growth, and satisfactory adjustment.

Slavson feels that milieu therapy is suitable for persons whose deviant behavior is a reaction to unfavorable life conditions.[78] If the milieu, or environment, is carefully planned so that deviant adaption will not be needed, fostered, or encouraged, delinquent behavior will be modified or eliminated. Kane feels that the milieu consists of everything happening to the child in his therapeutic environment, whether it is the institution, a halfway house, or some other controlled setting.

> It is as subtle as the attitudes of staff and the kinds of controls administered and the purpose of those controls, constructive or punitive. If one is to single out the essence of a therapeutic milieu, I would say that it is found in the quality of relationships between the children and the direct contact staff.[79]

Because their environment is, in fact, the therapeutic setting, daily activities, including both failures and successes, are the topics of discussion between the client and those persons who are a part of his milieu. Fenton and others define the correctional milieu and the goals of milieu therapy in this setting:

> The correctional community is a method of social therapy in which staff and inmates make a conscious effort to utilize all the experiences in all areas of the group existence in a therapeutic manner. This program bridges a communication gap between staff and inmates typically found in correctional institutions and also utilizes inmate peer influence—the self-help concept—to help inmates gain self-awareness and a more responsible outlook. Inmates who live and work together meet with the staff regularly with an expressed goal of improving post-release performance. By employing, under staff direction, open communication, confrontation, as well as other treatment methods, inmate participants can model and adjust their behavior through learning, testing, and fixating newer and more effective modes of perceiving and relating to others.[80]

[77] *Ibid.,* p. 523.

[78] S. R. Slavson, *Reclaiming the Delinquent* (New York: The Free Press, 1965), p. 17.

[79] Joseph H. Kane, "An Institutional Program for the Seriously Disturbed Delinquent Boy," *Federal Probation,* 30 (September 1966), pp. 42–43.

[80] Norman Fenton, *et al., Explorations in the Use of Group Counseling in the County Correctional Program* (Palo Alto, Calif.: Pacific Books, 1962).

Milieu therapy takes a more general orientation to treatment than guided group interaction, group therapy, social casework, and the other methods because it focuses on the total environment of the individual and is viewed as the major therapeutic agent. Milieu therapy is generally utilized in controlled or semicontrolled environments where the client's behavior, actions, and experiences can be somewhat regulated. The many other techniques discussed in this chapter, such as casework and group therapy, can be used to supplement the milieu therapy approach.

SOCIAL ENVIRONMENT THERAPY

An approach similar to *milieu* therapy is social environment therapy. Also referred to as the living unit concept, Haley mentions that the therapy has been used by the Canadian Penitentiary Service in recent years with great success. Custodial officers are used as treatment agents, providing counseling to a number of inmates who live together in the same section of the institution. The custodial officers, under supervision, provide a natural communication link with the inmates, integrating their custodial duties with their therapeutic help. Advocates of this approach

argue that a treatment approach to delinquency should focus on the creation of a controlled environment ih order to modify the inmate's social behaviour. Within this setting an atmosphere is created in which staff and inmates endeavor to solve problems in order to teach the inmates social skills and values. These concepts should be applied within the living units of the institution so that the natural tendencies to form social relationships can be utilized. As many inmates as possible should be involved in this process so that although committees are sometimes used, they are to facilitate rather than replace contacts with all those concerned. On the basis of these formal and informal meetings, staff and inmate barriers break down; treatment plans are developed and implemented; and the entire institutional environment becomes the forum [for treatment].[81]

DIRECT HOME INTERVENTION

Attempts have been made to treat aggressive youngsters in their own homes by training their parents to deal with the behavioral problems. The Oregon Research Institute initiated a series of investigations using the direct home intervention approach with Patterson, Reid, and Hendriks elaborating on many of the methods and techniques.

Techniques can range from teaching the parents child management procedures to offering financial inducements for successful handling of their chil-

[81] Hugh L. Haley, "Social Environment Therapy: A Treatment Approach for Correctional Institutions," *Canadian Journal of Criminology and Corrections,* Vol. 16, No. 3 (July 1974), p. 268.

dren. Much emphasis of this approach has been with youngsters who were stealing. The conclusions drawn by Patterson and Reid were

> that a successful treatment of stealers will have to evolve at least the following steps: An initial external incentive for the family to change; extensive training in intra-family relations of a general nature; training the parents to monitor or track their children; and finally programs to alter the stealing itself. At this time, we are still experimenting with variations on the home intervention approach. Until a way can be found to get more of the referred families to actually enter and participate in treatment, the conclusions reached (in this paper) must remain speculative.[82]

Reid and Hendriks have evaluated this approach and report that there was a reduction in deviant behavior of children referred to the program.[83]

FAMILY CRISIS COUNSELING

Sacramento County, California, has a diversion project to deal with juveniles involved in status offenses like runaway and incorrigibility. Intensive short-term family counseling therapy is used so that the youngster can stay in the family in lieu of going through the formal process of the juvenile justice system. Specialists trained in family counseling provide almost immediate assistance to the youngster within the constellation of his family. The project has four main goals:

1. To reduce the number of cases going to court.
2. To reduce the number of repeat offenses.
3. To decrease overnight detentions.
4. To accomplish these goals at a cost no greater than required for regular processing of cases.[84]

Referral to the program can originate from several different sources, such as the police, school, or even the family, and the first session with the family begins within hours of the referral. The problem is not only dealt with immediately, but the parents are made aware that the difficulty the youngster is having is the responsibility of the whole family.

---

[82] G. R. Patterson and J. B. Reid, "Intervention for Families of Aggressive Boys: A Replication Study," *Behavior Research and Therapy,* Vol. 11 (1973), p. 389.

[83] John B. Reid and A. F. C. S. Hendriks, "Preliminary Analysis of the Effectiveness of Direct Home Intervention for the Treatment of Pre-delinquent Boys Who Steal," in *Behavior Change: Methodology, Concepts and Practice,* Leo Hamerlynck, *et al.,* Eds. (Champaign, Ill.: Research Press, 1973), p. 218.

[84] U.S. Department of Justice, "Family Crisis Counseling: An Alternative to Juvenile Court," Sacramento County Probation Department, Law Enforcement Assistance Admin., National Institute of Law Enforcement & Criminal Justice (Washington, D.C.: U.S. Government Printing Office, 1975), p. 3.

The sessions usually last from one to two hours, although they could last longer. The maximum number of sessions is five; and the parents, as well as the youngster, are encouraged to contact the counselor by telephone, if necessary.

The project staff, which consists of a supervisor and six counselors, has been effective in providing intensive counseling to youngsters and their families.

> During the first year of the project, only 3.7 percent of the youths had court petitions filed. The cost of handling, detention, and placement for each project youth was approximately half of that for youths cared for under conventional procedures.[85]

Because of the success of this program, the Law Enforcement Assistance Administration recommends that other communities use this type of approach in dealing with youngsters in trouble.

SUMMARY

This chapter has described some of the specific methods that are used in handling the juvenile. One or all of these methods could technically be utilized in one large program. Just because several methods have been described doesn't necessarily mean that the method is successful in helping the youngster adjust to his environment. Chapter 10 will discuss the research findings relative to some of the therapies discussed. Suffice it to say that, to date, there have been pessimistic appraisals of many of the therapeutic techniques currently used.

> Treatment programs for delinquents have been notoriously unsuccessful, as indicated by the high recidivism rates usually reported. Efforts to keep delinquents free of crime are hampered by a strong peer culture which maintains the delinquent behavior. Even those treatments which are successful on a short-term basis have usually failed to document any long-term difference over similar nontreated youth in such variables as number of offenses. As such, the treatment of delinquent youth represents one of the greatest challenges to the fields of psychology, psychiatry, and social work.[86]

QUESTIONS AND PROJECTS

Essay Questions

1. Compare the advantages and the disadvantages of individual treatment versus group treatment.

[85] *Ibid.,* p. 1.

[86] K. Daniel O'Leary and G. Terence Wilson, *Behavior Therapy: Application and Outcome* (Englewood Cliffs, N.J.: Prentice-Hall, Inc., 1975), p. 1976.

2. What treatment method do you think is most appropriate for juvenile delinquents?

3. Why have "conventional" treatment approaches not been effective with juvenile delinquents?

4. Why can't all youngsters benefit from a group treatment experience?

5. Why are there so many different methods of treatment?

Projects

1. Attempt to identify the major treatment methods of the various agencies within your community.

2. Develop a list of criteria that will facilitate determining the effectiveness of a particular treatment method.

3. Develop a coordinated educational program for the professionals in the juvenile justice system to acquaint them with the various methods of treatment in your community.

chapter 10

The Need for Research in Delinquency Prevention and Treatment

Vigorous research is necessary to identify the many variables related to the phenomenon of juvenile delinquency. Meaningful research will contribute to the establishment of theoretically sound treatment, prevention, and control programs. Research can provide a sound basis on which successful programs can be replicated in different environments and communities.

At present no adequate data base exists that can provide the necessary information about the relative merits of the many available programs or the alternatives most applicable to the many different types of delinquent behavior syndromes.

Research efforts have to be directed in areas that have heretofore been neglected. In addition, scientists from many different disciplines should participate in delinquency research to make it complete. Empey and Lubeck provide some helpful suggestions, and list the following steps for an effective delinquency research process:

1. Define the target population. Decide whether it is to include the young children, a middle-range group, or older, convicted offenders.

2. Conduct a pilot study by which to identify and describe the particular children who fit the general characteristics of the target population.

3. Define objectives for the program. Include administrators, practitioners, and research people in the defining process.

4. Write a contract specifying the obligations and roles of each of these three sets of people.

5. Derive an intervention strategy based upon the general leads provided by the theory and the findings of the pilot study.

6. Establish a research strategy based on the same principles and guidelines and concerned with studying the characteristics of the subject population, the program itself, and its outcome.[1]

Much more effort has to be made toward more sophisticated evaluation and research procedures if successful programs are to be perpetuated and replicated and unsuccessful ones eliminated or improved. Evaluation and research should be an integral part of any program established to assist the delinquent.

It is common to hear from social scientists that more research is needed and it is probably not much less common to hear from practitioners that research is usually inconclusive and that it is more important to get underway with action programs. But whatever its implication, long term development of delinquency control measures requires the kind of knowledge that only comes from systematic research efforts. Three specific types of research now seem required. National statistical data are necessary for long term planning and for keeping the public informed. There is a desperate need for description and evaluation of alternative programs of prevention and control and the techniques which will aid in the development of such programs. Finally, theoretical research is needed to provide a base for the creation for more meaningful and theoretically sound action programs.[2]

Research means many different things to different people and often "strikes terror" into the hearts of practitioners when it is proposed. Research is merely a tool, which can take many different forms, to assist in defining problems and developing methods for their solution.

Research is many kinds of activity. It is gathering and analyzing facts. It is conducting and evaluating operational experiments. It is searching for the motivations of human behavior. Obviously there is a need here for a wide variety of talents. Sociologists, lawyers, economists, psychiatrists, psychologists, physical scientists, engineers, statisticians, mathematicians—all these and more are needed. There is likewise opportunity for a wide variety of organizations and institutions. Too little is known about the various uses and limitations of different methods of organizing for research to permit the prescription of any one mold for future research efforts. Indeed it is essential that such efforts take many different forms.[3]

---

[1] Lamar T. Empey and Steven G. Lubeck, "Delinquency Prevention Strategies," U.S. Department of Health, Education and Welfare, Social and Rehabilitation Service, Youth Development and Delinquency Prevention Administration, 1970.
[2] Stanton Wheeler, Leonard Cottrell, Jr., and Ann Romasco, "Juvenile Delinquency—Its Prevention and Control," in *Task Force Report Juvenile Delinquency and Youth Crime*, The President's Commission on Law Enforcement and the Administration of Justice (Washington, D.C.: U.S. Government Printing Office, 1967), p. 424.
[3] *Ibid.*

Since World War II massive research efforts have been undertaken to determine the causes of and the solutions to crime and delinquency. Assumptions have been drastically modified, practices have changed, much has been learned, but the surface of the problem has hardly been scratched. Many promising courses have been embarked on only to be abandoned as time proved them ineffective, inefficient, too costly, or unpopular. No aspect of the criminal justice system has received more attention than juvenile and adult corrections. Yet, there prevails at present a decided pessimistic attitude toward correctional research. In the words of Robert Martinson, "correctional research is about nine-tenths pageantry, rumination, and rubbish, and about one-tenth useful knowledge."[4]

However pessimistic his statement, Martinson cannot but affirm the value of good research in problem solving. Moreover, rising crime and delinquency, crowded institutions, fear for public safety, budgetary problems, and the spread of new management methods into social agencies have all created strong pressure for evaluative research. The public at large is demanding to know what is being done to reduce the crime rate, whether the measures employed are effective, and what they are costing them in tax dollars. The answers to these and other critical questions can come only from continued research. To be effective, however, the research of the future will have to proceed from a sound theoretical base, employ realistic and not necessarily "classical" methodologies, and be translated into practice by administrators open to experimentation and innovation.

History

Since adult and juvenile corrections have been the subject of such considerable research efforts, a summary of the history of correctional research will afford significant insight into the development of research in parallel components of the criminal and juvenile justice systems. Correctional research is, moreover, of particular relevance to juvenile delinquency. In addition most of the "vigorous" criminal justice research has been done in institutionalized correctional populations. This was done for the obvious reason of having the subject in a controlled setting.

Accounts and statistics have been maintained from the early nineteenth century in housekeeping, budgeting, and audit. These data were used as reports for funding sources and in planning for future needs. With an expanding offender population, the need for the increased accuracy of analytical techniques became acute. The advent of relatively accurate statistical analysis brought with it some penetrating questions regarding professional practice. The data suggested, for example, that the costs of imprisonment might be reduced by the increased use of probation and parole and other community treatment approaches. This raised the question of public safety. If relatively large numbers of offenders were to be

[4] Robert Martinson, "California Research at the Crossroads," *Crime and Delinquency* (April 1976), p. 183.

set free or not incarcerated at all, small-scale experimentation had first to establish whether a considerable negative impact on public safety would ensue. The acceptance of the need for experimentation before large-scale changes in correctional practice could be undertaken established the principle of the continuity of statistical analysis.

For many years, the effectiveness of correctional programs has been evaluated by counting the convicted offenders who return to criminal behavior. This return is termed "recidivism" and understanding its scope is essential to operational control. The statistics on recidivism are extremely difficult to obtain, however; correctional agencies are, for the most part, not equipped to gather accurate data on recidivism. A greater hindrance to the collection of recidivism data is the fragmented nature of the criminal justice system: the police, the courts, correctional agencies, do not always cooperate effectively with one another.

Last, recidivism of this type is only the return to criminal behavior that is *officially* noted. In other words, officially noted recidivism is only a rough measure of objective recidivism, a certain percentage of which is always undetected.

Statistical data taken alone, however, by no means provide adequate information. They provide a numerical count or a numerical comparison. The numbers must be interpreted and strategies to improve results must be devised. Thus research and statistics are interdependent.

The earliest empirical research in corrections, that of Sheldon and Eleanor Glueck in the thirties,[5] examined the experience of offenders who had been exposed to various rehabilitative programs. Their basic approach has remained the one most frequently employed up to the present. A considerable amount of research data, which has had a significant impact on correctional programs, has accumulated. Perhaps the most dramatic finding of correctional research has been that incarceration cannot be shown to produce any positive effect on offender behavior. Thus incarceration seems incompatible with rehabilitation, regardless of the treatment program. This conclusion has been arrived at with amazing consistency and has led to an interest in developing community-based alternatives to incarceration. These offer more hope of rehabilitation and are also considerably cheaper. Present consensus maintains that institutionalization should be employed only in the cases of those offenders who pose a direct and obvious threat to the public. This position has resulted in the complete reorganization of adult and juvenile correctional services in some states.

Experiments conducted in the late fifties and early sixties have demonstrated the relative feasibility of various alternatives to incarceration such as community treatment, halfway houses, work release, and probation subsidy. Evidence seems to show that these programs do in fact reduce recidivism *if* the choice of participant is fortunate, that is, if only those offenders are chosen to participate who seem predisposed to success. Establishing the objective criteria, however, which indicates that an offender is favorably predisposed to various

[5] Sheldon and Eleanor Glueck, *500 Criminal Careers* (New York: Knopf, 1930).

treatment alternatives constitutes the most critical need of research today, since if anything is obvious at this juncture it is that different offenders react in a variety of ways to treatment. Thus, the overall premise that a community-based, nonpunitive program is appropriate to *all* offenders is as erroneous as the age-old punitive and incarceration approach to *all* offenders.

Changing Offender Behavior

Experimentation in the changing of offender behavior is of recent origin. It is based on *three* groups of theories which derive from the limited general range of socialization theory. The *first* group promotes the belief that human behavior is most profoundly affected by the rewards and punishments that accrue to various behaviors. The whole present criminal justice system, with its incarceration, limitation of freedom short of incarceration, fines, and so on, is based on it. The *second* group of theories supports the notion that effective socialization derives from the acquisition of insight and self-awareness, the lack of which results in defective socialization or criminal behavior. This position is applied in the practice of many types of therapy and counseling. The *third* and least developed group of theories hold that the corrective change to be sought is in the nature of the offender's relation to the community rather than a change in the offender himself. The emphasis is therefore placed on the interaction between the offender and his surroundings. The attempt is made to "reintegrate" him into the community in a better position than the one he had occupied before turning to delinquent behavior.

Experimentation thus far has not uncovered a theory of sufficient power to guarantee the restoration to society of large numbers of offenders. Moreover, the present state of corrections seems to work at cross-purposes to this objective.

Redefinition of Recidivism

Major current research is concerned with a redefinition of recidivism and, on the positive side, with a definition of offender success. For example, an offender may not have been convicted of further crimes but may be on the welfare rolls, a school dropout, a patient in a mental hospital, or an alcoholic on skid row. While technically not a failure, he is also not a success. A further concern is a need to relate success in some demonstrable way to a specific strategy or technique. Because of the correctional preoccupation with rehabilitation, the effects of punishment and incapacitation have yet to be studied for their practical relevance. The increasing clamor for accountability creates the need for research into quality control. Agency improvement, the modification of old programs, and the introduction of new programs can only result subsequent to research and experimentation.

Academicians continue to debate whether the poor yield thus far from criminal justice research is attributable to a *poverty of theory, a dearth of methodology*, or to the *lack of practical relevance* of the research. As research in criminal justice matures, however, there is every reason to believe that all three areas will receive greater attention and will experience a proportionate degree of refinement.

Research Methods and Strategies

A research method or technique consists of a series of tasks or procedures designed to systematize inquiry and to maintain objectivity, insofar as this is possible, into an area of experience—either for the purpose of simply adding to present knowledge or to solve a pressing problem. In addition to the terms *research method* and *research technique*, one also often hears the term *research model*. Generally speaking, a model represents or translates something into a physical, conceptual, or mathematical framework for the purpose of comparing or measuring. Research models are grouped into the broad categories of methodological models, subject-matter models, actor-oriented models, goal-oriented models, broad strategy models, and academic or industrial models.

The methodological models have the most general relevance in criminal justice research; therefore, the bulk of our discussion will concern them. Some examples of methodological models in current use in criminal justice delinquency research are nonexperimental, quasiexperimental, and controlled-experiment models.

Nonexperimental studies are the most numerous in criminal justice research, comprising eighty to ninety percent of all studies. There is a consensus among researchers that nonexperimental studies also have the most impact, resulting in the most important research-based policy changes. One reason for their popularity is that they can be applied with relative rapidity and ease as opposed to the cumbersome controlled experiment, for example. Moreover they are cheaper and easier to communicate to nonspecialists because they are more tangible and less abstract. Disadvantages in their use include subjectivity, lack of standardization, and uncertain reliability; they are also often difficult to interpret.

Some of the more common types of nonexperimental studies include the following. The case study examines in depth a person, group, place, event, program, or experience to determine what exists, what is happening and, if it transcends the purely descriptive, the case study perhaps even delves into causes.

Surveys of various kinds systematically collect data of similar nature from several sources. They may be collected by telephone, by mail, by distributing a form, by interview, or by any combination of these. The data collected are primarily descriptive although they can be evaluative if comparisons constitute an advanced step of the process. Events are measured at periodic intervals in an attempt to assess trends. They demonstrate increases, declines, breaks, displacements, fluctuations, and stabilities.

Cohort analysis is a special kind of time series evaluation that examines the record of performance of a group or cohort over a period of time. Cohorts are artifically constructed groups that share similar characteristics relating to time. They may have been born in the same year, for example, or arrested in the same year, released from an institution or a halfway house in the same year, and so on. They can be compared for performance pattern, performance level, performance distribution, and comparative performance.

Before-after studies attempt to evaluate the condition or status of a group before involving them in some experience and subsequent to its application. Changes which result may be attributed to the experience.

The *quasiexperiment* is most often used to evaluate a treatment process by comparing two groups of subjects, who were chosen for comparison because of similar or shared characteristics or experiences. The latter usually bear some relationship to the desired outcomes of the treatment in question. One group is subjected to evaluation of the treatment, while the other is not. Any measurable differences in performance later may be then attributed to the effects of treatment. The quasiexperiment is employed when a "rigorous" evaluation is sought under conditions which preclude the use of a controlled experiment. These conditions can be political, an insufficient control of a multiplicity of variables, time pressure, or, the treatment program to be evaluated may no longer be in existence. Quasiexperimental procedures (1) identify the treatment group, (2) isolate the personal and social characteristics of the group, (3) discover a comparison group with similar characteristics, and (4) compare the performances of the two groups in equatable posttreatment periods of time and situations.

The *controlled experiment* evaluates a treatment experience by measuring differences in the behavior of "experimental" and "control" groups, who have been selected randomly rather than for a similarity of characteristics, as in the quasiexperiment.

For example, in the Fremont Experiment, a short-term residential treatment project operated by the California Youth Authority, boys randomly selected for the program were exposed to both small-group treatment and a work program. This was supplemented with home visits and other activities. This experimental group of Fremont youngsters was compared with a similar control group in a regular institutional program. The control group was not given the same intense exposure to treatment and programming. After a two-year follow-up study, no statistically significant differences emerged between the experimental and the control groups.[6]

Another example is the Fricot Ranch study. Fricot Ranch is a training school operated by the California Youth Authority. Youngsters at the school were divided into an experimental group and a control group. Those youngsters in the experimental group were exposed to frequent contacts with both their peers and staff members. As a result of comparing boys in the control and experimental groups, there were some interesting findings. Even though the boys who were in the experimental group remained out of trouble for longer periods of time than those in the control group, 80 percent of both the treatment and

[6] Joachim P. Seckel, *The Fremont Experiment, Assessment of Residential Treatment at a Youth Authority Reception Center,* Department of the Youth Authority (Sacramento, Calif., 1967).

the control groups experienced difficulties within the three-year follow-up period.[7]

Other studies have also attempted to compare experimental and control groups to determine the effectiveness of the various treatment approaches. In many cases the research findings are confusing, and often specific conclusions cannot be drawn because many variables and extenuating circumstances interfere with effective evaluation.[8]

It is only in the implementation and testing of the randomization procedure that the controlled experiment varies from the quasiexperiment. One method of randomization is to list the eligible subjects in alphabetical order and to assign every other one to the experiment; the rest automatically become controls. The same procedure can be carried out with numbers, the intervals can be varied to each third eligible, for example, and so on. The controlled experiment has been actively and widely employed over the past twenty years and has not, in general, lived up to its initial promise. Experiments with youth programs have been more productive than those with adults. However, the impact of controlled experiments has been of considerably less effectiveness than that of the looser and "softer" designs like nonexperimental studies. Responsibility for the relatively low productivity of the controlled experiment can be attributed to its expense, the time it takes to carry it out, its susceptibility to biasing, selection problems, the effect of external events, data instability, as well as other factors.[9] Experience seems to indicate that the controlled experiment is perhaps more a researcher's instrument than a management aid. Thus it has probably outlived its usefulness as an agent of change in these times of incredibly rapid transition.

Money Criterion. With increasing frequency the money criterion (or the cost of the program) has been applied in the evaluation of criminal justice programs. The monetary values considered may be costs, returns, or both. The advantages of the monetary criterion are many: (1) several programs have been shown to produce behavioral results which are no worse than those of considerably more expensive programs and thus prove more desirable vis-à-vis the expenditure of scarce resources; (2) the monetary criterion reduces unmanageable behavioral data into economic consequences, which are easier to analyze; (3) it speaks the language of the policy-maker and of the manager and addresses the problem of accountability. For these reasons, the monetary criterion will undoubtedly grow in importance. For example, financial considerations are of prime importance in the following types of program evaluations.

[7] Carl F. Jesness, *The Fricot Ranch Study*, Department of the Youth Authority (Sacramento, Calif., 1965).
[8] Edwin Powers, "An Experiment in the Prevention of Delinquency," *Annals, American Academy of Political and Social Science*, (1949), p. 77; Stuart Adams, "The PICO Project," in *Sociology of Punishment and Corrections*, Norman Johnston, Leonard Savitz, and Marvin Wolfgang, Eds. (New York: John Wiley & Sons, Inc., 1962), pp. 213–24; and LeMay Adamson and H. Warren Dunham, "Clinical Treatment of Male Delinquents: A Case Study in Effort and Result," *American Sociological Review*, 21 (June 1956), pp. 312–20.
[9] See Donald T. Campbell, "Reforms as Experiments," in *Quasi-Experimental Approaches*, James A. Caporaso and Leslie L. Roos, Jr., Eds. (Evanston, III.: Northwestern U. Press, 1973), pp. 187–225.

Cost analysis places a cost on each of the correctional or criminal justice actions or services involved in dealing with offenders. By applying business office or auditor techniques, the various actions are translated into "units," which are then assigned a cost. The "units" can represent such agency objectives as "the cost of rehabilitating a juvenile gang" or "the cost of correcting a youthful offender," and so on.

Cost comparisons compare two or more cost analyses. *Cost-benefit comparisons* compare costs with benefits when benefits other than cost reduction have high priority and when data on the benefits are available or can be estimated with some degree of accuracy. Cost-benefit comparisons are most valid when derived from the follow-up evaluations of experiments and quasiexperiments.

Operations research describes and analyzes an operational system in order to provide information which will facilitate the optimal use of the processes, people, materials, and resources that are already available. It seeks to measure input, process, and outcome and their interrelationships in an attempt to improve and control them. In corrections, for example, the input would include a heterogeneous mixture of offenders, physical facilities, staff, equipment, and supplies. The processes consist of work, job training, education, counseling, incapacitation, depersonalization, and punishment. The desired outcomes are law observance, social adjustment, economic productivity, self-esteem, and the capacity for personal growth. Operations research attempts to analyze these phenomena and to provide an information base for decision making.

Systems analysis differs from operations research insofar as it attempts to identify alternative means of achieving objectives. It examines not only actual assessments but also hypothetical estimates of performance, costs, and risks. Operations research can constitute a component of systems analysis, which focuses on a larger entity, requiring a comparison of programs and/or systems. Systems analysis is more concerned with selecting from among alternatives than operations research. Contemporary thinking makes this distinction of the utmost importance; crime and delinquency are increasingly being thought of as a problem of systems rather than of people. The problem is thought to be rooted in the system or in the complex of systems beginning with the family, and proceeding through the neighborhood, the school, and the society. This line of thought contends that it is futile to look for solutions to crime and delinquency in the individual; the system is at the root of the problem, hence the powerful raison d'être for systems analysis vis-à-vis treatment analysis. Systems analysis and operations research as well as nonexperimental studies of numerous varieties hold promise of greater impact on the criminal justice system than do the traditional "strong design" studies like the controlled experiment.

Simulation attempts to predict future trends, events, and behavior by creating similar conditions artificially and observing their development. It is designed to anticipate, evaluate, and improve control over the phenomena being simulated. War games are simulations of war, rehearsals are simulations of dramas and concerts, scrimmages and skull practice are simulations of actual football games. Population projection is also a type of simulation. The computer has rendered simulation much more accurate and useful. It will undoubtedly be used with increasing frequency in the future. The National Center for Juvenile Justice, for example, has launched an effort to develop a computer simulation model of a juvenile justice system. It is hoped that the model will be able to assess the impact of new juvenile justice programs before they are widely implemented as well as to evaluate present programs.

Research Findings

Research findings to date show with relative clarity that

there is not now nor will there be in the foreseeable future either one general solution to delinquency or a multiple number of strategies which will either prevent or control all delinquency. One often has the impression that many of the most concerned with delinquency yet believe that an answer to this problem lies "just around the corner." Some deviancy, however, seems to be an inevitable price which our society must pay for freedom from undue social restraint, for allowing youth a relatively long period for preparation for adult society, and for our material affluence.[10]

Despite the depressing tenor of the above statement, there continues to prevail a note of optimism that a certain percentage of juvenile delinquency can be treated and prevented. Although only an extremely small number of delinquency and youth development programs are ever evaluated—and, even when evaluated, an even smaller number demonstrate significant results—the research has shown some strategies to be more effective than others. Still others, too new to have been evaluated sufficiently, indicate a hopeful level of potential. The following paragraphs will discuss the research regarding all three.[11]

Probation is currently the most widely used response to juvenile delinquency. Probation usually entails some form of control over the youth plus individual counseling. Although it may be attributable to the nature of the youths selected for probation, this group has less serious recidivism rates than boys remanded to training schools. "Unofficial probation," which consists of giving a warning and release, seems to be the most effective. Random assignment of boys to both types has not resulted in court record differences in studies that have compared the two groups. However, unofficial probation costs less and seems to produce more positive attitudes toward the probation experience. Apprehension and contact with a probation officer seem to contribute to an increase in future delinquency rates.

[10] J. Toby, "The Prospects for Reducing Delinquency Rates in Industrial Societies," in *Society, Delinquency and Delinquent Behavior*, H. Voss, Ed. (Boston: Little, Brown and Company, 1970), pp. 454–458.

[11] These summaries were gleaned from Chapter 3, "Results: Findings From Empirical Studies" in Michael C. Dixon and William E. Wright, *Juvenile Delinquency Prevention Programs* (Nashville, Institute on Youth and Social Development, The John F. Kennedy Center for Research on Education and Human Development, George Peabody College for Teachers, 1974).

Some courts combine group counseling with probation. Group counseling has not been shown to decrease recidivism rates. It does seem to decrease the number of weeks a youth spends on probation, however, and, by influencing his personality development, to minimize the number of petitions against him while he is on probation. Group counseling also seems more cost efficient than individual casework.

Volunteers in probation, variously called "buddies," "partners," "big brothers," "Y-pals," "advocates," and so on replace the probation officer in monitoring the delinquent youth. In addition to decreasing costs and the caseloads of probation officers, the volunteers minimize the stigma of labeling. The program seems generally to produce beneficial results although the data concerning it are subjective and must therefore be viewed with caution.

Individual and *group counseling* techniques, when applied as the only mode of treatment, have not proven effective in reducing future delinquent behavior.

In extensive follow-up studies, neither child guidance therapy nor social casework could be shown effective in reducing serious delinquency. Indeed there are strong indications that intensive social casework results in a form of labeling that may have a negative effect on youngsters, and may even stimulate further delinquent behavior.

Street-corner workers make contact with delinquent juvenile gangs, seeking to gain their confidence and subsequently to direct their energies into socially acceptable channels. Street-corner programs have not only not reduced delinquent behavior; they seem, on the contrary, to have promoted pride in the gang (a gang with its own worker must be particularly "bad"), enhanced gang cohesiveness, and perhaps even stimulated it to engage in more notorious exploits.

Although the data are sparse and of questionable reliability because of the newness of the concept, Youth Service Bureaus, which seek to coordinate existing youth services and to provide nonexistent but needed services for youth, continue to demonstrate relatively positive results.

Educational programs for youths considered by their teachers as "headed for delinquency," consisting of intensive counseling and special classroom attention, could not be shown to reduce delinquency or disruptive school behavior.

Work-study programs, which entail a half-day of classroom work and a half-day of supervised work, are generally viewed negatively by participants, who may perceive themselves as members of "work gangs" and as having very low status. Those programs which provide job training as opposed to remedial education demonstrate more success if applied with fifteen- and sixteen-year-olds. They are less effective with younger groups.

In evaluations of Neighborhood Youth Corps programs in four cities, data revealed that the projects were not successful with either males nor with Caucasian females. They did result in fewer police contacts, less unemployment, greater attitude changes, and a higher proportion of continued education after dropping out of school than the comparison group for black females, however.

Studies of guided group interaction programs, such as the Highfields project in New Jersey, report less delinquency in the treatment than in the control groups. As in many other cases, however, the data are subject to question; among other reasons, there is a possibility of bias in the selection procedures employed. As was stated above, however, community treatment of any kind is in all cases at least as effective as incarceration and is considerably less expensive. It seems destined to greater application in the future.

A research effort that used learning principles to condition delinquent subjects to dependable and prompt attendance at a part-time job resulted in significantly fewer arrests than a comparison group during a three-year follow-up period.

There exists no evidence that professional social work and intervention, including social work plus counseling and psychotherapy, have any effect whatsoever. Psychotherapy alone has had equally little impact on neurotic adults and children.

The mixed or sketchy findings of some program evaluations would seem to warrant further research. Falling into this category are vocational training programs, programs which use volunteers, community treatment projects, and youth service bureaus.

Research with Impact

One of the objectives of research is to bring about change. Some research has had a broad impact on practice, other research has had none at all. Most of it could be placed somewhere on a continuum between these two extremes. In addition to stimulating change in criminal justice practice, research can have theoretical and methodological consequences, as well. The heaviest impact to date seems to come from the simplest design: the field survey. The controlled experiment seems to produce the least impact. More inquiry into the relation between impact and research characteristics must be done. There are indications, however, that research planners stimulate more impact than research specialists.

Following are some examples of studies that had impact: they resulted in change in the handling of offender populations.[12]

In 1956 the California Special Study Commission on Correctional Facilities and Services studied the sixty county probation departments in the state to evaluate the status of the probation process, to note problems and deficiencies in it and to make relevant recommendations to the state legislature. Employing a field survey design, various types of instruments and strategies were used to secure descriptive and judgmental data from probation department staff and county judges. Research staff added their evaluations, which were based on generally accepted professional criteria.

---

[12] These examples were taken from Stuart Adams, Ph.D., "Research with Impact: Six Case Studies," in *Evaluative Research in Corrections: A Practical Guide* (Washington, D.C.: U.S. Department of Justice, Law Enforcement Assistance Administration, National Institute of Law Enforcement and Criminal Justice, 1975), pp. 12-14.

One of the recommendations emanating from the survey report was that counties should be provided with a subsidy by the state to enable them to upgrade their operations so that they would better conform with professional standards.

This recommendation did not pass the assembly in 1957. A later survey, similar but on a smaller scale, stimulated the same recommendation. However, this time it was modified to tie payments to the county to rates of diversion of convicted offenders from state institutions to county correctional programs. This added incentive convinced the legislature and the measure passed. It has been estimated that 40,000 adult and juvenile offenders were diverted from California penal institutions in the first eight years of its operation.

In 1959 an exploratory study of the impact of the California Youth Authority's Preston School of Industry on its male delinquent inmates was undertaken. A series of interviews at two-week intervals were held with fifteen selected youths during a six-week stay at the Northern Reception Center Clinic and at two-month intervals at Preston. Delinquency identification, attitudes toward authority, peer relationships, values, goals, criminal language, and skills were examined with a view toward assessing the influence of the clinic and the training school on changes in these phenomena. At the completion of the study, the researcher judged that the net effect was probably unfavorable to the youths and to the communities, to which they eventually returned. It was subsequently recommended to the Youth Authority that a controlled experiment be conducted to compare the effects of institutional and community treatments. The recommendation was accepted by the Youth Authority executives even though the results might prove the Youth Authority obsolete. This impact is indeed significant in view of the normal tendency of bureaucracies to reject anything that threatens their existence.

The decision to proceed with the experiment resulted in the now famous Community Treatment Project, which continued from 1961 to 1974 in three different phases, funded by the National Institute of Mental Health. The impact of the Community Treatment Project in the treatment and handling of juveniles has been momentous. It is largely responsible for rendering diversion and community treatment the wave of the future.

Most research does not result in this kind of impact. There are several reasons for low research payoff, regardless of the field. Research in high technology, for example, is successful only five percent of the time. There is no reason to believe that expectations for criminal justice research should be any more optimistic. Much research is of doubtful quality. There is often an incongruence between researcher styles and the pressing and practical needs of administrators; researcher priorities at higher levels of theory and purity of method clash with the administrator's need for advice in uncertain situations. Moreover,

many administrators do not welcome change; their anxieties, personal views and preference for order and tranquility in their institutions may turn them against innovation, even when it appears reasonable, constructive and buttressed by scientific evidence. Others exist in precarious balance, and the operationalizing of new, even though tested, concepts increases the difficulty of their position. Still others have seen many promising new ideas come and go, leaving disillusion in their wake. Finally, new ideas may call for increased budgets, and the skepticism of legislative committees about budget expansion in corrections cuts deeper than research ire.[13]

Fortunately, however, research in delinquency prevention and treatment is receiving increased funding and emphasis. The Coordinating Council on Juvenile Justice and Delinquency Prevention has listed the following priorities for federal research:

A short-term study of offender careers in two cities. This would be a follow-up of all juveniles first arrested during 1968 in two major metropolitan areas. Such a study would constitute an inexpensive and relatively quick method of increasing our knowledge regarding the development and maintenance of delinquent careers.

A double replication of the Wolfgang cohort study. These studies would replicate the cohort study directed by Dr. Marvin Wolfgang in Philadelphia which focused on the arrest histories of males born in that city in 1945. Replications of this study (with some modification) focusing on youths born a decade later would allow testing for changes in rates and patterns of delinquency over time.

A major prospective cohort study. This research effort would entail following a large sample (perhaps nationwide) of very young subjects over a long period of time (10–15 years) in order to examine the development of delinquent and non-delinquent careers. Such a study would permit examination of a broad range of factors related to delinquency, and a variety of intervention approaches.

The cohort and offender career studies are all structured to answer the same set of questions: What types of delinquent behavior portend serious future criminality? What patterns of behavior are best understood as isolated deviations that do not predict future criminality? How does the juvenile justice system operate? Do different types of juvenile justice system responses to youth crime lead to different patterns of future crime and delinquency?

The relationship between youth crime and family economic opportunity. Studies in this area might focus on "income maintenance" and serious youth crime, or test the hypothesis that constraints on economic opportunity increase the rates of property crime. Another proposition to examine is whether serious youth crime is committed by groups that are immune to opportunities provided by fluctuations in the economic cycle.

Comparative studies of juvenile delinquency preventions strategies. These might encompass supported work, public housing, the school context, youth development approaches, defensible space, control of handgun avail-

[13]*Ibid.*, p. 34.

ability, and an examination of "conforming" behavior; that is, a focus on approaches designed to enhance the likelihood of youth conformity as opposed to reducing the deviance.

Special studies of youth violence. These studies might focus on robbery, homicide, and aggravated assault, and involve examination of patterns of youth violence over time. Special attention might be given to the increasing use of guns and to the characteristics of particular cities that have experienced the sharpest increases in rates of youth violence.

An annual compilation of data on youth crime. This volume would be a single comprehensive summary of data pertaining to the youth population in the U.S., delinquent behavior, youth arrests, juvenile courts, probation, community corrections and institutions housing young offenders. Presentation of these and other data would permit discussion of patterns and trends in youth crime, and the identification of knowledge gaps.

The relationship between delinquent gangs and youth criminality. In addition to research on the nature and distribution of juvenile gangs in U.S. cities, research in this area might examine the correlation between gang participation and violence. Other research might address the etiology of gangs and mechanisms of recruitment into their membership and intervention approaches.

A comparative study of juvenile courts. Such a study might involve collecting data on disposition in a fairly large and representative sample of cases; determining by offense and offender type rates of different kinds of dispositions; comparing offenses recorded by the police with behavior listed by the court as the basis for its jurisdiction; and examining the emergence of particular types of dispositions.

Studies of the impacts of different juvenile justice intervention techniques. Such studies might include diversion strategies, case dismissal, community placement, arbitration models, and other innovative approaches related to the administration of juvenile justice. These studies should examine the impact of such approaches on delinquent careers and the juvenile justice system.

Special studies of the relationship between hard narcotics and delinquency. These studies would explore whether a causal relationship exists between use of hard narcotics and youth crime. Attention might be given to this relationship in the context of juvenile gangs. An hypothesis that appears worth testing is that hard narcotics increase crimes of prey by creating needs for higher levels of illegitimate earnings and by recruiting youth into antisocial life styles.[14]

SUMMARY

Research consists of gathering and analyzing facts, conducting and evaluating experiments, devising methods for testing the effects of change, searching for the

[14] First Comprehensive Plan for Federal Juvenile Delinquency Prevention, Office of Juvenile Justice and Delinquency Prevention, Law Enforcement Assistance Administration (Washington, D.C.: U.S. Government Printing Office, 1976), pp. 45-47.

motivations of human behavior, and so on. Since World War II massive research efforts have been undertaken to determine the causes of and the solutions to crime. The pressure for continued research, especially evaluative research, has never been greater.

Perhaps the most dramatic finding of adult and juvenile correctional research has been that incarceration cannot be shown to produce any positive effect on offender behavior. This conclusion has led to an interest in developing community-based alternatives to incarceration, which, in addition to holding more promise for rehabilitation, are also considerably cheaper.

Experimentation in the changing of offender behavior, which is of recent origin, derives from the limited general range of socialization theory. It has thus far not uncovered a theory of sufficient power to guarantee the restoration to society of large numbers of offenders.

Major current research is concerned with a redefinition of recidivism and on the positive side, with a definition of offender success. Of further concern is the need to relate success in some demonstrable way to a specific strategy or technique. Increasing emphasis on accountability is creating a need for ever more evaluative research.

Currently employed in criminal justice research are several different research models. Of the methodological models, which have the most general relevance, the *nonexperimental* study is the most widely used and also has the greatest impact. Case studies, surveys, time series, cohort analysis, and before-after studies are types of nonexperimental research. The *quasiexperiment* is most often used to evaluate a treatment process by comparing two groups of subjects, who were chosen for comparison because of similar or shared characteristics. One group is subjected to the treatment being evaluated, while the other is not. Results are then compared. *Controlled* experiments vary from the quasiexperiment only in that they employ a randomizing procedure in their choice of subjects rather than the characteristic-matching procedure of the quasiexperiment. Experiments with youth programs have been more productive than those with adults. In general, however, they have not lived up to their initial promise.

With increasing frequency, the money criterion has been applied in the evaluation of criminal justice programs. Cost analysis, cost comparisons, and cost-benefit comparisons are methods which employ the money criterion.

Operations research describes and analyzes an operational system in order to provide information which will facilitate the optimal use of available resources. Systems analysis differs from operations research insofar as it attempts to identify alternative means of achieving objectives. Systems analysis and operations research as well as nonexperimental studies of numerous varieties hold promise of greater impact on the criminal justice system than do the traditional "strong design" studies.

Simulation attempts to predict future trends, events, and behavior by creating similar conditions artificially and observing their development.

Research findings have shown that there is no hope of finding one, single, universally applicable solution to juvenile delinquency. Some strategies have been shown to be more effective than others, however. Still others are too new to have been evaluated sufficiently but they indicate a hopeful level of potential. Boys placed on probation, for example, show less serious recidivism rates than boys remanded to training schools. (Note: Boys placed in training schools are usually more serious offenders than boys placed on probation. In addition most boys in training schools were on probation at some time in their "careers.") Group counseling has not been shown to decrease recidivism rates. Volunteers in probation seem generally to produce beneficial results. Individual and group counseling techniques, when applied as the only mode of treatment, have not proven effective in reducing future delinquent behavior. Neither child guidance therapy nor social casework could be shown effective in reducing serious delinquency. Street corner programs have not only not reduced delinquency behavior; they seem even to promote it. Youth Service Bureaus continue to demonstrate relatively positive results. Educational programs could not be shown to reduce delinquency or disruptive school behavior. Work-study programs, which provide job training as opposed to remedial education, demonstrate success if applied with fifteen- and sixteen-year-olds. They are less effective with younger groups. Neighborhood Youth Corps programs seem to result in success only with black females. Guided group interaction programs report less delinquency in the treatment than in the control groups. Neither professional social work nor psychotherapy in any combination can be shown to have any effect whatsoever on delinquent behavior.

Probation Subsidy, the Preston Impact Study, and the Community Treatment Project in California are examples of research that have resulted in major impact. These studies were largely responsible for rendering diversion and community treatment the wave of the future. Most research does not result in this kind of impact.

The importance of adequate evaluative research cannot be overstated. Without proper evaluation and research, new programs cannot be initiated or old programs eliminated or improved. Most delinquency programs have not been evaluated by vigorous research methods. Only through long-term longitudinal studies can the effects of various prevention efforts be determined and evaluated.

Development of sound public policy regarding all aspects of delinquency prevention and control requires adequate information upon which to base the decisions. National planning will have to depend on statistical studies of trends in the amounts and types of delinquency. There is need for detailed information on the reasons for referrals to juvenile court and the time spent in detention facilities, on the reasons for the dispositions made by the court, on the personnel who work with juvenile delinquents and on the character of the training schools and other facilities. All these things call for a collection of local, state, and regional data in a national center which can provide statistical analysis and report the results—we are still nearly as deep in ignorance regarding the effects of programs and the conditions producing the effects as we were before the programs were launched. We can only hope that a high priority is given to research in future projects so that we can begin to develop the knowledge base that is essential to the creation of successful programs.[15]

QUESTIONS AND PROJECTS

Essay Questions

1. Why is research necessary in almost all types of problem solving?

2. Why are statistics on recidivism difficult to obtain and tabulate?

3. Why are nonexperimental studies most frequently employed in criminal and juvenile justice research?

4. What are the advantages and disadvantages of the controlled experiment?

5. Why is "cost analysis" becoming increasingly popular as a research method?

Projects

1. Choose a research method for a delinquency area that you would like to know more about. Justify your choice.

2. Design a nonexperimental study.

3. Design a quasiexperiment.

4. Design a controlled experiment.

---

[15] Stanton Wheeler, Leonard Cottrell, Jr., and Ann Romasco, "Juvenile Delinquency—Its Prevention and Control," in *Task Force Report, Juvenile Delinquency and Youth Crime,* p. 424.

chapter 11

An Example: Community-Based Treatment Programs

A community-based prevention and treatment program can be defined as any program that attempts to mobilize the resources of the community in an effort to prevent and treat delinquency. Resources are based in the community, and most of the youngster's time is spent participating in community activities and utilizing those agencies and institutions that are a part of the community. The program that we will discuss specifically, a halfway house, is an example of both a prevention and treatment program. A youngster who is in the halfway house has already been in contact with the juvenile justice system, and therefore a halfway house is not a pure or primary prevention program. If the treatment that takes place is successful and future delinquent behavior ceases, however, then the halfway house can be considered both a treatment and a prevention program.

An example of a halfway house that is a community-based treatment and prevention program will facilitate the tying together of many of the principles that have been discussed thus far. The establishing of a program is not a simple process, and more than a knowledge of delinquency causation is necessary (Chapter 2). We have seen that juvenile delinquency is only a subcategory of the overall concept of deviancy (Chapter 1) and that it is a manifestation of youngsters who are adolescents (Chapter 4). It is necessary to understand both concepts, deviant behavior and adolescent behavior, to understand the theories of causation. It also logically follows that knowledge of prevention programs (Chapter 8) and treatment therapies (Chapter 9) is necessary to best serve the clients. All these factors revolve around the handling of youngsters within the juvenile justice system (Chapter 6).

The question could be asked, Why community-based treatment and prevention? This question was probably not asked or answered soon enough because community-based treatment on a large scale is a relatively new concept and could be one of the major breakthroughs that has occurred in the last several years.[1] Community-based treatment and prevention programs have become popular today, because, through research and observation, it has been determined that institutions are artificial and do not provide the type of atmosphere where the youngster can learn to work out his problems in a realistic manner. Even though institutions are needed for some youngsters, as a last resort and final alternative, they have been utilized too frequently.

Vinter et al., in their extensive study of juvenile corrections, point out that the states spent $300 million for the operation of juvenile correctional institutions, camps, and ranches during fiscal 1974. This was:

> ten times the amount spent on community-based programs and over thirty times the amount spent on foster care. The average offender-year cost of these services was $11,657, with three states spending less than $5,000 and four spending over $19,000.
>
> ...While it is apparent that the total number of group homes, halfway houses, etc., has greatly increased since the late sixties, community-based residential facilities are not—in the overwhelming majority of states— handling juvenile offenders on a scale consistent with either the recom- mendations of several national commissions and advisory bodies or the opinions of state correctional executives themselves. Our survey identified an aggregate average daily population of 5,663 in state-related community- based residential programs during 1974. This is about one-fifth the number of youth assigned to institutions.
>
> The average daily populations assigned to community programs ranged from 0 in six states and 3 in one state, to a high of 800. The average across the states was 110, compared with 560 for institutions, camps, and ranch- es. If we repeat the exercise of extrapolating hypothetical national average daily population figures for community-based facilities on the basis of states' highest and lowest rates, the two figures we arrive at are 41,656 and 0. Once again a remarkable variation.
>
> The forty-three reporting states together spent slightly less than $30 million to operate their community programs during fiscal 1974. This sum is about one-tenth that spent on institutions, camps, and ranches, and clearly shows that these facilities are not receiving significant proportions of state juvenile corrections budgets. One state spent almost $5 million, but the overall average was $596,000, and half the states spent less than $300,000.
>
> Consistent with a basic argument of those who advocate wider use of this

---

[1] Oliver J. Keller, Jr., and Benedict S. Alper, *Halfway Houses: Community Centered Corrections and Treatment* (Lexington, Mass.: D. C. Heath & Company, 1970), p. 174.

alternative, the offender-year cost averages less than half of that for institutions—approximately $5,500.[2]

Even though a greater emphasis was supposed to be placed on community-based programs most states still assign more youngsters to residential-type facilities than to community-based programs. Furthermore, even when states utilize community-based programs this does not necessarily mean that their institutional population will decrease.

> Deinstitutionalization rates for the forty-eight reporting states indicated that only four states assigned as many youth to community as to institutional settings, that thirty-six states had rates of less than 25%, and that the average national rate was only 17.7%. Despite substantial deinstitutionalization achieved by states as varied as Massachusetts, South Dakota, Oregon, Maryland, and Utah, the majority have not embraced such a policy . . .

> . . . Overall there is *no* correlation between states' per capita average daily populations in institutions and those in community-based programs. This lack of relationship indicates that the increased use of community services is *not* accompanied by lower-than-average use of institutions. Naturally there are several exceptions, but generally as the number of offenders in community-based facilities increases, the *total* number in all programs also increases.[3]

Community-based control, treatment, and prevention programs can be much more effective in integrating the individual into his home community and enabling him to adapt to his environment because treatment personnel will be familiar with the community resources available, such as educational and employment opportunities. Treatment can be based on the utilization of community resources. With help from professionals and volunteers, the offender can become acquainted with community resources and receive support and guidance as he adjusts to his community and faces its pressures and responsibilities. The mobilization of community resources of both private and public agencies as well as the assistance of professionals and nonprofessionals will help integrate the delinquent into the community processes. In the artificial institution setting, the delinquent more often than not loses touch with his community and the resources available and does not learn the problem-solving process that will contribute to his personal and social adjustment.

In addition to academic and employment facilities, many resources within a community can help the youngster. Innovative approaches have been taken by local, state, and federal governments to help control, prevent, and treat delin-

---

[2]Robert D. Vinter, George Downs, and John Hall, *Juvenile Corrections in the States: Residential Programs and Deinstitutionalization*, A Preliminary Report, National Assessment of Juvenile Corrections, The University of Michigan, 1976, p. 68.
[3]*Ibid.*, p. 73, 77.

quent behavior. For example, vocational rehabilitation provides academic, vocational, and on-the-job training services to persons who are culturally, economically, and socially disadvantaged, including persons convicted of crime or judged delinquent.

In sum, community-based treatment centers and other prevention, treatment, and control programs located near population centers permit the flexible use of community resources and enable the delinquent, in cooperation with treatment personnel, to establish new community ties which will assist him not only in becoming satisfactorily integrated into the community but also in developing new social, educational, and employment skills.

HALFWAY HOUSES

The use of halfway houses in delinquency prevention and treatment is becoming increasingly popular. The halfway house is a community-based program small enough to facilitate individualized treatment but still large enough to necessitate a knowledge of theories of causation, deviant and adolescent behavior, treatment therapies, prevention concepts, and procedures and methods for handling juveniles.

History

Even though halfway houses have only recently been used on a large scale, the halfway house concept is not a new one. As early as 1916 the Hebrew Orphan Asylum in New York established a home for adolescent girls who had been discharged from the asylum but were unable to adjust in their own homes, with foster families, or on their own.[4]

Although there have been exceptions, such as Pioneer House, established in Detroit in 1946, and Highfields, established in New Jersey in 1950, little actual development of this type of treatment facility took place until after 1960. In comparison with such other methods of treatment as the training school, aftercare, and probation, the halfway house is still in its infancy.

Halfway houses have been described in various ways. "The trend has been to name these facilities group homes, pre-release guidance centers, transitional homes and the like."[5]

The main idea behind the halfway house concept is that it should help bridge the gap between the confinement of the institution and the total freedom of the community. The halfway house can be used for many different purposes. McCartt and Mangogna, in their federal government publication on guidelines and standards for halfway houses, describe the various clients that can benefit from this type of program.

[4]Martin Gula, *Agency Operated Group Homes*, U.S. Department of Health, Education, and Welfare (Washington, D.C.: U.S. Government Printing Office, 1964), p. 2.
[5]Kenneth Carpenter, "Halfway Houses for Delinquent Youth," in *Children*, U.S. Department of Health, Education, and Welfare, November–December 1963, p. 224.

Mandatory Releasee and Parolee—The mandatory releasee or parolee who is in need of a transitional center, and the range of series it offers has always been and still is being served by the community treatment center.

The Probationer—Many halfway houses are increasingly accepting persons placed on probation. Probationers are referred to a halfway house under two sets of general circumstances: First, the court may consider the individual too much of a risk to simply place them on probation to be supervised by an already overworked probation officer, who will be unable to give the needed time and attention to the prospective probationer. At the same time, the court may recognize that the individual in question does not need incarceration in the traditional institutional setting.

The Pre-releasee—For several years, Federal law, and more recently, the laws of several states, have allowed for the release of prisoners to halfway houses or community treatment centers prior to their actual mandatory release or release on parole.

Study and Diagnostic Services of Offenders—Depending on their level of sophistication, many halfway houses are now capable of offering study and diagnostic services to courts. Such services are rendered prior to final disposition in court.

The Juvenile—Neglected and Delinquent—Halfway houses, or group homes, as they are often called, are being utilized increasingly for the child who is neglected or delinquent. The establishment of such group homes has been increasing at an extremely rapid pace. Many times in the past, the neglected child was placed in detention facilities or training schools along with delinquent children, simply because there were no other resources to draw upon.

Use of Halfway Houses for Individuals with Special Difficulties, such as Drug Abuse, Alcoholism and Psychiatric Problems—Halfway houses or community treatment centers are being utilized for target populations with special difficulties such as drug abuse, alcoholism or psychiatric problems. Due to the nature of the problems being treated, the length of stay in such centers is usually much longer than in those servicing the general offender population, often for as long as eighteen months.

Use of Halfway Houses for Individuals Released on Bail Prior to Final Disposition—Bail reform has been spreading rapidly in the United States. Federal and many state and local jurisdictions have enacted bail reform measures.

Use of the Halfway House for Diversion from the Criminal Justice System—Halfway houses or community treatment centers can be utilized in the future to divert individuals from the criminal justice system.[6]

---

[6] John M. McCartt and Thomas J. Mangogna, *Guidelines and Standards for Halfway Houses and Community Treatment Centers,* U.S. Department of Justice, Law Enforcement Assistance Administration, Technical Assistance Division, (Washington, D.C.: U.S. Government Printing Office, 1973), p. 22-29.

Types of Youth Served

According to Carpenter, the youths to whom halfway house programs seem to give the most help are those

who have no home to return to, those whose parents are sufficiently inadequate or rejecting to give them the necessary guidance and support for successful adjustment, those whose parents may be fostering their delinquent behavior or those whose parents live in neighborhoods in which the youth are unable to cope with the many pressures they would face upon return to their home community.[7]

Use of Structure

Structure is an important aspect of halfway house programming. Rabinow lists some factors that must be considered in the structure of the halfway house program:

1. A living situation that has limits to which the child can relate.

2. Adults who reflect maturity in their behavior.

3. A peer group that does not have too much extreme in age or behavior.

4. Living quarters that provide some degree of privacy.

5. Community resources such as schools, recreational facilities, and work opportunities that do not make overwhelming demands upon him.

6. Professional assistance to help in dealing with personal problems, family relationships, and peer relationships.

7. The security of knowing that food, clothing, financial aid, medical care, etc., are always provided for him no matter what his behavior.

8. The security of knowing that he will have competent assistance to aid in making plans for the future when he leaves placement.[8]

Personnel

Competent staff personnel are an important aspect of the total halfway house program and structure.

The opportunity to live closely with adults whose behavior can be a model to emulate and from which to take strength is a unique one for most of the adolescents in placement. Immature, undisciplined, and inconsistent behavior by house staff can have a most destructive effect.[9]

[7]Carpenter, *op. cit.,* p. 224.
[8]Irvine Rabinow, "The Significance of Structure in the Group Release Program," *Journal of Jewish Communal Service,* 38, No. 3 (Spring 1962), p. 302.
[9]*Ibid.,* p. 301.

Location of the House

The location of a halfway house can have important ramifications and should be given careful consideration. The halfway house should be located in a metropolitan area near the resources of the community. It should also be located in a neighborhood where it will be accepted by the residents and where there will not be animosity between the community and the program.

There should be schools and recreational facilities available and places of employment that are within a reasonable distance. Chapter 2, "Theories of Delinquency Causation," discussed the importance of the environment and institutions like the school in preventing delinquent behavior.

Economic Benefit

The halfway house program is much less costly for the taxpayer than other programs. Even though the cost per resident may be the same as the cost at an institution, or even slightly higher, the halfway house returns the youngster to society sooner, making the cost per individual treated much lower. In New Jersey eight out of ten releasees from the Highfields project were "successful" for one year after release as opposed to five out of ten releasees from the training school at Annandale. The costs per inmate per day were approximately equal. "On a strict per capita basis the Highfields project cost one-third as much as the traditional program for each boy treated."[10] The reason is that the average term of treatment at Highfields was approximately five months, whereas the average term of treatment at Annandale was slightly over a year.

Halfway Houses in Michigan

Because Michigan is one of the leaders in the nation in halfway house development and utilization and also because the author of this textbook was a director of a halfway house in Michigan for a period of time, the example presented will be taken from his experiences in the halfway house program. Halfway houses in Michigan are operated by the Department of Social Services and serve children between the ages of thirteen and nineteen, with the average term of residence being six months. Although halfway houses have been utilized on a limited basis in the past, there are plans for expansion so that most juveniles who are committed to the Department of Social Services will be able to profit from this community-based treatment method. Only those youngsters who are unable to tolerate the closeness and pressures of the community will be sent to institutions.

---

[10] H. Weeks, "The Highfields Project," in *Juvenile Delinquency: A Book of Readings,* Rose Giallombardo, Ed. (New York: John Wiley & Sons, Inc., 1966), p. 530.

Administration and Programming

Halfway houses in Michigan are staffed by a caseworker, who is the director, and five child-care workers (boys' or girls' supervisors) who work on an eight-hour-shift basis. The houses, which have a capacity of twelve wards each, are programmed to provide both school and work experience. In the *academic program*, those wards who are motivated and capable of further academic training are given an opportunity to continue their education. A ward also has the opportunity to enroll in a joint academic and work program, which allows him to continue his education, obtain some work experience, and achieve some financial independence. In the *work program*, wards who are not capable of, or not interested in, furthering their formal education are given the opportunity to work full time.

PROBLEMS INVOLVED IN OPERATING
A HALFWAY HOUSE PROGRAM

Although the halfway house program that will be described was operated by the Department of Social Services, the development of new techniques and methods was highly flexible at the time the author was director because of the newness of the operation.

The Treatment-Custody Dilemma

The major problem that exists in correctional programs employing a wide variety of professionals is a communication breakdown between the college-educated and the noncollege-educated staff. This is merely a symptom of the age-old treatment-custody dilemma. This phenomenon occurs in a number of institutional and parainstitutional settings, and a review of the literature in this area reveals that this is a universal problem in the treatment of juvenile offenders regardless of the type of facility.

This dichotomy usually exists because institutional staffs have historically been segregated—first by function, and second by training. On the one hand, the custody staff, who have the function of controlling (guarding) the clientele, usually have no formal training. On the other hand, the treatment staff, whose function it is to "treat" (however this is interpreted), usually have extensive formal training. Also implied in the treatment-custody dilemma is the treatment staff's decision-making power in the institution. The custody individual is typified by his role of "watchdog" and "inhibitor of privileges," while the treatment individual is the "giver of privileges." Animosity can obviously exist in such a situation. This conflict of roles not only affects the relationship between the custody and the treatment personnel but also has implications in their relationship with the clientele. The dilemma affords a natural and opportune situation for the clientele to manipulate the staff and turn them against one another, which can have a decided negative effect on the total administration of the treatment program. Also, because of basic philosophical differences that often exist between occupational groups working in the juvenile justice system, the custodial staffs of institutions and even the noncollege-educated staffs of smaller programs like group homes and halfway houses are usually oriented criminologically to the classical school of criminology and the classical view of organization, whereas treatment personnel subscribe to the positive school of criminology and the human relations view of organization.

Several questions can be asked: Is the treatment-custody dilemma inevitable? Will it always exist because of the division of labor by function and training? What can an administrator do organizationally to alleviate this problem? These questions and others will be answered later in the chapter.

The Type of Clientele

Another problem that exists in correctional facilities is the type of clientele served. Persons adjudicated delinquent do not usually voluntarily seek treatment for their problems; on the contrary, they often attempt to perpetuate their condition. Unlike neurotics and psychotics who are plagued by anxiety and distress, most delinquents are unaware that they have problems. Because of their psychological makeup and learned social behavior, delinquents can be expert manipulators and effective con men, and this is often an integral part of their value system. Manipulation is more than merely a prized and desired asset, it is a tool with which most delinquents "ply their trade." Hence, they have an extraordinary ability to manipulate people, and the treatment-custody dilemma plays right into their hands and perpetuates this pathological process.

This major clinical difference between the delinquent and the neurotic or the psychotic necessitates not only a knowledge of deviant behavior but also an awareness of therapies available for the treatment of the different diagnostic categories.

Generally, neurosis and psychosis are manifestations of an excessive amount of guilt and anxiety. Conversely, the delinquent's pathology is many times directly attributable to a lack of guilt and anxiety. The delinquent, throughout his entire life, has not had positive identification models who could transmit the values of the larger society. The result is that a social and moral void exists in his conscience structure. Hence the attitude "take what you can get" and "it's only wrong or immoral if you get caught."

If, then, the delinquent is different from the neurotic or the psychotic, should the techniques for treatment be different or the personnel performing the treatment be different?

Serving a Human Being

The "commodities" that are being produced and served in correctional settings are not inanimate objects, but human beings, and human beings have the innate ability to affect one another in many ways. For example, an assembly line worker operating under classical organization theory receives instructions and orders from his supervisor and then performs his task of riveting the right front fender of a new automobile. The fender does not respond in a manner that can cause an emotional reaction in the worker. However, something quite different happens when the worker (the child-care staff member) is dealing with a human being (the delinquent). The worker may get his instructions and advice from his supervisor, but a second element is involved in the process—the worker not only performs an action, but the object on which he performs the action is capable of producing a reaction in the worker. Thus a reciprocal emotional situation evolves. The delinquent can accentuate an emotional reaction in others because of his aggressiveness and antisocial attitude. He often exhibits behavior that is boisterous, aggressive, and cocky to disguise his feelings of worthlessness, fear, and insecurity. In effect, he actively attempts to antagonize society so that he will be rejected, thus reinforcing his self-concept that he is worthless and a social outcast. He has been hurt emotionally and hence does not want to take the chance of being hurt again. The dynamic of rejecting before being rejected is a defense against getting close to people. Because serving human beings is different from producing a material product, organizational assumptions have to be altered to consider the human factor, an important reason why classical organization theory cannot be easily transposed to situations where the "product" is human and not material.

The questions to be asked are: How can positive communication be facilitated between the staff and the boys? What effect does an emotionally charged situation have on both the boys and the staff? What techniques can be utilized to keep negative reinforcement and reactions at a minimum?

Personnel

Persons attracted to the correctional field can present certain problems. This is not to imply that all persons attracted to this field are negatively motivated, but it is important to mention that some of them are, and it is in reference to these individuals that this section attempts to raise some questions.

The child-care staff, since they are on the "firing line" and in constant contact with the boys, are in a position to exert a great amount of influence as identification and authority models. Whether this influence is positive or negative depends on the individual staff member.

People satisfy their emotional needs in a variety of ways. In most instances, delinquents are vulnerable to displaced hostility and negative reinforcement from persons working in correctional settings. An "energy surplus" exists in the work situation—the worker has more energy left than is needed to perform his job, and much of this energy is psychological and is manifested in the work group. Where the "product" is human, the surplus energy can be focused on the clients as well as on the work group. It is possible that some persons are attracted to this field because they can overassert their authority and direct their energy into negative channels.

Conversely, an individual can mask his intense hostility by being over-permissive and oversolicitous even to the point where he encourages the delinquent to act out. The staff member, if he also has a problem accepting authority, can experience vicarious satisfaction when the delinquent acts out against society and specifically against the correctional administration. Deviant behavior by staff members in such instances can become commonplace.

Some questions to be asked at this point are : How do delinquents affect persons who are negatively motivated and attracted to the correctional field, and in turn how does this affect the treatment-custody dilemma? Do some staff members prefer and even perpetuate the treatment-custody dilemma? What are the ways in which staff members can be used most effectively?

The Treatment Concept

Another problem in correctional administration is the defining of the word *treatment.* Many times treatment personnel are not clear as to what is meant by the concept and what it entails. Treatment usually varies with the treater and the situation. Many different approaches can be used, depending on the orientation of the agency and the academic and personal preferences of the therapist or the counselor (see Chapter 9). Can *treatment* personnel expect *custody* personnel to understand and accept the treatment concept if, in fact, it is not clearly defined and it changes like a chameleon depending on the circumstances? Does treatment mean being extremely permissive? Is treatment dependent on the treater's ability to use superfluous psychological jargon? Is it necessary that treatment be practiced in a clinical setting? Isn't the definition of treatment really a definition of the particular organization's purpose and goals? Isn't is possible to transform theoretical concepts into manageable and practical terms for the line staff?

Training

The area of training can present sizable problems for the administrator. The training concept has implications for the treatment goals. If the goals and purposes of the organization are clearly defined and if the staff understands the criminological and organizational orientation of their organization and the assumptions that its operation is based on, then the treatment techniques and the training methods needed will be a logical consequence.

Just as training will have to fit the goals and purposes of the organization, so will the trainer have to be acquainted with the problems peculiar to that organization. It is one thing for the trainer to impart certain concepts, methods, and techniques on how to react in a certain volatile situation and another thing for the trainer to experience the actual aggressiveness. Can the trainer, who is usually the college-educated treatment person, summarily chastise a staff member for reacting negatively to being called a derogatory name if he has not experienced the situation himself? (This does not mean the trainer has to agree with the negative reaction, but it is mandatory that the potential emotional ramifications be recognized.) Or should the trainer stay away from the firing line so as not to taint his humanitarian image?

The Community

The relationship to the community can also pose certain problems. In the halfway house operated in Michigan, there was often a direct correlation between the amount of aggression exhibited in the house and the amount of negative behavior exhibited in the community. Those boys who would verbalize and rebel in the house would not act out in the community. Therefore, our general philosophy was that it was better for the boys to act out in the house because the problem could be dealt with on the spot, and hence there would be less of a tendency for them to displace their aggression onto the community. This did not mean that the boys were free to express themselves in any manner they desired. They could not, for example, destroy the furniture; they could, however, express verbal anger and discontent to the staff.

Concomitant with this philosophy, our major emphasis was not on regimentation. On various occasions boys would rebel by not making their beds or doing other assigned chores. The house, however, usually never looked any worse than it would have if a normal group of teenagers had been living in it. (Chapter 4, "The Adolescent," provided background on what is considered "normal.")

It was interesting to note that even though visitors to the house seemed to accept our integrated organizational philosophy of "controls but not regimentation," they usually expected to see the "shiny institution" characteristic of classical organizational theory. Their disapproval and surprise could often be observed by staff members, who were presented with a role conflict that made them uncomfortable. On the one hand, they were attempting to play their roles according to the norms on which the program had been established, but on the other hand, they were being evaluated according to normative criteria with which the philosophy of the program did not adhere. What effect could this organizational paradox and role conflict have on the operation of the program? How could this situation be alleviated?

SOLUTIONS TO THE PROBLEMS: DEVELOPING A NEW ORGANIZATIONAL AND PHILOSOPHICAL (CRIMINOLOGICAL) SYSTEM

In the halfway house operated in Michigan, it was felt that the staff should not have to be dichotomized into treatment and custody. In other words, there did not have to be such strict division of labor and emphasis on specialization, two key principles of the classical view of organization. The same person could play the role of both "giver" and "taker," "controller" and "liberator." In effect, with adequate staff selection and training, one person could make the decision as to the proper treatment technique at any given time, which is congruent with the human relations view of participation in decision making.

Employing staff members who will perform what some people consider a dual function (treatment and custody) implies certain alterations in classical organizational theory concepts, namely, the decentralization of authority and decision making from the caseworker (administrator) to the line staff.

It was felt that if the new concept of decentralization of authority, which involved participation in decision making by the entire staff, was introduced into the halfway house program, the child-care staff would see their role more favorably and would feel a part of, and identified with, the total treatment program, which would increase the congruent normative orientation of all concerned. This would specifically result in better communication between the caseworker and the staff, a more effective treatment program, and the solidification of the group—with corresponding social rewards for the group members.

It was also assumed that each staff member would be given authority commensurate with his responsibility and that authority and communication would be a two-way process. Even though the major decisions would be made by the entire staff at the weekly staff meeting (group participation in decision making), day-to-day decisions would still have to be made by the particular staff member who was on duty. His decisions would never be reversed by the caseworker, and if a difference of opinion arose, the problem would be discussed either privately or publicly at the staff meeting. In addition, the staff members were kept informed and were involved in every phase of both the house operation and the boys' status in terms of past, present, and future diagnosis, treatment, and planning. Hence the necessity for all staff to have knowledge of deviant behavior, theories of causation, therapies, and adolescent behavior.

Finally, because the boys had also witnessed the treatment-custody dilemma before coming to the halfway house, it was thought important that some tangible administrative responsibility (a form of division of labor and specialization) be given to each staff member to reinforce the concept that the entire staff was involved in decision making and also to increase the status of the child-care staff. Each staff member was therefore given a major administrative responsibility; for example, one staff member was responsible for all monetary transactions in the house and another staff member was responsible for programming all house activities.

Organization Structure

The organization chart took a new shape. Previously the chart had resembled and had typified the classical organizational model shown on p. 336.

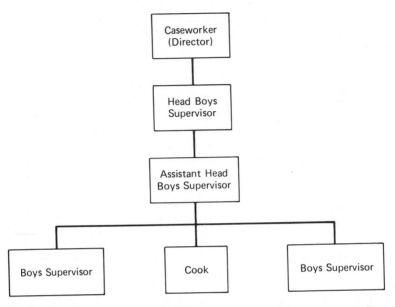

Under this system the head boys' supervisor did most of the actual staff direction, but the caseworker made most of the decisions. The decisions were meant to be categorized into treatment decisions (made by the caseworker) and house management decisions (made by the child-care staff). This was a very hazy line, however, and conceivably the caseworker could (and sometimes did) reverse a decision made by the child-care staff by rationalizing that it was a treatment decision. For example, if a boy was involved in a drinking escapade within the house and the child-care staff restricted him to the house, the caseworker could reverse the decision on treatment grounds (because he exercised his authority according to the classical principle) and allow the boy to go on a home visit because "the boy's drinking was the result of an excessive amount of pent-up frustration and anxiety." A situation like this can obviously affect the morale and the motivation of the child-care staff and the treatment of the boy. The staff would undoubtedly feel powerless in their roles, the boys would be able to utilize the situation for manipulating, and most importantly the normative bonds that have to exist for effective functioning would be nonexistent.

As seen on p. 337, the new organizational chart of Pine Lodge was much more decentralized, with a "flattened" hierarchy. In this chart, the caseworker was the director and was responsible for supervising the staff, providing casework for the boys, and administering the total program. However, the total administrative and social structure of the house was considered the major therapeutic agent. This means that house management activities and house controls were considered as much a part of the treatment program as were direct casework services. There was an integrated approach to both the organizational structure (combining classical and human relations principles) and the treatment structure (combining positive and classical principles).

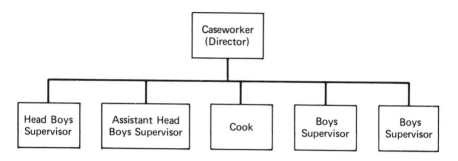

Differences in Treatment. Treatment techniques in correctional settings have to be different because the clients are different. Treatment of the boys in the halfway house was a twenty-four-hour-a-day job. In a typical clinical or psychiatric setting, a client might tell the therapist that he was involved in a "beer blast" at home. The therapist would discuss the situation with the client and would try to determine the etiology of the problem and the psychological dynamics present. In the halfway house, the staff did not have the luxury of merely discussing the problem in a second-hand manner. In addition to being concerned with the psychological dynamics of the client, the staff had to be concerned with controlling the client. Obviously, the boys could not be allowed to have a "beer blast," especially on state property.

Because the treatment program was viewed as involving the boys' total life process within the organization structure, it was not feasible or desirable that the house staff be specialized into treatment areas and house management areas. Hence, decision making could not be dichotomized into decisions made by the caseworker and decisions made by the child-care staff. The entire staff had to participate in all decision making that affected the boy and the operation of the house.

This, however, did not necessarily mean that there was no division of labor or specialization of duties according to the staff members' position as determined by their Civil Service classification. There was still a hierarchy of responsibilities, the head boys' supervisor having more responsibility, and so on. The responsibility, however, related to objective administrative functions, such as making out the staff payroll and being responsible for calling repairmen, not to decisions concerning the boys. The division of labor referred more to differences in responsibility for house management, not to differences in power or authority over the boys.

The more pronounced the hierarchical structure, the more the boys will have the opportunity to manipulate the "boss" against the "staff," and the more they will, in fact, manipulate. A flattened hierarchical structure with equal decision-making power for all eliminates much of this manipulation and thus interrupts one of the boys' major pathological processes.

Even though treatment objectives should be specifically defined, the techniques for attaining these specifically defined goals should be kept flexible to encourage the staff to use their own initiative and personal assets. This would also facilitate decision making because the staff member would not have to be concerned about using the "right" technique. The "right" technique could apply in an industrial organization operation if under classical principles, but not in a situation where managing and dealing with human behavior was a major variable. Staff members could try innovative techniques, and this would eliminate their need to try new methods through devious means (see Chapter 9).

There were, however, specific guidelines under certain circumstances. For example, if a boy was placed on restriction by the entire staff, a staff member could not make the decision on his shift to allow the boy to go out on "free time." This, however, referred more to the concept of consistency in decision making than it did to flexibility in the particular technique applied. If an individual staff member deviated from the norms established by the rest of the staff, the informal sanctioning process was very effective. Because the size of the staff was small, and the problems the boys presented difficult and frustrating, the individual staff member needed the support of his peers. Hence informal sanctioning by the staff, which many times meant withholding of social rewards (participation in social activities and other forms of socialization), was very effective. Formal sanctioning, like firing and administrative reprimand for deviations that were more serious, although infrequent, nevertheless had to be resorted to on occasion.

Another point should be clarified. Even though each staff member had the authority to make decisions about problems that would arise on his shift, he could always telephone another staff member for advice (usually the caseworker). At first the staff did this constantly, but when they became confident and comfortable with their decision-making ability and the normative orientation of the organization, consultation by telephone decreased.

Staff members were also informed that treatment did not necessarily mean a clinical setting and the use of psychological jargon. Treatment could be taking a boy shopping for clothes, giving him advice on dating, or helping him with his homework. Treatment could take place over a pool table or at the dinner table. In other words, treatment was considered anything that related to the boys' total life process. The importance of understanding all aspects of adolescent behavior was also emphasized. If staff members understood "normal" adolescent behavior, it was felt that they would be less critical of the boys when they manifested normal adolescent "symptoms" like being loud, boisterous, moody, secretive, and defiant.

The Treater: Facilitating Communication

People are attracted to certain types of work and organizations for many reasons, psychological, educational, monetary, social, and so on, and individuals working with juvenile delinquents are no exception.

It was mentioned earlier that since the delinquent was usually clinically different from the neurotic or the psychotic, it followed that the treater did not need the same clinical experience—the clinical difference between the delinquent and the neurotic or the psychotic was that the delinquent lacked an adequate conscience structure as a result of inadequate identification models. (Chapters 2 and 3 illustrated this.) At the halfway house it was felt that because positive identification models were so important, the major treatment device would not be the using of clinical jargon and knowledge to alleviate guilt and anxiety, since the client had a minimal amount of both, but would be the providing of positive identification models. Making this assumption would be a logical conclusion if theories of delinquency causation were understood and made effective by translating them from theory into practice. Because positive identification models could be found in every walk of life, we did not look for persons with a particular educational background—according to our definition and requirements, formal education was not a prerequisite to being an effective therapist. Not emphasizing a particular educational background would facilitate the combining of the classical and positive schools of criminology because the person we were looking for had to be cognizant of social and psychological factors that contribute to delinquency (the positive school) but had to be practical with an emphasis on personal responsibility and free will (the classical school). In addition to being a positive identification model, it was therefore mandatory that the person be mature and understand his own personal dynamics as well as psychological and social dynamics contributing to human behavior. This would enable him to transmit to the boy that he was honestly concerned and understood extenuating circumstances and variables. If a staff member's actions toward a boy were inappropriate, it was important to determine if he was displacing negative feelings from other persons or situations onto the boy. Staff members therefore had to understand psychological dynamics and be constantly introspective.

Persons were employed who liked children and had the ability to (1) tolerate and understand aggressive and demanding behavior, (2) give of himself emotionally and mentally without expecting or demanding something in return, (3) work with other staff members, and (4) be understanding and flexible yet firm and consistent in the enforcement of house rules.

It was observed that certain boys were attracted to, confided in, and communicated with specific staff members. This natural attraction was encouraged because of the importance of the relationship with a positive identification model in helping the boy to modify his socially deviant behavior. This positive relationship with a particular staff member was beneficial because it not only accelerated the treatment process but also gave the boy someone he could emulate and please through socially acceptable behavior. In effect, we utilized and perpetuated the natural channels of communication, unlike the authority structure in classical organization theory with communication structured between layers, ranks, and positions. The caseworker would still provide supervision (unity of command principle) to the particular staff member, but the actual casework was being performed by the staff member the boy trusted and had chosen as his friend. The caseworker's supervision mainly involved interpreting the meaning of various behavior patterns and helping the staff member understand what dynamics were present and operating in the boy. Because of the small size of the staff, span of control was not a factor.

Because one specific kind of formal education or one specific kind of personality was not required for work in Pine Lodge, the staff consisted of a variety of personality types. A person's positive personality characteristics were used to the program's best advantage. For example, an athletic staff member would program athletic events for the boys, and this could literally mean altering the organization to fit the employee. Altering the organization to fit the employee was done by choice in this instance, but it was also sometimes done by necessity. If some staff members had negative personality characteristics, these could also be utilized to the program's advantage. For example, a staff member who had difficulty exerting even minimal controls for fear that he would lose his "nice guy" image could be put on a shift that had the greatest amount of flexibility in regard to controls. He could also be used effectively to perform duties that involved being "nice" to the boys. Conversely, a staff member who was excessively controlling could be used effectively in another phase of the program where, for example, the setting of the controls and limits would be beneficial to the program.

Like other delinquents, the boys at the halfway house had reached adolescence with many of the same likes, dislikes, and pressures as normal adolescents, but they had fewer social, intellectual, and occupational skills. They had experienced little success in life. The staff attempted to intervene in their life process and acquaint them with positive life experiences.

Staff members were encouraged to react spontaneously. If a staff member was angy at something a boy had done, it was much better to express the anger than to suppress it, displace it, and have it come out in a subtle punitive, passive-aggressive manner that the boy could neither accept nor understand. (Chapter 3 pointed out the negative effects of inconsistent discipline and passive hostility in child rearing.)

Staff members involved themselves personally. They took the boys job hunting and on recreational activities, and they gave advice on social amenities. Even when staff members were looking for a new car or shopping for clothes, they often took boys with them.

Because the boys were impulsive, hedonistic, and unable to tolerate much frustration, they needed constant support and encouragement to stay on their jobs, to stay in school, and to refrain from acting out behavior.

Staff members were always willing to give a boy a ride to and from work, advance money from the house fund until he received his first paycheck, and allow him much freedom in purchasing, with his pay, such items as record players, guitars, bicycles, and radios.

This action not only supported the boy while he was experiencing the first few frustrating days on the job, it helped satisfy his need for immediate gratification and showed him that by means of employment it was possible to acquire pleasurable items legitimately. The staff should be aware of the clinical differences in delinquents, such as their impulsiveness and low frustration tolerance level, because this understanding provides a basis for developing a treatment plan and orientation. Our constant support of the boys as they moved out into the environment was predicated on the clinical peculiarities of delinquents.

It was not naively assumed that a boy who had already utilized almost every state and local service available would suddenly succeed in the community because of some deep psychological insight into the nature of his behavior. If he refrained, for example, from shoplifting, it was probably because of the money in his pocket earned from a job to purchase the items rather than because of any insight into the nature of his "oedipal problem."

The approach with the boys was direct, always emphasizing the reality of the situation. The method of reality therapy was the basis of treatment (see Chapter 9). Reality therapy emphasizes individual responsibility for actions, which is similar to the classical school of criminology's concept of free will. Psychological and sociological variables, principles of the positive school of criminology, were considered, but these variables were combined with the concept of free will through the use of reality therapy. The unconscious was not probed, mainly because of the type of boy treated, with his impulsivity and need for immediate gratification. Time was also a factor.

If, for example, a boy had the urge to steal a car, the reality of the situation rather than the boy's "unconscious conflict with authority" was emphasized. Stealing the car was the important event. There was not time to—nor did the boy want to—look introspectively at the unconscious conflict. The present event and its consequences had to be dealt with because otherwise, unlike the neurotic who would have had an anxiety attack, the boy would have acted out in the community and would have been in conflict with the law.

It was also important for the boy to please an adult with whom he had a positive relationship (the identification process) so that if the adult was mainly concerned with obtaining information relating to the psychodynamics of the boy, then the boy would naturally attempt to please the adult by giving him such information. If the adult was too eager to explain to the boy the reason why he went wrong, the boy might too eagerly accept this way of avoiding reality.[11] When the reality of the situation was emphasized, many of the boy's attempts to manipulate by means of psychological jargon in the interview were eliminated. The boy was encouraged to look at the situation and its consequences, and his guilt was not dissipated, which could have been a motivating factor for change.

The structure of the house was constantly utilized in the treatment of

[11] William Glasser, *Reality Therapy* (New York: Harper & Row, Publishers, 1965).

the boys. There were not many rules, but the ones there were were consistently and firmly enforced using as a basis the works of many of the authors who were discussed earlier (see Chapter 3, "The Family and Juvenile Delinquency").

The boys also had the opportunity to go on home visits. This assisted them in experiencing home and community pressures in a less-intensified manner. It gave them the opportunity to test out new skills and attitudes and then return to the halfway house to share their experience with staff members. The staff not only supported them in their responsible home behavior but also assisted them in seeking and implementing alternative socially acceptable solutions to problems. In addition, staff members involved themselves in community activities so that they could influence "social engineering" and help change environmental conditions that contribute to delinquent behavior.

Orientation

Prior to training staff members it is important to have an orientation procedure to familiarize the new staff member with the operation. McCartt and Mangogna have devised an appropriate orientation procedure. The following is extracted from their report on guidelines and standards for halfway houses:

A. *Orientation*

  1. *Introduction of the staff member,* student or volunteer to the immediate environment in which they will be working:

      a. To staff members who will be responsible for supervising them.
      b. To staff members with whom they will be collaborating.
      c. To clients with whom they will be working.
      d. To physical environment of the agency, and the neighborhood in which it is located.

  2. *Clear identification of new staff member's role* in the agency:

      a. His responsibilities and duties, as outlined in a job description and job specification.
      b. The responsibilities and duties of other staff members in the agency, both those supervising him and those with whom he will be collaborating, as outlined in job descriptions and specifications.

  3. *Presentation of a thorough overview* of the agency and its functions. If the agency operates more than one program, the staff member must learn what relationships, if any, exist between the various programs and how he can utilize other components of the agency for the benefit of his clients. If the agency has an organizational chart, this will be helpful to the new staff member to gain insight into the agency's operations.

4. *Presentation of philosophy, goals, objectives and techniques* utilized by the agency.

5. *Introduction of basic policies and procedures* of the agency. This should include such matters as personnel and travel policies, intake policies and procedures, special requirements which may be imposed by law, funding or contract agencies. This section should also be used to introduce the staff member to the *shalls* and *shall-nots* established by the agency, and to give him a clear understanding of the latitude he has in which to function.

6. *Introduction of basic forms* the staff member will be required to use and some practical exercises in completing such forms.

7. *Introduction of the Criminal Justice System as a whole and corrections in particular.* Concurrently, the staff member must have a thorough understanding of the relationship of the halfway house to the Criminal Justice System and to the correctional system, including both its formal and informal relationships.

8. *Introduction to collateral agencies and community resources* with which the staff member will be working, and which he will be utilizing, including, but not limited to:
   a. Probation departments.
   b. Parole departments.
   c. Jails.
   d. Penal institutions.
   e. Courts.
   f. Mental health agencies.
   g. Medical agencies.
   h. Vocational training agencies.
   i. Educational facilities.
   j. Recreational facilities.
   k. Welfare agencies.
   l. Family service agencies.
   m. Employment agencies.
   n. Any other agencies utilized by the halfway house.

   It should be noted that the new staff member should not only be introduced to the services provided by these agencies, but also the method of obtaining such services for his clients, as well as methods for developing new resources to cope with unexpected problems. In addition, the new staff member should be introduced to workers at such agencies, at the line level, and given the opportunity to develop a relationship with them. It is important to start with line staff in collateral agencies, for they are usually responsible for intake and service delivery, on a day-to-day basis.

9. *Assignment of tasks* to the new staff member which are within his immediate capabilities and skills, with the assignment of increasingly complex and difficult tasks as his knowledge and skills grow. It is crucial that close supervision be provided to the staff member during

the entire orientation period, and that orientation itself be goal- and task-oriented training, with intermediate objectives set out to attain those goals.

10. *Introduction to treatment framework* of the agency, if such a framework has been adopted. If not, then introduction into a few basic types of treatment modalities, acceptable and compatible with the agency's program.

11. *Planned opportunities* for the new staff member to give and receive feedback as well as to ask questions and clarify any issues which are not thoroughly understood. Feedback should also include evaluation of the orientation program itself, by both the trainee and trainer. In retrospect, trainees can be extremely helpful in evaluating what was helpful to them, and what was not, what needed more emphasis, what less, what should have been included, and what should not.

Once orientation has been completed, the process of training has only begun. Continuous in-service training, at regular intervals with continual supervision, is absolutely essential if the worker is to continue to grow in knowledge and skills, and be able to adapt to new situations and challenges.[12]

Training

Utilizing the personal assets of the staff also had implications for staff training. Even though staff training was usually geared to impart certain general principles and techniques for the entire staff, training also had to be geared to individual needs and abilities. In the halfway house some staff members had innate, intuitive, and empathetic qualities that assisted them in relating positively to the boys and reacting appropriately to emotion-laden situations. Others did not have these innate personal assets and in effect had to be "conditioned" to act in a certain manner even though they did not "feel like it." Of course, it was not merely a matter of either having the qualities or not having them. It should be viewed on a continuum, with some individuals having both more innate assets and a better ability to be introspective. Training can accentuate a person's positive traits and provide him with new skills.

One of the trainer's major responsibilities should be the transforming of theoretical concepts into practical terms to make them more acceptable to the staff. Working with delinquent boys could be frustrating, and the staff might often need something tangible to look at in terms of their accomplishments. The trainer would be much more effective if he pointed out to the staff that a particular boy had improved a great deal because he was staying in school or on the job regularly for the first time in his life, instead of saying that the boy had increased "frustration tolerance" and "impulse control." This would eliminate one of the major criticisms and problems of many theories, namely,

[12] McCartt and Mangogna, *op. cit.,* pp. 59–61.

that they were impractical and their propositions not easily translated into practical application.

The trainer should also be realistic and able to empathize with the staff. The director should cover at least one shift a week so as to have an opportunity to observe what takes place "on the firing line." After having experienced various situations, at different times of the day and night it is easier to be more tolerant and less judgmental of a staff member who might have reacted angrily in a particular situation. Such an experience affords the trainer new insights into the dynamics of human behavior and helps eliminate many of the problems inherent in staff-line relationships.

In relation to the caseworker's covering a shift, many persons mistakenly believe that the "treatment person" should not become involved in the areas of disciplining and controlling. If the thesis concerning the staff (including the caseworker) acting as parental substitutes is extended, in how many families is one parent the "good guy" and giver and the other parent the "bad guy" and disciplinarian? The same parent can perform both functions effectively, and the child readily accepts and wants this. Why then can't parental substitutes perform the same dual function? It realistically illustrates to the boys that adults play many roles and perform many functions, some pleasing and some displeasing, and it is an honest approach to child rearing (see Chapter 3).

Extending the analogy between parents and parental substitutes, just as teenagers in "normal" families "act up" and become aggressive, so do delinquent teenagers in a halfway house setting. The difference is that delinquents act up to a greater degree, and their acting up is much more difficult for the staff (parental substitutes) to tolerate because, even though the staff members are parental substitutes, there is not as great an emotional bond between them and the boys as there is between a parent and a child. Because of the different backgrounds and personalities between the boys and the staff, there is bound to be more of a chance for a personality clash than in a normal family. Different types of behavior by the boys will affect individual staff members differently. Hence the necessity of staff members' understanding their own psychological dynamics and motivation as well as normal adolescent behavior.

If it was felt that a particular boy who had been referred to the house might present a particular problem to a certain staff member, the staff member would be involved in the interview with the boy regarding his being accepted by Pine Lodge. The boy was usually at his best when he was being interviewed, and therefore it was unlikely that he would make a negative impression. The staff member was usually in favor of accepting the boy. After the boy had been accepted and was a resident of the house, he began to "learn the system" and his particular idiosyncrasies began to emerge. At this point the staff member might become very irritated with the boy. Because he had been involved in the acceptance process, however, he would be less likely to insist prematurely that the boy be returned to the Boys Training School.

In effect, involving the staff in the selection of boys encouraged the staff member to work a little harder, be more tolerant, and try to determine why this particular boy caused an exaggerated and inappropriate reaction within him.

Learning the System

After the boys had been in residence for a few weeks, they began to learn the organizational and social system. Some aspects of the Pine Lodge system were kept unpredictable (unlike classical organizations) because otherwise the boys would have spent much of their time trying to "beat the system" and little of their time trying to positively increase their social and personal functioning. The structure of the house, with its consistent enforcement of the rules, was an asset, but a system that was completely predictable could eliminate all anxiety and place a premium on conformity and "playing the game" to attain a release.

It is important to point out that the organization and the organization's system should be constantly evaluated in terms of the implications the system might have for the program.

In the case of the Pine Lodge system it was unlike that of the classical institution because a premium was not put on rationality, conformity, and regimentation. However, the boys quickly learned what was emphasized, namely, expression in the house rather than in the community, and some of them began "playing the game" in regard to this system. In other words, they were expressing themselves in the house so as to elicit the response, "Well, at least you must be improving because you are able to express yourself directly (in lieu of displacement) in the house." These same boys might also be "expressing" themselves in the community, however, and much of their energy might be expended in playing "our game." Thus the need for constant organizational evaluation, updating, and innovation.

Relation to the Community

It was mentioned that there were many community visitors to the halfway house. This in itself was not a problem. The problem arose when the visitors transmitted to the staff surprise and disappointment that there was not more uniformity and regimentation, which typifies most institutions that operate under the classical philosophy.

Quite naturally the staff wanted to operate within the philosophy of the program, but they were also concerned that the visitors would interpret the lived-in look as being a symptom of poor functioning. There was a role conflict.

Even though much of the negative communication from the visitors could not be dispelled, the problem took care of itself. As the staff became more identified with the treatment program and more committed to the philosophy of the program, they became less concerned with negative comments and more enthusiastic about the program and the special techniques that were used in the treatment of the boys. This increased enthusiasm, and *esprit de corps* and normative transmission made a positive impact on the visitors, with the result that fewer negative comments were made about the lack of uniformity and regimentation. In other words, the visitors, because of good public relations work and commitment by the staff, began evaluating the program in terms of content rather than in terms of what could be seen (shiny floors, regimentation, and so on). This is not to imply, however, that the staff did not attempt to "tidy up" the house when a particular influential person who was "institution oriented" visited. This is merely astute organizational management and perception of the reality of the need for public support if the program is going to succeed.

Conclusion

Throughout the chapter, involvement of the entire staff in the total program, and especially in decision making, has been emphasized. This does not mean, however, that there was not a central figure to give guidance and direction. The caseworker (administrator) was responsible for directing and supervising the staff. To be effective, the caseworker must be the "boss" in that he provides direction, guidance, and support, but he must not be so "bossy" that he squelches individual initiative and thinking.

EVALUATION OF THE PROGRAM

Although some of the boys may not have developed any additional insight into the etiology of their behavior, they did experience some success and gratification in the areas of employment, education, and recreation. They have been able, with the support of the staff, to delay immediate gratification and tolerate unpleasant situations even though the temptation to become involved in deviant behavior is always present.

In effect, the boys have demonstrated to themselves that it is, for example, possible to go downtown without shoplifting because there are other means, namely, through employment, to acquire pleasurable items. Also, it is possible to get "chewed out" by the boss without quitting the job because the boys realize from previous experience that the paycheck received will be a source of much gratification.

During the evaluation period in the early stages of the program eighty boys were accepted by Pine Lodge. Eleven boys were returned directly to the Boys Training School after a short stay, twelve were residents at the time of the evaluation, and the remaining fifty-seven were released to the community.

Of the fifty-seven boys released from Pine Lodge to their home communities after an average stay of seven and one-half months, eleven (19.3 percent) were released to independent living arrangements, three (5.3 percent) enlisted in the armed forces, twenty-seven (47.4 percent) were released home, and sixteen (28 percent) went to live with relatives or at a foster home.

Eleven of the fifty-seven (19.3 percent) had contact with law enforcement officials, necessitating a return to the Boys Training School or some other form of incarceration (an adult institution, a jail, etc.). The remaining forty-six boys (80.7 percent) did not become involved in future negative behavior in the community. At the time of the evaluation some of the boys had been released for up to three and one-half years.

The question will arise, and rightfully so, as to whether the positive results have taken place in spite of the program rather than because of it. This is possible, but it should be remembered that these boys had previously utilized almost every available state and local service, but to no avail. It must, however, be mentioned in all fairness to the various state and local facilities that a halfway house program has the advantage of being community based and able to maintain control over the boy while providing him extensive support and guidance as he moves into the community to face its pressures and responsibilities. Furthermore, the program was established and operated on a sound framework and a knowledge of deviant behavior, delinquency causation theory, organizational theory, adolescent behavior, clinical therapies, and prevention programs.

Results of Pine Lodge Program

	Number of Boys	Percent of Total
Returned to Boys Training School	11	13.7
Remained as residents of Pine Tree	12	15.0
Released to the community	57	71.3
Boys involved in the evaluation of the program	80	100.0
Released to independent living arrangements	11	19.3
Enlisted in the armed forces	3	5.3
Released to previous home	27	47.4
Released to relatives or to foster homes	16	28.0
Boys who were released to the community	57	100.0
Number of boys who were reincarcerated	11	19.3
Boys who did not exhibit negative behavior	46	80.7
Boys who were released to the community	57	100.0

GUIDING PRINCIPLES FOR OPERATING
A HALFWAY HOUSE

1. A competent staff dedicated to the philosophy that delinquents are persons worth helping.

2. Active involvement of the entire staff in the treatment process.

3. A sound administrative structure with clear lines of communication.

4. A minimum of rules and regulations, both the firm and consistent enforcement of the existing ones.

5. A refined selection process for accepting clients to the program. Each client's individual needs as well as the group interaction and the problems that can result from either overplacement or underplacement should be considered.

6. Adequate programming and good working relationships with such agencies as the police and the schools.

McCartt and Mangogna provide specific recommendations for standards and guidelines for community-based programs. The following are their recommendations:

RECOMMENDATIONS FOR STANDARDS AND
GUIDELINES FOR COMMUNITY-BASED
PROGRAMS

Program

1. The community-based treatment center should be located in an area reasonably close to public transportation, employment and vocational opportunities, medical, psychiatric, recreational and other community resources and agencies to be utilized by the center for its clients.

2. The agency will clearly state in writing its purposes, programs, and services offered. This will be done in a form suitable for distribution to staff, clients, referral sources, funding agencies and the general public. Its program and services must have a direct relationship to its stated purposes as they appear in the agency's constitution, articles of incorporation, by-laws or statutes, if the agency is part of a public entity. The program and services must be based upon identified needs in the community in which it is located.

3. An agency operating a community-based treatment program will provide the following services:

- shelter.
- food service.
- temporary financial assistance.

- individual counseling.
- group counseling.
- vocational counseling.
- vocational training referral.
- employment counseling and referral.

4. The agency, if it does not provide the service itself, will see that its clients have ready access to:

- medical services, including psychiatric and dental care.
- psychological evaluation.
- psychological counseling or therapy.
- vocational training.
- vocational and/or employment evaluation.
- employment placement.
- academic upgrading, e.g., G.E.D. college courses, etc.
- any other services as needed by the type of program operated, and the particular need of an individual client.

5. In general, the agency will provide clearly identified resources that are relevant and essential to the successful conduct of its programs and will utilize the resources of other agencies in order to provide services needed by its clientele but which cannot or should not be provided by the agency operating a community-based treatment program.

6. The agency will establish clearly defined and written intake policies and procedures. Such policies and procedures will state the type of client acceptable for admission to the program.

- intake policies will be disseminated to all referral sources.
- clearly defined age limits for admission to the program will be established by the agency.
- any category or categories of potential clients not eligible for admission into the program must be clearly stated in the intake policies.
- prospective clients ineligible for admission for services and their referral sources must be informed of the reasons for their ineligibility. When possible, the ineligible clients should be referred to other agencies for services.

7. Program goals and services to be offered will be discussed with each individual client.

8. The individual treatment program established will be done with a maximum degree of client involvement.

9. The agency will develop procedures for the evaluation of its clients in order to determine client progress in the program. Conferences, formal or informal, will be held regularly to review such progress and to alter or develop further treatment plans. For the greatest effectiveness, clients must be involved deeply in their own evaluation process.

10. The agency should participate actively in community-planning organizations as they relate to the agency's field of service and should conduct a program of public information, using appropriate forms of communica-

tion – such as the news media, brochures, speaking engagements, etc., to encourage understanding, acceptance and support of its program.

11. The agency will maintain accurate and complete case records, reports and statistics necessary for the conduct of its program. Appropriate safeguards will be established to protect the confidentiality of the records, and minimize their possibility of theft, loss or destruction.

12. A single case record for each client admitted to the program or served by the agency will be maintained so as to communicate clearly, concisely and completely, appropriate case information.

13. Individual case records will be maintained on a current basis, and will include:

- identification data.
- reports from referral sources.
- pertinent case history.
- diagnosis when appropriate.
- problems and goals.
- referrals for service to other agencies.
- evaluation or progress reports.
- correspondence pertinent to client's case.
- record of any significant incidents, both positive and negative.
- signed release of information form, where appropriate.
- current employment data, including place of employment, date of employment, job title, rate of pay, record of client earnings.
- discharge report, including summary statement.
- other information necessary and appropriate to the program and/or individual client's case.

14. Agencies operating community treatment center programs will establish methods and procedures for evaluating the effectiveness of the programs.

15. Evaluation must measure the outcome of the program and services in relation to the agency's stated purpose and goals. Program and service effectiveness must be measured by recognized evaluation techniques, and when possible, by formal research.

16. The results of evaluation and research should be reviewed on a systematic basis by the staff and governing body to determine:

- the effectiveness of program and services in fulfilling the stated purposes and goals of the agency, and
- as the basis for change, modification or addition to the program and services offered by the agency.

Personnel

1. The agency must employ competent and qualified staff to provide the services essential to achievement of program goals and client needs.

2. The agency must provide competitive salaries and benefits in order to attract and retain competent personnel.

3. Minimum qualifications for professional staff will be four years of college plus two years of experience in social service, or a Master's Degree in one of the behavioral sciences. Experience may be substituted for educational background, but the ratio of such substitutions must be spelled out clearly in job qualifications. However, when standards of qualification have been established by recognized professional groups, the agency will not adopt less than those as minimum standards for its professional staff.

4. The agency will establish standards of qualification for its para-professional personnel.

5. When standards of qualification have not been established by an organization or group for a particular position, the agency must establish reasonable qualifications and an on-going assessment of competence in job performance.

6. A balance of professionals, para-professionals and ex-offenders is the preferred staffing pattern.[13]

SUMMARY

Halfway houses are no panacea for the treatment of the delinquent. They cannot serve all children, especially those who need a good institutional treatment program with more stringent controls and at least partial separation from community pressures, but the halfway house does introduce a new resource that seems to be a better answer for certain children.[14]

There are some problems, however, in operating community-based programs, such as a lack of coordination both intraorganizationally and interorganizationally. Negative public attitudes can affect the operation of the program, and jurisdictional disputes between community agencies can hinder and even destroy the program. The next chapter will describe a process whereby these problems can be minimized and even alleviated.

QUESTIONS AND PROJECTS

Essay Questions

1. How can the treatment-custody dilemma be mitigated?

2. Why is proper personnel selection so important for agencies working with juvenile delinquents?

3. Why are programs for delinquents often very regimented?

---

[13] *Ibid.,* pp. 260–65.
[14] Martin Gula, *Agency Operated Group Homes,* U.S. Department of Health, Education, and Welfare (Washington, D.C.: U.S. Government Printing Office, 1964), p. 29.

4. *Is a halfway house suitable for all youngsters?*

5. *Why do you think halfway houses were not utilized more in the past?*

Projects

1. *Develop an approach for convincing community residents that a program like a halfway house will not "contaminate" them.*

2. *Develop a set of rules and regulations that could be implemented in a halfway house in your community.*

3. *Describe how you would go about financing a halfway house.*

chapter 12

Delinquency Prevention through Citizen Involvement

Juvenile delinquency prevention is one of the least refined areas of criminology. The juvenile delinquency phenomenon is extremely complex not only in itself, but because of the profusion of information available on theories of causation, the allocation of resources to combat it, and the number of assumptions as to how to treat it.

Most of the programs established under the guise of prevention are often "after the fact." They attempt to work with the youngster after he has made contact with the formal processes of the juvenile justice system. Many different programs exist, ranging all the way from informal probation to institutionalization. There are also programs such as Job Corps and Employment and Manpower projects, which work with youngsters who have not been adjudicated delinquent. Most of these programs however have as their major objective providing opportunities for youngsters of the community, not necessarily the prevention of delinquency. The prevention of delinquency is often a secondary objective and result.

In addition to the many attempts at prevention through the establishment of specific programs, there are also many psychologically-oriented treatment approaches, therapies, and strategies, as well as sociologically-oriented "social engineering" projects.

The question might be asked, Why with all the resources and the theories from the many different disciplines available have attempts at delinquency prevention been, for the most part, unsuccessful?

The answer to this question is not a simple one. The conditions that contribute to crime and delinquency are complex, and long-range solutions to such problems as unemployment, inadequate housing, and unequal opportunity will not take place overnight. A massive amount of "social engineering" will be necessary, as well as a commitment by the total community to alleviate these social problems.

Furthermore, it has been naively assumed that theories, manpower, and resources are automatically translated into action programs. For any program or organization to operate effectively, there has to be more than theories, resources, manpower, and good intentions; there must be an adequate *structure* to the program or organization, as well as a *process* that facilitates cooperation, integration of functions, and orderly procedure for goal achievement.

Developing an organizational structure, or even a process, is not difficult if the organization has well defined specific goals. Establishing a *structure* and a *process* is not so simple, however, if goal achievement is dependent on a complex system of organizations.

Even though one of the stated goals of the organizations and agencies of the juvenile justice system is delinquency prevention, the structures and processes of the individual agencies are often not conducive to interagency cooperation and goal achievement. The philosophical and operating ideologies of the various agencies often conflict with one another, and this leads to interagency bickering, attempts at boundary maintenance, and perpetuation of individualized approaches to delinquency prevention problem solving. The expertise of the numerous disciplines represented in the various agencies is not coordinated or integrated for the common good and welfare of the community.

The core of the problem is developing a *process* that will coordinate and involve the many agencies and community residents so that there will be a normative goal orientation to problem solving and a blending of ideas, expertise, and cooperative effort. The issue of developing and presenting a process that contributes to this end will be discussed shortly. First, however, some of the factors that have contributed to the need for a calculated and formal problem-solving process will be mentioned.

THE PRESENT INEFFECTIVENESS OF INFORMAL SOCIAL CONTROL

The importance of the family as an institution for transmitting the positive norms of the community is readily acknowledged. Either directly or indirectly, the family influences the behavior of its members and can have a great impact on controlling their behavior. When many families are blended together to form a cohesive community, the impact of influencing the behavior of community members becomes even greater. Ideally, then, the community, through its natural interdependent processes which satisfy individual and group needs, is the most potent force for influencing behavior and preventing deviance.

Because of urbanization, mobility, and many other factors, present-day communities are not as cohesive as they were in the past. Hence, they no longer exert the degree of influence over individuals that they did in the past. Before the growth of our complex urban communities, much crime and delinquency was effectively prevented through informal normative influence. Even if the youngster did come in contact with a formal community agency, such as the police, the matter was often handled informally because the police officer on the beat knew his community and its residents.

The complexity of present-day communities has reduced the impact and effectiveness of the police officer on the beat. The informal communication process between the police officer and the community no longer exists; and because of this lack of face-to-face contact, the police officer is no longer able to empathize with the community, understand the life-styles of its members, or exert informal influence.

In the past, most of the activities of the community residents revolved around community institutions like the family, the church, and the school. Most of the primary relationships and friendships were within the immediate boundaries of the community or neighborhood. The local businessmen knew their customers and community members knew their neighbors, and public and private agency personnel lived in the community.

The interdependence and informal network of relationships that existed effectively complemented the formal institutions. Because of this network of interdependent relationships, if a youngster did happen to become involved in some form of delinquent activity, he could easily be identified as a community resident. His actions would be made known to his parents, most of the time through informal channels, by the police officer or someone else in the community.

The police officer, or even a private citizen, knew that the youngster would usually be reprimanded by his parents. The community could also affect the youngster's future behavior through the influence it could transmit through its various institutions, of which the youngster was usually a member.

The preceding description of the community's power over the actions of its members does not mean to imply that crime and delinquency did not occur or that the social environment was devoid of unemployment, poverty, and discrimination. Crime, delinquency, and negative social conditions did exist, but these factors were often counterbalanced by the positive influence exerted by a strong cohesive community and the effectiveness of its institutions of control.

Today, the same negative social conditions exist, but without the strong normative community bonds to counteract unpleasant social conditions. Furthermore, increased mobility and urbanization have contributed to the impersonality of both private and public service organizations. Community residents no longer feel that they can effectively exert influence through their community organizations and institutions. The present process of citizen influence usually has to be formal, impersonal, and time consuming, often with little assurance of success. This bureaucracy contributes to apathy and to an unwillingness of citizens to become involved in the community problem-solving process.

Contemporary communities are not conducive to encouraging citizen involvement in problem solving or coordinating the efforts of the many community organizations for a common purpose or toward a common goal. The intra-community and interorganization ties are no longer as binding. As a result, operations by community organizations and agencies have grown more independent and individualized; often with a minimum of citizen input and involvement.

CITIZEN INVOLVEMENT

In their volume, titled *State of the Nation*, William Watts and Lloyd A. Free report on an attempt to elicit the opinions of average citizens with regard to what can be done to reduce the crime rate. Various solutions were proposed and respondents were asked to list their preferences. Responses showed a generally-perceived need for stricter parental discipline, a citizen responsibility. However, none of the remaining preferred solutions promoted community involvement or citizen action, even though the most popular solution recommended "cleaning up social and economic conditions in our slums and ghettos that tend to breed addicts and criminals."[1] Respondents were proposing that this overwhelming task be left to the "professionals"!

The present tendency is either to blame or to strengthen the professional crime-fighting element in the face of rising crime rates. Without citizen involvement, however, there can be no hope whatsoever for improvement. The National Advisory Commission on Criminal Justice Standards and Goals, Task Force on Community Crime Prevention makes the assumptions that:

1. Citizen apathy and indifference contribute to the spread of crime;

2. Private and public agencies outside the criminal justice system influence rises and declines in crime rates; and

3. Community crime prevention efforts include demonstrable benefits for existing institutions and agencies organized toward the achievement of other primary goals.[2]

The primary task of those alarmed at the increased prevalence of crime is to awaken the general citizenry to the reality that without citizen initiatives, cooperation, and involvement, more crimes will be committed, more will go undetected, and the increased inability of the "professionals" to cope with crime will provide even more encouragement to the lawbreaking element to persist in illegal activity.

Until relatively recently, as pointed out earlier, crime prevention was considered the duty of every citizen. Even today, in more closely-knit societies, in-

---

[1] William Watts and Lloyd A. Free, Eds., *State of the Nation*, a report by Potomac Associates (Universe Books, 1973), pp. 118–120.
[2] National Advisory Commission on Criminal Justice Standards and Goals, *Community Crime Prevention* (Washington, D.C.: U.S. Government Printing Office, 1973), p. 1.

dividuals are considered responsible not only for their own actions, but for those of their neighbors as well. When a crime is either observed or known to have been committed, the citizen is expected to raise a "hue and cry" to arouse other community members, all of whom are obligated to pursue the criminal.

With the migration to the cities, the extended family unit and, thus, the tightly-knit community were broken up in industrialized societies. Cooperation and mutual responsibility were replaced by greater affluence, greater mobility, and greater alienation. As everyone began "doing his own thing," agencies of professionals had to be created to perform the duties that were previously considered common responsibility: the care of orphans and neglected children, care of the aged, illegitimacy, public health, and so on, *and* crime.

Law enforcement agencies were created as specialized units to deal with crime. Total specialization came gradually, however. As recently as a generation ago, crime fighting specialists and citizens cooperated quite closely with one another. With the advent of greater complexity in urban life, the widespread use of the automobile, the replacement of verbal gossip by radio and television, mobility and rootlessness as the path to affluence, citizens became alienated from one another, as well as from their public agencies. Police departments, as a part of the greater society, shared the general trends; police officers often no longer come from the communities that they serve, and, developing specialization to the point at which their duties can be handled impersonally and dispassionately, the police operation has become dehumanized, alienating the police from the society that they serve. These developments have led to an increased inability of the police to deal with crime and an unwillingness of an alienated citizenry to become involved in crime detection and prevention, all of which has resulted in a situation in which crime does indeed pay.

In full recognition of the present undesirable state of affairs, the Community Crime Prevention Task Force of the National Advisory Commission on Criminal Justice Standards and Goals recommends "a more balanced allocation of law enforcement duties between specialists and citizenry—for citizens to reassume many of their discarded crime prevention responsibilities."[3] It further recommends the establishment of neighborhood citizen councils that exercise decisive control over the delivery of public services, including those related to crime prevention, as provided for by an act of the Indiana Legislature in 1972.

Citizen efforts at crime prevention in the past have often been mere sporadic reactions to a particularly heinous crime. With the exacerbation of the crime problem in America, however, citizen efforts are becoming more informed, more concerted, and of greater durability.

Just about everyone is able to contribute to crime prevention efforts in the course of his everyday life. Gambling, for example, is widespread; gambling proceeds are often an important source of funds for organized crime rings, who use them to import illegal drugs. (There is a high correlation between drug addiction

[3] *Ibid.*, p. 8.

and robbery.) Citizen antigambling efforts can be effected in many ways: through block or neighborhood crime prevention associations; by applying pressure in churches, social clubs, fraternal organizations, or civic associations. An employer or employee can press to stop gambling on company premises.

Trade associations, educational institutions, political parties, unions, charities, foundations, and professional societies provide ready-made organizations for citizen crime prevention efforts. Member can insure that community crime prevention efforts receive appropriate consideration in their organization's charitable donations.

Direct crime prevention efforts, such as security councils and tenant patrols, are practical efforts that can be instituted with relative ease. Of greater importance, however, is individual citizen and organization support of programs that attack the root causes of crime, programs designed to increase the employability of the jobless, programs furthering the education of the dropout, programs providing adequate medical treatment for the alcoholic and drug addict, and programs organizing constructive activities for youth, whether they are recreational or job related.

Currently, citizen crime prevention efforts include educational, employment, recreational, counseling and treatment efforts, police-related activities, court and corrections-related activities, and efforts to insure official integrity.

Citizen volunteers encourage dropouts to complete their education by insuring that they have adequate clothing and school supplies, by providing tutors for students who need special help. Others provide alternative educational opportunities, such as street academies or vocational programs. Kiwanis International distributes a free 16-page booklet, titled "You and the Law," to teen-agers. Many parents regularly donate their services to schools, preparing instructional materials, and assisting teachers in the classroom. Other citizens assist schools in counseling young people on drug use, pregnancy, family breakdown, employment, and so on. Fraternal organizations provide scholarships for needy students.

Citizens of the business community attempt to place disadvantaged youths in part-time jobs during the school year or the summer. The Urban Coalition has induced some companies to fill a certain percentage of new jobs with the hardcore unemployed and to modify their eligibility standards. Other groups are promoting on-the-job training programs, which enable people who are otherwise unemployable to secure employment. Still others provide job counseling and training and disseminate job opportunity information in high unemployment areas.

Citizen organizations finance and operate summer camps for disadvantaged youngsters and organize sports activities and tournaments. Families in rural areas take in city youths for the summer. Individuals volunteer to take youths to sporting, entertainment, and cultural events. Some groups have founded youth centers, established and refurbished parks and other recreational facilities, developed nature trails and nature demonstration centers and induced urban youth to make use of them. Citizens have organized talent shows, arts and crafts classes, and special interest programs in automobile repair, aviation, weather, motorcycle safety, music, and dancing. Citizens in some areas have banded together to hire gang members to build parks, and so on.

Citizens have established hotlines to counsel those with drug-related and other problems. The YMCA acts as a referral agent to community agencies that provide medical and mental health services, drug rehabilitation, planned parenthood counseling, juvenile and legal aid services. Volunteers counsel children and parents in an attempt to bring them closer together. Others assist professionals in drug and alcohol treatment, support and conduct anti-drug-abuse educational campaigns. Citizen groups often provide the primary financial support for treatment centers of various kinds.

Citizens support the police by reporting crime themselves, and promote better crime reporting by the public by encouraging fellow citizens to protect their homes and businesses with improved locks, bolts, bars, and lighting. One organization encourages informers by offering sizable rewards for information leading to the arrest and conviction of lawbreakers. Citizens band together with alarm systems, which, when activated, alert all members of the cooperative. Citizen organizations provide speakers who answer questions on security matters. Many individuals have joined police reserve units. Block mothers provide a haven for harassed children. The Indianapolis, Indiana, Crime Crusade was successful in reducing crime significantly in some areas through a street-lighting campaign. Business groups sponsor clinics on shoplifting and robbery prevention and projects to reduce automobile thefts. Citizen Crime Commissions provide a prestigious and effective body for the reduction of crime and the policing of law-enforcement agencies. "Deskbook on Organized Crime," published by the United States Chamber of Commerce, advises businessmen on measures that can be taken to counter the attempted incursions of organized criminal elements into legitimate business. Several organizations have furnished funds or have lobbied for increased police manpower, more equipment, higher police salaries, and better educational opportunities and training for officers.

Probably the largest group of citizen volunteers to be found is assisting the court component of the criminal and juvenile justice systems. Most of them are active in the very successful Volunteers in Probation program. Citizen volunteers in this program act as advisory council members, arts and crafts teachers, home skills teachers, recreation leaders, coordinators or administrators of programs, employment counselors, foster parents, group guidance counselors, information officers, court support services workers, neighborhood workers, clerical and secretarial office help, one-to-one counselors of probationers, professional skills volunteers, public relations workers, community education counselors, record keepers, religious guidance counselors, tutors, and educational aides.

Court watching is another activity of court volunteers. The latter observe the performance of judges and prosecutors, determine reasons for delays and continuances, note the presence of bail bond solicitors, and record the consistency of sentences for comparable offenses. Others aid those who have been jailed by reporting and attempting to resolve cases of error and delay and by securing the admission of some offenders into community programs. Some citizens spearhead diversion efforts between arrest and trial. Others facilitate communication between lawyer and client. Still others study court procedures with a view toward making courts more efficient. Family courts employ volunteers who counsel families in trouble, explain the court process to them, gather information about them to assist the judge in his determination, and help them secure aid from community agencies.

Citizen volunteers aid corrections programs by offering medical and legal aid to inmates. They also conduct inspections and surveys of jails, prisons, and institutions for juveniles. Some volunteers, acting as friends, visit an inmate assigned to them at least once a month and write regular letters to him for the duration of his prison term. Through study and discussion groups, volunteers prepare inmates for release. They also act as counselors, listeners, and as intermediaries between inmates and their families. Some citizen organizations provide needed friendship, support, recreation, transportation, and emergency food, furniture, and clothing to families of inmates. Others press for correctional legislation and educate the public concerning the problems of inmates and correctional institutions. Halfway houses, homes for runaways, foster homes, and group homes and their respective programs are often financed by citizen organizations. Citizens help ex-offenders readjust by providing information, counseling, and job placement and by helping ex-offenders obtain welfare, medical and legal aid, and adequate clothing and shelter. Citizens also refer ex-offenders with alcohol, drug, or family problems to appropriate community agencies. Business associations provide job-training programs. The use of volunteer probation officers is increasing because of its proven effectiveness.

The number of ways in which citizens can help in the fight against crime is legion. The preceding discussion listed only some of the more frequent manifestations of citizen involvement.

ORGANIZING CITIZEN EFFORTS

As a result of poor organization many a well-intentioned citizen effort has met with failure or died of attrition after initial successes. Citizen motivation is more often than not sparked by some spectacular event, usually a particularly heinous crime. Initial response usually consists of forming an organization. A new organization is only appropriate if there is none in existence which might already have the charge to deal with the area proposed to be covered by current citizen interest. If a new organization is perceived as essential after researching existing organizations, its organizers must proceed in full realization of the possible reactions to their efforts.

Since the mid-1960s, citizen participation has come to be identified with the civil rights movement, advocacy movements, such as the thrust to save the environment, and so on. The brand of political activism demonstrated by these movements has posed significant threats to the interests of middle- and upper-class segments of society. The new organization may elicit considerable negative reaction if it is perceived as a challenge to established power relationships.

The difficulties involved in motivating large numbers of alienated citizens have been explored. Even when engendered, motivation and participation are difficult to sustain over extended periods of time. Public administrators seldom view citizen efforts, which they consider uninformed and amateurish, favorably. Foot-dragging and even sabotage can sometimes be expected from this quarter. The new effort will also have to deal with all the problems endemic to any organization: leadership and staffing concerns, funding problems, controls, red tape, and so on. The greatest problem of all is posed by the crime prevention effort itself. No single effort has been shown beyond reasonable doubt to be a foolproof method for preventing crime. There are efforts, to be sure, that show considerable promise, as discussed by other authors on research, but the citizen group will first and foremost have to identify an area of prevention on which it can realistically hope to have an impact. Objectives have to be narrow enough to make short-term successes possible; these will reinforce and, thus, maintain citizen motivation. The rationale or philosophy of the objectives should be non-judgmental, broad enough to appeal to many segments of society, and, above all, should not conflict with those of the professional crime fighters. To have any hope of success, the citizen effort must be buttressed by resources, both human and material, solicited from many sources. As such, it will be perceived as a complement, rather than a challenge to the city administration.

Forrest M. Moss has developed a blueprint for a citizen crime prevention effort with the broad goal of preventing crime through enhanced employment opportunities for youths and offenders. Included are a number of subgoals:

A. *Information-gathering*: Establish a task force to determine
   1. Youth population, by area;
   2. Number of youths employed;
   3. Extent of delinquency and subdelinquent behavior;
   4. Community-wide employment opportunities and existing programs;
   5. Extent of job preparation training, if any, and relationship to job market;
   6. Extent of local, state, and federal funding for use in employment projects and manner in which it is being used;
   7. Nature of nonofficial community or neighborhood resources being employed, if any;
   8. Specific problems experienced by youth, delinquents, probationers, or parolees relative to

  a) Job placements:

  (1) Prejudice against past record,

  (2) Prejudicial state licensing requirements,

  (3) Lack of bonding acceptability,

  (4) Poor verbal skills,

  (5) Unacceptable appearance,

  (6) Racial discrimination,

  (7) Poor performance of prior employees,

  (8) Prejudice against youth,

  (9) Lack of occupational skills, and

  (10) Lack of general educational skills, and

  b) Job retention:

  (1) Poor punctuality and transportation problems,

  (2) Lack of acceptance by the public being served,

  (3) Prejudicial attitude of other employees,

  (4) Personal information or habits reflecting poorly on company,

  (5) Poor adaptability to increased responsibility,

  (6) Resistance to supervision or authority,

  (7) Poor self-discipline, and

  (8) Lack of trustworthiness, and

  c) Promotion:

  (1) Inability to accept increased responsibility,

  (2) Prejudice of management, and

  (3) Employee resistance;

9. Extent of diversion within the formal juvenile justice system (for example, employment training or counseling in lieu of pressing charges of formal trial);

10. Focus of responsibility for diversionary programs and basis of funding;

11. Existence of diversionary programs within the community youth service bureau or the police delinquency bureau or division; and

12. Number of probationers or parolees within the community, expressed needs of probation and parole officers, and specific problems of the individuals they supervise (lack of suitable clothing for job interviews, lack of study areas at home, and transportation expenses, for example).

B. *Conferences*: Motivate community groups and citizens to create or direct resources already in existence to solve the problem by

1. Relating the problem to the economic welfare of community safety, and increasing earning within a particular area;
2. Challenging existing social, fraternal, religious, professional, and business groups to sponsor a number of youths, preparing action alternatives, and making manning proposals;
3. Determining potential resources and attempting to enlist business-men for the purpose of advocacy.

C. *Specific tasks:*

1. Job market analysis and job development:
   a) Establish a job bank,
   b) Obtain commitments to hire,
   c) Get endorsements from satisfied employers, and
   d) Insure full use of established employment agencies.
2. Training:
   a) Develop training courses in specific needed skills in neighbor-hood schools, church groups, and community colleges,
   b) Provide occupational counseling,
   c) Make arrangements for occupational sampling, and
   d) Establish supportive services while in training.
3. Placement:
   a) Match interests and skills to job,
   b) Provide supportive meetings and counseling,
   c) Provide new opportunities stimulation, once employed, through
      (1) Night school,
      (2) Community service,
      (3) Neighborhood councils, and
      (4) Big Brothers and drug abuse counseling,
   d) Do periodic follow-up, and
   e) Recruit successful probationers, parolees, and youth as spokes-men and for training in community responsibility.[4]

The above list could be continued almost *ad infinitum*. Its true advantage lies in subgoals that cover so many areas that just about any citizen group could find at least one of interest.

Once a citizen task force has made the decision to organize and has estab-lished priorities, its next step is to choose a method of operation that will insure success. The following section describes such a method.

---

[4] Robert C. Trojanowicz, John M. Trojanowicz, Forrest M. Moss, *Community-Based Crime Prevention* (Pacific Palisades, Calif.: Goodyear Publishing Co., 1975), pp. 128–130.

A MODEL FOR ACTION:
NORMATIVE SPONSORSHIP THEORY

The *normative sponsorship theory* approach to community problem solving has been used to assist communities in developing programs for the prevention and control of crime and delinquency. The theory was originated and developed by Dr. Christopher Sower, professor of sociology at Michigan State University.

Simply stated, normative sponsorship theory proposes that a community program will only be sponsored if it is normative (within the limits of established standards) to all persons and interest groups involved.

When attempting to initiate community development and prevention programs it is of major importance to understand how two or more interest groups can have sufficient convergence of interest or consensus on common goals to bring about program implementation.

Each group involved and interested in program implementation must be able to justify and, hence, legitimize the common group goal within its own patterns of values, norms, and goals. The more congruent the values, beliefs, and goals of all participating groups, the easier it will be for them to agree on common goals. The participating groups, however, do not necessarily have to justify their involvement or acceptance of a group goal for the same reasons.[5]

Whenever areas of consensus are being identified between groups with a different normative orientation, it is important not to deny the concept of self-interest, because it cannot be expected that all groups will have common or similar motivations for desiring program development. Self-interest is not dysfunctional unless it contributes to intergroup contest or opposition and diverts energy that should more appropriately be directed at problem solving.

Programs that follow the tenets of normative sponsorship will undoubtedly be more likely to succeed than those that do not. Violation of the normative sponsorship process usually results in apathy or even concerted subversion and resistance to program development.

An example of a community that has been successful in utilizing this approach will be given, and the normative sponsorship process will be explained. This method has been most successful in communities where there are several interest groups and a diverse orientation to problem solving and the expression of needs. For example, in describing a riot in Detroit, the Kerner Report states that

> As the riot alternately waxed and waned, one area of the ghetto remained insulated. On the northeast side the residents of some 150 square blocks inhabited by 21,000 persons had in 1966 banded together in the Positive Neighborhood Action Committee (PNAC). With the professional help

[5] Christopher Sower et al., *Community Involvement* (Glencoe, Ill.: The Free Press, 1957).

from the Institute of Urban Dynamics, they had organized block clubs and made plans for improvement of the neighborhood. In order to meet the need for recreational facilities, which the city was not providing, they had raised $3000 to purchase empty lots for playgrounds [challenge instead of conflict].

When the riot broke out, the residents, through the block clubs, were able to organize quickly. Youngsters agreeing to stay in the neighborhood participated in detouring traffic. While many persons reportedly sympathized with the idea of rebellion against the "system," only two small fires were set—one in an empty building.[6]

The PNAC neighborhood was organized and its positive programs developed by using the concepts of normative sponsorship theory. The excerpt illustrates that when people are actively involved in the community problem-solving process and have some control over their own destiny, they will respond positively and effectively to the implementation of community development programs.

The quotation also illustrates two other important concepts of normative sponsorship orientation to community development.[7] First, the role of the Institute of Urban Dynamics was one of providing technical assistance. The technical assistance concept is different from many contemporary assistance roles. Too often assistance means (either directly or indirectly) paternalism or co-optation of community problem solving.

Effective technical assistance recognizes the vast amount of human resources within the community and the residents' willingness to develop positive community programs if their efforts are appreciated and if they are meaningfully involved in the problem-solving process.

Technical assistance, according to our definition, does not mean co-optation. It means making assistance readily available so that the community can "plug in" to *available* and appropriate resources. Technical assistance is provided only upon community request. After the specific assistance is rendered, the technical assistance unit withdraws until further requests are made. It is interesting to note that as the community becomes aware of available resources and learns the problem-solving process (which many of us take for granted), their requests for assistance decrease. It takes a special type of professional to operate effectively in a technical assistance role. He must be competent and knowledgeable in the areas of resource identification and problem solving, yet he must avoid a do-gooder or a paternalistic approach. He is not expected to save the world, but only to help make it run more smoothly.

The second important concept illustrated by the excerpt is that challenge is more effective than conflict as a means of program development. Normative sponsorship theory postulates that programs that challenge the skeptics through

---

[6] *Report of the National Advisory Commission on Civil Disorders* (New York: Bantam Books, Inc., 1968), p. 96.
[7] Also see Robert C. Trojanowicz, "Police Community Relations: Problems and Process," *Criminology*, February 1972.

involvement, participation, and cooperative action will be more effective than programs that are conflict oriented. Not only do the skeptics and the cynics gain support when there is a conflict, interest groups polarize their positions. For example, the community may make unreasonable demands, while the community agencies react by overjustifying their position and actions. The longer and more intense the conflict, the less chance there is to identify and develop consensus points from which viable programs can be implemented.

In sum, the technical assistance role is undoubtedly more conducive to community involvement and participation than contemporary approaches. Many contemporary "experts" who have attempted to provide "expertise" to community problem solving have "come under fire" from both the community and such community professionals as the police. The community feels that external "experts" often expect the community to act as a human laboratory. The "experts," however, do not have a stake in the community and are frequently unconcerned about the frustration and disruption they create when they fail to keep promises.

The police often feel that the outside "expert," although teaching communication and stressing empathy, is unwilling himself to empathize with the police and understand that the police are merely a reflection of the larger power structure of which the "expert" is also a part. The police, as well as other agency professionals, believe that if the "expert" would provide them with alternatives for action, rather than merely castigate them, they would be more receptive to constructive criticism and to "new and radical" ideas. A technical assistance unit should assume a *neutral* position in problem solving, emphasizing cooperative action, not disruptive verbalizations. Cooperation can be an elusive concept if normative sponsorship theory is not utilized as a model.

Contemporary crime prevention programs strongly suggest that *normative sponsorship* can work throughout a community.[8] Perhaps the best example of a normative sponsorship type of approach is Indianapolis, where a coalition of women's clubs throughout the city formed an anticrime crusade in 1962. The coalition was prompted by the death of a ninety-year-old at the hands of a purse-snatcher. The interests and actions of the crusade, which, over time, has included an estimated sixty thousand volunteers, were expanded to lend support to almost every area of crime prevention—the functioning of the formal justice system, the education and return to school of dropouts, rehabilitation efforts, drug abuse treatment, employment opportunity programs, job training and placement, and so on. A review of the crusade's history and progress by the National Advisory Commission on Criminal Justice Standards and Goals sets out some of the elements that may account for its outstanding successes.

> Organizationally, the Crusade is a federation, but one with no dues, by-laws, constitution, budget, government financing or membership list. A

---

[8]Some of the material in this section was written by Forrest M. Moss and extracted from *Community-Based Crime Prevention*, Robert C. Trojanowicz, John M. Trojanowicz, and Forrest M. Moss (Pacific Palisades, Calif.: Goodyear Publishing Co., 1975), pp. 134–144.

woman does not become a member of the Crusade; she participates as a *volunteer worker* in it. The emphasis is on *action*. . .

Delegation of responsibility far down into the organization is consistent with sound decision making and this contributes significantly to *meaningful participation, sustained interest,* and *continued momentum*. . .

The women spent six months studying the crime problem and setting priorities. They avoided plunging. . . .

Committees of two contacted all agencies of local government whose activities had a bearing on crime reduction—from educators to law enforcement officials . . . they probed areas that others had overlooked, or that experts had neither time nor money to address adequately. . .

The Crusade avoided another common mistake *by deciding to tackle each problem on a modest, pilot basis.* [They] "curbed one crime, put one dropout back in school, got one bright light on one dark street, sat one day in court to observe, helped one problem child, assisted one father to get a job." . . .

The Crusade has operated on the premise that it should avoid areas in which public officials already have the resources to do the job. When necessary, volunteers spur officials to perform the tasks for which tax payers have already provided the supplies, equipment and salaries. . .

It has sought and welcomed assistance from such groups as the local chamber of commerce, Jaycees, Rotarians, Kiwanis, and Optimist and Exchange Clubs. . . .

Selection of chairmen . . . for various divisions or program areas was *based on the interest* exhibited by volunteers. . .

Strong media support . . . was of great assistance . . . continued media backing for the group has proved to be a major factor in attracting volunteers. . .

One year, for example, the dropout program required $4,000. Volunteers *generated* funds through bazaars, chile suppers, benefits, book reviews, and speaking engagements.[9]

This quotation points out many of the qualities so desperately needed in a positive approach to community crime prevention—information gathering, pragmatic goal setting, cooperation, self-initiative, a minimum of organizational layering, and goals that can be attained. People welcome the opportunity to be independent and to construct alternatives and implement actions over which they have control. They are happiest when they are contributing to their social existence, whether in the family, their occupation, or the community environment.

A contemporary critic of community action for delinquency prevention has written,

---

[9]National Advisory Commission on Criminal Justice Standards and Goals, *Community Crime Prevention*, pp. 25–26.

Community action is distinguished by the insistence that the causes of delinquency are many, all interrelated, and that they need broad based action to be removed. But its most striking difference is the willingness to substitute *conflict tactics* for accommodation and cooperation which are trade marks of traditional community organization. Such tactics are a logical outgrowth of a bureaucratized, and unresponsive system and that officials no longer listen to the very real complaints of the poor, or if they do listen, it is only to anticipate and forestall any constructive change.[10]

This statement, made in 1971, is probably still true in many communities. It is true because political and social activists have often sought to realign the existing power balance in the guise of delinquency and crime prevention. It is true because much of the contemporary social literature provides a poor guide to action and an improper level of cynicism. It is probably also true because cooperation and challenge require more homework, more sensitivity, and a modification of grandiose schemes in terms of the complex realities of modern social life. Yet, community action programs yielding positive dividends in crime reduction are being initiated and hold out high potential. The Indianapolis Crusade is but one example.

KEY ELEMENTS: A GUIDE TO ACTION

Every community is unique, and no one plan of action will guarantee success in all communities. Riedel's maxim that "the appropriate form of citizen participation is the one that works" is in effect a plan for community delinquency and crime prevention.

Program Organizers

The structure and specific role of the organization for crime prevention may be critical to the success of the effort. Who will comprise the initial cadre—city officials, community leaders, or an ad hoc committee of interested citizens? Are these individuals acceptable to the larger community (that is, do they have the social capability to motivate citizen participation in the initial stages of action, such as conferences and information gathering)? Where can the most innovative approaches be anticipated? Is consensus in the community strong enough so that broad goals can be stated with certitude? Does this apply to subgoals? Where does the direction and impetus for action in the community arise? How will the priorities of goals or subgoals be assigned?

In general, the organization that can remain most responsive to the perceived needs of citizens, that can act as a catalyst in promoting direct action at the citizen level, will probably have the most success. Such an organization

[10] Edwin M. Lemert, *Instead of Court* (Rockville, Md.: National Institute of Mental Health, Center for Studies of Crime and Delinquency, 1971), p. 86. Italics added.

should have as few levels as possible—usually a board of directors, program leaders, and volunteers. Programs that are established, coordinated, and directed from top levels will usually not promote the necessary citizen motivation and may, in fact, alienate many segments of the community.

The theory of normative sponsorship assumes that the role of organizations in delinquency and crime prevention will be as enabling agencies—organizational leaders will coordinate and integrate the goals, needs, and capabilities of action groups; serve as a central information-gathering and dissemination agency; provide a nexus for promoting official acceptance and cooperation with the various efforts; and plan for fund-raising or logistical needs of the whole range of subgoal programs. The board of directors should be comprised of a wide mixture of private and official leaders, as well as representatives from many community areas. Its primary role should be to remain responsive to the information, material, and technical needs of the action groups. Procedures should be kept to a minimum in favor of action, and the entire community should have immediate access to the board. Ideally, a board of directors will prevent action groups from jumping at "glamor issues" in crime prevention and channel the actions of all groups toward goals they are most capable of attaining. The directorship of such an organization should, in short, determine the normative priorities of the community and, within that framework, provide the action groups with the support necessary to translate those priorities into action.

Initial Steps

*Step 1, Information Gathering—*Crime and delinquency are talked about a great deal, but members of a community usually do not have any precise measure of the degree of delinquency and criminal behavior, its cost to the community, or the resources available to treat the problem. Crime reporting can provide a beginning point, but it should be expanded to include an estimate, by area and by type, of unreported crime. This type of information can often be gained from neighborhood organizations, sampling of citizens, the medical profession, and church functionaries. Rape crisis centers, drug abuse "hotlines," and the like are excellent means of gaining a closer approximation of the real extent of crime in a community.

A comparison of crime rates in different areas with the physical realities of the areas often suggests immediate remedies, such as increased lighting, increased police patrols, block organizations, and citizen patrols. These apparently simple solutions should not be passed over on the assumption that any clear problems would already have been acted upon by public officials. Public officials operate in a climate of high demand and limited resources. They usually react only to blatant problems that immediately threaten public equilibrium. Action groups should be sensitive to this limitation and attempt to provide complementary action, if it is appropriate.

Step 2, Analysis of the Community—It is highly improbable that an outsider to the community could rationally organize a community crime prevention effort. It would first be necessary to become intimately familiar with the community, its history, its process of development and past conflicts, and its current politics and problems. All these factors influence the attitudes of the citizens and the acceptability of various problem-solving techniques. Consideration in analyzing the community should include the following:

1. Economic base:
   (a) Single-industry or business center base,
   (b) Expansion plans,
   (c) Community attitudes toward expansion,
   (d) Labor-management crises,
   (e) Present and future job market.

2. Cultural aspects:
   (a) Single or multicultural community,
   (b) Class lines and prior conflict, if any,
   (c) In multiculture community, nature of equilibrium, if any, or strife,
   (d) Official response to cultural situation, in terms of favoritism, distribution of services, alignment of elected officials,
   (e) Mobility patterns.

3. Social organization:
   (a) Extent and nature of social, fraternal, and church organizations,
   (b) Conflict, cooperation, or coalition, if any, for common cause,
   (c) Reactive organizations, if any,
   (d) Political affiliations of organizations and attachments to particular social movements,
   (e) Existing social programs and projects,
   (f) Potential for creation of new organizations.

4. Official functions:
   (a) Punitive formal justice agencies,
   (b) Nonpunitive approaches created or supported by formal agencies,
   (c) History of attempts to create programs or supplement official crime prevention programs,
   (d) Current coordination and planning—fragmented or centrally assumed,
   (e) Inter- and intra-agency conflict or cooperation; attitudes of formal justice and social agencies toward each other.

5. Crisis handling:
   (a) Natural disasters and social crises that have influenced attitude formation,

(b) Racial strife and its resolution or nonresolution,

(c) Sensational crime, by neighborhood or area; presence of organized crime, if any,

(d) Public perceptions of adequacy of officials in responding to past crises, especially regarding major crime.

Step 3, Relevant System Identification—Before programs that necessitate cooperation of more than one group can be implemented, it is necessary to identify the relevant interest groups—the *relevant systems*. The major relevant systems concerned with delinquency prevention would be the community, the police, the court, the social work agencies, the legislature, and the other private and public agencies and business organizations in the community.

The technical assistance unit whose services are secured by the relevant systems is not a relevant system itself because it is usually not an integral part of the community. It is, rather, *a neutral external resource.*

In effect, all components of the community that can contribute any resources to delinquency and crime prevention should be identified. In addition to the official agencies, businessmen's groups, clubs, and church groups, special emphasis should be placed on gaining input from youth, neighborhood, block, occupations, drug and alcohol treatment, and informal interest groups. Press club representation is important for necessary publicity, as well as for the extensive contacts the press can activate in support of such a program. Ad hoc committees formed to deal with prior problems should be identified for potential reactivation. For the public agencies present in the community, information should be gathered about their charter or public mandate, jurisdiction, budget, current programs, physical and manpower resources, federal and state project endorsement, organizational structure, proposed future programs and budget requests, emphasis, expressed needs (media, budget requests), and operational limitations based on professional abilities, case load, and past performance.

This list is a much abbreviated approach to the planning process. It must be complete and comprehensive to insure that false starts are avoided. With this information, a schema depicting social, economic, and normative links between various institutions, neighborhoods, and groups can be constructed. This schema should indicate the relative strength or potential strength of various positions to guide the planner in determining whether support exists for different tentative approaches to delinquency and crime prevention. Social situations are enormously changeable, however, and a prevention program must not only be founded on a thorough analysis of existing factors, but also remain in touch with change. Modern communities are extremely complex social systems, which do not normally respond well to attempts at manipulation. The identification of and appeal to basic values holds out the greatest promise of effective community prevention.

Step 4, Identification of Leadership—There is no clear guide to the appropriate selection of leadership in prevention programs. In one community, civic, business, and government leaders may have the public support and confidence necessary to set goals and to execute action alternatives. In another, a high degree of skepticism will greet efforts by these leaders. In the main, it appears that most successful efforts at community delinquency and crime prevention utilize a coalition of established community leaders, who are genuinely interested in innovation and action, a leadership emerging from neighborhoods, and a variety of social groups. Persons identified from within the relevant system are better able to reflect the system's norms, values, and goals and are knowledgeable about how it functions. They also exert considerable influence, and their opinions and suggestions are respected and implemented.

They may hold a position in the formal structure of a community organization, such as officer in a block club, or they may hold a command rank in the police department or an administrative position in a social work agency. However, they may not have a formal position in either a community organization or a community agency, yet exert influence through the informal structure.

Identification of these leaders is accomplished through a process of sampling members of the relevant organizations and asking such questions as "Whom do you or most of the people in the organization go to for advice on problem solving?" and "Who in the organization is respected, has power and influence, and has the reputation for getting things done?"

After the sampling process is completed, it is possible to construct a list of those individuals whose names have been mentioned most often as leaders. The sampling process is important for leadership identification. It should not be assumed that sampling is not necessary because leaders are already known. Leadership is not static, and those persons *assumed* to be leaders because of their formal or informal position are not necessarily the major source of power or influence. The identification of true leadership is mandatory, if the process of program development and implementation is to be successful.

The Indianapolis Crusade selects leaders from those who volunteer and express an interest in a particular action program. Regardless of the method of selection, leaders in a delinquency and crime prevention program should exhibit many of the following characteristics:

1. An ability to relate personally to the action program, preferably by living in the neighborhood involved, or through close cultural or class ties to the individuals most affected by the problem.

2. An orientation to problem solving as opposed to rhetoric.

3. An ability to identify with the people involved and, ideally, recognition by that group as a natural spokesman.

4. The ability to get things done, coupled with a realization that crime prevention is a long-term effort, fraught with frustration, that may not be successful under the best of conditions.

5. The ability to innovate, inspire action, and stimulate continued and widespread citizen participation.

6. The ability to encourage citizen response from all segments of the community.

There are several groups not normally involved in community crime prevention that can supply leadership and volunteer services. Youth should be challenged to organize action programs in delinquency prevention, drug-abuse treatment, and restorative education. The youth of any community usually have time to spend in such programs and are an invaluable source of creative thinking and energy. The aged also need desperately to be reintegrated into community life at all levels. Older citizens often possess the diplomatic abilities and strong sense of purpose that would lend great stability and status to a prevention program. Their experiences and commitment should be directly sought and extensively utilized. Prior offenders and citizens who profit from such action programs should also be encouraged to assume leadership and volunteer roles. They are in an excellent position not only to identify with those with social problems, but also to supply badly needed role models for offenders already being treated by the formal juvenile justice system.

Step 5, Bringing Leaders of Relevant Systems Together—After leaders have been identified in each relevant system, the next step is to bring the leaders together for a meeting. They should be told that they have been identified by their peers as influential leaders interested in the prevention of delinquency and crime. The initial meetings (the meetings are chaired by a technical assistance adviser) will be somewhat unstructured. The major objectives of the initial meetings will be to

1. Facilitate the expression of feelings about the apparent problem.

2. Encourage relevant systems to exchange perceptions about each other. (There is often much suspiciousness between the agencies and between the citizens and the agencies.)

3. Produce an atmosphere conducive to meaningful dialogue so that the misperceptions can be identified and the constellation of factors contributing to the causation of the problem can be discussed.

4. Identify self-interest, pointing out that from the self-interest standpoint of all systems, cooperative problem solving to prevent crime and delinquency will benefit everyone. The community agencies will have smaller case loads and more time to provide services; while the citizens will be better protected from threats and offenses against life and property.

It is not the purpose of the initial meetings to produce attitude changes or develop a "love relationship" between the relevant systems. Negative attitudes will change when positive perceptions between the relevant systems increase and when meaningful involvement and positive behavioral action is initiated and carried out through program development and implementation.

Whenever diverse interest groups assemble, they will often have biased opinions, misinformation, and negative perceptions toward one another. If there is extensive defensiveness by the relevant systems and if an atmosphere of freedom of expression does not prevail, the initial stages of the process will be hindered, and this can have unfavorable implications for future cooperation and program implementation.

In our experience with groups that have assembled to discuss delinquency prevention problems, initially many mutual accusations are made by the various relevant systems. The police, for example, are accused of authoritarianism and aloofness, while the community is accused of complacency and lack of cooperation. Agency professionals also exhibit intergroup hostility and negative perceptions. The social workers may call the police "hard-headed disciplinarians," and the police may retaliate by calling the social workers "permissive do-gooders." If there is a too hasty denial of the accusation, if elements of truth in the accusations are not handled in an honest manner, if the constellation of factors that contributed to the perceptions are not identified, and if these perceptions are not discussed, then the communication process will be shallow and the total problem will not be understood.

The technical assistance adviser can play an important role in these early stages. He can help control the meetings so that they are not monopolized by one interest group or so that expression of feelings does not become inappropriate and offensive to the point of disruption and ultimate disbanding of the group. He can also help clarify the issues and provide insight into the problem and the reasons for its existence.

The admission of the obvious truth of some of the accusations by the relevant systems will be helpful in establishing an atmosphere of trust and credibility. This will facilitate understanding and cooperation.

The communication process between the relevant systems should be more than merely the denial or the admission of fact. It should include a discussion of the constellation of factors that can contribute to misperceptions. For example, the citizens could be informed of the policies of the various agencies and the effect these policies have on the delivering of services to the community. Insight in this area may be helpful in explaining that certain administrative considerations have to be weighed and certain priorities have to be established. Citizens could also share with the agencies the reasons why they become frustrated with the apparent lack of concern and impersonality of large agency structures. This will facilitate the agency personnel's empathizing with the citizens, and vice versa. Interagency misperceptions can also be neutralized through the process of sharing problem-solving approaches and reasons why an agency takes a particular orientation.

The increased empathy between relevant systems will help destroy misperceptions and provide the relevant systems with new insights into individual and organizational behavior. This will establish a basis for future understanding and cooperation.

The first few meetings are usually typified by (1) the unstructured expression of feelings and perceptions, (2) the admission of "reality facts," (3) the discussion of the constellation of contributing factors, (4) the facilitation of understanding, and (5) the increased number of positive perceptions. The sessions then begin to take a more focused and less emotional orientation. If the initial meetings have achieved their objectives, the stage is set for the next phase of the process, the identification of areas of consensus and disagreement in the prevention of crime and delinquency.

Step 6, The Identification of Areas of Consensus and Disagreement—In the third stage of the process, the matrix method is utilized for the identification of areas of consensus and disagreement. In dealing with this kind of methodology, Ladd has made an important contribution.[11] He obtained the following kinds of information for each of the major positions of the small society that he studied. This same information will be helpful in understanding the relevant systems involved in crime and delinquency prevention:

1. What are the prescriptions of expected behavior?
2. Who makes these prescriptions?
3. To what extent is there consensus about the prescriptions?
4. Who enforces them?
5. What are the rewards for compliance?
6. What are the punishments for deviance?

As illustrated in Table 1, this kind of information, as well as additional information, can be assembled into a matrix pattern for the analysis of any system or set of systems.

This method serves as a vehicle for visually and objectively comparing the perceptions among and between relevant systems. For example, the perception the police have of their role can be compared with the perception the community has of the police role, and vice versa. This comparison can also be made with the other relevant systems—police with social workers, social workers with the community, and so on.

The perceived roles of the systems can also be compared with the actual behavior of both systems, and then an evaluation can be made regarding whether the behavior is deviant or normative, functional or nonfunctional. Finally, the statement of alternatives for problem solving of each system can be compared with the perceived expected alternatives. It may be learned, for example, that the alternatives contemplated by each system are not incompatible or as different from each other as originally perceived.

As a result of the intrasystem and intersystem comparisons, it is easy to compile the information about how each system expects and perceives both its own members and members of the other systems to behave. From this it is not a difficult research task to classify the categories of information as either normative (as they should be) or deviant (different than they should be) to the relevant systems.

[11] John Ladd, *The Structure of a Moral Code* (Cambridge: Harvard University Press, 1957).

The use of the matrix method results in the realization that many programs already exist and are unknown to much of the community, that there is more consensus than anticipated about basic values and needs, and that a good deal of honest effort fails because it occurs in isolation from the potential support of the larger community.

Comprehensive media coverage for the prevention project should be obtained. Normative priorities, goals and subgoals, proposed action programs, resources required, and calls for leadership and volunteers can thus be publicized. Even if some of the programs appear controversial, this should pique public interest and invite dialogue. Media coverage should challenge local community organizations to fund, organize, and take responsibility for action programs. Initial efforts might well be spent in pilot programs to determine the corrective potential of a particular approach, the extent of the resources that would have to be expended in such an effort, the normative priorities of the community, and the total known resources. Results of pilot programs should be presented in public forums and cooperation encouraged between citizens and groups throughout the community.

*Step 7, Program Implementation—*After areas of consensus and disagreement have been identified, a program can be developed that will incorporate the areas of consensus so that the program will be normative to *all* systems. The systems will not necessarily agree in all areas, but there will usually be enough common areas of agreement so that cooperation and sponsorship will be predictable.

It will be surprising and enlightening to the relevant systems, after using the matrix method, to learn how many areas of consensus are present, which at first glance, after a subjective evaluation, may not be apparent. There generally will be consensus on major goals, such as the need for delinquency prevention programs, for more positive and effective communication, and for cooperation between the systems. Areas of consensus may decrease as specific techniques for problem solving are identified and alternatives for program implementation are suggested by each system. This will be a minor problem, however, because if the normative sponsorships process has been followed, an atmosphere of cooperation will prevail and compromise will be facilitated.

*Step 8, Quality Control and Continuous Program Development and Updating—*As with any viable program, there is a constant need for quality control and continuous program development and updating. There should be meaningful feedback, the testing of new theories, and reciprocal involvement and program evaluation by the relevant systems, as well as individual and system introspection.

There is also a need for scientific research, not only on basic causes of crime, but also on the effectiveness of the system. Evaluation of each action program should be undertaken to determine its effectiveness. This may provide a guideline for the better allocation of official resources and an indication of which services the official juvenile justice system and the community can best provide. Considerations should include (relative to, for example, drug abuse among youth):

TABLE 1. Diagram of the Matrix Method of Identifying Areas of Consensus and Disagreement

Norms and Behavior Perceptions Held by:	Norms and Behavior Perceptions Held About:					
	The Police	The Community	Social Workers	Businesspeople	Legislators	Other Agencies and Organizations

The police	Self-Concept
	1. Perceived norms and expected behavior as it relates to delinquency prevention
	2. Description of actual behavior
	3. Defined as:
	  a. Normative
	  b. Deviant
	4. Statement of alternatives for problem solving
		1. Perceived norms and expected behavior as it relates to delinquency prevention
		2. Description of actual behavior
		3. Defined as:
		  a. Normative
		  b. Deviant
		4. Perception as to what alternatives the other systems will select for problem solving
			*	*	*	*

	The community (including youth groups)	Social workers	Businesspeople	Legislators	Other agencies and organizations
The community (including youth groups)	Self-Concept 1. Perceived norms and expected behavior as it relates to delinquency prevention 2. Description of actual behavior 3. Defined as: a. Normative b. Deviant 4. Perception as to what alternatives the other system will select for problem solving	Self-Concept 1. Perceived norms and expected behavior as it relates to delinquency prevention 2. Description of actual behavior 3. Defined as: a. Normative b. Deviant 4. Statement of alternatives for problem solving	*	*	*
Social workers	*	*	Self-Concept	*	*
Businesspeople	*	*	Self-Concept	Self-Concept	*
Legislators	*	*	*	Self-Concept	*
Other agencies and organizations	*	*	*	*	Self-Concept

*Use the same criteria that are presented in the cell showing the Police Department's perception of the community.

1. What is the drug overdose rate now in relation to when the program started?

2. What is the current and past arrest rate for trafficking and abuse? In this regard, make sure that the organizational posture of the official agencies is taken into consideration. The establishment of a special narcotics squad at the city or county level inevitably increases the arrest rate, even during an effective community attack on drug use.

3. What is the trend in drug use—from marihuana to amphetamines, to acid, and so on, or the other direction? Programs must insure that by attacking the use of marihuana (for example) they do not encourage drug abusers to turn to more dangerous substances.

4. What is the current state of drug use and trafficking in the local intermediate and high schools? Have sufficient youth been mobilized at those locations?

5. What is the current state of youth participation at the established drug abuse treatment clinics? Is the increase or decrease indicative of the effectiveness of the program? For example, an increase in the number of participants in a drug abuse clinic may be an indication that more youth are genuinely interested in decreasing their drug intake, or that, because of decreased availability "on the street," the drug rehabilitation center is the best place to make a "contact."

6. What effect has the problem had on the incidence of other crime (burglary, armed robbery, theft, and so on), if any, in the community, and by neighborhood?

7. What collateral problems have been discovered, during the course of the program that indicate potential for treatment, and by whom?

8. Do the known or anticipated results justify the expenditure of resources, or could those resources (citizen time, funds, expertise, formal justice system emphasis, and so on) be better employed in another area? How can this be clearly shown to be the case?

9. What is the relative restorative effect of the citizen "prepunitive" efforts (for example) in relation to the punitive efforts of the police?

10. Are *all* the community efforts in the area of drug abuse providing a mutually complementary product, or are some aspects at "cross-purposes?" How can this problem be approached?[12]

These are but a few of the considerations relative to one subgoal—drug abuse, totally apart from the causation of drug abuse itself. Evaluation techniques must be devised to insure effective programs by providing a rational basis for decision making and for the use of limited resources.

---

[12] Developed by Forrest M. Moss and taken from *Community-Based Crime Prevention* by Robert C. Trojanowicz, John M. Trojanowicz, and Forrest M. Moss (Pacific Palisades, Calif.: Goodyear Publishing Co., 1975).

CONCLUSION

The normative sponsorship method can be used to link the university to the community through extension courses in the community. The extension course can serve the same general purpose as the community meeting, if the course has a wide variety of participants. The same type of problem-solving process, as it relates to delinquency prevention that was described earlier, can be facilitated in the classroom. The classroom is conducive to meaningful communication and the transmission of ideas and feelings because the organizational constraints and pressures that often inhibit the communication process in an interorganizational meeting are less evident. The instructor can function in the same technical assistance role described earlier. Community improvement projects such as crime and delinquency prevention can be initiated in the community through a cooperative team effort. The team (which is composed of representatives of all relevant systems) can return to the classroom periodically to provide feedback and receive inputs and an objective evaluation of their project by the instructor and class peers.

An effective prevention program results only through a cooperative first-hand experience of all relevant systems in the problem-solving process. A maximum of active involvement and a minimum of shallow verbalization will facilitate cooperation and mutual understanding among the relevant systems.

The most effective means of motivating people is to transmit to them that their opinions will be valued, that they will have a voice in decision making, and that they will be involved in the problem-solving process. Programs will be sponsored and perpetuated, if these criteria are adhered to because the parties who comprise the relevant systems have a personal investment in the process. Involved action by the relevant systems will be mutually beneficial and will increase understanding and cooperation between them.

> The nature of the group (and group goal) serves to fulfill certain needs of its members, and the satisfaction of these needs is its function. Through the symbolic system of the group, its roles, role-systems, and norms, individual behavior is differentiated and at the same time integrated for the satisfaction of needs, and the fulfillment of its function.[13]

SUMMARY

Effective prevention includes more than a knowledge of theory, extensive resources, and good intentions. All of these are necessary, but they only become translated into action when there is cooperative involvement in the problem-

[13] Scott A. Greer, *Social Organizations* (New York: Random House, 1955), p. 24.

solving process by the community residents and the maze of agencies and organizations both internal and external to the juvenile justice system. This chapter has presented a process that can facilitate the translation of theory, resources, and good intentions into action programs.

The following are some additional considerations that will need to be taken into account if cooperation and problem solving will ever be facilitated.

1. Police officers must no longer be the only representatives of the community who consistently respond to social problems twenty-four hours a day. This situation places the police in an untenable position and convinces many citizens that the only "after-hours" community responsibility is a punitive one. Many social agencies do respond to emergencies, if notified, but this is a haphazard and uncoordinated effort.

2. A community response team, consisting of the police and representatives from various community organizations (AA, crisis centers, drug centers, youth services, welfare, religious groups, neighborhood representatives, etc.), must be manned on an around-the-clock basis. Since the police have the greatest information-gathering resources and receive most citizen requests for aid, such a team might operate out of police facilities and respond to calls along with the police.

3. Representatives of all organized social welfare agencies must be convinced of the importance of the social problems that lead to criminal and delinquent acts and must be fully integrated into the team effort. New local resources must be developed. Fraternal, business, and social organizations must be encouraged to lend their full support to a program of nonpunitive diversion, and team workers must be recruited from their memberships.

4. City management and every element within the formal criminal justice system must be made to see the rationale for such an approach and must provide moral and legal sanction for it. This will require great skill and effective diversion programs, so that the community continues to feel protected.

5. A system of case follow-up and review must be established and rigorously pursued, and a rigorous system of data collection must be initiated, so that the effectiveness of the program can be gauged and techniques expanded or discarded. The opportunity for social research, especially relating to causation theories, must not be ignored.

6. The program must be organized so that the possibilities for favoritism or other abuse are minimized, information is collected for community feedback, research data are collected, and adequate, confidential case documents are maintained. At the same time, bureaucratic tendencies must be avoided, innovation encouraged, and new resources developed and integrated. Membership and employment must include all class, racial, religious, and ethnic groups.

7. Maximum effort must be expended to insure that the program remains person-oriented and does not become a platform for political activism.

8. Full and periodic disclosure of the results, problems, and needs of the

program must be made to the public, in settings that guarantee the widest possible community participation. Legitimation for the program must be gained through the widest possible public participation.[14]

Action programs that help prevent juvenile delinquency and involve all community interest groups will be successful because the interest groups will have a stake in both the process and the "product." Although this action involvement by community interest groups to prevent delinquency will not be the same as the informal community processes that were so effective in influencing human behavior in the past, it will be a step in the right direction.

QUESTIONS AND PROJECTS

Essay Questions

1. Why is it difficult to mobilize the efforts of community residents to prevent delinquency and crime?

2. Why is informal social control not as effective today as it was in the past?

3. Is the normative sponsorship *approach realistic for very large cities?*

4. Why are resources, theories, and "good intentions" not enough to effectively prevent and reduce juvenile delinquency?

5. Why is it mandatory that the entire community be involved in crime control and delinquency prevention?

Projects

1. Identify all the interest groups in your community that would have to cooperate for effective juvenile delinquency prevention, control, and treatment.

2. Develop a present-day alternative to the police-officer-on-the-beat concept.

3. Develop a rationale for convincing adults that youngsters in the community should be actively involved in problem solving and decision making.

---

[14]Trojanowicz, Trojanowicz, and Moss, *Community-Based Crime Prevention,* pp. 162–163.

chapter 13

Critical Issues– A Look to the Future*

Maybe the only thing growing faster than the rate of crime is fear of crime. To say that the general public views crime and delinquency as primary concerns is an obvious understatement. In most public opinion polls, crime is at or near the top of the list of domestic priorities.

Yet harnessing the citizens' fear of crime into support for prevention and control programs becomes more difficult as the situation gets worse. As crime statistics climb, existing programs appear to be failing. So not only is the general public's fear of crime growing, there is also increasing frustration at what appears to be society's inability to stem the tide. This frustration manifests itself in anger and frustration that can turn to apathy—or extremism.

Extremism stems from the deep schism in society between the two opposing views of how the criminal should be treated, both positions being locked into a polarizing struggle for supremacy. For the past few years, the public has been handed a lot of information, supposedly emanating from social science research, that contends the solution to all crime problems lies in a humanistic approach based on the contention that all criminals and delinquents can be rehabilitated, and that crime will disappear if the root causes (poverty, urban blight, and so on) were eliminated by social action. It could be called the *there is no such thing as a bad boy* approach.

While proponents of this position argue persuasively that this approach was never adopted on a broad enough scale to get a fair trial, the apparent failure of this orientation in solving the problem has spawned an onslaught of

*Assistance in the final draft was obtained from Bonnie Pollard, associate editor, *Michigan Farmer*, Lansing, Michigan.

criticism from vocal adherents of the opposite position that say punishment as a deterrent never had its fair trial either.

Gaining credence daily is the view that the rising crime rate is directly attributable to the "coddling" of offenders as practiced by "bleeding heart liberals" during the sixties. The new conservatism instead contends that crime can be controlled by the adoption of harsh methods, at whatever price necessary in terms of the loss of protection of individual rights. This might be called the *people are good only if the penalties for straying are high enough* school of thought.

In the center lies a confused and angry populace whose allegiance shifts between the simplistic solutions offered by both sides. Now the pendulum is shifting away from rehabilitation, back toward punishment, as evidenced in a recent market opinion research poll that showed that 64 percent of citizens surveyed now favor the death penalty for first-degree murder, kidnapping, and terrorism. In addition, 72 percent said wiretaps should be used to investigate organized crime, while 73 percent agreed wiretaps should be used to investigate suspected drug dealers.[1]

The difficulty lies in the fact that rational and realistic programs, combining the best elements of both philosophies, are the least likely to be heard above the clamor created by both extremes. Since this middle position doesn't promise immediate results, it doesn't gain instant converts.

And there is a middle ground that contends that the approach to solving crime problems should be geared toward the person and the type of crime involved. There is indeed a small percentage of repeat violent offenders so dangerous and so unlikely to respond to efforts toward rehabilitation that they should be removed from the community. On the other hand, those who can potentially be reached by more humanistic approaches should have the chance to change through interaction with alternative programs.

This sort of dual approach demands cooperation and support from the community to be successful, yet it is the polarization of the citizenry that allows this middle ground to get lost in the shuffle. For instance, it becomes almost impossible to achieve revision of the juvenile or criminal codes in most communities. Any move to legalize prostitution or betting on sports brings an outcry from both extremes. Legalizing marihuana is always a "hot" issue. The jury is still out on whether marihuana is indeed safe to use, but advocates of legalization or decriminalization argue positions that range from saying marihuana is no worse than alcohol to claiming it is beneficial. On the other hand are vocal opponents who charge that marihuana is not only detrimental, but sinful. To be in the middle urging substantive change to deal with the problem more effectively is to be virtually alone. Yet without grass roots community support, change cannot occur.

Another obstacle in the path of gaining community support for efforts

[1] *The Michigan Public Speaks Out On Crime,* 4th Ed., A Study by the Office of Criminal Justice Programs, Market Opinion Research Co., April 1976, p. 64.

against crime is that fear of crime also means fear of contact with known offenders. Community-based treatment has proven to be one of the best alternatives currently available, yet many citizens react negatively if it means having offenders next door. These fearful citizens worry about further exploitation, as well as an increase in social problems and deterioration of the neighborhood. Yet it takes community support for such efforts to succeed.

In summary, there are innumerable studies that show citizens are concerned about crime, and suggestions about what to do are countless. There is nothing really new in the growing conservatism toward dealing with crime and criminal offenders. But the point to remember is that the public does see crime as a very serious problem, yet new and innovative programs will be difficult to initiate unless concern is translated into support. The community must be convinced that the program will indeed remedy the situation—but not at the expense of harm to people and property within the community.

JUVENILE CRIME

Statistics on juvenile crime are staggering. Persons under the age of 18 account for 45 percent of all arrests for serious crime, 23 percent of arrests for violent crime. Burglary and auto theft are overwhelmingly youth crimes. There are 12 arrests for every 100 juveniles between the ages of 15 and 17.[2]

While the number of minors in the total population rose only 10 percent from 1969 through 1974, crimes committed by this group rose 35 percent. Most criminal and juvenile justice practitioners and academicians know, however, that there are many reasons involved in this continuous rise.

Part of the increase is the result of more sophisticated methods used to gather data, and many things reported as crimes today might not have been deemed crimes in the past. But what remains is that today more youngsters are involved in delinquent behavior and there is concern about the serious nature of the delinquency problem. Also of concern is what often appears to be the system's unwillingness to deal with those few involved in the more serious offenses (this will be dealt with later in the chapter).

And, juvenile crime is no longer just a problem limited to congested inner-city areas. It permeates almost every section of the country, state, and community.

In fact, juvenile crime is one of the most serious problems facing rural areas today. To many, it remains an enigma because rural areas are still expected to have a more traditional set of values, a stronger family structure, and a more cohesive community—a climate where crime would be less likely to flourish. But the problem is there, and growing worse, and many factors have contributed to the dynamics of this increase, so rural crime deserves a closer look.

[2] *Federal Juvenile Delinquency Programs, First Analysis and Evaluation,* Vol. 1, Office of Juvenile Justice and Delinquency Prevention, LEAA. U.S. Dept. of Justice (Washington, D.C.: U.S. Government Printing Office, 1976), p. 1.

Rural Crime

The phrase "boys will be boys" still rings as true today as it did twenty years ago. But society has changed drastically in the meanwhile.

When Dad was a boy, if he got caught tipping over a neighbor's outhouse, his victim knew just what to do to insure swift and certain punishment. Dad was marched home so that his family could administer immediate justice.

If a boy today commits a "prank," the system is much more likely to be harsh. Chances are the youngster will collide head-on with the juvenile justice system.

In most cases, it is not that boys today are that much different, but that the system and its complexities have created different ways of dealing with the problem. Fast, informal punishment was meted out to yesterday's perpetrator, usually by the community, and most directly by the parents. Today, if the son is caught, the reaction is less benign.

One factor involved is that young people are more mobile than in the past. Rural youngsters today can easily go to the big city, become lost in its confusion, and, in many cases, end up a crime statistic.

Rural juvenile crime is in many ways attributable to the cumulative effect of increased mobility (cars) and mass media (television and movies) on rural teen-agers. They are no longer isolated from the urban way of life. Rural adults may find what they see on television about city life *appalling*, but to their teen-agers, seeking an escape from boredom, that urban life-style seems *appealing*. And since human beings are quicker to take advantage of strangers than friends, these rural teen-agers are therefore much more likely to abuse one of "them" in the city, than one of us at home in the country.

Away from home, the youth knows his chance of getting caught is less because there is less chance he will be recognized. But that's a two-edged sword, since if he is caught, this means he doesn't have the informal connections, means, or contacts in the community far from home that he would have in his home community. Therefore, he is often treated more harshly because he is an outsider.

So, if country-bred Johnny rips off somebody in the big city, the victims won't know that's Johnny Jones, from such-and-such street, so that they can go to talk it over with Johnny's mother and dad—they don't know who the hell Johnny's parents are, and therefore they have no assurance his parents would cooperate. As a result, Johnny gets labeled, becomes a statistic, and has his first contact with the formal system and all the negative ramifications that implies.

The reverse, of course, is just as true for the city boy who goes to the country to "have fun/cause trouble" (depending on your point of view). So many factors tie into the phenomenon of rural crime—outsiders coming in, insiders going out, insiders incapable of handling pressures from conflicting life-styles who react with hostility in their own communities.

For there is still a conflict between rural and urban life-styles, though cars and television have blurred the boundaries—Mrs. Walton still wouldn't find much in common with Rhoda or Maude. And when these two value systems conflict, it is most often the rural teen-ager who is caught in the middle.

One key to the rural crime problem may be that it resembles what happened when immigrants came to this country in the early 1900s. Immigrant parents had a lot of difficulty with their children, and there was a lot of delinquency. The children were, on the one hand, being socialized by immigrant parents, yet when they went to school, they had to contend with a different, looser value system. Many children didn't know how to resolve the conflict.

Rural teen-agers face a similar situation. Rural areas still do have an explicit value system that teaches children to treat others altruistically. Rural parents transmit certain concepts, like "treat your neighbor fairly." If your neighbor should hit you on the side of the head, you can hit him back, but then you forget about it. Because they share common goals and problems, one farmer will help another rebuild his barn after a fire, because his might burn tomorrow. There is a deep sense of interdependence.

But when that rural kid gets to the city, in city-type situations, whether it is in school, at athletic events, or when he goes to the university, he usually finds a value system far different in terms of how others should be treated. It is "business is business, and that's too bad, kid." This can make him resentful of his upbringing. "Hey, I haven't been equipped to deal competitively with that big, bad world out there. You have cloistered me in my small-town environment." Trying to compete, he overcompensates, and often performs in negative, often deviant ways—perhaps cheating or stealing.

Competitive Society.   Though it doesn't excuse the behavior, the increased competitiveness in society is a pressure that may well be an important root cause of much of today's teen-age turbulence. It is harder for kids today to compete than it was in the past, and many times parents can't comprehend the peer pressure kids face, or the pressure the system exerts upon them.

A society that is competitive may well be a dog-eat-dog place, but adults are better equipped to deal with that view of reality than teen-agers. Often, adults feel they have no control over decisions that affect their lives, their jobs, their community, and the national political scene, but at least most are socialized into a value system that encourages self-discipline and restraint. Adults are less likely to think "I'll rip off that gas station to get back the $100 my boss gypped me out of" because they have been socialized not to act out.

But when adults transmit this sense of loss of control to kids, even indirectly through conversations about how messed up the system is, those youngsters internalize the message differently. Not having the same background, discipline, and experience as an adult, the teen-ager's ability to find alternatives that are socially acceptable is limited.

A boy who steals a car and drives 100 miles an hour down the expressway, passing adults, has no doubts that he has seized control. When a teen-ager holds a gun at someone's head while robbing a gas station, he has total control of his world. It is negative control, to be sure, but each individual needs to feel he has some control over his own destiny, and the teen-ager often sees fewer ways to express that need.

Digging further into this problem it is evident that personal and social guilt/responsibility are no longer instilled in the young to the degree they were in the past. Yet personal and social guilt provide an important function in society if we are to work and live together effectively.

If fear of detection is the only restraint against an antisocial impulse, it is not enough. Refraining from a hostile act because of a personal moral code or because of inculcation of the concept that society would collapse if everyone did likewise means that there does not have to be a cop on every corner. As a result of the lack of personal and social guilt, many people have lost confidence because the system cannot work without it. There is therefore no assurance that cooperative solutions to problems can be found.

One of the worst commercials ever produced was the one that admonished people not to leave their keys in their cars, titled "Do you want to make a good boy go bad?" The idea was that adults made kids go bad by not taking their keys with them. It implied no individual responsibility for the action on the part of the youngster, and when this happens, adult society transmits pessimism. We transmit weakness. "You have no control over what you do."

That commercial says directly that if adults are dumb enough to leave the keys, it's not the kid's fault, in fact he's being smart if he does steal the car. Blame is shifted from the perpetrator of the crime onto the victim, turning the thief into a mere pawn.

Personal and social responsibility are part of maturity, as pointed out in earlier chapters. Just because a youngster is physically mature does not mean he has the psychological wherewithal to deal with complex social problems.

It is ironic that a society that labels positive results as "individualism" labels negative results as the fault of the system. If a person makes it, becomes famous, makes a lot of money, becomes a success, it is because he's a great guy with wonderful individual characteristics. But if he fails, it is not the individual's fault, it's the system's failure. Constant system blame, as pointed out several times in these chapters, perpetuates negative behavior, excuses deviation, and never lets the youngster deal with the part he plays in any action.

To deal effectively with rural juvenile crime, as with city crime, the family remains the key. Professionals have also made the mistake of transmitting the impression that they have all the answers. The family is the key; the professionals play no more than a supporting role. It is better to be honest and tell the family that it is doing a good job 95 percent of the time, and that the professional is there to help during the 5 percent of the time things don't work. The support systems in the community, professional or paraprofessional, are there to help deal with serious, stressful situations where the family needs extra assistance.

But, society must be helped to understand that not everyone can be cured. There is a very small percentage who just cannot be reached, the small group involved in violent behavior. One priority should be to get that kind of person off the street.

We rationalize that we cannot be humane and, at the same time, lock people up. We must get rid of that idea.

And for the others, that larger group which *can* be helped, we must find alternatives, deal with them, work with them.

Drawing the line between a prank and a crime is not easy. Perhaps it is not too glib to suggest that a prank is something your child does to others, while a crime is something someone else's child does to you. It is fashionable to argue that society coddles criminals, as long as the criminal is not your 13-year-old daughter shoplifting a blouse, or your son dipping into a neighbor's gas tank.

The problem of juvenile crime, whether rural or urban, is complex—and so are the answers. There are as many views on juvenile crime as there are people involved. And almost everyone is involved, either as victim, potential victim, teacher, police officer, social worker, minister, parent, and that very special person—the juvenile offender. The remainder of this chapter will deal with critical issues that must be faced if the problem of juvenile delinquency is to be recognized, understood, and ultimately resolved.

JUVENILE JUSTICE ADMINISTRATION

Agencies that handle juveniles are often referred to as components of a system. By calling this process a system, a certain coordination is implied as being an integral part of the system's operation and function. But, too often, that label is a misnomer. Coordination, and even cooperation, do not always exist.

Mason P. Thomas specifically points out that

> legislatures have passed laws to establish a separate court system for children under certain ages because youths should not be held accountable under the same standards as adults, and because there may be a better chance of reform or rehabilitation with young people. While these concepts contain assumptions that might be questioned, the separate system idea has never been tried with adequate resources and personnel—thus, while our separate juvenile corrections system may be more myth than fact, it seems clear that professionals involved must develop new strategies to work cooperatively as management teams. In the past, the judge has been the star, with the administrative control and other powers over the rest of the system. The challenge for today is whether the separate parts of the system, when available, can develop a team concept to help juvenile corrections to function as a system in a positive way upon the lives of those children who have no choice about being pushed through the various parts of the system.[3]

[3] Mason, P. Thomas, "Juvenile Corrections, Five Issues to be Faced." *Popular Government*, May 1971, Institute of Government, The University of North Carolina at Chapel Hill.

The federal government, through the Office of Juvenile Justice and Delinquency Prevention, has attempted to establish a more rational approach to juvenile justice problems, processing, programming, and treatment. Major problems identified included failure to provide consistency in treatment; housing status offenders in facilities with serious repeat offenders; lack of coordination among the several agencies that could be working with a single delinquent; and a lack of uniformity in procedures and programs, so that accountability in leadership often takes a back seat to expediency, system maintenance, and system perpetuation.

At the heart of the problem of lack of coordination in many juvenile justice systems is a lack of built-in accountability. If the duties, responsibilities, services, and functions of each component are clearly spelled out, not only can accountability be determined, the process of defining itself improves coordination.

For too many juveniles, processing through the system is more dependent upon the individual's economic situation than the offense and its seriousness. Some method of accountability would contribute not only to more effective processing, but it would insure that services are dispensed rationally and equitably.

Lack of consistency in the juvenile justice system may not only be unfair, it may actually be depriving youngsters of due process of law. Dr. Charles Thomas, a sociologist, believes that the variation in sentencing has serious implications. He has found that juvenile judges "take into consideration a youth's dress, sex and race, whether the parents are present, how submissive a child is, whether he is still in school, and other factors when determining sentencing."[4]

Because of such abuses, there has been a need for a concerted effort at federal, state, and local levels to establish a system of justice more rational, consistent, and fair. In too many states, departments of welfare, education, mental health, public health, and divisions of probate court act independently, with no common guidelines, facilities, or programs to exchange and share. Administrative responsibilities are fragmented, which lead to duplication of service. This creates a situation in which a child can encounter various and conflicting methods of treatment throughout his exposure to the system. Competitive struggles among various departments occur too often, and there are often no separate bureaus of child welfare, or offices for family, children, or youth services.

To begin dealing with such problems, the Juvenile Justice and Delinquency Act (Public Law 93-415) was enacted in September 1974. This act created "for the first time, a uniform national program to deal with juvenile delinquency prevention and control. The Congress passed the act because existing federal programs had not provided the direction, coordination, resources, and leadership required."[5]

[4] *Juvenile Justice Digest,* Washington Crime News Service, February 13, 1976, p. 5.
[5] *Federal Juvenile Delinquency Programs, op. cit.,* p. 1.

Several provisions in the act were specifically designed to insure a coordinated interagency and interdisciplinary approach to delinquency problems. Besides establishing overall objectives and priorities, the act also created both a coordinating council and an advisory committee on juvenile justice and delinquency problems. The coordinating council is comprised of representatives from other federal agencies and is chaired by the Attorney General. The advisory committee is composed of private citizens appointed by the President, with four members required to be under the age of 26.

Increased efforts to solve problems, provide coordination, set priorities, and use more logical procedures are being developed at the federal level.

In addition, having one organizational unit for children and youth at both the state and local levels enhances the opportunity for improved planning and programming. Each state would then be responsible for establishing priorities and policies that local jurisdictions can use to develop rational approaches to the problem. Also, accountability is increased, so that "revolving door" justice is minimized. The same standards must be applied to local jurisdictions so that there is an increase in uniformity, and a resulting decrease in fragmentation.

Several states have used this approach to deal with the problem, and Michigan, for example, has established a juvenile service training council. It provides a forum for key youth service system administrators to deal with 'raining and related needs on a statewide basis. Through assistance, consulta-on, and coordination, services are provided to agencies and institutions. Money for training is also provided to staffs that work with delinquent and predelinquent youth. Expanded fiscal support is being sought for other areas, such as programming and treatment.

The focus of this statewide system is to (1) identify gaps in youth service training, (2) eliminate unnecessary duplication of training efforts in youth service units, (3) establish a central coordination and communication point for all youth service staff training in the state, (4) direct technical and financial support for training efforts to the areas of greatest need, and (5) subsidize training efforts and insure adequate quality and fiscal controls.[6]

Even though this Michigan effort is focused only on training, delivery of services and programming could be handled on a statewide basis using the same structure to provide accountability, coordination, and consistency of services provided to youths. Such a system makes decision making more rational and policies and programs more useful in helping troubled youth. The point is that it takes a coordinated effort to deal adequately with the problem. Accountability is an important issue and some administrator has to be responsible if the "system" concept is ever to be a fact rather than a rhetorical statement. On the adult criminal justice level the *sheriff* has the best opportunity to secure a true "system" because he has responsibility and accountability for both police operations and corrections functions. He arrests and in most cases is expected to rehabilitate the offender.

[6] Juvenile Services Training Council, Annual Report, 1974–75, Michigan Department of Social Services, p. 1.

Coordination, centralization, and accountability, however, are not the only solutions to the problem, since, as mentioned earlier, some youngsters do not even have to be processed by the system, in particular those involved in status offenses.

STATUS OFFENSES

Status offenses are "crimes" only because of the status (minor) or age of the person committing the act. These include such offenses as running away, violating curfew, and truancy.

In the past, status offenders were often handled improperly and were incarcerated not only with repeat juvenile offenders, but too often with hardened criminals as well.

That sort of error resulted in bad publicity that has helped make status offenses into a very thorny problem for contemporary society. Status offenses have in essence become a political football, and such political hassling interferes with the likelihood that realistic legislation to deal with the problem effectively will be passed. Whenever there is an attempt to revise the juvenile code and address the problem of status offenses, political pronouncements tend to cloud the issue, preventing necessary delivery of services so that the young people with problems receive needed help.

The problem is that many people contend that status offenses should be wiped from the books, since such acts would not be crimes if the offender were merely older. This would have the positive impact of eliminating labelling and the stigma attached to becoming involved with the juvenile justice system.

This sounds logical and well-meaning, but the problem is that status offenses are likely to be symptoms of deeper problems. To eliminate such offenses from juvenile codes without providing realistic alternatives to provide these troubled young people with help is relinquishing an important societal responsibility.

To deal effectively with status offenders, there must be realistic alternatives, such as programs for runaways, counseling for disturbed youth, and assistance for youngsters on the street in the wee hours of the morning with nothing to do, or nowhere to go.

Mere removal of the offense from the books may cut the "crime" rate, but this is too simplistic an approach to a complex problem. Without a means, a handle, to justify intervention, and without alternative services to deal with the problem, the status offender would merely be left to proceed to committing more serious offenses, thereby losing an important and vital opportunity to intervene at a more benign level. The problem may stem from difficulties within family relationships or problems in relating to the community, but if the young person's problem is not dealt with, intervention is just delayed until the time a more serious offense occurs.

Legislators must be careful not to eliminate the role police can play as preventive agents who can interact with young people, and status offenses provide a common reason to intervene. A properly trained police officer, with an attitude of caring, has great value in a preventive role. Eliminating him from this position could have dire consequences if no provision is made for alternative help.

For instance, the police officer is the person who notices young people out late at night, or in situations where their welfare may be threatened. Police intervention, usually on an informal basis, is often the key allowing community, family, and school to grapple with the problem youngster whose behavior indicates further, more serious problems down the road.

Unfortunately, there are those who believe police should not be involved with youngsters, even on an informal basis. They perceive the police officer's role as strictly law enforcement, and they argue social agencies should handle all other responsibilities.

Many police officers might happily relinquish this extra responsibility of dealing with status offenders, but only if alternative social programs existed. This means the social program must be designed not only to identify young people with problems, but it must have the justification to intervene. Then the program must also provide follow-up to the initial contact. Perhaps the family has multiple problems. Maybe the child is abused or neglected. This might be a case where the family is having difficulty controlling the youngster and the first indication of serious problems occurs when the child runs away.

Unfortunately, most social agencies are not open 24 hours a day. The police department then becomes the only agency whose schedule permits this kind of around-the-clock community observation. The majority of status offenses do not become apparent, or do not become offenses at all, until after agency hours.

So the question arises: if social agencies were designed to provide that initial contact, then why haven't they at least been available for support to the police now? Realistically, it will take this kind of double-barreled approach from police and social agencies to deal effectively with the problem. If the alternative is to eliminate status offenses without providing another means of dealing with these symptoms of more serious problems, then nothing at all will be done to help the juveniles in trouble until more serious offenses are committed.

FUTURE DIRECTIONS

B. J. George, Jr., distinguished legal scholar, has made some interesting observations about possible directions the juvenile court and system of juvenile justice should go.

He believes the reasons for the existence of the juvenile court are now obsolete. When the court was established, he points out, it was probably not envisioned that there would be the extreme proliferation of administrative agencies, such as social service departments, mental health departments, and other treatment and rehabilitation organizations.

Administrative agencies now intervene in people's lives to a greater degree than the court can. Most key decisions about young people are made by school social workers, case workers in welfare departments, and persons in other administrative organizations. Specifically, decisions about status offenses, and neglect and abuse cases, are made prior to any court involvement.

He states,

> Hence, the principle function of the juvenile court in most instances is simply to confirm, or inform, what has already been decided. If this is so, why not recognize that it is the responsibility of the various offices and agencies to make administrative decisions, subject to the mandates of administrative due process, well-delineated in a number of fields of administration, state and federal. Such a formal recognition of a responsibility to adjudicate administratively should force juvenile service agencies to regulate their procedures for handling the claims and liabilities of juveniles and their families. Among other things, it might promote the creating of qualified hearing examiners, qualified paralegal advocates to help citizens, in their negotiations with social service agencies, and adequate agency administrative review systems. If these were accomplished, then the role of the court system (in this instance, through the circuit courts) would be precisely what it is in other fields of public administration, in which citizens are satisfied or dissatisfied with the activity or inactivity of public agencies: the satisfied can seek legal endorsement to overcome the reluctance of other administrators to abide by an earlier administrator's decisions, and those dissatisfied with official activity can attack it on the basis of either legal impropriety or abuse of administrative discretion.[7]

George also states that administrative agencies should have the power to compel participation in programs, so that services can be delivered and affected persons will utilize the services.

George also recommends that all persons of a given age and above (he uses 14 since it is established in traditional criminal law) be processed exactly the same as adults, regardless of age or status. This way, status offenses would disappear, and he points out that if people were dealt with in the same way, problems for law enforcement would lessen, and clearer guidelines would emerge for law enforcement officers to handle these persons.

The system of juvenile justice is also becoming increasingly more adversary. If there are no changes in the court structure, according to George, this means the system for processing young people will differ from the way adults are handleu in name only, anyway. Why not instead recognize the increased adversary situation and process juveniles in the same way, with administrative safeguards, and, of course, legal due process?

> Development along these lines might also force early development of adequate guidelines for screening and diversion. The police department

[7] Statement by B. J. George, Jr.

should be able to establish adequate guidelines for disposing of younger offenders as well as adult defenders. Preconviction probation can be accomplished as well in the case of the younger offenders as older offenders. By not fragmenting screening and diversion systems on a happenstance basis of age, a much more effective plan of screening and diversion might be achieved, than if juvenile and adult justice systems go their separate, uncoordinated ways.[8]

If the system operated regardless of age, George feels there would be a more coordinated approach toward handling offenders and more efficient use of resources, with no need for separate intake and probation staffs. Reception and diagnostic centers could be centralized, institutional programs made realistic in terms of delivery of services, rather than the present uncoordinated and arbitrary nature because of age restrictions.

George admitted that his recommendations would be met with resistance by several groups, probably on both ends of the continuum. On the one hand, civil libertarians would see drawbacks for youngsters associated with a process now considered adult and criminal. On the other hand, more reactionary elements would feel justice and sanctioning would be greatly reduced for young juvenile offenders because they would be the least serious of the criminal population, merely put back into the community to continue their "wayward ways" until the offenses became so serious they would be removed from the community.

Realistically, however, as pointed out earlier, the juvenile justice system is becoming more adversary, and if the trend continues, it will be almost indistinguishable from the adult process anyway. In light of this, serious attention should be paid to George's suggestion that the two systems be combined, centralizing most of the dual functions, recognizing that administrative agencies like social welfare make most decisions anyway. This would give them the responsibility and authority to make critical decisions that affect young people. It would facilitate early intervention, and thereby, it is hoped, avert more serious deviant behavior in the future.

It is probable that the preceding discussion of the future of juvenile court and administrative agencies will be no more than just that in most communities. Whether or not it is agreed that administrative agencies should have new major roles, and the influence of the juvenile court thereby diminished, most would agree that diversion from all formal court processes, regardless of the jurisdiction of the court, is by far the more acceptable alternative for most juveniles.

DIVERSION

Diversion has become a popular method of solving juvenile problems in recent times, primarily because it shows the greatest promise of success.

The National Advisory Commission on Criminal Justice Standards and Goals defines diversion as "halting or suspending, before conviction, formal criminal

[8] *Ibid.*

proceedings against a person on a condition or assumption that he will do something in return."[9]

This definition was expanded by the following:

Diversion provides society with the opportunity to begin the reordering of the justice system, by redistributing resources to achieve justice and correctional goals . . . to develop truly effective prevention, justice, control, and social restoration programs . . . perhaps the single biggest contribution that diversion can make during the next decade is to make society more conscious and sensitive to the deficiencies in the justice system, and hence, to force radical changes within the system so that appropriate offenders are successfully diverted from the system, while others are provided with programs within the system that offer social restoration instead of criminal condemnation.[10]

Diversion is designed to keep juveniles away from involvement with traditional juvenile and criminal justice systems "in order to reduce adjudication rates in courts, to reduce recidivism rates of these youths by providing alternative methods of handling, and to concentrate resources on those youth considered to be at the greatest risk of unnecessarily penetrating the juvenile justice system."[11]

In more simple terms, diversion means that instead of putting the youngster into more formal channels, he is diverted into other programs that help his specific problem. For some it could be a job, for others drug programs, education programs, counseling programs, or any other program designed to help the child adjust. It could also be a program designed to provide a support service for the family so that the family can work on the problem together with the child, to help him become a productive citizen.

Diversion can occur at many different levels. For example, the police can divert youngsters they contact. However, guidelines are needed for police officers so that after a youngster is diverted to a community agency, regardless of whether it is a mental health agency or the social service department, there is a follow-up so that the officer can see results. This is vital so that the youngster does not just become another administrative statistic, without delivery of some practical service.

Status offenses, such as runaway, curfew violation, incorrigibility, are situations where diversion should be employed in almost all cases. The only exceptions might be where the status offense occurs in conjunction with a more serious offense, such as breaking and entering or car theft.

But in most cases, a general rule of thumb for law enforcement officers should be to refer status offenders to noncourt youth agencies if they are

[9] National Advisory Commission on Criminal Justice Standards and Goals, *Courts* (Washington D.C.: U.S. Government Printing Office, 1975), p. 27.
[10] National Advisory Commission on C.J. Standards and Goals, *Corrections,* 1973, p. 94.
[11] First Comprehensive Plan for Federal Juvenile Delinquency Programs, LEAA, U.S. Department of Justice (Washington, D.C.: U.S. Government Printing Office, 1976), p. 13.

available. Policies and procedures should be developed so police can work in conjunction with these agencies, especially in the case of status offenses.

Not only must there be guidelines for making diversion referrals, there should be standards within the agency regarding what procedures will be used, what services will be available, and what administrative guidelines will exist to insure effective handling. Without adequate criteria for referral and handling, the system can become sloppy, thereby harming the youngster as much or more than if he were sent through the formal court process.

In terms of standards that should be used, the following model has been established:

> *Factors that should be considered favorable to diversion are:*
>
> the relative youth of the offender,
>
> the willingness of the victim to have no conviction sought,
>
> any likelihood that the offender suffers from a mental illness, or psychological abnormality which was related to his crime, for which treatment is available,
>
> any likelihood that the crime was significantly related to any other situation, such as unemployment, or family problems that would be subject to change by participation in a diversion program,
>
> the likelihood of the accused to accept the voluntary service,
>
> the availability of adequate diversion programs,
>
> school and family strengths.
>
> *Among the factors that should be considered unfavorable for diversion are:*
>
> any history of the use of physical violence toward others, and/or prior offenses,
>
> involvement with organized crime,
>
> a history of anti-social conduct, indicating that such conduct has become an ingrained part of the offender's lifestyle and would be particularly resistant to change,
>
> any special need to pursue criminal prosecution as a means to discouraging others from committing such offenses,
>
> the unavailability of treatment.
>
> *Guidelines for making diversion decisions should be established cooperatively by police, schools, courts, prosecutors and representatives of public and private youth-serving agencies. These guidelines should be made public.*[12]

Youth service bureaus (as mentioned in chapter 8) are an appropriate diversion agency that can make a significant impact on the reduction of delin-

---

[12]Criminal Justice Goals and Standards, State of Michigan, Michigan Advisory Commission on Criminal Justice, 1975, pp. 32-33.

quency by providing services for youngsters in need. Such bureaus are particularly useful for status offenders, or those involved in less serious, nonviolent criminal acts.

Referrals can be made by police, schools, mental health agencies, or any other community agency. In some cases, the court may even use the bureau because the youngster is not considered likely to benefit from court services.

Youth service bureaus offer alternatives both in terms of programming and as a method of helping the youngster avoid arrest or processing. The obvious advantage is that the youngster is not just processed or warned and released without follow-up. The youth service bureau can provide adequate follow-up and make close determinations about the kind of service the youngster needs. This could range from psychological counseling all the way to employment assistance. If the bureau itself doesn't provide this range of service, its staff people should have broad awareness of what resources are available in the community.

Funding for the program can be either private or public, but interlocking support is helpful in promoting community support.

Youth service bureaus should be organized as independent, locally operated agencies that involve the widest number of people of the community, including youth, in the solution of youth problems. The most appropriate local mix for decision making should be determined by the priorities set among the goals, but in no case should youth service bureaus be under the complete control of the justice system or any other one agency. It should be governed by a local citizen board that does cooperate with other private agencies, the Juvenile Court, schools, and the township or municipality.

— A bureau should be operated with the advice and consent of the community it serves, particularly the recipients of its services. This should include the development of youth responsibility for community delinquency prevention.

— A coalition, including young people, indigenous adults and representatives of agencies and organizations operating in the community, should comprise the decision-making structure. Agency representatives should include juvenile justice policymakers.

Youth service bureaus should make needed services available to all young people in the community. Bureaus should make a particular effort to attract diversionary referrals from the juvenile justice system.

— Law enforcement and court intake personnel should be strongly encouraged, through immediate policy changes and ultimately through legal changes, to make full use of the youth service bureau in lieu of court processing for every juvenile who is not an immediate threat to public safety and who voluntarily accepts the referral to the youth service bureau, and for which the youth service bureau has access to an adequate program.

— Specific criteria for diversionary referrals should be jointly developed and specified in writing by law enforcement, court and youth service bureau personnel. Referral policies and procedures should be mutually agreed upon.

— Diversionary referrals should be encouraged by continual communication between law enforcement, court and youth service bureau personnel.

— Referrals to the youth service bureau should be completed only if voluntarily accepted by the youth.

— The juvenile courts should only refer but may not order youth to the youth service bureau.

— Cases referred by law enforcement or court should be closed by the referring agency when the youth agrees to accept the youth service bureau's service. Other dispositions should be made only if the youth commits a subsequent offense. Follow-up should be conducted to insure the service is being provided.

— Referring agencies should be entitled to and should expect systematic feedback on initial services provided to a referred youth by the bureau. The youth service bureau, however, should not provide justice system agencies with reports on counseling content but may indicate if the child is still in treatment.

— Because of the voluntary nature of bureau services and the reluctance of young people who might benefit from them, the youth service bureau should energetically strive to provide its services to youth. This should include the use of hotlines and outreach or street workers wherever appropriate.[13]

Citizens and public servants who are truly interested in attacking the crime and delinquency problem will have to develop alternatives to punitive handling of offenders. One such approach would be the initiation of a primary, operational linkage between the full scope of all Criminal Justice II agencies and Criminal Justice I at the police level.[14]

The National Advisory Commission on Criminal Justice Standards and Goals labels the formal traditional process as Criminal Justice System I. Criminal Justice System II is described as follows:

Many public and private agencies and citizens outside of police, courts, and corrections are—or ought to be—involved in reducing and preventing crime, the primary goals of criminal justice. These agencies and persons, when dealing with the issues related to crime reduction and prevention, plus the traditional triad of police, courts, and corrections make up a

---

[13] *Ibid.,* pp. 35, 36, 37.
[14] Figures 1, 2, and 3 were developed by Forrest M. Moss and are found in *Community-Based Crime Prevention* by Robert C. Trojanowicz, John M. Trojanowicz, and Forrest M. Moss (Pacific Palisades, Calif.: Goodyear Publishing Co., 1975), pp. 158–161.

larger criminal justice system, a system which this commission calls Criminal Justice System II . . . Whatever the difficulties of obtaining cooperation among the various interests of Criminal Justice System I, they are immeasurably greater in Criminal Justice System II.[15]

It is the police who start the formal process. It is the police, working in full cooperation with the nonpunitive agencies, that can assure that only those offenders not treatable in the larger society are introduced to the punitive system.

Figure 1 sets forth the traditional process of reacting to criminal behavior. Such a system, essentially punitive in orientation, may be useful in societies with strong cultural homogeneity and a high consensus of opinion about right and wrong. America has neither. The notion of crime and delinquency prevention by treatment of the causes has resulted in the recognition that a multitude of social agencies and private citizens can aid in the process. Criminal Justice System II can be conceptualized as shown in Figure 2.

Efforts within Criminal Justice System I to reduce the punitive nature of the system, or to moderate it in selected cases, has led to a revitalization of diversion after arrest. (See Figure 3.)

But while the bulk of juvenile offenders would best be served by alternative social programs like diversion, the fact remains that some juveniles commit crimes so violent it would be foolish to risk employing such alternatives.

They are the small percentage of violent youthful offenders who show no indication that intervention will change their violent behavior in the near future. In their case, they cannot be allowed to remain in society, because the risk to others if they are left on the street far outweighs any consideration of what stigmatization would do to the juvenile.

Crime is so serious in some cities that people have changed their whole life-style because they fear leaving their homes. The elderly, the least capable of protecting themselves, become easy prey. In some cities, juvenile gangs roam the streets, completely occupying a specific geographic territory they claim as their own.

The problem is so acute in these cases that it allows no time to delve into the "why" of such animalistic behavior. In such cases, the only answer is removing the violent youth from the streets and dealing with him in humane, but cloistered, environments.

YOUTH VIOLENCE

Violence by youthful individuals and gangs has reached what must be called crisis proportions in some cities. Dr. Walter B. Miller, in a study of gangs in some

---

[15] National Advisory Commission on Criminal Justice Standards and Goals, *Crim. Just. System* (Washington D.C.: U.S. Government Printing Office, 1975), p. 1.

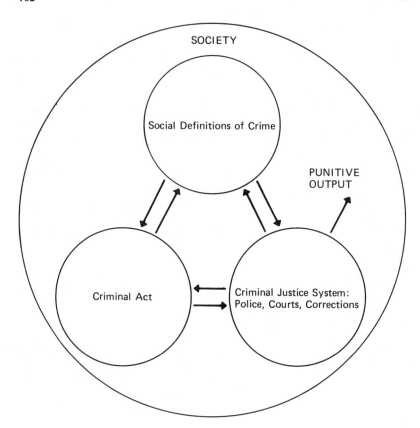

FIGURE 1. Traditional Response to Criminal Deviance

of the nation's largest cities (New York, Los Angeles, Chicago, Philadelphia, Detroit, and San Francisco), said there could be as many as 2,700 gangs, with 81,500 members, in these six cities alone.[16] These are not social clubs or groups, but gangs that carry weapons, including handguns, involved in a wide range of aggressive behavior.[17] And Dr. Miller sees no sign of improvement. He predicts a continuing increase in gang activity during the next five to ten years.[18]

In some cities, gangs have gotten out of control to the point that the regular activities in the community are disrupted. Armed bands of young gang members board buses and physically force passengers to give up wallets and other personal items. Gang members are getting so bold that not only do they show total disregard for their fellow man, but they have no fear of police or any formal consequence for their actions.

Gang violence and youth misbehavior became so serious in Detroit, Michigan, that the Michigan State Police were commissioned by the governor to

[16] LEAA Newsletter, Vol. 5, No. 10, May 1976, p. 6.
[17] *Ibid.*
[18] *Ibid.*

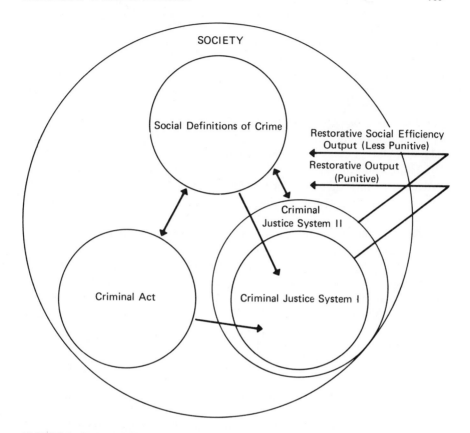

FIGURE 2. Expanded, But Traditional, Response to Criminal Deviance

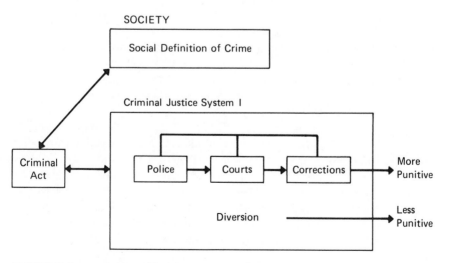

FIGURE 3. System-Centered Diversion

patrol the highways and freeways within city limits. This had been done in Michigan before only during the urban riots.

When curfews were imposed in some major cities in an effort to curb gang violence, civil libertarians complained it was unconstitutional. Yet the zip guns, handguns, knives, chains, and other weapons displayed proudly by these violent young people made residents so fearful there was little constitutional guarantee of their right to "life, liberty, and the pursuit of happiness." The situation had deteriorated to the point at which many residents, especially the elderly, found it impossible to act freely in their own communities.

Increased gang and youth violence also sparked sales of weapons to private citizens who buy them for protection. Obviously, when entire communities become armed camps, many accidents occur and innocent people are hurt. The problem has become so serious that citizens don't know where to turn, and even law enforcement authorities admit they cannot control the situation.

A great part of the terror from teen-age violence comes from the fact that much of it is random and unprovoked. It is not necessarily directed at a particular person, nor is it performed for the purpose of stealing money or goods. Examples of this wanton violence appear in the newspapers every day. For instance, Rosalyn Brown, a 15-year-old Detroit girl, was sitting in the parlor with her boyfriend when she was killed by random gunshots. Others nearby were injured from this random display of firepower.

Violence is so pervasive in many cities that it defies description.

Violence in Schools

Since young people spend so much time in school, this has become the place where the increase in violence is most evident. Its awesome fury is directed at the facilities, the teachers, and fellow students.

Disgruntled students a few years ago set a fire that caused a million dollars in damages in a New York high school.

Dr. Miller reported it is a commonplace activity for gang members to shake down schoolchildren for money before they will allow them to walk the hallways safely.

The Los Angeles school district provided pamphlets telling teachers how to avoid gunfire by tactical moves.

A recent report points out that there are 75,000 serious physical assaults on teachers each year, with many more injuries. As many as 100 murders were committed in 1973 in the 757 districts surveyed. "Other survey results show that between 1970 and 1973 only, reported assaults on teachers jumped 77.4 percent, reported assaults on students went up to 85.3 percent, reported robberies of students and teachers increased 37 percent, reported rapes and attempted rapes went up almost 20 percent, and the number of dangerous weapons confiscated from students was up by almost 55 percent."[19]

[19] *Juvenile Justice Digest,* Jan. 30, 1976, p. 2.

Public education cannot function in an atmosphere of violence and intimidation. Very serious crimes are not uncommon—arson, rape, and even murder have become commonplace occurrences in several schools in the United States. The increase in vandalism alone costs already overburdened school districts money that would otherwise have paid for educational programs. When vandalism is coupled with attacks on teachers and students, the whole process of education is threatened with extinction.

It is the teachers who are the most inviting targets for much of this rising youth violence. In some schools their lives are threatened. The teachers' reaction to such situations has been described as "battle fatigue." Some teachers show such psychological and physical strain they have been transferred from one school to another, just for rest and recuperation.

This danger has led to the unfortunate spectre of armed guards in hallways, among other security measures.

A study finished recently provided insight into reasons for the massive increase in the school crime problem. It said,

> All school rules are eventually questioned, including classroom decorum, seating, attendance, proper language, course content, tests, and grades . . . students express their anger through defiance of teacher's authority, tardiness, absences, acts of vandalism, robbery, noise, and attacks on teachers . . . teachers express their anger by resorting to disciplinary measures to keep order, or by expelling disruptive students. The ultimate punishment, of course, is to go through the motions of teaching, even though no one pays attention . . . Students express anger towards peers by name calling, threats of violence, painting ethnic slurs on walls, and shaking down and beating up weak students.[20]

Next to the family, the school is the most important socializing agent. Yet without the proper atmosphere, education becomes impossible.

> It is important for those concerned with the future of our young people to appreciate both the gravity of the situation, and the obstacles these problems raise for the education of our children. For millions of children, public education should present one of the most meaningful and realistic opportunities to become productive citizens. Too often, however, youngsters arriving at our public schools today are not finding the quiet atmosphere of instruction, enrichment, and encouragement, but instead an environment dominated by fear, chaos, destruction, and violence. For these young people, public education becomes only a lesson in the cruelty of promises unfulfilled.[21]

Teachers today often find little time to teach and instead become disci-

[20] "Learning Stops When Violence Walks School Halls," Salvatore Didato, Gannett News Service, *Lansing State Journal,* Aug. 26, 1976.
[21] *Juvenile Justice Digest,* April 11, 1975, p. 2.

plinarians, controllers, and security guards. And no area of the country appears to be immune. Senator Birch Bayh's subcommittee report on youth violence said that in the Northeast, homicides in schools increased 20.1 percent between 1970 and 1973. In the South, student assaults on school personnel increased an incredible 316.4 percent. In the West, robberies rose 93 percent. And in the North Central region, rapes and attempted rapes went up 60 percent.[22]

Frightening though those figures are, data on the seriousness of the problem are often inaccurate because of poor recordkeeping and reporting systems, and, very likely, because of indirect reluctance on the part of many school administrators who fear the community would become outraged at such apparent poor administrative control.

The problem has become so serious that legislation is, of course, being written to try to help. But it will take awareness by the general public and a commitment to make changes to provide the millions of dollars it will take to renovate buildings, provide security, protect teachers, and, it is hoped, thereby develop an atmosphere in which education can take place.

Priorities

Society must come to grips with youth violence. It will require stringent methods to deal with those youthful perpetrators of violence who have no regard for life or property.

However, the sad fact remains that while politicians, public officials, and community leaders are quick to voice disgust when their communities are overrun by violent youngsters, few have the courage to support the needed action—getting those violent young people off the streets. Few community leaders will admit that that's what it will take. Most are too afraid of being criticized as conservative, traditional, and authoritarian. Yet in a sense, those leaders merely reflect the views of the larger community that is apparently not ready to take such stringent measures.

For the fact is that few violent youthful offenders are ever institutionalized. "Between July 1973 and June 1974, only 4.4 percent of 5,666 juveniles arrested for violent crimes in New York City were ever sent to an institution, according to a study just completed by the Office of Juvenile Services, New York Division of Criminal Justice Services."[23] Those serious crimes were murder, manslaughter, rape, attempted rape, kidnapping, assault, sodomy, arson, robbery, and possession of dangerous weapons—a frightening litany that would seem to indicate that you can get away with murder—if you are young enough.

It seems inconceivable that society is not so fed up that it is demanding strong and more stringent types of handling for the relatively small percentage of youngsters involved in these violent crimes. It seems unthinkable that community leaders would even hesitate to endorse getting these young people off the streets.

[22] *Ibid.*
[23] *Juvenile Justice Digest,* May 7, 1976, p. 2.

The argument heard most often is that since sending youngsters to institutions or training schools doesn't provide them with beneficial treatment or rehabilitation, there is no benefit in sending them away.

Unfortunately it is true that rehabilitation programs have not proven very successful in changing violent youthful offenders into productive citizens. Studies just out also show probation doesn't work as well as hoped. "A sampling of juveniles put on probation in Maryland for the first time during 1971 and then tracked for the next four years revealed 45.5 percent became repeat offenders."[24]

Given the current state of the art of social science, it appears there are no simple guidelines to follow that inspire violent juveniles to mend their ways.

But to argue therefore that there is no benefit in institutionalizing them ignores the fact that there is indeed a very real benefit to the community when such juveniles are removed simply because when they are removed they cannot pillage and assault people anymore. Even if the institutions lack ways of helping the serious offender, the community is served merely by his absence.

It can also be argued that when the consequences of violent behavior are so obviously negligible that there is seldom anything done to those who commit violent crimes, others are encouraged to participate, or those already involved are led to believe they can get bolder with impunity.

Another effect is that it makes it more difficult to get people to testify. Certainly some refuse because they "don't want to get involved," but others justifiably fear reprisals when so few violent juveniles charged are ever removed from the community, and even those who are institutionalized typically spend only a very short time away.

The community has a right to protection. Unfortunately, the community must be willing to demand what it takes to provide protection. To be protected, they must be willing to risk criticism that will arise if they demand that violent juveniles be removed. To do less implies society has become so decadent as to tolerate savagery in the community rather than face the unpleasant task of removing people from the community. If that is indeed the case, perhaps society will get what it deserves.

John Greacen, head of the National Institute for Juvenile Justice and Delinquency Prevention, predicts it will be almost impossible, even with more money, to curb juvenile crime during the next few years. He said "about 15% of these youths whom we would call delinquent should be handled in a pretty strong way. They should be locked up."[25] Likewise, he agreed that these "kids" should not be locked up on the basis that they will get better treatment in an institution—they should be locked up because they are dangerous and they are hurting people.

The wisest trend in the future would be for the courts to deal more severely with hardened young criminals and remove them from the streets,

---

[24] *Juvenile Justice Digest,* Jan. 30, 1976, p. 10.
[25] *Juvenile Justice Digest,* Sept. 12, 1975, p. 4.

while providing diversion and other types of community programs for those involved in less serious offenses, and those who are first-time offenders.

Judge Irving Kaufman said, "it has become increasingly apparent that our traditional system of juvenile justice is a failure. It neither safeguards society from violent juveniles, nor provides adequate protection for the alarmingly large number of children reared in brutal environments—which breeds hostility and failure."[26]

The Juvenile Justice Standards Commission urged the following:

— juveniles aged 16 and 17 who commit violent crimes should be processed as adults, subject to the longer sentences now reserved for adults.

— definite and, in some cases, longer prison sentences should replace indeterminate sentences which have been criticized for being too lenient for violent offenders, too strict for nonviolent juveniles, and not evenly applied to offenders committing similar crimes.

— juvenile justice process should be changed from a quasi-civil, secret, nonadversay proceeding, in which reform of the child is the main goal, to a public, adversary, trial process in which punishments play a greater role. As part of this change, juvenile defendants would be provided with lawyers.

— status offenders would be removed from court jurisdiction, and handled instead by social agencies, or by the family, free of the stigma of being certified delinquent.[27]

The Juvenile Justice and Delinquency Prevention Act of 1974 proposes to improve treatment for status offenders. It also provides finances for the states to come up with programs as alternatives to prison and jails for youths. Community-based facilities are emphasized and money is already being dispensed. Some communities are already taking more stringent steps to deal with violent youngsters. In New York, Governor Hugh Carey has proposed that juveniles who commit violent crimes such as murder and rape be sentenced to longer prison terms.[28]

Prevention

The chapters in this book have tried to emphasize that the best way to deal with the total juvenile delinquency crime problem is prevention. When prevention doesn't work, then diversion is the best approach for youngsters who can benefit from community social programs, while incarceration may well be the only realistic means available today to deal with violent juveniles offenders.

---

[26] "Coming: Tougher Approach to Juvenile Violence," *U.S. News and World Report,* June 7, 1976, p. 65.
[27] *Ibid.,* p. 65.
[28] *Ibid.,* p. 66.

But prevention, if successful, would make both diversion and removal from society unnecessary, by dealing with problems by preventing them before they occur.

As pointed out in Chapter 3, the family is still the most important socializing agent for youngsters, and when there is a strong family, chances are minimized that the youngster will become involved in violence and criminal activity.

This means the family must work together to help the youngster adjust to society and become a productive citizen. But the contemporary family unit is a very different thing from the traditional family. Divorce, broken homes, psychological and physical abuse, and neglect have all become common problems in today's families.

More than ever it has become difficult to keep the family intact, not only because of social problems, but because of the increased number of mothers in the labor force. Working mothers in themselves do not contribute to delinquency. But society has not completely adjusted to this fact so that a working mother is sometimes allowed to impair the family's functioning as a unit. This can have a deleterious effect if it interferes with giving preschoolers the support and encouragement needed from at least one parent during the day.

Overall, in contemporary society, more and more parents are relinquishing their responsibilities to community institutions. The most important of these these is the school, since the youngster spends more time there than in any other social institution. School violence was discussed earlier, and it should be noted that much of the violence and hostility that erupts there is probably the result of misdirected feelings of anger the children have toward their parents. In school, they manifest the resentment they feel toward parents who don't spend enough time, show concern, or develop guidelines for value orientation that can help youngsters survive in today's complex society.

Because the school has had to assume many parental responsibilities, not only does violence emerge, but less time is left for teaching basic skills such as reading, writing, and arithmetic.

The obvious result is that many young people emerge from school ill-prepared for today's demanding world. The frustration caused by this lack of preparation can manifest itself in many deviant ways. Research is confirming more and more that children who become delinquents or who have behavioral problems also have some kind of reading or schoolwork-related problem. A recent study showed that "80% of the inmates of prisons may be there because they have had a childhood problem called dyslexia, a neurological disorder that causes persons to see letters and numbers backwards. Frustration that arises from an inability to learn in a traditional manner could account for juvenile delinquency and anti-social behavior.[29]

That the skill levels of school-age children are declining has been documented in many studies. Since children show decreased writing abilities, it has

---

[29] *Juvenile Justice Digest,* Dec. 4, 1975, p. 6.

been suggested that the schools get back to basics and teach writing, spelling, punctuation, and other basic mechanics necessary to survive in the work world.

Not only are youngsters unable to write coherently, it has been estimated that "over 1 million American juveniles, aged 12 to 17, can't read or write at even the fourth grade level."[30] This report, by the Department of Health, Education, and Welfare, classifies these individuals as functionally illiterate. Ironically, it is a cyclical pattern that violence reduces the time to teach, while failing to impart needed skills to youngsters may increase the likelihood of their violent behavior.

Another problem in schools, as pointed out in a study released by the Children's Defense Fund, is that school systems discriminate against different kinds of children. The report found that

> if the child is not white, or white but not middle class, does not speak English, is poor, needs special help in seeing, hearing, walking, reading, learning, adjusting, growing up, is pregnant, or married at age 15, is not smart, or is too smart, then in too many places, school officials decide that school is not the place for that child. It is as if many school officials have decided that certain groups of children are beyond their responsibility and are expendable. Not only do they exclude these children, they frequently do so arbitrarily, discriminatorily, and with impunity.[31]

The situation isn't entirely hopeless, however. As mentioned earlier, the federal government is providing money to communities to help with school violence problems, and, in addition, other legislative efforts are being made to deal with the situation. Legislation and laws, however, will not solve the problem. Only through community and individual effort can these serious problems be met.

School Programs

Several communities have attempted to deal with the delinquency problem and several programs have been discussed in this book. Some communities have used the school as the focal point and have tried alternative schools as an answer for troubled young people.[32] Youngsters having difficulty in regular school can become involved in alternative youth programs, and they can be given counseling, help in finding jobs, and receive any other assistance that might be helpful.

An example of this kind of center is the Teen Center in White Plains, New York. Students there can earn high-school credit through the program, and they can also receive remedial help and tutoring in basic skills.

---

[30] *Juvenile Justice Digest,* June 1974, p. 5.
[31] *Juvenile Justice Digest,* Jan. 3, 1975, p. 2.
[32] Delinquency Prevention in Focus, Oakland County Youth Assistance Program, Pontiac, Michigan, 1974, p. 5.

A fulltime psychologist, a social worker, and four guidance counselors provide personal, educational, vocational, family, and group counseling services to the students. They come from a cross-section of socio-economic groups and since 1967, 830 students have attended the program. Of these, 232 have graduated, 100 have gone to college, and 31 have enrolled in technical and vocational training programs.[33]

Washington, D.C., has a program for underachievers who also have behavioral problems and who are in trouble with the school system. As pointed out earlier, these problems often go together because those with behavioral problems often cause difficulty in school, and this can be a result of not learning properly or not being interested in the material. The Washington program contains three elements—Math and English, to provide basic skills, and a third component designed to help develop interpersonal skills. Students receive points for completing skill units, and they also get points for cooperative behavior. Students lose points if their behavior is not acceptable—for example, if they are disruptive in the classroom. The point system both encourages positive behavior and discourages negative behavior that inhibits learning. The children are helped to identify the dysfunctional behaviors that cause them problems in the classroom, and then they are helped to alter that behavior so learning will be facilitated.

Preliminary findings indicated that the program is successful and that many youngsters learn both basic skills and interpersonal skills.[34]

The California Youth Authority has a school in Whittier that works with small groups of youngsters who have difficulty reading. The program emphasizes the use of tutors. Wards of the institutional program not only receive tutoring help, they provide it in turn to persons who have even less ability than they do. This peer-to-peer tutoring approach seems to be working well.[35]

In St. Louis, Missouri, there is an educational program that has significantly reduced recidivism in delinquent community youngsters. Of those who completed the program, 62 percent were either employed or enrolled in public vocational schools, with 16 percent unknown, and only 22 percent have been in further difficulty that resulted in institutionalization.

The Providence Educational Center is a nonresidential school and re-socialization center for adjudicated delinquents. It accepts 12- to 16-year-old boys with learning problems who have committed high-impact crimes as well as youth with a history of lesser offenses. By improving classroom performance and reversing negative attitudes, the program aims to help juveniles hold down jobs or successfully reenter high school after leaving

---

[33] "Alternative School of Troubled Youth," *Target,* International City Managers Assoc., July 1976, Vol. 5, Issue 5, p. 2.
[34] *Juvenile Justice Digest,* May 1974, p. 7.
[35] *Juvenile Justice Digest,* April 25, 1975, p. 5.

the Providence Educational Center. It is this approach, combining an emphasis on counseling and treatment with individualized instruction and supported learning, that makes Providence unique.[36]

These are among several examples of what communities can do to help youngsters who are involved in delinquent behavior, have dropped out, or whose behavioral problems in the classroom were such they could no longer be tolerated. The reason these programs seem to be as involved with school and education as with delinquency problems is because there is a close correlation between delinquent behavior and a youngster's inability to adapt to a classroom. These programs attempt to provide counseling, private tutorial assistance, and individualized attention to help the young person acquire better skills. This makes them less likely to be frustrated in the classroom, and they are able to learn more easily in a more accepting environment.

One key to reducing delinquency will be improving services to young people, especially in the school setting. Alternative educational programs, referral services, and other innovative approaches have proven successful in communities that are truly looking out for the welfare of their young people.

Other communities have even established elaborate child-care and day-care programs for preschool children. Those formative years are very important, and many times, when both parents are working, or when there is a separation or other family difficulty, young people are not well cared for. These day-care centers therefore can provide needed services and act as substitute parents until the family heals or has more resources with which to deal with the child more effectively.

Several public schools now provide day care to families where both parents work or problems exist. Working with young people at early developmental ages often inhibits the negative life-cycle process. It provides at least basic security and environmental conditions that get youngsters off to a good start toward a productive life.

Many schools are also developing vocational education curricula within the secondary school system. This gives youngsters an important alternative. If they aren't academically inclined, providing vocational alternatives enhances opportunities for more interest and motivation, and this in turn increases the youngster's desire to stay in school.

The ideal public education system would provide an environment flexible enough to induce learning, while helping young people become aware of themselves and the world, but not at the expense of the basic skills—reading, writing, and arithmetic.

Schools also must work closely with employment agencies and other community agencies that can provide jobs. Unemployment, especially for teen-agers, is very high. And, when unemployment escalates, so does the rate of juvenile

---

[36] Providence Educational Center, U.S. Dept. of Justice, LEAA (Washington, D.C.: U.S. Government Printing Office, 1976), p. 1.

delinquency. Crime rates are 50 to 100 times greater in areas of high unemployment than in similar areas where unemployment rates are low.[37] Unemployment rates for black youth are as high as 40 percent in some areas—this has obvious results in terms of juvenile crime problems.

Patrick Murphy, president of the Police Foundation and former Commissioner of Police for New York City, stated that

> staggeringly high unemployment rates for young people condemn them to something like a modern-day debtors' prison. Idleness is not enforced behind walls, but in alleys and hallways of the central cities, and backwater pockets of rural poverty. For these unemployed, there is idle time to watch television, and see portrayed all the material objects they cannot obtain. For these unemployed, there is idle time to consider venting frustrations in crime or by obtaining by criminal means the material things that are denied them.[38]

To make matters worse, cities plagued by high unemployment have budgetary problems that result in cutting the police force to the bare minimum. This can only entice violence and criminal activity on the part of the element that knows all too well the increased vulnerability of inner-city residents when police protection is cut.

Jobs are critical and the schools must work more closely with employment agencies and other agencies that can help. Beyond that, the Department of Labor said that it feels both the quantity and quality of jobs for young people just out of high school needs improvement. Unemployment for youths 16 to 19 years old is three times that for workers 20 years old and over. The proportion of unemployed workers who are young has increased from 15.8 percent, in 1955, to 28.5 percent, in 1973.[39]

According to the Department of Labor, part of the problem is that employers are not in touch with school officials and therefore do not know what young people can offer to the work world. Conversely, schools have not stressed vocational counseling or occupational assistance, so there is not a good link for graduating seniors between school and the world of work.

To get that first job often takes family connections—relatives with influence or connections in the business community. Unfortunately, inner-city youngsters who most desperately need jobs are also those least likely to have these connections.

But here again the picture isn't completely gloomy. Some communities have dealt with the unemployment problem. Harbor City Learning Center in Baltimore, Maryland, an alternative school program established by the city's board of education and operated in conjunction with the mayor's office of

[37]*Juvenile Justice Digest,* May 23, 1975, p. 4.
[38]*Ibid.*
[39]"Youth Employment Problems," U.S. Dept. of Labor (Washington, D.C.: U.S. Government Printing Office, 1973).

manpower service, has attempted to deal both with education problems and unemployment problems. The program is jointly funded by the federal government and local sources. It has a variety of programs, providing a mix of education and career development.

Students are usually referred by the school system or by themselves. They continue their education while at the same time learning skills for careers in fields such as medical technology, telecommunications, general business, and building trades. Students also take the basic educational curriculum of English, social studies, math, and science, but, as much as possible, these studies are linked to the work world.

The Baltimore program also has cooperative arrangements with community agencies. In particular, an arrangement with Johns Hopkins Hospital allows students studying medical technology to gain practical, on-the-job experience. Perhaps it is the practical experience, tied to the educational program, that is the most enticing aspect of the program. It has had the effect of motivating young people to stay in school.

In addition, the Baltimore center also acts as a referral source for jobs, even odd jobs. Jobs are advertised on radio and television as public service announcements. The program has what it calls a job bank where jobs are catalogued and stored, so that a likely referral can have ready access to the information and very quick placement, if desired. Special emphasis is given to summer jobs, encouraging many young people to use their idle time constructively. As many as 10,000 Baltimore young people are employed each summer as a result of the program.

The program involved youth counselors, educational specialists, employment specialists, and community volunteers. It is a total community effort to deal with an educational problem and an employment problem, linking education to work in a coordinated fashion.[40]

SUMMARY AND CONCLUSION

This chapter looked at many aspects of juvenile crime and delinquency with an eye toward what will, and should, happen in the future.

There was an examination of a new and troubling problem, rural juvenile crime. An effort was made to explore the dynamics behind this problem, along with the part played by the increased competitiveness of society. The phenomenon of rural juvenile crime has implications for the future, not only because it can be expected to get worse, both in numbers and degree, but because an analysis of the underlying causes for this increase may provide important insights into the whole problem of juvenile crime and delinquency.

Then the chapter's focus shifted to the juvenile justice system as it exists

[40]"Coordinating An Emphasis on Jobs and School," *Youth Reporter,* March 1975, Dept. of H.E.W. (Washington, D.C.: U.S. Government Printing Office), pp. 1–10.

today, and what must be done immediately for it to deserve the designation "system." It is apparent that to function responsibly and effectively, the system must address itself to the need for increased coordination, accountability, and consistency of treatment.

But if juvenile justice is designed to serve the needs of juveniles who stray, perhaps this calls into question the whole structure of the existing system. Efforts should be made to tailor the system to the juvenile and the type of crime involved. Status offenders, first-time offenders, and those involved in less serious crimes should ideally be dealt with outside the stigmatizing formal system. Police officers could be the initial preventive agent who would then deliver the offender to a social agency that could handle the specific problem. If this process of diversion is to work, it will require more and varied social programs within the community, along with improved follow-up and communication with police.

But at the same time this more liberal and humanistic approach shows the best promise of dealing effectively with the bulk of juvenile offenders, a more hard-line approach is needed to deal with that handful of juveniles who commit serious, violent crimes. Society must make the commitment to provide incarceration and longer sentences, for those juveniles whose continued existence in the community is itself a threat. Since the current level of social science expertise does not afford a way to insure change, these juveniles must be removed, not for their own benefit, but for the relief that it would provide the community.

Going still deeper into the problem of how to handle juvenile crime and delinquency, it cannot be denied that the optimal method of attack is to get at the roots of the problem with primary prevention. This means developing ways of dealing with initial symptoms, before there are serious consequences either for the youngster or society. This is the wisest course of action a civilized society can take, yet it would be naive not to admit that there are serious obstacles in the way.

Often parents are unwilling to allow an agency to intervene early because intervention is viewed as interference. And typically the youngsters who will potentially have the most serious future problems come from families in which parents are the least willing to confront the situation responsibly.

Communities, too, show great reluctance in getting involved in primary prevention. It would mean identifying conditions and problems in the community that show signs of leading to maladapted behavior and then taking corresponding action early enough to prevent problems.

But many things must change before primary prevention stands a healthy chance of success. Legislative support and funding will be needed. Social scientists must provide better tools for early detection and prediction of symptoms that show which youngsters will have problems in the future. But perhaps the most important component still missing is cooperation and a spirit of compromise on the part of individuals and groups in society. Each must be willing to give up some short-term autonomy to gain long-term results.

The family remains the main socializing agent for the youngster, yet parents have relinquished many of the responsibilities to outside agencies, most specifically schools, where youngsters spend the greatest share of their time outside the home.

Unfortunately, by shifting this burden to the schools, thereby asking them to do double-duty, less time is left in which to teach basic skills. This creates a cyclical problem in which young people who lack the basics have their negative self-attitudes reinforced when, after graduation, they find themselves ill-prepared to deal with adult society and the world of work.

Parents, teachers, and community agencies must work together to insure that children receive the basic education they must have in order to compete. At the same time, schools must become flexible enough to allow for individual differences. Parents, too, must become open enough to accept suggestions from trained school personnel who identify early problems that show signs of further, more serious problems developing in the future.

This requires compromise by everyone, along with a willingness to be innovative and flexible. Yet at the same time there remains a need for structure to provide children the security they need. It will take this total and coherent approach on the part of those who interact with children to produce a primary prevention program that has any chance of altering the grim picture painted by today's juvenile crime and delinquency problem.

Every time a young person commits a crime society loses. It is necessary on the one hand to improve services and systems needed to cope with today's teen-agers in trouble, but it will take an even greater spirit of cooperation and support, on the other hand, to stand a chance of preventing tomorrow's problems before they begin.

Bibliography[*]

INTRODUCTION

This bibliography attempts to provide the student of juvenile delinquency with a *sample* of recent literature relating to various aspects of the phenomenon. The works cited herein describe the problem in the United States and abroad, and discuss causes, treatment strategies, prevention, and professional training, among other topics. They reflect a number of differences of opinion in these areas, differences which are especially great in the areas of causes and ways of dealing with delinquency.

The varieties of thinking in relation to the problem can best be illustrated by comparing some of the following views. Sheldon and Eleanor Glueck,[1] for example, maintain that certain individual characteristics are associated with delinquency to such an extent that delinquency can be predicted on the basis of these characteristics. Schur,[2] on the other hand, feels that delinquency involves a good measure of chance in that the youth who is labeled delinquent is often the youth who just happened to be caught doing what other youths—nondelinquents—were also doing. In another example contrast the views of Shaw,[3] who maintains that compassion and understanding are the keys to reforming the errant youth, to those of Loble and Wylie,[4] who adopt a "get-tough" stance which holds youth responsible for their delinquent acts.

[*]The annotated bibliography was written and compiled by Suzann M. (Pyzik) Jude, Michigan State University, East Lansing, Michigan.

[1] Sheldon and Eleanor Glueck, Eds., *Identification of Predelinquents* (New York: Intercontinental Medical Book Corporation, 1972); Sheldon and Eleanor Glueck, *Toward a Typology of Juvenile Offenders* (New York: Grune and Stratton, 1970).

[2] Edwin M. Schur, *Radical Nonintervention: Rethinking the Delinquency Problem* (Englewood Cliffs, N.J.: Prentice-Hall, Inc., 1973).

[3] Otto L. Shaw, *Prisons of the Mind* (New York: Hart Publishing Co., 1974).

[4] Lester H. Loble and Max Wylie, *Delinquency Can Be Stopped* (New York: McGraw-Hill Book Company, 1967).

Some trends in the literature, however, are apparent. They include the trend toward solving the problem of juvenile delinquency in the community and enlisting the aid of the local citizenry, instead of automatically resorting to the treatment institution. Only a few works are devoted mainly to explaining delinquency; the tendency is more toward practical knowledge—how to train social workers and police officers in dealing with delinquents, how to equip the juvenile institution, and how to gather empirical data for use in developing specialized prevention programs.

Each title and accompanying description is followed by the Library of Congress call number, which is utilized by large libraries.

The decision to include books published since 1965 was based on both an attempt to provide an in-depth treatment of the literature chosen and to focus on recent works. It is hoped that the titles and descriptions will aid in furthering the student's knowledge in the area of juvenile delinquency.

Afsaruddin, Mohammad. *Juvenile Delinquency in East Pakistan.* Afsaruddin, 1968. 103 p.

Provides an overview of the juvenile delinquency problem in East Pakistan, which the author feels is related to the social disorganization of a society in transition. Discusses extent and distribution, definition, characteristics of offenders, causes, treatment, and prevention.

HV 9200.5 .A6 E3

Ahlstrom, Winton M., and Robert J. Havighurst. *400 Losers.* San Francisco: Jossey-Bass, Inc., 1971. 246 p.

A report of a combined work-experience and modified academic program involving eighth-grade students who were studied until ages eighteen or nineteen. In addition to reporting specific experimental findings—mainly that the work-experience program was related to improved social adjustment in some of the boys—the book's main emphasis is on describing the actual life situations to which the boys successfully or unsuccessfully adapted.

HV 9106 .K2 A64

Ahmed, Salahuddin. *Studies in Juvenile Delinquency and Crime in East Pakistan.* Dacca: College of Social Welfare and Research Centre, 1966. 143 p.

The author views juvenile delinquency as a byproduct of the change which is currently characteristic of East Pakistan. Stresses the importance of the family as a major factor in prevention, and the importance of probation and aftercare.

HV 9200.5 .A6 E314

Amos, William E., and Jean Dresden Grambs (Eds.). *Counseling the Disadvantaged Youth.* Englewood Cliffs, New Jersey: Prentice-Hall, Inc., 1968. 438 p.

Written for students and practicing counselors, the articles in this work define the term *disadvantaged* as the absence of middle-class experiences which prepare youths to function successfully in society. Included are discussions of the problems facing the counseling profession, the role of the nonprofessional, goals and methods of counseling, and counselor characteristics.

HF 5382.5 .U5 A717

Amos, William E., and Raymond L. Manella (Eds.). *Delinquent Children in Juvenile Correctional Institutions.* Springfield, Illinois: Charles C Thomas, 1966.

The book contains eight articles dealing with the juvenile reception and diagnostic center. Contributors discuss staffing; contributions to be made by research, clinical psychiatry and psychology, education, and social work; the physical plant of the center; and the juvenile court and diagnostic services. The orientation of the book is practical rather than theoretical. Included are descriptions of the facilities of twelve states having reception and diagnostic centers.

HV 9104 .A796

Amos, William E., and Raymond L. Manella (Eds.). *Readings in the Administration of Institutions for Delinquent Youth.* Springfield, Illinois: Charles C Thomas, 1965. 212 p.

Collection of readings intended for individuals responsible for planning and administering juvenile correctional institutions. The readings deal with the mission of the treatment-oriented institution, its administrative organization, role of committees in management, training as the "key to institutional improvement," physical plant standards and design, reception and orientation programs, education, vocational programs, cottage life, clinical programs, religious programs, clothing and food services, problems of programming, discipline and security, prerelease planning, and relationships between the state agency and the institution.

HV 9104 .A8

Amos, William E., Raymond L. Manella, and Marilyn Southwell. *Action Programs for Delinquency Prevention.* Springfield, Illinois: Charles C Thomas, 1965. 137 p.

Deals with community-level programs for the prevention of juvenile delinquency and stresses the importance of community input into formulation of prevention strategies. Includes examples of working programs from various localities in the United States.

HV 9104 .A795

Amos, William E., and Charles F. Wellford (Eds.). *Delinquency Prevention: Theory and Practice.* Englewood Cliffs, New Jersey: Prentice-Hall, Inc., 1967. 254 p.

Contains thirteen articles which summarize prevention efforts and suggest future actions, especially through mobilization of forces in the community. Discusses basic concepts, the role of prediction in prevention programs, and the nature of the socialization process. Included is an examination of the roles of family, religion, school, recreation, economic structure, police, and the judicial process in the prevention of juvenile delinquency.

HV 9069 .A68

Arnold, William R. *Juveniles on Parole: A Sociological Perspective.* New York: Random House, 1970. 177 p.

Presents a sociological analysis of the parole system. Discusses the interrelationship of its components (parolees and their peers, parole officers and their peers, parents of parolees, and others), and the importance of the characteristics and roles of each. The author believes such analysis provides the best understanding of the behavior of those in the system in order to effect changes in that behavior. He suggests that the behavior of others in the system may need modification before parolees' behavior can be changed. Includes specific changes that might be made in the parole system to improve its effectiveness.

HV 9104 .A85

Bakal, Yitzhak (Ed.). *Closing Correctional Institutions.* Lexington, Massachusetts: Lexington Books, 1973. 186 p.

The readings in this work present the case for closing correctional institutions, discuss some of the problems involved, and suggest specific alternatives. Contributors cite the failure of institutions to rehabilitate, and suggest that community-centered measures are more humane and effective as well as closer to the problem.

HV 9069 .C518

Barr, Hugh. *Volunteers in Prison After-Care.* London: George Allen and Unwin, Ltd., 1971. 167 p.

Report of a project which explored ways to involve the ordinary citizen in aftercare. Includes information on the organization and training of volunteers and implications for future projects.

HV 9348 .L6 B36

Beard, Belle B. *Juvenile Probation.* Montclair, New Jersey: Patterson Smith 1969. 219 p.

Reprint of a 1934 analysis of 500 cases of juveniles on probation in Boston. Considers such variables as quality of home life, physical and mental health, companionship, work, recreation, and education.

HV 9106 .B7 B4

Beattie, Jeann. *And the Tiger Leaps.* Toronto: McClelland and Stewart, Ltd., 1971. 216 p.

Personal narrative of a nonprofessional who becomes involved in work with delinquents and an antidelinquency group in Toronto.

HV 9108 .B4

Bernstein, Saul. *Alternatives to Violence.* New York: Association Press, 1967. 192 p.

The author relates civil rights movements, antipoverty programs and urban riots to "alienated youth," which he defines as youth with a weak self-image, lacking in self-confidence and trust, and who perceive the world as hostile. Each of the three phenomena is presented and evaluated both sympathetically and critically in terms of its success or failure to help alienated youth. Society's responsibility for overcoming poverty, prejudice, and violence is stressed.

HV 9104 .B425

Boss, Peter. *Social Policy and the Young Delinquent.* London: Routledge and Kegan Paul, 1967. 102 p.

Traces the development of policy relating to processing of the young offender. Presents historical background and examines the court, prevention efforts, and policy influences.

HV 9146 .B6

Boyle, Hugh. *Delinquency and Crime.* Westport, Connecticut: Pendulum Press, 1969. 61 p.

Examination of the causes of juvenile delinquency, with emphasis on influences of the home and society, especially the absence of pride and concern in society. Advocates preventive efforts rather than treatment programs, which are doomed to failure.

HV 9104 .B68

Bremmer, Robert H. (Ed.). *Children in Confinement.* New York: Arno Press, 1974. 324 p.

Collection of five articles on the detention of youthful offenders in the United States, which was originally published in the years 1877–1944.

HV 9104 .C44

Brennan, James J., and Donald W. Olmstead. *Training Police in Delinquency Prevention and Control.* East Lansing: Michigan State University, 1965. 280 p.

Report of a training program aimed at acquainting police with methods of delinquency control, extending their knowledge of the individual delinquent, and furthering coordination of their efforts with those of other agencies; and a report on a subsequent evaluative study designed to measure such changes. Examines such areas as police handling of delinquents, amount and kind of information gained on each offender, and attitude changes. Includes procedures and design of the study, analyses of data, and outlines of educational materials.

HV 9104 .B7

Bureau of Prisons, U.S. Department of Justice. *Differential Treatment . . . A Way to Begin.* Washington, D.C.: Bureau of Prisons, 1970. 120 p.

A practical work intended for the correctional worker. It examines the goals and operations of the Robert F. Kennedy Youth Center; presents the case for differential treatment of offenders, with analogies to the treatment of the physically ill; and emphasizes classification of offenders, with assignment to appropriately-matched staff.

HV 9106 .M62 R6

Caldwell, Robert G., and James A. Black. *Juvenile Delinquency.* New York: The Ronald Press Co., 1971. 354 p.

Summary of thinking on juvenile delinquency in the contemporary United States, including a definition of the problem and discussions of causation, treatment, and prevention.

HV 9104 .C248

California Youth Authority. *A Comparative Study of the Community Parole Center Program.* Research Report No. 63. Sacramento: California Youth Authority, January 1973. 79 p.

Report of a program utilizing seven parole centers located in areas of high juvenile delinquency, each of which serves all CYA parolees in the area. An important aspect of each center's work is the use of reduced caseloads.

HV 9103 .C2 C2 1973 #63

California Youth Authority. *Follow-Up of Wards Discharged from CYA During 1965*. Research Report No. 64. Sacramento: California Youth Authority, February 1973. 16 p.

Report of a study addressed to three concerns: the proportion of CYA wards who had committed offenses after discharge, the relationship between behavior while a CYA ward and post-discharge behavior, and the demographic characteristics related to post-discharge behavior.

HC 9103 .C2 C2 1973 #64

Carney, Frank J., Hans W. Mattick, and John D. Callaway. *Action on the Streets*. New York: Association Press, 1969. 160 p.

A "handbook for inner city youth work" which grew from the experience of the Chicago Youth Development Project (1960–1966), a three-fold attack on juvenile delinquency consisting of street club work with youth, community organization work with adults, and use of informal facilities. Contains a description of the project, its goals and organization, and the functions of outreach workers.

HV 9106 .C4 C37

Carter, Robert M. *Middle-Class Delinquency: An Experiment in Delinquency Control*. Berkeley: School of Criminology, University of California, 1968. 66 p.

Report of a project carried out in Contra Costa County, California, with goals of determining the nature and extent of delinquency in the suburbs, and developing a program to prevent and control delinquency which directly involved young people. The project was significant in that it was initiated by the communities involved.

HV 9105 .C2 C37

Cavan, Ruth Shonle, and Jordan T. Cavan. *Delinquency and Crime: Cross-Cultural Perspectives*. Philadelphia: J. B. Lippincott Co., 1968. 244 p.

An intensive study of delinquency and crime in fourteen societies, which contrasts rural and urban areas and notes the effects of social change. The study is based on published rather than original research. The authors conclude that crime is international, that it spreads across borders, and that it is defined in terms of each society's cultural values.

HV 9069 .C34

Cicourel, Aaron V. *The Social Organization of Juvenile Justice*. New York: John Wiley and Sons, Inc., 1968. 345 p.

Presents the case for the study of social organization, contending that social organization influences both community policy toward juveniles and those who implement policy. Those who implement policy bring attitudes and expectations to their work which also exert an influence on policy. Because the end result of policy is the labeling of certain youngsters as delinquent, the social organization is as worthy of study as is the phenomenon of juvenile delinquency.

HV 9069 .C512

Coffey, Alan R. *Juvenile Justice As a System*. Englewood Cliffs, New Jersey: Prentice-Hall, Inc., 1974. 152 p.

A survey of the juvenile justice system intended for students and workers in the system. Summarizes the scope and impact of juvenile delinquency; theories of causation; historical background of the juvenile court; diversion, prevention, and control; the neglected and abused child; intake, rights versus needs of youth in the system; detention; probation; treatment; institutions; parole; and the future of the juvenile court.

HV 9069 .C528

Cohen, H. L., I. Goldiamond, J. Filipczak, and R. Pooley. *Training Professionals in Procedures for the Establishment of Educational Environments.* Silver Spring, Maryland: Educational Facility Press, 1968. 102 p.

Presents procedures for training professionals in establishing effective learning environments for juveniles and applying the available behavioral technology; and reports on an intensive training session involving a combination of theory and specific techniques used at the National Training School for Boys. The book is meant to serve as a handbook for future programs.

HV 9081 .T72

Cohen, Harold L., and James Filipczak. *A New Learning Environment.* San Francisco: Jossey-Bass, Inc., 1971. 192 p.

Describes a project in "contingency management" carried out at the National Training School for Boys, in which boys were given monetary and material rewards for improved social behavior and academic performance. The project involved a 24-hour learning environment and establishment of an economy based on academic achievement and work for the administration; essentially it included choices and compensations available to wage-earning members of society. It was found that increased academic skills and positive attitudinal changes resulted.

HV 9106 .W32 N353

Cole, Larry. *Our Children's Keepers.* New York: Grossman Publishers, 1972. 152 p.

Cole is critical of juvenile correctional institutions, viewing them as both a result and a cause of problems. He traces the development of institutions, provides detailed portraits of several institutions, and presents specific cases through interviews with staff and inmates. Following this, he speculates on the reasons for the situation as it is and provides specific suggestions for positive change.

HV 9104 .C56

Committee on Mental Health Services Inside and Outside the Family Court in the City of New York. *Juvenile Justice Confounded: Pretensions and Realities of Treatment Services.* National Council on Crime and Delinquency, 1972. 124 p.

Examination of the treatment services available to the court for children adjudged delinquent or in need of supervision. Concludes that resources are least available for those in greatest need of them. The court is faced with community "pathology," manifested through denial of treatment services, in addition to the pathology of the troubled child and his family.

HV 9105 .N7 A49 1972

Conger, John J., and William C. Miller. *Personality, Social Class and Delinquency.* New York: John Wiley and Sons, Inc., 1966. 249 p.

Report of a study of boys in various academic grade levels which investigated whether certain personality traits were related to future delinquency and whether the nature and extent of these relationships varied according to the social class or intelligence of the individual. The study was exploratory rather than predictive. Researchers found differences in personality characteristics and behaviors even in early school years. They conclude that juvenile delinquency in general and certain forms of delinquency in particular are aggravated by changes in the structure of society. They also emphasize that juvenile delinquency is complex and not simply the result of socioeconomic status, cultural deprivation, or social disorganization.

HV 9069 .C58

Cortes, Juan B. *Delinquency and Crime: A Biopsychosocial Approach.* New York: Seminar Press, 1972. 468 p.

Review of biological, psychological, and social factors associated with juvenile delinquency and crime.

HV 6025 .C65

Coulter, Ernest K. *The Children in the Shadow.* College Park, Maryland: McGrath Publishing Company, 1969, 277 p.

Reprint of a 1913 work which maintains that three delinquents exist: the child, the parent, and the community. Presents causes and cures of delinquency; asserts that love, kindness, and friendship should be shown to delinquents; and considers the juvenile courts the "greatest social clinics in the world."

HV 9106 .N6 C7 1969

Cowie, John, Valerie Cowie, and Eliot Slater. *Delinquency in Girls.* New York: Humanities Press, 1968. 220 p.

Briefly summarizes earlier studies of delinquency in girls and conclusions derived from them; and reports on a new inquiry which examined age, intelligence, home and family, and psychiatric record. Concludes that differences exist in these areas between delinquent and nondelinquent girls and between delinquent girls and delinquent boys.

HV 6046 .C68

Cressey, Donald R., and David A. Ward. *Delinquency, Crime and Social Process.* New York: Harper and Row, 1969. 1151 p.

A collection of readings dealing with the statistical distribution of crime and delinquency, and the process by which individuals behave in a criminal or delinquent manner. Cressey and Ward maintain that criminality is a status conferred on certain individuals for certain acts at certain times and in certain places. They support an explanation of crime and delinquency involving epidemiology and individual expression, and maintain that the two concepts are interrelated.

HV 6028 .C67

Davies, Martin. *Probationers in Their Social Environment.* London: Her Majesty's Stationery Office, 1969. 204 p.

A study of male probationers which attempted to identify environmental variables related to reconviction. Includes analyses of living conditions, personal relationships, work, money, position in peer groups, leisure time, girlfriends and wives, and relationships with supervising officers of those reconvicted within twelve months.

HV 9146 .D3

De Fleur, Lois B. *Delinquency in Argentina.* Pullman: Washington State University Press, 1970. 164 p.

The author's work was originally an attempt to "test," cross-culturally, Albert Cohen's formulations concerning the delinquent subculture, but it resulted in a new contribution. An important finding was that marginal participation in major social institutions may be a key factor related to juvenile delinquency. De Fleur concludes that theory must be built upon each specific society.

HV 9130 .C6 D4

Diamond, James et al. *Sociological and Educational Factors in the Etiology of Juvenile Delinquency.* Syracuse: Syracuse University, 1966. 95 p.

Summary of a two-year study sponsored by the U.S. Office of Education which attempted to isolate the factors which contribute to a pattern of delinquent behavior, and to assess the role played by the school in reinforcing this behavior. Stresses the importance of the school as the most "stable and intrusive" factor in a child's life outside of the family.

HV 9076.5 .S63

Dickson, M. G. *Young Offenders in Sarawak and Sabah.* Kuching, Sarawak: Borneo Literature Bureau, 1965. 51 p.

Presents statistics on 100 young offenders from Sarawak and Sabah, states within the Federation of Malaysia. Deals with such characteristics as age, offense, previous conviction, home background, and personality.

HV 9080 .S37

Donovan, Frank R. *Wild Kids.* Harrisburg, Pennsylvania: Stackpole Books, 1967. 287 p.

Examines how concepts of juvenile delinquency have changed from primitive cultures, Greek and Roman times, and so on through the post-World War II period to the present.

HV 9065 .D6

Downes, David M. *The Delinquent Solution.* London: Routledge and Kegan Paul, 1966. 284 p.

Deals with gangs in Great Britain, examines American and British theories on the "delinquent subculture," and distinguishes between uses of the term by various researchers.

HV 9060 .D6

Eisner, Victor. *The Delinquency Label: The Epidemiology of Juvenile Delinquency.* New York: Random House, 1969. 177 p.

Eisner is critical of current methods of dealing with juvenile delinquency. He suggests an epidemiological approach in which the relative risks of becoming delinquent in an environment are analyzed. Emphasizes the importance of labeling, and of treating causes as well as effects. Specific recommendations include reducing alienation among different groups in society, focusing less on punishment and more on rehabilitation, allowing a wider range of behaviors to be acceptable, and finding a place for adolescents in society.

HV 9104 .E5

Eldefonso, Edward. *Youth Problems and Law Enforcement.* Englewood Cliffs, New Jersey: Prentice-Hall, Inc., 1972. 128 p.

This is a practical resource intended to aid in training police in the area of youth problems. Eldefonso feels that police are primarily responsible for enforcing the law and only indirectly responsible for resolving the social problem of juvenile delinquency. He presents legal and administrative definitions of juvenile delinquency; discusses differences between delinquents and nondelinquents, dependent, neglected, and abused children; methods of measurement; causes; the purposes, function, and operation of the juvenile court; juvenile law; and police handling of juveniles from arrest to disposition, with special emphasis on the problem of drug abuse.

HV 9060 .E52

Elliott, Delbert S., and Harwin L. Voss. *Delinquency and Dropout.* Lexington, Massachusetts: Lexington Books, 1974. 264 p.

In an investigation of the problem of school dropout, the authors propose that delinquency and dropout are alternative responses to failure and alienation. They suggest, and the study supports, that delinquency leads to dropping out of school, and further, that movement out of school reduces both frustration and delinquent behavior. The authors relate a number of variables to delinquency, not all of which are supported by the study, and question current antidropout campaigns.

HV 9104 .E44

Emerson, Robert M. *Judging Delinquents.* Chicago: Aldine Publishing Company, 1969. 293 p.

Report of a study conducted in a juvenile court in a large metropolitan area. The study analyzed the nature and consequences of the court's effort to implement treatment as an organizational goal, the practices it used in dealing with the cases brought before it, and the nature of the delinquent's contacts with court personnel and their effect on assessments made of his character.

KF 9709 .E44

Empey, Lamar T. and Maynard L. Erickson. *The Provo Experiment.* Lexington, Massachusetts: D. C. Heath and Company, 1972. 321 p.

Report of one of the first attempts to provide a community alternative to incarceration for habitual delinquents. The authors present the underlying assumptions of the experiment, discuss the impact of the program on offenders, and describe the experimental operation.

HV 9106 .P93 E56

Fenton, Norman and Ernest A. Taron (Eds.). *Training Staff for Program Development in Youth Correctional Institutions.* Sacramento: Institute for the Study of Crime and Delinquency, 1965. 180 p.

Report of a training program for institutional middle-management staff, the goal of which was to prepare all classes of employees to work together as a team in the treatment program of the institution.

HV 7428 .F45

Fleisher, Belton M. *The Economics of Delinquency*. Chicago: Quadrangle Books, 1966. 127 p.

Fleisher, an economist, attempts to discover the relationships between economic factors and delinquency, and to identify and evaluate the influences of non-economic factors. He concludes that economic factors are intimately related to delinquency, and presents implications for policy development.

HV 9069 .F5

Fourth Annual Seminar on Juvenile Delinquency Prevention and Control, A Report. Lawrence, Kansas: Governmental Research Center, The University of Kansas, 1966. 58 p.

Report of a seminar which brought together individuals from a variety of disciplines concerned with juvenile delinquency. Discusses roles of police and the juvenile court, juvenile legislation, and coordination of efforts of the disciplines which handle juveniles.

HV 9058 .S45 no. 4

Frankenstein, Carl. *Varieties of Juvenile Delinquency*. London: Gordon and Breach Science Publishers, 1970. 252 p.

Deals with the types of juvenile delinquency and their causes and symptoms. The author emphasizes "waywardness"—because the largest number of delinquents are of this type—and psychopathy—because of its "disquieting" nature.

HV 9060 .F685

Franklin, Marjorie E. (Ed.). *Q Camp*. The Planned Environment Therapy Trust, 1966. 68 p.

Report of the activities of Hawkspur Camp, a therapeutic camp for young offenders and those unable to adapt to society. Summarizes characteristics of treatment, including a valuation for individual personality, sincerity, and love; internal government of the camp; and daily camp life.

HV 9146 .Q2

Giallombardo, Rose (Ed.). *Readings in Juvenile Delinquency*. New York: John Wiley and Sons, Inc., 1966. 565 p.

Collection of forty-four articles with a sociological orientation dealing with the following topics: definition and measurement, causes, delinquent groups, the juvenile court, treatment, and prevention.

HV 9060 .G445

Giallombardo, Rose. *The Social World of Imprisoned Girls*. New York: John Wiley and Sons, Inc., 1974. 317 p.

Report of a study which suggests that the inmate social system reflects the system of the outside society, not merely the values and attitudes of those who enter the institution. Further implications are that the goal emphasis of the institution has an impact on the inmate organization; thus the informal social system can aid or hinder treatment.

HV 9104 .G5

Gibbens, T. C. N., and R. H. Ahrenfeldt (Eds.). *Cultural Factors in Delinquency.* London: Tavistock, 1966. 201 p.

Report of a meeting of an international group representing a variety of disciplines which met to discuss the contribution of cultural factors to juvenile delinquency. Participants discussed definitions of delinquency, male versus female involvement, age, social class, role of the police, subcultures, internal controls, comparability of statistics between countries, learning and unlearning delinquency, trends in delinquency in various countries, research, and the difficulty of reaching agreement on programs for action.

HV 9069 .G46

Gibbons, Don C. *Changing the Lawbreaker.* Englewood Cliffs, New Jersey: Prentice-Hall, Inc., 1965. 306 p.

Gibbons describes this work as a "primer on treatment theory," which emphasizes that type of treatment must be tailored to type of offender. A major problem of treatment is reversing the learning process, in effect, "unlearning" delinquent behavior. Typology is important, as are the nature and forms of treatment, and obstacles to treatment, especially the workings of social patterns within correctional institutions.

HV 9275 .G5

Gibbons, Don C. *Delinquent Behavior.* Englewood Cliffs, New Jersey: Prentice-Hall, Inc., 1970. 276 p.

Gibbons uses existing data on delinquency to present a general overview of the problem. Although sociologically oriented, the work does identify ways in which psychological and sociological factors interact. Covers definitions, laws, statistics, police and court dealings with delinquents, "official delinquency," causes, forms of delinquency, international perspectives, and corrections. The author emphasizes that what is needed is further research aimed at a judicious combination of the various lines of thought into a coherent body of knowledge.

HV 9104 .G53

Glueck, Sheldon, and Eleanor T. Glueck. *Delinquents and Nondelinquents in Perspective.* Cambridge, Massachusetts: Harvard University, 1968. 268 p.

Presents findings of a detailed follow-up inquiry into the conduct of the matched juvenile offenders and nonoffenders of *Unraveling Juvenile Delinquency* through adolescence and adulthood. Some of the factors examined included health, academic achievement, vocational training, domestic relations, work history, economic conditions, interests, and ambitions. The authors also present theoretical and practical implications of their work for prevention.

HV 9069 .G537

Glueck, Sheldon, and Eleanor T. Glueck (Eds.). *Identification of Predelinquents.* New York: Intercontinental Medical Book Corporation, 1972. 150 p.

The book is an outgrowth of a session on identification of predelinquents at the Sixth International Congress of Criminology in 1970. Various facets of identification are explored in the articles. According to the editors, prediction is the most fruitful concept in criminology.

HV 9069 .G539

Glueck, Sheldon, Eleanor T. Glueck, and Franco Ferracuti. *Replication of Unraveling Juvenile Delinquency in Puerto Rico.* Cambridge, Massachusetts: Harvard University, Cooperative Research Programs of the Office of Education, U.S. Department of Health, Education, and Welfare, 1966. 321 p.

The authors discuss an attempt to replicate the work described in *Unraveling Juvenile Delinquency.* They summarize the design of the study; analyze similarities and differences between results of the original studies in Boston and the studies in Puerto Rico; and draw inferences for further investigations and for practical, constructive changes in educational, social welfare, and family guidance programs.

HV 9069 .G55 1966

Glueck, Sheldon, and Eleanor T. Glueck. *Toward a Typology of Juvenile Offenders.* New York: Grune and Stratton, 1970. 203 p.

The authors discuss the concept of "type," present a sample of typological approaches, and describe typology. In their view, the types can be arranged along a continuum from those whose prognosis is most favorable to the "core type" delinquent. Data from their earlier works are used as foundations for development of treatment strategies.

HV 9069 .G545

Gold, Martin. *Delinquent Behavior in an American City.* Belmont, California: Brooks-Cole, 1970. 150 p.

Report of a study conducted in Flint, Michigan, which attempted to obtain a clear picture of delinquent behavior. Gold stresses the distinction between delinquency and delinquent behavior, and concludes that present knowledge about juvenile delinquency may not apply to delinquent behavior. Furthermore, varying degrees of delinquency exist. Since almost everyone breaks the law, the idea of "the delinquent" is invalid.

HV 9104 .G63

Goldman, Ronald. *Angry Adolescents.* London: Routledge and Kegan Paul, 1969, 119 p.

Account of a group of adolescents and their establishment of a youth club near London, England.

HV 1441 .G7 G64

Goshen, Charles E. *Society and the Youthful Offender.* Springfield, Illinois: Charles C Thomas, 1974. 167 p.

Goshen attempts to redirect attention to the majority of cases of delinquency which are routine and undramatic. He maintains that the criminal justice system is not designed for such offenders. His suggested changes include redirection of attention to the victims of crime, professionalism of law enforcement and correctional personnel, investigations of the responsibilities of and alternatives to prison, emphasis on prevention, reorientation of the system of occupational entry, programs designed for the multiproblem family, and revision of the allocation of responsibilities among components of the criminal justice system.

HV 9069 .G66

Graubard, Paul S. (Ed.). *Children Against Schools.* Chicago: Follett Educational Corporation, 1969. 376 p.

The book is intended for students and individuals with responsibilities for the education of delinquent, disturbed, and disruptive children. Its purpose is to reduce the time which exists between research findings and classroom applications; to convey specific skills to practitioners; and to define and attempt to solve problems. Included are sixteen articles which deal with the social context of problem behavior, development of approaches to education, and practical applications.

HV 9081 .G7

Hahn, Paul H. *The Juvenile Offender and the Law.* Cincinnati: The W. H. Anderson Company, 1971. 416 p.

Hahn attempts to give police an understanding of juvenile delinquency. He stresses the importance of teamwork between the police, the courts, and corrections, and the need for police to be at least as knowledgeable about juvenile delinquency as the other components of the criminal justice system. He provides a thorough introduction to the subject, discussing such topics as classification of offenders, causes of delinquency, types of delinquent manifestations, drugs, alcohol, prevention, the police approach to juvenile offenders, the philosophy and procedures of the juvenile court, and treatment.

HV 9069 .H23

Hardt, Robert H., and George E. Bodine. *Development of Self-Report Instruments in Delinquency Research.* Syracuse, New York: Syracuse University Youth Development Center, 1965. 33 p.

Report of a conference convened to investigate the self-report technique—direct questioning of adolescents about their delinquent activities—as a tool in gathering statistical data about juvenile delinquency.

HV 9104 .H26

Hardy, Richard E., and John G. Cull. *Climbing Ghetto Walls: Disadvantagement, Delinquency and Rehabilitation.* Springfield, Illinois: Charles C Thomas, 1973. 195 p.

The book is written for psychologists, social workers, and counselors who work with delinquents. Hardy and Cull discuss causes of delinquency, stressing the importance of family environment; indices of prediction; and suggestions for treatment, including counseling of parents, guided group interaction, and objectives of institutional treatment.

HV 9069 .H315

Hardy, Richard E., and John G. Cull. *Fundamentals of Juvenile Criminal Behavior and Drug Abuse.* Springfield, Illinois: Charles C Thomas, 1975. 258 p.

The authors take a multidisciplinary stance in discussing current trends in rehabilitation of the delinquent, the delinquent's environment, reasons for his behavior, and specific case studies. Included is information on the types of drugs, their effects, and drug terminology.

HV 9069 .H316

Hardy, Richard E., and John G. Cull (Eds.). *Problems of Adolescents: Social and Psychological Approaches.* Springfield, Illinois: Charles C Thomas, 1974. 278 p.

Written for professionals who work with adolescents, the fifteen articles discuss the male and female juvenile delinquent, importance of the family, prediction of delinquency, environmental factors, runaway behavior, the drug problem, use of college students as volunteers, development of employment opportunities, and rehabilitation. Because a practical approach is taken to the problems of adolescents, much emphasis is placed on the drug problem and runaway behavior. The contributors discuss the effects of drugs, the drug abuser and his language, and his rehabilitation. Case studies are included, and suggestions for working in each of the areas discussed are presented.

HV 9069 .H3168

Hardy, Richard E., and John G. Cull. *Psychological and Vocational Rehabilitation of the Youthful Delinquent.* Springfield, Illinois: Charles C Thomas, 1974, 248 p.

The book includes articles by the authors and nine other contributors which describe the delinquent, types of delinquent behavior, and approaches to rehabilitation, including behavior modification, guided group interaction, and development of employment opportunities. It contains both theoretical and practical information, and is intended for both student and practitioner.

HV 9069 .H317

Haskell, Martin K., and Lewis Yablonsky. *Crime and Delinquency.* Chicago: Rand, McNally and Company, 1970. 517 p.

The authors attempt to describe the nature and extent of crime and delinquency and to provide specific recommendations for reducing its occurrence. They discuss causes, the juvenile court, juvenile delinquency and the socialization process, the gang as a near-group, and treatment and control.

HV 9069 .H327

Hawes, Joseph M. *Children in Urban Society.* New York: Oxford University Press, 1971. 315 p.

Hawes traces juvenile misbehavior from colonial days to the present, emphasizing that juvenile delinquency is not a recent phenomenon. In attempting to present a complete narrative of American responses to the problem, he makes the following observations: (1) the trend toward more humane treatment is part of a general concern in Western countries; (2) the history of juvenile delinquency is basically a history of the city, since the city concentrates individual antisocial acts and lends increased visibility to them; and (3) government agencies and institutions and city government as a whole are inadequate to deal with the problem. Individual cases are presented to support these observations.

HV 9104 .H35

Hirschi, Travis. *Causes of Delinquency.* Berkeley: University of California Press, 1969. 309 p.

Hirschi criticizes strain, control, and cultural deviance theories, advocating instead a social control theory which views the delinquent as a person lacking the aspirations and beliefs which hold most individuals to a law-abiding life.

He stresses the importance of constructing a theory which is compatible with empirical data.

HV 9096 .U5 H56

Hirschi, Travis, and Hanan C. Selvin. *Delinquency Research: An Appraisal of Analytical Methods.* New York: The Free Press, 1967. 280 p.

An examination of published analyses of quantitative data on delinquency, which emphasizes that the most important part of a study is analysis. When approaching data the researcher is advised to be in the proper frame of mind, with objectivity, vigilance, and sympathy.

HV 9068 .H5

Hoenig, Gary. *Reaper: The Story of a Gang Leader.* Indianapolis: The Bobbs-Merrill Company, Inc., 1975. 168 p.

In-depth case history of a delinquent in Brooklyn which recounts the events leading to his gang involvement. Includes the author's comments on the social situation on the street.

HV 9106 .N6 H63

Hopewell, John A., and Frances K. Kernohan. *Out of Sight–Out of Mind.* New York: Community Service Society of New York, 1968. 56 p.

Report of an examination of New York state training schools by the Committee on Youth and Correction of the Community Service Society of New York. Included are a brief summary of the juvenile justice system, a historical view of juvenile delinquency, and a number of case studies.

HV 9105 .N7 H6

Hughes, Helen MacGill (Ed.). *Delinquents and Criminals: Their Social World.* Boston: Allyn and Bacon, Inc., 1970. 211 p.

Twenty readings on the subjects of delinquency, crime and deviance, most of which relate to delinquency. In addition to providing a description of delinquency, they discuss the nature of the problem and the process by which a young person becomes delinquent; the behavior choices available to the young person before committing a crime; kinds of delinquent behavior and the consequences of a lack of moral support from the family; delinquency and social status; and middle-class delinquency.

HV 9104 .H9

Hussain, Syed. *Juvenile Delinquency.* Madras: Madras Book Agency, 1967. 83 p.

Deals with juvenile delinquency in India, discussing definition; the most prevalent types of delinquent behavior; causes, including economic factors, home environment, and personal factors; and treatment. Hussain maintains that the present form of the problem is a result of urban, industrial society.

HV 9069 .H85

International Penal and Prison Commission. *Children's Courts in the United States.* New York: AMS Press, Inc., 1973. 203 p.

Reprint of the 1904 report of the International Prison Commission which was submitted to the U.S. Congress. The report strongly recommended and supported the juvenile court, citing its paternal attitude as an indication of a new spirit in corrections. Contains reports of courts established and operating in eight states at the time in addition to summaries of juvenile court laws in various states.

HV 9091 .I6 1973

James, Howard. *Children in Trouble.* New York: David McKay Company, Inc., 1970. 340 p.

Through presentation of specific cases, James raises doubts about what the juvenile justice system is now doing to combat delinquency and offers recommendations. He is critical of institutions, viewing them as "damaging"; and of the process by which those employed in institutions come to see them as "normal" environments.

HV 9104 .J34

Jurjevich, Ratibor-Ray M. *No Water in My Cup: Experiences and a Controlled Study of Psychotherapy of Delinquent Girls.* New York: Libra Publishers, Inc., 1968. 185 p.

Discussion of "relationship therapy," an individualistic psychotherapy characterized by a genuine interest in helping and re-education. Jurjevich includes examples from his work at a training school for girls. He presents results of a comparison of test scores which showed significantly larger psychological and behavior improvement in institutionalized delinquent girls treated in individual psychotherapy than in those exposed only to institutional training.

RJ 503 .J8

Juvenile Delinquency: A Report on State Action and Responsibilities. Chicago: The Council of State Governments, 1965. 96 p.

The report was prepared for the Governors' Conference Committee in 1962, and is supplemented with material based on returns from questionnaires circulated among state authorities in 1964. It deals with practical rather than theoretical aspects of prevention, treatment, and control of juvenile delinquency, emphasizing the role of the states in these areas. Recommends coordination of programs and services and development of leadership.

HV 9104 .C6 1965

Kassebaum, Gene G. *Delinquency and Social Policy.* Englewood Cliffs, New Jersey: Prentice-Hall, Inc., 1974. 186 p.

The book is concerned with the way in which youth are defined as delinquent, the manner in which official agencies deal with them, and the resulting effects. Emphasis is on the social process by which juveniles are arrested, adjudicated, supervised, and instructed. Kassebaum feels that delinquency is built into society; most conflict which is labeled juvenile delinquency arises from child-adult conflict which cannot be understood apart from social conflict.

HV 9069 .K36

Kenney, John P., and Dan G. Pursuit. *Police Work with Juveniles and the Administration of Juvenile Justice.* Springfield, Illinois: Charles C Thomas, 1970. 423 p.

A manual for police departments with juvenile units. It emphasizes that police must work closely with other components of the criminal justice system and that police have a responsibility for the welfare of children and youth. Contains information on the juvenile justice system, law, the police role, processing of the offender, and prevention programs.

HV 9069 .K3 1970

Khanna, J. L. (Ed.). *New Treatment Approaches to Juvenile Delinquency.* Springfield, Illinois: Charles C Thomas, 1975, 157 p.

Contains papers given at a workshop on treatment approaches. The topics discussed include the extent of officially-labeled juvenile delinquency; prediction and prevention; and contingency management of delinquent behavior. Participants discussed the use of token economies, the reversal of contingencies which maintain delinquent behavior, forms of behavior modification, and examples of new treatment approaches.

HV 9104 .N38 1975

Klare, Hugh J. *Delinquency, Social Support and Control Systems.* London: The London School of Economics and Political Science, G. Bell and Sons, Ltd., 1966. 30 p.

Klare examines the relationships of four social support and control systems to juvenile delinquency: the personal social services, penal social services (institutions, probation, and aftercare), courts, and government. He stresses their interdependence and calls for increased coordination between penal and social services, and the development of new concepts of social work. Klare also discusses self-help efforts and calls for a better-informed public to aid in combatting juvenile delinquency.

HV 7428 .K57

Klein, Malcolm W. (Ed.). *Juvenile Gangs in Context.* Englewood Cliffs, New Jersey: Prentice-Hall, Inc., 1967. 210 p.

Contains fifteen articles on juvenile gang delinquency by practitioners, researchers, and scholars in the area. Included are descriptions of gang delinquency, police contacts, and treatment programs.

HV 9069 .J8

Klein, Malcolm W. *Street Gangs and Street Workers.* Englewood Cliffs, New Jersey: Prentice-Hall, Inc., 1971. 338 p.

Klein presents current knowledge about gangs, information on gang workers and programs, and a report of a project carried out in California which combined action and research to gain more information about the gang. He believes that current approaches to reducing gang delinquency are unproductive; the gang member has numerous opportunities for getting into trouble while the gang worker is almost devoid of resources necessary to reduce those opportunities.

HV 7428 .K6

Knight, Doug. *Delinquency Causes and Remedies: The Working Assumptions of California Youth Authority Staff.* Research Report No. 61. Sacramento: California Youth Authority, 1972. 163 p.

Report of a survey of California Youth Authority staff. Researchers attempted to use staff experience in developing a statement about implications for reducing juvenile delinquency, and to understand the working assumptions held by staff members. Staff agreed that causes are complex; diversion from the criminal justice system should be a priority; the problem should be solved in the community; and the California Youth Authority should be both a social-policy advocate and a direct-action prevention agency.

HV 9103 .C2 C2 #61

Korn, Richard R. (Ed.). *Juvenile Delinquency.* New York: Thomas Y. Crowell Co., 1968. 257 p.

Contains excerpts from *Wayward Youth; The Gang; The Jack-Roller; Street Corner Society; Children Who Hate; The Addict in the Street; Manchild in the Promised Land;* and *Rivers of Blood, Years of Darkness.*

HV 9061 .K67

Leinwald, Gerald, and Carol West. *Crime and Juvenile Delinquency.* New York: Washington Square Press, 1968. 159 p.

An introduction to crime and delinquency in urban areas. Some of the topics discussed are the amount, definition, and distribution of delinquency; its causes; treatment; and the difficulty of the police role.

HV 6789 .L44

Lemert, Edwin M. *Instead of Court.* Chevy Chase, Maryland: National Institute of Mental Health, Center for Studies of Crime and Delinquency, 1971. 95 p.

Lemert feels that too many children are processed by the juvenile court and that the harm done to them outweighs any benefits. He examines a number of alternatives for diverting youth from the courts, among which are the school, welfare agencies, police, and community organizations. A major problem with these agencies is the phenomenon of labeling, whereby a juvenile comes to see himself as delinquent and subsequently behaves according to expectations. According to Lemert, new ways of perceiving the concept of prevention must be developed which consider the consequences of agency policies and actions. All children engage in delinquent behavior; therefore efforts should be made to control rather than prevent such behavior. Forms of juvenile delinquency are defined into existence; therefore they can be defined out of existence.

HV 9065 .L4

Lemert, Edwin M. *Social Action and Legal Change: Revolution Within the Juvenile Court.* Chicago: Aldine Publishing Co., 1970. 248 p.

Account of the revision of California's juvenile court laws in 1961 and an analysis of the social action behind the revision. The study, conducted through interviews, committee reports, questionnaires, and examinations of files, was addressed to the question of how law develops, the specific processes which produce revolutionary change, and the extent to which legislation affects the direction of change.

KFC 1177 .L4

Lerman, Paul (Ed.). *Delinquency and Social Policy.* New York: Praeger Publishers, 1970. 488 p.

Contains forty-two articles dealing with the major issues in prevention and control of juvenile delinquency—its definition and legal basis, control and guidance of police handling of delinquents, assuring fairness in the administration of justice, correctional practices, and social planning to prevent and control delinquency.

HV 9104 .L37

Loble, Lester H., and Max Wylie. *Delinquency Can Be Stopped.* New York: McGraw-Hill Book Company, 1967. 148 p.

The authors are highly critical of the leniency inherent in the present juvenile law, methods of dealing with juvenile offenders, and those who process juveniles through the criminal justice system. The law is seen as overly idealistic and obsolete; youths are treated as disadvantaged instead of criminal; and practitioners are ignorant of the effects of their permissiveness, the current juvenile "crime wave." The authors recommend that juvenile proceedings should not be hidden; that offenders should be made publicly answerable for their crimes; and that attention should be paid to the victims of crime. They emphasize that it is not society that is responsible for crime, but the offender who commits it.

HV 9105 .M9 L6

MacIver, Robert M. *The Prevention and Control of Delinquency.* New York: Atherton Press, 1967. 215 p.

MacIver states that the causes and solutions to the problem of juvenile delinquency are complex and emphasizes the need for a centralized strategy based on research to deal with it. He criticizes a number of theories of causation while calling for investigation into the conditions under which delinquency occurs more frequently, and the groups most affected by it. Emphasizes the importance of reaching youth before they become delinquent, since research has shown prevention to be more successful than rehabilitation.

HV 9069 .M26

Martin, John M., Joseph P. Fitzpatrick, and Robert E. Gould. *The Analysis of Delinquent Behavior: A Structural Approach.* New York: Random House, 1970. 208 p.

The authors advocate the use of structural analysis in understanding delinquent behavior and in developing programs to deal with delinquency. This method of analysis considers the historical antecedents as well as situational causes of a given delinquent act. Juvenile delinquency is related to the organization of the total urban community. The authors maintain that the causes of delinquency lie in social and political inequality, and further, that gross inequalities exist in police, judicial, and correctional systems.

HV 9104 .M26

McArthur, A. Verne. *Coming Out Cold.* Lexington, Massachusetts: Lexington Books, 1974. 131 p.

The book is concerned with the situation confronting the offender as he is released from a state reformatory. Through interviews with thirty-four youthful offenders and their mothers conducted from one week prior to release to four weeks after release, the author explores the problems of community reentry as experienced by the offenders and as shaped by institutional procedures. He concludes that the situation awaiting the released offender virtually insures that he will fail to become a productive, law-abiding citizen, and he raises serious questions about the criminal justice system's neglect of the people entrusted to it.

HV 9104 .M18

Manzanera, Luis Rodriguez. *La Delinquencia de Menores en Mexico.* Mexico: Ediciones Botas, 1971. 343 p.

Deals primarily with juvenile delinquency in Mexico City. Includes discussions of causes, kinds of delinquency, treatment, and prevention.

HV 9111 .A5 R6

Mennel, Robert M. *Thorns and Thistles: Juvenile Delinquents in the United States 1825-1940.* Hanover, New Hampshire: The University Press of New England, 1973. 231 p.

Traces the history of prevention, control, and explanation of juvenile delinquency in the United States from 1825 to 1940, with a very brief summary of developments since 1940. Concludes that economically disadvantaged youths have been stigmatized to a greater degree than the affluent; institutions also stigmatize their populations and lead them into adult criminal behaviors; and that change will occur only when the social structure is reorganized.

HV 9104 .M45

Monger, Mark. *Casework in Aftercare.* London: Butterworth, 1967. 218 p.

Monger outlines the ways in which casework can be used in aftercare with adult and juvenile offenders. He discusses the method of casework, its applicability to aftercare, and its use within and without the institution.

HV 9346 .M68

Moore, Arthur E. *The New Justice for Children and Families.* Oxford, Michigan: Camp Oakland, Inc., 1965. 111 p.

The author, a former judge, describes the programs of Camp Oakland for delinquent and neglected children and youth, and emphasizes the importance of family in both causes and cures of juvenile delinquency. He feels that the court should be a leader in prevention and should not be punitive.

HV 9105 .M52 C3

Moore, Joe Alex. *First Offender.* New York: Funk and Wagnalls, 1970. 214 p.

Describes a program in Royal Oak, Michigan, involving citizen volunteers who work with delinquents on a one-to-one basis under guidance of professionals.

HV 9106 .R62 V65

Morse, Mary. *The Unattached.* Baltimore: Penguin Books, 1965. 228 p.

Report of a three-year project carried out by the National Association of Youth Clubs in Great Britain to reach youth unattached to any kind of youth organization. Discusses the unattached youths, how they were contacted, and the goals the workers attempted to achieve within the local communities.

HV 1441 .G7 M6

Mueller, O. W. *Delinquency and Puberty.* New York: New York University
School of Law, 1971. 123 p.

A study of "hidden" juvenile delinquency—law violations which do not
come to the attention of authorities—which traces the movement of a fad
involving theft across the United States.

HV 9104 .M8

Mukherjee, Satyanshu Kumar. *Administration of Juvenile Correctional Institutions.* New Delhi: Sterling Publishers Private Ltd., 1974. 304 p.

Report of a study of juvenile correctional institutions in India. The study
focused on policy and legislation, institutional services, problems in administration, and practical solutions developed by administrators.

HV 9199 .D45 M84

Murphy, Patrick T. *Our Kindly Parent-The State.* New York: The Viking Press,
1974. 180 p.

A criticism of the juvenile justice system by a lawyer who maintains that the
system does more harm than good. Murphy traces the history of the juvenile
court, claims that numerous abuses exist, and cites specific cases to illustrate
his charges.

HV 9104 .M87 1974

National Council on Crime and Delinquency. *Citizen Action to Control Crime
and Delinquency.* New York: National Council on Crime and Delinquency,
1969. 63 p.

Contains a list of projects for prevention and control of juvenile delinquency
which can be implemented by citizen groups.

HV 7431 .N3 1969

National Governors' Conference on Juvenile Delinquency, Summary. New York:
The Council of State Governments, 1967. 35 p.

Presents summaries of participant addresses and discussion sessions of the
conference, which was concerned with the significance of recent court
decisions, federal-state relations, and new trends in dealing with delinquency.

HV 9058 .N3

Neighborhood Gangs: A Case Book for Youth Workers. New York: National
Federation of Settlements and Neighborhood Centers, 1967. 55 p.

Presents case studies for use in staff training. The studies involve a variety
of situations actually faced by workers, together with background, the
worker's report, and questions for discussion.

HV 7428 .N3

Oklahoma Council on Juvenile Delinquency Planning. *A Summary of Recommendations.* 1971. 18 p.

Summary of the recommendations presented in *Youth In Trouble—A Shared
Concern.*

HV 9105 .05 A45 Summary

Oklahoma Council on Juvenile Delinquency Planning. *Youth In Trouble—A Shared Concern.* 1971. 231 p.

Report of a two-year study by the Council which presents specific recommendations for improvement in the areas of delinquency prevention and control; rehabilitation of those already enmeshed in the criminal justice system; such special problems as drug abuse, overrepresentation of minority groups in the delinquent population, and staff training; and responses of the citizen, the media, agencies and lawmakers to the problem of juvenile delinquency. The report also presents the background and evolution of the project.

HV 9105 .05 A45

Palmer, Theodore B. *An Evaluation of Community Treatment for Delinquents.* Seventh Progress Report, Part 3. California Youth Authority, 1968. 33 p.

Deals with the process of decision-making in the California Youth Authority's Community Treatment Project. Researchers questioned whether decisions to revoke or restore to parole varied as a function of the experimental or control status of each offender involved in the project, and whether such differential decision making could be justified. The report presents and compares types of offenses committed by experimental and control offenders, establishes that differential decision making does exist in the project, summarizes the factors related to it, and examines the relationships between given decisions and the objective of favorable discharge from the authority.

HV 9105 .C2 C2 No. 9 Pt. 3

Pathak, Sumitra. *Social Background of the Delinquent Child.* Agra, India : Agra University Press, 1967. 171 p.

Presents case studies of sixty delinquents. Considers the influences of such factors as home and family, environmental conditions, and the community.

HV 9190 .P37

Pearson, John W., Sharlene E. Haire, and Theodore B. Palmer. *The Group Home Project—A Demonstration Project: Differential Treatment Environments for Delinquents.* Research Report No. 2. Sacramento: California Youth Authority, 1968. 135 p.

Report of a project designed to determine the feasibility of establishing five types of group homes, each differing in attitudes and handling of wards, and maintaining an environment specific to the needs of particular types of delinquents. The project also attempted to classify the attributes of each environment, and to evaluate the impact of each home upon its wards.

HV 9105 .C2 P4

Pickett, Robert S. *House of Refuge.* Syracuse: Syracuse University Press, 1969. 217 p.

Documents in detail the history of the refuge movement in the United States. The author feels that present-day sociologists and other practitioners in the field have an ignorance of history, and attempts to remedy this situation. He believes that the ideas which shaped the refuge movement underlie current notions about both causes and treatment of juvenile delinquency.

HV 9105 .N77

Platt, Anthony M. *The Child Savers.* Chicago: The University of Chicago Press, 1969. 230 p.

Platt links contemporary programs of delinquency control with the child-saving movement of the late nineteenth century. He studies the origins, nature, and achievements of the movement in an attempt to understand the relationship between social reforms and concomitant changes in the criminal justice system; the methods by which communities have an input in regulating crime; and the gap between the ideal and the actual in the implementation of change. Emphasis is placed on the development of the juvenile court in Illinois, theories of criminology, the value of punishment, and the civil liberties of youth.

HV 9104 .P53

Polsky, Howard W., and D. S. Claster. *The Dynamics of Residential Treatment.* Chapel Hill: University of North Carolina Press, 1968. 223 p.

Report of a study of residential cottages at Hawthorne Cedar Knolls School, a treatment center for disturbed and delinquent boys and girls. Through observation of specific interactions and behavior patterns, the study examined differences in cottage-care orientation and management and their resulting impact on peer-group organization and treatment.

HV 9106 .H35 P6

Pond, Esther M. *The Los Angeles Community Delinquency Control Project: An Experiment in the Rehabilitation of Delinquents in an Urban Community.* Research Report No. 60. Sacramento: California Youth Authority, 1970. 51 p.

The study questioned whether first offenders assigned to the Community Delinquency Control Project would perform as well (as measured by parole performance) as comparable youngsters assigned to the regular institutional and parole program. The CDCP program included intensive individual, family, and group counseling; tutoring; and school and employer liaison services; in addition to the use of a reduced caseload. No significant differences were found between the programs on parole performance measures; but it was found that the CDCP program was shorter, more economical, and equally effective in the rehabilitation of offenders in low income areas.

HV 9103 .C2 C2 1970 #60

Poston, Richard W. *The Gang and the Establishment.* New York: Harper and Row, Publishers, 1971. 269 p.

Poston describes an attempt by gang members to help other ghetto youth through elimination of poverty, establishment of job programs, day-care programs, etc. With support from private foundations, the Office of Economic Opportunity, business firms, city government and police, the youths formed an organization aimed toward constructive neighborhood development. The author tells of the problems associated with the attempt—which included failure to get neighborhood youth involved, in-fighting, and squandering of grant money—describes its ultimate failure, and gives suggestions for constructive use of grant funds.

HV 6795 .N5 P68

Powers, Edwin, and Helen Witmer. *An Experiment in the Prevention of Delinquency*. Montclair, New Jersey: Patterson Smith, 1972. 649 p.

Report of a study which investigated the idea that delinquency can be prevented through "sustained and directed friendship." Powers and Witmer suggest that a major cause of juvenile delinquency is the lack of such attachment, especially in the home. The study was longitudinal and offered one group of boys an additional measure of friendly and supportive counseling over the ordinary social services received by the other group.

HV 9069 .P73 1972

President's Commission on Law Enforcement and Criminal Justice. *Task Force Report: Juvenile Delinquency and Youth Crime*. Washington, D.C.: U.S. Government Printing Office, 1967. 428 p.

Contains twenty-two articles which deal with the administration of juvenile justice and the understanding and prevention of juvenile delinquency. Includes the Gault decision, a survey of juvenile courts and probation services, and an exploration of some of the difficulties within the juvenile justice system, accompanied by suggestions for improvement. The contributors also present statistics on juvenile delinquency, and relate affluence, the youth culture, importance of identity, family relationships, the school, economic factors, and recreation to juvenile delinquency. Also discussed are assessment and prediction, and prevention and control.

HV 6789 .A33

Proceedings of the Third Annual Conference on Juvenile Problems. Savannah, Georgia: The Community Services Department, Armstrong State College and the Chatham County Juvenile Court, 1967. 86 p.

Proceedings of the conference, which was concerned with, among other things, the qualifications of a probation staff; constitutional rights of the juvenile offender; the increase in juvenile delinquency in the United States; public misunderstanding of probation, courts, and detention; involvement of parents of delinquents in rehabilitation; use of groups in treatment; and practical suggestions for prevention.

HV 9058 .C6 No. 3

Pursuit, Dan G. et al. (Eds.). *Police Programs for Preventing Crime and Delinquency*. Springfield, Illinois: Charles C Thomas, 1972. 490 p.

Seventy readings which deal with the following subjects: law enforcement's role in crime prevention, programs for community relations, prevention programs for specific offenses, educational programs, recreational programs, technological programs, and funding resources and requirements. The editors' criteria for selecting the programs included the following: the programs were innovative, used evaluative procedures, used officer time efficiently, involved volunteers and citizens effectively, were applicable to various communities, were applicable to youths of different ages, and/or tended to improve the police image.

HV 8031 .P58

Quay, Herbert C. (Ed.). *Juvenile Delinquency: Research and Theory*. Princeton, New Jersey: D. Van Nostrand Co., 1965. 350 p.

Nine articles which deal with incidence, history, etiology, and definition of juvenile delinquency; social disorganization and delinquent subcultures; family interaction and juvenile delinquency; intellectual functioning; personality; prediction; community action; treatment in institutional settings; and the educational system. According to Quay, theory and research are closely related, since theory must be tested.

HV 9104 .Q3

Reckless, Walter C. *The Crime Problem.* New York: Appleton-Century-Crofts, 1967. 830 p.

A criminology text which deals with the characteristics, causes, and correction of crime and juvenile delinquency in the United States.

HV 6025 .R46 !967

Reckless, Walter C., and Simon Dinitz. *The Prevention of Juvenile Delinquency: An Experiment.* Columbus: Ohio State University Press, 1972. 253 p.

The experiment described in this work consisted of four phases: development of theory—that self-concept acts as an insulator against delinquency—and testing of the theory; development of a school-based prevention program at the sixth-grade level in certain schools; implementation of the program at seventh-grade level in all inner-city schools; and evaluation through an annual follow-up of all participating students and home interviews with a sample of participants. The authors view juvenile delinquency as an inherent part of our social system and as an entity much affected by the family, the community, and the value structure. Findings showed few differences between participants and nonparticipants in the program. The authors offer possible explanations for such findings and suggest directions for further research.

HV 9069 .R413

Richette, Lisa. *The Throwaway Children.* Philadelphia: J. B. Lippincott Co., 1969. 342 p.

Richette is concerned with the juvenile court and its problems, and with the welfare of children and the difficulties they have in dealing with adults, society, and agencies designed to help them. She notes a sense of frustration in the court due to public demands for control and punishment rather than treatment and rehabilitation.

HV 9106 .P5 R5

Rosenberg, Bernard, and Harry Silverstein. *The Varieties of Delinquent Experience.* Waltham, Massachusetts: Blaisdell Co., 1969. 165 p.

Report of a study which attempted to dispel the typical stereotype of the delinquent, and to oppose specifically the theories of Robert K. Merton and Oscar Lewis. The study questioned whether cultural differences exist between groups in similar economic circumstances and whether these differences determine juvenile delinquency; and explored the concept of anomie. In interviewing 133 adolescents, the researchers discovered that most had committed delinquent acts while only a few were officially labeled delinquent. They thus conclude that most adolescents commit delinquent acts; juvenile delinquency is not a lower-class phenomenon; there is no "culture of poverty" which correlates with delinquent behavior; and however anomic or alienated a person may be, he never totally lacks a sense of good and evil.

HV 9104 .R63

Rosenquist, Carl M., and Edwin I. Megargee. *Delinquency in Three Cultures.* Austin: University of Texas Press, 1969. 554 p.

Report of a detailed cross-cultural investigation involving interviews, psychological testing and medical examinations of the differences between delinquents and nondelinquents in three cultural groups: Anglo-Americans and Mexican-Americans in the United States, and Mexican nationals in Mexico.

HV 9106 .S33 R6

Rubenfeld, Seymour. *Family of Outcasts.* New York: The Free Press, 1965. 328 p.

A highly theoretical discourse which presents the author's "psychocultural theory" of causation. Somewhat similar to the containment theory of Reckless, psychocultural theory takes into account both internal and external controls on behavior. Rubenfeld emphasizes the importance of the family in determining behavior and stresses the interdependence of forces behind both individual and societal behavior.

HV 9069 .R8

Rubin, Sol. *Crime and Juvenile Delinquency.* Dobbs Ferry, New York: Oceana Publications, Inc., 1970. 234 p.

Discusses the definition of juvenile delinquency; the question of parental responsibility for delinquency; authority, procedures, and requirements of the juvenile court; treatment of youthful offenders; and the need for "scientific" research. Includes a criticism of *Unraveling Juvenile Delinquency.*

HV 9104 .R77 1970

Sanders, Wiley B. (Ed.). *Juvenile Offenders for a Thousand Years.* Chapel Hill: University of North Carolina Press, 1970. 453 p.

Contains 124 readings tracing the handling of juvenile offenders from the year 688 to 1900 in England, Scotland, Australia, and the United States. Sanders concludes that children who have broken the law have generally been treated more leniently than adults.

HV 9065 .S25

Schafer, Stephen, and Richard D. Knudten. *Juvenile Delinquency: An Introduction.* New York: Random House, 1970. 394 p.

The book provides a broad introduction to the problem of juvenile delinquency, first by defining and describing delinquency and discussing its extent in the United States and abroad. It also gives a brief history of the problem; and summarizes theories of causation, with emphasis on the sociological. The authors discuss variations in patterns of delinquency; characteristics of the youthful offender; society's responses to the offender; and sociocultural influences, such as family, culture conflict, environment, socioeconomic status, education, and physical and mental health. Also considered are the police role in control of juvenile delinquency; the history, development, and procedures of the juvenile court; treatment theories and programs; the lack of a treatment philosophy in most institutions; sentencing alternatives; prevention; and speculation on the future in view of current court decisions.

HV 9069 .S35

Schasre, Robert, and Jo Wallach (Eds.). *Readings in Delinquency and Treatment.* Los Angeles: The Delinquency Prevention Training Project, Youth Studies Center, University of Southern California, 1965. 104 p.

Nine articles which the editors feel reflect "planned change." They define "planned change" as involving rational planning for social change which is aimed at ameliorating social problems, in this instance, juvenile delinquency. The articles are devoted to areas in which planned change is needed and examples of operating programs. Some of the topics discussed are: deficiencies in current treatment programs, the relationship of employment to delinquency, the problem of resistance to education and difficulty of educating individuals beset by numerous problems, and corrections and its needs.

HV 7428 .S35

Schur, Edwin M. *Radical Nonintervention: Rethinking the Delinquency Problem.* Englewood Cliffs, New Jersey: Prentice-Hall, Inc., 1973. 180 p.

Schur feels that current policy on juvenile delinquency is ineffective. He advocates a radical change of major institutions and prevailing cultural values, and an acceptance of greater diversity in behavior. In his view, many youths engage in misconduct and law-breaking but escape the delinquency label; the delinquent is the youth who is caught in this behavior. Schur further emphasizes that creation of programs for prevention should be based on research.

HV 9104 .S328

Sellin, Thorsten, and Marvin E. Wolfgang (Eds.). *Delinquency: Selected Studies.* New York: John Wiley and Sons, 1969. 161 p.

Collection of readings dealing with measurement of delinquency, distance of residence from place of offense, areas of high delinquency, group delinquency, the offender who participates in gangs or groups, police disposition of juvenile offenders, and indices of offenses.

HV 9061 .S45

Shaw, Clifford R. *The Jack-Roller: A Delinquent Boy's Own Story.* Chicago: University of Chicago Press, 1966. 205 p.

A sociological life history of one male delinquent, originally published in 1930. The author stresses the value of the intensive case history as a method of sociological inquiry, presents the boy's social and cultural background, a history of his behavioral difficulties, and summarizes treatment of the youth.

HV 9105 .I3 S5 1966

Shaw, Clifford R., and Henry D. McKay. *Juvenile Delinquency and Urban Areas.* Chicago: University of Chicago Press, 1969. 394 p.

Based on investigations focusing on the Chicago area, the authors relate juvenile delinquency to the physical structure of a city. They postulate that delinquency rates are high in urban areas characterized by a disrupted social order and a lack of organized community effort to deal with disorganization. The implications for prevention and treatment are discussed and linked to changes in economic and social conditions of the urban area.

HV 9069 .S52 1969

Shaw, Otto L. *Maladjusted Boys*. London: George Allen and Unwin Ltd., 1965. 135 p.

A description of England's Red Hill School, a residential treatment facility, and its operation, illustrated with specific cases. The basic approach used in treatment is understanding. American edition published under the title *Youth in Crisis*.

HV 9148 .E22 R47

Shaw, Otto L. *Prisons of the Mind*. New York: Hart Publishing Co., 1974. 243 p.

Shaw stresses the importance of understanding and compassion in the treatment of maladjusted and delinquent boys. The diagnosis of each youth's problems must be supplemented by the removal of temptation. Specific cases described are drawn from the work of Red Hill School.

HV 9148 .E22 R473

Shaw, Otto L. *Youth in Crisis: A Radical Approach to Delinquency*. New York: Hart Publishing Co., Inc., 1966. 135 p.

A description of England's Red Hill School, a residential treatment facility, and its operation, illustrated with specific cases. The basic approach used in treatment is understanding. British edition published under the title *Maladjusted Boys*.

HV 9148 .E22 R47

Short, James F., Jr. (Ed.). *Gang Delinquency and Delinquent Subcultures*. New York: Harper and Row, 1968. 328 p.

A collection of readings describing delinquent gangs and delinquent subcultures, and examining data and theories concerning delinquent subcultures. Short stresses the need for additional testing of theory.

HV 9069 .S53

Short, James F., Jr., and Fred L. Strodtbeck. *Group Process and Gang Delinquency*. Chicago: University of Chicago Press, 1965. 294 p.

The authors describe a detached worker program conducted in Chicago. They discuss the theory on which the study was based, implications of the data for various theories of gang behavior, and relationships of self-conceptions and cultural and structural factors to behavior. Finally, they summarize the development of a group-process perspective and place it in the context of recent theoretical formulations.

HV 9104 .S45

Slavson, S. R. *Reclaiming the Delinquent*. New York: The Free Press, 1965. 766 p.

Slavson describes a study of group psychotherapy in residential treatment of delinquent boys. The study was designed to test Slavson's Activity and Analytic Group Psychotherapy, to obtain staff responses to such procedures, and to determine the effect of such procedures on the total institutional community. The author emphasizes the importance of discovering the underlying motives for and causes of delinquent behavior and feels that delinquents will only reveal motives when in therapy in the secure climate of the group. He includes case histories and recommendations for practitioners.

HV 9069 .S59

Sparks, R. F., and R. G. Hood (Eds.). *The Residential Treatment of Disturbed and Delinquent Boys.* Cambridge, England: Institute of Criminology, 1968. 76 p.

Contains papers presented at a conference on treatment of seriously maladjusted and disruptive boys. The papers deal with the nature of the resident population, implications for treatment, the educational role of training schools, and limits of the therapeutic method.

HV 9146 .C72

Spergel, Irving A. *Community Problem Solving: The Delinquent Example.* Chicago: University of Chicago Press, 1969. 342 p.

Spergel formulates a general framework for community problem solving, especially in the inner city, in a theoretical work intended for the social work student. He analyzes various kinds of organizational strategies and intervention tactics, describes community characteristics and processes which determine the course of juvenile delinquency, discusses methods for modifying and influencing organizational behavior, and presents policy recommendations.

HV 7428 .S58

Spergel, Irving A. *Street Gang Work: Theory and Practice.* Garden City, New York: Doubleday and Co., Inc., 1967. 300 p.

Report of a study undertaken to examine what the street worker does and should do, in an attempt to present guidelines for acceptable performance. According to Spergel, standards of good practice are the same for beginning and experienced workers; yet each worker must develop his or her own style of work which combines sound principles, training and experience, and his or her own personality.

HV 7428 .S6 1967

Stapleton, W. Vaughn, and Lee E. Teitelbaum. *In Defense of Youth.* New York: Russell Sage Foundation, 1972. 243 p.

A study of the role of attorneys in the juvenile court which combines legal analyses with social science methodology and interpretation. The authors discuss the history and philosophy of the juvenile court and maintain that the introduction of defense attorneys changed the proceeding into an adversary process. They also discuss the consequences of this process through observations from two cities.

KF 9709 .S7

Stephenson, Richard M. and Frank R. Scarpitti. *Group Interaction as Therapy.* Westport, Connecticut: Greenwood Press, 1974. 235 p.

The authors describe a program designed to intervene in the processes of juvenile delinquency and rechannel behavior into more acceptable dimensions. Using the Essexfields project as an example, they discuss the methodology of the project, its accompanying evaluative research, and comparative research on similar programs.

HV 9275 .S73

Stokes, Sewell. *Our Dear Delinquents.* London: Heinemann, 1965. 198 p.

Report of an investigation carried out by nonprofessionals to determine what is being done to rehabilitate delinquents in Great Britain. Includes a subtle attack on institutions which do not help their residents.

HV 9146 .S69

Stratton, John R., and Robert M. Terry (Eds.). *Prevention of Delinquency: Problems and Programs.* New York: The Macmillan Company, 1968. 334 p.

The authors attempt to provide the student with a broad overview of current topics in prevention. The thirty-one articles illustrate a lack of agreement on the problems involved in formulating and implementing prevention programs and their general failure to prevent juvenile delinquency. Topics discussed include: the prerequisites for prevention, identification of potential delinquents, problems in implementing prevention programs, the role of existing community agencies and institutions, and prevention through community reorganization. Reports on existing programs are included.

HV 9069 .S785

Street, David, Robert D. Vinter, and Charles Perrow. *Organization for Treatment: A Comparative Study of Institutions for Delinquents.* New York: The Free Press, 1966. 300 p.

Report of a study of six juvenile institutions with differing organization, executive strategies, staff-inmate relations, etc. The study examined the consequences of commitment to different beliefs and goals, and the conditions under which organizations can sustain or adapt old models or develop new ones. Attempts were also made to modify the institutions through an intensive staff training seminar. Findings were mixed and inconsistent, with only one institution showing major change.

HV 9104 .S84

Sullivan, Clyde E., and Wallace Mandell. *Restoration of Youth through Training.* New York: Wakoff Research Center, 1967. 393 p.

This is the final report of the Restoration of Youth through Training Project, a research project which provided vocational training for certain inmates serving time in the New York City jail and evaluated their postrelease job performance and social adjustment. The report includes a history of the project, which was riddled with problems involving staff turnover and morale and sponsorship of the program, in addition to the expected difficulties in working with inmates and correctional staff. The bulk of the report is devoted to method and findings, the most basic of which is that the program does make a positive difference in subsequent job performance and social adjustment, and to perspectives and recommendations.

HV 9106 .N5 S8

Szurek, S. A., and I. N. Berlin (Eds.). *The Antisocial Child: His Family and His Community.* Palo Alto, California: Science and Behavior Books, Inc., 1969. 224 p.

Eighteen articles written by psychiatrists and psychologists which deal with the origins of antisocial behavior, treatment efforts, and mental health consultation with juvenile courts and other agencies.

RJ 499 .S97

Teele, James (Ed.). *Juvenile Delinquency.* Itasca, Illinois: F. E. Peacock Publishers, Inc., 1970. 461 p.

This textbook for undergraduate classes presents various points of view in discussing the causes, prevention, and treatment of juvenile delinquency. Included are discussions on the amount of delinquency in the United States, the labeling process, and the relationship of self-perception to delinquency.

HV 9104 .T44

Tomaino, Louis. *Changing the Delinquent.* Austin: University of Texas, 1969. 110 p.

Intended to be a training manual for probation and parole officers, the book presents a practical approach to changing the delinquent's behavior. Tomaino discusses the probation officer in relation to the juvenile court, background of the court, processing through the court, and work strategies with the delinquent. He also maintains that the delinquent is responsible for his own behavior.

HV 7428 .T65

VanDyke, Henry Thomas. *Juvenile Delinquency.* Boston: Ginn and Company, 1970. 119 p.

A brief introduction to the problem of juvenile delinquency. VanDyke discusses definition, the scope of the delinquency problem, some characteristics of the delinquent, causes, relationship of modern society to delinquency, prevention, and corrections.

HV 9069 .V27

VanWaters, Miriam. *Youth in Conflict.* New York: AMS Press, 1970. 293 p.

Reprint of the 1925 edition of the book, which discusses the case of youth in conflict with the authority of the home, the school, industry, and the community. Individual cases are presented to illustrate the types of conflict and to support the view that such conflict is inherent in and caused by society. The author's goal is to provide insight into the problem for social workers, parents, and teachers.

HV 9069 .V3 1970

Vaz, Edmund W. *Middle-Class Juvenile Delinquency.* New York: Harper and Row, 1967. 289 p.

Contains nineteen articles with a sociological orientation which discuss the adolescent youth culture, the relationship between socioeconomic status and juvenile delinquency, patterns of middle-class delinquency, and theories. The articles suggest that all adolescents break the law, and that they commit different types of offenses. Differences in values are associated with various behavior patterns. Middle-class delinquency is generally pleasure-seeking and a quest for status or masculinity.

HV 9069 .V38

Vedder, Clyde B., and Dora B. Somerville. *The Delinquent Girl.* Springfield, Illinois: Charles C Thomas, 1970. 166 p.

Vedder and Somerville attempt to provide insight into the phenomenon of female juvenile delinquency. They report on a questionnaire sent to all state institutions for delinquent girls to ascertain the offenses which lead to institutional commitment, and discuss the results of the questionnaire. They also discuss theoretical considerations, briefly summarize the literature on female delinquency, and give case histories of females who were runaways, incorrigible, sex-delinquent, probation-violators, or truant, the most common offenses of females.

HV 6046 .V4

The Vocational Rehabilitation of the Youthful Offender. Springfield, Massachusetts: Springfield Goodwill Industries, Inc., 1967. 146 p.

Report of a project which attempted to develop a method of improving employment stability and reducing recidivism using the work process as a rehabilitative process.

HV 9106 .M3 S78

Vodopivec, Katja (Ed.). *Maladjusted Youth, An Experiment in Rehabilitation.* Lexington, Massachusetts: Lexington Books, 1974. 275 p.

Final report of a project concerned with the introduction of new methods of educating maladjusted and delinquent youth in a small institution in Yugoslavia. The staff developed a permissive and understanding relationship with inmates through the use of group counseling, individual therapy, and use of the entire setting as a therapeutic environment. The report stresses the importance of special training and counseling of staff. Vodopivec concludes that permissive educational methods do not result in inmates who are greater threats to society after release, and that institutions can deal with various kinds of disturbed inmates.

HV 9191.6 .D6 M34

West, D. J. *The Young Offender.* London: Gerald Duckworth and Co., Ltd., 1969. 333 p.

West defines the term "young offender," gives statistics on types of offenses and ages of individuals who commit them, discusses the social background of offenders, and briefly reviews theories of causation. He also discusses prediction and classification; the involvement of girls, sex, drugs, and violence; the penal system; and treatment, control, and prevention.

HV 9146 .W4

West, D. J., and D. P. Farrington. *Who Becomes Delinquent?* London: Heinemann, 1973. 265 p.

Report of a study which investigated the development of juvenile delinquency and compared delinquents with nondelinquents. A sample of boys was chosen, information about them was collected for ten years, and differences between those who became delinquent and those who did not were noted. Researchers concluded that differences did exist between delinquents and nondelinquents, noting especially that the family background and personal characteristics of delinquents were much less fortunate than those of nondelinquents. Some possible reasons for these findings are discussed, along with thoughts on prevention.

HV 9069 .W422

Wheeler, Stanton (Ed.). *Controlling Delinquents.* New York: John Wiley and Sons, Inc., 1968. 332 p.

Contains thirteen articles based on empirical study which deal with the control of juvenile delinquency. Each contribution is concerned with some aspect of the interaction between offenders and those who work with them. The articles deal with examination of organized systems of control, problems arising between control agencies and delinquents, and community casework and prevention programs.

HV 9069 .C59

Wheeler, Stanton, and Leonard S. Cottrell, Jr., with Anne Romasco. *Juvenile Delinquency: Its Prevention and Control.* New York: Russell Sage Foundation, 1966. 54 p.

In a report prepared for the U.S. Department of Health, Education and Welfare, the authors deal with perspectives of prevention and control, analyses of current programs and suggestions for further action, importance of the labeling process, the police, the juvenile court, rehabilitation efforts, research, personnel training and development, and organization of prevention and control efforts. A summary of main points to be used as a basis for development of new programs is included.

HV 9104 .W48

Wies, Louis B. *From the Probation Officer's Desk.* New York: Exposition Press, 1965. 84 p.

Wies presents case histories of delinquents with analyses of causes and cures. He emphasizes that parents cause juvenile delinquency by the ways in which they treat their children. Children are victims of circumstances they cannot control, to which they respond with delinquent acts.

HV 9104 .W44

Wills, W. David. *The Hawkspur Experiment.* London: George Allen and Unwin Ltd., 1967. 193 p.

Wills describes the operation of Hawkspur Camp, an experiment in residential rehabilitation of wayward adolescents in Great Britain. The camp, which existed from 1936 to 1940, employed group therapy, shared responsibility, and affection in attempting to rehabilitate delinquents. The author, who was camp chief, presents individual cases and some autobiographical material.

HV 9146 .W54 1967

Wills, W. David. *Spare the Child.* Baltimore, Maryland: Penguin Books, 1971. 153 p.

An account of the process of converting a British approved school into a therapeutic community, with emphasis on eliminating a hierarchical and repressive structure.

HV 9146 .W55

Winslow, Robert W. *Juvenile Delinquency in a Free Society.* Belmont, California: Dickenson Publishing Co., 1968. 237 p.

Contains selections from the seventeen-volume report of the President's Commission on Law Enforcement and Administration of Justice. Deals with the concept of juvenile delinquency, ecological or spatial patterning of delinquency, the juvenile justice system, treatment, and a national strategy for prevention and control.

HV 9103 .A63

Wolfgang, Marvin E., Robert M. Figlio, and Thorsten Sellin. *Delinquency in a Birth Cohort.* Chicago: University of Chicago Press, 1972. 327 p.

The authors provide a statistical description of juvenile delinquency through studying the history of delinquency among a group of youths born in the same year. They analyze all available official data on nearly 10,000 boys from ages ten through eighteen, noting the age of onset of delinquency, and its progression or cessation. They then relate these data to personal or social characteristics of delinquents, and compare the characteristics with those of others in the cohort who have not become delinquent.

HV 9106 .P5 W64

Wright, Jack, Jr., and Ralph James, Jr. *A Behavioral Approach to Preventing Delinquency.* Springfield, Illinois: Charles C Thomas, 1974. 146 p.

According to the authors, juvenile delinquency is learned and maintained in the same manner and by the same principles that control other behaviors; therefore, prevention and control of delinquency must focus on the learning process. Each chapter demonstrates how behavioral techniques may be applied by various institutions, such as the court, the home, and the school, and by individuals who deal with children. The authors differentiate between "ivory tower" theory and reality.

HV 9069 .W75

Index

Abrahamson, David, 74
Abusing parents
  addictive, 191–92
  arrest of, 196
  characteristics of, 190, 192
  and child-rearing patterns, 190
  criminal-sadistic, 191
  disciplinarians, 191
  emotionally immature, 190
  mentally deficient or uninformed, 191
  neurotic or psychotic, 190
  versus neglectful parents, 189
Academic resources in community, use of,
  in treating delinquents, 325
Ackerman, Nathan W., 104
"Acting out," 80
Action for Appalachian Youth, 230–31
Activity therapy, 297–98
Adams, W. Thomas, 83
Adaptive behavior (See Behavior, adaptive)
Adjudication, formal, undesirability of,
  for juveniles, 173–76
Adolescence
  cultural perspective of, 95–99
  erratic and hostile behavior in, 100–101
  in industrialized and technologically
    advanced countries, 96
  physical changes of, 94, 99
  in primitive societies, 96
  problems in early stages of, 99–100
  problems in transition from early stages
    of, 100
  psychological changes of 94–95, 99–101,
    102–6
  in United States, 96
  vacillation of behavior during, 102
Adolescent, the
  American, 95, 96, 97
  general status of, in society, 106
  normal, 99–102
  use of external resources for guidance of,
    87–88

Adolescent, the (*cont.*)
  working with, 108–10
    requirements for success in, 109
Adolescent gang, 97–98
  rites of passage of, 97
Adolescent period, as transition from
    pleasure to reality, 103
Adult behavior codes, adolescent submission
    to, 100
Adult values, adolescent questioning of,
    85–86
Affluence, social problems resulting from,
    86–87
Aggression, unsocialized, 76
Aggressive casework method, 272–74
Aichhorn, August, 57–58, 70, 74, 75–76,
    81–82, 266–67
Alateen, as delinquency prevention pro-
    gram, 239
Allen, James E., 292–93
Alternative behavior, 45–47
American Correctional Association,
    definition of counseling, 287
Amphetamines, 123–24
  sources of, 118
Analysis, transactional, 258, 277–79
Andry, R. G., 74, 77
Anger, dangers of parental repression of,
    87–88
Anomie theory, 38–40
  in relation to deviant behavior, 39–40
  social structure and, 38–40
Anthony, James, 109–10
Anxiety during adolescence, 100
Ardrey, Robert, 62–63
Arrest rates for persons under age 18, *table,*
    27
"Attitude set" as cause of human behavior,
    90
Authority figures, freshness against, 100

Bandura, Albert, 77, 82

Barbaro, Joseph S., 293–94
Barbiturates, 124–25
  sources of, 118
Barker, Gordon H., 83
Bash, Carrie, 214
Beccaria, Cesare, 30
Becker, Wesley C., 73, 83
Behavior
  adaptive, 39, 41, 45
  antisocial, 61
  delinquency, "ultimate cause" of, 61
  dissocial, 57
  manifestations of, during adolescence, 101
  modification, 281–82, 285
  reinforcement of, 282–84
  socially acceptable, obstructions to, 59
Behavior adaption, conflict subculture, 46
Behavior therapy, 281–84
Behavioral adaption, retreatist subculture, 46
Behavioral contracts, 285–86
Berman, Sidney, 70
Berne, Eric, 276–77
Big Brother organization, 163
Biological determinism (*See* Determinism, biological)
Biology, criminal, 34
Block, 87–88
Boy Scouts, as delinquency prevention effort, 238
Brienton, M., 33
Broken homes, 73–75
  age of child at breakup, 73
  effect of, in producing delinquency, 73–74
  events preceding formal breakup in, 74
Bronner, A., 58–59
Browning, Charles J., 73

California State Aid to Probation Services Program, 256
California Youth Authority, 313, 317
Caplan, Gerald, 84, 85, 110
Carpenter, Kenneth, 325, 327
Carson Pirie Scott EE Program, 224–25
Casework method, 270–73
  delinquents' resistance to, 271–72
  parents resistance to, 271–72
Cavan, Ruth S. and Jordan T., 95, 96, 99
Central-Harlem Street Club Project, 223–24
Change, acceleration of social and technological, 84
Child abuse and neglect, the problem of
  causes of, 188–94
    abusing parents, 189–94 (*See also* Abusing parents)
  child protective services, 197–98
    Bowen Center, 202
    Child Abuse Listening Mediation, 203
    Children's Aid Society, 202
    Children's Protective Services Center, 200
    crisis nursery, 202
    foster grandparents, 201
    history of, 198–99
    lay therapists, 201
    methods and programs, 199–203
    Odyssey House, 201–2
    parent aides, 201
    Parents Anonymous, 202
    temporary shelter-home program, 201
  and law enforcement, 196–98
  prevention, 203–6
  primary cause of childhood death, 186
  psychiatric implications of, 193–94
  relationship between adolescent and adult criminality and, 186–88

Child abuse and neglect, the problem of (*cont.*)
  sexual abuse, 194–95
Child as "love object," 80–81
Childhood development, 102–6
Child-rearing process, factors affecting, 71
Children's Bill of Rights, 200
Child's self-perception, 81
Chromosome makeup, study of, in offenders and nonoffenders, 32–34
Citizen involvement, 357–61 (*See also* Community problem-solving)
  causes for failure of delinquency prevention programs, 354–55
  guide to action 369–80
    analysis of the community, 371–72
    bringing the leaders together, 374–76
    identification of leadership, 372–74
    identifying areas of consensus and disagreement, 376–77
    information gathering, 370
    program implementation, 377
    program organizers, 369–70
    quality control and continuous program development and updating, 377–80
    relevant system, identification, 372
  ineffectiveness of informal social control, 355–57
  normative sponsorship theory 365–69
  organizing citizen efforts, 361–64
    blueprint for, 362–64
Citizens' Probation Authority, 249
Civil rights for juveniles, 26, 166–68
Class mobility and family environment, 68
Class status and delinquency, 44–50
Classical criminology (*See* Criminology, classical)
Classical organization theory (*See* Organization, classical view of)
Cloward, Richard, 40, 45–47, 53
Cocaine, 123
Codeine, 119
Cohen, Albert, 40, 44–45, 47, 53
Cohesiveness, family, 66
Coleman, James S., 98, 103–4, 108
Coming of Age in Samoa, 95
Communication, lack of, between parents and adolescent, 106–7
Communication of feelings, adolescent hesitation of, 101
Community
  force of, in influencing behavior, 355
  past and present, compared, 355–57
  relationship of, to halfway houses, 333
Community-based prevention and treatment programs 323–34 (*See also* Delinquency, treatment of, community-based programs)
  defined, 325
  reasons for establishing, 326–28
Community problem-solving
  involvement of youth in, as prevention measure, 106
  normative sponsorship approach to, 365–69
    defined, 365
    identification of areas of consensus and disagreement in, 376–77
    identification of leadership in, 372–74
    program implementation of, 377
    quality control and continuous program development and updating in, 377–380
  use of, in university extension courses, 381
  programs for mobilizing community residents in, 223–24, 361–64

Community resources
lack of, 25
mobilizing for combating delinquency,
327–28, 361–64
Community Youth Citizen Project, 239
Comprehensive Drug Abuse Prevention and
Control Act of 1970
control of sedative drugs by, 119, 123,
125
penalty for possession of LSD under, 123
Conflict subculture (*See* Behavior adaption,
conflict subculture)
Conflicts during adolescence, 103
Conformity, 39
Conscience structure, 64, 77
inadequate, 77, 79
"Containment theory," 64
Control
inner, 64
outer, 64
personal, 71–72
social, 3–9, 71–72
Control structures, role of family in, 72
Cooperative Extension Service, prevention
of delinquency by, 221
Counseling (*See also* Delinquency, treatment
of)
family crisis, 302–3
individual and group, 287–90
use of, in rehabilitating addicts, 130
vocational, 279–81
Counselor, school, 290
Court, juvenile 151–82 (*See also* Juvenile
justice system)
Cressey, Donald R., 29, 43
Crime, adult, and juvenile delinquency,
22–23, 54
Crime causation, 54
Crime prevention measures, 260
Crime rates, 54
Criminal behavior, process of learning, 43
Criminal enterprises, 39
Criminal patterns, 53
Criminal statistics (*See* Statistics, criminal)
Criminality
contemporary theories of, 35–36
motivation for, 36
psychological theories of, 54–63
sociological theories of, 36–53
Criminological inquiry
beginning of scientific, 29
by psychiatry, 29
by psychology, 29
Criminologist, defined, 265
Criminology
classical, 30–35, 51–52, 349
adherence of police to, 51
pleasure-pain principle in, 30
punishment in, 30
rationalism in, 30, 31
positive, 30–35, 51–52, 349
adherence of social workers to, 51, 349
negation of free will in, 31
treatment in, 31
Crisis intervention (*See* Delinquency, treatment of, crisis intervention)
Cultural change, stages of, 22
Cultural factors in deviance, 9–11
Cultural goals, 38
Cultural transmission (*See* Delinquency,
cultural transmission of)
Customs Agency Service, drug control by,
117

Decision-making
guidance in, 90–91
parental avoidance of, 83

Dederich, Charles, 128
Delinquency
cultural transmission of, 41–43
and drift, 50–52
group, 40–41 (*See also* Gang theory)
group approach to treating, 263, 264
legal definition of, 24
obstacles to handling, 25–26
official records of, 69
psychological theories of, 54–66
punishment, as treatment for, 263–64
as self-expression, 58
social definition, 24
transmission of, 53
treating causative factors of, 334
Delinquency causation, theories of, 29–66
Delinquency prevention
classification of, 213
community support for, 216
evaluation and research, 211–60
identifying relevant systems for, 372
middle-range-type efforts of, 215
problems hindering, 211–12
Delinquency prevention, pure
community-based programs
Action for Appalachian Youth, 230
Carson Pirie Scott EE Program, 225–26
Central-Harlem Street Club Project,
224–25
Chicago Area Project, 221
Fuld Neighborhood House, 227
HARYOU Act, 231–32
Henry Street Settlement House, 226
Houston Action for Youth, 230
Los Angeles Youth Project, 223–24
Louisville Red Shield Boys Club, 225
Midcity Project, 221–22
Mobilization for Youth, 228
Quincy Community Youth Develop-
ment Project, 223
South Central Youth Project, 222–23
Syracuse Crusade for Opportunity, 228–
29
United Planning Organization, 229–30
educational programs, 235–39
Community Youth Citizen Project,
237–38
Personality Improvement Program,
236–37
federal government efforts, 217–21
Department of Agriculture, 219
Department of Health, Education, and
Welfare, 217–18
Department of Justice, 218–19
Department of Labor, 219–20
Office of Economic Opportunity, 220–
21
lack of evaluation of, 216–17
"officer friendly" concept, 234
police-school liaison programs, 234–35
criticism of, 234
effectiveness of, 233–34
evaluations of, 234–35
objectives of, 233
Delinquency prevention, rehabilitative
programs, 215, 239–261
defined, 214
Family Treatment Program, 256–57
Focus program, 260–61
foster homes, 251
Fremont Experiment, 311
Fricot Ranch Study, 311–12
halfway houses, 251–52
Highfields Project, 259–60, 331
juvenile institutions, 240–47
alternatives to, 247–60
probation, 247–51

Delinquency prevention, rehabilitative
    programs (*cont.*)
  Provo Experiment, 258–59
  research on approaches to, 261
  VISTO, 257–58
  Youth Advocacy Program, 260
Delinquency, treatment of (*See also* Com-
    munity-based prevention and treat-
    ment programs)
  activity therapy, 297–98
  behavioral contracts, 285–86
  behavior therapy, 281–84
  blending of approaches, 264–65
  casework method, "directed friendship,"
    274
  community-based programs, 323–34
  counseling
    major goals of, 287
    technique of, 287–88
  crisis intervention, 286–87
  direct home intervention, 301–2
  family crisis counseling, 302–3
  group
    counseling, individual and, 287–92
    psychotherapy, 290, 295–97
    as "social laboratory," 294
    therapy, 290–93
    work, "detached" group, 294
  guided group interaction, 298–300
  halfway houses, 326–27
  milieu therapy, 300–301
  psychologists' approach to, 265
  psychotherapy, 265–71, 288
  reality therapy, 274–77, 288
    criticism of, 276
    in halfway houses, 341
    objectives of, 276
  :ocial casework, 271–74, 288
  social environment therapy, 301
  social group work, 293–95
    defined, 293
  sociologists' approach to, 265
  transactional analysis, 277–79, 288
  vocational counseling, 279–81
Delinquent, as ambiguous term, 24–26
Delinquent adolescent, 108
Delinquent behavior
  effect of economic status on, 42
  effect of environment on, 42
  parental approval of, 82
  socialized, 76
  variable nature of, 5–8
Delinquent subculture, 45
Delinquents
  fantasies of, 268
  feelings of omnipotence in, 268
  providing alternatives for, 270
Demerol, 119
Denton, Clifford, 129
Department of Health, Education, and
    Welfare, 122, 217–18
Department of Justice, 122
Department of Social Services, 329
Dependence-independence conflict in
    adolescence, 103, 106–8
Dependency, negative ramifications
    of prolonged, 106–8
Depressants, 124–25
Deprivation
  and delinquency, 59
  physical and psychological, 73
"Detached" group work method,
    294
Determinism
  biological, 31–32
    Hooton's study of, 32

Determinism (*cont.*)
  in positive criminology, 31
    Sheldon's study of, 32
  social, 31–32
    beyond, 64–66
Deviance, 2
  biological, 20
  legal, 19–20
  moral, 20
  normative, 21–22
  social, 1–28 (*See also* Social deviance)
Deviancy rates, effects of social structure
    on, 38
Deviant acts
  adventurous, 7
  defensive, 7
Deviant behavior, 1
  effectiveness of casework method in
    altering, 271–72
  process of learning, 44
Dextroamphetamine, 123
Differential association, 43–44
Dinitz, Simon, 2, 59–60, 184
"Directed friendship," use of, in treating
    adolescents, 274
Direct home intervention, 301–2
Directness, importance in treating
    delinquents, 269
Discipline
  erratic, 79
  as expression of love, 88–89
  lax, 79, 88
  love-oriented, 79
  overly-strict, 88–89
  punitive, 79
Divorce, influence of, on delinquent behav-
    ior, 73, 76 (*See also* Broken homes)
Double standards, conflict of, during
    adolescence, 100
Doyle, Vincent P., 130
Dressler, David, 282, 293
Drift, 50–52
"Drift" process, 53
Drug abuse
  adolescent, 111–31
    amount of, 111–13
  assumptions about, 115
  child's exposure to prevention of
    by mass media, 129
    by parents, 129
    by schools, 129
  cost of, to addict, 112–13
  defined, 112
  economic loss from, 113
  hard-core, 115, 116
  hippie, 116
  inadequacy of severe penalties in con-
    trolling, 116
  peer influence in, 113
  personal loss from, 113
  reasons for, 113–14
  rehabilitation as means of controlling,
    117, 126–31
  situational, 115
  social loss from, 113
  spree, 115
Drug abuser, 114–16
  psychotherapy for rehabilitation of, 128
Drug addict
  care of, after release from hospital, 122
  rehabilitation available to, in communi-
    ties, 122
Drug control, 116–17
Drug dependence, development of, 114–115
Drug Enforcement Administration, 111,
    112, 115–16, 117, 118, 128

Drug prevention education, 129–31, 235
Drug prevention and rehabilitative programs, 126–31
  federal efforts, 129
Drugs
  legal, 118
  parental use of, as factor in adolescent drug abuse, 90–91, 113–14
  types of, 117–26
Durkheim, Emile, 38, 41, 42, 44, 47, 53

Economic Opportunity Act, 219
Economic status, effect of, on handling delinquent, 25
Ectomorph, 32
Education, formal, social problems caused by, 81
Ego, 55
"Ego states," 277
Emotional confusion during adolescence, 100
Emotional deprivation, 76
  early, 70
Emotional discomfort, as factor in delinquency, 58
Emotional stability, parental, 80–82
Emotionally disturbed states among delinquents, 54
Empey, Lamar T., 299
Employment, improving delinquent attitudes toward, 279
Employment project, 352
"End justifies the means" doctrine, 39
Endomorph, 32
Environment, 53 (*See also* Delinquency, treatment of)
  and criminality, 35–36
  and delinquency, 50–51, 53–61
  of the family, 72–84
Escobedo v. *Illinois* decision, application of, to juveniles, 167
Eskimo society, lack of delinquency in, 99
External resources, use of, by parents for child guidance, 87–88

Family
  contemporary, 84–91
  economic status of, effect on delinquent, 83–84
  environment of, 72–84
  importance of, in shaping behavior, 86
  role of, in delinquency, 69
  as significant factor in delinquency, 68–70
  stable, 73
  vital role of, for adolescent, 114
  younger children in, 73
Family crisis counseling, 302–3
Family economics, as factor in delinquency, 83–84
Family structure, cohesive, 114
Family tension and delinquency, 74–76
Family Treatment Program, 256–57
Father
  as aggressive identification model, 82
  hostile, 77
  as identification model, 77
  role of, in delinquency, 77–78
Federal Bureau of Customs, prevention of smuggled drug flow by, 117
Female-based households, effects of, on social identification, 48
Female delinquency
  nature and extent of, 132–33
  new directions in handling, 147–49
    Feminist Movement, 148

Female delinquency (*cont.*)
  theoretical explanations of, 133–38
    differences in opportunities, 136
    social control, 136–38
    socialization patterns, 135–36
Female delinquents in the juvenile justice system, 138–47
  chivalry factor, 139–40
  dispositions, 141–42
  institutional programs for, 142–43
    family contacts, 144–45
    institutional programming, 145–46
    institutional staff, 145
  juvenile detention, 140–41
  juvenile parole, 146–47
Fenton, Norman, 300
Ferguson, Elizabeth A., 271, 293
Focus program, 260–61
Foster homes, 250
4-H program, prevention of delinquency by, 219
Freedom of expression, attitude of, 90
Freeman, Beatrice, 80
Free will, 30–31
Fremont Experiment, 311
Freud, Sigmund, 54, 55
Fricot Ranch Study, 311–12
Friedlander, Kate, 267
Frustration tolerance, 64, 90
Fuld Neighborhood House, 227
Future of juvenile crime prevention, 384–416
  directions in, 394–96
  diversion, 396–401
  juvenile justice administration, 390–93
  rural crime, 387–90
    competitive society, 388–90
  status offenses, 393–94
  youth violence, 401–14
    prevention of, 408–10
    priorities, 406–8
    school programs, 410–14
    in schools, 404–6

Gang, The, 40
Gang delinquency, 47–48
Gang delinquent activity, 45
Gang group worker, requirements for, 294–95
Gang theory, 40–41
Garrison, Karl C., 85
Gault decision, legal safeguards provided by, 156, 177
Gazda, George M., 290
Generation gap, 84–87
  exaggeration of, 108–9
  positive secondary effects of, 91–92
  reduction of negative effects of, 91–92
Gibbons, Don C., 69, 78, 92–93
Gideon v. *Wainwright* decision, application of, to juveniles, 168
Glueck, Bernard, 56
Glueck, Sheldon and Eleanor, 34, 60–62, 73, 75, 77, 78, 81
Goals, failure to achieve, 42
Gold, Martin, 69, 73, 135–36, 149
Group delinquent activity, 45
Group for the Advancement of Psychiatry, 84, 85, 86
Group homes, 250
Group psychotherapy, 290, 295–97
Group therapy, 290–93
  use of, in rehabilitating addicts, 130
Group unity, difficulty of developing, 295–96
Guided group interaction, 298–300

Guilt, reduction of, through activity
    therapy, 297

Halfway houses, 251–52, 323–51 (See also
        Delinquency, treatment of)
    academic programs, 330
    administration and programming, 330
    authority, decentralization of, 335
    differences in treatment of clients, 337–38
    direct approach of treatment, 341
    economic benefit, 329
    evaluation, 347–48
    guiding principles for operating, 348–50
    history of, 326–27
    home visits, 341–42
    learning the system, 345–46
    location of, 329
    in Michigan, 329, 330, 334
    orientation, 342–44
    personnel, 328–51
    positive identification models, 339
    problems in operating, 330–34
        community, 334
        personnel, 332–33
        serving a human being, 331–32
        solutions to, 334–48
        training, 333–34, 344–45
        treatment-custody dilemma, 330–31,
            333
        type of clientele, 331
    relation to the community, 346
    reorganization of structure, 335–36
    staff
        as parental substitutes, 345
        spontaneous reactions of, 340
        utilizing personal assets of, 344–45
    staff-trainer, requirements for, 344–45
    treater in, 338–42
    types of youth served by, 328
    use of structure, 328
    work programs, 330
Hallucinogens, 122–23
Hard-core addict (See Drug abuse, hard-
    core)
HARYOU Act, 231–32
Haskell, Martin R., 248
Health and safety rules, adolescent flaunting
    of, 100
Healy, William, 58–59, 60
Hebrew Orphan Asylum, 326
Henry Street Settlement House, 226
Heroin, 117, 118
    characteristics of addiction to, 119–22
High crime areas, prevention programs in,
    221–25
Highfields Project, 259–60, 331
    success of, 329
Hippies, 116
Hodges, Emory F., Jr., 83
Holmes, Donald J., 268–69
Home, characteristics of delinquent, 83
Homosexual groupings, adolescent, 101
Hooton, Ernest, 32, 34
Horizon House, crisis intervention
    technique at, 286
Hostility, parental, 70
Houston Action for Youth, 230
Human behavior and social control, 3–9
    conservative tendency, 3–8
    normative bias, 8–9

Id, 55
Identification, need for, during adolescent
    period, 97
Identification modeling, transmission of
    behavior through, 84

Identification models, 70–71
    in Aichhorn's theory, 57–58
    parents as, 72
    positive
        importance of, in problem-solving, 280
        provision of, in psychotherapy, 267
Immaturity, unrecognized, 89
Impulse control, instability of, in adoles-
    cence, 100
Incompetence to competence, adolescent
    transcendence from, 103
Inconsistency, parental, 70
Individual approach, 58–59
Individual-based theory, 55–57
    learned-behavior theory, 56
    psychoanalytic theory, 55–56
Individual rights, attitude of, 90
"Infantilizing" praise and punishment,
    revulsion toward, 100
Innovation, 39
Institute of Urban Dynamics, 366
Institutionalized means for goal achieve-
    ment, 38
Institutional rehabilitative prevention pro-
    grams, 239–46
Institutions
    artificiality of, 324
    juvenile, 240–47
Interaction, guided group, 298–300
Interpersonal relations, ambivalent, in
    adolescent, 100
Intersibling quarrels, 74
Intervention, direct home, 301–2

Jacobs, Patricia A., 33
James, Jessie, 233
Jenkins, Richard L., 76
Job Corps, 352
Josselyn, Irene M., 99, 100, 102, 103
Judge, in juvenile court, 172–73
Judicial system, English, and delinquency,
    22–24
Jurjevich, Ratibor-Ray M., 270
Juvenile court, 22–24, 152–62
    first, 22
    intake division, 172–75
    referral, 253
    role of, in perpetuating delinquency,
        183–84
Juvenile Court Act, 23
Juvenile court processing beyond intake,
    175–78
    additional legal safeguards for juvenile
        in, 158–60
    adjudication hearing, 177–78
    disposition hearing, 177–78
    dispositional alternatives, 177
    intake unit of probation department,
        172–76
Juvenile delinquency
    cultural factors in, 9–16
    as deviant behavior, 22–26
    as expression of animal territoriality,
        62–63
    reasons for increasing severity of problem,
        184–85
    role of school in perpetuating, 184
    and self-concept, 59–60
Juvenile delinquent
    decision points in probation handling of,
        figure, 171
    handling of, within juvenile justice sys-
        tem: case study, 179–82
    police options for handling, 163–64
    police procedure for handling, 162–71
    waiver of, to adult court, 171

Juvenile delinquent behavior, reduction of, 238–39
Juvenile justice system, 69, 151–87
assumptions of professionals in, 51
detaining and taking custody, 166–67
juvenile court, 23–24, 170–79
age of juvenile processed by, 172
organizational difficulties of, 170–71
origin and development of, 152–58
shortcomings of, 172
orientation of, in handling delinquents, 26
police and, 162–70
processing of delinquent in, 170–79
Juvenile offender
disposition of, after custody, 169–71
fingerprinting, 168–69
interviewing, 168
photographing, 168–69
records of, 168–69
taking custody of, 166–67
notification of parents after, 167–68
waiver of, to adult court, 170

Kamada, Samuel I., 268
Kane, Joseph, 300
Kaufman, Irving, 71, 82
Kent v. *United States,* legal safeguards stated in, 156
Kolb, Lawrence C., 265
Konopka, Gisela, 293
Kretschmer, 34

Labeling
ease in, 101
effect of, on deviant youth, 25
factors in, 7
by juvenile court, 184–85
by practitioner in juvenile justice system, 108
Ladd, John, 374
Law Enforcement Assistance Administration (LEAA), 218, 303
Learned-behavior theory, 56–57
Lebovici, Serge, 84–85, 110
Lejins, Peter, 214
Life-style, incorporation of delinquent role into, 53
Local government approaches to delinquency prevention, 325–26
Lombroso, Cesare, 31–32, 34
Long, Anna Marie, 268
Los Angeles Youth Project, 223–24
Louisville Red Shield Boys Club, 225
Love, importance of experience of, in psychotherapy, 267
Lower-class boy, delinquency of, 47–48
Lower-class structure and delinquency, 47–48
LSD, effects of, on user, 122–23
Lubell, Samuel, 108–9
Lying to child, 90
Lysergic acid diethylamide (*See* LSD)

McCarthy, James E., 294–95
McCord, William and Joan, 74–75, 79
McCrokle, Lloyd W., 298, 299–300
McKay, Henry, 41–43, 47, 53
McKeiver v. *Pennsylvania,* 156
Manpower project, 352
Marihuana, 125–26
mental effects of, 125–26
physical effects of, 125–26
psychological dependence on, 126
sources of traffic in, 118
Matza, David, 2, 50–52
Mead, George Herbert, 44, 53

Mead, Margaret, 95
Melville, M., 33
Mental health workers, use of casework method by, 272
Merton, Robert, 13, 38–40, 42, 47, 53
Mescaline, 122
Mesomorph, 32
Methadone, 119, 128
Methadone Maintenance Programs, 128
Methamphetamine ("speed"), 123
effects of prolonged use of, 124
Michigan juvenile laws, 166–67
Midcity Project, 221–22
Middle-class institutions, aggression against, 45
Middle-class juvenile delinquency theory, 48–50
Middle-class measuring rod, 44–45
Middle-class system, reaction against, 53
Milieu therapy, 300–301
Miller, Walter, 47–48, 53
Miranda v. *Arizona* decision, 167
application of, to juveniles, 168
Mobilization for Youth, 228
Modeling, effective, 77
Monahan, Thomas P., 73
Moral standards, vacillating, in adolescence, 100
Morphine, 119
Multifactor approach, 60–62
Murray, Ellen, 59–60

NARA (*See* Narcotic Addict Rehabilitative Act)
Narcotic Addict Rehabilitative Act, 122, 127
choices of treatment provided by, 122
Narcotic addict, treatment for, 122
Narcotic Control Act, establishment of drug-abuse penalties by, 119
Narcotics, 119, 122
abuse of, 119
use of, in medicine, 119
National Information Center on Volunteers in Court, 249
National Institute of Mental Health, studies of LSD by, 123
National Training School Project, 284
Negative attitudes, parental transmission of, 82
Neighborhood Youth Corps, 219, 281
Neurotic offender (*See* Offender, neurotic)
New Careers Program, 281
Nikelly, Arthur G., 266
Nonproductive vs. productive orientation in adolescence, 104
Normative sponsorship theory approach to community problem-solving, 365–69
Norm breakdown as cause of delinquency, 5–6
Norms (*See also* Anomie theory)
community, 71
as criteria of deviant behavior, 5–6
defined, 5
legal, 6
socio-legal, 64, 72
use of, in achieving goal, 38
Nye, F. Ivan, 69, 72, 75, 76, 78, 79, 88
Nyswander, Marie, 128

Offender
character disorder, 297
neurotic, 297
Offender behavior, changing, 309
Ohlin, Lloyd, 40, 45–47, 53

Omnibus Crime Control and Safe Streets
    Act, 218
One-to-one relations, threat of: to adoles-
    cents, 290
Opium, 119
    sources of illicit traffic in, 117–18
Opportunity, lack of, as factor in drug
    abuse, 113
Organic factors in delinquency, 54
Organization
    classical view of, 335–36
    failure of, in serving human beings, 332
    in halfway houses, 330, 333–36
    human relations view of, 337
        in halfway houses, 333
    integrated view of, 336
        in halfway houses, 333
    structuralist view of, 336
    traditional theory of, 334–36
Organizational perspective, 52–53
"Other-centered" versus self-centered
    activities in adolescence, 103–4
Overcompetitiveness, social problems
    caused by, 86

Paregoric, 119
Parens patriae, concept of, in juvenile court,
    24, 152, 156, 157
Parental absence (*See* Broken homes)
Parental control
    inconsistent, 79
    methods of, 78–80
    use of physical punishment in, 78
Parental emotional stability, 80–82
Parental hostility, 80
Parental jealousy, 80
Parental rejection, 76–78
    effect of, on conscience, 76
Parental relationship, poor, 113
Parental separation (*See* Broken homes)
Parental transmissions to child, 90–91
Parents
    alcoholic, 81
    child's perception of, 76, 81
    death of (*See* Broken homes)
    effects of attitudes of, 59–60
    emotionally disturbed, 81
    as identification models, 77
    as irrelevant models, 105
    lack of respect for, 79
    mentally retarded, 81
    role of, in delinquency, 59
    role of, in middle-class delinquency, 48–
        49
    type of role played in family by, 81
Park, Robert Ezra, 10
    and School of Human Ecology, 10
Parole, 248–49
Parole officers, 61
    use of casework method by, 272
Peer group, 108
    dictatorship of, 100
    and family environment, 68
    importance of, during adolescence, 104–5
    as primary source of influence, 114
    use of, in guided group interaction, 298–
        99
Peer group acceptance, 58
Peer group relationships, effect of
    authoritarian parents on, 78
Pep pills (*See* Stimulants)
Personality, structure of, 55
Personality Improvement Program, 236–37
Personality theory, 55
Peterson, Donald R., 73, 83
Peyote, 122

Pierce, F. J., 294
Pine Hills, 299
Pioneer House, 326
Play groups, 40
Police
    agencies, role of, in perpetuating delin-
        quency, 184
    athletic leagues as delinquency prevention
        effort, 239
    department, 151–52, 162–71
    dispositions, variables in, 69
Police officers, 51
Positive Action for Youth, 249
Positive criminology (*See* Criminology,
    positive)
Positive Neighborhood Action Committee
    (PNAC), 363–64
Poverty, 53
Powers, Edwin, 274
Present behavior, emphasis on, in reality
    therapy, 275
Prevention (*See also* Delinquency preven-
    tion)
    corrective, 213
    mechanical, 213
    punitive, 213
Prevention program, community-based (*See*
    Community-based prevention and
    treatment programs)
Principles of Criminology, 43
Priorities in parents' relationships with
    child, 89–90
Prison counselor, use of casework method
    by, 272
Probation (*See also* Delinquency prevention,
    rehabilitative programs)
    department, 151–52, 247–49
    officer, 61, 288
        function of, 248
        in juvenile court, 172–73
        as parental substitute, 257
        use of casework method by, 272
    requirements for child, 178–79
Provo Experiment, 258–59
Psychoanalytic theory, 55–56, 57–58
Psychological makeup, role of, in delin-
    quency, 50
Psychological theories of criminality (*See*
    Criminality, psychological theories of)
Psychologists and delinquency, 51
Psychology
    and the family, 70–71
    Freudian, 68
Psychopathology and crime, 54
Psychotherapeutic method, 270–71
Psychotherapy, 265–71
    defined, 265
    group, 295–97
    resistance to, 278
    use of, in rehabilitating addicts, 130
Punishment, unfair, 79

Quincy Community Youth Development
    Project, 223
Quinney, Richard, 1, 65

Rabinow, Irvine, 328
Rabow, Jerome, 299
Rationalism in classical criminology, 30
Reality
    perception, weakness of, in adolescence,
        100
    therapy, use of, 274–77, 288, 341
Rebellion, 39
Recidivism, redefinition of, 307–8, 309–10
Reckless, Walter, 59–60, 64, 96–97, 184

Recreational programs as delinquency prevention efforts, 239
Redl, Fritz, 100, 286
Reeducation as solution to delinquent behavior, 57, 242
Reformatories, 240
Rehabilitation (*See* Delinquency prevention, rehabilitative programs)
Reinforcers (*See* Behavior, reinforcement of)
Reiner, Beatrice S., 71, 82
Reiss, Albert J., Jr., 71, 83
Rejection
    fear of, 76
    mutual, 76
    parental, 70, 76–78
Research on delinquency prevention and treatment changing offender behavior, 309
    effective delinquency research process, 305–6
    history, 307–9
    methods and strategies, 310–14
    money criterion, 312–14
        cost analysis, 313, 320
        cost comparisons, 313, 320
        operations research, 313, 320
        simulation, 313–14, 320
        systems analysis, 313, 320
    recidivism, 307–8, 309–10
    research findings, 314–16
    research with impact, 316–19
Resistance
    to change, adult, 84
    to therapy, 109
    to treatment, 290–92
Responsibility, personal, 90
Retreatism, 39
Retreatist subculture (*See* Behavioral adaption, retreatist subculture)
"Rites of passage," 96
    of adolescent gang, 97
Ritualism, 39
Role
    need of, by adolescent, 98
    playing
        reverse, 289
        use of, in group counseling, 288–89
    theory, discrepancies in, 45–46
Runaways, homes for, 235–36

Sanctions, in halfway houses
    formal, 338
    informal, 338
Sarri, Rosemary C., 284
Savastano, George, 80, 290
Scarpitti, Frank, 59–60
School
    attendants, 61
    role of, in drug abuse prevention, 129–30
    role of, in perpetuating delinquency, 183
Schulman, Irving, 296
Schwitzgebel, Ralph, 283–84
Scientific management theory, 335–36
Sedatives (*See* Depressants)
Self-concept
    development of, 102
        in adolescence, 104
    effect of positive reinforcements on, 282–83
    and juvenile delinquency, 59–60
    negative, role of school in developing, 184
    positive, 64
    shifting, in adolescence, 100
Self-control, 64
    development of, 90
Self-image, 283

Self-image (*cont.*)
    negative, 60
    positive, 60
Self-maximization in adolescence, 109
Self-regard, low, during adolescence, 109
Self-role theory, 44
Sexual adequacy, doubt of, in adolescence, 109
Sexual identification, adolescent boy's, 48
Sexual misconduct and female delinquency, 137–38
Sexual stages in Freudian psychoanalysis, 55
Shah, Saleem, 282, 283, 284
Sharp, E. Preston, 288–89
Shaw, Clifford, 41–43, 47, 53
Sheldon, William H., 32, 34
Shepard, George H., 233
Slavson, S. R., 96, 106, 107, 109, 297, 300
Slocum, Walter, 73, 75
Slums, drug abuse in, 114–15
Social adequacy, doubt of, in adolescence, 109
Social behavior, erratic, during adolescence, 100
Social casework, 271–74
Social change, as cause of generation gap, 85
Social consciousness, 90
Social control
    agencies, lack of effective, 41
    ineffective, 53
    informal, 355–57
Social determinism (*See* Determinism, social)
Social deviance, 1–28
    categorization of, 18–22
        biological, 20
        legal, 19–20
        moral, 20
        normative, 21–22
    cultural considerations, 9–10
    inevitability of, 4–5
    juvenile delinquency as a form of, 22–26
    lack of central authority in, 15–16
    reduction of, by sanctions on, 4
    modification of, because of age, 4
Social engineering, 265
    need for, in delinquency prevention, 355
Social environment therapy, 301
Social group work, 293–95
Social investigation, use of, in handling delinquents, 178
Social psychologists, 36
Social structure, environment of, 54
Social work agencies, role of, in perpetuating delinquency, 184
Social workers, 51
    school, use of casework method by, 272
    translation of psychological and sociological theory into action by, 267
Socially disadvantaged area residents, prevention programs designed for, 220–32
Society, prolongation of adolescence by, 98
Socioeconomic classes, distribution of delinquency throughout, 69
Sociological theories of criminality (*See* Criminality, sociological theories of)
Sociology
    academic courses in, 29
    approaches used in, 36
    and the family, 71–72
Socrates, on adolescents, 110
South Central Youth Project, 222–23
Sower, Christopher, 365
"Speed" (*See* Methamphetamine)

State government approaches to delinquency
    treatment, 325-26
Statistics, criminal, 26-28
Status
    class, and family environment, 68
    socioeconomic, and family environment,
        68
Status offenses, 160-62, 393-94
Sterne, Richard S., 74
Stimulants, 123-24
Stone, Carol L., 73, 75
Strain, 53
Structuralist view of organization, 336
Subconscious, 55
Subculture
    autonomous, 50
    delinquent, and family environment, 68
Success goals and opportunity structures,
    45-47
Suicide rates, effects of culture on, 38
Sullivan, Clyde, 214
Superego, 55, 64
Sutherland, Edwin, 43-44, 53
Synanon, 128
Syracuse Crusade for Opportunity, 228-29
Szurek, S. A., 268

Tait, Downing, Jr., 84
Tappan, Paul W., 271
Tarde, Gabriel, 31
Teachers, effects of attitudes of, 60
Television, as transmitter of drug informa-
    tion, 113, 129
Theories of delinquency causation (See
    Delinquency causation, theories of)
Therapist
    as parental figure, 266
    trust between, and child, 267
    well adjusted, 268
Therapy
    activity, 297-98
    behavior, 281-84
    family, need for, in treating delinquent,
        296
    group, 290-93
    milieu, 300-301
    reality, 274-77, 288
    social environment, 301
Thorp, Ronald G., 282
Thrasher, Frederick, 40-41, 47, 53
Transactional analysis, 277-79, 288
Transference, in psychotherapy, 267
Treatment, 28 (See also Delinquency,
    treatment of)
    methods, theoretical orientation of, 263-
        64

Treatment (cont.)
    problems in defining term, 335
    programs, community-based, 323, 324-
        26

United Planning Organization, 229-30
United States v. Wade decision, application
    of, to juveniles, 171
Upward Bound Program, 220
Urban slum children, 69

Vaz, Edmund, 48-50, 53
Villeponteux, Lorenz, Jr., 288
Vinter, Robert D., 288, 290
VISTA, 219
VISTO, 257-58
Vocational counseling, 279-81
Vocational guidance programs, as delin-
    quency prevention efforts, 239
Vocational rehabilitation programs, as
    delinquency prevention efforts, 239

Walters, Richard H., 77, 82
Weeks, H. Ashley, 259-60
Weirman, Charles L., 232, 234
Wetzel, Ralph J., 282
Wilkins, Leslie T., 213
Will, as factor in delinquency, 50
"Will to crime," 50
Wineman, 286
Winship case, 157
Witmer, Helen, 274
Wolberg, Lewis R., 265
Wolfgang, Marvin E., 105
Wooton, B., 217
Working-class boy, 44-45

XYY man, 32-34

Yablonsky, Lewis, 248
YMCA, as delinquency prevention effort,
    239
YWCA, as delinquency prevention effort,
    239
Youth Advocacy Program, 260
Youth assistance programs, as delinquency
    prevention efforts, 239
Youth culture, 102
    delinquency in, 49
Youth opportunity centers, as delinquency
    prevention efforts, 239
Youth subculture, 108

Zola, Irving, 74-75, 79